RACE AND RACISM
IN THE WEST
CRUSADES TO THE PRESENT

Third Edition

Edited by Paul Sweeney
California State University, San Bernardino

Bassim Hamadeh, CEO and Publisher
Kassie Graves, Director of Acquisitions and Sales
Jamie Giganti, Senior Managing Editor
Jess Estrella, Senior Graphic Designer
Carrie Montoya, Manager, Revisions and Author Care
Kaela Martin, Project Editor
Natalie Lakosil, Licensing Manager
Berenice Quirino, Associate Production Editor

Printed in the United States of America

ISBN: 978-1-5165-1862-3 (pbk) / 978-1-5165-1863-0 (br)

www.cognella.com   800-200-3908

Contents

Introduction to the Third Edition

By D. Paul Sweeney, Jr.

Nearly seven years ago I started working on this text, and while not intending to look at every angle of racism, the goal was to establish an interdisciplinary baseline for students and instructors to work with, through case studies and comparative readings on a variety of related topics. The primary focus was to identify the foundations of white supremacy and the earliest notions of racial differences predicated on biological assumptions, especially the alleged purity of one's blood. In this third edition, Part III, *Historic Processes and Case Studies*, explores the concepts of race and the language of scientific racism in a new "medieval suite." Topics covered are the eighth century origins of Islamophobia, discussed in the context of the Iberian Conquest by Islamic armies in 711 C.E., as well as the process of social integration between Christians, Jews, and Muslims in southern Spain (*al-Andalus*). At the same time, cases of anti-Semitism overlapped with the anti-Islamic perspectives. Equally complex issues stem from examining literature of the period. For example, today there are two camps regarding Spain during the Islamic occupation: The first posits that *convivencia*, (the tolerance or relative peace), was a golden age of enlightenment, and that great scientific and artistic achievements are attributable to the Arabic influences.

Conversely, the second, more recent view, somewhat shaped by negative perceptions of Islam in the post-9/11 world, calls *convivencia* a contrite fiction, or the *Myth of al-Andalus*. Regardless of which side students or faculty may take on the matter, the real issues in Western thought still resound with us versus them tropes, and Spain's modern historic identity as a Christian nation contains symbols of a violent Reconquest, hostile to Islam and Judaism. Presently, festivals and relics associated with Spanish cultural identity are under review for their sensitivity to historical oppression, and debates on welcoming a Muslim minority population try to rectify the past with the European Union's politics of inclusion and multiculturalism. Serving as a modern case study, the issues are posed with arguments for and against inclusion, which strikingly resemble the ongoing immigration debate in the United States that reached a fevered pitch during the 2016 presidential campaign.

New to this edition is a dedicated medieval suite addressing the First Crusade (1096–1099), greatly expanding on the previous editions' readings on its origins and prosecution, and why crusaders attacked Rhineland Jews. Additionally, the section greatly expands the source material, and goes into great depth to show how the demonization process works culturally, contributing to viewing an "other" in ways ranging from religious hostility, notions of racial difference, the underlying propellant of prejudice, discrimination, bigotry, and racism: fear. Using available Arabic sources to shape the narrative somewhat, students will learn how the West's view of this significant event also distorts the events and motivations, as well as propagandizes to some degree. The *historiography* (the history of the history), is also critiqued and even Arabic sources are not immune to Western influences and tendencies. When the modern war on terror is evoked, it elicits different reactions in Western countries than it does in many Middle Eastern nations. While the First Crusade was not the first violent contact with Islam, it has dominated discourse ever since. Today the word *crusade* implies a holy war, but in the West's viewpoint, *jihad* is Islam's version of a holy war, and associated with Islamic terrorists. The meanings and uses of the word *jihad* have undergone change since the eleventh century, nevertheless, fear is still a leading concern with regard to Islam, especially immigrants from Muslim-majority countries.

As noted in the second edition, the original themes established in the first edition of *Race and Racism in the West: Crusades to Present* remain, but are enhanced significantly to assist students with suggested assignments. Additionally, there is more vocabulary in the glossaries to make newer material approachable, and there are also more comparative reading and discussion prompts to enhance learning outcomes and critical thinking skills. The process of racialization, and notions of difference along biological lines reflect Western civilization's Eurocentric notions, including how hierarchies and ranking races by type, color, and geographically evolved from medieval times through the early twentieth century. Employing both original research and carefully selected reading excerpts from a variety of authors on related topics, students and instructors can pick and choose the order of readings; the structure is not linear, but organized along thematic lines. Comparative reading and related exercises can be derived from the content, and some readers

might think that history seems cyclical based on the frequency of recurring beliefs and issues they encounter within the text. We recommend the readings addressing physiological assumptions about race and definitions of racism as starting points, however, so that students establish a foundation: racism is a system of advantages based on race. Comparisons can be conducted with readings from different sections. The variety of topics lends itself to comparative research, and periodic reviews of the literature should help students see through complex arguments that try to defend indefensible positions, such as a correlation between race and intelligence.

Chapter I, *What is Race? Science, Pseudoscience, and Dispelling Race As A Biological Fact,* gets readers acquainted with the academic background of racism, especially the problems associated with human classification systems, as well as reviewing scientific findings that refute long-standing assumptions that biological differences (i.e., biological determinism) are a fact. The discussion about human variation is important to follow closely because it reveals how folk taxonomies, such as *limpieza de sangre* (blood purity), discussed in Part III, entered politics and shaped social policies in many countries. But most importantly, it establishes that race is culturally and socially constructed. We explore a number of definitions of racism that have circulated for over thirty years, as well as an overview of how classification systems after Carl Linnaeus quickly racialized. This process of socially constructed racism informed the premises of nearly all studies in the nineteenth century, especially in European physical anthropology and its subdivision, archaeology. This chapter also discusses the role American anthropology took, under Franz Boaz, to change how humans were studied, and makes suggestions on how to prevent the perpetuation of racism through education.

Part II retains three reading selections from the original edition, along with a sophisticated analytical work to exam how crime, race, and punishment escalated in the United States after President Nixon declared the war on drugs in the 1970s. The prison system has expanded since

1974 and presently incarcerates more people than China and India together, though they have larger populations. Students and instructors may wish to compare the readings to Michelle Alexander's *New Jim Crow* thesis, as well as the extraordinary new documentary *13th* (2016). This section of the book also includes a definition of racism using David Wellman's 1977 model: power + prejudice = racism. Additionally, Peggy McIntosh defines and addresses her examples of how white privilege is realized on conscious and unconscious levels will show students that the pushback against privilege after the 2016 election of Donald Trump is a defining moment in the evolution of how racism's association with white privilege is viewed and taught in classrooms. Ultimately, the historic case studies found in Part III tie together the definitions of racism and race-based human classifications.

As previously mentioned in the second edition of the book, many contemporary social and cultural problems have long lineages, and the term *lineage* takes on a new meaning when examining the Spanish concept limpieza de sangre. Stemming from the gradual reconquest of the Iberian Peninsula, and loosely following the holy war model established in the First Crusade, Part III attempts to bring about an understanding of human behavior and actions with as balanced a perspective as possible. Because identifying some of the longest-lived racisms inevitably mixes with religion and politics, it is essential to understand that religious bigotry contributed to cultural anti-Semitism, Islamophobia, and racial identity based on biological notions that blood can be pure or contaminated. Avoiding "black legend" views of Spain as a violent colonizer, it is more useful instead to trace the origins of how the idea of purity of blood transferred to the Americas, as discussed in the reading from *Genealogical Fictions: Limpieza de Sangre, Religion, and Gender in Colonial Mexico* by María Elena Martínez (2008). The original text of Bartolomé de Las Casas's famous sixteenth century narrative, *The Devastation of the Indies: A Brief Account*, examines how attitudes formed during the Reconquista transferred to the Americas. De Las Casas demonstrated how the indigenous people were treated by the Spanish, but also reflects on how, despite a benevolent attitude, a subtle notion of inferiority crept in via paternalism. Moreover, he portrays the native peoples as weak, naïve, victims who need 'help' from the superior whites and Christianity to save them from paganism. The final section of Part III addresses scientific racism in the nineteenth century and its affect on Western thought, ultimately reaching its nadir with the rise and fall off Nazi Germany (1933–1945). Additionally, Alexander Alland, Jr.'s analytical essay reveals how the ongoing attempts to correlate race and intelligence continue to use flawed methodology, misconstrued numbers, and not so subtle attempts to influence social policies and funding for after school programs and minority education in the United States. Alland demonstrates, through numerous examples, how the ongoing bad science can be traced to the overt racism of the nineteenth century scholars discussed in Part I and Part III. In *Race and IQ*, Alland describes the weak premises of studies by Cyril Burt and Arthur Jensen, as well as the early 1990s book *The Bell Curve*, which briefly revived the race-based notions of intelligence the role of political implications in its publication.

The reading about Adolf Hitler reveals how this most reviled historic figure, which many feel embodied all that is hyperbolically evil, was psychoanalyzed in the past, and how modern sources question, but cannot refute the assertions of previous studies regarding his anti-Semitic views. The only remaining question about this last point is when Hitler actually applied racism towards Jews and others deemed a threat to Aryan purity, as the "Nation and Race" from *Mein Kampf* reveals in a rambling style. In *Mein Kampf* he claimed to have become a staunch anti-Semite as a teen in Vienna before the First World War (1915–1919). The open question is not that he was anti-Semitic, but did his views coincide with his start in politics? Or was it, as he claimed, possibly to impress his readers and followers, early in life? Regardless, the Holocaust expressed the ideology of Nazism in its darkest manifestation. Closely related, and heavily influenced by the Nazis and scientific racism, white supremacy movements have gained momentum, from the margins of America to the political mainstream under the moniker "Alt-Right," white nationalists, or even white separtists. The origins of these groups used to be associated with the Ku Klux Klan, motorcycle gangs, and skinheads, but recent evidence implicates the overlap and sympathizing of conspiracy theorists somewhat, with overtly racist groups. The readings by Pete Simi and Robert Futrell, *Contemporary Aryan Hate and Aryan Hate in the Home* describe up close and personal encounters after several years of fieldwork amongst such organizations in the United States. Looking at their core ideology, it is clear that many currently share some far right sentiments, even if they do not associate with these organizations. Another recent trend in 2017 is that white supremacy groups actively try to recruit students from university campuses. Valid questions include: Will their presence affect freedom of speech on campuses across the U.S.? And will their actions help or hinder discussions on racism? The violent events on Saturday, August 11, 2017 at the University of Virginia campus in Charlotsville is a significant event in modern understanding. Originally billed by white supremacy organizations and leaders, such as David Duke and Richard Spencer as a forum to discuss the removal of a statue of Robert E. Lee, it quickly devolved into a melee, and one woman was killed by a car deliberately driven into the crowd of counter-protesters.

Part IV contains two important excerpts by Aime Cesaire and Frantz Fanon, both of whom were raised in the former French colony of Martinique in the Caribbean. In the 1950s Cesaire, advocated for socialism as the only fair solution to the historical system of social controls and dominant colonialism, and that the colonized peoples of the world should unify in their effort to attain dignity and self-determination. Conversely, Fanon explains how violence is the inevitable outcome when the colonial power leaves, or when the chosen replacements from within the colony's elites perpetuate the discrimination and policies of their predecessors. Current events in the Middle East and North Africa after the "Arab Spring"

show how Fanon's model works. For example, in northern Nigeria the Islamist group Boko Haram has fought a long campaign to remove the current government and create an Islamic state, or caliphate, as a safe place for Muslims. In fact, the very name Boko Haram translates to "western education is forbidden" in the Hausa language. Some students should also explore the rapid changes in Egypt since 2011, changing from a military dictatorship to a democratically elected government led by the Muslim Brotherhood, and back to a military government. At the time of this writing social unrest between Muslims and the minority 10 percent Coptic Christian population led to bloody attacks on churches and neighborhoods, all of which were claimed by the Islamic State in Syria and Iraq (ISIS), itself currently under siege. Finally, Islamophobia dominates international headlines, and its relationship to colonialism and politicized Islam should be considered when looking at the problem of colonialism.

In early 2017 two separate attempts to apply a ban on immigrants from Muslim-majority nations, including Syria, were initiated by an executive order from the White House. Both measures, which aim to limit or restrict Muslim immigrants, are strongly denied as a 'Muslim ban' by the White House, but the wording and the seven (now six) nations listed in the text refute the denial. Looking further back, students may be interested in how scientific racism, eugenics, social engineering, and selective immigration policies prevailed in most western hemisphere countries. Immigration and migration are nearly always racialized, politicized topics in the United States, and lately Western Europe has experienced a wave of anti-immigrant movements and threats to the European Union's core values of inclusion.

Similarly, Part V examines how the Chinese were treated in the nineteenth century when they arrived in both the United States and Mexico. These case studies shed light on the ongoing rhetoric about foreigners and perceived threats to the established order. Embedded in the populist expression "Make America Great Again" (MAGA) are sentiments of exclusion, protectionism, isolationism, and thinly masked racism: The others are not welcome, are not a good fit, cannot assimilate, bring drugs, violence, and sexual misconduct. The resistance claims MAGA really means Make America White Again. It might surprise readers to learn that the very same things currently being said about Muslims were said about the Chinese, and the xenophobic 'Yellow Peril' reemerged along with political, economical, and military concerns regarding China in the late nineteenth century. It remains to be seen how this last pattern plays out, but restrictive legislation largely began with the Chinese Exclusion Act (1882), and this led to immigration quotas, deportations, and bans in the U.S. and many other Latin American nations. Even now renewed efforts to limit Asian students from admittance to Harvard and other universities is part of the initiative to end race-based admissions and Affirmative Action.

Finally, in Part VI, Latin America is examined though a variety of readings. First is a short excerpt from Jorge Amado's novel, *The War of the Saints,* which merges magic realism with deep-seated social antagonism in Brazil's blackest city, Bahia de Salvador. Also evident through the characters described in the novel is the internalized racism of a key character that displaces angst onto her niece, who is dating a young Afro-Brazilian lad. After Nigeria, Brazil is the second blackest country in the world, and contrary to its modern cultural identity as a racial democracy, equality is as disproportionate as the non-white population is to the privileged upper class. Since 2004 Brazil has experimented with affirmative action, which gradually spread through the country's university system. However, conflicts remain and racism lurks below the surface, and many deny or fail to see the societal issues regarding race and opportunity. The last reading, by Ariel E. Dulitzky, *A Region in Denial*, is an excellent guide to rhetorical denials of racism used by many Latin American governments, and sheds light on how ethnic minorities are diminished by seemingly harmless political language and terms. Simultaneously, these attitudes trivialize the plight of the underprivileged. Suggested comparative readings could examine the legacy of limpieza de sange and modern notions of beauty,

as well as how hidden histories of minorities in the countries discussed contribute to their non-representation in government.

Taken collectively, this third edition examines Western societies from the eighth century to the twenty-first, and illustrates the patterns and social forces that continue to create situations that discriminate along lines of ethnicity, religion, or biological notions that not all 'races' are equal or pure. What factors led to holy wars in the Holy Land and Spain? Why does anti-Semitism keep reappearing in times of economic decline and social unrest? Why does Islamophobia recur, often in close proximity to anti-Semitism? We answer some of these questions in the text, but as always, we encourage students to choose their sources carefully when conducing research, and to be selective so as not to perpetuate myths and erroneous conclusions. Moreover, colonialism cast a long shadow over many diverse societies that demonstrated patterns of inequality that show correlation to eugenics. Why, for example, do individuals in Jamaica, Nigeria, India, the Philippines, and many other countries engage in the phenomenon of skin bleaching? What created 'light privilege' in communities of color? Understanding how racism is infrastructural and affects non-whites in ways invisible to whites can help with the discussion that white privilege exists, and move the conversation about racism forward. Students and instructors alike can take the readings and revise or expand them as class or individual projects to enhance understanding of how racism is about power, and why there is so much resistance to changing a sociopolitical system that advantages one group over others.

1

Scientific Fallacies and Race as a Social Construct

What is Race?

Science, Pseudoscience, and Dispelling Race as a Biological Fact

By D. Paul Sweeney, Jr.

● ●

Explaining Human Variation

Race is a Biological Fact and Other Fallacies

What is race? The word itself is ambiguous, yet it remains a powerful social and political concept used universally to denote differences between one group and the next. Additionally, *race*, the word, is commonly used to refer to both biological and cultural variation. Moreover, it also implies geographical concerns, genetics, ancestry (genealogy), and even language or culture differences. To inform this study, the **geographic race concept** is tied to the "classic" three racial designations still utilized by forensic scientists today: Caucasoid, Mongoloid, and Negroid. As such, the corresponding geography of these three types also yielded color terms to describe each "race": white, yellow, and black respectively. Consider too that Africa was referred to as the "Dark Continent" well into the twentieth century. Further, geographic subdivisions also created sub-continental groupings, such as East Asian, Southeast Asian, and so on.[1]

While geographic concerns are a useful way to sort and organize race, and this concept crosses many disciplines, *it is not*, however, the best way to describe or study human biological variation. In this circumstance, the tendency is to focus on **phenotype**, the physical characteristics that demonstrate adaptive and clinal variations in *Homo sapiens*. This is an ever expanding field of study, and modern scientists now explore sets of genetic markers rather than erroneous classic definitions of race that focused primarily on the **phenotypic traits**: skin color, hair texture, craniometrical dimensions, and related considerations. Nevertheless, the area of inquiry most studied is the global distribution of specific phenotypic traits, especially skin color variation and craniometric traits (skull shape, size, and capacity).[2]

Linnaeus and the Five Geographic Races, 1735. The first concern of this chapter is to explore the following question: How did we arrive at this point? In 1735, Carl Linnaeus (1707–1778), in his taxonomic fascination, "originated" four distinct groups of *Homo sapiens*, largely based on what was known about the world in the early eighteenth century. He established the basis for further taxonomies (**taxa**) by introducing Latin terminology, including *Americanus, Europeus,*

---

1 John H. Relethford, "Race and Global Patterns of Phenotypic Variation," *American Journal of Physical Anthropology* 139, (February 2009): 16.

---

2 Ibid.

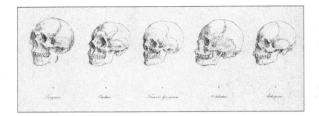

Figure 1.1: Blumenbach's Five Races

Asiaticaus, and *Afer* (Africa). Linnaeus, as best as it can be determined, was not motivated by an overtly racist sense of superiority when he compiled this taxonomy. It was not long after his classifications of the species, however, before overt racist thinking entered the discussion on human variation.[3]

As discussed, skin color especially factored into virtually all racial classification systems historically. While descriptive terms such as "brown," "black," and "white" are common, in reality the distribution of human skin color is *continuous*, which means that categories containing a finite number of shades are irrelevant. Nonetheless, this is an ongoing preoccupation that bordered on the pathological in Medieval Spain before and after the conquest of the New World, and later in Nazi Germany. Further, social implications regarding race often lead to political considerations, as well as the armchair theories of cultural elites and academics. For example, "Caucasian" is generally used to delineate light-skinned people from Europe, Western Asia, and even North Africa, but why is the word used if it derives from a mountain range deep in southern Russia?[4]

The term Caucasian was invented in 1795 by the German naturalist J. F. Blumenbach (1752–1840), who provided two reasons for selecting this descriptor: first, the "maximal beauty" of the people from this relatively small region was assumed to be a superior trait, and second, he assumed that in all probability humans must have originated from the area. Further, Blumenbach's work on racial classification set a standard in the taxonomy of European

Figure 1.2: Great Chain of Being

racial discourse. In the manner now so familiar to US citizens filling out applications and census forms, the word "Caucasian" really means "white," which often imbues positive social characteristics to those who fit this racial designation. Nevertheless, when Blumenbach devised a new taxonomy for humanity in 1795, he modeled it after Linnaeus but expanded the original four groups into five. What set his new taxonomy apart, though, was that the five groups were named accordingly by *both* geographic location and physical appearance.[5]

In short, the "Caucasian variety" emphasized the light-skinned inhabitants of Europe and adjacent areas. Eastern Asian inhabitants, including the people of China and Japan, were designated the "Mongolian variety," and the "Ethiopian variety" referred to the dark-skinned peoples of Africa. Additionally, Blumenbach devised an "American variety" to explain the native populations in the Americas (New World), and finally, the "Malay

---

3 Stephan Jay Gould, *The Mismeasure of Man, Revised and Expanded Edition* (New York, NY: W.W. Norton, 1996), 404–405.

4 Gould, *Mismeasure of Man*, 401–402; Relethford, "Race and Global Patterns," 16–17.

5 Gould, *Mismeasure of Man*, 401–402.

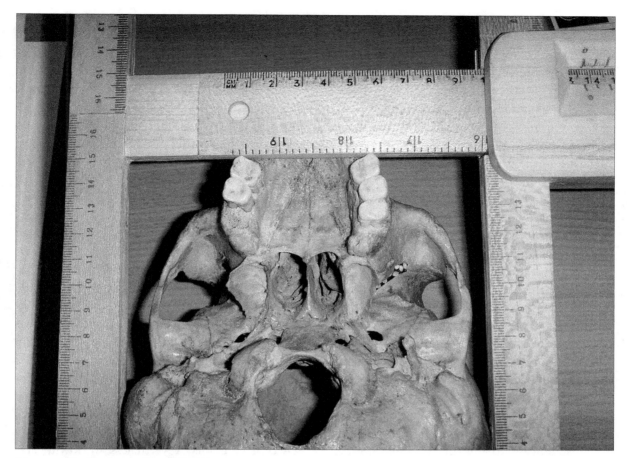

Figure 1.3: Anthropology/Craniometry

variety" explained the Pacific Islanders, particularly the Polynesians and Melanesians, as well as the Australian aborigines [see Fig. 1.1].[1]

While Linnaeus is credited with taxonomic criteria, Blumenbach is recognized as the father of *racial classification* because he shifted the former's four-race model into a Caucasian ideal that topped both the geographic and racial hierarchies. Further, adding the Malay category was the key "achievement" for Blumenbach, and it marked another departure from the original model established by Linnaeus in 1735. Ultimately, the species *Homo sapiens* was arranged loosely by geography, with variations of the three descriptive words once used by Linnaeus to identify color, temperament, and stance.[2] The next section will guide the learner through the complexities of human genetic variation.

Human Genetic Variation and Skin Color. What is certain in matters of race and factors that are assumed to be differences in human genetic variation is that skin color has been especially calculated into virtually all racially based classifications. As mentioned above, continued use of descriptive color terms ignores that the distribution of human skin color is continuous, but this last consideration is a fairly new finding in comparison to the discussion at hand. If this is true, then what accounts for such variation? Ultimately, the Darwinian term **natural selection** can account for complexion, and it reveals a very high correlation between skin color and latitude because it suggests adaptability to the intensity of ultraviolet rays.[3] Therefore, regional variation in skin color, when associated with latitude, leads some people to correlate geography as well, but many studies found that there are no identifiable

1   Ibid., 402.
2   Ibid., 403–404.

3   Relethford, "Race and Global Patterns," 16–17.

clusters due to the continuous nature of human skin tone variations. This, in turn, shows that skin color demonstrates a classic pattern of **clinal variation.**[4]

The Fascination with Craniometrics. If the phenotypic trait skin color is indicative of clinal variation, how do global patterns of **craniometric variation** fit the present study? It is generally accepted that some traits are correlated with climate (latitude), but this only minutely affects cranial variations found in *Homo sapiens*. Can "race" then be attributable to whether or not craniometric variation forms recognizable clusters? Some studies found that long clusters (long skulls) are evident in the six geographic regions sampled by Howell (1973, 1989, 1995, 1996), and this reflects that craniometric variation *is* geographically structured. While Howell's findings are still reassessed and debated, the real issues are how the numerous numbers and measurements are calculated, and more importantly, *interpreted*. In a 1972 study by Lewontin, it was concluded that differences among humans are much too small and insignificant to inform accurate classification. However, like the Howell studies, this report too had limitations, as did others that followed. Further, using craniometrics and multivariate methods was generally perceived to be the best way to test another forensic anthropologist's (Sauer, 1992) findings, according to Ousley et al. (2009). Ousley et al. found that the multivariate classifications of craniometrics within traditional race categories (Caucasoid, Mongoloid, and Negroid) did reveal significant variability, but failed to factor environmental concerns or use large populations in the studies. After the testing of the Sauer hypothesis, it was determined that "proving" the existence of biological races might be limited only by the number of samples in a given study. However, this interpretation contradicts the classic viewpoint that there are only a few discrete biological races.[5]

Related studies to those cited above showed that global patterns of craniometric variation indicate an underlying genetic relationship pattern, which also reflects a correlation to geography. The relevant finding, though, is that there is an association between skull shapes and sizes and geography. This means that if populations exist farther away from one another, they will be less similar to populations grouped in close proximity. One probable reason to explain such biological differences is the continental origins of blacks and whites. Additionally, Ousley et al. speculated that **institutional racism** in the United States could be one reason assertive mating (miscegenation) between these two groups shows such little progression even today. Further, much information regarding Spanish colonialism and other historic factors has surfaced to partially explain morphological heterogeneity, but *time* is another consideration that is often overlooked. For instance, time is a variable to show differences from past to present in terms of nutritional improvements, healthcare, and hygiene, to name but a few considerations. Nevertheless, worldwide craniometric variation does show strong geographic patterning, but there are far too many possible distinctive variables that challenge a conclusive study on racial differences. To quote Livingstone (1962), "there are no races, only populations." Ultimately, these considerations can yield flawed assumptions or conclusions, but generally speaking, using geographic race to describe the geographic structuring of human biological variation is a "crude method," according to Relethford.[6]

When racial classification is applied to geographically structured variations in craniometrics, it can produce numbers via measurements to confirm that such variations exist. Further, to cite Howell's study of six discrete regional studies, this would on the surface appear to be a valid consideration. However, subdivisions were not factored into any of the Howell studies, which exposed

---

4 Ibid., 17.
5 Relethford, "Race and Global Patterns," 17–18; Stephen Ousley, Richard Jantz, and Donna Freid, "Understanding Race and Human Variation: Why Forensic Anthropologists

are Good at Identifying Race," *American Journal of Physical Anthropology* 139, (February 2009): 72.
6 Livingstone, quoted in Relethford, "Race and Global Patterns," 19; Ousley, Jantz, and Freid, "Understanding Race and Human Variation," 73–74.

a number of problems in his conclusions. For instance, anticipating how a relationship between racial units and classification accuracy comes into play, and oversimplifying the findings, also complicates this discussion. While geographic patterning is evident, can this really be used to describe race? No, states Relethford, partly because "crude" labeling has entered political ideology for far too long. Therefore, the underlying variation, although continuous in actuality (like skin color), is discretely summarized and categorized in these examples.[7] Too often, broad grouping descriptions about race are not biologically sound, and semantics sometimes dodge the use of the word "race" by instead substituting "geographic regions," "ancestry," or "social class."

Forensic Anthropology and Human Variation

Can Craniometrics Identify Race? As discussed, the 1992 Sauer study declared that the reason American forensic anthropologists are so good at identifying the race of decomposing remains is "because of a concordance between social race and skeletal morphology in American whites and blacks." Sauer was cautionary, however, and stressed that the concordance he observed "*did not* [italics added] validate the classic biological race concept of physical anthropology that there are a relatively small number of discrete types of human beings."[8] Additionally, other studies that used both craniometric and molecular data show strong geographic patterning of human variation, even with overlap in the distributions identified in these studies. Furthermore, Ousley et al. tested Sauer's findings meticulously using the methods described already, and their analysis found that humans *could* be accurately classified into geographic origin using craniometrics, even if there is overlap (human variation) among groups.[9] As is usually the case with published peer-reviewed empirical research, rebuttals and revisions of previous studies are a certainty, and very few findings

are free of limitations. Still lacking, though, is evidence to show humanity is not based on variation.

Common Misconceptions and Patterns When Discussing Race

Problem One: The Habit of Classification and Folk Taxonomy. In *Anthropology and Race* (1994), Eugenia Shanklin explored the human habit of classifying things and thinking in terms of opposites, such as the following paired words: us/them; black/white; in/out; hot/cold, and so on. The idea that one or more groups is "out," as in outside humanity as defined by a particular group also leads to the excluded becoming "others." In short, the human habit of classification is referred to as **folk taxonomy**, and it is culturally relevant, as well as regionally specific within a particular society. Such classifications do not always follow the logic of Linnaeus, and sometimes they are mutable, ever changing with the times. Outside of socially constructed taxonomies are several schools of thought on biological classifications, as well as a historic shift from century to century.[10]

Semantics and Other Hedging Tactics. *Taxon* is usually the term used to denote the members of a biological classification, but it is common today for sociologists and anthropologists to avoid using the term "race" even though it is prevalent in courts of law, political debates, and nightly news programs. To avoid using this word, social and philosophical theorists use wordplay and other hedging devices to create different names for two kinds of language. For example, there is ordinary everyday or practical language, and secondly, theoretical language that attempts to be transcultural by employing Latin names. Therefore, this theoretical language becomes ubiquitous in the "pure" or hard sciences as well as the applied and social sciences.[11]

Because most words, in the ordinary usage sense, have multiple meanings, they are changing at different rates due to multiple variables and

7 Relethford, "Race and Global Patterns," 20–21.
8 Ousley, Jantz, and Freid, "Understanding Race and Human Variation," 68.
9 Ibid.
10 Eugenia Shanklin, *Anthropology and Race* (Belmont, CA: Wadsworth 1994), 1–3, 67.
11 Michael Banton, "The Naming of Social Categories," *Theoria* 60 (September 2013): 1–2.

circumstances. Conversely, scientific or theoretical language emerged from empirical experimentation, but social sciences sometimes struggle to develop such a recognized standard due to slower progress in this regard. For instance, students who simultaneously study psychology, sociology, and anthropology may at times encounter a theory or situation with matching considerations, but they must apply genre or discipline-specific names for the same phenomena. The foundation for this dilemma was established when Linnaeus developed the biological classification system in 1735, because it created taxonomic structures that contemporary social scientists try hard not to repeat when it comes to race. After all, human "specimens" cannot be organized into neat, orderly, and fixed or immutable categories.[12]

The Monogenist Perspective on Race. In Europe, up until the middle of the eighteenth century, the biblical Adam and Eve were believed to be the first humans on earth and created in God's image. Further, Adam's descendants served as an explanation of differences between races, especially Noah's accursed son Ham. This thought process led to the belief that some groups are "cursed," as reflected in the views of some pre-Christian Jews and developed further by early Muslims. Additionally, this system of belief was institutionalized in medieval Europe to justify serfdom, and later, African slavery.[13]

This pattern of thought is called a **genealogical explanation.** The "logic" of it stipulated that black Africans were "naturally" born to be slaves because they *must* be the cursed descendants of Ham (also spelled Cham), who was turned dark or black as a punishment for disrespecting his father, Noah. Ham was ostracized from civil society and cast out.[14] Further, as the word "race" integrated into Western European languages, possibly via Spain's adoption and corruption of the Arabic word *raza*, which meant a kind or type of animal (taxonomic), it evolved to become synonymous

with genealogical implications (see the Martínez excerpt in this book for how this concept works). In addition to meaning genealogy or ancestry, race implied a vertical relationship in nature and society (Fig. 1.2, The Great Chain of Being) as well as a horizontal relationship with regard to the nature of distinctiveness culturally and geographically.[15]

The Process of Racialization. Early in the seventeenth century, writers in Britain and France described the citizens of each nation as separate races. This phenomenon is called **racialization,** a mode of racial classification created via a social process that creates for those in power a privileged status. What contributes to this process? Legislative acts, social science, and in modern times, media tendencies to racially classify people, according to Webster.[16] Another idea emerged in the 1700s that postulated "Englishmen" descended from the "German race," but centuries later, some elites still debated whether this was a biological or cultural certainty. Nevertheless, prior to Charles Darwin's *Origin of Species* (1859), the species *Homo sapiens* had already been divided into five semi-permanent types (by Blumenbach). Regardless of how such taxonomic designation was employed, race clearly reflected *class*, which meant it had political connotations by the early nineteenth century.[17]

As the meaning of words evolved through racialization and other processes, certain connotations led to coupling words, such as "negro" and "slave," "black slaves," "Blackmores," and "negroes" (for slavery) in colonial North America by the late seventeenth century.[18] Additionally, folk taxonomy also created the "One-Drop Rule," amongst other political and legal considerations regarding who was white and who was considered black, and its premise implied that one's status was secured in society only if their blood was undiluted. Therefore, operating on the assumption of

---

12   Ibid., 2–3.
13   Ibid., 3–4.
14   Winthrop D. Jordan, *White Over Black: American Attitudes Toward the Negro, 1550–1812.* (Chapel Hill, NC: University of North Carolina Press, 1968), 60, 62 footnote.

---

15   Banton, "The Naming of Social Categories," 3–4; Gould, *Mismeasure of Man*, 396–400.
16   Yehudi O. Webster, *Racialization of America* (1992. Reprint, New York, NY: St. Martin's Press, 1993), 2–3.
17   Banton, "The Naming of Social Categories," 4–5.
18   Webster, *"Racialization of America,"* 106–109; Jordan, *"White Over Black,"* 60–63.

a five-race taxonomic model to explain biological differences, many early scientists and social elites later evolved to favor the single species, or **monogenist** conclusion. Ultimately, racism and many sociopolitical factors inhibited this presumption at least until the 1930s.[19] The next section will explain related scientific classification systems.

Problem Two: Three Key Differences Between Pheneticism and Phylogenetic Classification

Phenetic classifications are ahistorical, meaning they define *taxa* in terms of similarity between members, but not genealogical relations between these organisms. Conversely, **phylogenetic classifications** *are* historical because they define *taxa* using terms from evolutionary history.[20] Because pheneticism uses similarity alone to define its *taxa*, it differs from the premise of the phylogenetic concept that considers similarity *as evidence* for group membership, but defines *taxa* differently. Finally, the third significant difference between these two systems is that the pheneticist classification is supposedly theory neutral because those who utilize it do not want to colorize or shape the thing being classified. Phylogenetic classifications, however, are theory dependent because their aim is to consider all patterns and processes of evolution. Therefore, evolutionary theory is very integral to the phylogenetic process.[21]

The key issue, though, is that while both schools of thought claim to be fact objective, only the phylogeneic classifications fit this description. Why? Objectivity is maintained because phylogenicism uses processes independent of human classifying practices, which theoretically frees it from socially constructed ideas and pitfalls. Conversely, the main problem with pheneticism is that it purports to maintain objectivity by also taking into account all of the properties relevant to each individual process. For example, what

counts as a character? For every organism there is an infinite number of possible traits, such as phenotypic, genotypic, and behavioral. Further, there are countless traits within each type, so these considerations can reveal the limitations of the pheneticism approach to classification.[22]

As revealed, scientific classifications are not always clear-cut, even in the most structured environment; therefore, folk taxonomy is equally unstable and inconsistent. While the preceding examples can be confusing for some students, advanced research data indicate that many findings are relevant to refute two premises of racism: that not all "races" are equal and some are *inherently* inferior. Thus, if there is no such thing as biological race, why is that fact so hard to understand and accept for some people? The conversation now shifts to how **cognitive dissonance**, the psychological term for discordant belief systems conflicting, leads to feelings of guilt when race matters and white privilege enters the conversation.

Cognitive Dissonance as a Hindrance to Accepting that Race is a Social Construct

Cognitive dissonance is a manifestation of **white privilege** being exposed, and the resultant guilt comes to the fore when debunking race as a biological category conflicts with existing paradigms in some individuals. As addressed in the Tatum excerpt found in this book, white students in the United States sometimes experience a sequence of emotions ranging from guilt to anger.[23] Not all whites accept that they have a privilege simply by being born white in the Western world, nor do some accept that the US and other societies are *very* taxonomic. Much like the Great Chain of Being did in the medieval world, where feudal society believed God made the aristocracy special and the other groups had to follow blindly and obey, modern governments use science to inform their perspectives, but inequality sometimes

19   Jordan, "*White Over Black*," 170; Banton, "The Naming of Social Categories," 5.
20   Robin O. Andreasen, "Race: Biological Reality or Social Construct?" *Philosophy of Science* 67 (2000): S655–S656.
21   Andreasen, "Race: Biological Reality or Social Construct?" S656.

22   Ibid.
23   Beverley Daniel Tatum, "*Why Are All the Black Kids Sitting Together in the Cafeteria?" and Other Conversations About Race* (1997. Reprint, New York, NY: Basic Books, 2003), 3–10.

still exists.[24] It takes careful explanation to first establish that race is not a biological fact and that racism is a system of advantages based on race. When paired, power and prejudice equate to racism. All else is bigotry, bias, and prejudice without infrastructural power.

Confronting this form of ignorance is the primary goal of this book, but rather than point out that institutionalized racism exists, it is important to explain step by step how Western Civilization views itself and its achievements, and how it measures these achievements for the rest of the world. Furthermore, it is important to understand that scientific racism enhanced folk taxonomy, which in turn influenced academia and then the social elites of many societies, who in turn often hold the reigns of power in Western societies. Because of how biological race considerations shaped politics and social structures, it is equally important to know how and when challenges were brought, albeit flawed initially, which rejected racist views and influenced change in social sciences, especially physical anthropology in the early twentieth century.

European and American Anthropology in the Early Twentieth Century

Throughout the nineteenth century and well into the twenty-first, race was and still is widely believed to be a biological "fact." Despite arguments and evidence to the contrary, as briefly covered in the preceding section, **constructivist** theories about race *assume* that biological realism and social contructivism are incompatible views about race, but both can be compatible if both perspectives can be explained fully and placed in context.

Physical Anthropology, Craniometrics, and Anthropometry

Prevailing Attitudes About Race and Science. In 1918, Ales Hrdlicka (1869–1943) founded the *American Journal of Physical Anthropology* at a

time when the **eugenics** movement and European-style racial anthropology competed for relevancy in academic journals. It was a landmark because it was the first time "the science of race" was part of mainstream anthropology, whereas previously the nineteenth-century **polygenist** American school had been predominant. Additionally, and equally important, during the First World War (1914–1918) the American Anthropology Association was dominated by Franz Boas (1858–1942), and later his students also influenced the academy by challenging the predominant race concept that had existed in academia since the 1890s. Boas and associates were primarily interested at that time in Native American language, culture, and archaeology because the indigenous movement was also the preoccupation of Western Europe and some Caribbean nations.[25] However, tensions between physical anthropology and the so-called American anthropology pitted the former's European racial approach against the latter's more liberal application and commitment to progression.[26]

As things developed, the "Boasian" influence created a new category with the field: biological anthropology. Boas continuously challenged the concept of race, and at least in American anthropology, this was perpetuated after his death. Specifically, the field focused on the processes that underlay human variation from a biologically informed perspective. The challenge, however, was that in 1918, physical anthropology in the United States was in its infancy, and it took an anthropologist named Earnest A. Hooton (1887–1954) to steer it properly with category-specific training in a PhD program at Harvard in 1925. In time,

---

24 Jean Halley, Amy Eshelman, and Ramya Mahadevan Vijaya, *Seeing White: An Introduction to White Privilege and Race* (Lanham, MD: Rowman & Littlefield, 2011), 2–4.

25 Bettina Arnold, "'*Arierdämmerung*' Race and Archaeology in Nazi Germany." *World Archaeology* 38 (March 2006): 12–14.

26 Rachel Caspari, "1918: Three Perspectives on Race and Human Variation." *American Journal of Physical Anthropology* 139 (February 2009): 5; Amos Morris-Reich, "Project, Method, and the Racial Characteristics of Jews: A Comparison of Franz Boas and Hans F. K. Günther." *Jewish Social Studies: History, Culture, Society, n.s.* 13, no. 1 (Fall 2006): 138–140.

Hooton's twenty-eight students spread his influence to other institutions across the country.[27]

Originally, the "new science" that physical anthropology was anticipated the institution of standardized procedures as well as the gradual development of regular instruction in the field. Additionally, this new, peer-reviewed approach would find a vehicle for publication and distribution though the *American Journal of Physical Anthropology*. The first areas of interest centered on Native Americans and Eskimos, but the strong influences of the polygenist European school of thought took time to fully identify and refute.[28]

Polygenists, Primivitism, and Eugenics. During Hrdlicka's tenure, race was fundamental to the new discipline, especially how it was applied when studying Native Americans. Because of the dominant European influences, as well as existing studies on polygenism that "explained" how the US and the New World were originally peopled, race factored into early discussions. Using the Morton method of data collection, the main focus of physical anthropology before 1918 was based on racial description (phenotypic variety) like everywhere else at that time.[29]

Other issues of the day played a role too. Because scholarly focus centered on a "more primitive" human race and its presumed subdivisions, it revealed much European influence, although a certain level of professionalism was devised. Another hot topic after the First World War was the outcome(s) of **miscegenation**, especially between blacks and whites and whites and Indians (Native Americans). Additionally, with social changes due to immigration resuming after being placed on hold during the war years, a drive to institute immigration quotas was at the forefront of sociopolitical discourse. Hrdlicka, in particular, was concerned with the possible negative effects of European immigration on American

society. Further, immigrants from "non-white" countries were even more discriminated against, as the assumption was that they carried diseases and were less desirable physically and intellectually to assimilate into society. In short, **eugenics** was not the only preoccupation of the era, the *zeitgeist* (world spirit); it also applied to how physical anthropologists informed the premises of their studies.[30]

While the other preoccupations of the day raged in political and academic circles, Hooton, conversely, was interested in craniometric and other measurements when studying humans. For instance, he believed that the Eskimos showed physical characteristics that were not "racial," but rather, *functional*, because two different "races" that adapted to similar sub-arctic environments shared them. This set off a wave of international comparisons to determine if the variations found in Eskimos was attributable to nonmetric similarities in Icelanders, possibly because of the frequency of interbreeding, it was hypothesized.[31]

Hooton's conclusion, therefore, assumed that race mixture was possible between Eskimos and Icelanders (who were considered Nordic or Aryan in Europe), and "it was more probable that the similarities were shared physiological responses due to their 'fish and flesh' diet and the habitual chewing of very tough food." Ultimately, Hooton's use of the word race was not focused or consistent, but he felt that races could occur at any level in a sub-specific hierarchical classification; this revealed continuity with the overt racism infiltrating science by the late nineteenth century.[32]

By emphasizing that traits could be measured, Hooton and others in this period felt a "correlation" between the traits could be established if a percentage of the samples displayed certain combinations

27 Caspari, "1918: Three Perspectives on Race and Human Variation," 5–6; Morris-Reich, "Project, Method, and the Racial Characteristics of Jews," 138–140, 143–145.
28 Caspari, "1918: Three Perspectives on Race and Human Variation," 6.
29 Caspari, "1918: Three Perspectives on Race and Human Variation," 6; Arnold, "'*Arierdämmerung*' Race and Archaeology in Nazi Germany," 8–10.

30 Caspari, "1918: Three Perspectives on Race and Human Variation," 8; Joseph Nevins, *Operation Gatekeeper and Beyond: The War on "Illegals" and the Remaking of the U.S.-Mexico Boundary*, (New York, NY: Routledge, 2010): 34-37.
31 Caspari, "1918: Three Perspectives on Race and Human Variation," 9.
32 Ibid.

of features. However, his methodology did not include a biometric approach to correlation, nor did he address why or what the significance of correlation was. Therefore, Hooton's approach to inquiry was *inductive* because he concluded that features were functional because they were not racially based. For Hooton, racial features were phylogenetic, not just inherited traits. In essence, traits shared by Eskimos and Icelanders were **heritable**, but *not* inherited from a common ancestor. Thus, they were homoplasies, not homologies; hence, they were not racial. In essence, the "evolutionary polygenist" perspective of the day postulated that race could be explained by divergence from a very early common ancestor. From this perspective came Hooton's phylogenetic classification of race, and a polygenist viewpoint that "once pure" races had separate evolutionary histories. Nevertheless, a limitation to this point of view was a very limited understanding of the importance of human variation. Essentially, this process left far more questions unanswered than science could answer.[33]

Franz Boas and the Boasians

Where Franz Boas made a mark is how he departed from his predecessors' ways of thinking. Unlike Hrdlicka and Hooton, Boas focused on variability, both within and between European types. In particular, he studied the distribution of traits in twenty-five Swedish provinces. Using maps to trace perceived variables, such as conspicuous obstacles, Boas illustrated gradual changes in traits, but this method also demonstrated sharp distinctions in both features and variability. Unable to reach full concordance in explaining the irregularity of the distribution of traits, he realized that maybe the *cause* of the variability in different regions was an important area for further inquiry.[34]

It was this last consideration that inspired Boas to critique the long-standing idea of discrete or fixed racial types. A major contribution of the so-called Boasian school of thought was the introduction of more scientifically sound methods, including empirical research, cross-sectional and longitudinal studies, and focusing on human variation in non-racial ways. Boas, ultimately, was more interested in explaining the impact of the environment (including culture) on biology, which included learned behaviors, rather than the effect of biology (race) on culture. This new philosophy is known today as **cultural determinism**.[35]

One of the conclusions Boas reached in his book *Mind of Primitive Man* (1911) is that "differences between different types of man are, on the whole, small as compared to the range of variation within each type." In retrospect, Boas challenged both **biological determinism** and the validity of discrete types, thereby shifting the direction of American anthropology away from the influences of European scientific racism after 1918.[36]

Ruth Benedict and the First Discussions About Racism in the US

Among other notable students of Franz Boas, Ruth Benedict (1887–1948), made her impact in anthropology when she wrote two influential books, including *Patterns of Culture* (1934 & 1952) and the *Chrysanthemum and the Sword* (1946). Lesser known, however, was her second book *Race: Science and Politics* (1940), which marked the shift in American society to focus on race and racism. While her work bore the imprint of racial distinctions through the construction of biological race under the tripartite Caucasoid, Mongoloid, and Negroid, it still addressed many existing contradictions within American notions of egalitarianism and assimilation. Additionally, Benedict looked at "American exceptionalism" through an approach that traced a *cultural history* of racism. Her legacy is not without some bleak moments, though, as her work for the government during the Second World War (1939–1945) showed. Further, she was still in the pitfalls of folk

---

33 Ibid.
34 Caspari, "1918: Three Perspectives on Race and Human Variation," 10; Morris-Reich, "Project, Method, and the Racial Characteristics of Jews," 144–146.

35 Caspari, "1918: Three Perspectives on Race and Human Variation," 11; Alexander Alland, Jr., *Race in Mind: Race, IQ, and Other Racisms* (New York, NY: Palgrave, 2002): 160.
36 Caspari, "1918: Three Perspectives on Race and Human Variation," 11; Alland, "*Race in Mind*," 160.

science by using religion to mask racism when coauthoring a wartime pamphlet called *The Races of Mankind* (1943), which instructed US troops on the essential oneness of human kind.[37]

Regardless of an imperfect method early on, where the Boasian influence challenged scientific racism and biological determinism (social Darwinism) was the claim that significant differences between humans derived from cultural factors exclusively. Therefore, Benedict utilized a constructionalist perspective regarding racism in the United States that pointed to a historic pattern of oppression, along with a discussion on racial conflict using cultural tools. In particular, she and fellow Boasians criticized the discriminatory race concept and all of its labels. Although the term *racism* existed in the nineteenth century, it was not commonly known in the 1930s. While Benedict affirmed that distinct races existed, she adhered adamantly to the belief that claims of superiority by some races had no validity.[38]

In her book on race, Benedict offered this definition of racism: it was a product of modernity, a "modern superstition" that did not fully develop until the twentieth century (Nazism come to mind here). Further, her "natural history" is less definable as a series of processes than as a genealogical account that identifies multiple overlapping points of origin. Even if present-day anthropologists disown this aspect of her philosophy, which was indicative of the late 1930s, they sometimes approve of Benedict's attempt to explain how racism developed through analysis of a particular group's philosophy, belief(s), dogma, and any hierarchies based on biological differences. Finally, Benedict's contribution to antiracism was to challenge notions of "other" groups being inferior and attempts to "prove" their inferiority by using spurious claims and false science.[39]

How Race is Defined Politically, Socially, and Academically

Discarding Race and Confronting Racism

One important issue in the conversation about race is that simply saying or denying the biological fallacy about differences between "races" is ineffective because all previous attempts to classify groups along phenotypical or cultural lines still sort them into **typological frameworks**. In turn, these frameworks often carry implicit notions of inferiority and superiority, but overturning two or more centuries of such beliefs *is* the root of the problem when confronting racism. Additionally, removing "scientific" concepts of race does not always separate science from folk taxonomies, and time has not been kind in keeping the two in separate lanes.[40]

Another valid question concerns itself with why anthropology rejects race as a valid scientific concept, yet concedes that racism is still an ongoing social problem globally. In other words, why has the discipline of anthropology sidestepped these concerns in the present? Shanklin provides the following scenario about an anthropologist at an undisclosed "major university" who tested students for racist ideas before and after teaching a course on race and racism. The results, according to this apocryphal tale, showed that the instructor was horrified because the students expressed even more racist beliefs that multiplied rather than diminished during the term. Despite careful explanations of the differences between human groups, the following possible interpretations were devised to explain the student learning outcomes (SLOs):

1. Students became aware of the scientific validity of "racial" differences.
2. Students felt more relaxed about admitting their prejudices.

37 Mark Anderson, "Ruth Benedict, Boasian Anthropology, and the Problem of the Colour Line." *History and Anthropology* 25 (September 2013): 395–397; Alland, "Race in Mind," 180–181.
38 Anderson, "Ruth Benedict, Boasian Anthropology," 398–400.
39 Ibid., 400–401.
40 Shanklin, *Anthropology and Race*, 98.

3. The instructor did a poor job of getting the anthropological message across.
4. Admitting the existence of physical differences between groups leads or allows people to assign their own, other people's, or their society's meaning to those differences, despite cautions to the contrary.
5. Teaching of anthropological viewpoints is dangerous because it feeds the fires of racist thinking.

This story circulated during the 1970s, when the first interpretation above was the perspective in vogue in academia. By the 1990s, the fourth interpretation may have been the most favored, possibly because "political correctness" allowed an extension that stipulated merely mentioning physical or other differences was taboo. Nonetheless, the exact meaning of the preceding anecdote is open to many speculations, but as Shanklin suggests, by discussing racist thinking, contemporary anthropology has not focused on the most important problem: Why do "humans so easily divide themselves into groups and then believe in or even fight for the existence of these groups?"[41]

The Power of Ethnocentrism. The conversation on race now turns to **ethnocentrism**, the belief that one's group or society is superior to all others, and what social scientists, not limited to anthropologists, know about this topic. Consider that a cultural myth (or three) surrounds each society's views of others on the outside, and vice versa. In this instance, *racism* can be understood as an extreme form of ethnocentrism, which also includes religious bigotry, cultural prejudice (and cultural racism), and class biases. All of these concepts are addressed in this book, but the challenge remains: In what ways can "people be socialized as group members without identifying targets to persecute?"[42]

The Many Definitions of Racism

Race is more of a sociocultural concept than a biological one because its usage follows social patterns significantly more than biological differences. Another way to express this is that a particular group of people may be assigned a racial category (racialization) regardless of their genetic traits. Consider the "One-Drop Rule" in its present context: children of mixed or biracial parents in the United States are considered "black" despite being equal to both parents genetically. This process led to a definition of racism posited by Nelson and Jurmain (1991), that "[r]acism is a cultural phenomenon that has no genetic basis[,] [and] [t]hat one race is mentally superior or inferior to another has yet to be demonstrated."[43]

Conversely, Bernard Campbell (1992) "defines racism as the belief in the superiority of one or more races over others." In this version, the word *superior* takes precedence. Nevertheless, a proposed cultural and linguistic solution is reaching parity between cultural and linguistic differences, and by dissolving those racial differences racism too will fade into insignificance.[44] Campbell's definition is not accepted, however, by most anthropologists, according to Shanklin, Why? Because some authors skirt the concept of race in preference for describing the human fossil record and evolutionary concerns instead. Additionally, some authors address race by defining it as "a group of populations sharing certain traits that make them distinct from other groups of populations. The concept of race," states Relthford (1990), "is difficult to apply to patterns of human variation."[45]

Shanklin's simple definition of racism "is the belief that humans are subdivided into distinct hereditary groups that are innately different in their social behavior and mental capacities and

---

41 Ibid., 98–100.
42 Ibid., 100.

43 Nelson and Jurmain (1991), quoted in Shanklin, *Anthropology and Race*, 100–101.
44 Bernard Campbell (1992), quoted in Shanklin, *Anthropology and Race*, 101.
45 Relthford (1990), quoted in Shanklin, *Anthropology and Race*, 101; for a discussion on how the academy has contributed to these views see Alland, Jr., *Race in Mind*, 7–12.

that can therefore be ranked as superior or inferior. The presumed superiority of some groups and inferiority of others is subsequently used to legitimize the unequal distribution of the society's resources, specifically, various forms of wealth, prestige, and power."[46] Another general definition is that "racism is a special kind of prejudice, directed against those who are thought to possess biologically or socially inherited characteristics that set them apart."[47]

As discussed in the Tatum excerpt elsewhere in this book, many people use the terms *prejudice* and *racism* interchangeably, but this is not an accurate application. Additionally, David Wellman (1977) defines racism as a "system of advantages based on race," and the relevant topic of white privilege addressed in this book will offer how this definition is but one aspect in tackling this difficult subject (see both Tatum and McIntosh for details). This definition is also useful in explaining the infrastructural racism that exists in many societies, and this includes culturally specific messages, beliefs (folk), and actions taken by individuals. The second most useful definition of racism does not depart from the first, but it does tie together the following relationship: power + prejudice = racism.[48]

What is clear from these samples is that some textbook authors are almost too casual in addressing race and racism, and at times they are negligent in their discussions of both topics. To gain an understanding of the issues that resurfaced in the 1990s, read the Alexander Alland, Jr. excerpt on "Race and IQ" in this book, as well as the first few pages of the introduction to the Adolf Hitler selection "Race and nation."

Racism's Many Forms in Cultural Context: A Cuban Case Study

Whitewashing Cuban History, 1895–1902

The Cuban Struggle for Independence: An Overview, 1868–1898

From the mid nineteenth century until its end, the push to liberate Cuba from Spanish sovereignty always came from the island's easternmost province, Oriente. Before the Ten Years' War (1868–1878) and La Guerra Chiquita, or Little War (1879), tensions built up as Spain's former colonies had largely become independent and abolished African slavery. Cuba, however, still operated in full swing with shiploads of slaves arriving well past the 1840s to offset the overwhelming world demand for sugar. Technological advances and mechanization of the process led to higher yields of sugar and staggeringly high profits in a strong market. In 1846 approximately thirty-six percent of Cuba's population lived enslaved, and free persons of color comprised an additional seventeen percent of the population. Lurking, however, in the shadows of the imagination of whites lay the fear of a successful black uprising on the scale of the Haitian Revolution. Ever vigilant, the planters built larger and larger sugar mills, known as *ingenios*, with watchtowers and cadres of professional slave hunters always at the ready. Despite the financial success of the planter class, an internal bias that favored the western side of the island where Havana lay created a rift in time because planters in the east and central provinces were limited in their access to slaves and political power. Disgruntled, many planters in Oriente freed and armed their slaves and launched a ten-year conflict on October 10, 1868, but Spain ultimately won, largely because it had no other enemies in the world to fight at that time.[49]

46 Marger (1995), quoted in Shanklin, *Anthropology and Race*, 105.
47 Ibid.
48 David Wellman (1977) quoted in Tatum, "*Why Are All the Black Kids Sitting Together in the Cafeteria?*" 7–8.

49 Ada Ferrer, *Insurgent Cuba: Race, Nation, and Revolution, 1868–1898*, (Chapel Hill, NC: University of North Carolina Press, 1999), 1–3; Paul Sweeney, "The Connectors of Two Worlds: Chano Pozo, Dizzy Gillespie, and the Continuity of

The abolition of slavery was among the many social issues after the conflicts, but Cuba also had a very large population of free persons of color, mixed blood (pardos), and growing numbers of indentured Chinese laborers who arrived as a transition from slavery to wage labor began even as the population of slaves reached epic heights as late as 1867. Discontented with this slow process, Cuba experienced a further indignity when Spain levied a high tax to pay for the two wars. Additionally, the surviving leaders of the rebellion were either in hiding or exile, including Maximo Gomez, José Martí, and Antonio Maceo, but toward the end of the nineteenth century a new drive for independence took form. Writing from afar about the equality and fraternity of all Cubans, regardless of their skin color, Martí returned to Cuba secretly, assembled the former leaders of the earlier wars of independence, and plotted the path to attain "Cuba Libre" (free Cuba) in 1895. Martí, however, did not see the defeat of Spain because he was cut down at the front in July 1896. With the spiritual leader of the movement dead, it fell upon Gomez and other leaders, including the mixed-race General Maceo to keep the dream and drive alive.[50]

Martí's philosophy "if you can die you can vote" informed the message even after death that everyone belonged in the struggle for independence and deserved a free Cuban government where the relationship between race and citizenship would never be held to scientific racism's hierarchical measures. Antonio Maceo in particular was a leading figure in the insurgent armed forces. He rose through the ranks after he joined the original resistance movement in 1868, and his role emphasized the profound effect that African slaves and their descendants had on the character of the rebels. Further, Maceo spoke frequently about antiracism, and the fraternal nature of the insurgency was the very model of the term *Cubanidad*, or what

it meant to be Cuban.[51] Nevertheless, one lesson that Maceo learned early in the 1895 war was that if he continued to speak about race, it would raise barriers against national unity during the struggle and after. After all, he stood accused of racism by some on his own side, who alleged that he favored and promoted black soldiers before whites in his army. Therefore, Maceo had to be more careful and censured what he said because one source of this allegation dogged him for almost thirty years. Part of this issue stemmed from his own experience of being unrewarded for his achievements because merit often led to obstacles centered on race matters and political power.[52]

Maceo, ever mindful of future political and social ramifications if he promoted too many black or mulatto officers, appointed a white Puerto Rican-born general to replace him when he advanced on Havana province in early 1897. Whatever he might have achieved was cut violently short when his forces were ambushed by Spanish troops. Both Maceo and Maximo Gomez's son were killed in action, and immediately conspiracy theories and rumors circulated about all aspects of his death, including betrayal. Maceo's body was saved from Spanish retribution, however, so threats of turning his beard into a broom never reached fruition. Regardless, even in safe hands his body would later suffer further indignities.[53]

Changes in the Curriculum at the University of Havana, 1898–1904

Cuba entered the United States' sphere of influence after Spain's defeat and subsequent expulsion in the War of 1898 (often called the Spanish-American War, to Cuba's dismay). In the aftermath, many changes occurred rapidly in Cuban society, at the political level as well as socially and racially. Even before the US got involved in Cuban affairs a shift was taking place that emphasized cultural

Myth Through Afro-Cuban Jazz." (Master's thesis, California State University, San Bernardino, 2005), Ch. 1 & 2.

50 Ferrer, *Insurgent Cuba*, 18; Aline Helg, *Our Rightful Share: The Afro-Cuban Struggle for Equality, 1886–1912*, (Chapel Hill, NC: University of North Carolina Press, 1995), 55–59, 88.

51 Helg, *Our Rightful Share*, 1–2.

52 Ferrer, *Insurgent Cuba*, 166–167.

53 Ferrer, *Insurgent Cuba*, 167–168; Alejandra Bronfman, *Measures of Equality: Social Science, Citizenship, and Race in Cuba, 1902–1940*, (Chapel Hill, NC: University of North Carolina Press, 2004), 1.

"whitening" through selective immigration, another manifestation of the eugenics movement. The preferred immigrants were often enticed with monetary privileges, and recruitment centered on the historic region of Andalusia in Spain. Further, racism toward black Cubans, hereafter referred to as Afro-Cubans, was rampant and escalating. Compounding their situation was the entrance of the North Americans who brought their racism and Jim Crow-style segregation that further distanced Afro-Cubans in the two-tier race model that characterized Cuba at that time. In effect, Afro-Cubans were persecuted along lines of their syncretic religious beliefs, such as *regla de ocha* (commonly known today as *santería*) and *palo*, as well as discriminatory laws and hiring practices.[54]

If the concept of race is a flexible category throughout time and place, and not a fixed biological classification, the latter consideration was the predominant belief by social elites. On the eve of the transformation from a Spanish colony to a fledgling republic under the ever-watchful eye of the Americans, change and reorganization also affected the University of Havana's Anthropology Department. Changes in academia were concurrent with pressure exerted by the occupying military government on elite white Cubans to both reassert their whiteness and claim membership in the "Latin race."[55] As discussed earlier, such racism was largely informed by social Darwinism, which utilized theories that survival of the fittest also fit societal classifications. Because the War of 1898 was considered a racial struggle between Anglo-Saxons and Latins (as well as the black and white struggle Spain claimed prior to the entrance of the US), the aftermath of the war involved a non-violent "civilizing invasion" by North Americans who demoted the social status of white Cubans unless they united with the "pure" white Spaniards who lived in Cuba. This created a dilemma in elite circles: Should they try to resist the US by demonstrating their whiteness, and therefore competency and civilization, or should they submit to the threat of indefinite occupation stipulated in the Platt Amendment (1904–1934)?[56]

Effectively faced with no choice, white Cubans and Spaniards reached an understanding, but in the eyes of the occupiers they could never be "white enough" to gain the full respect of the North Americans. One manifestation of this subtext was a joint undertaking between the US military government and Cuban scientists at the University of Havana. Together, although credit was unequal, they created a series of academic departments and appointed their chairs in late December 1899. In particular, anthropology was considered "unprofessional" under Spanish rule, so the new Americanized department supplemented the Museum of Anthropology in Havana. The sub-field of anthropology featured both North American and Cuban scientists who worked mutually on the presumption that biological and measureable differences existed amongst the races. To illustrate how rapidly change was effected, the definition of **anthropometry** was detailed in a period manual as "the systematized art of measuring and taking observations on man, his skeleton, his brain, or other organs." Additionally, the stated objective was "to ascertain whether and how its human stock is progressing or regressing." In Cuban society, this translated to *equality* being measured socially at the ballot box, in criminal cases, and museum displays.[57] In this regard, Cuban anthropology continued the inherent biases exhibited by the French founder of anthropometry, Paul Broca, who assumed that human races (and gender) could be ranked biologically, and in a linear scale along lines of intelligence.[58]

Eugenics and Immigration. Selective immigration, much as it was practiced in North America and other Latin American nations was

---

54 Louis A. Pérez, Jr., *The War of 1898: The United States and Cuba in History and Historiography*, (Chapel Hill, NC: University of North Carolina Press, 1998), xii–xiii; Bronfman, *Measures of Equality*, 1; Helg, *Our Rightful Share*, 131–132; Ferrer, *Insurgent Cuba*, 196–200; Sweeney, "The Connectors of Two Worlds."
55 Bronfman, *Measures of Equality*, 5–7.
56 Helg, *Our Rightful Share*, 104; Louis A. Pérez, Jr., *Cuba Under the Platt Amendment, 1902–1934*, (Pittsburgh, PA: University of Pittsburgh Press, 1986), xv–xvii.
57 Bronfman, *Measures of Equality*, 5–7.
58 Gould, *Mismeasure of Man*, 118–119.

one avenue elites and political figures in those societies took to "improve the race," and this tactic was advocated early on by the Cuban anthropologist Fernando Ortíz. The premise was that only North Europeans, especially Germans, would "sow among us the germs of energy, progress, [and] life." Any other groups, or races, he believed, would only increase criminality and degenerate behavior in Cuba. Therefore, by asserting Cuban Latin heritage against the Anglo-Saxons, it also heightened how some sectors of the white population perceived Afro-Cubans, who were ranked low socially. This situation undoubtedly led to the internalization of racism amongst some mixed-bloods, because "true Cubans" originated from Spain, and were therefore "white." Moreover, pushed by this shift in perspective to the margins of society, Afro-Cubans were viewed as a type of "bastard" race, partly African and partly Cuban. Thus, in the standpoint of European scientific racism, they were doomed to decrease, and possibly vanish in time because their original purity had regressed by miscegenation.[59] It was this last consideration that prompted the three anthropologists from the recently reorganized department at the University of Havana to exhume and examine Antonio Maceo's remains.

How Anthropometry "Determined" the "Race" of General Maceo, 1900–1902

In 1900, a national commission initiated a study to examine Maceo's remains at the university using the new departmental methodology as a measure, and they were eager to demonstrate to the occupying Americans that they were competent and professional. The entire premise was symptomatic of the Cuban elites' state of mind as they hoped for self-determination in the post-war period. The conflict, however, centered on the ancestry (race) of Cuba's most successful and popular war hero, General Maceo, and it stemmed from the rigid racial theories about miscegenation and hierarchical ranking's inability to rectify the fact

of Maceo's existence as a non-white, but brilliant military thinker. Clearly liberties took place in the methodology when the scientists finally published a report of their findings after a two-years study. Informed by implications of racial differences, they also pondered how Maceo "fit" essentially fixed ideology. Affecting their bias prior to the inquiry, though, was the empiricist and positivist desire to place him culturally and historically in the hierarchical sense where a Cuban hero was idealized to be: at the top.[60]

The "available" racial categories at this time (most scientists still envisioned Blumenbach's five-race model, but some also leaned toward Gobineau's tripartite model), ruled out all but white and black, which contrasted two extremes such measurements would conform to: civilization and savagery. Maceo's skull was placed in the former camp by the use of craniometrics and anthropometry-specific methods. The published study was entitled *El craneo de Maceo: Estudio antropológico* (*Maceo's Skull: An Anthropological Study*). In it, the authors concluded the following: Maceo's "white" heritage kept his blackness subordinated based on his skull and *probable* brain measurements (because it was decomposed already).[61] Further, what made Maceo a Cuban hero was that his "white" brain gave precedence to his battlefield savvy, and when combined with the strength of the "black" limb proportions, it gave him the strength and fortitude indicative of a "truly superior man." In this manner, Antonio Maceo and Cuban history were whitewashed simultaneously by shoddy science.

Additionally, the liberal alteration of factual reality was also on display in these findings because the study concluded that Maceo "... approached more the white race, he matched it, [and] he even surpassed it in the general confirmation of his head, the probable weight of his brain, [and] his skull capacity." Common at this time was a tendency to downplay or even ignore African ancestry in a family or society, and in Cuba, Puerto Rico,

---

59   Helg, *Our Rightful Share*, 104; Gould, *Mismeasure of Man*, 383.

60   Bronfman, *Measures of Equality*, 1–2; Helg, *Our Rightful Share*, 104–105.

61   Helg, *Our Rightful Share*, 104–105; Bronfman, *Measures of Equality*, 1; Ferrer, *Insurgent Cuba*, 168.

Mexico, and elsewhere in Latin America, it was the norm by 1900. However, this notable omission of Maceo's blackness was necessary to conclude that his superiority was on account of his whiteness. If Maceo's "whitening" scientifically typified the early republic years, Cuba's first national opera *Yumuri* was inspired by aboriginal themes and Italian music that promoted impossible origins and the *haute* culture of Europe. Like Europe, Cuba, Puerto Rico, and the Dominican Republic preferred to diminish blackness in favor of a Taino-Arawak indigenous lineage that was next to impossible to find amongst any Caribbean population.[62]

One motivation to "scientifically" alter the social reality that Maceo represented centered on reassuring the Americans that Cuba was civilized and its people *were capable* of self-rule.[63] The problem with this conclusion, however, was that the early photographs and artwork that depicted Maceo clearly indicated he was a black man phenotypically-speaking. Ultimately, in the days before Photoshop, whitening campaigns worked hard to affect the racial composition of Cuba and "improve the race" by encouraging more light-skinned babies. Maceo too was whitened culturally: by an artist's brush. Depending on where in Cuba, Maceo's image could range from dark to light brown, or even as white as a Spaniard. Therefore, the preoccupation with race and social order was rampant in the first twenty years of the Cuban republic, and racial tensions came to a violent conclusion via a coordinated attack staged by the Cuban military in Oriente in 1912. The attack eliminated the only black political party, and thereby limited black political power and representation in what was supposed to be a democratic government. Political relevancy for Afro-Cubans then was stifled indefinitely. Furthermore, after the 1912 massacre, Afro-Cubans experienced alternate periods of repression and backhanded praise for their "folkloric" contributions to *Cubanidad* (what it means to be Cuban). Until the 1959 Fidel Castro-led Social Revolution, the status of black Cubans was precarious. Despite its

claims, though, the Cuban Revolution's ideology did not end the legacy of racism on the island. After all, deep-seated matters such as racism are not so easily erased.

Strategies to Confront Racism

A Classroom Divided: The Elliott Eye Color Experiment, 1968

In the wake of the landmark Civil Rights Act (1964), Jim Crow segregation in the South was unconstitutional and collapsed, but its demise did not end discrimination or racism on the black-white color line in the United States. Then, the turbulent 1960s bore witness to the escalating Vietnam War and political assassinations, including President Kennedy (1963), his brother Robert (1968), Malcolm X (1965), and Dr. Martin Luther King, Jr. (1968). Perhaps motivated by these current events, Jane Elliott, a schoolteacher, devised an experiment that she conducted with her third grade class. The average age of the students was eight years old, and one of the questions she wanted to answer was if at this age children would demonstrate discriminatory behavior if empowered and told they were superior.[64]

Prosecuted over several years, the experiment was deceptively simple. Elliott divided her classes by eye color, blue or brown. On one day, the blue-eyed children were assigned the inferior role, but the situation was reversed the following day, when the brown-eyed kids were demoted. Other prompts Elliott gave to influence each group the day they were in the superior mode included assurances that they were more civilized and smarter than the "inferior" kids. Ultimately, the results horrified Elliott because when empowered the children *immediately* adopted the position of superiority, and they were equally adept at leveling abuse and disdain toward the children in the inferior role. When summarizing her observations, one of Elliott's reflections was "... there must be a way to keep children from growing up

---

62   Helg, *Our Rightful Share*, 105; Arnold, "'*Arierdämmerung*' Race and Archaeology in Nazi Germany," 11–14.

63   Ferrer, *Insurgent Cuba*, 168.

64   Shanklin, *Anthropology and Race*, 107.

into the kind of adult so many of us are, a way less drastic, less painful than this."[65]

Unfortunately, Elliott's and related experiments by others confirmed her alarming conclusions. By eight years old, children are fully capable of assuming "the role of a racial superior or inferior, no matter how whimsical the criterion for judgment [is] …"[66] Nevertheless, it is clear that children absorb their parents' and society's attitudes about racism, and teaching them not to discriminate or engage in racist activities is but one approach researchers advocate. For more reflection on this topic, a closely related variable is *internalized racism*. See the Tatum selection "Can We Talk?" located elsewhere in this book for more about this aspect.

On Solving Racism as Advocated by Ruth Benedict

When it came to solving racism in America, Ruth Benedict argued that like religion, it can only be understood along historic lines, especially as it exposes the product of culture. In essence, racism must be treated as a belief system because racism too has its slogans, stereotypical jokes, and justification for persecution. Benedict also summarized two principle reasons that racism exists: First, racism bears the stamp of scientific authority, informed by biased and often unchallenged legitimacy; and secondly, racial dogmas nearly always lean toward racial "purity" and how best to defend it, often at the expense of ethnic groups deemed "dirty" or "mongrelized." Further, her recommendation centered on looking beyond "race" to isolate the causes of underlying oppression, similar to an iceberg model, and investigate why persecution even exists. Inevitably, political considerations are intertwined with nationalistic rivalries, white privilege, poverty, unemployment, and even war.[67] Benedict's ultimate aim, prior to her death in 1948, was "[t]o minimize racial persecution … [by] … minimi[zing] conditions which lead to persecution[;] it is not necessary to minimize race."[68] While a biological approach to explaining race is almost never mentioned by anthropology today, Benedict's approach to explaining cultural specifics and histories that yield racism, persecution, or discrimination toward one group or another informs the interdisciplinary approach utilized in the writing and assembling of readings contained within this book.

Bibliography

Alland, Jr., Alexander. *Race in Mind: Race, IQ, and Other Racisms.* New York, NY: Palgrave, 2002.

Anderson, Mark. "Ruth Benedict, Boasian Anthropology, and the Problem of the Colour Line." *History and Anthropology* 25 [September 2013]: 395–414.

Andreasen, Robin O. "Race: Biological Reality or Social Construct?" *Philosophy of Science* 67 [2000]: S653–S666.

Arnold, Bettina. "'Arierdämmerung' Race and Archaeology in Nazi Germany." *World Archaeology* 38 [March 2006]: 8–31.

Banton, Michael. "The Naming of Social Categories." *Theoria* 60 [September 2013]: 1–14.

Bronfman, Alejandra. *Measures of Equality: Social Science, Citizenship, and Race in Cuba, 1902–1940.* Chapel Hill, NC: University of North Carolina Press, 2004.

Caspari, Rachael. "1918: Three Perspectives on Race and Human Variation." *American Journal of Physical Anthropology* 139 [February 2009]: 5–15.

Cho, Helen. "Lessons Learned: Teaching the Race Concept in the College Classroom." *Multicultural Perspectives* 13 [2011]: 36–41.

Constantine, Madonna G. and Derald Wing Sue, eds. *Addressing Racism: Facilitating Cultural Competence in Mental Health and Educational Settings.* Hoboken, NJ: Wiley, 2006.

Ferrer, Ada. *Insurgent Cuba: Race, Nation, and Revolution, 1868–1898.* Chapel Hill, NC: University of North Carolina Press, 1999.

---

65 Elliott, quoted in Shanklin, *Anthropology and Race*, 107–108.
66 Ibid., 108.
67 Anderson, "Ruth Benedict, Boasian Anthropology," 402.

---

68 Benedict quoted in Shanklin, *Anthropology and Race*, 102.

Gould, Stephen Jay. *The Mismeasure of Man, Revised and Expanded Edition.* New York, NY: W.W. Norton, 1996.

Halley, Jean, Amy Eshelman, and Ramya Mahadevan Vijaya. *Seeing White: An Introduction to White Privilege and Race.* Lanham, MD: Rowman & Littlefield, 2011.

Helg, Aline. *Our Rightful Share: The Afro-Cuban Struggle for Equality, 1886–1912.* Chapel Hill, NC: University of North Carolina Press, 1995.

Jordan, Winthrop D. *White Over Black: American Attitudes Toward the Negro, 1550–1812.* Chapel Hill, NC: University of North Carolina Press, 1968.

Morris-Reich, Amos. "Project, Method, and the Racial Characteristics of Jews: A Comparison of Franz Boas and Hans F.K. Günther." *Jewish Social Studies: History, Culture, Society, n.s.* 13, no. 1 [Fall 2006]: 136–169.

Mukhopadhyay, Carol C., Rosemary Henze, and Yolanda T. Moses. *How Real Is Race? A Sourcebook on Race, Culture, and Biology, Second Edition.* Lanham, MD: Rowman & Littlefield, 2014.

Nevins, Joseph. *Operation Gatekeeper and Beyond: The War on "Illegals" and the Remaking of the U.S.-Mexico Boundary.* New York, NY: Routledge, 2010.

Ousley, Stephen, Richard Jantz, and Donna Freid. "Understanding Race and Human Variation: Why Forensic Anthropologists are Good at Identifying Race," *American Journal of Physical Anthropology* 139, [February 2009]: 68–76.

Pérez, Jr., Louis A. *Cuba Under the Platt Amendment, 1902–1934.* Pittsburgh, PA: University of Pittsburgh Press, 1986.

Pérez, Jr., Louis A. *The War of 1898: The United States and Cuba in History and Historiography.* Chapel Hill: University of North Carolina Press, 1998.

Relethford, John H. "Race and Global Patterns of Phenotypic Variation." *American Journal of Physical Anthropology* 139 [February 2009]: 16–22.

Shanklin, Eugenia. *Anthropology & Race.* Belmont, CA: Wadsworth, 1994.

Sweeney, Paul. "The Connectors of Two Worlds: Chano Pozo, Dizzy Gillespie, and the Continuity of Myth Through Afro-Cuban Jazz." Master's thesis, California State University, San Bernardino, 2005.

Tatum, Beverly Daniel. *"Why Are All the Black Kids Sitting Together in the Cafeteria?" and Other Conversations About Race.* 1997. Reprint, New York, NY: Basic Books, 2003.

Webster, Yehudi O. *Racialization of America.* 1992. Reprint, New York, NY: St. Martin's Press, 1993.

Glossary of Terms

Anthropometry: The study of human body measurements, especially in a comparative manner.

Biological determinism: An interpretation of humanity that posits each human behavior, belief, and desire is a fixed genetic trait.

Clinal variation: A derivative of the biological term cline, it refers to a continuous, gradual variation of a trait.

Cognitive dissonance: The psychology term to explain feelings of guilt or stress caused when existing paradigms or concepts are in conflict with others that contradict previously held beliefs.

Constructivist: A theoretical style based on the premise that human experience creates active learning in any environment where the learner is a constructor.

Craniometric variation: A fascination of anthropologists when comparing species and human variation.

Craniometrics: Also called craniometry, it is a method to measure cranial capacity and the size of the skull, especially in relation to comparing "races" in nineteenth and twentieth-century scientific racism.

Cultural determinism: A belief that the culture people are raised in determines what the society becomes in terms of emotional and behavioral levels.

Ethnocentrism: A heightened form of discrimination that assumes one's culture or society is superior to others.

Eugenics: A social movement that assumed Darwin's natural selection would apply if populations discouraged miscegenation and selectively bred to "improve the race."

Folk taxonomy: The human habit of classification that is characteristic of any given society.

Genealogical explanation: Essentially a record or account of family or group ancestry and lineage.

Geographic race concept: Looking at race from a continental origins perspective and along hierarchical lines of classification.

Heritable: A gene or trait capable of being inherited or of passing by inheritance.

Human variation: The genetic differences both within and among populations, with multiple variations possible as evidence of adaptability and clinal variation.

Institutionalized racism: The social and legal structures relative to a given society that clearly favor a particular group, thereby creating a system of advantages based on race.

Miscegenation: The mixing of "races," especially between whites and non-whites through marriage or sexual intercourse.

Monogenist: Theorizes that humans descended from a single pair of people, Adam and Eve, for example, and this informs a single ancestral type.

Natural selection: The Darwinian term for survival of the species based on the premise that strong species will reproduce and weaker species will die off, also known as survival of the fittest.

One-Drop Rule: The seventeenth-century policy in US cultural history that stipulates even one drop of black blood makes a person black.

Phenetic classifications: Groups organisms together by overall similarity, not by evolution.

Phenotype: Observable physical traits or characteristics in humans.

Phenotypic traits: A distinct variation of any organism that may be inherited.

Polygenist: The theory of human origins that posits multiple human races have different origins (polygenesis), and it is the opposite of monogeny.

Phylogenetic classifications: An orderly arrangement of organisms (as taxa) or objects in a hierarchical series.

Racialization: a mode of racial classification created via a social process that creates for those in power a privileged status.

Social Darwinism: Based on survival of the fittest, but when applied to racial theory, it is biased toward "pure" races being dominant and progressive while inferior groups are regressive.

Taxa: A biological term that is the plural of taxon (L.), used for classification, or taxonomy.

Typological frameworks: A form of classification using linguistic theory to create a meaning in a given society, but when applied to racial classifications it is a fallacy.

White privilege: In Western nations, historic events interacted to create a system of advantages based on race, and the system always placed whites at the top of the hierarchy.

For Discussion

1. "Improve the race" or "improving the race"— what implications do these expressions reflect when taking the scope of this chapter into consideration?
2. From Shanklin's subsection, speculate on how "can people be socialized as group members without identifying targets to persecute"? What strategies would you suggest?
3. What did Franz Boas change that made scientific inquiry more responsible and distanced it from racist European physical anthropology methods?
4. What are some reasons given by Relethford in the text as to why even if geographic patterning is evident, this still cannot "prove" that multiple races exists?
5. In what ways can you list manifestations of *ethnocentricism* in American society? Does the notion of "American exceptionalism" fit this description?
6. In what ways does race become associated with politics? How does racialization work to further this notion?

Activity

Helen Cho (2011) advocates this exercise in her classrooms: "How do you determine race?" and "Based on your definition, what are the human races?" Make a list, but explain your criteria first (pp. 36–37).

Outcomes: Students should realize how many inconsistencies there are when defining what race and human variation are, and how these inconsistencies prevent the list from being anything but taxonomical. Are "Muslims" an ethnic group? How about the census term "Hispanic"? Be sure to discuss your findings with peers and identify the fallacies that surround biological classification of humans.

Image Credits

2

Can We Talk? Discussions on Racism and White Privilege

Defining Racism

"Can We Talk?"

By Beverly Daniel Tatum

● ●

Editor's Introduction

Just as the other selections in this anthology deal with specific issues and broader terms, Beverly Tatum asserts that racism "[is] a system of privileges based on race."[1] This excerpt should be read closely and compared with the Peggy McIntosh article on white privilege. The concepts of color-blind society also arise, and thus, another good match for Eduardo Bonilla-Silva's discourse on racism without racists.

One of Tatum's goals is to open the discussion on race and make it clear that racism is alive and well in American society. However, once awareness is reached, as well as recognition, change can begin, albeit slowly.

Notes

Tatum, Beverly Daniel. *"Why Are All the Black Kids Sitting Together in the Cafeteria?" And Other Conversations About Race.* New York: Basic Books, 2003, 7.

Early in my teaching career, a White student I knew asked me what I would be teaching the following semester. I mentioned that I would be teaching a course on racism. She replied, with some surprise in her voice, "Oh, is there still racism?" I assured her that indeed there was and suggested that she sign up for my course. Fifteen years later, after exhaustive media coverage of events such as the Rodney King beating, the Charles Stuart and Susan Smith cases, the O. J. Simpson trial, the appeal to racial prejudices in electoral politics, and the bitter debates about affirmative action and welfare reform, it seems hard to imagine that anyone would still be unaware of the reality of racism in our society. But in fact, in almost every audience I address, there is someone who will suggest that racism is a thing of the past. There is always someone who hasn't noticed the stereotypical images of people of color in the media, who hasn't observed the housing discrimination in their community, who hasn't read the newspaper articles about documented racial bias in lending practices among well-known banks, who isn't aware of the racial tracking pattern at the local school, who hasn't seen the reports of rising incidents of racially motivated hate crimes in America—in short, someone who hasn't been paying attention to issues of race. But if you are paying attention, the legacy of racism is not hard to see, and we are all affected by it.

The impact of racism begins early. Even in our preschool years, we are exposed to misinformation about people different from ourselves. Many of us grew up in neighborhoods where we had limited opportunities to interact with people different from our own families. When I ask my college students, "How many of you grew up in neighborhoods where most of the people were from the same racial group as your own?" almost every hand goes up. There is still a great deal of social segregation in our communities. Consequently, most of the early information we receive about "others"—people racially, religiously, or socio-economically different from ourselves—does not come as the result of firsthand experience. The secondhand information we do receive has often been distorted, shaped by cultural stereotypes, and left incomplete.

Some examples will highlight this process. Several years ago one of my students conducted a research project investigating preschoolers' conceptions of Native Americans. Using children at a local day care center as her participants, she asked these three- and four-year-olds to draw a picture of a Native American. Most children were stumped by her request. They didn't know what a Native American was. But when she rephrased the question and asked them to draw a picture of an Indian, they readily complied. Almost every picture included one central feature: feathers. In fact, many of them also included a weapon—a knife or tomahawk—and depicted the person in violent or aggressive terms. Though this group of children, almost all of whom were White, did not live near a large Native American population and probably had had little if any personal interaction with American Indians, they all had internalized an image of what Indians were like. How did they know? Cartoon images, in particular the Disney movie *Peter Pan* were cited by the children as

their number-one source of information. At the age of three, these children already had a set of stereotypes in place. Though I would not describe three-year-olds as prejudiced, the stereotypes to which they have been exposed become the foundation for the adult prejudices so many of us have.

Sometimes the assumptions we make about others come not from what we have been told or what we have seen on television or in books, but rather from what we have *not* been told. The distortion of historical information about people of color leads young people (and older people, too) to make assumptions that may go unchallenged for a long time. Consider this conversation between two White students following a discussion about the cultural transmission of racism:

"Yeah, I just found out that Cleopatra was actually a Black woman."

"What?"

The first student went on to explain her newly learned information. The second student exclaimed in disbelief, "That can't be true. Cleopatra was beautiful!"

What had this young woman learned about who in our society is considered beautiful and who is not? Had she conjured up images of Elizabeth Taylor when she thought of Cleopatra? The new information her classmate had shared and her own deeply ingrained assumptions about who is beautiful and who is not were too incongruous to allow her to assimilate the information at that moment.

Omitted information can have similar effects. For example, another young woman, preparing to be a high school English teacher, expressed her dismay that she had never learned about any Black authors in any of her English courses. How was she to teach about them to her future students when she hadn't learned about them herself? A White male student in the class responded to this discussion with frustration in his response journal, writing "Its not my fault that Blacks don't write books" Had one of his elementary, high school, or college teachers ever told him that there were no Black writers? Probably not. Yet because he had never been exposed to Black authors, he had drawn his own conclusion that there were none.

Stereotypes, omissions, and distortions all contribute to the development of prejudice. *Prejudice* is a preconceived judgment or opinion, usually based on limited information. I assume that we all have prejudices, not because we want them, but simply because we are so continually exposed to misinformation about others. Though I have often heard students or workshop participants describe someone as not having "a prejudiced bone in his body," I usually suggest that they look again. Prejudice is one of the inescapable consequences of living in a racist society. Cultural racism—the cultural images and messages that affirm the assumed superiority of Whites and the assumed inferiority of people of color—is like among in the air. Sometimes it is so thick it is visible, other times it is less apparent, but always, day in and day out, we are breathing it in. None of us would introduce ourselves as "smog-breathers" (and most of us don't want to be described as prejudiced), but if we live in a smoggy place, how can we avoid breathing the air? If we live in an environment in which we are bombarded with stereotypical images in the media, are frequently exposed to the ethnic jokes of friends and family members, and are rarely informed of the accomplishments of oppressed groups, we will develop the negative categorizations of those groups that form the basis of prejudice.

People of color as well as Whites develop these categorizations. Even a member of the stereotyped group may internalize the stereotypical categories about his or her own group to some degree. In fact, this process happens so frequently that it has a name, *internalized oppression.* [...]

Certainly some people are more prejudiced than others, actively embracing and perpetuating negative and hateful images of those who are different from themselves. When we claim to be free of prejudice, perhaps what we are really saying is that we are not hate-mongers. But none of us is completely innocent. Prejudice is an integral part of our socialization, and it is not our fault. Just as the preschoolers my student interviewed are not to blame for the negative messages they internalized, we are not at fault for the stereotypes, distortions, and omissions that shaped our thinking as we grew up.

To say that it is not our fault does not relieve us of responsibility, however. We may not have polluted the air, but we need to take responsibility, along with others, for cleaning it up. Each of us needs to look at our own behavior. Am I perpetuating and reinforcing the negative messages so pervasive in our culture, or am I seeking to challenge them? If I have not been exposed to positive images of marginalized groups, am I seeking them out, expanding my own knowledge base for myself and my children? Am I acknowledging and examining my own prejudices, my own rigid categorizations of others, thereby minimizing the adverse impact they might have on my interactions with those I have categorized? Unless we engage in these and other conscious acts of reflection and reeducation, we easily repeat the process with our children. We teach what we were taught. The unexamined prejudices of the parents are passed on to the children. It is not our fault, but it is our responsibility to interrupt this cycle.

Racism: A System of Advantage Based on Race

Many people use the terms *prejudice* and *racism* interchangeably. I do not, and I think it is important to make a distinction. In his book *Portraits of White Racism,* David Wellman argues convincingly that limiting our understanding of racism to prejudice does not offer a sufficient explanation for the persistence of racism. He defines racism as a "system of advantage based on race." In illustrating this definition, he provides example after example of how Whites defend their racial advantage—access to better schools, housing, jobs—even when they do not embrace overtly prejudicial thinking. Racism cannot be fully explained as an expression of prejudice alone.

This definition of racism is useful because it allows us to see that racism, like other forms of oppression, is not only a personal ideology based on racial prejudice, but a *system* involving cultural messages and institutional policies and practices as well as the beliefs and actions of individuals.

In the context of the United States, this system clearly operates to the advantage of Whites and to the disadvantage of people of color. Another related definition of racism, commonly used by antiracist educators and consultants, is "prejudice plus power." Racial prejudice when combined with social power—access to social, cultural, and economic resources and decision-making—leads to the institutionalization of racist policies and practices. While I think this definition also captures the idea that racism is more than individual beliefs and attitudes, I prefer Wellman's definition because the idea of systematic advantage and disadvantage is critical to an understanding of how racism operates in American society.

In addition, I find that many of my White students and workshop participants do not feel powerful. Defining racism as prejudice plus power has little personal relevance. For some, their response to this definition is the following: "I'm not really prejudiced, and I have no power, so racism has nothing to do with me." However, most White people, if they are really being honest with themselves, can see that there are advantages to being White in the United States. Despite the current rhetoric about affirmative action and "reverse racism," every social indicator, from salary to life expectancy, reveals the advantages of being White.

The systematic advantages of being White are often referred to as White privilege. In a now well-known article, "White Privilege: Unpacking the Invisible Knapsack," Peggy McIntosh, a White feminist scholar, identified a long list of societal privileges that she received simply because she was White. She did not ask for them, and it is important to note that she hadn't always noticed that she was receiving them. They included major and minor advantages. Of course she enjoyed greater access to jobs and housing. But she also was able to shop in department stores without being followed by suspicious salespeople and could always find appropriate hair care products and makeup in any drugstore. She could send her child to school confident that the teacher would not discriminate against him on the basis of race. She could also be late for meetings, and talk with her mouth full,

fairly confident that these behaviors would not be attributed to the fact that she was White. She could express an opinion in a meeting or in print and not have it labeled the "White" viewpoint. In other words, she was more often than not viewed as an individual, rather than as a member of a racial group.

This article rings true for most White readers, many of whom may have never considered the benefits of being White. It's one thing to have enough awareness of racism to describe the ways that people of color are disadvantaged by it. But this new understanding of racism is more elusive. In very concrete terms, it means that if a person of color is the victim of housing discrimination, the apartment that would otherwise have been rented to that person of color is still available for a White person. The White tenant is, knowingly or unknowingly, the beneficiary of racism, a system of advantage based on race. The unsuspecting tenant is not to blame for the prior discrimination, but she benefits from it anyway.

For many Whites, this new awareness of the benefits of a racist system elicits considerable pain, often accompanied by feelings of anger and guilt. These uncomfortable emotions can hinder further discussion. We all like to think that we deserve the good things we have received, and that others, too, get what they deserve. Social psychologists call this tendency a "belief in a just world." Racism directly contradicts such notions of justice.

Understanding racism as a system of advantage based on race is antithetical to traditional notions of an American meritocracy. For those who have internalized this myth, this definition generates considerable discomfort. It is more comfortable simply to think of racism as a particular form of prejudice. Notions of power or privilege do not have to be addressed when our understanding of racism is constructed in that way.

The discomfort generated when a systemic definition of racism is introduced is usually quite visible in the workshops I lead. Someone in the group is usually quick to point out that this is not the definition you will find in most dictionaries. I reply, "Who wrote the dictionary?" I am not being facetious with this response. Whose interests are served by a "prejudice only" definition of racism? It is important to understand that the system of advantage is perpetuated when we do not acknowledge its existence.

Racism: For Whites Only?

Frequently someone will say, "You keep talking about White people. People of color can be racist, too." I once asked a White teacher what it would mean to her if a student or parent of color accused her of being racist. She said she would feel as though she had been punched in the stomach or called a "low-life scum." She is not alone in this feeling. The word *racist* holds a lot of emotional power. For many White people, to be called racist is the ultimate insult. The idea that this term might only be applied to Whites becomes highly problematic for after all, can't people of color be "low-life scum" too?

Of course, people of any racial group can hold hateful attitudes and behave in racially discriminatory and bigoted ways. We can all cite examples of horrible hate crimes which have been perpetrated by people of color as well as Whites. Hateful behavior is hateful behavior no matter who does it. But when I am asked, "Can people of color be racist?" I reply, "The answer depends on your definition of racism." If one defines racism as racial prejudice, the answer is yes. People of color can and do have racial prejudices. However, if one defines racism as a system of advantage based on race, the answer is no. People of color are not racist because they do not systematically benefit from racism. And equally important, there is no systematic cultural and institutional support or sanction for the racial bigotry of people of color. In my view, reserving the term *racist* only for behaviors committed by Whites in the context of a White-dominated society is a way of acknowledging the ever-present power differential afforded Whites by the culture and institutions that make up the system of advantage and continue to reinforce notions of White superiority (Using the same logic, I reserve the word *sexist* for men.

Though women can and do have gender-based prejudices, only men systematically benefit from sexism.)

Despite my best efforts to explain my thinking on this point, there are some who will be troubled, perhaps even incensed, by my response. To call the racially motivated acts of a person of color acts of racial bigotry and to describe similar acts committed by Whites as racist will make no sense to some people, including some people of color. To those, I will respectfully say, "We can agree to disagree." At moments like these, it is not agreement that is essential, but clarity. Even if you don't like the definition of racism I am using, hopefully you are now clear about what it is. If I also understand how you are using the term, our conversation can continue—despite our disagreement.

Another provocative question I'm often asked is "Are you saying all Whites are racist?" When asked this question, I again remember that White teacher's response, and I am conscious that perhaps the question I am really being asked is, "Are you saying all Whites are bad people?" The answer to that question is of course not. However, all White people, intentionally or unintentionally, do benefit from racism. A more relevant question is what are White people as individuals doing to interrupt racism? For many White people, the image of a racist is a hood-wearing Klan member or a name-calling Archie Bunker figure. These images represent what might be called *active racism,* blatant, intentional acts of racial bigotry and discrimination. *Passive racism* is more subtle and can be seen in the collusion of laughing when a racist joke is told, of letting exclusionary hiring practices go unchallenged, of accepting as appropriate the omissions of people of color from the curriculum, and of avoiding difficult race-related issues. Because racism is so ingrained in the fabric of American institutions, it is easily self-perpetuating. All that is required to maintain it is business as usual.

I sometimes visualize the ongoing cycle of racism as a moving walkway at the airport. Active racist behavior is equivalent to walking fast on the conveyor belt. The person engaged in active racist behavior has identified with the ideology of

White supremacy and is moving with it. Passive racist behavior is equivalent to standing still on the walkway. No overt effort is being made, but the conveyor belt moves the bystanders along to the same destination as those who are actively walking. Some of the bystanders may feel the motion of the conveyor belt, see the active racists ahead of them, and choose to turn around, unwilling to go to the same destination as the White supremacists. But unless they are walking actively in the opposite direction at a speed faster than the conveyor belt—unless they are actively antiracist—they will find themselves carried along with the others.

So, not all Whites are actively racist. Many are passively racist. Some, though not enough, are actively antiracist. The relevant question is not whether all Whites are racist, but how we can move more White people from a position of active or passive racism to one of active antiracism? The task of interrupting racism is obviously not the task of Whites alone. But the fact of White privilege means that Whites have greater access to the societal institutions in need of transformation. To whom much is given, much is required.

It is important to acknowledge that while all Whites benefit from racism, they do not all benefit equally. Other factors, such as socioeconomic status, gender, age, religious affiliation, sexual orientation, mental and physical ability, also play a role in our access to social influence and power. A White woman on welfare is not privileged to the same extent as a wealthy White heterosexual man. In her case, the systematic disadvantages of sexism and classism intersect with her White privilege, but the privilege is still there. This point was brought home to me in a 1994 study conducted by a Mount Holyoke graduate student, Phyllis Wentworth. Wentworth interviewed a group of female college students, who were both older than their peers and were the first members of their families to attend college, about the pathways that lead them to college. All of the women interviewed were White, from working-class backgrounds, from families where women were expected to graduate from high school and get married or get a job. Several had experienced abusive relationships and other personal difficulties prior to coming to college. Yet their experiences were punctuated by "good luck" stories of apartments obtained without a deposit, good jobs offered without experience or extensive reference checks, and encouragement provided by willing mentors.

While the women acknowledged their good fortune, none of them discussed their Whiteness. They had not considered the possibility that being White had worked in their favor and helped give them the benefit of the doubt at critical junctures. This study clearly showed that even under difficult circumstances, White privilege was still operating.

It is also true that not all people of color are equally targeted by racism. We all have multiple identities that shape our experience. I can describe myself as a light-skinned, well-educated, heterosexual, able-bodied, Christian African American woman raised in a middle-class suburb. As an African American woman, I am systematically disadvantaged by race and by gender, but I systematically receive benefits in the other categories, which then mediate my experience of racism and sexism. When one is targeted by multiple isms—racism, sexism, classism, heterosexism, ableism, anti-Semitism, ageism—in whatever combination, the effect is intensified. The particular combination of racism and classism in many communities of color is life-threatening. Nonetheless, when I, the middle-class Black mother of two sons, read another story about a Black man's unlucky encounter with a White police officer's deadly force, I am reminded that racism by itself can kill.

The Cost of Racism

Several years ago, a White male student in my psychology of racism course wrote in his journal at the end of the semester that he had learned a lot about racism and now understood in a way he never had before just how advantaged he was. He also commented that he didn't think he would do anything to try to change the situation. After all, the system was working in his favor. Fortunately, his response was not typical. Most of my students leave my course with the desire (and an action plan) to interrupt the cycle of racism. However, this young man's response does raise an important question. Why should Whites who are advantaged by racism *want* to end that system of advantage? What are the *costs* of that system to them?

A *Money* magazine article called "Race and Money" chronicled the many ways the American economy was hindered by institutional racism. Whether one looks at productivity lowered by racial tensions in the workplace, or real estate equity lost through housing discrimination, or the tax revenue lost in underemployed communities of color, or the high cost of warehousing human talent in prison, the economic costs of racism are real and measurable.

As a psychologist, I often hear about the less easily measured costs. When I ask White men and women how racism hurts them, they frequently talk about their fears of people of color, the social incompetence they feel in racially mixed situations, the alienation they have experienced between parents and children when a child marries into a family of color, and the interracial friendships they had as children that were lost in adolescence or young adulthood without their ever understanding why. White people are paying a significant price for the system of advantage. The cost is not as high for Whites as it is for people of color, but a price is being paid. Wendell Berry, a White writer raised in Kentucky, captures this psychic pain in the opening pages of his book, *The Hidden Wound*:

> If white people have suffered less obviously from racism than black people, they have nevertheless suffered greatly; the cost has been greater perhaps than we can yet know. If the white man has inflicted the wound of racism upon black men, the cost has been that he would receive the mirror image of that wound into himself. As the master, or as a member of the dominant race, he has felt little compulsion to acknowledge it

or speak of it; the more painful it has grown the more deeply he has hidden it within himself. But the wound is there, and it is a profound disorder, as great a damage in his mind as it is in his society.

The dismantling of racism is in the best interests of everyone.

A Word About Language

Throughout this chapter I have used the term *White,* to refer to Americans of European descent. In another era, I might have used the term *Caucasian.* I have used the term *people of color* to refer to those groups in America that are and have been historically targeted by racism. This includes people of African descent, people of Asian descent, people of Latin American descent, and indigenous peoples (sometimes referred to as Native Americans or American Indians). Many people refer to these groups collectively as non-Whites. This term is particularly offensive because it defines groups of people in terms of what they are not. (Do we call women "non-men?") I also avoid using the term *minorities* because it represents another kind of distortion of information which we need to correct. So-called minorities represent the majority of the world's population. While the term *people of color* is inclusive, it is not perfect. As a workshop participant once said, White people have color, too. Perhaps it would be more accurate to say "people of more color," though I am not ready to make that change. Perhaps fellow psychologist Linda James Myers is on the right track. She refers to two groups of people, those of acknowledged African descent and those of unacknowledged African descent, reminding us that we can all trace the roots of our common humanity to Africa.

I refer to people of acknowledged African descent as Black. I know that *African American* is also a commonly used term, and I often refer to myself and other Black people born and raised in America in that way. Perhaps because I am a child of the 1960s "Black and beautiful" era, I still prefer

Black. The term is more inclusive than *African American,* because there are Black people in the United States who are not African American—Afro-Caribbeans, for example—yet are targeted by racism, and are identified as Black.

When referring to other groups of color, I try to use the terms that the people themselves want to be called. In some cases, there is no clear consensus. For example, some people of Latin American ancestry prefer *Latino,* while others prefer *Hispanic* or, if of Mexican descent, *Chicano.* The terms *Latino* and *Hispanic* are used interchangeably here. Similarly, there are regional variations in the use of the terms *Native American, American Indian,* and *Indian. American Indian* and *Native people* are now more widely used than *Native American,* and the language used here reflects that. People of Asian descent include Pacific Islanders, and that is reflected in the terms *Asian/Pacific Islanders* and *Asian Pacific Americans.* However, when quoting others I use whichever terms they use.

My dilemma about the language to use reflects the fact that race is a social construction. Despite myths to the contrary, biologists tell us that the only meaningful racial categorization is that of human. Van den Berghe defines race as "a group that is socially defined but on the basis of *physical* criteria," including skin color and facial features.

Racial identity development [...] usually refers to the process of defining for oneself the personal significance and social meaning of belonging to a particular racial group. The terms *racial identity* and *ethnic identity* are often used synonymously, though a distinction can be made between the two. An ethnic group is a socially defined group based on *culture* criteria, such as language, customs, and shared history. An individual might identify as a member of an ethnic group (Irish or Italian, for example) but might not think of himself in racial terms (as White). On the other hand, one may recognize the personal significance of racial group membership (identifying as Black, for instance) but may not consider ethnic identity (such as West Indian) as particularly meaningful.

Both racial and ethnic categories are socially constructed, and social definitions of these categories have changed over time. For example, in his book *Ethnic Identity: The Transformation of White America,* Richard Alba points out that the high rates of intermarriage and the dissolution of other social boundaries among European ethnic groups in the United States have reduced the significance of ethnic identity for these groups. In their place, he argues, a new ethnic identity is emerging, that of European American.

Throughout this [work], I refer primarily to racial identity. It is important, however, to acknowledge that ethnic identity and racial identity sometimes intersect. For example, dark-skinned Puerto Ricans may identify culturally as Puerto Rican and yet be categorized racially by others as Black on the basis of physical appearance. In the case of either racial or ethnic identity, these identities remain most salient to individuals of racial or ethnic groups that have been historically disadvantaged or marginalized.

The language we use to categorize one another racially is imperfect. These categories are still evolving as the current debate over Census classifications indicates. The original creation of racial categories was in the service of oppression. Some may argue that to continue to use them is to continue that oppression. I respect that argument. Yet it is difficult to talk about what is essentially a flawed and problematic social construct without using language that is itself problematic. We have to be able to talk about it in order to change it. So this is the language I choose.

For Discussion

1. What is the cost of racism according to Tatum? What does she cite as examples?
2. What are the differences between *active racism* and *passive racism*? Provide some examples.
3. Are all whites racist? Is racism exclusively the domain of whites in Western societies? What evidence does Tatum provide to refute or support these proactive questions?

4. Using the Peggy McIntosh reading as a reference, create your own list of how racism is a system of advantages based on race. Can you think of any societies where the dominant group is not "white," yet discrimination and racism exist as the model power + prejudice = racism explains?

5. At what age does the impact of racism begin? Compare Tatum's examples with the Elliot "Eye Color" experiment.

Activities: A Sequence for Advanced Discussions

1. "Think of your first race-related memory ..." asks Tatum. "How old were you?"

2. "What emotions can you attach to this first memory? Were you the observer or the object of observation?"

3. "Did you talk to anyone about what happened? Did you tell anyone how you felt?" If no, then why not? Had you already learned that race is a topic not to be discussed?

One-Week Diary Assignment

Keep a diary for one week. As you go through the day, what images or messages do you see or hear regarding race? Are stereotypes at play? Did someone tell an ethnic or racist joke? Did you laugh at it? Repeat it to others? Write down where and when you come into contact with matters of race, ethnicity, and racism. Tally the amount by category and compare with other students. What can you conclude from your findings?

Study Terms

Prejudice
Cultural Racism
Internalized Oppression
Racism
Racial Prejudice
White Privilege
Active Racism
Passive Racism
Racial Identity Development
Ethnic Identity
Ethnic Group

White Privilege

Unpacking the Invisible Knapsack

By Peggy McIntosh

Editor's Introduction

Often cited but seldom presented in its full form, this now-classic treatise on white privilege is embraced widely as a tool for anti-racist educators. As noted in the Beverly Tatum selection, whites seldom realize how they benefit from the invisible forms of privilege, but this article by Peggy McIntosh is one of the first written by a white person addressing this topic. Perhaps more than any other issue in the United States, the assumption that all are equal under the Constitution is refuted by institutionalized racism, unofficial policies at companies to follow non-whites while they shop, and a host of other considerations. Students should engage in open discussion on this matter and realize that the definition of racism as a system of privileges enjoyed knowingly and unknowingly by whites is vital to disseminating notions of a color-blind society.

References

McIntosh, Peggy. "White Privilege: Unpacking the Invisible Knapsack," *Peace and Freedom Magazine,* pp. 10-12. Copyright © 1989 by Peggy McIntosh

Through work to bring materials from Women's Studies into the rest of the curriculum, I have often noticed men's unwillingness to grant that they are over-privileged, even though they may grant that women are disadvantaged. They may say they will work to improve women's status, in the society, the university, or the curriculum, but they can't or won't support the idea of lessening men's. Denials which amount to taboos surround the subject of advantages which men gain from women's disadvantages. These denials protect male privilege from being fully acknowledged, lessened, or ended.

Thinking through unacknowledged male privilege as a phenomenon, I realized that, since hierarchies in our society are interlocking, there was most likely a phenomenon of white privilege that was similarly denied and protected. As a white person, I realized I had been taught about racism as something that puts others at a disadvantage, but had been taught not to see one of its corollary aspects, white privilege, which puts me at an advantage.

I think whites are carefully taught not to recognize white privilege, as males are taught not to recognize male privilege. So I have begun in an untutored way to ask what it is like to have white privilege. I have come to see white privilege as an invisible package of unearned assets that I can count on cashing in each day, but about which I was "meant" to remain oblivious. White privilege is like an invisible weightless knapsack of special provisions, maps, passports, codebooks, visas, clothes, tools, and blank checks.

Describing white privilege makes one newly accountable. As we in Women's Studies work to reveal male privilege and ask men to give up some of their power, so one who writes about white privilege must ask, "Having described it, what will I do to lessen or end it?"

After I realized the extent to which men work from a base of unacknowledged privilege, I understood that much of their oppressiveness was unconscious. Then I remembered the frequent charges from women of color that white women whom they encounter are oppressive. I began to understand why we are justly seen as oppressive, even when we don't see ourselves that way. I began to count the ways in which I enjoy unearned skin privilege and have been conditioned into oblivion about its existence.

My schooling gave me no training in seeing myself as an oppressor, as an unfairly advantaged person, or as a participant in a damaged culture. I was taught to see myself as an individual whose moral state depended on her individual moral will. My schooling followed the pattern my colleague Elizabeth Minnich has pointed out: whites are taught to think of their lives as morally neutral, normative, and average, and also ideal, so that when we work to benefit others, this is seen as work which will allow "them" to be more like "us."

I decided to try to work on myself at least by identifying some of the daily effects of white privilege in my life. I have chosen those conditions which I think in my case *attach somewhat more to skin-color privilege* than to class, religion, ethnic status, or geographic location, though of course all these other factors are intricately intertwined.

As far as I can see, my African American co-workers, friends, and acquaintances with whom I come into daily or frequent contact in this particular time, place, and line of work cannot count on most of these conditions.

1. I can if I wish arrange to be in the company of people of my race most of the time.
2. If I should need to move, I can be pretty sure of renting or purchasing housing in an area which I can afford and in which I would want to live.
3. I can be pretty sure that my neighbors in such a location will be neutral or pleasant to me.
4. I can go shopping alone most of the time, pretty well assured that I will not be followed or harassed.
5. I can turn on the television or open to the front page of the paper and see people of my race widely represented.
6. When I am told about our national heritage or about "civilization," I am shown that people of my color made it what it is.
7. I can be sure that my children will be given curricular materials that testify to the existence of their race.
8. If want to, I can be pretty sure of finding a publisher for this piece on white privilege.
9. I can go into a music shop and count on finding the music of my race represented, into a supermarket and find the staple foods that fit with my cultural traditions, into a hairdresser's shop and find someone who can cut my hair.
10. Whether I use checks, credit cards, or cash, I can count on my skin color not to work against the appearance of financial reliability.
11. I can arrange to protect my children most of the time from people who might not like them.
12. I can swear, or dress in second-hand clothes, or not answer letters, without having people attribute these choices to the bad morals, the poverty, or the illiteracy of my race.
13. I can speak in public to a powerful male group without putting my race on trial.
14. I can do well in a challenging situation without being called a credit to my race.

15. I am never asked to speak for all the people of my racial group.

16. I can remain oblivious of the language and customs of persons of color who constitute the world's majority without feeling in my culture any penalty for such oblivion.

17. I can criticize our government and talk about how much I fear its policies and behavior without being seen as a cultural outsider.

18. I can be pretty sure that if I ask to talk to "the person in charge," I will be facing a person of my race.

19. If a traffic cop pulls me over or if the IRS audits my tax return, I can be sure I haven't been singled out because of my race.

20. I can easily buy posters, postcards, picture books, greeting cards, dolls, toys, and children's magazines featuring people of my race.

21. I can go home from most meetings of organizations I belong to feeling somewhat tied in, rather than isolated, out-of-place, outnumbered, unheard, held at a distance, or feared.

22. I can take a job with an affirmative action employer without having co-workers on the job suspect that I got it because of race.

23. I can choose public accommodations without fearing that people of my race cannot get in or will be mistreated in the places I have chosen.

24. I can be sure that if I need legal or medical help, my race will not work against me.

25. If my day, week, or year is going badly, I need not ask of each negative episode or situation whether it has racial overtones.

26. I can choose blemish cover or bandages in "flesh" color and have them more less match my skin.

I repeatedly forgot each of the realizations on this list until I wrote it down. For me, white privilege has turned out to be an elusive and fugitive subject. The pressure to avoid it is great, for in facing it I must give up the myth of meritocracy. If these things are true, this is not such a free country; one's life is not what one makes it; many doors open for certain people through no virtues of their own.

In unpacking this invisible knapsack of white privilege, I have listed conditions of daily experience that I once took for granted. Nor did I think of any of these prerequisites as bad for the holder. I now think that we need a more finely differentiated taxonomy of privilege, for some of these varieties are only what one would want for everyone in a just society, and others give license to be ignorant, oblivious, arrogant, and destructive.

I see a pattern running through the matrix of white privilege, a pattern of assumptions that were passed on to me as a white person. There was one main piece of cultural turf; it was my own turf, and I was among those who could control the turf. *My skin color was an asset for any move I was educated to want to make.* I could think of myself as belonging in major ways and of making social systems work for me. I could freely disparage, fear, neglect, or be oblivious to anything outside of the dominant cultural forms. Being of the main culture, I could also criticize it fairly freely.

In proportion as my racial group was being made confident, comfortable, and oblivious, other groups were likely being made inconfident, uncomfortable, and alienated. Whiteness protected me from many kinds of hostility, distress, and violence, which I was being subtly trained to visit, in turn, upon people of color.

For this reason, the word "privilege" now seems to me misleading. We usually think of privilege as being a favored state, whether earned or conferred by birth or luck. Yet some of the conditions I have described here work systematically to over-empower certain groups. Such privilege simply *confers dominance* because of one's race or sex.

I want, then, to distinguish between earned strength and unearned power conferred systemically. Power from unearned privilege can look like strength when it is in fact permission to escape or to dominate. But not all of the privileges on my list are inevitably damaging. Some, like the expectation that neighbors will be decent to you, or that your race will not count against you in court, should be the norm in a just society. Others, like the privilege to ignore less powerful people, distort the humanity of the holders as well as the ignored groups.

We might at least start by distinguishing between positive advantages, which we can work to spread, and negative types of advantage, which unless rejected will always reinforce our present hierarchies. For example, the feeling that one belongs within the human circle, as Native Americans say, should not be seen as privilege for a few. Ideally it is an *unearned entitlement*. At present, since only a few have it, it is an *unearned advantage* for them. This paper results from a process of coming to see that some of the power that I originally saw as attendant on being a human being in the United States consisted in unearned advantage and conferred dominance.

I have met very few men who are truly distressed about systemic, unearned male advantage and conferred dominance. And so one question for me and others like me is whether we will be like them, or whether we will get truly distressed, even outraged, about unearned race advantage and conferred dominance, and, if so, what will we do to lessen them. In any case, we need to do more work in identifying how they actually affect our daily lives. Many, perhaps most, of our white students in the U.S. think that racism doesn't affect them because they are not people of color, they do not see "whiteness" as a racial identity. In addition, since race and sex are not the only advantaging systems at work, we need similarly to examine the daily experience of having age advantage, or ethnic advantage, or physical ability, or advantage related to nationality, religion, or sexual orientation.

Difficulties and dangers surrounding the task of finding parallels are many. Since racism, sexism, and heterosexism are not the same, the advantages associated with them should not be seen as the same. In addition, it is hard to disentangle aspects of unearned advantage which rest more on social class, economic class, race, religion, sex, and ethnic identity than on other factors. Still, all of the oppressions are interlocking, as the Combahee River Collective Statement of 1977 continues to remind us eloquently.

One factor seems clear about all of the interlocking oppressions. They take both active forms, which we can see, and embedded forms, which

as a member of the dominant group one is taught not to see. In my class and place, I did not see myself as a racist because I was taught to recognize racism only in individual acts of meanness by members of my group, never in invisible systems conferring unsought racial dominance on my group from birth.

Disapproving of the systems won't be enough to change them. I was taught to think that racism could end if white individuals changed their attitudes. But a "white" skin in the United States opens many doors for whites whether or not we approve of the way dominance has been conferred on us. Individual acts can palliate, but cannot end, these problems.

To redesign social systems, we need first to acknowledge their colossal unseen dimensions. The silences and denials surrounding privilege are the key political tool here. They keep the thinking about equality or equity incomplete, protecting unearned advantage and conferred dominance by making these taboo subjects. Most talks by whites about equal opportunity seems to me now to be about equal opportunity to try to get into a position of dominance while denying that *systems* of dominance exist.

It seems to me that obliviousness about white advantage, like obliviousness about male advantage, is kept strongly inculturated in the United States so as to maintain the myth of meritocracy, the myth that democratic choice is equally available to all. Keeping most people unaware that freedom of confident action is there for just a small number of people props up those in power and serves to keep power in the hands of the same groups that have most of it already.

Although systemic change takes many decades, there are pressing questions for me and I imagine for some others like me if we raise our daily consciousness on the perquisites of being light-skinned. What will we do with such knowledge? As we know from watching men, it is an open question whether we will choose to use unearned advantage to weaken hidden systems of advantage, and whether we will use any of our arbitrarily awarded power to try to reconstruct power systems on a broader base.

*This is an authorized excerpt of McIntosh's original white privilege article, "White Privilege and Male Privilege: A Personal Account of Coming to See Correspondences through Work in Women's Studies," Working Paper 189 (1988), Wellesley Centers for Women, Wellesley College, MA.

Been in the Pen So Long

Race, Crime, and Justice

By Michael K. Brown

● ●

The problem of crime among urban blacks is arguably the most visceral, emotional aspect of the debate about race in America today. Probably even more than welfare or affirmative action, the question of black violence has fueled a fundamental shift in the debate that began in the late 1960s and accelerated in the 1970s and 1980s. In these decades blacks lost the moral high ground in the eyes of numerous white commentators, including many former liberals. Between the flowering of the civil rights movement and the Reagan years, the image of black youth in particular underwent an extraordinary transformation: the brave little girl walking up to the schoolhouse door in the face of jeering white crowds was replaced by fearsome young black men coming down the street ready to take your wallet or your life. The cultural transformation of black youth from victims of injustice to remorseless predators was mirrored in public policies that quietly reduced funding for programs that had historically served minority youth. At the same time, lawmakers and legal authorities visibly cracked down on young people of color through tougher sentences, "zero tolerance" strategies in the schools and on the streets, and increased treatment of juvenile offenders as adults.

Conservative social scientists and other commentators have taken the lead in constructing this cultural and intellectual shift. Their analysis of black crime and the justice system both reflects this shift and seeks to justify it through a presentation that purports to be a straightforward recital of obvious, if troubling, "facts." The main argument, advanced repeatedly by conservative authors like James Q. Wilson, John J. DiIulio, John McWhorter, and the Thernstroms in *America in Black and White*, is that there is both good news and bad news on the crime front.[1] On the one hand, crime and violence, like other "behavioral" problems, are devastatingly high in many black communities. Indeed, the lawlessness helps to explain why so many blacks remain mired in poverty. Crime causes poverty, they contend, by scaring businesses away from black communities and by giving too many black men an alternative to honest work. On the other hand, there is no longer systematic racism in the criminal justice system. There used to be, conservatives agree, but that was in the past. Today black officials in black-dominated cities run many court systems as well as police departments, so how can racism still be a factor?

It is true, these writers acknowledge, that blacks are overrepresented in the jails and prisons. But that is because of a hard reality: blacks commit more of the kinds of crimes that get people behind bars. There is no credible evidence of systematic racial bias in the institutions of justice, they claim. Instead, the justice system simply responds to existing high levels of serious crime among blacks. The black proportion of the prison population, writes John McWhorter, "neatly reflects the rate at which they commit crimes. … One study after another, even by scholars expecting their results to reveal racism, shows … when prior records, gravity of the crime, and use of weapons is taken into account, there is no sentencing bias against blacks."[2] Conservatives do not say much about the origins of those high rates of crime. But the implication is that high levels of violence stem from the same sources as the other multiple pathologies of the so-called black underclass. And whatever those sources are, according to conservatives, they are clearly not economic. Rather, they must be cultural, since research fails to show any connection between economic disadvantage and crime.

For many racial realists, the idea that racial discrimination causes crime and leads to injustice in the treatment of blacks by the criminal justice system is itself part of the problem. The fashionable tendency to excuse black criminality as an expected and even morally tolerable response to discrimination, in the view of some writers, has helped to erode the sense of personal responsibility among blacks and has thus encouraged crime. Without fear of serious consequences or moral disapproval, the realists argue, black crime has been tacitly allowed to run rampant. The journalist Jim Sleeper, for example, acknowledges that racism against black defendants in the justice system has been "a great, historic wrong," which liberal activists and others did "much to curb" in the 1950s and 1960s.

> But lately liberals have been curbing systemic racism in favor of a racism that refuses to pay blacks the compliment of holding them to the same elementary civil standards as everyone else. With stunning callousness, "civil rights" attorneys from Kunstler to Cochran have goaded black juries into political, "send a message" acquittals of black assailants

of whites, never considering that not only are such acquittals morally indistinguishable from those of white assailants of blacks in the old South, they also encourage liberals' shameful neglect of black victims killed or raped by blacks.[3]

As with other realms of social life, the realist discussion of race and crime represents itself as simply a factual account, a hardheaded and sober examination of some troubling though inescapable realities. On closer inspection, however, it is actually a highly partisan, and oddly selective, manipulation of the evidence on the roots of crime in the black community and the workings of the justice system. The argument gains some superficial credibility because racial realists often choose to focus on soft and vulnerable targets. In this instance, the soft targets are liberals and black civil rights advocates who, according to the realists, insist that the vast numbers of blacks in the courts, jails, and prisons are simply innocents caught in the snares of a racist system. Having set up this convenient straw person, these writers proceed to knock it down by showing that social science research uniformly suggests that blacks have higher rates of serious offenses (for street crimes, though not, importantly, for white-collar crimes). They then move on from that thoroughly unremarkable finding to the much more sweeping assertion that racism is irrelevant for understanding black overrepresentation in the justice system—or in the crime statistics.

There is a cautionary note here. To the extent that some people still deny that violence in many black communities is a real problem, or who argue that black overrepresentation in the correctional system is only a reflection of the racist bias of police and courts, the realist argument appears to offer a sober, research-based corrective to soft-headed liberal ideology. That argument quickly crumbles, however, when their claims are put up against a more subtle and complex analysis that recognizes both the reality of high levels of black violence and the continued salience of racism. In this view, racism is both subtle and not so subtle, both direct and indirect, in breeding violence and shaping black Americans' experiences with the criminal justice system.

What is truly startling about the conservative assertion that liberal indulgence is responsible for black crime in America is that it comes after decades of the most rapid increases in the incarceration of black Americans in our history—a time of utterly unprecedented efforts by legislators and the courts to "get tough" on crime and drugs in the inner cities. Some of the numbers that describe this stunning change are by now numbingly familiar: at the close of the twentieth century, almost one in ten black men aged twenty-five to twenty-nine was in prison compared to one white in ninety. In California, black men are five times as likely to be in state prison as in state college. Nationally, 28 percent of black men will spend some time during the course of their lives in a state or federal prison, and between the mid-1980s and the mid-1990s, the number of black men sentenced to prison for drug offenses increased by more than 700 percent. The fastest growing segment of the imprisoned population is black women, who are incarcerated mainly for nonviolent offenses. This curious disconnect between the idea that blacks have been absolved of personal responsibility for their behavior and the reality of nearly thirty years of increasing harshness toward black offenders suggests that there must be something fundamentally amiss with the conservative argument. There is.

The conservative argument fails in two respects. First, the serious scholarly research on racial discrimination within the justice system—which is by now extensive—does not support the view that it operates in a completely race-neutral way. Indeed these studies provide consistent evidence not only that race still matters in the justice system but also that discrimination in the justice system has a rippling effect on blacks' life-chances across every other institution in American life. Second, the relationships between race, structural disadvantage, and crime—far from being irrelevant or unproven—are among the most consistent findings in the entire body of criminological research. In this chapter we analyze each of these issues in turn—paying more attention to the first one, since it is the linchpin of conservative discussions of race and crime.

Has Racism Disappeared from the Justice System?

No one seriously doubts that the level of overt discrimination in the criminal justice system has diminished since the civil rights era. But to say that racial discrimination has been expunged from the justice system—as conservatives do—provides an extremely misleading picture of what social science research really shows.[4] To understand why, some intellectual history is necessary.

In the past few decades, there have been basically three waves of social research on discrimination in the justice system. Wave 1 researchers, writing in the era before the civil rights movement had an impact on the behavior of courts and police, typically saw pervasive discrimination throughout the system, especially in the South. Blacks were found disproportionately represented at all levels of the criminal justice process, from arrest to imposition of the death penalty. Anecdotal evidence, legal research, and descriptive statistics all pointed to a pattern of systematically harsher responses to blacks, particularly if their victims were white.

In the massive study *An American Dilemma*, for example, researched in the 1930s and published during World War II, the Swedish social scientist Gunnar Myrdal and his associates validated a portrait of endemic racism in the southern justice system already sketched by a number of earlier researchers. They claimed to find less racial bias in the North, where, in Myrdal's view, blacks faced no special problem of getting justice in the courts beyond that encountered by poor people of all races (the police were another matter). But in the South, discrimination was the norm, and it worked in two ways. On the one hand, blacks were far more likely to be put under surveillance, arrested, and sentenced, especially in the lower courts, if their victims (or supposed victims) were white. According to Myrdal's collaborator, Arnold Rose, "The courts, particularly the lower courts, often seem to take for granted the guilt of the accused Negro. Negro defendants are sentenced upon scanty evidence. When the offender is a white man and the victim a Negro, a grand jury will often refuse to indict. ... When the offender is a Negro, indictment is easily obtained." At the same time, Myrdal and his colleagues found, the southern criminal justice system treated crimes against blacks casually, whether committed by whites or by other blacks: "As long as only Negroes are concerned and no whites are disturbed, great leniency will be shown in most cases. The sentences for even major crimes are ordinarily reduced when the victim is another Negro. The Southern Negro community is not at all happy about this double standard of justice in favor of Negro offenders. ... Leniency toward Negro defendants in cases involving crimes against other Negroes is thus actually a form of discrimination."[5]

The second wave of research appeared mainly during the 1970s and early 1980s, after the civil rights legislation of the 1960s and after a movement toward law enforcement professionalization had, presumably, substantially altered the racial character of American justice. This research painted a very different picture than the first wave. Applying more stringent social science methodology, the Wave 2 studies concluded that when other crucial factors were controlled, race was not important in shaping offenders' trajectories in the justice system, or at least not *very* important. Wave 2 researchers pointed out that most of the early findings on the pervasiveness of discrimination were based on studies that did not control for the level (or seriousness) of black offenses when explaining their disproportionate representation in the system. Instead, these researchers took the disproportion alone as an instance of discrimination. For the Wave 2 researchers, that made no sense. Any estimation of bias in the system, they argued, had to take into account things like the seriousness of the offenses blacks were committing relative to whites, the extent of their prior criminal records, and other "legally relevant" factors. When Wave 2 researchers took those factors into account, they often concluded that little, if any, of the racial disparity in sentencing was attributable to racism.

Probably the most influential piece of research in this wave was a well-known study by Alfred Blumstein of Carnegie-Mellon University. First published in 1982, this research compared black rates of arrest for violent crime with black imprisonment rates—reasoning that discrimination in sentencing would be shown only if the black rates of going to prison significantly exceeded the rates at which they were arrested. Once the high levels of black arrest for violent crimes were accounted for, Blumstein found that about 80 percent of the difference between black and white rates of imprisonment for crimes of violence disappeared. (Note, however, that even Blumstein's findings could not explain a significant 20 percent of the disparity.[6]) Similar findings appeared in several other studies.[7]

For some people, the apparent methodological sophistication of Wave 2 research settled the issue. A partial consensus emerged among some criminologists that systematic discrimination against black offenders had been eliminated. This consensus was ably summed up (and generally accepted, with important reservations) in a book by Michael Tonry of the University of Minnesota Law School in the early 1990s. "From every available data source," Tonry concluded, "the evidence seems clear that the main reason that black incarceration rates are substantially higher than those for whites is that black crime rates for imprisonable crimes are substantially higher than those for whites." Thus, it no longer made sense to try to "ferret out a willful and pervasive bias in a criminal justice system in which most officials and participants believe in racial equality and worry about the racial patterns they see every day."[8] (Importantly, Tonry made an exception for drug offenses, where discrimination seemed much clearer.)

For Tonry, who was deeply concerned about racial disparity in the prisons and jails, this meant criminologists should pay more attention to the forces that caused high levels of black crime in the first place. For many conservatives, however, whose argument rests largely on Wave 2–type research—to the extent it is based on evidence at all—this finding proves that racial discrimination no longer has much, if anything, to do with black overrepresentation in the criminal justice system. What these conservatives either do not know, however, or do not acknowledge, is that this evidence has been superseded by a newer wave of empirical research.[9]

The third wave, which has mainly emerged since the early 1990s, finds Wave 2 research too simplistic and often riddled with severe methodological flaws. This most recent wave includes careful studies by Donna Bishop and Charles Frazier at Florida State University; Darlene Conley, Robert Crutchfield, and George Bridges at the University of Washington; Darrell Steffensmier at Pennsylvania State University; and many others.[10] Wave 3 takes the connections between race, crime, and justice to a more sophisticated level, incorporating and going beyond some of the insights of both earlier waves of research. Wave 3 researchers do not deny that street crime is high in many poor black communities. Nor do they dispute that high levels of crime substantially account for the high levels of black incarceration. But this research also clearly demonstrates that racial discrimination in the justice system still exists, though it is usually more indirect and complicated than past discrimination.

Wave 2 tended to define discrimination too simply as overt racial bias. In contrast, Wave 3 is based on a much more nuanced conception of how discrimination operates. As a recent Human Rights Watch report on the enforcement of drug laws in Georgia puts it, "Contemporary racism in public institutions" is often "subtle, diffuse, and systemic, and less likely to be the result of the conscious prejudices of individual actors."[11] Indeed, the newer research clearly shows that discriminatory outcomes can be produced by actions that appear bureaucratically neutral or color-blind—sometimes even well intentioned, undertaken in response to concerns raised by minority communities. But in the world of structured racial disadvantage, these actions predictably work against blacks (and often Latinos as well). [...] Ironically, in a truly vicious cycle, these practices may ultimately contribute significantly to the rise of black crime. (Some of this research, however, also points to the persistence of more overt racial stereotyping and animosity, especially in certain jurisdictions.[12])

The Wave 3 studies reveal several fundamental methodological problems with the Wave 2 approach. One is what is sometimes called "over-aggregation" of the data on black-white disparities in incarceration. Taking another look at Alfred Blumstein's influential comparison of black arrests and imprisonment rates for violent crimes, for example, Robert Crutchfield and his colleagues showed that Blumstein's *national*-level comparisons obscure variations in black arrest and incarceration rates between different *states*. In some states, the proportion of blacks behind bars does indeed closely match the proportion of blacks arrested for certain serious offenses. In other states (including unexpected ones, like Mississippi) blacks appear to be imprisoned at a lower rate than would be predicted by their rate of arrests (perhaps reaffirming Myrdal's finding that black offenses against black victims are often treated leniently). But in other states, blacks wind up in prison at a rate far in excess of what would be predicted on the basis of their arrest rates. High black arrest rates explained less than half of the racial imbalance in imprisonment in Massachusetts, for example, and only 40 percent in Washington State. As the researchers put it, even measured in this blunt manner, it is clear that some states "deliver justice" less equitably than others.[13] If we look only at national-level averages, we lose sight of the harsher reality blacks face in many specific jurisdictions. To date, no one has seriously challenged this key finding.

A recent study of racially disproportional prison admissions in Pennsylvania confirms and elaborates this crucial insight. Between 1991 and 1995, according to Roy L. Austin and Mark D. Allen, only 42 percent of the racial imbalance in Pennsylvania's court commitments to state prisons was explained by racial differences in arrest rates. The proportions were especially small for lower-level crimes, where discretion in criminal justice processing is presumably greater (a finding that reappears often in recent research on racial disparities in sentencing). Thus, higher black arrest rates for drug offenses explained only 26 percent of the racially disproportionate drug sentences during those years. As with other recent research, that startlingly low percentage confirms that it is virtually impossible to explain away the stunning levels of black over-representation for drug offenses in the prisons of many states. But even when drug offenses are removed from the count, Austin and Allen found that black arrests explained only 70 percent of black overrepresentation in prison commitments.[14]

There is, of course, another problem with the strategy of assessing discrimination in the justice system by comparing rates of imprisonment with rates of arrest: it ignores the possibility that discrimination in police practices strongly influences who will be arrested in the first place. We will return to this issue in a moment. But for now, the key point is that the Wave 3 research makes a compelling case that discrimination still operates after arrest in the stages of detaining, diverting, and sentencing offenders. Racial conservatives and realists, for the most part, have simply ignored the research on which that increasingly strong case has been made. The Thernstroms, for example, argue that discrimination does not operate in sentencing by presenting raw figures from Justice Department studies showing that, overall, blacks who are charged with adult felonies are marginally less likely than whites to actually be prosecuted and, if prosecuted, are marginally less likely to be convicted. So there is, they say, no evidence of "greater zeal to punish African-Americans," adding, the "only hint of racial disparity was to the advantage, not the disadvantage, of blacks accused of crimes." But it is not possible to assess whether these raw figures indicate bias, or the lack of it, unless one controls for a variety of other factors that may help determine whether a given defendant is prosecuted or convicted. This is a fundamental social science principle that, curiously, the Thernstroms themselves invoke elsewhere in their discussion but abandon here.

Those sophisticated controls are precisely what distinguish Wave 3 research from most earlier efforts—and that may explain why the Thernstroms and other conservatives rarely mention it. Moreover, contrary to John McWhorter's assertion that "study after study" finds no discrimination in the justice system when other relevant factors are controlled, it turns out he is wrong. The vast bulk of recent studies that do use adequate controls produce consistent evidence of continuing discrimination.

This pattern begins with the differential treatment of juvenile offenders and continues, though perhaps less glaringly, into the treatment of adults. The fact that race has an especially visible and fateful impact in the juvenile justice system is another reason why studies that look for discrimination by assessing adult sentencing patterns at one point minimize the persistence and severity of racial disadvantage. By the time young blacks reach the adult justice system, discrimination has already had a serious impact. As a result, it appears that adult court processing is relatively bias-free.

The bare statistics reveal that as African Americans move more and more deeply into the juvenile justice system, a pattern of cumulative overrepresentation emerges. Thus, as of the late 1990s, black youth were

- 15 percent of the general population under age eighteen
- 26 percent of juvenile arrests
- 31 percent of referrals to juvenile court
- 44 percent of referred juveniles detained in custody
- 32 percent of youth judged delinquent
- 40 percent of youth in residential placement
- 46 percent of juveniles waived to adult criminal court
- 58 percent of youth admitted to adult state prisons[15]

The question is what to make of these figures. Many conservative writers, following Wave 2 logic, argue that these progressive disparities simply reflect the reality that black youth commit more serious offenses or commit them more often or both. More sophisticated research, however, strongly shows that differential treatment of juveniles by race is pervasive, even when such "legally relevant" factors are taken into account.

This research suggests that modern discrimination is not so much a matter of overt racial prejudice but rather of more subtle yet insidious processes that tend to accumulate over time. Small disadvantages at each successive stage in the justice process result in big disparities over the long run. Exacerbating this is the larger pattern of cumulative social disinvestment in black communities [...]. High unemployment, few effective public social programs, and the resulting pressure on black families all work to the disadvantage of black youth in the justice system. Because authorities perceive blacks as having fewer outside resources to help them achieve a crime-free life, the system is likely to define them as poor risks and to opt for custody over release to the community. In turn, this greater likelihood of incarceration further constricts the youths' chances upon release, thus contributing to another kind of self-fueling downward cycle.

For example, recent research finds that juvenile authorities tend to institutionalize youth that come from families they think are unable to provide sufficient support or supervision for them in the community. That choice is typically defined as race-neutral. But black youth that come from single-parent homes, or homes without an employed breadwinner, are more likely to wind up in institutional custody. Similarly, there is also a well-intentioned inclination to institutionalize troubled black children because that is seen as the only way to get them services that do not exist in their communities or that their families cannot afford, like mental health intervention or drug treatment. But this gives black youth a record of prior incarceration, which will almost certainly be used against them in their next encounter with the system. This in turn increases the likelihood that they will be incarcerated again and treated even more harshly.

The new studies do not indicate that the fate of black youth in the criminal justice system is unrelated to their actual level of offending. Far from it.

There is no real question that legally relevant variables like the seriousness of the offense and the youths' prior record carry the most weight. But the research shows that the relatively high level of serious crime among black youth is not the whole story. Something else happens to young blacks as they pass through the juvenile justice system, and that "something" operates independently of the extent and seriousness of the crimes they commit. Consider these examples:

- In a study of race and juvenile justice decision making in Florida, Donna Bishop and Charles Frazier found that nonwhite youth were systematically disadvantaged at "each successive stage" of the system, from intake to incarceration. As a result, the population in the system became increasingly darker the further the youth penetrated it. Nonwhite youth were 21 percent of the population aged ten to seventeen but 29 percent of those referred to intake and 44 percent of those incarcerated or transferred to adult court. When the researchers controlled for factors like the youths' prior records and the seriousness of their current offense, the disparities, unsurprisingly, were reduced, but they did not disappear. With all else accounted for, the chances of being committed to a juvenile institution or being transferred to adult court were nearly twice as high for nonwhites as for whites. Why were black youth subject to what the researchers call a "consistent pattern of unequal treatment" at every stage of the process? Interviews with juvenile justice personnel pointed to several explanations. Officials tended to define black youths' families as uncooperative or incapable of providing sufficient support or control. They also often believed that the only way to get drug treatment or mental health services to the black youth was to institutionalize them. The problem, of course, is that these decisions become self-perpetuating, a trap for minority youth. "What may begin with good intentions at an earlier stage ultimately becomes a self-fulfilling prophecy. The influence of race is [later] obscured as decisions to formally prosecute and detain in the past are used to justify more severe sanctions for youths returning to the system."[16]

- Similarly, a study of five midwestern counties by Madeline Wordes and Timothy Bynum found that black (and Latino) youth were consistently more likely to wind up in secure detention, even when such legally relevant factors as seriousness of offense, prior record, and carrying a weapon were taken into account. Moreover, the disparity in incarceration for minority youth persisted even when a number of other social factors were also considered. Other things equal, for example, youth from single-parent families were more likely to be put in detention, which worked to the disadvantage of young blacks. But even with family structure controlled, black youth were still more likely to be detained. Wordes and Bynum concluded that blacks were systematically disadvantaged indirectly, because they more often came from the social strata and family types most likely to be incarcerated, and directly, probably because stereotypes about dangerous minority youth meant they were charged with more serious offenses at the outset.[17]

- A recent study of probation officers' reports on juvenile offenders demonstrates that minority youth tend to be seen differently than whites by court authorities, even when they have committed similar offenses. George Bridges and Sara Steen found that probation officers in a western state were much more likely to attribute black youths' delinquency to internal problems—negative attitudes and personality traits. On the other hand, they were more likely to stress the influence of external, environmental pressures as causes for white youths to break the law. As a consequence, the probation officers were apt to conclude that the black youth were more dangerous and more likely to reoffend, which in turn influenced their sentencing recommendations.[18]

- Interestingly, one recent study, by Michael Leiber and Jayne Stairs, found that black youth in a midwestern state were both more likely to be detained by juvenile justice authorities than were whites and less likely to receive some sort of structured diversion program. The black youth, that is, were more likely to be sent on for tougher punishment and to be simply let go. The system apparently did not offer supportive intervention, outside custody, to black youth in trouble.[19] This raises, once again, an important, though inadequately examined, issue: racial discrimination in the justice system may be obscured, as it was in the segregation era, because the system's response to black offenders conflates both harshness (under certain conditions) and neglect (under others), depending on the nature of the offense and the race of the victim.

Differential treatment as juveniles propels blacks disproportionately into the adult criminal justice system. It also helps hide the way race works to shape the color of the adult prison population. Even at the level of adult sentencing, several recent studies have found persistent racial disparities that cannot be explained away by the frequency or seriousness of offenses or any other legally relevant factors. This is especially true for drug offenses, and—strikingly—it remains true despite the adoption by the federal system and a number of states of elaborate sentencing guidelines designed specifically to eliminate discretion. For example, a recent study by Christopher Hebert of federal sentencing of drug offenders found there was no clear pattern of racial bias in sentencing for drug offenses generally.[20] But for cocaine specifically (and to a lesser degree opiates) the disparities in sentencing, controlling for a host of other factors, were stark. Being black, other things equal, not only doubled the chance of going to federal prison for a cocaine-related offense but added, on average, forty months to the sentence. Celesta Albonetti, in another study of sentencing under federal guidelines, found that both blacks and Latinos were disadvantaged in sentencing decisions, relative to whites, when it came to drug offenses. These disparities were apparently produced by the differential use of what the federal system calls "departures" from the guidelines, especially those providing more lenient sentencing for offenders who furnish "substantial assistance" to prosecutors and who accept responsibility for their crimes. To the degree that federal sentencing guidelines allowed considerable discretion in the justice system, in other words, the discretionary possibilities typically disadvantaged minority defendants.

This pattern can be found at the state level as well. A Human Rights Watch study of Georgia drug enforcement found that black defendants were far more likely than whites to receive the harshest sanctions for drug offenses. During some periods, for example, Georgia drug laws allowed a potential life sentence for the second or subsequent drug offense, even if both offenses were minor ones. Between 1990 and 1995, of the 573 offenders given a life sentence under these Draconian laws, *only 13 were white*. The disparity was reduced, but not eliminated when the researchers controlled for the proportions in each race who were eligible for this harsh sentence under the state law because of the specific nature of their offense and their prior record. Three percent of whites who were convicted of a "qualifying" drug offense received a life sentence versus 15 percent of blacks. Thus "life-eligible" blacks were five times as likely to actually get a life sentence as "life-eligible" whites were.[21] Charles Crawford, Ted Chiricos, and Gary Kleck found a similar situation in a study of racial patterns in sentencing under a "habitual offender" statute in Florida in the early 1990s. Of nearly ten thousand offenders eligible to be sentenced as habitual offenders in 1992–93—which meant serving a much longer sentence than others—only about 20 percent were actually given that disposition. But with all else controlled, eligible blacks were between 36 and 69 percent more likely to be declared habitual offenders than eligible whites.[22]

Though drug offenses provide the most visible disparities, racial differences in sentencing are not confined to drugs. Crawford, Chiricos, and Kleck found that race also played a critical role in sentencing for property offenses. And in a study of race and incarceration in New York State, James Nelson discovered that—after controlling for the seriousness of the offense, county of jurisdiction, and other factors—roughly one in three blacks sentenced to jail would have received a more lenient sentence had they been treated the same as comparable white offenders.[23] Every year in the state, four thousand black defendants went to jail who would not have gone behind bars had they been treated the same as similarly situated whites. The disparity was less stark for admission to prisons, as opposed to local jails. Still, three hundred blacks went to state prison in New York annually who would not have gone to prison had they been white.

These disparities are, perhaps unsurprisingly, even greater when age and gender are combined with race. Because most studies lump all ages (and usually genders as well) together, comparisons of racial patterns in sentencing typically obscure the especially harsh outcomes for *young black men*. How much so is apparent in Darrell Steffensmier and colleagues' study of adult sentencing in Pennsylvania, a state with a system of sentencing guidelines that again, other things equal, should reduce the effects of legally irrelevant factors like race on sentences. The study found, as have others, that the severity of the offense and the defendants' prior records carried the most weight in determining whether they went to prison, and for how long. But with all else controlled, the odds of imprisonment for white men aged eighteen to twenty-nine were 38 percent less than those for black men the same age. And the prison sentences for white men, when they received them, were shorter by an average of almost three months. The racial disparities decreased at older ages, as both black and white men became less likely, other things being equal, to be sent to prison, making the odds for black and white men over fifty roughly similar. But putting race and age together changes the picture dramatically: the odds of going to prison for black men eighteen to twenty-nine were more than four times those of white men over fifty. Thus "the influence of race in the sentencing of males depends on the defendant's age."[24]

Why do younger black men so predictably get the toughest sanctions? On the basis of interviews with Pennsylvania judges, the researchers suggest that older offenders and women were often seen as more likely to be supporting a family and more likely to be holding down a steady job "now or in the future." Young black men, on the other hand, were not seen to have those stabilizing social bonds. They were also generally regarded as more dangerous to public safety, less reformable, and less likely to have suffered mitigating victimization of their own, like being coerced into crime at the hands of men or suffering from some psychological disorder. Some of the judges, moreover, "were reluctant to send white offenders to state prisons (whose populations were more than 65 percent black) for fear that whites would be victimized by black inmates." As the researchers point out, when one ignores how race, gender, and age interact to shape the fate of offenders in the justice system, we seriously underestimate the "high cost of being black, young, and male" specifically, and thus the "continuing significance of race in American society."[25]

Many of these studies are quite sophisticated, and they go a long way beyond the superficially convincing Wave 2 platitudes on which the conservative argument depends. Like their analysis of race and sentencing, the conservative discussion of race and the death penalty also neglects or misrepresents pivotal research findings. The Thernstroms, for example, spend considerable time analyzing a well-known study by David Baldus of the University of Iowa and his colleagues, which famously found that killers of whites were four times as likely to get the death penalty as killers of blacks were.[26] They counter these conclusions by pointing out that the findings surely must depend on the kind of murder involved. Killing a police officer, for example, is more likely to be a capital offense. Since more police officers are white than black, they reason, it is only logical that people get the death penalty more often for killing whites. Thus, there is no racial bias involved. Except for a minor comment late in the discussion, one would never know that Baldus and his colleagues did control for the factors (over two hundred) that differentiated between murders. And they found that, with nearly every possible variable controlled, killers are still more likely to be sentenced to death, all else equal, if they kill a white person. One would also never know that there have been numerous other studies in several other states since Baldus's research that show approximately the same thing. These studies are not obscure. The U.S. General Accounting Office recently surveyed them in a review.[27] A more up-to-date Philadelphia study by Baldus and colleagues showed, moreover, that at least in the City of Brotherly Love, an offender's race also strongly shapes the likelihood of a death sentence. Other things controlled, they found blacks far more likely than whites to be sentenced to death for potentially capital offenses.[28]

Race, Police Practices, and the "Vicious Circle"

The best research now available, in short, confirms—repeatedly—that race still influences whether someone who comes before a court will be sent behind bars, and for how long. It is not the only factor that matters, nor even the most important variable. But race remains the significant issue. And because going behind bars has such an enormous impact on future chances for a good job and a stable life, the powerful role race plays in funneling defendants deeply into the criminal justice system is obviously a significant part of the accumulated adversities that perpetuate racial disparities throughout every other realm of life.

Moreover, the exclusive focus on what happens *after* arrest understates these adverse effects because it ignores the issue of how and why so many people of color wind up getting arrested in the first place. Much of Wave 2 research was about sentencing. But a great deal, of course, happens before sentencing that shapes someone's chances of entering the system and, once in it, their progress to the sentencing stage. This is clearly a problem in studies like Blumstein's that measure the presence or absence of racial bias by comparing imprisonment rates with arrest rates. When those rates matched up reasonably well, that was taken as evidence that the justice system was not biased. (In fact, the rates did not match up all that well, even in Blumstein's study. The high black arrest rates for violent crime still left unexplained 20 percent of the black-white disparity in imprisonment across the country.) But that kind of conclusion is deeply flawed because it ignores the possible effect of discriminatory practices in creating the initial disparity in black and white arrest rates.

Conservatives downplay this possibility. Dinesh D'Souza, for example, along with the Thernstroms and others, invokes the findings of the victim surveys carried out regularly by the U.S. Department of Justice. These surveys ask samples of the general population about their experience of victimization by crime and, among other things, ask them about the race of the people who committed the crimes. Those studies do indeed show that victims of violent crime, including black victims, describe the perpetrators as black in proportions that far outweigh the black proportion of the population as a whole. And since the results of these surveys do not depend on the behavior of authorities, as do arrest statistics, they are often said to be free of racial bias. Following several Wave 2 researchers, many conservatives suggest that these findings demonstrate conclusively that racism has nothing to do with the disproportionate number of black arrests.

The point is an important one if it is not taken too far. But some Wave 2 researchers did take it too far, and so do some conservative writers. Though the victim surveys can offer at best only a very crude estimate of the prevalence of offenders in a given population, it is certainly true that they generally support the uncontroversial point that blacks commit a disproportionate amount of street crime. But these surveys cannot legitimately be used as evidence that the criminal justice system is free of bias because they tell us nothing about how blacks who encounter the justice system are actually treated. National-level survey data, for example, cannot get around the

overaggregation problem we mentioned above. Thus, the fact that blacks are a high proportion of offenders nationwide obviously cannot be used as evidence that the police in Los Angeles or New York do not engage in discriminatory street tactics. Nor can the victim survey findings tell us anything about the extent of discrimination in the way police handle most drug offenses, which are, in a sense, "victimless" and as such do not figure in the surveys. Because the number of black men sentenced to prison for drug offenses increased by more than 700 percent from 1985 to 1995 alone—and blacks constitute 80 percent or more of incarcerated drug offenders in seven states— that is, to say the least, a significant limitation.[29]

Some recent research makes it abundantly clear that aggressive police behavior toward minorities *cannot* be explained away simply as the natural result of higher levels of crime among them. A study of police stops of civilians in New York City, for example, done for the New York State attorney general's office, found that over a fifteen-month period in 1998 and 1999, blacks were stopped by police six times as often as whites were, and Latinos, four times as often. Blacks made up about 25 percent of the city's general population but 50 percent of people stopped by the police. Whites made up 43 percent of the general population but just 13 percent of civilians stopped by police. As with the studies of differential sentencing, the researchers did find that a substantial part of this disparity could be attributed to higher levels of offenses by blacks and Latinos—as measured by the frequency with which the stops were followed by an actual arrest—but by no means all of it. Blacks were stopped considerably more often than they were arrested, whites less so; blacks endured 1.5 stops for every arrest versus 1.2 for whites.[30]

And in fact the social science evidence on patterns of discrimination in police practices, though not extensive, is nevertheless both consistent and long-standing. Evidence from a variety of sources has shown for decades that such discrimination is systemic and widespread, even in police departments that are generally considered to be highly professional. Indeed, those discriminatory practices are not only tolerated but also frequently justified as good police work, in "color-blind" terms, by police themselves. Those practices, however, are often the first steps in a cumulative process through which people of color, and minority youth in particular, are funneled disproportionately into the criminal justice system.

In a classic and careful observational study of police responses to juveniles in a midwestern city in the 1960s, for example, Irving Piliavin and Scott Briar found starkly different treatment for black youth, even in a department widely noted for "the honesty and superior quality of its personnel."[31] Especially when it came to relatively minor offenses, where officers had a great deal of discretion in deciding what to do with a youth, the police were much more likely to give blacks the tougher dispositions (from an official reprimand to arrest and citation to juvenile court) and less likely to release them outright. Piliavin and Briar discovered that the officers' decisions were heavily based on cues that "emerged from the interaction between the officer and the youth [and] from which the officer inferred the youth's character": "Older youths, members of known delinquent gangs, Negroes, youths with well-oiled hair, black jackets, and soiled denims or jeans … and boys who in their interactions with officers did not manifest what were considered to be appropriate signs of respect tended to receive the most severe dispositions."[32]

These cues were so significant in determining police decisions that blacks and those otherwise fitting the delinquent stereotype were more likely to be stopped and interrogated "often even in the absence of evidence that an offense had been committed." And if offenses were found, they typically received "more severe dispositions [than] for the same violations" committed by whites. The fact that black youths were greatly overrepresented among those who had to be released for lack of evidence corroborated the researchers' observations.

Piliavin and Briar found that the police often based these racially targeted responses on departmental statistics showing higher rates of offenses among black youth. The police "justified their selective treatment" on "epidemiological lines";

they concentrated their attention on "those youths whom they believed were most likely to commit delinquent acts." As one officer put it to the researchers, "our delinquency problem is largely found in the Negro community and it is these youths toward whom we are sensitized." Indeed, Piliavin and Briar found these assumptions meant that the police targeted their surveillance "in areas frequented or inhabited by Negroes" in the first place, thus assuring that black youth would be more likely to be stopped by officers. But the obvious problem with this "epidemiological" approach to policing, the researchers pointed out, was that it "may well have self-fulfilling consequences." Black youth routinely stopped by the police might become hostile toward law enforcement and display the wrong kind of demeanor in encounters with them, thus vindicating the officers' prejudices and spurring more arrests. This, in turn, might lead "to closer surveillance of Negro districts, more frequent encounters with Negro youths, and so on in a vicious circle."[33]

More recent work by Darlene Conley and others suggests that similar patterns prevail today, even after another three decades of efforts in some jurisdictions to improve the racial record of the police. The newer research reconfirms that black (and Latino) neighborhoods are more likely to be the focus of heavy police monitoring and surveillance to begin with and that black and Latino youth are more likely to be defined by police as threatening or insubordinate, more likely to be stopped more often under various pretexts, more likely to get arrested than to receive a warning, and less likely to have charges dropped by police.[34]

Some recent research suggests that police are well aware of these racially structured practices but that they often defend them on one or both of two related grounds. On the one hand, just as Piliavin and Briar found in the 1960s, police still operate with an epidemiological or "actuarial" attitude toward their surveillance of young people. Since minority youth are statistically more likely to be carrying weapons or dealing drugs on the street, why would police not concentrate their limited time and resources on them? Why, realistically, would they spend as much time patrolling middle-class white suburbs looking for armed gang members? (As a police officer in a southern state put it to one of us recently, "I could spend my time jacking up elderly Asian ladies, but why would I?") Moreover, as Human Rights Watch found in their study of the racially bifurcated enforcement of drug laws in Georgia, the police most often operate as a reactive agency that responds to public outcry over crime and drugs, and that outcry is louder in the inner-city ghettoes and barrios where the worst open drug dealing and gang presence are found on the streets.[35] So that is where they go. How can it be called "racist," police often ask, to respond to the concerns of the law-abiding citizens in minority communities? (Especially since the police doing the responding may be minority too?)

But the result of this "actuarial" reasoning, of course, is to exacerbate the very differences that are invoked to justify the racially targeted practices in the first place. This in turn helps to cement the public's image, and the police's image, of the gun-toting gangster or drug dealer as black or Latino. And this confirms the validity of the police focus on youth of color, which then goes around and around in the same kind of vicious circle Piliavin and Briar described a generation ago.

The New Jersey attorney general's report on racial profiling by the state police provides some clear contemporary evidence of how this particularly insidious variety of circular reasoning works in practice. The New Jersey authorities discovered that the vast numbers of motorists subjected to traffic stops on the state's turnpikes were almost 60 percent white. A tiny minority of all stops—less than 1 percent—resulted in a vehicle search. But of those searched, "the overwhelming majority" (77 percent) were of minority motorists. Blacks in particular were 27 percent of those stopped but 53 percent of those searched and 62 percent of those subsequently arrested. In seeking to explain these disparities, the report notes that they probably result, in part, from "willful misconduct" on the part of a relatively few troopers, but much more often from "the tautological use of statistics to tacitly validate pre-existing stereotypes."[36] The state police, in other words,

search the vehicles of blacks and Latinos on the grounds that they are more likely to be carrying drugs or weapons, as determined by who has already been arrested and imprisoned for those offenses. By largely confining these searches to blacks and Latinos, they ensure that most of the people arrested for transporting guns or drugs on the freeways are black or Latino. This, of course, further validates the disproportionate scrutiny of minority drivers. "To the extent that law enforcement agencies arrest minority motorists more frequently based on stereotypes," the report concludes, they continue to "generate statistics that confirm higher crime rates among minorities which, in turn, reinforces the underpinnings of the very stereotypes that gave rise to the initial arrests."[37]

The vicious circle of intensified surveillance, the generation of statistics that support stereotypical conceptions of race and offenses, and on to still more heightened surveillance has arguably worsened in recent years because of the increasing adoption of aggressive, often paramilitary police responses to drugs and gangs in the cities. These strategies escalated in the 1990s with such practices as antigang injunctions that allowed police to target youths labeled, often vaguely, as gang members if they so much as stop to talk with a friend on the street. These practices have surely ratcheted up the role of the police in shunting minority youth into the criminal justice system in disproportionate numbers. Elliott Currie's research in one California county widely known for its extensive *white* drug-using counterculture found that 93 percent of youth sent to juvenile court for the offense of "possession of narcotics or controlled substances for sale" in the 1990s were Latino.[38] Of youth and adults arrested in 1998 in California for the recently enacted offense of "participating in a street gang," only 13 percent were white and non-Latino; almost 67 percent were Latino alone.[39]

It is abundantly clear, then, that race still helps to determine who will enter the formal justice system in the first place and thus powerfully shapes what will happen thereafter. And what the research shows clearly is how persistent racial stereotyping meshes with the effect of long-term structural disadvantages to ensure that blacks wind up more often in the criminal justice system. A legacy of adverse structural conditions causes blacks to have higher rates of offenses to begin with. The higher rates of offenses are then used to justify decisions by police to monitor blacks more intensively and by courts to sentence them more severely. Their greater levels of incarceration contribute to difficulties in getting steady jobs and maintaining stable families, which increases their risks of offending, which … and so on, in a tragic downward spiral.

Racial conservatives fail to acknowledge the destructive effects of that cycle, in part because they do not acknowledge that there are structural reasons for high black crime rates—an issue to which we will now turn.

Disconnecting Crime and Disadvantage

One of the most uncomfortable facts about race in America today is that intolerable levels of crime and violence wrack many black communities. And, as we have seen, no one now seriously doubts that this is what leads to the overrepresentation of black Americans in the criminal justice system. But where do those high rates of crime come from? A recurrent theme in much conservative writing on race is that high black crime rates cannot be caused by racism or by the structural conditions like poverty and extreme inequality that disproportionally afflict blacks. Instead, conservatives argue, high rates of crime, like many other inner-city ills, are produced by some kind of cultural or behavioral deficiencies internal to much of the black community.

In a 1998 issue of the *American Enterprise* magazine devoted to "Fresh Thinking on Race in America," for example, Karl Zinsmeister sums up this view: "Dangerous streets," he argues, like the rest of "our urban underclass problems, [are] not caused by race. They are caused by dysfunctional families and personal behaviors." In *America in Black and White*, the Thernstroms provide the clearest statement of this conservative argument.

They never provide a detailed alternative to the argument that high levels of ghetto violence have something to do with many generations of structural disadvantage. Rather, they suggest that, like other ills of the underclass, crime is a problem blacks have brought upon themselves—with, perhaps, the perverse help of the wrongheaded ideas of guilty white liberals and black demagogues. Ultimately, they suggest that, after all, crime is an individual failing, and one that, repeated over and over again, helps to doom the black underclass to economic stagnation.

This argument is never very clearly articulated, nor is it supported by carefully assembled social science evidence. It is usually presented mostly as unsupported assertions, sometimes backed by rather simplistic historical arguments about the trajectory of crime rates among black Americans. Dinesh D'Souza, for example, argues that there can be no significant connection between racism and high crime rates among blacks because racism has generally declined since the 1950s, while black crime rates have generally gone up. The Thernstroms, similarly, resurrect the shopworn argument (James Q. Wilson used it as far back as the 1960s) that crime cannot be connected to poverty (or unemployment) because crime fell during the depression, when millions of Americans descended into the ranks of the poor, and rose in the prosperous 1960s. That paradox (as Wilson used to put it) is offered as proof that the roots of crime are individual and cultural, not structural.[40]

The fallacy of the conservative argument is not their assertion that high rates of crime in some black communities reflect cultural or behavioral problems. That is true virtually by definition (indeed, the idea that crime is "caused" by "personal behavior" is essentially tautological; crime *is* personal behavior). The problem with this argument is that conservatives tend to detach cultural or behavioral troubles from the larger social context in which they are generated. The conservative position makes a sharp distinction between structural or systemic factors and cultural or behavioral ones. But the most compelling research shows that this distinction is simplistic and misleading.

Consider first the Thernstroms' argument that poverty and crime are not linked. Once again, they radically oversimplify what has been a subtle and complex discussion about the connections between crime and economic disadvantage. Criminologists have rarely argued that crime is caused simply by a lack of money. Instead, the bulk of criminological thought about the links between crime and poverty has run in one of two other directions, or sometimes in both.

The first is that crime is related more to relative than to absolute deprivation. Crime is most likely to grow, as in the so-called strain theories of social scientists like Robert Merton or Richard Cloward, when some people are doing very well while others, for a variety of reasons beyond their control, are left out of that prosperity. Thus, it is not very surprising that crime rose in the 1960s, when the economic fortunes of young unskilled men in the ghettos were plummeting relative to the fates of many other Americans, both white and black. A number of recent studies confirm this long-standing theoretical point. Gary LaFree and Kriss Drass of the University of New Mexico, for example, have shown that rising rates of violent crime among blacks since the 1950s were closely associated with the growth of economic inequality within the black population.[41] Studying a more recent period, Richard Fowles and Mary Merva of the University of Utah have demonstrated that rising rates of murder and assault in the 1980s closely track the growth of wage inequality among men during the same period.[42]

The second important line of criminological thought suggests that poverty and crime are closely linked, but the link is mainly indirect rather than direct. It involves the destructive impact of long-term deprivation and economic marginality on the stability and supportive capacity of institutions like families and local communities. This helps explain why crime could be worse among poor people in the 1960s than in the depression—and why crime among blacks could be worse today than in the 1950s, when there was more overt racism in America. Among other things, the black poor in the 1930s, especially migrants to the cities, had lost some of the supportive network of extended families and stable communities that sustained them, to some extent, in the face of the deep rural poverty of earlier decades. By the 1960s, that kind of social impoverishment had worked its cumulative ill effects on the lives of several generations of the urban black poor. Once again, social science evidence points to the powerful effects of a long-term process of disaccumulation that has shaped the current problems in inner-city communities, a process that conservatives seem not to comprehend.

This perspective also helps to explain the link between family disruption and crime, a link that conservative writers often invoke as an alternative to a more structural explanation. For many years criminologists have noted the impact family disruption has had in increasing the rate of crime in black communities. But a substantial body of research by Edward Shihadeh, Robert Sampson, Graham Ousey, and others confirms the unsurprising point that family disruption is itself often generated by structural forces, notably high levels of long-term joblessness.[43] Similarly, it is clear that, even more than to family structure, violent crime is also related to some problems of family functioning. But once again, economic insecurity and disadvantage strongly predict whether, and how badly, families will be afflicted by these problems. Severe child abuse and neglect, for example, is one of the most potent sources of later violent offending. The risk of severe abuse and neglect, however, is much greater in communities suffering from endemic joblessness and dire poverty.[44] Inadequate supervision of children by parents or other adults is also a fairly good predictor of delinquency. But poor supervision in turn is more likely when parents are forced into long hours of low-wage work to make ends meet and when few public or private community institutions are available to help take care of their children.[45]

The evidence for the relationship between crime and structural conditions, then, is both far stronger and far more sophisticated than conservatives suggest. The best criminological research on these issues makes it clear that the frequent conservative distinction between individual or cultural factors on the one hand and structural or economic ones on the other—between bad attitudes and externally imposed disadvantages as explanations of crime—is much too simplistic. This research confirms the fundamental sociological insight that the effects of social structure on people's behavior are cumulative and mutually reinforcing. These studies do not suggest that black people never behave badly—that is another straw person. They do tell us that bad behavior among black people, just as among white people, is more likely to occur when blacks are living under extremely adverse conditions, especially if they are caught in those conditions for generations. In short, subject people—white or black—to impoverished, limited, and stressful conditions for a long time, and they may begin to act in destructive or self-destructive ways. They may have trouble staying married, might beat their children or their wives, might use drugs heavily or drink too much, or might become depressed and find it difficult to cope or to parent well. Not all of them will respond in these ways, even under the worst social conditions. But the risks that some will are much greater. Over time, these responses may even crystallize and be passed on across the generations. It would be silly to deny that these things happen or that the risks of troubling behavior are very high in some black communities. Those risks, however, cannot be divorced from their roots in the corrosive impact of generations of hardship, segregation, community disinvestment, and restricted opportunities.

Again, it is not just a few pieces of recent research that make these links between deprivation (or joblessness) and crime. By now, most serious criminologists agree that these links are undeniable and enormously important. Acknowledging the complex and sometimes indirect quality of these connections does not diminish their importance. If anything, it is the opposite. Understanding that years of not having a job, and having no hope of getting one, may have the power to wreck one's personal relationships, for example, is powerful corroboration that economic forces can have a potent impact on personality and on human relationships.

The recent trajectory of crime rates in the United States, moreover, suggests that this process can be turned around: that the spiral of disadvantage, social exclusion, and violence can be reversed under more favorable economic conditions. Culture is real. But it is not set in stone. Rates of violence among black youth, for example, fell strongly after the early 1990s, in tandem with the long economic boom of the 1990s and the decline in unemployment and subemployment among the inner-city young. Research by Jared Bernstein and Ellen Houston of the Economic Policy Institute showed that crime among minority youth indeed fell fastest in those regions where opportunities for steady work for low-income young people grew the most. Just as there is powerful evidence that the loss of entry-level jobs through the 1980s helped drive violent crime rates higher, so there is now evidence that the extraordinary growth in new kinds of employment during the boom years helped to bring those rates down by pulling young men off the street corner and into the legitimate labor force.[46] There is no guarantee that these benign effects will endure: at this writing, violent crime rates have stabilized and in some places risen along with the economic downturn in the first years of the twenty-first century. They do, however, provide one more impressive indication of the capacity of structural forces to affect the behavior of people who are often described by conservatives as hopelessly mired in a "self-defeating culture."

There are other ways in which racial discrimination may affect the crime rate that, even though there is less research on them, clearly need mentioning. First is the impact of racially structured disinvestment in the public institutions that could intervene with people once they have a problem or begin to get in trouble. Discriminatory disinvestment in the public sector in minority communities—in such services as mental health care, child protection, or drug treatment—means that the kinds of problems that make people more vulnerable to crime and violence will be more widespread. It also means that people of color who are at risk will get less help. In other words, to the extent that public sector disinvestment is structured by race, the black youth with a potentially troublesome problem is going to have less chance of getting help than a white youth. The black child at risk of severe mistreatment by her parents is much less likely to get effective attention from stressed and underfunded child protective systems. The black mother suffering from chronic depression and unable to handle her kids is less likely to get help from the crumbling public mental health system than her white counterpart who can afford a good therapist. All of this substantially increases the chances that those children will become involved with delinquency and crime in a serious way.

Second, the discriminatory processes within the criminal justice system outlined above also contribute to the high crime levels in many black communities. That has probably always been true, but it is becoming increasingly so as the level of black incarceration has skyrocketed in recent years, utterly transforming poor black neighborhoods in the process.[47] Although it is not easy to quantify, there is little doubt that crime in the black community today has increasingly become an iatrogenic malady that reflects, in part, the destructive impact of mass incarceration on individual life chances, the family, and the local community. As Dina Rose and Todd Clear have shown, there is a point beyond which the removal of so many workers, parents, uncles, and other adults from the hardest-hit communities weakens their capacity to exert what sociologists call informal social control, thus countering any crime-reducing effect of high rates of imprisonment.[48] The enormous rise in incarceration has blocked a good part of several generations of black men from attaining steady work and has accordingly hindered the formation of stable families and increased the attraction of illegal ways to make a living.[49] The sociologist Bruce Western has found that the experience of incarceration as a juvenile reduces employment by about 9 percent among black youth. Being incarcerated as a juvenile is even more detrimental to black youths' future employment prospects than is dropping out of high school.[50] The still-faster rise in the incarceration

of black women has fractured families even more and left large numbers of children effectively without parents.

The growth of Draconian ancillary punishments for drug offenses in particular, like losing public assistance benefits and housing subsidies for life, has deepened the economic subordination and social impoverishment experienced by great numbers of black Americans. Voting restrictions for ex-felons have disenfranchised many others, rendering them less able to challenge adverse social and economic conditions through legitimate political action. An estimated 13 percent of adult black men are disenfranchised under these provisions. In ten states, as of the late 1990s, the number was more than 20 percent, and in Alabama and Florida 31 percent of all black men had permanently lost the right to vote.[51] Over the long run, all of these adversities contribute to high crime in black communities across the United States, and, barring changes in American criminal justice practices, will probably do so increasingly in the future.

More generally, there is a crucial sense in which the increasingly repressive responses to inner-city crime and drug abuse have been the flip side of the cumulative disinvestment in more positive strategies to reconstruct poor communities. Especially in these fiscally conservative times when there is limited scope for public investment, the diversion of billions of scarce public dollars to prisons and jails means that there will be that much less money available for child protection, dropout prevention programs, public colleges accessible to low-income young people, and a host of other public institutions that could operate as the front line in preventing crime. Since the early 1980s, the already meager and declining public investment in the social infrastructure of poor communities of color has been further eroded by the diversion of billions of dollars in scarce public spending to prisons and jails. Thus the incarceration boom has helped, in a truly vicious cycle, to aggravate the steady depletion of public and social capital available in communities already disabled by a heritage of poverty and segregation and abandoned by several decades of deindustrialization.

It is not accidental that the 1980s and 1990s were decades of both crumbling schools and bulging prisons (from the mid-1980s to the late 1990s, the state of California built twenty-two prisons and one college). Americans are now paying a steep price for that choice of priorities—in high rates of violence as well as of illiteracy, preventable disease, drug abuse, and other ills. And a sustained economic downturn could intensify that destructive tradeoff.

Race, Crime, and Disaccumulation: Ideology and the Politics of Social Policy

The conservative argument, then, distorts the reality of the black experience with crime and punishment in two ways, both of which impede our understanding of the causes of social troubles in the black community and hinder efforts to develop effective strategies to do something about them.

First, conservatives have diverted attention from the more subtle and complex, yet nevertheless quite destructive, problem of continuing racism in the institutions of justice. They have accomplished this by mis-characterizing the liberal view as one that sees the overrepresentation of blacks in the criminal justice system as *only* a reflection of racist police, prosecutors, and judges. This enables them to ignore a pervasive set of interlocking processes that not only help to explain the black predominance in the jails and prisons but also put all too many black Americans on a downward trajectory in every other realm of social life. For while there is a sense in which it is true that crime causes poverty, as conservatives often argue, it is also true that *imprisonment causes poverty*—indeed the whole host of difficulties such as joblessness or family problems that conservatives and racial realists often dismiss as behavioral ones. Discrimination in the justice system is not the only source of the crippling overrepresentation of black Americans in the prisons and jails. But it remains an important one, and one whose impact on black communities is pervasive and fateful.

Second, the conservative move to deny the links between black crime and black economic and social disadvantage flies in the face of decades of criminological research. It therefore leaves Americans without meaningful guidance on how, realistically, to combat the violence and drug abuse that continue to devastate poor communities of whatever color. Disconnecting these very genuine problems from their structural roots enables conservative ideologists to salvage their central idea that black problems in post–Jim Crow America simply reflect behavioral or cultural deficiencies and have little or no connection with discrimination, past or present. Thus the denial contributes to the belief that well-intentioned intervention by government is unlikely to help, and might hinder, black advancement. That argument cannot, however, stand even modest scrutiny. The evidence is overwhelming that high rates of crime and violence are one of the costs of a legacy of discrimination and of systematic disinvestment in black communities. And it suggests that Americans will not make enduring strides to minimize crime among African Americans unless and until that legacy is confronted more seriously and creatively than has been done so far.

3

Historic Processes and Case Studies

Medieval Anti-Semitism and Islamophobia

Introduction to Medieval Spain

Islamophobia, Anti-Semitism, and Orientalism

By D. Paul Sweeney

●●●

Islam's Origins, Spread, and Perception in the West

From Islam's seventh century early formation in the holy city of Mecca on the Arabian Peninsula, Muhammad (570–632 C.E.) called for men and women to reform their ways and submit to God. Viewed as a prophet, Muhammad's teachings emanated from divine messages and were compiled into a sacred book, the *Quran*, that symbolized separation from the other Semitic faiths, i.e., Judaism and Christianity. Shortly thereafter, Islam quickly spread throughout the Middle East and Persia and Muhammad founded an Islamic empire. From Egypt, the religion spread across North Africa, facilitated in part, by the efficient network of roads built by the Roman Empire. By this time (656–661 C.E.) early dissent and civil war occurred over leadership and whose authority would succeed Muhammad's. Initially, Muhammad's cousin, 'Ali ibn Abi Talib, married Muhammad's daughter, Fatima, and proclaimed himself *caliph* in Kufa, but conflicts arose with Basra (Iraq) and Syria. Although victorious, 'Ali was regarded with resentment by those who felt he compromised too much and his assassination soon followed. In the wake of rapid expansion and conquests, a centralized authority was established in Damascus, Syria to maintain the newly developed Islamic State (*caliphate*), by Mu'awiya, after 'Ali's elder son, Hasan, acquiesced. This marked an important second phase in Islam's growth, during which many Muslims regarded the first four caliphs as *Rashidun* (Rightly Guided). The caliphs became virtually hereditary and for many years thereafter, family members descended from an ancestor named Umayya controlled an area known to posterity as the Ummayad Caliphate.[1] While other caliphates rose and declined in later centuries, it was the Ummayads who continued the westward expansion.

Explaining Islam's Impact: Open Questions. How did the rapid Islamic conquests make a global impact, and to what extent did they open or close historically established patterns and paths of world trade? Additionally, how did each ethnic and religious group deal with the inevitable tensions between power and powerlessness? Further, how and why were certain social and intellectual boundaries created? Finally, when, why, or how were the boundaries crossed, and how did this heighten tensions socially, especially as it regarded

---

1 Albert Hourani, *A History of the Arab Peoples* (Cambridge, MA: Harvard University Press, 1991), 14–27.

the identities of Muslim, Christians, and Jews? These questions are important to consider when looking through the often-blurred filters of ideology, selective memory, socioeconomic agendas, and imperfect or revisionist histories.[2]

On the eve of the Iberian Conquest (694–710 C.E.), world trade flourished as it had during the *Pax Romana* (Roman Peace), but once the historic trade centers lay in Muslim hands, some scholars hypothesized, especially Henrie Pirenne, that a shared sense of community created by Imperial Rome no longer existed in Western Europe. According to Pirenne's economic-based assertions, the aftermath of Rome's decline led Europe to quickly shift to a pattern of ruralization. Most significantly, Europe adopted a moneyless economic model characteristic of the medieval feudal system, where barter, trade, and tribute to manor lords held sway until the thirteenth century.[3] In the Byzantine Empire the Greeks felt the loss of the Orient and a necessary economic dependence on Western Europe for raw materials. In response, they created a desirable market for goods unique to the East.

In essence, this reversal was the complete opposite of the trade and commerce that existed in Roman times, where the West was independent of the East economically speaking. Thus, by the tenth century, Muslims controlled many of the old trade routes and ports in the Mediterranean, from Syria to Morocco. This was not an impermeable barrier, however, and all neighboring states participated in a new world economy, occasionally infused by substantial quantities of gold from Sudan.[4]

Importance of Gold and Silver. Known as a bimetallic economic system, the extreme reaches of world trade were influenced by a desire for,

or a lack of gold and silver. A triangular trading system between the West, Byzantium in the middle, and the Islamic World in the East created an interdependent economic system, which was most pronounced by the flow of gold from Islamic lands via the Byzantines to the West, in exchange for raw materials otherwise unobtainable. The middle point in the trade triangle, in the markets of Constantinople (Istanbul), had the finest luxury items and spices for purchase. Of even greater importance to economic trade patterns, however, was the ratio in value of silver to gold throughout the middle ages, which differed in each of the three sectors. For example, gold generally moved from where it was less highly valued (e.g., Sudan) to where it was most desirable (Byzantium and Western Europe). Conversely, the flow of silver ran the opposite direction for the same reason. Together, gold and silver encouraged and contributed to the later development of monetary exchange systems. Regardless of a gold or silver standard, these patterns of flow help explain the prevalence of silver in early medieval Europe, and the infamous lust for gold during the Spanish Conquest of the Americas after 1492. The Byzantines had a penchant for gold accumulation (as typified by gold leaf iconography), but the bimetallic system found its first home in the Islamic territories. Refining the Pirenne thesis, it is evident that, while minds may have been closed, purses remained open, insofar as there was a steady East-West is evident that only minds were closed because a steady East-West trade system was maintained until the First Crusade in the late eleventh century. Significantly, long-distance trade with the Far East (i.e., China and India) typically passed through Islamic lands to Byzantium, and then into Europe.[5]

To summarize, Muslims inherited the eastern and African regions of the former Roman Empire and ancient networks of roads. Further, weak and non-unified opposition facilitated the rapid spread of Islam. Another point to consider is that following the conquest the Islamic states also inherited former Roman subjects, who represented a large

2 Kenneth Baxter Wolf, "Muhammad as Antichrist in Ninth-Century," in *Christians, Muslims, and Jews in Medieval and Early Spain: Interaction and Cultural Change,* edited by Mark D. Meyerson and Edward D. English (Notre Dame, IN: University of Notre Dame Press, 2000), xi–xxi; Thomas F. Glick, *Islamic and Christian Spain in the Early Middle Ages* (Princeton, NJ: Princeton University Press, 1979), 19–21; Roger Collins, *The Arab Conquest of Spain, 710–797,* (Oxford, UK: Basil Blackwell, 1989), 1–5.

3 Glick, *"Islamic and Christian Spain,"* 19–21.

4 Ibid.

5 Ibid., 20.

variety of ethnicities and religious faiths, including Christianity and Judaism. Generally speaking, the Arabs had a reverence for the ancients' (*al-'uual*) mastery of unknown technologies while displaying ambivalence and contempt toward Roman ruins.[6] In this setting the next step in the spread of Islam was the Iberian Peninsula, which was easily accessible via the narrow Strait of Gibraltar. The resulting occupation of southern Iberia led to the creation of a new region called *al-Andalus*, by the end of the eighth century, which resembled Islamdom. Its creation shaped ethno-religious exchanges, as well as historical and sociological patterns. Spain, in general, saw recurring patterns associated with the coexistence, or, *convivencia* of Islam and al-Andalus between 711 and 1492.[7] While an Islamophobic reaction was delayed in Northern and Eastern Europe, early incidences of Islamophopia corresponded with Judaeophobia as a result of the Iberian Conquest.

Early Anti-Semitism: A Jewish "Conspiracy"

Scapegoating is an unfortunate human behavior, and typically, it occurs in times of economic downturn, social change, or following a military defeat. For instance, France blamed its very small percentage of Jewish army officers for the bitter defeat dealt by Germany in the nineteenth century, which resulted in a loss of prestige and the Alsace-Lorraine territory. In this case of anti-Semitism, an army captain named Dreyfus stood accused of treason. The infamous Dreyfus Affair (1895–1906) was a well-documented event in a world growing closer to nationalistic conflict.[8] Similarly, Spanish historians blamed the weaker Jewish minority after the rapid and embarrassing collapse of the Visigothic kingdom in 711. The monumental defeat could only be partially attributable to infighting between two brothers, but incompetence may have played a role too. Was there a tangible reason for

the empire's loss to a combined force of Arabs and Berbers? The 'conspiracy' theory will be addressed here because of its sociological importance to patterns of cultural anti-Semitism in Europe, but first it is necessary to establish what pre-Islamic Spain looked like socially and politically.

Visigothic Spain on the Eve of Conquest. Prior to its demise, the Visigothic state in Spain was an ethnically stratified society with a fragmented political structure marred further by its depressed and imbalanced rural-based economy. On the local level, herding was their chief concern and life was quite unlike that of the northern European states. Roughly 200,000 Goths migrated from German lands and ruled the indigenous population of about eight million Hispano-Romans. The German-speaking overlords and Latin-speaking subjects had cardinal religious differences as well. For example, the Goths were a minority, who as Arian Christians, denied the divinity of Christ, whereas the majority of the population was Catholic, with pagan antecedents in rural areas, or ancient communities of Sephardic Jews.[9]

An interesting parallel to late medieval Spain was a provision forbidding intermarriage between Goths and Hispano-Romans that lasted until 652. In time Roman law was abolished, but when its dual legal system ended, social tensions heightened because the Hispano-Romans were now relegated to second-class status. Thereafter, the Visigoths enjoyed being elite minorities that ruled an ethnically diverse majority, similar to a definition of racism established in Chapter I, "a system of advantages based on race." Furthering the complexity was an apparent Gothic conversion to Catholicism for political reasons, and probably because they feared their more numerous subjects. What came next was a shift to the medieval feudal model where dukes created fiefs in autonomous provinces and ruled with a firm grip.[10]

In the years approaching the conquest, both agrarian and urban economies were in decay. Moreover, the Jews, although an extreme minority, were well represented in Visigothic trade, as well

6   Ibid., 21.
7   Wolf, "Muhammad as Antichrist in Ninth-Century," xiv.
8   Jacob Katz, *From Prejudice to Destruction: Anti-Semitism, 1700–1933*, (Cambridge, MA: Harvard University Press, 1980), 298–300.

9   Glick, *"Islamic and Christian Spain,"* 27–28.
10   Ibid., 28–29.

as some foreign interests. Next came an economic recession, which helped establish the pattern of blaming the Jews for the decline and a "regressive cycle of restrictive anti-Jewish legislation" that apparently further eroded and disrupted trade.[11] In short, the economic regression in Visigothic Spain conspired with an equally disjointed social organization to the extent that mobilizing to face a common threat was slow, thereby facilitating the relative ease with which the Islamic invasion pacified Iberia.

Fall of the Visigoths

Sometime in April in the year 711, although the exact date is unclear, Tariq ibn Ziyad led a mostly Berber army on a swift campaign that quickly crushed the Visigoths. While sources do not agree on the size of the invading Islamic force, perhaps 7–12,000 soldiers may have been involved, and the majority of whom had newly converted to Islam after the conquest of North Africa. This sudden influx of Muslims into southern Christian Europe gave rise simultaneously to a new phenomenon that ushered in equal measures of fear and hate: Islamophobia, or, the fear of Islam and its multi-ethnic believers. The other reaction in southern Spain, although it may have found its origins in later revisionist histories, was a 'necessity' to explain the rapid loss of land and prestige as a result of betrayal. Thus, a Jewish conspiracy took root. By demonizing the Jews and Muslims alike, a system of privilege emerged in the Christian lands where, after 1391, the Old Christians identified as 'white' and racially more pure (*limpieza de sangre*) than the Jews and the Muslims. This in turn created a social caste that steadily disadvantaged Jews, including those who converted to Christianity (*conversos*), and Muslim converts (*moriscos*) as well. However, the fall of southern Spain was blamed primarily on the Jews.[12] In the next section, dissecting this myth by examining claims and sources will help build

critical thinking for examination of the quality or validity of sources utilized to construct social and national histories.

A Matter of Sources

In the past historians primarily used Christian (Latin) and sometimes Jewish (Hebrew) sources to explain what happened, and they categorically ignored Arabic sources until much later. When these sources were finally examined, in the nineteenth century, Orientalist thinking influenced interpretations of events and created what some scholars today call the *Myth of al-Andalus*. Using limited sources with an inherent bias is always problematic, but claims that Jews had, as early as 694, "entered into an alliance with their more fortunate brethren in Africa, with the intention of overwhelming the Visigothic empire" took root in the literature and in Spanish national identity. Further, the claim stipulated that the Jews were probably aided and abetted by Muslims. One source claimed that all of the Jews of Spain were enslaved as punishment.[13] Note the similarity of the claim of a Jewish plot to take over world markets and governments, which correspond to two types of cultural anti-Semitism: economic anti-Semitism and political anti-Semitism. It is almost certain that later revisions of older chronicles plugged in the anti-Semitic attitudes and opinions of the revisionist authors, which reemerged in the nineteenth century. Interestingly, the primary Jewish source, published in English and German in 1894 and 1895, respectively, echoed the anti-Semitic tract fabricated in Czarist Russia, an infamous forgery known as *The Protocols of the Elders of Zion* that appeared around the same time. Still other accounts insinuated that Jews in Visigothic Spain resented persecution; evidence for this as the root of the conspiracy is often cited in the old texts. This same storyline appeared in English and Spanish sources.[14]

---

11   Glick, *"Islamic and Christian Spain,"* 30; Collins, *"The Arab Conquest of Spain,"* 11–12.
12   Norman Roth, "The Jews and the Muslim Conquest of Spain," *Jewish Social Studies* 38, no. 2 (1976): 145–146.

13   Roth, "The Jews and the Muslim Conquest of Spain," 145–146; Collins, *"The Arab Conquest of Spain,"* 1–5.
14   Roth, "The Jews and the Muslim Conquest of Spain," 146.

Stretching the truth even further validates the definition of a stereotype that posits, in part, incomplete or selective histories, including one claiming that Jews made up the majority of the invading Islamic army. Therefore, this unholy alliance of Judaism and Muhammedans was the reason southern Spain became al-Andalus until 1492. This supposed dichotomy between Christians on the one hand and the other two Abrahamic religions on the other, was clearly first constructed in early modern Spain, in the years following the expulsion of the Jews. By the sixteenth century the moriscos too were expelled from Spain, which fits the pattern of anti-Semitism and Islamophobia often rising and falling in close proximity, albeit at disproportionate rates.[15]

Reconstructing a Narrative

Navigating between facts and fiction, what is evident in this elaborate conspiracy theory disparaging Jews is that as early as 694 the Visigothic king, Egica (687–702), had policies of unrelieved persecution directed at Jews. However, he was apparently more liberal than his predecessors. Egica is described as comparatively more "benign and generous with the Jews, but they, [were] ungrateful to their benefactor. ..."[16] This composite stipulated that Egica, feeling slighted, accused Jews in his kingdom of conspiring with "Hebrews in the areas across the sea." It is not clear though whether the Jews really were punished, expelled, or enslaved as a consequence. It is clear, however, that a Visigothic law requiring or advocating forced baptism of all Jews in the kingdom received renewed interest during the reign of Egica's son Wittiza (694–710). By 711, Jews faced another concern: Would the Muslims be more tolerant than the Visigoths? In theory the Jews should enjoy a legal "protected status" under Muslims because they were *ahl al-Qitah*,

(people of the book).[17] Their fate seemed doubtful initially because even the prophet Muhammad had persecuted Jews and expelled them from all of Arabia. At the same time though, contradictory behavior revealed surprisingly benevolent treatment of ethnic and religious minorities as Islam spread through former Byzantine lands, Egypt, and Essentially, a class of people who had a protected status was created under a principle called ahl al-dimma. These people were hereafter referred to as dhimmi.[18]

Despite claims to the contrary, there is no firm evidence that Jews had illicit contact with the Berbers, nor did early historians acknowledge that if all of the Jews were allegedly slaves, they could not have been capable of such a plot. The most reliable sources of the era, long unknown or ignored, are the Arabic texts. They reveal that the Iberian invasion was planned as early as 676 or 677, and in no way is it ever suggested that Jews played a role in any capacity, much less sponsoring a "conspiracy." Therefore, through the perpetuation of this myth and stereotype it is clear that a classic psychological displacement occurred to simultaneously explain defeat and demonize the Jews for religious reasons (Judaeophobia).[19]

Final Nail in the Coffin: The Treachery at Toledo Myth

While actual dates, months, and years are murky, the Arabic calendar's year 92 A.H. corresponded to the Western calendar's 711 C.E. Period Christian and Jewish sources are either incomplete or unreliable, heavily biased, and often written centuries after the events took place, providing another twist in how the Judaeophobic strain wove its way into the texts by the late medieval period. This version, or reinterpretation, posited that the fall of the Visigoth capital, Toledo, coincided with Palm Sunday while the townspeople were "out in the field" observing

15   Roth, "The Jews and the Muslim Conquest of Spain," 147; Edward Said, *Orientalism*, (1978. Reprint, New York, NY: Vintage, 1994), 27–28.
16   Roth, "The Jews and the Muslim Conquest of Spain," 149.

17   Ibid.
18   Roth, "The Jews and the Muslim Conquest of Spain," 149–150; Hourani, "*A History of the Arab Peoples*," 47–48.
19   Roth, "The Jews and the Muslim Conquest of Spain," 149–150; Collins, "*The Arab Conquest of Spain*," 23–24, 68–71.

religious practices. While engaged in their religious observances, the Jews allegedly informed the invaders that this would be the perfect time to attack, and the so-called spring or April narrative evolved into the "treachery at Toledo myth." This is preposterous for many reasons, not the least of which is geography. How would an invader penetrate so deeply into Spain without word preceding it? Further, this myth is easily dissolved by the Arab historian and chronicler Ibn al-Atir. Toledo fell in 92 A.H., on a day corresponding to October 18, 711.[20] This alone renders the suspiciously specific Palm Sunday libel both impossible and irrelevant to the defeat. Nevertheless, the damage of such lies, falsified facts, and creative reworking of history heightened Islamophobia and Judaeophobia in Westerners' imagination, narratives, and discourse, through perpetual discrimination, intolerance, and sometimes violence.

Occupation and Socialization. After enjoying early victories, the Berber armies established the practice of entrusting the Jews to run captured cities, if Jews dwelt there, and this pattern became an almost general procedure. Old Christian histories are understandably heavily biased on this detail, in addition to being fragmented, incomplete, and at times, unreliable. However, researchers face problems like these when reconstructing the past, especially when Jewish sources from the same period are absent or equally unreliable. Fortunately, untranslated Arabic chronicles partially fill in the gaps. The Arabic chronicles question why the Visigoths collapsed so quickly, if the cause was not treachery by the Jews?[21] A glimpse into the past first appeared in the fifteenth century after the expulsion of Jews from Spain in 1492. This Jewish text describes a bitter quarrel between Julian and Roderic, Witteza's sons, on the eve of conquest. Because of the infighting between the brothers, it divided their attention and contributed to mutual downfall. Interestingly, the narrative implied that the conquest took place during Holy Week (roughly, in April) and that both Córdoba and Toledo were taken unawares on Palm Sunday. It appears that the treachery at Toledo myth outlived the Jewish expulsion. This source may have been shaped by a converso. Clearly it was manufactured to fit a particular narrative, but it is easily refuted by the long shunned Arabic texts. What is true about April 711, however, is that the invasion began that month, but the capitulation of Toledo occurred in mid-October.[22] More probable is that the six-month campaign was more than the defeated Visigoths could bear psychologically, and so they displaced the humiliation by concocting a Jewish conspiracy.

Ultimately, a long-standing special hatred of the Jews contributed to falsification of events and perpetuated anti-Jewish propaganda that escalated with each retelling and rendering into print. As is often the case, a convenient scapegoat is found in minority populations within a greater society, serving to divert attention away from the real source of shame: the Visigoths were defeated because of bad leadership.

Al-Andalus and Christian Iberia

New Codes of Governance. After most of Iberia was occupied, its cities experienced a shift in daily life after the Muslim rulers imposed a code of governance that affected every aspect of law, policy, and social activity in al-Andalusan society. A certain amount of compliance was required from the indigenous population in Islamic Spain, which is more accurately termed 'al-Andalus' in order to avoid conflict with shariah law.[23] Exactly how much the new governments impinged on the indigenous population depended on whether the inhabitants lived in cities or the rural areas. While precise census records were not kept, the majority of the population lived in the vast mountainous expanses surrounding the cities and towns. What occurred next is often debated, but a revisionist

20 Roth, "The Jews and the Muslim Conquest of Spain," 152–157.
21 Roth, "The Jews and the Muslim Conquest of Spain," 154–155; Collins, "The Arab Conquest of Spain," 23–24.
22 Roth, "The Jews and the Muslim Conquest of Spain," 156–157; Collins, "The Arab Conquest of Spain," 17–18.
23 Richard Hitchcock, "Christian-Muslim Understanding(s) in Medieval Spain," Hispanic Research Journal 9, no. 4 (2008): 315.

twist found its way into the popular narrative, informed by Orientalist thought in the late nineteenth century. It posited that the rapid acquisition of Iberia established a "… tolerant attitude towards the Christian religion …"[24] Regarded as the *convivencia*, this fairly modern notion painted an idyllic and highly romanticized vision of rolling pastoral scenes and people of three faiths living harmoniously with one another, or at the very least, it was a relative peace.

The toleration, as it is also termed, created a freedom of exchange, for example intellectual and commercial exchange, which permitted a certain amount of assimilation between Christian and Muslim communities. Importantly, in the aftermath of the conquest a relative peace and trade between al-Andalus and non-unified Christian kingdoms in the north occured. For Christians, converting to Islam opened doors to upward mobility, and in time, even intermarriage between groups became more common. "[Becoming] a Muslim meant comparative freedom from the burden of taxation [*jizya*]."[25] The question is whether 'relative peace' was really possible with intertribal disputes during the early centuries in al-Andalus, and later feudal rivalries.

Christian Kingdoms in the North. In the northern kingdoms prior to the eleventh century, warfare was constant between feudal states. The primary difference is that before the Reconquista, war that broke out between Christians and al-Andalusan states was less motivated by religious differences, than desire for territory and tribute. It was not until the years following the First Crusade (1096–1099) that anti-Islamic sentiments reappeared, but Spain was somewhat insulated geographically from the rest of Europe and papal authority at that time.[26]

Dhimmi Status for People of the Book. Although the Jews initially worried about their well-being in an Islamic state, they had some familiarity of a practice conferred towards 'people of the book', which included Jews and Christians, from their connections in North Africa. In essence, dhimmi status permitted Jewish and Christian groups to retain religious practices in return for an annual tax based on Byzantine codes called the jizya. Protected by four schools of law, or *mdhuab*, all forms of worship were permitted under the Umayyad caliphate (756–976). Some stipulations allowed for the construction of new churches and synagogues, provided they lay one mile outside the outer wall of the urban centers. There was no policy of eradication of rival beliefs, as previously feared by religious groups (e.g., forced conversions, beheadings for aposty), but the dhimmi were expected to adapt to life in an Islamic state.[27]

There were documented instances of civic punishments meted out for violation of the *shariah* codes. For example, between 850–859 C.E. fifty-one Christians faced public blasphemy charges, thereby violating the dhimmi agreement, and were punished with the death penalty. While no Arabic records relate this situation, it is consistent with legal codes to try the accused before publically executing them for blasphemy. Nonetheless, it is important to understand that while there was no systematic or sustained anti-Christian policy in Córdoba during the Umayyad period, the limits of tolerance were tested, and will be addressed later in this chapter. Ultimately, enjoying the benefits and protections offered by the dhimmi was contingent upon staying civil, albeit at the price of second-class citizenship.[28]

Rural Populations in al-Andalus. In general, rural populations still operated under existing feudal codes and were not subject to the same dhimmi regulations or the corresponding jizya taxation. Instead, they paid tribute to landlords and lived off the land as their ancestors had.

---

24 Hitchcock, "Christian-Muslim Understanding(s) in Medieval Spain," 315; Dario Fernandez-Morera, "The Islamic Warriors' Destruction of a Nascent Civilization: The Catholic Kingdom of the Visigoths in Spain (A.D. 589–711)," *Modern Age* 53: nos.1/2 (2011): 6–7. Taking an Orientalist approach, the author has been accused of promoting "scholarly Islamophobia" by some academics.
25 Hitchcock, "Christian-Muslim Understanding(s) in Medieval Spain," 316.
26 Ibid.

27 Hitchcock, "Christian-Muslim Understanding(s) in Medieval Spain," 316; Collins, "*The Arab Conquest of Spain*," 41; Hourani, "*A History of the Arab Peoples*," 47–48, 68–69.
28 Hitchcock, "Christian-Muslim Understanding(s) in Medieval Spain," 318.

Little archaeological evidence supports any claims that Christianity was more dominant in the outlying areas than the cities, towns, and villages with churches and monasteries. If anything, many peasants may not have known about Islam's presence for a long time, nor were they obligated to comply or convert. Even for Christians in the remote areas of al-Andalus, Islam was considered a distant secular authority.[29] Therefore, it is difficult to know how women in rural areas lived compared to those in the areas directly under the shariah codes, subject to codes governing gender.

Women and Shariah in al-Andalus

In recent times, as discussion about immigration continues, much has been made about Muslims imposing shariah law in the West. The tone is clearly hostile and deeply rooted in religiosity, so an overview of what shariah meant for women, as well as the other dhimmi in al-Andalus, is needed. Western accounts, heavily influenced by the dual edge of Orientalism, cite diminished status for women in Islamic societies, along with restrictive social proscriptions.[30] However, similar restrictions existed in Judaism and Christianity. Even Islamic practices demonstrated varying degrees of permissiveness and conservatism, depending on time and place. What would women in Islamic Iberia have experienced during the first few hundred years after conquest? The next sections give an overview and outline the gender roles in respective societies.

Shariah's prevailing legacy placed women in the roles of daughters and wives who, if obedient, stayed within domestic settings and were discouraged from attending mosques or embarking on the *hajj*, the sacred pilgrimage to Mecca.[31] Assuming total subordination to men is not an accurate description of medieval Spain, particularly after the 1100s when the Islamic mysticism known as *Sufism* arrived in al-Andlaus. More open to women's participation, it may have given some women legal avenues to dictate marriage contracts, or restrict their husbands from taking a second wife. As is often the case with human behavior, official rules were not always applied to the letter of the law.[32]

Patriarchal Societies and Women. Comparatively speaking, the medieval period not a significant departure from other pre-modern codes, including Roman and Persian law, which heavily influenced Islamic law in the eighth and ninth-centuries. In general, men in the dominant social group (i.e., the patriarchal group) enjoyed full legal rights whereas the legal status of outside groups (dhimmi) was diminished at varying levels. The outside groups could include slaves, members of minority groups, other religions, women, and minors. However, despite a lower social status, women and the other were exempt from certain obligations, provided they behaved well and did not jeopardize the social contract.[33] What counted as exemptions? Christians and Jews were excluded from compulsory military service under the codes, and they enjoyed some legal and physical protection from the authorities. These protections were contingent, however, on an ability to pay the head-tax (*jizya*), though all dhimmi were obligated to show respect and defer to Muslims.[34]

Married Muslim women were protected by their husband and unmarried women by a wali (a guardian). The family provided for a woman's financial needs until she married, then the responsibility transferred to her husband. "Protection" also meant the person was not a full member of society. Briefly, women and non-Muslims were all considered second-class citizens and treated as such. For example, their presence and obtrusiveness in public spaces was supposed to be limited. Similar restrictions prevented Christians and Jews from building new houses of worship in city

---

29 Ibid.
30 Sonya Fernandez, "The Crusade Over the Bodies of Women," *Patterns of Prejudice* 43, nos. 3–4 (2009): 269–271.
31 Jessica A. Coope, "An Etiquette for Women: Women's Experience of Islam in Muslim Spain," *Essays in Medieval Studies* 29 (2013): 75; María Jesús Fuente, "Christian, Muslim and Jewish Women in Late Medieval Iberia," *Medieval Encounters* 15 (2009): 321.

32 Jessica A. Coope, "An Etiquette for Women," 75.
33 Ibid., 76.
34 Coope, "An Etiquette for Women," 77; Hourani, "A History of the Arab Peoples," 47–48.

limits, and they had to refrain from public processions or rituals. Finally, etiquette for women also dictated rules for how a woman should dress and where she could walk on the street (covered and off to the side), and non-Muslims too had to stay out of the way of Muslim men and authorities.[35]

Importance of Dress Codes. Ultimately, strict dress codes stressed group identification to prevent non-Muslims (and Muslim women) from passing themselves off as Muslim males. However, the code governing non-Muslim men may not have been well enforced in al-Andalus. Regardless of occasional lax enforcement, dress codes reveal the anxiety of their authors, which leads them to try to prevent members of a lower caste from infiltrating a higher caste. These place-setting laws that affected women, slaves, Christians, and Jews were not unique in the ancient world.[36]

Marriage and Upward Mobility. Despite the restrictions set by shariah, universal application and compliance was inconsistent. Jews and Christians often dressed like Muslims and some served in the military. Additionally, in certain areas enforcement may not have been as strict for women as the codes stipulated, particularly in larger cities such as Granada. Even the terms and conditions of marriage contracts were not as binding and restrictive. The best examples from surviving records show that a woman could opt for divorce if her husband tried to take a second wife, had a female slave who gave birth to his child, or was absent from home more than six months, unless he had embarked on the *hajj*. While society privileged Muslim men, wives sometimes held the upper hand in shaping their lives.[37]

Social Restrictions on Women. Holding a political office or a cultural position, or even engaging in matters of economics was barred from women in the stricter areas. Their primary role, defined culturally, was to raise children and maintain the household. However, domestic servitude belied the power women sometimes held outside of their household duties, especially when it came to cultural continuity, separatism, or cultural integration. The norm was that women in each faith were expected to be passive, submissive, and silent in their respective religious spaces. Nevertheless, the domestic space was extremely important to society and the economy, despite its lack of salary. Further, domestic slaves, who were mostly Muslims born in captivity or captured in war, also contributed to households. Some even conducted their master's business for him, and if freed, sometimes married into the family. There was a strong preference for female slaves, however, who were often subjected them to the owner's sexual appetites.[38]

Common jobs for women included housekeeper (*criada*), weaving, trading, and lending, all within the domestic context. Outside of the home women functioned as midwives (*porteras*) and nurse maids (*modrizas*), sheepherders, common laborers, and prostitutes. Less common, and often forbidden, were women who worked in some aspect of culture, medicine, or religion. As mothers, women's primary function was educating the youth. All three religious traditions placed this task on mothers, who also conveyed gender roles, rituals, and related cultural practices to their children. For instance, Jewish and Muslim rites required cleanliness, so purifying baths were mandated, especially at the time of menstruation, and before marriage. Ultimately, ritual bathing was a distinguishing factor and signifier of minority status amongst non-Christian women in the late medieval period, as one *morisca* named Madelena discovered when she was caught bathing and accused of false conversion.[39]

Cultural Preservation. Perhaps the most significant roles women played regardless of faith included preservation of the birth and death rituals their traditions dictated. Besides child rearing, they prepared kosher or halal meals for Passover and Yom Kippur, or Ramadan, respectively.

---

35   Coope, "An Etiquette for Women," 77; Hourani, "*A History of the Arab Peoples*," 117, 119–122; Fernandez, "The Crusade Over the Bodies of Women," 269–271.

36   Coope, "An Etiquette for Women," 77–78; Hourani, "*A History of the Arab Peoples*," 116–117.

37   Coope, "An Etiquette for Women," 78–79.

38   Fuente, "Christian, Muslim and Jewish Women," 321; Hourani, "*A History of the Arab Peoples*," 116–117.

39   Fuente, "Christian, Muslim and Jewish Women," 321–322.

Later, when such activities became illegal for converses and moriscas, women secretly conducted prayers and read from the *Torah*, or taught the Law of Muhammad to their children. After the fifteenth century, moriscos who still practiced Islam secretly almost always indicated that they learned the religion from a mother, grandmother, or mother-in-law when they were discovered practicing Islam secretly. Therefore, while societal proscriptions occurred after the conquest, it is clear that women perpetuated cultural memory by teaching their children in secret when necessary.[40]

Endogamy, Exogamy, and Social Stratification

When Visigothic Spain collapsed the social order also changed, particularly in the larger towns and cities. Unique to al-Andalus, when compared to the Christian kingdoms in the north, was stratification by groups, for example the Arab and Berber groups, to which membership was more among kinship lines than economics. Other commonalities shared by members of a group included ethnicity and religion, which solidified kinship ties. Compared to the Christian West, class structure was less sharply rigid, which greatly facilitated fluid economic mobility. Both Christianity and Islam in Spain shared the notion of kinship.[41]

The Arabs and Berbers that conquered Iberia were not isolated groups of warriors or opportunists. Rather, most of them functioned as members of organized tribal groups who were both agnatic and patrilineal. This aspect created a segmentary social system where individuals belonged to a hierarchy of progressively inclusive segments at a clan level, then upward to a tribal confederation. Briefly, a basic tribe contained several hundred families linked agnatically, which means the kinship system only shows importance to relationships through males. This in turn creates a system of *endogamous* marriages that are ideal because *endogamy* ensures that power, prestige,

and wealth are consolidated for the benefit of the agnatic group. A cross-cousin marriage, for example, is *exogamous* because the offspring will gain a different lineage. The key to a tribe's strength, however, is its ability to attract more women from the outside, thereby losing fewer women from the inside, and benefiting from the endogamous outcome.[42]

Indeed, this pattern of tribal or sub-tribal groups settled into the occupied al-Andalus under the common denominator of Islam, and the groups increased power and prestige through endogamy and constant testing of the groups' strength (i.e., warfare) versus their rivals'. Considering how medieval Christian kingdoms fought amongst themselves, this common characteristic was a social reality from the ninth century onward.[43]

Sub-Regional Distinctions. Ultimately, the dispersion of various clans lent sub-regional uniqueness to the cultural geography of al-Andalus, and the names of the towns or landscape features can denote Berber or Arab Diaspora. When it came to politics, the Arab and Berber tribes found strength by organizing confederations or alliances. To become stronger, for example, one group needed to diminish another, so allies were practical when aggressive tendencies were a societal norm. Further, the socialization of the children within a tribe was essential, so encouraging sibling rivalry and competitive behavior early on translated to bellicose actions against those outside of the agnatic group later. Another typical division separated entire ethnic groups in moieties, which results in a sociopolitical system where any conflict involves only two parties. Still, tribal infighting along of moiety lines, and over perceived slights, could result in feuds lasting as many as seven-years. Nevertheless, societal

---

40 Ibid., 322–324.
41 Glick, "*Islamic and Christian Spain*," 135–137; Hourani, "*A History of the Arab Peoples*," 104–108.

42 Glick, "*Islamic and Christian Spain*," 137–138. The complexity of tribal and clan organization led the U.S. military to recruit sociologists and anthropologists to compile lineage charts in a program called Human Terrain Systems. It was controversial because the maxim 'do no harm' was violated often and the charts were used to target local leaders for assassination in Iraq and Afghanistan.
43 Glick, "*Islamic and Christian Spain*," 138; Hourani, "*A History of the Arab Peoples*," 106–107.

evolution led to tribes yielding to clans as a primary social organizational unit. This process, in turn, evolved to a more familiar client-patron type of relationship where linear progression is less symptomatic as tribes settled into sedentary and urbanized societies.[44] Next, we compare the kinship patterns of the Christian realms to illustrate how social and religious differences affected relationships, and how they later heightened tensions.

Christian Kinship Systems in Spain

In contrast, kinship patterns and relations in the Christian regions of Spain never had the same sharply *patrilineal*, agnatic structure found amongst the Arabs and the Berbers. That is not to say that no such thing existed, but class differentiation in kinship relations is a principle variation between Christendom and al-Andalus. Extended families were more deliberately planned along socioeconomic lines. Further, the prestige of the family had certain privileges afforded by social and economic advantages, as well as ideological support from the Church. The second primary difference between Islamic and Christian areas in Spain is that Islam provided a framework that legitimized tribal values by giving them religious importance. Christians, however, emphasized the development of interpersonal (individualistic) relationships rather than intergroup (collective) bonds. Christian Spain had both patrilineal and matrilineal kinship systems in the north, as well as bilateral patterns that combined the other types, courtesy of Germanic influences.[45] While the notion of extended families is evident, this convention declined by the tenth century, except for the nobility class, who maintained it slightly longer. Compared to al-Andalus, the need to prevent *honor code* violations that often resulted in family blood feuds led various rulers and authorities to gradually diminish the social importance of extended families. Concurrently,

the Church and the appearance of guilds and military organizations combined with urbanization and colonization, resulting in a society that steadily mobilized. Finally, the feudal system also changed and disrupted previously self-contained kinship circles.[46]

To summarize, until the Christian states gradually stabilized through unification they were at a distinct disadvantage compared to the more fluid and flexible agnatic kinship systems found in al-Andalus. While 'honor' amongst tribal societies is directly connected to agnatic feeling, if attacked, however, or unified, a severe sense of honor lost occurs for the Muslims. Conversely, the Christians viewed honor as variable dependent on one's social status rather than whether an individual was embedded in a certain class. For instance, a poor man could greatly increase his honor by marrying a wealthy woman of higher social standing, although such opportunities would be very rare indeed. By contrast, in agnatic societies, a wife who originated outside (exogamous) the group cannot embrace her husband's prestige, even if she had considerable wealth.[47] These were the social conventions in the Christian north and al-Andalus in the south on the eve of the First Crusade (1096–1099) and the subsequent Reconquista.

A Shift Towards Islamophobia

Eulogins of Cordoba: A Case Study. Around 850 C.E., a monk named Eulogins attempted a pilgrimage from his home in Córdoba to Germany, but a combination of political unrest and banditry at the borders of Spain diverted him to a monastery in Leyre, near Pamplona. In the marketplace he found a rare manuscript for sale, written by Anonymous (this was common in medieval times to avoid repercussions). It was a four-page biography of Muhammad called *Istoria of Mahomt's*, written by a Christian. Regardless, it demonstrated some familiarity with the prophet's

44 Glick, "*Islamic and Christian Spain,*" 138–140; Hourani, "*A History of the Arab Peoples,*" 108–109.
45 Glick, "*Islamic and Christian Spain,*" 141–143.
46 Ibid., 143.
47 Ibid., 144–145.

life and origins. However, it painted a decidedly negative and heretical profile by attributing Muhammad's revelations as "the spirit of error" that induced countless others to follow his lead. While whoever authored it distorted reality such that any Christian who read it could not possibly overlook it Islam was unequivocally equated with evil. Nor would a Muslim recognize any of the "verses" attributed to the *Quran*. Apparently uncritical, Eulogins returned to Córdoba with a hostile view of Islam.[48]

Testing the Limits of Tolerance. One of Eulogins' acquaintances in Córdoba was an influential nobleman named Isaac, who regularly mediated between the Muslim authorities and the Christian community. After reading the manuscript, Isaac adopted the anti-Islamic work and then stayed at a nearby monastery for one-year for reasons unclear. Upon return Isaac initiated a public discussion about Islam and deliberately blasphemed against Muhammad, which was a serious violation of shariah codes. Predictably, Isaac was granted a chance to recant his statements, and it was even insinuated he could claim innocence by temporary insanity or intoxication. This offer was surprisingly tolerant considering that blasphemy was a capital offence. Isaac, however, refused the offered clemency and decided to take a stand, saying he meant what he said. Naturally, he was summarily decapitated and his remains were displayed to deter others from blasphemy.[49]

A Series of Martyrs. The Córdoban officials were very surprised that Isaac's execution did not have the desired affect, because within two-days, six more Christians followed his example, and more blasphemed against Islam publicly in the following weeks. All were put to death, unrepentant, but in the Christian community their resistance against the rulers was considered martyrdom. If the situation had been solely about Isaac, the officials probably would not have given the code violation a second thought, however, they realized

that something bigger was afoot as more martyrs followed, albeit at a slower rate over the following weeks turned into months. The emir considered "killing all Christian men and dispersing their women by selling them into slavery." Wisely, to maintain the peace, the emir retracted and avoided giving the Christian minority population a possible cause for rebellion.[50]

Retribution came in other ways though, when the emir dismissed all Christians from the civil service. Then he deprived Christian soldiers of their pensions, raised the jizya, and targeted local churches for destruction. Eulogins documented the fifty martyrs' names, but he too was eventually arrested for harboring an apostate from Islam (Christian convert). In 859 Eulogins denounced Islam and paid the price. His primary concern, as revealed in his writings, was that Christians were too cozy with the Islamic leadership in all of al-Andalus. Another problem was that this fraternizing with Islam came at the expense of their faith, because too many Christians were eager for upward mobility by serving in the civil service or military. While this movement ceased after his death, Eulogins' resistance planted a seed of dissent in Córdoba and other cities in al-Andalus. But it took at least two hundred more years to materialize.[51]

The Conquest of Toledo in 1085 and Social Change

The Crown of Castile Expands. By the eleventh century, warfare between neighboring states yielded to a new process of territorial expansion and colonization. While the First Crusade was still a decade away, King Alfonso VI of Castile initiated a successful campaign that ended with the capture and subsequent defense of Toledo in 1085. In the aftermath, this drive south had profound political and social implications. First, the city itself was heavily fortified and protected on its southern edge by merging rivers. However, the fertile lands that surrounded the area were the real prizes. The second important result came

48   Chris Lowney, *A Vanished World: Muslims, Christians, and Jews in Medieval Spain*, (2005. Reprint, New York, NY: Oxford University Press, 2006), 55–56.
49   Lowney, "*A Vanished World*," 56–57; Hourani, "*A History of the Arab Peoples*," 65–67.

50   Quote from Lowney, "*A Vanished World*," 57–59.
51   Ibid., 57–58

from being the first permanent incursion into al-Andalusan territory. Moreover, after several hundred years of Arabicization, the Arabacized Christians, or *mozarab*, found themselves in the midst of social upheaval. Although they had technically preserved their Christian faith, one clear marker of their cultural hybridization was use of the surname–mozarab by some.[52]

City Life in Toledo and Social Change. One of the first changes that occurred in Toledo was the conversion of the grand mosque into a cathedral. One feature of city life in the previous order was that Muslims and Christians lived amongst each other, often in neighboring homes, and some, but not all Jews lived in a separate quarter of the city. However, by the late twelfth century steady changes diminished the social status of Muslims and Jews, even more so by the thirteenth century, when the epic work of Spanish literature appeared, *Poema de mio Cid*.[53]

Significance of El Cid. Epic poems in medieval times were often performed publicly at feasts and festivals as chanted verse or else sung by the professional praise singers known as *troubadours* and *jongleurs*. El Cid's most significant aspect was that it reflected changing attitudes towards Muslims in the years after the First Crusade (1096–1099) and the gradual process of reclaiming Iberia. In it too was a new lexicon, the sweeping use of the term *moros* (Moor) that became a general descriptor applied to all Muslims in Iberia. For instance, *moros* could mean either a friend or a foe, and its use did not distinguish separate ethnic designations within the Islamic world.[54] Today, *moro* is a pejorative term.

Consistent with the influential religious designations that appeared in *Poema de mio Cid*, Castilian Christians viewed the mozarabs

as political enemies on account of their "alien names, language, and habits."[55] Even earlier in the eleventh century, warfare against the Almohads (1012–1013) created a notion that gained traction: Muslims were a religious foe that needed to be defeated and driven back. Therefore, when the city Alcaraz was captured later in 1213, the pattern established at Toledo consecrated the victory through the archbishop holding mass in the newly appropriated grand mosque. Perhaps encouraged by the success of the First Crusade, Pope Honorius III charged Archbishop Rodrigo with organizing a holy war against Muslims around 1217. The attempt was short-lived, however, and foundered by 1220. This slow reconquest characterized an era where separate campaigns by different kingdoms gradually moved southward.[56]

Change of Racial Status for *Mozarabs*

The evolution of Islamophobic thought continued in Iberia organically, through sociopolitical events, regional warfare, literature, and external influences such as the crusades and papal advocacy for holy war against Islam. Within the new territories gained from Muslim principalities, the three religious groups had to readjust to new legal codes, attitudes that changed often, as well as a steady shift to racialize the citizens not identified as Christian. Frequently under observation, the mozarabic population in Toledo ran afoul of Archbishop Rodrigo who felt that their Arabic-inflected language did not fit in the new order, nor were their Arabic surnames particularly welcomed or compatible with his faith. Therefore, Rodrigo sought to eradicate mozarabic legal status through legitimate, but deliberate policies of discrimination. Further, Rodrigo's writings were often cited and the word *mozarab* quickly evolved into a 'pejorative slur'. This may also have been the first time a distinct racial category was applied in Castile; the archbishop also referred to mozarab as *mixti Arabes*, (mixed blood Arabs)

---

52 Hitchcock, "Christian-Muslim Understanding(s) in Medieval Spain," 318; Glick, "*Islamic and Christian Spain*," 191–193.
53 Hitchcock, "Christian-Muslim Understanding(s) in Medieval Spain," 318–319; Lowney, "*A Vanished World*," 119–121, 128–142. The life of Rodrigo Diaz de Vivar, the real El Cid, is described in great detail and his cultural significance on the *Reconquista* cannot be emphasized enough; Glick, "*Islamic and Christian Spain*," 173.
54 Hitchcock, "Christian-Muslim Understanding(s) in Medieval Spain," 320; Lowney, "*A Vanished World*," 120–121.

55 Hitchcock, "Christian-Muslim Understanding(s) in Medieval Spain," 320.
56 Ibid.

who were indistinguishable from Arabs. The term also reinforced that mozarabs, like Jews, were contaminated, by blood.[57]

Long-Term Affects on the Mozarabs. Ultimately, Archbishop Rodrigo's contempt and subsequent defamation of the mozarabic character led to their diminished second-class status in Castile. By the thirteenth century, the steady process of discrimination finally led to legislated expulsion from Christian lands.[58] We disagree with Hitchcock's claim that social issues led to the mozarabic's status as *personae non gratae* and not escalation of racially-based prejudice. While Hitchcock asserts that political motives removed any influence the Arabicized Christians may have had, similar pressures soon befell the Jews. It is plausible though that religious discrimination paved the way for early race-based designations, and contributed to *limpieza de sangre*.[59]

Daily Life in the Tri-Ethnic Christian Cities

Slaves and the Slave Trade. Slavery has been a scourge of history, and its prevalence throughout the literature follows the rise and fall of great empires. It appears that someone somewhere was enslaved because of gender, ethnicity, religion, punishment for crimes, being born into servitude, or the misfortune of being on the losing side. The Romans had a practice of documenting a slave's origins, but generally slavery was not racially based as it was after the fifteenth century in the Americas. This case study briefly examines the terms of sale related to four Muslims in thirteenth century Barcelona on the Mediterranean coast. Because it was a port city, Barcelona was an extremely important trade center for the realm of Aragon-Catalonia, and for the Mediterranean as a whole. As noted earlier, the Reconquista made slow but steady progress southward, and as Christians obtained more territory, they also brought more *mudejar* (Muslim) communities under their jurisdiction. Incidentally, Muslim slaves, sometimes referred to as *Saracens* in texts, made up at least 21% of Barcelona's household population. Moreover, this astonishingly high percentage was symptomatic of cultural interchanges between Islam and Christendom throughout the thirteenth century. In general, the unpublished Latin contracts indicated that Jewish entrepreneurs facilitated the slave trade, at least in Christian lands.[60]

A Preference for Light-Skinned Women. Interestingly, however ironic, the slave trade brought the tri-ethnic communities together socially and culturally. Sales contracts and other literature allude to a widespread preference for lighter-skinned (white) Muslim women, and indicated their intended role for domestic settings. However, the documents show that "black" Muslim men, although the minority in the slave population, were also traded between Christian and Jewish households. One key difference in the northern Christian realms is that Muslim slaves were not traded directly by fellow Muslims as it occured in southern regions.[61]

It cannot be emphasized enough that female slaves were preferred, and on all available documents in the Burns study (1999) all four contracts bore Jewish signatures. Jews also appear to be the initiators of the bills of sale. In Catalonia, the region where Barcelona lay, most Muslims who were encountered daily were foreign traders or slaves. So in effect, there was no free *mudejar* population. Further, the preference for women as household slaves escalated by the middle of the thirteenth century when a pronounced feminization occurred, particularly in Barcelona. Compared to the other areas in Spain and Europe where social prestige through owning slaves was common to the noble, artisan, and merchant classes, it is the averageness of slave owners in

---

57 Hitchcock, "Christian-Muslim Understanding(s) in Medieval Spain," 320; Glick, "*Islamic and Christian Spain*," 191–193, 277–281.

58 Hitchcock, "Christian-Muslim Understanding(s) in Medieval Spain," 320; Glick, "*Islamic and Christian Spain*," 191–193.

59 Hitchcock, "Christian-Muslim Understanding(s) in Medieval Spain," 320–321.

---

60 Robert I. Burns, "Interactive Slave Operations: Muslim-Christian-Jewish Contracts in Thirteenth-Century Barcelona," *Medieval Encounters* 5, no. 2 (1999): 135.

61 Ibid., 136.

Barcelona that differentiated ownership from notions of class.[62]

Origins of the Slaves. Where did the slaves come from before the Atlantic Slave Trade? In the period of gradual reconquest and seasonal warfare the spoils of war would be a reasonable guess. However, during the thirteenth century slave origins had no correlation to warfare and instead centered more on commerce. As the century progressed the cost per slave rose as well. The slaves themselves represented every class or category in the medieval world, but one primary difference was that those hailing from more affluent backgrounds could be released upon remittance of a ransom. The movement of Muslim slaves into Christian lands was an involuntary mass migration. Similarly, the slave trade existed simultaneously in al-Andalus and North Africa. In the Muslim territories, Christians and Muslims were being sold as slaves, mirroring the trade in Christian lands. While some Jews also found themselves enslaved in the south, it was far less common.[63]

As the late medieval period approached, Christians and Jews alike engaged more readily in the slave trade, and more often than not sales were between the two groups. Therefore, a Muslim slave could very likely have served in houses of both faiths. Although officially instructed not to, Jews regularly converted their slaves to Judaism. Moreover, each sales contract examined followed the letter of the Roman Law regarding slaves' origins and gender. Additionally, each contract was written to withstand any legal scrutiny or challenge. Again, in a tri-ethnic society, the experience was interactive because slaves were almost exclusively Muslim whereas Jews and Christians were always free in Christian societies.[64]

In Part II the background of the First Crusade will be examined and comparative reading between how tri-ethnic communities coexisted in Spain until 1492 and how Jews were regarded in Northern Europe reveal patterns of cultural anti-Semitism. These patterns escalated from doctrinal differences

(Judaeophobia or religious anti-Semitism) to demonization, and finally a shift towards being labeled subhuman. It is also significant how Islam was viewed in the eleventh century, and how similar the rhetoric is today when discussing Muslim immigration to the United States and migration to Europe. The origins of Islamophobia are rooted in medieval thought, but the recurrent themes, like those accusing Jews of 'blood libel' are heavily rooted in distortions of stereotypes, fear of the 'other' taking control of the West, religious discrimination, and patterns of racism and racial profiling. Presently, some scholars claim that 'liberal thought' watered down or somehow apologized for the aggressive actions of Christians, while claiming Islam is 'a religion of peace'. In the next section consideration of all perspectives are presented so readers can understand and decide for themselves which narrative of events is more revisionist or accurate based on the limitations of the sources.

In Part III the story returns to Spain to discuss the social changes and patterns of discrimination that may have been the first documented case of racism to fit both definitions: Power + prejudice, and, a system of advantages based on race. In particular, we explore religious shifts and return of a monetary system in the thirteenth century, combined with *Millenarian* expectations and other human tendencies to disadvantage Muslims and Jews by compelling them to convert to Christianity in order to assimilate. What occurred next was a combination of socioeconomic and sociopolitical events in a rapidly changing society, marked by a violent but gradual campaign to reclaim al-Andalus from Islam. The final section bridges the past and the present, to examine cultural history and identity in an age of multicultural inclusion, marred by recurring patterns of Islamophobia, anti-Semitism and racism.

---

62   Ibid., 136–138.
63   Ibid., 139, 149–150.
64   Burns, "Interactive Slave Operations," 150–151; Glick, "*Islamic and Christian Spain*," 171–172.

The First Crusade

Holy War and the Problem of Interpretation

By D. Paul Sweeney

Introduction to Common Themes

Holy War and Crusading. The word *crusade* today has many implications and meanings in various contexts, and its significance is interpreted differently in Western societies than in the Middle East. For some, images of mounted knights in shining armor, with a cross emblazoned on their garments, pennants, and shields, create a sense of romantic chivalry. For others, particularly in Arab and Muslim countries, *crusade* implies a holy war against Islam and a crusader or Zionist plot to steal and colonize land and natural resources, especially water and oil. Similarly, modern tropes view *jihad* as holy war, but offensive, not defensive. This text does not attempt to explain all of the nuances of jihad, but a comparison between how holy war is viewed in modern times and how it was viewed in the eleventh-century is worth considering. Finally, the literature on the expedition to Jerusalem between 1096 and 1099 almost always begins, as will this section, with a discussion about the catalyst, the speech in November 1095 delivered by Pope Urban II in Clermont, France.

The exact content of the speech, as evaluated in the present, is a composite of three separate witnesses or chroniclers who wrote about it, in some cases, well after the event took place. What is clear though is that the concept of holy war is a Western idea,[1] and Urban II proclaimed it as a Christian duty. But did he say to reclaim the Holy Land and create safe passage for pilgrims? Despite romanticism and arguments over historiography and what the original intent and justification were, the short-term results of the First Crusade are outlasted by hundreds of years of mixed reactions. A current trend is taking a more defensive position that Christians were justified in waging the campaign, and that liberal scholars have unkindly blamed greed and desire for colonies as the real motivation for the holy war.[2] The often-overlooked Arab perspective of the same events paints another picture with equal measures of

---

1 Lloyd Steffen, *Holy War, Just War: Exploring the Meaning of Religious Violence*, (Lanham, MD: Rowman & Littlefield, 2007); Michael David Bonner, *Jihad in Islamic History: Doctrines and Practice*, (Princeton, NJ: Princeton University Press, 2006), xv–xviii.

2 Rodney Stark, *God's Battalions: The Case for the Crusades*, (New York, NY: Harper Collins, 2009). Stark's lack of a theoretical approach also weakens the claims that Islam was first aggressor and Christendom was justified to save Western Civilization.

propaganda, sensationalism, and valor of combatants, but it also helps fill in missing pieces of information about why certain actions and decisions were made.[3]

Concurrent with the themes in this collection of interchangeable chapters on medieval Spain, the growing animosity towards Jews and Muslims will be examined. While some of the situations are similar to what occurred in Spain, the Ashkenazi Jews of the Rhineland were demonized for reasons somewhat unique to the regions where they immigrated. Finally, the parallels of the past to present us versus them casting of Islam as the enemy within, or outright attempts at banning admittance via immigration all have their origins in Western civilization. Frequently, these Islamophobic and anti-Semitic patterns recur when economic downturns spark nationalistic fervor, and political shifts to the right and far right promote expulsion or discriminatory policies. Part Two provides an overview of European and world events that preceded Pope Urban II's proclamation, but also focuses on how the "othering" process works and how racism (power + prejudice, or, a system of advantages based on race), stereotypes, and prejudice contributed to discriminatory thinking and actions.

Pope Urban II and Northern Europe

The Setting Prior to 1095. Drawing heavily from the chronicle of the First Crusade, Fulcher de Chartres wrote his history *after* events concluded, chiefly with the successful capture of the Holy City of Jerusalem. Through Fulcher and other period sources, the task of reading between the lines of propaganda, opinion, and judgment is not easy, however, every story has an origin. The difficulty lies in explaining how a continent perpetually at war with itself suddenly experienced a religious awakening and put aside petty rivalries to attack a

common foe: Islam. The real background is more complex, so examining the medieval mindset unique to Northern Europe is necessary. What common themes existed in regions that spoke different languages, had cultural identities, different monarchies, and a feudal manor system? Unlike Spain where tri-ethnic groups interacted with varying degrees of animosity and tolerance, France, Germany, Italy, England, and other countries were primarily Christian with a Jewish minority in certain cities.

Sin: A Societal Fear. One societal commonality in Latin Christendom was the biblical concept of *sin*. Sin and temptation were everywhere, and only by confessing sins to a priest could alleviate the anxiety and guilt socially instilled by the Church. Penance, the act of cleansing away sins after confession, was assigned by the priests, and it could range from saying certain prayers to lighting candles, giving alms, or, in extreme cases, such as a knight taking a life, undertaking a pilgrimage.[4] Pilgrimage could mean many things, but in most cases the destination was far away from home, particularly if it meant going to the Holy Land. Moreover, natural human impulses, such as hunger, lust, and pride were common contributors to sin, so a seemingly endless cycle of searching for inner peace was a common pursuit for those able to do so. The ideal Christian lifestyle existed theoretically, but constant contact with contamination marred the true path to purity and perfection. Some chose the monastic life and served as laypersons, monks, or nuns in their attempt to conquer earthly desires through vows of celibacy and constant prayer. Ultimately, achieving the pinnacle of the religious experience was equated to walking the path towards perfection. Sainthood was often attributed to those who found perfection and successfully denied the self (e.g., St. Francis).[5]

For reasons not entirely clear, Urban II chose the monastic path, possibly because he was a

3 Amin Maalouf, *The Crusades Through Arab Eyes*. Translated by Jon Rothschild, (New York, NY: Schocken Books, 1985); Alex Mallett, "Islamic Historians of the Ayyubid Era and Muslim Rulers from the Early Crusading Period: A Study in the Use of History," *Al-Masaq* 24, no. 3 (2012).

4 Stark, "*God's Battalions*," 116–118.
5 Thomas Asbridge, *The First Crusade: A New History, the Roots of Conflict Between Christianity and Islam*, (2004. Reprint, New York, NY: Oxford University Press, 2005), 7–11.

younger son and not eligible for inheritance despite noble origins. Knighthood was generally barred to all but firstborn sons, and whether for this or another reason, Urban moved from his native France to a monastery in Ostia, Italy. Around 1080 the standing pope noticed him and Urban was ordained cardinal-bishop of Ostia, which was a powerful ecclesiastical office, but also very close to a tumultuous dispute within the Vatican.[6]

The Papal Legacy. In essence, the eleventh-century papacy claimed an unbroken descent from St. Peter, the first Bishop of Rome, who was ascribed in scripture as empowered by Christ to make God's will manifest on earth. After Peter, popes enjoyed apostolic power considered immune to dilution, and newly appointed popes were conferred with refreshed divine authority. Some even believed they were entitled to absolute control over the Latin Church of Europe. However, the papacy in Urban's time did not exactly exhibit the acclaimed authority. For example, the pope could not entirely manage central Italy's spiritual affairs, much less mediate all of Western Christendom, due to internal abuses, power struggles, and physical dislocation between the individual realms of kings. When Pope Gregory VII (1073–85) was appointed, his first task was to reestablish the divine authority and the position held over all kings through censure and threats of excommunication.[7]

Gregory VII's Precedence. Pope Gregory VII was not powerful militarily and he quickly overplayed his hand intervening in neighboring states. Still, the concept of *crusading* can be traced to his tenure as pope, which found continuity through his successor, Urban II. One of the most significant ideas Gregory propagated and spread throughout Europe was the that of *fideles* (faithful). He envisioned an expedition to the Holy Land to reclaim it from Muslims, who he equated with *infideles* (unfaithful), but the holy war did not materialize in his lifetime because Europe was too internally divided. Regardless, Gregory conjectured the idea that holy war would 'defend'

the Christian faith by aiding the eastern Byzantine kingdom in their stand against Islamic aggression and expansion. Moreover, such an action would be construed as charitable. Thus, "charity" really meant "defensive action," which in turn would justify it. Nonetheless, the complicated precedence that launched the First Crusade found its accelerant in Urban II, whose proclamation at Clermont firmly established himself, and successive popes, as the divine authority in Europe.[8]

Urban II, the Man and His Motivations

Born (c. 1035) into the de Lagery family from Châtillon-sur-Marne in northern France, Odo, his baptismal name, followed the papal tradition and broke with the past by selecting the name Urban II at his coronation. In his fifties by 1085, Urban embraced the Vicar of Christ role wholeheartedly, but his decisions and attitudes reflect the period in which he was raised. After all, he was born into French aristocracy, a violent warrior-class that often thrived on interfamily blood feuds, campaigns for ransom, extortion and related intrigues. Therefore, his speech was primarily directed towards the aristocracy in spite of France being historically divided, north from south with two languages, Languedor and Languedoc respectively. Collectively, however, a singular term emerged to categorize pre-modern France: 'Franks.'[9]

Endless Cycles of Violence. Urban's concern stemmed from his familiarity with the latent destructiveness of medieval Europe as a whole. Even the comparably peaceful nobles occasionally dabbled in rapine and plunder. Despite this backdrop of violent episodes, Urban grew up immersed in the Christian faith that reflected the ongoing medieval anxiety about sin and absolution. While it seems contradictory in light of frequent bloodshed, the years approaching the millennium were a very spiritual age. God's absolute power was manifest in every aspect of

---

6 Ibid.

7 Ibid., 7–13.

8 Asbridge, "*The First Crusade*," 7–13; Steffen, "*Holy War, Just War*," 192.

9 Asbridge, "*The First Crusade*," 3–5.

life, the *Great Chain of Being*, and constant display of providence was interpreted as miracles. For instance, a blind man's sudden cure after prayer was proof of divine grace. Other cause and effect relationships too were attributed to divine justice, such as a murderer being smitten by lighting. While such matters today are interpreted largely as natural phenomena, eleventh-century Europe was governed by a dogma, whose cornerstone cemented a human reaction: fear. Fear of sin, but also fear of the final judgment when repented and unrepented souls would be divided. The pure would enjoy everlasting paradise, but the impure would suffer eternal torment in the fires of Hell.[10] These were the conditions in Latin Christendom when Urban II left Rome to attend the ten-day Council of Clermont in mid-November, 1095.

The Council of Clermont

Whenever a pope called for a council (e.g., Trent, Worms), it meant that something important was afoot: A schism, doctrinal issues, heresy, or establishing authority. The question of why the Council of Clermont occurred can be answered by turning to Fulcher de Sartres. As mentioned previously, seemingly endless conflicts between rival kingdoms, such as Henry in Germany and Philip in France, as well as perceived vacillating faith, would all be valid reasons for a summons.[11] Further, Urban II wanted to elevate the Latin Church's status ever higher in European affairs, thereby privileging papal authority. There were internal problems, however, that took two forms in Urban's view: The clergy on one hand, and the laity on the other. Plus, the princes of the lands never experienced any long-lasting peace. Other offenses cited by Fulcher included growing incidences of theft, kidnapping for ransom or imprisonment, and a general malaise caused by "three evils[:] … hunger, thirst, and cold. …" Sacred places too were under siege figuratively

and literally, and collectively they contributed to a spirit of derision that attacked and infected humanity.[12] Another reason Fulcher claimed for convening a council was the spread of Muslim Turks into parts of Romania, which concerned Urban II, and necessitated the summons be sent via messengers in all directions.

Proclamation for Holy War

Was There an Imminent Threat? It is important to note that Urban's actual speech was not fully documented, so the accounts by Fulcher, Robert the Monk, and Raymond de Auguiler are garbled compilations gleaned from memory, or in Fulcher's case, it is not entirely clear if he was present or not.[13] What can be ascertained confidently though is that Urban specifically asked for military assistance in Byzantium. Liberating Jerusalem may or may not have been the primary objective, but central to any crusading movement was ensuring the existence of Byzantium. Long viewed as the last bastion and frontier of Christendom in the east, the Greek Empire was also the first adversary of Islam in an ongoing conflict that began in the seventh-century. While it is speculation, some accounts suggest that Alexius I sent an embassy in March 1095, to meet with Urban II in Italy and apparently implored him to send aid because bellicose Seljug Turks led by Kilij Arslan, had infringed on territorial holdings in Anatolia. Furthermore, the Levant (i.e., a region comprised of Turkey and Syria) was considered a natural extension of Christendom, which Christian pilgrims traversed after sailing across the Bosphorus from Constantinople. Highway robbery was a common threat for pilgrims and merchants alike, but was there aggression solely directed at Christians by Muslims? This is hard to correlate or prove. What is clear, from Arab and as Christian sources, is that internal intrigues and expansions by Muslim rulers, in addition to the

10 Asbridge, "The First Crusade," 5–6.
11 Fulcher de Sartres. *A History of the Expedition to Jerusalem, 1095–1127*. Translated by Frances Rita Ryan, (New York, NY: W.W. Norton, 1969), 61.

12 Ibid.
13 Peter Lock, *The Routledge Companion to the Crusades*, (New York, NY: Routledge, 2006), 298; Fulcher, "A History of the Expedition to Jerusalem," 18–19; Asbridge, "The First Crusade," 1–2.

young Kilij Arslan, were elevating the importance of their respective capitals in Antioch, Damascus, Aleppo, and Mosul.[14]

The Speech: Textual Analysis

Because it is the most consolidated, the text provided by Thomas Asbridge is an abridged version of the longer transcript originally found in Robert the Monk's *Historia Iherolintana*. The ten-day Council of Clermont concluded with this dramatic and passionate proclamation:

> *"A race absolutely alien to God has invaded the land of the Christians, has reduced the people with sword, rapine and flame. These men have destroyed the altars polluted by their foul practices. They have circumcised the Christians, either spreading the blood from the circumcisions on the altars or pouring it into the baptismal fonts. And they cut open the navels of those whom they choose to torment with loathsome death, tear out their most vital organs and tie them to a stake, drag them around and flog them, before killing them as they lie prone on the ground with their entrails out. What shall I say of the appalling violation of women, of which it is more evil to speak than keep silent?*
>
> *On whom, therefore, does the task lie of avenging this, of redeeming this situation, if not on you, upon whom above all nations [France] God has bestowed outstanding glory in arms, magnitude of heart, litheness of body, and strength to humble anyone who resists you."*

On the last Tuesday of November 1095, Urban's apocalyptic account of alleged atrocities against pilgrims en route to the Holy Land, and threat of imminent invasion by Muslims with malicious intent met with an enthusiastic response by all in attendance. Holy war was proclaimed as an armed expedition to the Holy Land. Thus, to receive penance (and credit from Purgatory) the knights of France rallied because of spiritual conviction, and the notion that *dishonor* required *vengeance*, which in turn *justified* a violent action against savage Muslims.[15]

Holy War, Just War and Justification. The phrase "expedition to Jerusalem" highlights the intent, justification, and objective of the holy war. While the term 'crusade' was not applied until centuries later, the First Crusade was set into motion. After implying that recent calamities in the East occurred, Urban II implored Christendom to muster and arm posthaste. Another consideration of his motives was to keep Christianity from destroying itself, as found in Fulcher's account: "… oh sons of God, you have promised Him to keep peace among yourselves … faithfully sustain the rights of [the] Holy Church more sincerely than before, there still remains for you, newly aroused by Godly correction, an urgent task … ."[16] By creating a sense of threat (which justifies action), and an identifiable enemy, the Turks (i.e., Muslims), Urban shifted the onus of the appeal for reprisal as a Christian duty ("on whom, therefore, does the task lie of avenging this …")? Even in Constantinople, the Byzantine notion of holy war shared certain attributes, including clemency for any soldiers who shed blood on Christianity's behalf, whether fighting Islam or heresy. However, crusading as an armed pilgrimage was Latin Christendom's contribution to the prosecution of holy war.[17]

Justification and Prosecution of Holy War. How did a holy war rectify the inherent ruthlessness and violence of medieval warfare? Urban II not only preached it, he condoned the violence that followed because it simultaneously encouraged unity through an expression of pious devotion and applied unity through sanctified warfare. In this construct

---

14 Lock, *"The Routledge Companion to the Crusades,"* 298–299; Asbridge, *"The First Crusade,"* 15; Amin Maalouf, *"The Crusades Through Arab Eyes,"* 3–5; Stark, *"God's Battalions,"* 95–98.

15 Asbridge, *"The First Crusade,"* 1–2.

16 Fulcher, *"A History of the Expedition to Jerusalem,"* 65–66; Steffen, *"Holy War, Just War,"* 233–238.

17 Fulcher, *"A History of the Expedition to Jerusalem,"* 66; Asbridge, *"The First Crusade,"* 1–2; Lock, *"The Routledge Companion to the Crusades,"* 299.

Christians became good, while Muslims were viewed as evil: "Wherefore with earnest prayer I, not I, but God exhorts you as heralds of Christ to repeatedly urge men of all ranks whatsoever, knights as well as foot-soldiers, rich and poor, to hasten to exterminate this vile race from our lands and to aid the Christian inhabitants in time."[18] The binary good versus evil dichotomy received the papal blessing and legitimacy, which in turn imposed divine sanction and simplified the justification. But where did the idea for necessitating warfare originate in Western thought? It is possible that the necessity of warfare became ingrained socially because throughout Ancient Rome's lifespan, bellicosity was symptomatic of mere existence? Significantly, however, the root of holy war also appears in the writings of St. Augustine of Hippo (354–430 C.E.), who argued that war could be legal and justified, as long as it was conducted in strictly controlled conditions.[19]

Three Prerequisites for Waging a Just War. First, according to St. Augustine, just war (*jus ad bellum*) must be proclaimed by someone with legitimate authority, such as a king, prince, or bishop. Secondly, it needed a just cause, which was not solely limited to the recovery of lost lands or property, or fending off enemy attacks. Finally, just war required that the war be fought with a right intention (*jus in bello*) towards the enemy. In principle the last point meant warfare without excessive cruelty or bloodshed. Collectively, the three Augustinian principles formulated the crusading ideal. While this theory never saw action prior to 1095 outside of crushing heresy, to sanctify violence required adding elements such as promising a heavenly reward or eternal life to warriors. Gregory VII paved the way by conditioning eleventh-century Latin Christians to accept papal sponsored warfare, but wielding uncompromising papal authority was Urban's contribution. Until Clermont, the laity was slowly transformed to embrace being 'soldiers of Christ', and fideles emphasized incumbent service and

vassalage for all Latin Christians, not just those in ecclesiastical service.[20]

With Muslims dehumanized and a direct threat to Christianity invoked, all Christians had a duty to become pilgrims. In return for any wrongs committed, a remission of sins would be granted. Given the sense of urgency he instilled, Urban II clearly needed those present in the cathedral to spread the word quickly. He also escalated the rhetoric by heightening fear, especially fear of divine punishment for not taking action (implied sin) and fear of Islam spreading westward. Fulcher wrote of Urban: "oh what a disgrace if a race so despicable, degenerate, and enslaved by demons should overcome a people endowed with faith in Almighty God and resplendent in the name of Christ!"[21]

Aftermath of the Speech: Mobilization

Word spread quickly from Clermont in the weeks and winter months that followed. It was generally understood that armies could not march or sail with success in the winter, but an estimated 100,000 men and women from all strata of medieval society took up the call and rallied to the pope. The unified cause brought together peasants and paupers and feudal knights with a feverish desire to extract punishment on the enemy. Recent scholarship challenges the mass rally, however, and one study claimed that 85–90% of the Frankish knights and princes stayed behind. Still, in order to establish peace between former enemies, an oath was taken by all princes called the Truce [of God] according to Fulcher. Additionally, the symbol of the cross (*cruce signati*) was fashioned from fine silks and gold-covered cloth and other materials considered beautiful. Sewn onto garments, and painted on shields, the cross became a badge of identification and a source of motivation to realize inner peace and outward protection.[22]

18 Asbridge, "*The First Crusade*," 21–22; Urban II quoted in Fulcher, "*A History of the Expedition to Jerusalem*," 66.
19 Asbridge, "*The First Crusade*," 21–24; Christopher Tyerman, *God's War: A New History of the Crusades*, (Cambridge, MA: Harvard University Press, 2006), 27–51.

20 Asbridge, "*The First Crusade*," 21–28; Steffen, "*Holy War, Just War*," 236; Tyerman, "*God's War*," 27–51. Tyerman goes into great depth on how 'defending the faith' was conducted.
21 Fulcher, "*A History of the Expedition to Jerusalem*," 66.
22 Asbridge, "*The First Crusade*," 2; Fulcher, "*A History of the Expedition to Jerusalem*," 67–68; Stark, "*God's Battalions*," 114.

Significance of the First Crusade. Although justified by Urban, he had two agendas: First, to unify Europe so internal warfare would cease, and secondly, driving the 'pagans' out of Christian lands, even though the Holy Land had not been in Christian hands for four hundred years. The First Crusade was not the first war between Christians and Muslims, as evidenced by the conquest of Spain, but it symbolized a resurgence of deep-seated Islamophobia. The ill will can still be measured, and at times academia and revisionist history revive the old rhetoric of us versus them, good versus evil, and more recently, discrimination against Muslim immigrants and refugees because of fear evoked by the "Clash of Civilizations" thesis.[23]

Another consideration is that in March 1095 Urban II made many assurances to the Byzantine envoys that aid would come to help fight the Turks. Interestingly, he even took an oath of allegiance to the emperor (Alexius I) to stand in solidarity against the 'pagans.' In short, Asbridge wrote, "the call to arms made at Clermont *was not* directly inspired by *any* recent calamity or atrocity in the East [my italics]." Instead, the holy war was a proactive, not reactive undertaking, and it did not attempt to evangelize the Muslims (i.e., conversion). The widespread response must have surprised Urban II, but in the mob-like mentality, some think opportunists took the Islamic 'other' to mean another 'other' living in their midst: the Ashkenazi Jews.[24]

The First Holocaust? The Rhineland Jews and Crusaders in 1096

Perception of the Jews in Germany: Doctrinal Differences. Compared to the Sephardic Jews who lived primarily in areas occupied or heavily influenced by Islam, the Ashkenazi Jews migrated to Germany via the river valleys between 500–1000 C.E., with the majority settling in the

Rhineland cities of Metz, Mainz, Worms, Speyer, and Köln (Cologne). In many cases, key rulers perceived Jews as useful settlers and made attractive enticements to draw them northward from Spain, France, and Italy.[25] The Ashkenazi tradition is most associated with Northern and Eastern Europe and they maintained an orthodox messianic doctrine that stood apart from the Sephardic Diaspora. Fundamentally, the Ashkenazi paralleled Islam's view of Christianity as idolatrous due to the existence of graven images in Catholicism. In contrast, some Spanish Jews had less apprehension about this perspective, which may explain why they were less resistant to converting to Christianity.[26]

Maintaining the comparative study, an assertion long perpetuated by Yitzhak F. Baer posited that a supposed fidelity and purer, authentic Jewish tradition existed in Germany, as opposed to a 'watered down' form in Spain. For example, Baer's thesis, which has held sway since 1966, speculates that racial mixing (e.g., Christian and Jewish intermarriage) was more common in the southern country, whereas the Ashkenazi were generally non-assimilated. The conflicts between Christians and Jews in Northern Europe prior to the First Crusade, and the steady process of demonization that led to pogroms and massacres in 1096 will be examined in depth here. For example, when crusader mobs attacked Jews in May 1096, was forced conversion their primary objective, or was violence the main goal with offers of conversion to the survivors as an afterthought? Additionally, to what extent did greed motivate the crusaders? Baer suggested that voluntary sacrifice was the method used by the Ashkenazi to avoid apostasy, and today it serves as a euphemism for suicide. Similarly, Robert Chazan's "assimilate or annihilate" model has long helped explain the violent actions against the

---

23 Fulcher, "*A History of the Expedition to Jerusalem,*" 68–69; Asbridge, "*The First Crusade,*" 2. Stark's thesis is heavily loaded with the decline of the West if Islam won imagery.
24 Asbridge, "*The First Crusade,*" 10, 17–21.

25 Martin Gilbert, *The Routledge Atlas of Jewish History, Eighth Edition,* (New York, NY: Routledge, 2010), 31; Robert Chazan, "*In the Year 1096*": *The First Crusade and the Jews,* (Philadelphia, PA: The Jewish Publication Society, 1997), 5–6; David Malkiel, "Destruction or Conversion: Intention and Reaction, Crusaders and Jews, in 1096," *Jewish History* 15 (2001): 258.
26 Ibid., 258–259.

Jews. Still, would conversion, voluntary or forced, have saved life and property in reality? Another consideration is this: Was seizing Jewish wealth and property the original intent of some groups in the People's Crusade to help finance their journey to the Holy Land?[27]

Demonization and Dehumanization of the Jews

Accusations of Ritual-Murder. While content in medieval literature and artwork depict daily life, also present are accusations against the Jews, which often reinforced a stereotype that they performed ritual-murder in preparation for Passover. This ritual-murder viewpoint took deep root in the areas where Ashkenazi settled, primarily the larger cities of Europe. Further, the Passover narrative established a repeated claim that prior to Passover, which often coincided with Easter on the calendar, Jews took their victim's blood, usually a child's, to make unleavened bread, and performed magic ceremonies with poison and witchcraft. Therefore, Jews were often associated with everything anti-Christian and considered satanic. Ritual-murder, in particular, had a long life in its retelling and revision throughout the middle ages in Norwich, England (1144), Western and Eastern Europe (1191), Spain (1491), and again in Syria (1840). How the accusations perpetuated is an open question, but it is worth considering *that* the accusations were continuous.[28]

The premise of ritual-murder centered on the torture, mutilation, disembowelment, or alleged crucifixion of a Christian child during or before Passover. The exact origin is nebulous, but the recurrence of this form of libel is associated with economic downturns and social unrest. Moreover, these persistent patterns throughout time and across contexts contributed to cultural anti-Semitism, especially by conditioning the thinking about Jews as sinister, murderers of Christian children, and especially as 'Christ killers.' Further, the escalation of murder-ritual stories and related defamation shared another common pattern. They implied ritual, but emphasized, blood accusations, which taken together are called *Blood Libel*.[29]

Blood Libel Origins. As noted, every time a claim that 'ritual-murder' occurred, it had very little to do with Passover itself, but the occasional overlap with Easter and the implication of Christ's crucifixion bridged the two ideas, which is very evident in surviving literature. More damaging to the Jews, however, was the wide acceptance of such claims in the Christian communities because fantasy and fiction became fact rather quickly: "Jews *crucified* Christian children, usually during Passion Week, in order to reenact the crucifixion of Jesus and to mock and insult the Christian faith." This type of Judaeophobia became a predominant theme through the twelfth-century.[30]

If ritual-murder seems antagonistic, blood accusations almost went over the top in imagination. For instance, pervasive beliefs in the ancient world also extended to the middle ages, and conveyed that blood was necessary for medicine and magic, with a special emphasis on the latter being occult ('demonic'). Moreover, the stories are always very detailed in how blood was removed and stored in jars, and every rendition thereafter illustrated this stock charge, which also points to a limited stereotypical variety regarding the gory details.[31]

Sorcery and the Black Arts. Blood it seems, had many real or imagined uses for medicine, as a component for many types of poison vital to witches' rituals and sorcery, and of course, writing a contract with the Devil. The last detail becomes interesting and contradictory when

27 Malkiel, "Destruction or Conversion," 258–259; Shmuel Shepkaru, "Christian Resurrection and Jewish Immortality During the First Crusade," *Speculum* 89, no. 1 (2014): 1–6; Robert Chazan, "Medieval Anti-Semitism." In *History and Hate: The Dimensions of Anti-Semitism*, ed. David Berger, (Philadelphia, PA: The Jewish Publication Society, 1986), 52–56.
28 Joshua Trachtenberg, *The Devil and the Jews: The Medieval Conception of the Jew and Its Relation to Modern Anti-Semitism*, (Philadelphia, PA: The Jewish Publication Society, 1993), 127–129; David I. Kertzer, *The Popes Against the Jews: The Vatican's Role in the Rise of Modern Anti-Semitism*, (New York, NY: Knopf, 2001), 84–105.

29 Trachtenberg, "The Devil and the Jews," 127–129.
30 Ibid., 127–131.
31 Trachtenberg, "The Devil and the Jews," 141; Kertzer, "The Popes Against the Jews," 86–89.

only Jewish blood was considered sufficient for satanic treatises as a 1784 witchcraft trial in Hamburg illustrated. The women stood accused of murdering a Jew specifically so they could harvest his blood for use in their rituals. Nevertheless, the association of Jews with the Devil found a twist in many medieval tales, such as how Richard the Lion-Hearted of England, a famous crusader, was counseled by a Jewish doctor about how to treat the leprosy he suffered from. His cure required taking a bath in the blood of a newborn child to reverse the skin condition, but the internal cure entailed eating the still warm heart, raw. Ultimately, it is a nice story to reinforce negative stereotypes, but its absurdity lies in one simple detail, Richard never had leprosy.[32]

Despite the prevalence of such tall tales, blood accusations and alleged use of human parts for nefarious purposes was generally accepted as both true and accurate throughout the medieval world. This steady demonization process made it easier to blame Jews for unexplained events, such as the Black Death.

Worms, May 5, 1096: Prelude to Violence? By May 1096 the ripple effect of Pope Urban II's proclamation inspired not only the princes of Europe, but also generated five separate People's Crusades. While two of the groups led by Peter the Hermit and Walter the Penniless made their way towards Constantinople in the later spring months, three German crusader groups that resembled unruly mobs enacted an orgy of violence, not against Muslims, the 'race alien to God', but against the Rhineland Jews. What precipitated this unprecedented and seemingly spontaneous violence that murdered Jews, looted their properties, forced conversions, and created a phenomenon of suicide to avoid aposty?

Perhaps the 'ultimate combination' partially explains the violence towards the Jews in Rhineland cities, such as Worms. The aggressions overlapped, but essentially they entailed accusations against Jews for murder, blood, magic, poison, and a grand alliance whose aim

was to destroy Christendom. Although by 1096 there was a story, short on facts and credibility, that a specific incident may have been the catalyst that incited mob violence led by Count Entioch. This time, however, blood libel coincided with the call for holy war and within a month after Easter. In Worms, on May 5 it was purported that a corpse buried for a month (which would correspond approximately to Passover or Easter, falling in early-mid April), was exhumed and paraded around the city, accompanied by criers who claimed that Jews had killed a Christian, and first boiling him, then poisoning local wells with his remains (implied usage of blood and entrails). Exactly how an allegedly "boiled corpse" that further decomposed for a month underground could be displayed never entered the discussion, but apparently it contributed to the townspeople violently attacking the Jews on May 18. By May 20, the Jews of Worms were no more. Similar pogroms spread to other Rhineland cities in the days and weeks that followed, and the surviving Jews were forced to leave and moved further north and east, deeper into Germany, Poland, Lithuania, Latvia, and Russia.[33]

The Rhineland Case Study, Early 1096

Motivations of the Crusaders. Over and above the curious timing of the blood libel claims, there were clearly more forces at work that contributed to the bloodletting in many Rhineland cities. The violence started so suddenly and spread so quickly from town to town that Jews were often caught unawares or else had little time to hide, often in the cathedrals hoping the local archbishops could protect them. It appears that the Jews of France were aware of the papal call and to protect themselves, may have given provisions to Peter the Hermit. He apparently expected the German Jews to follow suite when his People's Crusade arrived as they made their way east, but Peter's group is not believed to have participated

---

32 Trachtenberg, "*The Devil and the Jews*," 140–142.

33 Trachtenberg, *The Devil and the Jews*, 144–145; Gilbert, *The Routledge Atlas of Jewish History*, 38; Chazan, *In the Year 1096*, 30–32.

in the assaults that swept through many cities, including Mainz, Metz, Speyer (May 3), Köln, Worms (May 18), and Sivan (May 27). Crusaders under Volkmar carried out similar actions further to the east in Regensburg as well, and later in Prague and Bohemia, as one massacre against Jews followed another.[34] Religious anti-Semitism is partially attributable to what occurred because the then thousand-year vendetta against Jews can best be characterized by the German word *blutrache* (vengeance), which specifically implies "… the extraction of justice through the spilling of blood."[35] Additionally, the literal references to Islam in Pope Urban II's speech assigned campaign objectives, and it also mentioned that equated rival faiths with "paganism" or said that they were alien. Despite this specific definition of the 'enemy' to Christendom, the Jews were the first casualties, and many thousands were killed by various bands of crusaders and local mobs.[36]

Toward a Theory of Displacement. Another interpretation precipitating the violence at Mainz and elsewhere posits that fervent preachers who simply lost control may have worked up crusaders. Latin texts acknowledge the resultant rioting and murders, but seems to downplay them. Not surprisingly, the events were not widely reported, although contributing authors to the annals and records did make a note of them. The only certainty in the literature on the First Crusade is that the papal call had a significant response in Western Europe, and a cross-section of medieval society mobilized. Some groups, led by nobility, were highly organized and disciplined, but other groups appeared unmanageable, with assorted short and long-term goals. The following descriptions of the violence come from both Christian and Jewish sources, some of which were not written by eyewitnesses at the time, but later by. … Additionally, both traditions tended

Figure 7.1: Massacre of Jewish People in Metz

to write "… their accounts in the context of their own theological and social agendas."[37]

Shmuel Shepkarau (2012) hypothesized that the best way to interpret the Rhineland massacres is through the psychological definition of *displacement*. What motivations contributed to attacking Jews in the West, despite Urban's call to fight Muslims in the East? Essentially, the Jews were a convenient substitute for Muslims, and various groups may have considered such actions sufficient to fulfill their crusading obligations, effectively, displacing their obligation from Muslims to Jews. One of the challenges given the limitations of the sources from that era is that it requires reading between the lines and identifying possible agendas. Christian and Hebrew literary styles are similar at times, and distortions of interpretation and agendas may have been inevitable. However, a reasonable middle ground can be assessed, compared, and evaluated accurately with all available works.[38]

Greed, Conversion, or Wanton Violence? Most modern texts about these events focus on the primary objectives of the violence, which often relate to one factor: *Greed*. Was greed attributable to debt dodging, or perhaps a way to finance the mission? Or, could religious idealism related to Millenarianism have shaped the view that like Muslims, Jews were also enemies of God,

---

34 Gilbert, "*The Routledge Atlas of Jewish History*," 38; Shmuel Shepkaru, "The Preaching of the First Crusade and the Persecutions of the Jews," *Medieval Encounters* 18 (2012): 93–94; Chazan, "*In the Year 1096*," 27–29; Tyerman, "*God's War*," 94–99.

35 Malkiel, "Destruction or Conversion," 260.

36 Shepkaru, "The Preaching of the First Crusade," 93–94.

37 Shepkaru, "The Preaching of the First Crusade," 94; Malkiel, "Destruction or Conversion," 263.

38 Shepkaru, "The Preaching of the First Crusade," 93–94.

which could have become a rationale for the attackers to distort Urban's intent?[39] Moving away from greed momentarily, another valid question is whether violence preceded attempts to force conversion, or follow the attempts if they failed? According to the records, most Jews preferred death, even by suicide, to avoid becoming apostates. The final questions examine the extremely graphic violence enacted against the Jews, and in the ongoing discussion of anti-Semitism, whether it was premeditated or symptomatic? While some writers have suggested there were political motives, they also describe it as an "obscene cocktail" of overlapping concerns that contributed to the crusaders' failure to distinguish between Muslims and Jews as the enemy.[40]

Religious factors? Other religious factors are similar to those described earlier regarding Jews as demonic and doctrinally flawed. One factor includes revenge (honor code), based on the vivid descriptions of how Muslims allegedly mistreated Christian pilgrims and defiled sacred places. This immediate spark would easily have been consistent with the long-standing cornerstone of religious anti-Semitism, that Jews killed Christ. Could this regional violence be explained as cause and effect of a messianic, apocalyptic, or millennial expectation? After all, a critical prerequisite for the Rapture to occur required the mass conversion of the Jews. Could these considerations have prompted the massacres after attempts to convert failed? Finally, was this the same pattern of behavior that led to the deaths of the Jewish population in Jerusalem in 1099, most of whom were burned alive in a synagogue?[41]

Hebrew texts similarly portray violence as preceding martyrdom and strongly emphasized this, perhaps to enhance the heroism of the martyrs

above the rapacious crusaders. There is, however, evidence that some, such as Godfrey of Bouillon, swore to avenge the blood of Christ before embarking on the pilgrimage East. Another theory credits Count Ditmar making a similar statement, but in addition to avenging Christ, he felt that killing even a single Jew would absolve all of his sins.[42]

Neither a Remnant, nor a Residue. While avarice cannot entirely be ruled out as a motivation, the hyper-violence that preceded the pillaging and looting of Jewish properties resembled blutrache. The vengeance appears to have been driven by the infectious zeitgeist bubbling through Europe by early 1096. When it combined with aspects of cultural anti-Semitism, it sparked the near total annihilation of Rhineland Jewry. Further, as an act of ethnic cleansing, the crusaders forced the surviving Jews to move elsewhere. Depending on which Latin text is examined, one view is that Jews were killed, but it was not originally planned, protracted, or foreseen. A second view suggests that Jews were killed for resisting baptism and conversion, but only if this choice was rebuffed. This, however, was in clear violation of Roman and German churches with policies that did not advocate victimization of the Jews, and canon law explicitly prohibited forced conversions. While some of the forced conversions were overturned later, the damage was done. A third implication drifted for the first time in Northern Europe towards racial anti-Semitism because while the deaths of 1,014 Jews in Mainz was attributed to their refusal to convert, the authors also regarded them in a subhuman context: Jews were an "execrable race."[43]

A fourth body of Latin sources supports Shepkarau's displacement argument in which mobs displaced their inability to reach the Holy Land on to the Jews, but 'paid' the price for their wanton mayhem by suffering violent deaths themselves on the Hungarian border. For example, the especially murderous group led by Count Entioch was almost annihilated by the king of Hungary,

39 Ibid., 95.
40 Ibid., 96.
41 Shepkaru, "The Preaching of the First Crusade," 96; Asbridge, "The First Crusade," 84–88; Lock, "The Routledge Companion to the Crusades," 141; Maalouf, "The Crusades Through Arab Eyes," 50–51; Richard H. Popkin, "Jewish Christians and Christian Jews in Spain, 1492 and After," Judaism 41, no. 3 (1992): 248; Fulcher does not mention Jews being killed in his history, although he stated many Saracens died atop the Temple of Solomon, 120–122.

42 Malkiel, "Destruction or Conversion," 266.
43 Malkiel, "Destruction or Conversion," 263–264; Asbridge, "The First Crusade," 86.

who did not appreciate their mannerisms and threat to peace. It is clear that many cities did have pogroms, but this fourth interpretation of events seems to justify the violent behavior, while acknowledging that the perpetrators deserved "divine punishment."[44]

Therefore, a medieval-style cause and effect relationship played itself out in reverse because of the pope's justification for holy war. In this case, the various groups and actors who initiated the massacres exhibited *wrong* authority, *unjust* prosecution and *wrongful* intent. In the viewpoint of Albert (Annales S. Disibodi), all Jews should convert and that was the original intent, and they should be forced to convert, if necessary. It was this dilemma that led to the suicides and slaughter. Conversely, William of Tyre (ca. 1130–1185) described the excess of the crusaders not simply as intentional, but homicidally intentional. Moreover, violence with malicious intent is only slightly downplayed by 'Anonymous' in the Mainz text where conversion was the primary motive. Nevertheless, the conclusions of many sources generally premised murder as the primary goal, and only the survivors were given a choice to convert.[45]

A social-theological context should also be considered in this analysis considering that the mobs were mostly composed of illiterate peasants and villagers: Did they understand the mission goals as liberation of the towns along their path east to mean being free of the infidel Jews? Further, pillaging properties might also have contributed to validating the mobs' convictions in a rapidly changing Christian society. Finally, the pretext of a pure Christian society may have inspired the "cleansing" of the Jews close to home, as well as the intention to evict Islam from the Holy Land.[46]

Violence and Its Interpretations

It was clear in his proclamation that Urban II expected immediate action to remove paganism and usher in a Christian time driven by apocalyptic imagery of the antichrist. The first problem for all crusaders was distance: Reaching the Holy Land entailed travelling hundreds of miles, obtaining permission from many kingdoms along the way to pass through their lands, purchasing provisions, and finally, confront the deadly enemy.[47] It is plausible that many crusaders realized what a logistical nightmare it would be, and like Peter the Hermit, demanded that French Jews in local cities remit payments or provisions to support the cause. In some cases the Jews complied, and some even said prayers in support of the holy pilgrimage, according to the Mainz Anonymous. Moving into German lands may also have seen local cooperation, although Peter the Hermit's fiery sermon on Easter in Köln not only excited the listeners to join his People's Crusade, but could have incited the violence toward Jews, the nearest 'other', a few weeks after he left town, despite their protection from the local bishop.[48] What is strangely clear is that the extreme aggression and violence mirrored the gory descriptions detailed in Urban's speech. For example, Jews were disemboweled and left to rot in the streets unburied, after being dragged about the cities. If the corpse was someone who committed suicide the belief was they could not be removed from the front door, so using windows or punching holes in the walls sufficed to leave their remains in the streets. It was a sin to kill oneself and burial was denied to anyone who committed suicide.[49]

Did Jews prefer martyrdom to conversion? Conversion is also interpreted as assimilation into Christian society, which begins with baptism, but it also meant converts were no longer part of the rabbinical traditions. The texts are confusing at times because both traditions show that original sources were revised, altered and updated. It is clear, for instance, when handwritten documents are changed because of varying handwriting styles and types of ink used. Confusing though is how parallel both Hebrew and Latin chronicles

---

44 Malkiel, "Destruction or Conversion," 263–264; Shepkaru, "The Preaching of the First Crusade," 93.
45 Malkiel, "Destruction or Conversion," 265–271.
46 Shepkaru, "The Preaching of the First Crusade," 97.

47 Ibid., 101–103.
48 Chazan, "*In the Year 1096*," 28–30.
49 Malkiel, "Destruction or Conversion," 260–262; Shepkaru, "Christian Resurrection and Jewish Immortality," 1–6.

point to common contextualizing. For example, both traditions indicate that martyrdom followed violence, although some depart with the variations discussed previously. The 'displacement theory', however, does not seem challenged by the evidence.[50]

While Worms and Mainz remain especially symbolic today for Jews, there are still open and valid research questions: Was it murderous intent or missionary zeal that diverted some crusaders from the task of liberating the Holy Land? It does appear, however, that both literary traditions downplayed what they may not have wanted to acknowledge at the time: Baptism was a choice, and it may have been proposed first in some locations, but slaughter followed because aposty was the bigger threat to messianic traditions of German Jewry.[51]

Final Summary of Displacement Theory. Displacement in general can indicate personal shortcomings or inadequacies can be factors causing anyone to displace their aggressions, and such human behaviors are entirely possible in any population across time and space. Christians may have been frustrated that Jews did not share their religiosity and elated expression for holy pilgrimage, and directed their frustrations and anger on the weaker citizens in their societies. All of the aforementioned motives could very well have emerged in the context of ideology and the holy war mentality. In particular, the cruelty and violence correlated with the details spread by Urban II's short letter after November 1095. In the letter it reiterated the implications of the speech, especially the hyper-violence, with words such as savagery and 'tyranny used to describe the Christian condition in the Orient. Again, punishment emerged as the key response required by Christians, to avenge misdeeds that caused Christians to suffer. Regardless of the religious perspectives, it is clear that avarice was symptomatic with violence in Köln where

many Jews were decapitated or seriously injured. Further, that the mobs made a point of looting all Jewish synagogues and properties and divided the spoils, then killed another 200 Jews with no offer for clemency implied the crusaders felt they had sufficiently 'punished' the 'other.' Displacement fits because the Jews were a convenient target and substitute for Muslims.[52] In the end, the local populations achieved another goal because there was 'neither a remnant nor a residue' of Jewry left in the Rhineland.

Arab Reactions to the Jerusalem Expedition

The People's Crusade in the Levant: First Encounter, Summer 1096. Initially, the news of the Franks' arrival spread slowly through the lands of the Turks and Syria, but the People's Crusade, led primarily by Peter the Hermit, arrived unannounced and unwelcomed outside Constantinople on August 1, 1096. The disheveled mass and their behavior shocked Alexius I, the leader of the Byzantine Empire, especially their tendency to take what they wanted from the citizenry, so he immediately banned them from entering the city. Also gathering outside his walls were more scattered groups of crusaders from Italy, France, Germany, and Peter's professionally armed contingent commanded by Walter Sansavoir. For a few days Alexius and Peter had civil relations, especially since the latter did his upmost to keep the masses in line, so the emperor agreed to provide supplies. Alexius also cautioned them to wait for the larger, better armed, and more orderly second wave to arrive, but Peter was determined to take action immediately. To avert the inevitable disorder, the emperor decided to deport them and provided ships to take the People's Crusade across the Bosphorus Straits to Anatolia, but in such a way as not to arouse the suspicions of his Turkish enemy, Kilij Arslan.[53]

---

50 Malkiel, "Destruction or Conversion," 260–262; Shepkaru, "The Preaching of the First Crusade," 134–135; Shepkaru, "Christian Resurrection and Jewish Immortality," 1–10.

51 Malkiel, "Destruction or Conversion," 265–271; Tyerman, "God's War," 100–106.

52 Shepkaru, "The Preaching of the First Crusade," 98–99, 103–106.

53 Maalouf, "The Crusades Through Arab Eyes," 1; Asbridge, "The First Crusade," 100–101.

On August 7 the People's Crusade landed in the Levant, and while Alexius continued to send provisions, they were isolated, and the emperor provided no intelligence about the Turks, their combat tactics, or how to find allies and exploit divisions within Islam. Positioned only two-days' march from the capital in Nicaea, Arslan thought the *franj*, as the Arabs referred to the crusaders, did not pose a significant threat. However, open war broke out quickly after Alexius deposited them because were highly motivated to act out Urban's call for action against Islam.[54] According to the Arab sources, was Peter the Hermit's group, the 'innumerable multitude', a complete surprise when they appeared in the Levant? No.[55]

The Turkish Encounter. In July, a month before the People's Crusade arrived, Kilij Arslan's informants learned of a large mass of *franj* en route to Constantinople from the West. Because his territory was the closest to Byzantium, he would potentially be the first to contend with any action that followed. Naturally alert and suspicious, Arslan felt an ominous premonition that no good would come of an armed encounter once they arrived in the Orient. Though he was only seventeen years old, his sultanate already ruled over swaths of Asia Minor, including lands recently captured from the Greeks. This partially explained his suspicion about Alexius's intentions, and also why Alexius sent envoys to Pope Urban II in March 1095 seeking assistance. Moreover, Arslan's capital city, Nicaea, was a former possession of Byzantium and contained more cathedrals than mosques. Even the population was numerically more Greek than Turkish. Therefore, he was on the alert for indications his population's loyalties would create a fifth column inside the city. The young sultan also understood that his enemy often used foreign auxiliaries to fight wars and wondered if this new force coming towards him fit that description.[56]

While pilgrims sometimes travelled with well-armed escorts the size and composition of the approaching group was reason enough to be cautious. By August 1096 Arslan grew more concerned after it was clear Alexius had aided in transporting and supplying the pilgrims. Because he did not know their intent, Arslan sent spies who easily infiltrated the undisciplined camp to learn more, which had the potential to help avoid a needless conflict. It was prudent as well to get an assessment of a potential enemy's strength and numbers, so the spies gathered information quickly. What they reported was alarming: the People's Crusade wanted 'to exterminate Muslims'. Additionally, they numbered between 30–40,000 (the best sources claim 20,000 but more enemies always sounds better), although clearly with the large numbers of women (some of whom did take up arms and fight), children, and elderly, not all were combatants. Still, Peter's force posed a viable threat, so the sultan prepared to strike them in Civitot, a day's march from his capital.[57]

The End of the People's Crusade. Waiting until September, Kilij Arslan counted on the heat and arid conditions to whittle down the *franj*, who by then resorted to looting and pillaging from local villages to feed the masses. They did not spare the Christian towns from massacres either, and the theft of the fall harvest was devastating to the populace. Despite keeping a close eye, Arslan was caught completely off guard when the mob appeared outside his walls one morning while he was away dealing with a rival. Knowing his reputation and prestige was at stake Arslan counseled his emirs to wait because revenge would be assured once they had a sense of the *franj* combat methods, which would help assess any weaknesses to exploit. Additionally, the Turks noticed the tendency for the crusaders to fashion strips of cloth into a cross on the back of their clothing, but its significance was not yet understood.[58]

54 Asbridge, "*The First Crusade*," 101.
55 Maalouf, "*The Crusades Through Arab Eyes*," 1–3.
56 Ibid., 3–5.

57 Maalouf, "*The Crusades Through Arab Eyes*," 3–6; Jala Salameh, "European Women During the First Crusade in the Holy Land," 12, no. 28 (2014): 2733-2734.
58 Asbridge, "*The First Crusade*," 101; Maalouf, "*The Crusades Through Arab Eyes*," 4–6; Tyerman, "*God's War*,"

The first blood and victory went to the People's Crusade, and emboldened they struck again two-weeks later and captured an isolated fortress called Xerigordon. Better prepared now, Kilij Arslan laid siege knowing that Xerigordon was devoid of water inside its walls, all he had to do was wait for thirst and hot weather to takes its toll. It was not a surprise when some of the *franj* surrendered, and to spare their lives they converted to Islam and fought alongside the Turks.[59] The rest were either held as captives or put to the sword, very few escaped. While this small victory removed 6,000 crusaders from the calculus, the majority remained unfought so the crafty sultan plotted another trap. Spies again were deployed to Peter's camp to inform them that their vanguard had successfully captured Nicaea, and a great treasure trove awaited them. However, the Latin view is that word reached Peter about the disaster at Xerigordon, and the enraged crusaders vowed revenge, but recklessly made their way towards Nicaea and fell right into Arslan's ambush. Despite a cadre of disciplined knights employing what was called a *fighting march*, a hollow square with a certain number of cavalry and infantry, the terrain, Turkish tactics, arrows, and use of the rising sun in the east to blind their opponents contributed to the Turkish victory.[60] So great was the annihilation that followed the defeat, very few of Peter the Hermit's followers were rescued by Alexius (including Peter) and carried back to Constantinople.

Interestingly, the Latin and Arabic sources reveal similar details, especially about the bloody slaughter of Peter's forces and subsequent allusions to homosexuality when not only young girls were spared, but also "beardless and beautiful young men." Regardless, the sultan was elated by the victory and may have developed victory

Figure 7.2: Survived Soldiers of Peter the Hermit and Godfrey of Bouillon

disease that marred his judgment when the real armed threat arrived early in 1097.[61]

A Brief Account of the Campaign for Jerusalem

The Price of Victory Disease. Rarely in the course of history has a decisive victory resulted in a catastrophic loss for those who won it. To his folly, Kilij Arslan ignored new reports of *franj* movements in the West, especially the details that this was an even more viable threat than before. Arslan assumed that Alexius I was sending another wave of amateurs to soften him up. When the new groups arrived in Constantinople in 1097, the Greek emperor was considerably more cordial and helpful. Cautious of the vast and well-armed crusading armies outside his walls, Alexius only permitted a handful of Franks into the city at any given time. Also eager to move them along to prevent infighting and theft of property, Alexius crafted a plan. By emptying the royal treasury he appeared to generously gift the crusaders the monies needed to buy tack and provisions, but naturally, the money returned quickly in the form of taxes. He was also more forthcoming with intelligence, especially how to avoid entrapment

59 Nicholas Morton, "The Saljug Turks' Conversion to Islam: The Crusading Sources," *Al-Masaq* 27, no. 2 (2015): 109–110; Tyerman, "God's War," 98–99.

60 Matthew Bennett, "The Crusaders' 'Fighting March' Revisited," *War in History* 8, no. 1 (2001): 1–2; Asbridge, "The First Crusade," 101–103; Maalouf, "The Crusades Through Arab Eyes," 7–8; Tyerman, "God's War," 99–100.

61 Asbridge, "The First Crusade," 103. Asbridge cited Albert of Aachen for this quote; Maalouf, "The Crusades Through Arab Eyes," 7–8.

by the Turks, and that Christian allies lay all along the way to Jerusalem (Armenians, for example), and that Islam was polarized by Sunni kingdoms in Syria and the Shia Fatamid Caliphate in Egypt. Moreover, Alexius neglected, purposely, to mention his alliance with the Fatamids up front, nor did he inform the Fatamids initially of the Franks' intentions because Jerusalem lay in Palestine, one of their territories.[62]

Total War. Lax in his attention to the West, Kilij Arslan learned in April 1097 that the new franj army crossed the Bosphorus and vastly outnumbered the previous group. Caught off guard, the sultan was again away from Nicaea fighting a rival when he learned the franj had his capital surrounded. Striking a truce with Danismend I, he gathered his forces to confront the new enemy, but failed to break the siege and conceded defeat. He also lost a large portion of territory along with prestige. One tactic that Muslim princes sometimes employed when faced with destruction was to issue a call for jihad, which invokes defending Islam. However, too many princes had used this approach in the past, so calling for *jihad* lost its meaning somewhat, and no one came to assist Kilij Arslan.[63] Ultimately, the *franj* army employed new tactics recommended by Alexius, as well as a better-executed version of the 'fighting march' that restricted the Turks' favorite maneuvers, albeit with a bloody learning curve. This led to victory after victory in almost every engagement, although the weather and terrain still favored the Turks. However, the crusaders kept coming, column after column. When news of the Turkish defeat swept the Middle East, genuine panic and anxiety spread.[64]

Syrian Campaign. The largest city in Syria, Antioch, found itself besieged on October 21 and fear gripped the inhabitants. Who could save them? The invaders appeared confident and their

war machines weakened the defenders' resolve psychologically. Again a local ruler invoked jihad by sending messengers east to Mosul. He also expelled all Christian men for fear of sedition, but promised to protect their families (along dhimmi terms), although he also expected them to report back about the franj. This time the call for jihad was heeded since the threat posed by the franj was understood. Similarly, the ruler of Mosul, Karbuqa, was already aware the invaders defeated his Turkish rival. The primary issues though included distance and the time needed to muster a sizable force, but then more bad news arrived, the franj captured the Armenian city of Edessa. Moreover, the prince who took it, Baldwin of Boulonge, planned on turning it into a crusader state. In the meantime, however, internal intrigues and betrayals led to the demise of Antioch's ruler, and this was in spite of the half-starved franj barely lifting their weapons. Nor did the summons for jihad reach fruition, as Karbuqa's force was divided and subsequently conquered.[65]

By 1098 the Frankish armies resumed their march south, hugging the Mediterranean coastline, which was necessary to maintain supply lines, but also because many of the existing roads through the rugged terrain left them no choice. Atrocities followed as more cities fell, including accusations that the crusaders committed acts of cannibalism when a period of starvation beset them. The long-standing implications of those massacres have created issues of mistrust and bad memories in the Arab world. Conversely, the franj considered themselves *anthrophagi* (benevolent conquerors).[66] Unbeknownst to the Arabs was a crisis of leadership within the enemy camp. Princes had competed and even fought one another at times for territory and loot despite a common foe and final objective. Nor did the road to Jerusalem prove as easy as many thought initially. Numerous sieges, seemingly endless enemies, hot weather, a perpetual shortage of water

62 Asbridge, "*The First Crusade,*" 103–116; Maalouf, "*The Crusades Through Arab Eyes,*" 8–16.

63 Maalouf, "*The Crusades Through Arab Eyes,*" 16–28; Bonner, "*Jihad in Islamic History,*" 1–4.

64 Maalouf, "*The Crusades Through Arab Eyes,*" 16–28; Bennett, "The Crusaders' 'Fighting March' Revisited," 1–2; Stark, "*God's Battalions,*" 142–148.

65 Asbridge, "*The First Crusade,*" 149–152; Maalouf, "*The Crusades Through Arab Eyes,*" 28–36; Stark, "*God's Battalions,*" 136–146,148–154,

66 Asbridge, "*The First Crusade,*" 249–250; Maalouf, "*The Crusades Through Arab Eyes,*" 36–39.

and food, and rugged terrain created conditions for a nasty mood in the crusaders' camps.

By January 1099 the clash between Arabs and the franj intensified, as one of the last cities in line to Jerusalem, Md'arra, fell and all opposition seemed to melt away. The anxiety of who would be next was partially solved when the invaders crossed the *Nahr al-Kalb*, the River of the Dog. This river was the boundary of the Fatamid Caliphate, who by then was informed by Alexius of the crusaders' intentions and target. On one hand, the Fatamids had little love for the Sunnis who were being defeated kingdom by kingdom, nor did they care for the Turks, but the success of the franj, on the other hand, implied their ally, the *Rum* (Greeks), were losing sway in Asia Minor. The question then was, what of Jerusalem?[67]

The Battle for Jerusalem. After a Fatamid delegation was sent to create a non-aggression pact with the franj, the possibility of establishing a partition was on the table. The franj, they proposed, could have northern Syria, which was already largely in their hands, while the Fatamids would retain southern Syria and Palestine. The problem remained, however, because Jerusalem was located in Palestine. While some of the crusaders did not overtly desire Fatamid territory, Jerusalem was the point of the pilgrimage. The negotiation went cordially, but no firm agreement was met, plus individual rivalries between princes would not guarantee a general agreement could be kept. Until Jerusalem was taken the princes had to work together, so they openly declared war on the Fatamids by crossing the River of the Dog on May 19. The road to Jerusalem led to a succession of Fatamid controlled cities falling or remaining under siege, including Beirut, Tyre, Acre, and Sidon whose leaders pledged allegiance, but only if Jerusalem was captured. The remaining towns and villages evacuated from their path until nightfall on June 7 and the franj erected their tents outside the walls of the Holy City. Preparations included building two enormous siege towers, and the Egyptian garrison inside the city walls had already stored enough foodstuffs to sustain

a long siege. The only concern, however, was the plugged hole in the northern wall the Egyptians made capturing the city previously.[68]

By parading around the city walls on July 15, 1099, the franj demonstrated their confidence, but the defenders also wondered at the display put on by the priests who chanted and sang loudly in a tongue they did not understand. This made them speculate just how *fanatical* the crusaders were, which is still one of the long-term perceptions of Christianity in the Middle East. Although not the only cause of the deterioration of relations between Christianity and Islam, the first and subsequent crusades made substantial and significant contributions that harmed a sense of trust and goodwill.[69] After a few initial attacks to detect weaknesses in the defense failed, the fateful day came when the walls of the city were breached on the north side, exactly where the defenders feared. Honoring an agreement, the Egyptian garrison was allowed safe passage, but the Muslim inhabitants of the city were massacred. Christian sources acknowledge that 10,000 at least were killed, whereas Arab sources claim as many as 70,000 perished. Despite the Arab source's suggestion of franj savagery, of which they are not entirely innocent, Muslim refugees escaped the sack of Jerusalem and may have reestablished themselves in Damascus. Surprisingly, Rodney Stark (2009) approved of the "no quarter" policy that states if no prior arrangements are made all would be killed. The victims of the attacks were the Jews. Oddly silent or downplayed in the Latin texts was the demise of the Jewish population in Jerusalem. Driven into their own quarter of the city, the Jews were all burned alive inside the main synagogue by the Franks.[70] Therefore, it seems that what occurred in the Rhineland in 1096,

---

67 Maalouf, "*The Crusades Through Arab Eyes*," 39–46.

68 Lock, "*The Routledge Companion to the Crusades*," 142–143; Maalouf, "*The Crusades Through Arab Eyes*," 47–48; Asbridge, "*The First Crusade*," 298–310.

69 Norman Housley, "The Crusades and Islam," *Medieval Encounters* 13 (2007): 189.

70 Daniella Talmon-Heller and Benjamin Z. Kedar. "Did Muslim Survivors of the 1099 Massacre of Jerusalem Settle in Damascus? The True Origins of the al-Salihiyya Suburb." *Al-Masaq* 17, no. 2 (2005): 165–166; Maalouf, "*The Crusades Through Arab Eyes*," 49–51; Asbridge, "*The First Crusade*,"

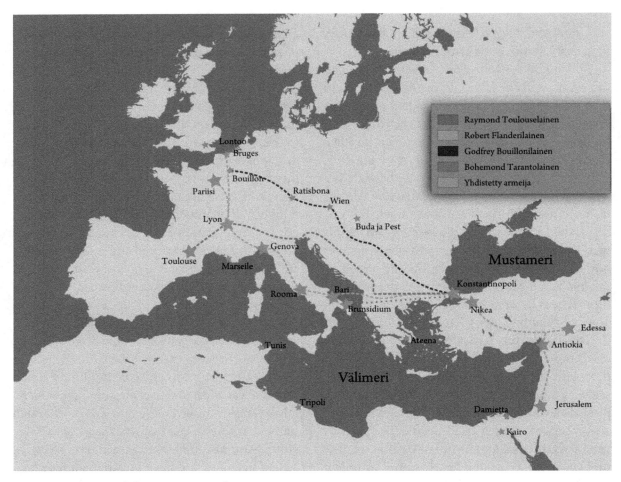

Figure 7.3: Map of the First Crusade

perhaps for the same reasons analyzed previously, was perpetuated at the conclusion of the First Crusade.

Afterword

While the element of surprise contributed to the fall of Jerusalem, the uninhibited violence and looting marred any sanctification or justification for holy war. Because the memory remains and continues to fuel hostility when the word 'crusade' is invoked, however naively at times, other problems associated with Orientalist perspectives also enhance the us versus them binary of Christianity and the West versus Islam and the Middle East.

Furthermore, for all its vainglorious bravado, the capture of Jerusalem and the foundation of a Frankish country around Tripoli and a few other cities, such as Antioch and Edessa, were all eventually lost to independent efforts by Turkish and Arab forces. Additionally, Pope Urban II died on July 29, 1099 without ever knowing the holy war he proclaimed had succeeded, albeit for a short time.[71] Another future conflict that emerged from the view that Alexius and Byzantium were duplicitous allies eventually led to future crusaders attacking Constantinople and creating a rift between the Holy Latin Church and Eastern Orthodoxy. Even today the division has not been resolved despite recent attempts from Popes John Paul

---

310–319; Fulcher, "*A History of the Expedition to Jerusalem*," 120–122; Stark, "*God's Battalions*," 157–158.

71 Lock, "*The Routledge Companion to the Crusades*," 142–143.

II, Benedict XVI, and Francis. From 1102 onward, instability among Frankish leadership hampered coordination, and more campaigns, defeats, and atrocities characterized the years after the First Crusade concluded.[72]

While the Levant was secured, seemingly endless attacks by the Turks and Arabs eventually broke down resistance, but this was eventually overshadowed by the rise of a new champion for Islam, Saladin, who gained allies and sufficient forces to push back and recover Jerusalem by October 1187. Pope Urban III is said to have died on October 29 after receiving word of Jerusalem's fall, and his successor, Gregory VIII, called for another crusade. Europeans did not access Jerusalem again, however, until the early twentieth-century. The city continues to be a source of pride and dispute between the three faiths whose holy relics, mosques, and temples lie within its walls.[73]

The idea and procedure of holy war and crusading took root in Spain after the eleventh-century, and Part Three analyzes the social and racial implications that emerged as Christian kingdoms unified and incorporated more of al-Andalus. Regions where the tri-ethnic communities once lived somewhat peacefully with one another gradually shifted to policies of exclusion, segregation, and racialization along lines of ethnicity and religion, predicated on purity of blood.

Image Credits

72 Lock, *"The Routledge Companion to the Crusades,"* 142–143; Stark, *"God's Battalions,"* 137–138.

73 Lock, *"The Routledge Companion to the Crusades,"* 71–72

Societal Changes in Aragon and Castile-León After 1391

By D. Paul Sweeney

Santiago Peregrino and Santiago Matamoros: The Dual-Imaged Symbol for Reconquest. Throughout the medieval period, Spain's patron, Saint James (Santiago), serves as the best symbol and metaphor for the schizophrenic social changes that occurred from the thirteenth century on. Second only to Rome, the popular thousand-year-old pilgrimage winds through the mountainous regions of northern Spain to the coastal town of Santiago de Compostela, the final resting place of the saint's earthly remains. On one level, St. James evokes the plight of the pilgrims, and he appears in some images clad in simple garments, holding a walking stick. This serene and peaceful manifestation is referred to as *Santiago Peregrino* (St. James the Pilgrim). At the shrine, pilgrims receive a blessing, and often cite miracles after inserting their hand into a worn recess in the column supporting his statue.[1] The biblical law of charity, "love thy neighbor as self" symbolized the saint's attributes, and Spain's tri-ethnic population revered the maxim because it implied reconciliation and good will.

The polar opposite images portray St. James astride a warhorse, swinging a mighty sword. At the bottom of St. James's statues are cowering or dead and decapitated turban-wearing, dark-skinned figures who represent Moors (Muslims). This violent, crusading incarnation of the saint is called *Santiago Matamoros* (St. James the Moor Slayer, killer of Muslims). Whereas Santiago Peregrino symbolizes concordance, Santiago Matamoros spearheaded religiously grounded hatred for Islam, and in Part Four, some long-term issues associated with this imagery and history will be discussed. To clarify, the bipolar nature of St. James in Spanish traditions and cultural history had nothing to do with the saint's life or legacy. Rather, it had everything to do with his devotees, who experienced the anxieties of the Reconquest and subsequent social changes it ushered in, and focused their hate primarily on Islam.[2]

---

1   Chris Lowney, *A Vanished World: Muslims, Christians, and Jews in Medieval Spain*, (2005. Reprint, New York, NY: Oxford University Press, 2006), 10–11; Glick, "*Islamic and Christian Spain*," 11, 117.

2   Lowney, "*A Vanished World*," 10–14; Javier Domínguez García, "St. James the Moor-Slayer, A New Challenge to

The Growing Role of Santiago Matamoros.
Animosity toward Islam had an early start as it regarded the pilgrimage destination of Santiago de Compostela. In 997 C.E. a professional Muslim army led by Almanzor attacked the Christian site with intentions "to send down confusion and disappointment on the obdurate unbelievers."[3] His target was well chosen because the small city had no standing army, but the industry of catering to pilgrims made it quite wealthy. Moreover, the attack itself was audacious, penetrating so deeply into Christian lands from Córdoba, over four hundred miles to the south. Despite the difficult terrain, Almanzor successfully sacked and obliterated the city. The only structure left standing housed Santiago's tomb, which was apparently spared by strict orders from the commander. The victors divided the substantial loot and prepared for the long journey home. However, no souvenir was more substantial or befitting than appropriating Compostela's cathedral bells! On the backs of Christian captives sold into slavery the bells were hoisted over hills and mountains until they reached Córdoba. In commemoration of the victory, the bells were hung in the great mosque where they stayed for over two centuries until they were recovered. Nonetheless, the lost honor and religious hatred percolated, and this scenario best characterizes the evolution of *Santiago Peregrino* to *Santiago Matamoros*.[4]

Unification Preceded Reconquest. Gradual unification from the twelfth century onward occurred with regularity as Spain's separate kingdoms slowly coalesced. Asturias, the realm where Santiago de Compostela lies, was incorporated into the kingdom of León, which in turn became part of Castile. Before the Reconquista ended in the late fifteenth century, Castile had merged with Aragon and formed a superpower state. Prior to this, however, the gradual victories and territories gained around Toledo cast a more violent and

bellicose mood that precipitated holy war and the push south. Furthermore, as the various Christian kingdoms consolidated, they encountered larger numbers of Muslims and Jews in their midst, which sparked social exclusions, slavery of Muslims, and as outlined in the next sections, initiated a toxic period for Spain's Jews.[5]

Fourteenth Century Roots of Spanish Anti-Semitism

Power Struggles in Castile-León. Part One of this chapter revealed that patterns of anti-Semitism follow significant economic downturns or social upheavals. Both of these conditions occurred in the thirteenth century with the reintroduction of a monetary system and power struggles between and within coalescing kingdoms. Such was the situation by the mid-fourteenth century in Castile-León when Count Enrique of Trastámora, one of ten bastard sons of King Alfonso XI 'The Wise,' brutally stabbed his brother, King Pedro IV, to death one evening in his tent. Assuming the Castilian crown in March 1369, the Trastámora dynasty began. Where Pedro had a sordid reputation and earned the moniker 'The Cruel', his demise was poetic because his heinous and violent acts in life were sometimes perpetrated against family members, so Enrique's primary motive must have been revenge. However, Enrique's reputation for political agitation and Judaeophobia started much earlier in life when an outbreak of the Black Death swept Europe in 1348. Over one-third of Europe's population perished during its three-year duration that ended as suddenly and mysteriously as it began.[6]

Just as they were accused of "the treachery at Toledo," Jews in Castile-León were blamed for causing the plague, perhaps through sorcery gone awry, and served as scapegoats of convenience. In Spain, Enrique's reputation for Judaeophobia took root in this era, and upon ascension to his brother's throne twenty years later, he circulated anti-Semitic messages to damage the privileged

Spanish National Discourse in the Twenty-First Century," *International Journal of Iberian Studies* 22, no.1 (2009): 69–78.

3 Lowney, "A Vanished World," 79; Glick, "Islamic and Christian Spain," 49–50, 111, 117.

4 Lowney, "A Vanished World," 84–88.

5 Ibid., 43–53.

6 Ibid., 227.

positions many Jews enjoyed during Pedro's reign. Succinctly, Enrique's real motive was to systematically dismantle Pedro's powerbase, which included Jews and conversos. Then, Enrique's successor, his thirteen-year-old grandson Enrique III, upended the Spanish tradition where monarchs defended Jews in times of social and religious tension. Thus, by 1391, the worst pogroms against the Sephardic Jews escalated, first in Seville's ghetto where thousands of Jews were murdered as the young, powerless king stood by and acquiesced to the rioting mobs.[7]

Pogroms and the Racialization Process. For Jews especially, but in Christian Spain as a whole, 1391 was a pivotal year that ushered in the racialization process where one's purity of blood determined social standing, and a concerted effort to rid society of mozarabs, Judaism, Islam, and all antecedents of those faiths, as well as any heretical histories within families. Therefore, when the social fabric snapped in Seville, a systematic unraveling of Jewry in Spain occurred, and terminated one hundred years later with expulsion in 1492. First, however, the pogroms spread quickly to Toledo, Madrid, Córdoba, Burgos, Valencia and Barcelona. When the blood lust subsided, many thousands of Jews were dead. The rapidity with which the mobs in the cities fell upon the Jews reflected the anger and fear heightened by catalysts such as an early economic recession following the switch to a new monetary system after centuries of trade and barter, Millenarianism, plus recurring visitations of the plague. Regardless, what elevated 1391 to extraordinary heights was the cause and effect relationship the pogroms elicited: Targeted mob violence prompted the phenomenon of mass conversion by Spanish Jews to Christianity. Were these events that brought about the first appearance of racism *and* racial anti-Semitism, and the process of racialization that followed, premised on purity of blood?[8]

Conversos and Social Change. The first significant wave of Jews who converted, and the subsequent communities of conversos quickly ran into conflict with the Old Christians and the Jewish community. While Jews had converted previously in the kingdom of Aragon for personal and legal reasons, such as avoiding debts and getting a fresh start in life, the fear of violence had a far different effect in Spain compared to its effect on the Ashkenazi Jews in Germany in 1096. Ultimately, tens of thousands of Jews in Aragon and Castile-León sought the protection afforded by submitting to baptism, because baptism symbolized assimilation into the dominant Christian societies.[9]

Further, conversion opened doorways previously closed to Jews. For instance, conversos could finally live outside of the segregated Jewish quarters in the cities (*juderías*). In addition, they no longer had to wear the distinctive clothing and badges identifying them publicly as Jews. Perhaps most importantly, previously closed paths for public and ecclesiastical offices opened to them. Such opportunities also permitted intermarriage between conversos and Christians, thereby breaking the mutual endogamous tendencies of Christian and Jewish societies. Initially, the Church accepted the newly converted although some immediately doubted the sincerity of conversos in light of the recent social unrest that prompted the reaction. Until the early fifteenth century, proselytizing in the Jewish communities also created a boundary between Christians, conversos, and the Jews. Between 1412–15 more aggressive missionary work yielded more converts but attempts to curtail the residential, social, and cultural ties to the *juderías*, the Jewish quarters, largely failed.[10]

---

7   Lowney, "*A Vanished World*," 227–229; Glick, "*Islamic and Christian Spain*," 172–174.

8   María Elena Martínez, *Genealogical Fictions: Limpieza de Sangre, Religion, and Gender in Colonial Mexico*, (Stanford, CA: Stanford University Press, 2008), 27; Lowney, "*A Vanished World*," 227–229; David Nirenberg, "Conversion,

Sex and Segregation: Jews and Christians in Medieval Spain," *American Historical Review* 107, no. 4 (2002): 1065–1066; Glick, "*Islamic and Christian Spain*," 173–174.

9   Alexandra Guerson, "Seeking Remission: Jewish Conversion in the Crown of Aragon, c. 1378–1391," *Jewish History* 24 (2010): 33–34; Martínez, "*Genealogical Fictions*," 27.

10   Martínez, "*Genealogical Fictions*," 25–27; Martha G. Krow-Lucal, "Marginalizing History: Observations on the Origins of the Inquisition in Fifteenth Century Spain by B.

Birth of Racism and Racial Anti-Semitism?
When the first purity of blood statutes (*limpieza de sangre*) appeared, the Spanish Inquisition was symptomatic of the race-based discrimination that reflected shifts in Christian society. The Inquisition's role was both internal housecleaning of the clergy in Christian territories and to ferret out crypto-Judaism. Academics still question if this dramatic shift was the birth of racism. In the reading selection contained in this book, Martínez mentions this possibility, but careful reading reveals her hope that scholars can find evidence that this occurred previously, somewhere other than Spain. For now, however, the evidence does implicate the purity of blood statutes as compelling evidence of racially distinguishing Christians from Jews and Muslims by flimsy measures of blood purity and contamination. A wave of dehumanizing tactics accompanied the violence experienced all over Iberia against Jews, except this time blood accusations and 'blood libel' were less common than they were in Northern Europe. Nevertheless, by the late fourteenth century, Jews were demonized through a combination of Church imagery and iconography, as well as public reenactments of the Passion during Holy Week. Additionally, cultural anti-Semitism found its way into literature and popular Christian mythology.[11]

Three Patterns Identified. What social, political, and economic factors contributed to fomenting the decidedly anti-Jewish laws and violence? A few developments have been identified: First, social and class tension heightened as the previous barter and trade economic model transitioned into a bimetallic monetary system. Second, the Black Death wrought so much havoc

and destruction throughout Europe that Jews faced widespread blame for the unexplainable calamity. Worse, Jews were likened to filth and lice, which implied that they caused the succession of plagues between 1347 and 1351, and again between 1388 and 1391. The third significant factor was the violence that encouraged mass conversions by Jews to preempt persecution. The deeply embedded Judaeophobia, primarily along religious lines, possibly driven by Millenariansm, evolved into more blatant racial anti-Semitism predicated on purity of blood, with legislation to enforce it.[12] This last shift fits both definitions of racism: Power + prejudice and a system of advantages based on race.

What Were the Purity of Blood Statutes?
From their first appearance in Spanish law codes, the slow spread of complicated and often piecemeal purity of blood statutes was a drawn out process. Unlike Nazi Germany's Blood and Honor laws enacted against Jews under the notion of *Rassenschande* (race polluted or race defilement),[13] some statutes faced intense scrutiny and were vigorously challenged, occasionally rescinded, but later reinstated. Stretching well into the sixteenth century, past the scope of this chapter, but tying into the Martínez reading on limpieza de sangre elsewhere in the book, both religious and secular institutions created and enforced purity of blood concerns in Spanish society. Significantly, these attitudes and statutes persisted for centuries and proliferated at precisely the same time Iberians colonized and organized societies in the Americas.[14]

The race-based blood purity statutes influenced both religious and social dynamics in New Spain and other regions in the Americas. Their long-term affects can still be measured today in areas that exhibit the most adherence to eugenics, but the immediate implication of limpieza de sangre was fastidious record keeping, particularly

Netanyahu," *Judaism* 46 (1997): 48–49; Guerson, "Seeking Remission," 34–37.

11 Martínez, "*Genealogical Fictions*," 26–27; Ronald Madden, "The Passion of the Christ: A Modern Mystery Play," *Journal of Religion and Health* 43, no. 3 (2004): 248–250; Nirenberg, "Conversion, Sex and Segregation," 1065–1066; Elizabeth Lapina, "The Mural Paintings of Berzé-la-Ville in the Context of the First Crusade and the *Reconquista*," *Journal of Medieval History* 31 (2005): 318–321.

12 Martínez, "*Genealogical Fictions*," 26–27.
13 Frank Caestecker and David Fraser, "The Extraterritorial Application of the Nuremberg Laws: *Rassenchande* and "Mixed" Marriages in European Liberal Democracies," *Journal of the History of International Law* 10 (2008): 35–40.
14 Martínez, "*Genealogical Fictions*," 25.

focused on genealogical lineage. What started as legal codes quickly evolved into an ideology of almost pathological obsession with race, degrees of whiteness by percentage, and the later complex *sistema de castas*, a typological organization of racial types and results of mixing (miscegenation). The driving force in Spain was the notion that blood was the vehicle through which positive religious attributes were transmitted (e.g., Christian = pure, Jew/Muslim = impure). It also established a baseline to differentiate Old Christians from New Christians, and heavily relied on female sexuality and reproduction to maintain purity and social order. Bloodlines were documented meticulously in this complex system, and the honor system, especially sexual honor, was elevated to promote a newly defined endogamy. Therefore, to regulate the process, maintaining familial and public records was necessary to prove ones purity, particularly when it came to legal matters or applying for a civic or Church service position.[15]

Racial Concerns and Sex. Similar to white supremacy that believes in racial purity and that its alleged benefits can only be achieved through strict endogamy, a renewed interest in the 'wrongs' of miscegenation focused on preventing minority men from having sexual relations with Christian women, especially prostitutes. Such violations of the sexual honor codes required that for any "… Jew or Muslim male […] found lying with a Christian woman, the Jew or Muslim should be drawn and quartered and the Christian woman should be burned, in such a manner that they should die."[16] In this situation, violence as a penalty for violating endogamy gained ecclesiastical backing. For example, in 1215 the Fourth Lateran Council sought to ban miscegenation, which was its chief concern, by justifying dress codes to aid in the process of segregation and identification, despite it being such an inconsistent measure.

Regardless, it is easy to see that converts benefited because eliminating the dress code's limited sartorial options was a public display of belonging and inclusion in Christian society. By contrast, Muslim men (and slaves) were compelled to adopt particular hairstyles and faced similar dress code restrictions, all of which combined to create the visual representation of sexual boundaries. As noted, transgression of these boundaries often led to unpleasant consequences.[17]

Why Sex? Horse breeding influenced early concepts of human biology that fixated on blood and bloodlines, and these presumptions stipulated that children born to a Christian parent the children were considered Christian. However, racial integrity may not have been included in the initial blood statutes or their motivation for criminalizing miscegenation. In a thirteenth century letter written by King Alfonso The Wise of Castile, we can see the attitudes of the day from the top of society: "Since Christians who commit adultery with married women deserve death, how much more do Jews who lie with Christian women, for these are spiritually espoused to Our Lord Jesus Christ by virtue of faith and baptism they received in His name … shall receive the same punishment as the Christian woman who lies with a Muslim."[18] What this letter states implicitly is that married or not, any Christian woman (including prostitutes) is the bride of Christ, and the act of miscegenation "becomes the cuckolding of Christ." The allusion to a 'sexualized God' in this and related period writings is interesting. Thus, the dishonor and subsequent shame of the feminine body was representative of the collective shame of the group (Christians), and honor could only be restored by punishment.[19] Even if the transgression were conducted in secret, the host would know at communion and mete out divine punishment, as illustrated in some paintings in cathedrals. This is a common theme in late

15   Martínez, "*Genealogical Fictions*," 25–26.
16   David Nirenberg, "Religious and Sexual Boundaries in the Medieval Crown of Aragon." In *Christians, Muslims, and Jews in Medieval and Early Spain: Interaction and Cultural Change*, ed. Mark D. Meyerson and Edward D. English (Notre Dame, IN: University of Notre Dame Press, 2000), 142.

17   Nirenberg, "Religious and Sexual Boundaries," 142–143.
18   Nirenberg, "Conversion, Sex and Segregation," 1067–1068; Nirenberg, "Religious and Sexual Boundaries," 144.
19   Nirenberg, "Conversion, Sex and Segregation," 1068; Nirenberg, "Religious and Sexual Boundaries," 144–145.

fourteenth century liturgical art in Spain, and it helped dictate the mores and expectations regarding Christian behavior.

Fear of Race Pollution. The fear of blood pollution was not originally a concept invented by eugenics or the Nazis. The purity of blood statutes used metaphors of the body, but fear of blood defilement through sexual activity quickly motivated introduction of new laws and proscriptions on fraternization between the tri-ethnic groups. Regardless, some neighbors in mixed communities witnessed plenty of drinking and gambling with no adherence to strict secular and religious laws. Because so many Jews converted after the 1391 pogroms, the next step in discriminatory legislation used *limpieza de sangre* to elevate the Old Christians. Old Christians were those who assumed themselves completely free of Jewish or heretical antecedents, or had ever converted to Islam for at least four generations. New Christians, conversely, were viewed as opportunists, "less pure," and their socially minded ambitions equated political and economic rivalry. It appears that what started as a "Jewish problem" soon became a "converso problem" when the 1449 Toledo statute sparked a rebellion.[20]

Converso Exclusion in Toledo After 1449. Toledo contained a very large population of conversos who had, in most cases, done quite well for themselves after being liberated from the dress code stigma. Many married Christian women and held key governmental positions, such as tax collectors. When the social and political exclusions outlined in the purity of blood statute were revealed, it was clear that conversos were targeted specifically, and the legal attempt to push them from or diminish their comfortable lifestyles induced riots and promulgated renewed violence against Jews and conversos alike. Therefore, exclusion by law encouraged persecution, first by the Old Christians, then later from the Inquisition.[21] Using a biological concept, the

1449 statute was withdrawn after the violence, but in 1467 a second, refined version passed through legislation in Toledo. What drove this desire for social exclusion? Jealousy of rapid ascension in society by conversos cannot be overlooked as a motivation for laws that first restricted, and then specifically discriminated against the conversos, who frequently acquired the best jobs, possibly because of the higher rates of literacy in Jewish societies. In order to limit their access, the Inquisition investigated any converso accused of judaizing, who was then legally described as a *marrano*, someone secretly practicing Jewish rites while outwardly posing as a Christian. These crypto-Jews were outed by torture typically, and thorough examination of their genealogical records traced lineage and bloodlines. However, neither statute succeeded at fully removing conversos from their offices, nor were they compelled to become "sincere practitioners of Christianity."[22]

The Inquisition, 1481–85. In the film *History of the World, Pt. 1* (1981) director Mel Brooks poked fun at the Spanish Inquisition through an elaborate song and dance to emphasize the application of torture to derive confessions and admissions from the morranos. The Inquisition appeared in Toledo around 1485 as a reactionary measure, but was quickly institutionalized throughout Iberia, including Portugal, and fixated on removing *conversos* who were not 'pure.'[23] Despite initial setbacks and large numbers of conversos escaping the snares, the international aspects of the Inquisition in the sixteenth and seventeenth centuries illustrated how the obsession with *limpieza de sangre* shaped the colonial

20   Nirenberg, "Religious and Sexual Boundaries," 243.

21   Dayle Seidenspinner-Núñez, "Conversion and Subversion: Converso Texts in Fifteenth Century Spain," in *Christians, Muslims, and Jews in Medieval and Early Spain: Interaction and Cultural Change*, edited by Mark D. Meyerson and Edward D. English (Notre Dame, IN: University of Notre Dame Press, 2000): 259–260.

22   Krow-Lucal, "Marginalizing History," 49–50; Linda Martz, "Relations Between Conversos and Old Christians in Early Modern Toledo: Some Different Perspectives," in *Christians, Muslims, and Jews in Medieval and Early Spain: Interaction and Cultural Change*, edited by Mark D. Meyerson and Edward D. English (Notre Dame, IN: University of Notre Dame Press, 2000), 220–221

23   Toby Green, "Policing the Empires: A Comparative Perspective on the Institutional Trajectory of the Inquisition in the Portuguese and Spanish Overseas Territories in the Sixteenth and Seventeenth Centuries," *Hispanic Research Journal* 13, no. 1 (Feb. 2012): 8.

experience. Significantly, however, by 1544 both the Spanish Crown *and* the papacy approved of continuing the blood statutes. This time though, the motivation was not driven by accusations of judaizing, but along lines that included "undesirable personality traits, occupations, lineage, and other *sins* inherited from [Jewish] ancestors."[24]

Granada and the Jewish Expulsion, 1492

Millenarianism as a Motivation? Theological Considerations. Once Europe's most Jewish and Muslim country, the Muslim Conquest probably saved Iberia's Jews from forced assimilation or expulsion. In the years leading up to 1492 the Reconquista gradually captured and incorporated former al-Andulasan territories and cities. Where social changes and expectations discussed earlier took place, Old Christians generally privileged themselves over the unconverted Jews, Muslims, and especially the New Christians.[25]

In a manner similar to the contemplation of elevated spiritualism prior to the First Crusade, a swelling tide of Millenarian and Messianic speculation could have motivated the combined crowns of Castile-Aragon to view the final victory at Granada and the subsequent expulsion of Jews who did not convert as fortuitous. The third element came in early 1493 when news of a New World inspired beliefs that Spain had providential blessing and many hoped this was the harbinger of the End of Days. Significantly, waves of conversions by Muslims and Jews followed each victory as al-Andalus fell, kingdom by kingdom.[26] Unlike the Christian realms, Jews in southern cities and smaller towns did not live in segregated quarters by decree, although some lived in close proximity to specific neighborhoods to facilitate Sabbath ceremonies and be near synagogues.[27]

Missionary Activity. By the fourteenth century the Millenarian attitude gathered intensity and some scholars believe this was one of the underlying themes in 1391 when intense pressure on the Jewish communities in Toledo and elsewhere yielded conversions en masse. In essence, Millenarian revivals have characterized many expectations of the Second Coming of Christ, and references in the book of Revelations suggested, perhaps even required, the conversion of the Jews as a prerequisite to the Rapture.[28] Coinciding with the Reconquista, missionary campaigns by friars made strides to convert Jews and Muslims in all the newly acquired areas, resulting in growing numbers of conversos and moriscos. As noted earlier, the Old Christians were suspicious of the motivations and authenticity of the conversions, especially as conversos moved up socially and economically. Interestingly, the dilemma stemmed from Pope Gregory I (540–604 C.E.), who officially outlined restrictions against forced baptisms, and this became canon law. Finally, one important detail remained as the most significant in Spain: Once baptized, a convert must remain a Christian.[29]

Therefore, by 1410 missionaries realized much success converting Jews, and even entire communities submitted to baptism. Concurrent with their efforts, resentment grew toward the remaining unconverted Jews in Aragon, especially between 1412–16. The shrinking Jewish population compelled most rabbinical leaders to flee Spain for North Africa. This combination of internal and external factors may have contributed to early self-deportation by Jews unwilling to assimilate. When the Spanish Inquisition appeared, its primary objectives were to police the New Christians and weed out judaizing, and other forms of heresy. Not surprisingly, conversos quickly found themselves outsiders. On one hand they were forbidden by canon law from reverting back, and on the other hand, Jews viewed them as sellouts with no hope of ever returning to Judaism.[30]

---

24 Martz, "Relations Between Conversos and Old Christians," 220–221.
25 Norman Roth, "The Jews of Spain and the Expulsion of 1492," *Historian* 55, no. 1 (1992): 17–19.
26 Richard H. Popkin, "Jewish Christians and Christian Jews in Spain, 1492 and After," *Judaism* 41, no. 3 (1992): 248.
27 Roth, "The Jews of Spain and the Expulsion," 17–19.

28 Popkin, "Jewish Christians and Christian Jews," 249.
29 Roth, "The Jews of Spain and the Expulsion," 20–21.
30 Roth, "The Jews of Spain and the Expulsion," 20–23; François Soyer, "Enforcing Religious Repression in an Age

Late Fifteenth Century. Because full assimilation required genuine conversion, animosity towards the New Christians was even more intense by the late fifteen century, partly rooted in fear of the conversos' growing power. Similarly, using the harshest condemnations, Jews were described as members of the "synagogue of Satan … and therefore must be avoided with the greatest care" (Revelations 3:2, 2:9). These beliefs contributed to the creation of the Inquisition and purity of blood statutes, and Jews and *conversos* were officially considered a race (*raza*) based on Jewsih ancestry. Furthermore, restrictions placed upon conversos essentially grandfathered in Old Christians with acknowledgement that Jewish blood "irreconcilably corrupted" the individual down to the fourth generation. This held true even if the New Christian married into Old Christian families. Thus, the four-generation restrictions barred significant numbers of conversos from holding important jobs.[31] Accounting for these circumstances, it is easy to see why the main title of Maria Elena Martínez's book is *Genealogical Fictions*. Fraudulent documents could have helped some escape all but the most in-depth examination of claimed lineage.

While the obsession with 'purity of blood' became almost pathological, at the time of their unification, both Isabel and Fernando had large numbers of Jews as friends, investors, and key administrators vital to their kingdoms in 1474. Additionally, the Pope set strict rules limiting the supervision of the Inquisition (by bishops), and how many Inquisitor generals (2–3 maximum) should be appointed. For instance, the Inquisitors had to be masters of canon law and follow strict procedural rules. But the king and queen categorically ignored the Pope. Soon thereafter, a pattern emerged: heretics were targeted, but the majority of them were marranos accused of judaizing. First, they extracted a confession by torture, and then forced the victim to implicate others, although torture did not always elicit the truth.

Theoretically, the Inquisition did not have authority over the Jews, who were viewed as property of the crowns' treasuries, so its chief concern until 1491–92 lay primarily with investigating New Christians.[32]

Blood Libel in Spain: Holy Child of La Guardia

The First Step Towards Expulsion. In 1491 the Inquisition uncovered an episode of blood libel similar to the examples discussed in Part Two. Known as the Holy Child of La Guardia, five people, including two Jews, were burned alive in a public display that was customary and central to the institution's reputation. That immersion of Jews in the blood accusation marked a change in direction by the leadership within the Inquisition, and appears to have been of the Jews' own initiative. A crime was confessed by a Jew, allegedly deceived by an inquisitor posing as a rabbi. A Christian child, fifteen years prior, was abducted on Good Friday and supposedly crucified, then, his blood and heart were mixed into the holy host at a nearby church. The subsequent use of blood and witchcraft introduced a wave of rabies that swept the land. The societal hysteria that followed this fabrication diminished both conversos and Jews, even though evidence could not support that a child was ever reported missing. Significantly, the curious timing of this blood accusation contributed to the Expulsion Edict the following year.[33]

Three Different Expulsion Edicts. The 'blood libel' charge was symptomatic of the Millenarian spirit, and the shifting focus of the Inquisition from conversos to the Jewish communities contributed to legislation governing the expulsion of Jews who declined conversion after the fall of Granada in early 1492. While the edicts contained the desired outcome to control the Jews, the first

---

of World Empires: Assessing the Global Reach of the Spanish and Portuguese Inquisitions." *History* (2015): 331.

31 Roth, "The Jews of Spain and the Expulsion," 21–23; Martínez, "*Genealogical Fictions*," 4–7.

32 Roth, "The Jews of Spain and the Expulsion," 24–26; Joseph Pérez, *History of a Tragedy: The Expulsion of the Jews from Spain*. Translated by Lysa Hochroth. (Urbana and Chicago, IL: University of Illinois Press, 2007), 83.

33 Pérez, *History of a Tragedy*." 83–84; Roth, "The Jews of Spain and the Expulsion," 26–27.

version was composed by the Inquisitor general, Torquemada, and revealed how deeply involved the Inquisition was in the process. The second text was generated in Aragon, but it watered down the Torquemada doctrine by declaring the Jews "are ours," which meant the monarchy assumed jurisdiction over the decision. The third edict, from Castile, was the most austere when compared to the harsher subtext of the Argonese document. In general, the Castilian text advocated segregated living, then, sending in the Inquisition, followed by full expulsion from Andulasia. The final edict was (deliberately) delayed by a month, and essentially gave Jews three months notice to leave the country, but the delay left only two months to make arrangements and comply.[34]

Although stated enigmatically in the combined Edict of Expulsion (1492), the crown would "be content with the Jews leaving Andulasia." A precedent had been set previously when Fernando expelled all Jews from Zaragosa, but some evidently reappeared. While large numbers of Jews converted after the edict was released so they could remain, those facing the looming deadline could not always realize the sale of properties or attain their full value. Often, they were forced to sell for ridiculously low ball offers on account of the short notice. Norman Roth (1992) acknowledged that there is evidence to refute the belief the Jews were expelled penniless and without material possessions. In theory, the monarchy ensured that any debts owed by Christians would be repaid and vice versa, even if the payment came later to wherever the Jews moved.[35] Joseph Pérez (2007), however, indicated that theory did not always meet reality, and claimed that collecting debts from Christians was not so simple, and many lawsuits remained unresolved or settled in a way that disadvantaged absentee Jews.[36] Another detail was how Jewish owned community property was viewed and handled during the expulsion process. Roth believed all synagogues and cemetery lands were confiscated, whereas Pérez

partially agrees, adding that any sales that did occur were far below actual value. Nonetheless, the departure of the Jews did not bankrupt Spain, despite the premises of some myths', but it did symbolize the official end of *convivencia*.

Where Did the Jews Go? If conversion was not considered, all Jews had to go, so many from Castile chose the nearest country, Portugal, which charged entry fees, although some officials accepted bribes. The move was short-lived, however, and the option dried up in a matter of years after Portugal also adopted a policy of expulsion. For others, North Africa was the best option because so many ancient Jewish communities thrived in the Mediterranean areas. They used family connections to get reestablished, or took a leap of faith into the unknown if no such opportunities existed. Some moved to England or Flanders in Northern Europe, and some went to cities with Jewish populations in France or Italy. Interestingly, Turkey, then part of the Ottoman Empire, welcomed Jews. Their inevitable reluctance to return to dhimmi status may have been overridden by the knowledge that practicing their faith was not restricted, aside from the taxes. To the present day, the descendants of the Sephardic Jews in Turkey speak a form of Spanish more akin to the medieval lingua than the modern Castilian form.[37]

The long-term implications of the Jewish expulsion can be viewed in terms of ethnic cleansing, which began as early as 1480 in Toledo when Jews and Muslims were relocated into segregated areas. Similarly, by the sixteenth century, the moriscos also faced the Inquisition and were expelled, thereby establishing the modern identity of Spain as a Christian country. Significantly, however, when Christopher Columbus brought back news and samples as evidence that a New World existed, some believed, well into the times of Thomas Jefferson, that the Lost Tribes could be found there. This belief completed a trilogy of fortuitous Millenarian-premised events: First, there

---

34 Quote from Pérez, *"History of a Tragedy."* 83–86; Roth, "The Jews of Spain and the Expulsion," 27–35.
35 Roth, "The Jews of Spain and the Expulsion," 27–30.
36 Pérez, *"History of a Tragedy."* 87–88.

37 Martin Gilbert, *The Routledge Atlas of Jewish History, Eighth Edition*, (New York, NY: Routledge, 2010), 46–47; Pérez, *"History of a Tragedy."* 87–90; Roth, "The Jews of Spain and the Expulsion," 30.

was the successful conclusion of the Reconquista, second was the expulsion of the unconverted Jews, and finally, a New World. Another consideration regarding the New World was preparing for the Second Coming by converting the heathens (Indios) in the Americas. Twelve Franciscan missionaries were dispatched to ensure this would occur. Following the example of St. Paul, spreading the Gospel worldwide and converting Gentiles was the modus operandi of Spanish and Portuguese colonies, theoretically.[38]

Race in the Americas. On the heels of the Spanish conquest of the Americas came both the Spanish and Portuguese Inquisitions to police the colonies for heresy, and ensure that only peninsular-born Old Christians obtained the most important administration positions. Limpieza de sangre took on a new meaning with the creation of the sistema de castas in New Spain (Mexico) between the sixteenth and eighteenth centuries. To see how these events and concepts moved away from Iberia into the Caribbean (Indies) and New Spain, comparative reading with the de Las Casas and Martínez selections in this book are suggested. These readings can enhance understanding of how human behavior led to privileging those identified as white, (Old) Christian, and literate. By creating the complex and inconsistent typological system based on purity of blood and degrees of whiteness, the racialization of the Americas began shortly after 1492 when miscegenation and the introduction of African slaves by the early 1500s created new 'races' or castas. For example, by the late sixteenth century, a certain Fray Prudencio de Sandoval held a negative view of Jewish antecedents in the blood of *conversos*, and held similar views about the Africans (*negros*) in New Spain. He questioned whether "in the descendants of Jews remains and lasts the bad inclination of their ancient ingratitude and failed beliefs, like in blacks the inseparable accident of their negritude? For if one thousand times they are with white women their children are born with the dark skin of their parents." Equating

these groups essentially painted the story of race relations in the Americas because he construed Jewish and black ancestries as ineffaceable strains that threatened Old Christian lineages (*lineaje*). Moreover, Sandoval revealed the anxiety of sexual honor codes and negative views of black men and white women having sexual relations.[39]

Ultimately, the Atlantic slave trade accelerated from 1504–1888, which connects other topics in this book regarding race and IQ, notions of criminality being associated with race, biological determinism, discussed in Chapter One, and social factors in Latin America regarding ethnicity and identity. Each of these topics are directly associated with the attitudes on the Iberian Peninsula that transferred socially and politically during the Spanish Conquest.[40] Another important consideration is how and why these attitudes perpetuated, and where the intersection of modern notions of beauty collides with deeply rooted manifestations of white supremacy and colorism. Finally, was New Orleans the birthplace of colorism in the United States after the Spanish introduced the sistema de castas between 1763–1803?[41]

---

38 Popkin, "Jewish Christians and Christian Jews," 249–250.

39 Quotation by Fray Prudencio de Sandoval from Martínez, "*Genealogical Fictions*," 158.

40 Carter G. Woodson, "Attitudes of the Iberian Peninsula," *The Journal of Negro History* 20:2 (1935): 196–198; Matthew Restall, *Seven Myths of the Spanish Conquest*, (New York, NY: Oxford University Press, 2003), 51.

41 Andrew N. Wegman, "The Vitriolic Blood of a Negro: The Development of Racial Identity and Creole Elitism in New Spain and Spanish Louisiana, 1763–1803." *Journal of Transatlantic Studies* 13:2 (2015): 204–208.

Medieval Traditions and Hegemonic Conflicts in Modernity

By D. Paul Sweeney

● ●

Explaining Santiago Matamoros Today: Islamophobia and the 'War on Terror'. After over five hundred years of representing the Reconquista and divine sanction, the government announced in 2006 they were removing the statue of *Santiago Matamoros* from the cathedral in Santiago de Campostela, leading to a public outcry regarding Spain's cultural identity. The postmodern discussion regarding the dominant hegemonic iconography of Spain's medieval period finds many who identify with and believe in the images, despite the narratives being constructed to fit a particular perspective, and those who view the relics as harmful to policies of inclusion. Further, many feared more terror attacks, especially after the incident in Madrid on March 11, 2004 (referred to as 11/4). Historical memory and continuity, however, are powerful forces, which leads to the following question: Is Santiago Matamoros a symbol of hate or a mythologized 'fact' of history with significant cultural identity associations?[1]

Moreover, Islamophobia has been at the forefront of the Western imagination ever since the September 11, 2001 (referred to simply as 9/11) attacks on the World Trade Center, the Pentagon, and other targets. Additionally, since 2015, many more attacks have occurred in France, the United States, and Belgium with association to radicalized Islam, particularly the Islamic State (IS, ISIL, ISIS, or *daesh*) currently under siege in Iraq and Syria. It was 9/11, however, that shaped the current conception of a "war on terror," a trope that on one hand, states that terror comes from Islamist extremists, but on the other, tries to assure Muslim nations it is not really a war on Islam. One problem, besides interpretation, is wading between truth and fiction. In the case of Spain, the struggle is how to rectify a modern identity shaped by violent medieval imagery and historic representation privileging Christianity, and the historical symbols are not limited to Santiago Matamoros. The other side of the coin is that history must also reflect social change because this is a key to human development. On March 11, 2004, a terror attack by *al-Qaida* killed 191 people in Madrid's central train station, and this provoked

---

1 Javier Domínguez García, "St. James the Moor-Slayer, A New Challenge to Spanish National Discourse in the Twenty-First Century," *International Journal of Iberian Studies* 22, no. 1 (2009): 69–70.

fear and anger that Islam threatened Spain's identity. One of the immediate responses, however, was for officials to cover the base of the statue with a white cloth. Why? Earlier in the chapter it was explained that the base of this, and many statues like it, always depict the decapitated heads of Muslims that emphasize the retribution-oriented nature of Santiago Matamoros. Covering up the base was the first step by officials who hoped the effort would stave off more terror attacks, but when the discussion shifted to removing the statue altogether, it sparked an intense backlash.[2]

The Debate. The Church in Campostela notified the media that the decision to remove the statue was important because they did not want to upset the 'sensitivities of other ethnic groups'. They denied that the timing had any correlation to the recent 11/4 attack or threats made against the Danish newspaper in early 2006 for publishing a cartoon depicting Muhammad, but this was met with a derisive response. The hegemonic discourse views assimilation as an act by a newly arrived minority to fit into the dominant society, but critics and Euroskeptics questioned whether the Church and government were themselves assimilating in reverse. Suddenly, Santiago Matamoros was central to a national discussion of cultural meanings, especially the symbols of Christianity and an ideology where values are never neutral (e.g., the Moors' violent deaths are celebrated). Additionally, symbolic meanings are privileges that become manifest in a given culture, and the statue was useful to the political right's nationalistic identity. Conversely, centrists and left-leaning political parties viewed the statue as a dated relic of the past and harmful to politics of inclusion. Immigration is central to the current debate, as it is in much of Europe and the United States, especially if it is from nations associated with Islam.[3] Ultimately, public pressure prevailed and officials rescinded the decision to remove the

statue, but a compromise was reached: Today the base is covered in flowers.

The Romanticization of History

Zacatecas, Mexico's 'Morismas de Bracho'. Mexico's rich cultural history stems from its diverse indigenous traditions that were never entirely extinguished or altered significantly by the Spanish Conquest. Cultural appropriation was a two-way street, and while the dominant Spanish society imposed its will, religion, and values for hundreds of years, today the blend of traditions can be witnessed in many events throughout Mexico. In particular, the annual *Morismas de Bracho* festival celebrates St. John the Baptist, the patron saint of Zacatecas, with a backdrop of elaborately staged mock battles pitting ornately costumed actors representing Christians against actors representing Moors. The final victory often features the simulated beheading of a Moorish king. While it commemorates 1492 it also reflects the original intent by Spanish officials in the sixteenth or seventeenth century to impose hegemonic symbolism. Today the occasion combines multiple events, including Charlemagne's (770 C.E.) defeat of the Islamic invasion in France, and the Christian victory over the Ottomans in the naval battle of Lepanto in 1571.[4]

The original purpose of the festival was to project Christianity's superiority to Islam and the 'paganism' in indigenous religions. To reinforce notions of white superiority, the original 'actors' representing the Moors were battalions of local natives and African slaves. Not limited to annual celebrations, in 1526 a mock battle was staged to honor Cortéz's return to Mexico City from business abroad.[5] If such traditions can be marked in the twenty-first century, when did they begin?

2 Domínguez García, "St. James the Moor-Slayer," 70–71; Chris Lowney, *A Vanished World: Muslims, Christians, and Jews in Medieval Spain*, (2005. Reprint, New York, NY: Oxford University Press, 2006), 108–112.

3 Domínguez García, "St. James the Moor-Slayer," 71–75; Lowney, *"A Vanished World,"* 108–112.

4 Max Harris, *Arabs, Moors, and Christians: Festivals of Reconquest in Mexico and Spain*, (Austin, TX: University of Texas Press, 2000), 57; Matthew Restall, *Seven Myths of the Spanish Conquest*, (New York, NY: Oxford University Press, 2003), 67–71.

5 Max Harris, *"Arabs, Moors, and Christians,"* 1–3; Restall, *"Seven Myths of the Spanish Conquest,"* 51, 75–76, 104–105.

Origins of the Mock Battles in Spain. Digging deep enough into the origins of the *moros y cristianos* traditions in Spain reveals that their battles signify more than yearly reminders of history. Until the mid-fifteenth century the mock battles were exclusive to territories held by Aragon-Catalonia. Around 1462, close to the period of unification, the traditions were introduced to Castile-León. Known as the *juego de cañas* (Game of Canes), they featured Christian knights against the Moors in an "equestrian exercise." In actuality the prosecution of the mock battle resembles a joust, with all its inherent dangers, but the 'horses' are really elaborate hobbyhorses, and this tradition continues to the present. In Barcelona the ceremonies merged at some point when celebrating the city's patron, St. Sebastian. In their retelling, it is the 'Turks' who caused his martyrdom, although in reality, the Romans killed Sebastian. Regardless, hegemonic narratives were affected by key events, such as the catastrophic fall of Constantinople (1453) to the Turks, and the reconquest.[6] Ultimately, the moros y cristianos tradition is being reevaluated, but the meaning of al-Andalus becoming Andalusia will be discussed in the context of Islamophobia and its cultural expressions.

The Festival of the Moors and the Christians

Commemorating 1492. As noted, throughout Spain annual festivals commemorate a combination of cultural, religious, and historic events. While different types of mock battles have been discussed already, there is a decidedly anti-Muslim expression in many of the cultural affairs, and this, like the Confederate flag and the removal of statues of Confederate generals debate in the United States, have experienced significant push-backs recently. Because Spain promoted Islamophobia and because of the symptomatic anti-Semitism throughout the Reconquista, there

is a conflict with Spain's Christian identity and a growing population of African and Muslim immigrants. One of the flashpoints is the "Festival of the Moors and the Christians" that draws tourists to many southern Spanish cities to commemorate the final victory at Granada.[7]

The grand spectacle of brightly colored costumes features two large armies confronting one another in and around the towns where they take place. Prior to 2006 these festivals typically concluded with the burning of both Muslim and Jewish effigies. Additionally, a large turban-clad puppet, *Mahoma* (Muhammad), had its head filled with gunpowder and was detonated by a lit cigar to signify the close of the festivities. The finales in such events also featured simulations of converting Moorish leaders to Christianity and publicly baptizing them immediately thereafter. The traditions described have been continuous since the early sixteenth century, but in 2006 a significant change took place. Already mentioned was the Danish newspaper threatened for depicting the prophet in an unflattering light. In the aftermath came mass protests for and against Islamophobic imagery. Further, bomb threats, and mob violence spread throughout Europe. It prompted a public apology from the newspaper, and ever since then an unofficial ban exists by all media from using any illustrations of Muhammad. The most recent provocation came in early January 2015 when the French satire magazine Charlie Hebdo pushed the envelope and Muslim extremists launched a deadly attack on their Paris office. The response in 2006 was to prevent exactly what happened in France. As a precaution, festival organizers in Valencia decided it was prudent to tone down the event. In another location the organizers chose to drag *Mahoma* through the streets instead of the customary explosion and effigy burning. However, further controversy arose because in almost all cases, the reenactment of Moorish conversion remained in the program.[8]

6 Max Harris, *"Arabs, Moors, and Christians,"* 54–63; Roger Crowley, *1453: The Holy War for Constantinople and the Clash of Islam and the West*, (New York, NY: Hyperion, 2005), 1-7.

7 Mikaela Rogozen-Soltar, "Al-Andalus in Andalusia: Negotiating Moorish History and Regional Identity in Southern Spain," *Anthropological Quarterly* 80, no. 3 (2007): 863.

8 Rogozen-Soltar, "Al-Andalus in Andalusia," 863–864.

A Multicultural Conflict. Understandably, most criticism of the "Festival of the Moors and the Christians" came from Spain's Muslim immigrant population. In a juxtaposition between the past and current trends of Islamophobia after the 11/4 Madrid bombing, growing national concern centered on how Muslim immigrants would fit in a country that identified as Christian. Many defended the content of the festivals as both accurate and significant to cultural history, whereas Andalusia struggles to portray itself as secular, Western and modern. The dilemma stems from the threat of Islamic extremists violently retaliating for the disrespectful use of the prophet's image, but it also ignores or else does not acknowledge, that the local Muslim population is offended by such displays.[9]

The situation described here highlights popular notions in Spain that imagine Muslims as extremists first, not fellow citizens, and this effectively casts them as the "other" and a potential enemy within. Historic events still shape modern laws in Córdoba. For example, Muslims are forbidden from praying at the former grand mosque, long since converted into a cathedral (the bells were returned to Santiago de Campostela on the backs of Muslim slaves after the city was retaken), but there is a movement to overturn these discriminatory laws. Similarly, on June 22, 2015, a small Spanish village in the province of Burgos, located in the former kingdom of Castile-León, dropped its historic name, Castrillo Mata de Judíos (Camp kill the Jews, or Fort kill Jews). Although the population only numbered 71 inhabitants, a referendum approved by the regional government sanctioned the name change to something less offensive. The next morning anti-Semitic graffiti appeared around town in protest.[10] While such conflicts with history seem grounded in religious differences on the surface, cultural intimacy enters the imagery and traditions of southern Spain. Ultimately, it took Arab and Muslim history and influences to create al-Andalus, however, an open question remains: What role does cultural ambivalence play in accepting change?

Literary Origins of the al-Andalus Myth Debate

In addition to local initiatives and tourism concerns, the revival of the myth of al-Andalus poses an interesting twist because the myth's origins are from Arabic literature. The most cited work came from al-Maqqari of Tlencen (1577–1632) who descended from Muslims in Granada. Originally, it was European Orientalists who locked onto this "forgotten" history, which sparked renewed interest in tracking down more Arabic sources. The problem stemmed from the Spanish Arabists being heavily influenced by Orientalism's concerns, and perspectives of Islam and the Orient being backwards yet exotic, and so on. Therefore, some feel that the presumptions of Orientalists were an attempt to rebuild the history of al-Andalus, however clumsily. By 1992, the 500th anniversary of the fall of Granada symbolized what most Spanish accepted as truth, and from this emanated renewed interest in architecture, and most relevant to this discussion, the notion of convivencia, the symbol of tolerance. As the prior examples show, while idealizing the past, Spain is simultaneously conflicted by their religious identity and cultural tolerance for the "other" again in their midst.[11]

---

9 Ibid.

10 http://www.atlasobscura.com/places/castrillo-matajudios

---

11 Maria Jesús Rubiera Mata and Mikel de Epalza, "Al-Andalus: Between Myth and History," *History and Anthropology* 18, no. 3 (2007): 269–270; Edward Said, *Orientalism*, (1978. Reprint, New York, NY: Vintage, 1994), 43–44, 57.

The Spanish Conquest and Race Relations

The Devastation of the Indies

A Brief Account

By Bartolomé de Las Casas

• •

Editor's Introduction

Like Christopher Columbus, whose writings he edited, few figures in the early history of the Spanish Conquest have inspired as much praise or fallen into as much disrepute. Bartolomé de Las Casas, the polemic figure blamed by Spain for almost single-handedly creating the Black Legend of Spanish cruelty, was published widely and translated into many languages. This latter aspect provided the English with the rationale and justification to invade Spanish territories in the Caribbean. Falling into obscurity after this publication, Las Casas was resurrected in the middle nineteenth century in a favorable light as part of the White Legend created by revisionist historians in Spain and her remaining colonies: Cuba, Puerto Rico, and the Philippines.

The White Legend reinstated both Las Casas and Columbus as proof of Spain's humanity and bridged the gap between Old and New Worlds. After all, Las Casas, while bishop of Chiapas, was bestowed the title "Protector of the Indians" by the Crown. His legacy, however, does not always include his early advocacy of escalating African slavery to replace the exploited indigenous labor on Spanish encomiendas (land grants with obligatory labor laws). His role in the slave trade was recanted on his deathbed.

Throughout this excerpt, Las Casas's views of the native peoples, although sympathetic and passionate, cannot refrain from Eurocentric interpretations and exudes paternalism. Las Casas, like many during this time and after, felt that Indians were like children and inferior, but if they accepted the white man's religion, they could enjoy reasonable amounts of help and protection.

References

Las Casas, Bartolomé. *A Short Account of the Destruction of the Indies*. Translated by Nigel Griffin. New York: Penguin, 1999.

Restall, Matthew. *Seven Myths of the Spanish Conquest*. New York: Oxford, 2003.

Schmidt-Nowara, Christopher. *The Conquest of History: Spanish Colonialism and the National Histories in the Nineteenth Century*. Pittsburgh: University of Pittsburgh Press, 2006.

The Indies[1] were discovered in the year one thousand four hundred and ninety-two. In the following year a great many Spaniards went there with the intention of settling the land. Thus, forty-nine years have passed since the first settlers penetrated the land, the first so-claimed being the large and most happy isle called Hispaniola,[2] which is six hundred leagues in circumference. Around it in all directions are many other islands, some very big, others very small, and all of them were, as we saw with our own eyes, densely populated with native peoples called Indians. This large island was perhaps the most densely populated place in the world. There must be close to two hundred leagues of land on this island, and the seacoast has been explored for more than ten thousand leagues, and each day more of it is being explored. And all the land so far discovered is a beehive of people; it is as though God had crowded into these lands the great majority of mankind.

And of all the infinite universe of humanity, these people are the most guileless, the most devoid of wickedness and duplicity, the most obedient and faithful to their native masters and to the Spanish Christians whom they serve. They are by nature the most humble, patient, and peaceable, holding no grudges, free from embroilments, neither excitable nor quarrelsome. These people are the most devoid of rancors, hatreds, or desire for vengeance of any people in the world. And because they are so weak and complaisant, they are less able to endure heavy labor and soon die of no matter what malady. The sons of nobles among us, brought up in the enjoyments of life's refinements, are no more delicate than are these Indians, even those among them who are of the lowest rank of laborers. They are also poor people, for they not only possess little but have no desire to possess worldly goods. For this reason they are not arrogant, embittered, or greedy. Their repasts are such that the food of the holy fathers in the desert can scarcely be more parsimonious, scanty, and poor. As to their dress, they are generally naked,

with only their pudenda covered somewhat. And when they cover their shoulders it is with a square cloth no more than two varas in size.[3] They have no beds, but sleep on a kind of matting or else in a kind of suspended net called *hamacas*. They are very clean in their persons, with alert, intelligent minds, docile and open to doctrine, very apt to receive our holy Catholic faith, to be endowed with virtuous customs, and to behave in a godly fashion. And once they begin to hear the tidings of the Faith, they are so insistent on knowing more and on taking the sacraments of the Church and on observing the divine cult that, truly, the missionaries who are here need to be endowed by God with great patience in order to cope with such eagerness. Some of the secular Spaniards who have been here for many years say that the goodness of the Indians is undeniable and that if this gifted people could be brought to know the one true God they would be the most fortunate people in the world.

Yet into this sheepfold, into this land of meek outcasts there came some Spaniards who immediately behaved like ravening wild beasts, wolves, tigers, or lions that had been starved for many days. And Spaniards have behaved in no other way during the past forty years, down to the present time, for they are still acting like ravening beasts, killing, terrorizing, afflicting, torturing, and destroying the native peoples, doing all this with the strangest and most varied new methods of cruelty, never seen or heard of before, and to such a degree that this Island of Hispaniola, once so populous (having a population that I estimated to be more than three millions), has now a population of barely two hundred persons.

The island of Cuba is nearly as long as the distance between Valladolid and Rome; it is now almost completely depopulated. San Juan[4] and Jamaica are two of the largest, most productive and attractive islands; both are now deserted and devastated. On the northern side of Cuba and Hispaniola lie the neighboring Lucayos[5] comprising more than sixty islands including those called

---

1   Caribbean Islands.
2   Present-day Dominican Republic and Haiti.

3   A *vara* is an old Spanish unit of length.
4   Puerto Rico.
5   Bahamas.

Gigantes, beside numerous other islands, some small some large. The least felicitous of them were more fertile and beautiful than the gardens of the King of Seville. They have the healthiest lands in the world, where lived more than five hundred thousand souls; they are now deserted, inhabited by not a single living creature. All the people were slain or died after being taken into captivity and brought to the Island of Hispaniola to be sold as slaves. When the Spaniards saw that some of these had escaped, they sent a ship to find them, and it voyaged for three years among the islands searching for those who had escaped being slaughtered, for a good Christian had helped them escape, taking pity on them and had won them over to Christ,[6] of these there were eleven persons and these I saw.

More than thirty other islands in the vicinity of San Juan are for the most part and for the same reason depopulated, and the land laid waste. On these islands I estimate there are 2,100 leagues of land that have been ruined and depopulated, empty of peopled.[7]

As for the vast mainland, which is ten times larger than all Spain, even including Aragon and Portugal, containing more land than the distance between Seville and Jerusalem, or more than two thousand leagues, we are sure that our Spaniards, with their cruel and abominable acts, have devastated the land and exterminated the rational people who fully inhabited it. We can estimate very surely and truthfully that in the forty years that have passed, with the infernal actions of the Christians, there have been unjustly slain more than twelve million men, women, and children. In truth, I believe without trying to deceive myself that the number of the slain is more like fifteen million.

The common ways mainly employed by the Spaniards who call themselves Christian and who have gone there to extirpate those pitiful nations and wipe them off the earth is by unjustly waging cruel and bloody wars. Then, when they have slain all those who fought for their lives or to escape the tortures they would have to endure, that is to say, when they have slain all the native rulers and young men (since the Spaniards usually spare only the women and children, who are subjected to the hardest and bitterest servitude ever suffered by man or beast), they enslave any survivors. With these infernal methods of tyranny they debase and weaken countless numbers of those pitiful Indian nations.

Their reason for killing and destroying such an infinite number of souls is that the Christians have an ultimate aim, which is to acquire gold, and to swell themselves with riches in a very brief time and thus rise to a high estate disproportionate to their merits. It should be kept in mind that their insatiable greed and ambition, the greatest ever seen in the world, is the cause of their villainies. And also, those lands are so rich and felicitous, the native peoples so meek and patient, so easy to subject, that our Spaniards have no more consideration for them than beasts. And I say this from my own knowledge of the acts I witnessed. But I should not say "than beasts" for, thanks be to God, they have treated beasts with some respect; I should say instead like excrement on the public squares. And thus they have deprived the Indians of their lives and souls, for the millions I mentioned have died without the Faith and without the benefit of the sacraments. This is a well-known and proven fact which even the tyrant Governors, themselves killers, know and admit. And never have the Indians in all the Indies committed any act against the Spanish Christians, until those Christians have first and many times committed countless cruel aggressions against them or against neighboring nations. For in the beginning the Indians regarded the Spaniards as angels from Heaven.[8] Only after the Spaniards had used violence against them, killing, robbing, torturing, did the Indians ever rise up against them.

---

6   blank [*sic*].

7   His numbers are spurious, but depopulation was rampant.

8   Part of a cultural myth begun by Columbus in his writings.

Hispaniola

On the Island Hispaniola was where the Spaniards first landed, as I have said. Here those Christians perpetrated their first ravages and oppressions against the native peoples. This was the first land in the New World to be destroyed and depopulated by the Christians, and here they began their subjection of the women and children, taking them away from the Indians to use them and ill use them, eating the food they provided with their sweat and toil. The Spaniards did not content themselves with what the Indians gave them of their own free will, according to their ability, which was always too little to satisfy enormous appetites, for a Christian eats and consumes in one day an amount of food that would suffice to feed three houses inhabited by ten Indians for one month. And they committed other acts of force and violence and oppression which made the Indians realize that these men had not come from Heaven. And some of the Indians concealed their foods while others concealed their wives and children and still others fled to the mountains to avoid the terrible transactions of the Christians.

And the Christians attacked them with buffets and beatings, until finally they laid hands on the nobles of the villages. Then they behaved with such temerity and shamelessness that the most powerful ruler of the islands had to see his own wife raped by a Christian officer.

From that time onward the Indians began to seek ways to throw the Christians out of their lands. They took up arms, but their weapons were very weak and of little service in offense and still less in defense. (Because of this, the wars of the Indians against each other are little more than games played by children.) And the Christians, with their horses and swords and pikes began to carry out massacres and strange cruelties against them. They attacked the towns and spared neither the children nor the aged nor pregnant women nor women in childbed, not only stabbing them and dismembering them but cutting them to pieces as if dealing with sheep in the slaughter house. They laid bets as to who, with one stroke of the sword, could split a man in two or could cut off his head or spill out his entrails with a single stroke of the pike. They took infants from their mothers' breasts, snatching them by the legs and pitching them headfirst against the crags or snatched them by the arms and threw them into the rivers, roaring with laughter and saying as the babies fell into the water, "Boil there, you offspring of the devil!" Other infants they put to the sword along with their mothers and anyone else who happened to be nearby. They made some low wide gallows on which the hanged victim's feet almost touched the ground, stringing up their victims in lots of thirteen, in memory of Our Redeemer and His twelve Apostles, then set burning wood at their feet and thus burned them alive. To others they attached straw or wrapped their whole bodies in straw and set them afire. With still others, all those they wanted to capture alive, they cut off their hands and hung them round the victim's neck, saying, "Go now, carry the message," meaning, Take the news to the Indians who have fled to the mountains. They usually dealt with the chieftains and nobles in the following way: they made a grid of rods which they placed on forked sticks, then lashed the victims to the grid and lighted a smoldering fire underneath, so that little by little, as those captives screamed in despair and torment, their souls would leave them.

I once saw this, when there were four or five nobles lashed on grids and burning; I seem even to recall that there were two or three pairs of grids where others were burning, and because they uttered such loud screams that they disturbed the captain's sleep, he ordered them to be strangled. And the constable, who was worse than an executioner, did not want to obey that order (and I know the name of that constable and know his relatives in Seville), but instead put a stick over the victims' tongues, so they could not make a sound, and he stirred up the fire, but not too much, so that they roasted slowly, as he liked. I saw all these things I have described, and countless others.

And because all the people who could do so fled to the mountains to escape these inhuman, ruthless, and ferocious acts, the Spanish captains, enemies of the human race, pursued them with the fierce dogs[9] they kept which attacked the Indians, tearing them to pieces and devouring them. And because on few and far between occasions, the Indians justifiably killed some Christians, the Spaniards made a rule among themselves that for every Christian slain by the Indians, they would slay a hundred Indians.

The Kingdoms That Once Existed on the Island Hispaniola

On the island Hispaniola there were five very large principalities ruled by five very powerful Kings to whom almost all the other rulers paid tribute, since there were other princes in distant provinces who recognized no one as their superior. There was a kingdom called Magua, the last syllable accented, which name means "The Realm of the Fertile Lowlands." This land is among the most notable and admirable places in the world, for it stretches across the island from the southern sea to the northern sea, a distance of eighty leagues. It averages five leagues in width but at times is eight to ten and is of very high altitude from one part to another and is drained by more than thirty thousand rivers and creeks, twelve of the rivers being as large as the Ebro and Duero and Guadalquivir combined. All the rivers flow from the western highland, which means that twenty or twenty-five thousand of them are rich in gold. For in those highlands lies the province of Cibao, where are the famous Cibao mines harboring a fine and remarkable pure gold.

The King who ruled this realm was called Guarionex. Great lords were his vassals, one of them having assembled an army of sixteen thousand men to serve Guarionex, and I know or knew some of them. That virtuous King Guarionex was by nature very pacific and was devotedly obedient to the Kings of Castile and in certain years gave them, through the nobles under his command, a generous amount of gold dust. Each man who had a house was given for this purpose a spherical bell, or rather, a spherical grain measure resembling a bell. This was stuffed full with gold dust (brought down by the rivers) for the people of this realm did not have the skill to work the mines. When there was not enough, some years, to fill the measure, then it was cut in half and one half was filled. This King Guarionex proclaimed himself ready to serve the King of Castile with a labor force that would be brought to Santo Domingo from the city of Isabella, the first Christian settlement, fifty leagues distant, and said, with reason, that they should not have to pay in gold because his vassals did not know how to procure it. That labor force, he said, would work the mines with great heartiness and their labor would be worth to the King of Spain, each year, more than three million castellanos.[10] And had that labor force been so employed, there would be, today, more than fifty cities the size of Seville, on this island.

The recompense they gave this great and good Indian ruler was to dishonor him through his wife, who was raped by a Christian officer. And King Guarionex, who, in time, could have assembled his people to avenge him, chose instead to go alone into hiding and die exiled from his kingdom, deprived of his rank and possessions, placing himself under the protection of the chieftain of the province called Ciguayos, one of his vassals.

When his hiding place was discovered, the Christians waged war on Ciguayos, massacring a great number of people until they finally took the exiled King and, in chains, put him on a vessel that was to take him to Castile. But the vessel was lost at sea and with it were drowned many Christians along with the captive King, and in this shipwreck was lost a quantity of gold dust and gold nuggets weighing the equivalent of 3,600 castellanos. Such was God's vengeance for so many terrible injustices.

Another kingdom on the island was called Marien and is now called Puerto Real. It is situated at the end of the fertile lowlands toward the north and is larger than Portugal, although much more suitable for development and settlement.

---

9   Bull Mastifs were commonly employed in this capacity.

10   A unit of measure based on refined ore (gold).

Many mountain chains exist here, which are rich in copper and gold. The King of this province was called Guacanagari, many of whose vassals were known to me. It was this King who welcomed the Admiral[11] when he first landed in the New World and set foot on the island of Hispaniola.

The welcome extended by this King to the Admiral and all those accompanying him could not have been more cordial and generous, even had it been the voyagers' native land and their own King greeting them with food and provisions of every kind, everything that was needed, which was a great deal, for the vessel on which Columbus had voyaged was lost here.

I know all this from conversations with the Admiral.

Well, that same King, while fleeing to the mountains to escape the cruel persecutions meted out to him and his people by the Christians, died, having been stripped of his rank and possessions by those same Christians, and all his vassals perished in the tyrannical persecutions and enslavements which I shall later on describe.

The third kingdom on the island of Hispaniola was Maguana, where the best sugar in that island is now made. The King of that realm was called Caonabo and in condition and importance he surpassed all the others. The Spaniards captured this unhappy King by using great and wicked subtlety, laying hands on him while he was in his house. Afterward, they put him on a ship outward bound for Castile. But while still in port with six other outward-bound vessels, God desired to manifest Himself against this great iniquity and sent a violent storm that sank all the vessels and drowned all the Christians on board, along with the shackled King of Maguana.

This native ruler had three or four brothers, who, like him, were strong and fearless. When their brother and lord was taken captive and his subjects killed or enslaved, these brothers, upon seeing the slaughter being carried out by the Christians, took up arms in revenge. The Christians met their attack with cavalry (horses being the most pernicious weapon against the Indians) and in the battles that followed half the land was laid waste and depopulated.

The fourth kingdom was that of Xaragua and it was like the marrow and medulla of the island, its sovereign court. Its King surpassed all the other princes in eloquence, refinement, and education and good breeding. Likewise, his government was the best ordered and the most circumspect. At his court there was a multitude of nobles whose beauty and elegance excelled all others.

Behechio, the King of Xaragua, had a sister, by name Anacaona. Together, the brother and sister rendered great services to the Kings of Castile and afforded great benefactions to the Christians, helping them to avoid countless mortal dangers. After the death of her brother the King, Anacaona continued to rule the land.

Then, one day the Christian Governor[12] of the island arrived with a cavalry force of sixty horses and three hundred foot soldiers. The cavalry alone could lay waste the land. Having been promised safe conduct there soon arrived three hundred Indian nobles. These, or most of them, were tricked into entering a very big Indian house of straw where they were shut in and burned alive when the house was set on fire. Those who did not perish in the conflagration were put to the sword or the pike, along with a countless number of the common people. As a special honor, the lady Anacaona was hanged.

And it happened that those Christians, either out of piety or cupidity, took some boys to shield them from the slaughter and placed them on the croup of their horses. But other Spaniards came up from behind and ran the boys through with their pikes. When the victims fell from the horses the Spaniards cut off their legs with a sword.

Some of the nobles who managed to flee from this inhuman cruelty took refuge on a small island nearby, about eight leagues out to sea. And the said Christian Governor condemned all those who had gone there to be sold as slaves because they had fled the butchery.

The fifth kingdom was called Higuey and its ruler was an aged queen who was called Higuanama. They hanged her. And there were

---

11   blank [*sic*].

12   blank [*sic*].

countless people that I saw burned alive or cut to pieces or tortured in many new ways of killing and inflicting pain. They also made slaves of many Indians.

Because the particulars that enter into these outrages are so numerous they could not be contained in the scope of much writing, for in truth I believe that in the great deal I have set down here I have not revealed the thousandth part of the sufferings endured by the Indians, I now want only to add that, in the matter of these unprovoked and destructive wars, and God is my witness, all these acts of wickedness I have described, as well as those I have omitted, were perpetrated against the Indians without cause, without any more cause than could give a community of good monks living together in a monastery. And still more strongly I affirm that until the multitude of people on this island of Hispaniola were killed and their lands devastated, they committed no sin against the Christians that would be punishable by man's laws, and as to those sins punishable by God's law, such as vengeful feelings against such powerful enemies as the Christians have been, those sins would be committed by the very few Indians who are hardhearted and impetuous. And I can say this from my great experience with them: their hardness and impetuosity would be that of children, of boys ten or twelve years old. I know by certain infallible signs that the wars waged by the Indians against the Christians have been justifiable wars and that all the wars waged by the Christians against the Indians have been unjust wars, more diabolical than any wars ever waged anywhere in the world. This I declare to be so of all the many wars they have waged against the peoples throughout the Indies.

After the wars and the killings had ended, when usually there survived only some boys, some women, and children, these survivors were distributed among the Christians to be slaves. The repartimiento or distribution was made according to the rank and importance of the Christian to whom the Indians were allocated, one of them being given thirty, another forty, still another, one or two hundred, and besides the rank of the Christian there was also to be considered in

what favor he stood with the tyrant they called Governor. The pretext was that these allocated Indians were to be instructed in the articles of the Christian Faith. As if those Christians who were as a rule foolish and cruel and greedy and vicious could be caretakers of souls! And the care they took was to send the men to the mines to dig for gold, which is intolerable labor, and to send the women into the fields of the big ranches to hoe and till the land, work suitable for strong men. Nor to either the men or the women did they give any food except herbs and legumes, things of little substance. The milk in the breasts of the women with infants dried up and thus in a short while the infants perished.

And since men and women were separated, there could be no marital relations. And the men died in the mines and the women died on the ranches from the same causes, exhaustion and hunger. And thus was depopulated that island which had been densely populated.

I will speak only briefly of the heavy loads the Indians were made to carry, loads weighing three to four arrobas,[13] Christian tyrants and captains had themselves carried in hammocks borne by two Indians. This shows that they treated the Indians as beasts of burden. But were I to describe all this and the buffetings and beatings and birchings endured by the Indians at their labors, no amount of time and paper could encompass this task.

And be it noted that the worst depredations on these islands in the New World began when tidings came of the death of Her most Serene Highness, Queen Isabel, which occurred in the year one thousand five hundred and four. Because, up to that time, only a few provinces on the island of Hispaniola had been destroyed in unjust wars, but not the entire island, since, for the most part, the island was under the royal protection of the Queen and she, may God rest her, took admirable and zealous care of these people, their salvation and prosperity, as we saw with our own eyes and touched with our hands.

---

13 A unit of measure, approximately 26 pounds.

Another rule should be noted: in all parts of the Indies, wherever they have landed or passed through, the Christians have always committed atrocities against the Indians, have perpetrated the slaughters and tyrannies and abominable oppressions against innocent people that we have described, and have added worse and more cruel acts, ever since God allowed them most suddenly to fall into dishonor and opprobrium. …

The Island of Cuba

In the year one thousand five hundred and eleven, the Spaniards passed over to the island of Cuba, which as I have said is at the same distance from Hispaniola as the distance between Valladolid and Rome, and which was a well-populated province. They began and ended in Cuba as they had done elsewhere, but with much greater acts of cruelty.

Among the noteworthy outrages they committed was the one they perpetrated against a cacique, a very important noble, by name Hatuey, who had come to Cuba from Hispaniola with many of his people, to flee the calamities and inhuman acts of the Christians. When he was told by certain Indians that the Christians were now coming to Cuba, he assembled as many of his followers as he could and said this to them: "Now you must know that they are saying the Christians are coming here, and you know by experience how they have put So and So and So and So, and other nobles to an end. And now they are coming from Haiti (which is Hispaniola) to do the same here. Do you know why they do this?" The Indians replied: "We do not know. But it may be that they are by nature wicked and cruel." And he told them: "No, they do not act only because of that, but because they have a God they greatly worship and they want us to worship that God, and that is why they struggle with us and subject us and kill us."

He had a basket full of gold and jewels and he said: "You see their God here, the God of the Christians. If you agree to it, let us dance for this God, who knows, it may please the God of the Christians and then they will do us no harm." And his followers said, all together, "Yes, that is good,

that is good!" And they danced round the basket of gold until they fell down exhausted. Then their chief, the cacique Hatuey, said to them: "See here, if we keep this basket of gold they will take it from us and will end up by killing us. So let us cast away the basket into the river." They all agreed to do this, and they flung the basket of gold into the river that was nearby.

This cacique, Hatuey, was constantly fleeing before the Christians from the time they arrived on the island of Cuba, since he knew them and of what they were capable. Now and then they encountered him and he defended himself, but they finally killed him. And they did this for the sole reason that he had fled from those cruel and wicked Christians and had defended himself against them. And when they had captured him and as many of his followers as they could, they burned them all at the stake.

When tied to the stake, the cacique Hatuey was told by a Franciscan friar who was present, an artless rascal, something about the God of the Christians and of the articles of the Faith. And he was told what he could do in the brief time that remained to him, in order to be saved and go to Heaven. The cacique, who had never heard any of this before, and was told he would go to Inferno where, if he did not adopt the Christian Faith, he would suffer eternal torment, asked the Franciscan friar if Christians all went to Heaven. When told that they did he said he would prefer to go to Hell. Such is the fame and honor that God and our Faith have earned through the Christians who have gone out to the Indies.

On one occasion when we went to claim ten leagues of a big settlement, along with food and maintenance, we were welcomed with a bounteous quantity of fish and bread and cooked victuals. The Indians generously gave us all they could. Then suddenly, without cause and without warning, and in my presence, the devil inhabited the Christians and spurred them to attack the Indians, men, women, and children, who were sitting there before us. In the massacre that followed, the Spaniards put to the sword more than three thousand souls. I saw such terrible cruelties done there as I had never seen before nor thought to see.

A few days later, knowing that news of this massacre had spread through the land, I sent messengers ahead to the chiefs of the province of Havana, knowing they had heard good things about me, telling them we were about to visit the town and telling them they should not hide but should come out to meet us, assuring them that no harm would be done to them. I did this with the full knowledge of the captain. And when we arrived in the province, there came out to welcome us twenty-one chiefs and caciques, and our captain, breaking his pledge to me and the pledge I had made to them, took all these chieftains captive, intending to burn them at the stake, telling me this would be a good thing because those chiefs had in the past done him some harm. I had great difficulty in saving those Indians from the fire, but finally succeeded.

Afterward, when all the Indians of this island were subjected to servitude and the same ruin had befallen there as on the island Hispaniola, the survivors began to flee to the mountains or in despair to hang themselves, and there were husbands and wives who hanged themselves together with their children, because the cruelties perpetrated by one very great Spaniard (whom I knew) were so horrifying. More than two hundred Indians hanged themselves.

And thus perished a countless number of people on the island of Cuba.

That tyrant Spaniard, representative of the King of Spain, demanded, in the *repartimiento*, that he be given three hundred Indians. At the end of three months all but thirty of them had died of the hard labor in the mines, which is to say only a tenth of them had survived. He demanded another allocation of Indians, and they also perished in the same way. He demanded still another large allocation, and those Indians also perished. Then he died, and the devil bore him away.

In three or four months, when I was there, more than seventy thousand children, whose fathers and mothers had been sent to the mines, died of hunger.

And I saw other frightful things. The Spaniards finally decided to track down the Indians who had taken refuge in the mountains. There they created amazing havoc and thus finished ravaging the island. Where had been a flourishing population, it is now a shame and pity to see the island laid waste and turned into a desert.

Study Terms

Black Legend
White Legend
Paternalism
Eurocentrism
Ethnocentrism
Repartimiento
Encomienda

Introduction

from *Genealogical Fictions: Limpieza de Sangre, Religion, and Gender in Colonial Mexico*

By María Elena Martínez

● ●

Editor's Introduction

In this selection by María Elena Martínez, the Spanish concept *limpieza de sangre* (purity of blood) is examined, and also how it evolved during the *Reconquista*, played a role in the Spanish Inquisition, and ultimately, continued in the Americas well into the eighteenth century. What is clear is that near-pathological obsession with purity of blood led to families keeping meticulous genealogical histories. What makes this more fascinating is that the practice was mandated "by the state, church, Inquisition, and other institutions in colonial Mexico ..."[1]

What can be learned here is how folk taxonomy [...] was instilled on a grand scale, and its legacy can still be traced today, even if the *sistema de castas* (system of caste) disappeared after Mexico's independence from Spain in the nineteenth-century.

Notes

María Elena Martínez. *Genealogical Fictions: Limpieza de Sangre, Religion, and Gender in Colonial Mexico*. Stanford: Stanford University Press, 2008, quoted from the back cover.

Problem and Objectives

This book charts the rise of categories of *limpieza de sangre* ("purity of blood") in Spain and their journey from the Iberian Peninsula to the Americas, where they eventually took on a life of their own. Having originated in late medieval Castile, the concept of purity of blood and its underlying assumptions about inheritable characteristics had by the late seventeenth century produced a hierarchical system of classification in Spanish America that was ostensibly based on proportions of Spanish, indigenous, and African ancestry, the *sistema de castas* or "race/caste system." This use of the concept would probably have surprised the Spaniards who first deployed it against Jewish converts to Christianity, the *conversos,* or "New Christians." They defined blood purity as the absence of Jewish and heretical antecedents and, as of the middle of the fifteenth century, they increasingly wielded the notion to deprive the conversos of access to certain institutions and public and ecclesiastical offices. The concept acquired greater force during the next one hundred years, as limpieza de sangre statutes—requirements of unsullied "Old Christian" ancestry—were adopted by numerous religious and secular establishments in Castile and Aragon, the Spanish Inquisition was founded to identify "secret Jews" and root out heresy, and the category of impurity was extended to the descendants of Muslims. By the middle of the sixteenth century, the ideology of purity of blood had produced a Spanish society obsessed with genealogy and in particular with the idea that having only Christian ancestors, and thus a "pure lineage," was the critical sign of a person's loyalty to the faith. Descent and religion—"blood" and faith—were the two foundations of that ideology, and the same would be true in Spanish America.

The transfer of the Castilian discourse of limpieza de sangre to Spanish America did not mean, however, that it remained the same in the new context. As much as Spaniards tried to recreate their society in "New Spain" (colonial Mexico), they had to face circumstances, peoples, and historical developments that inevitably altered their transplanted institutions, practices, and cultural-religious principles. The survival of native communities and part of the pre-Hispanic nobility, the importance of the conversion project to Spanish colonialism and to Castile's titles to the Americas, the introduction of significant numbers of African slaves into the region, the rapid rise of a population of mixed ancestry, the influx of poor Spaniards seeking to better their lot if not ennoble themselves, and the establishment of a transatlantic economy based largely on racialized labor forces—these and other factors ensured that the Iberian concept of limpieza de sangre would be reformulated and have different implications than in Spain. In Castile, for example, it did not produce an elaborate system of classification based on blood proportions as it did in the colonies, though signs that such categories might develop appeared in the sixteenth century, particularly in the Inquisition's

genealogical investigations. Furthermore, in Spanish America, the notion of purity gradually came to be equated with Spanish ancestry, with "Spanishness," an idea that had little significance in the metropolitan context. The language of blood and lineage also underwent modifications. Nonetheless, at the end of the colonial period, the concept of limpieza de sangre was still partly defined in religious terms. What were the implications of this religious dimension for colonial categories of identity, racial discourses, and communal ideologies? [...]

More to the point, the book seeks to expose the connection between the concept of limpieza de sangre and the sistema de castas. Although a number of scholars of colonial Mexico have referred to this connection, they have not fully explained it. They have not clarified how a concept that had strong religious connotations came to construct or promote classifications that presumably were based on modern notions of race. Exactly when, how, and why was the notion of purity of blood extended and adapted to the colonial context? This critical question has received little attention in the literature because, until recently, most historical studies of the sistema de castas have focused on the eighteenth century (when notions of race were starting to become secularized) and in particular on the problem of the saliency of "race" versus "class" as mercantile capitalism expanded. The privileging of the late colonial period in the historiography has meant that both the origins of the system and its relation to the concept of limpieza remain unclear. Works that do refer to the system in the early colonial period generally link the concept of purity of blood to race without elaborating on what exactly either of these terms meant at that time. Furthermore, they normally describe its rise as a function of the displacement of main peninsular status categories (noble, commoner, and slave) onto the three primary colonial groups (respectively, Spaniards, Indians, and blacks) and explain the disruption of this tripartite order by the growth of populations of mixed ancestry. This rendition of the emergence of the sistema de castas is seductive because of its simplicity; but it is also deceptive because it deprives the process of its contingency, does not explain why more than one category of mixture was created, and obscures the religious dimension of limpieza de sangre and therefore also its implications.

This [...] provides an analysis, first, of the linkages between the concept of limpieza de sangre and the sistema de castas with special consideration to the role of religion in the production of notions of purity and impurity, the historical specificity of Castilian categories such as *raza* (race) and *casta* (caste), the intertwined nature of peninsular and colonial discourses of purity, and the fluidity and ambiguities that characterized the system of classification throughout the colonial period. It is informed by critical race theory and in particular by scholarship that posits that race is not merely a consequence of material interests (an "effect" of class) but rather is linked in complex ways to economic, political, and ideological structures; social conditions; and systems of signification. Philosopher Cornel West has termed this approach "genealogical materialist." He has stressed the importance of investigating the origins and trajectory of racial ideas within specific cultural and historical traditions and their dynamic interaction with both micro- and macrolevel processes, including those related to political economy (local and global), the reproduction and disruption of power (say, through particular languages, idioms, or representations), and the construction of notions of self. West chose Nietzsche's concept of genealogy because he wanted to underscore the importance of undertaking deep and careful excavations of the meanings of race within the particular cultural-historical context in which it develops and of explaining its connections to different levels of existence.

In this study, the concept of genealogy is central both because it alludes to the process of historicizing race and because in the early modern Hispanic world it was ubiquitous and consequential, the foundation of a multitude of practices and identities that helped mold historical memory at both the individual and collective levels. It does not presuppose the automatic deployment of the concept of limpieza de sangre against colonial

populations and simple displacement of peninsular status categories onto them. Nor does it assume that the meanings of early modern notions of purity and race are self-evident, a mistake that can lead to the tautological argument that the system of classifying "blood mixture" arose because "race mixture" occurred, an argument that reproduces the idea of races as biological givens rather than challenging it by interrogating why categories arise, become reified, and get contested. Instead, this book prioritizes analyzing the discursive tradition that the concepts of limpieza and raza were part of and which, together with certain practices, those two notions helped to constitute. It begins by addressing the following questions. What exactly did the concepts of limpieza de sangre and raza mean in Spain, when and why did they first start to be deployed in Mexico, and how were they adapted to the colonial context? Was their growing usage related to events in the metropole, Spanish America, or both? Which institutions adopted purity-of-blood requirements and when did they begin to target people of mixed ancestry? Did definitions of limpieza de sangre change over time, and if so, how? And what practices and identities did the ideology of purity of blood promote? These are the questions that constitute the first of three main lines of inquiry in the book.

A second line of investigation pertains to the connections of the concept of limpieza de sangre to gender and sexuality. The book argues that these connections were strong not just because of the centrality of biological reproduction (and by extension, female sexuality) to the perpetuation of community boundaries and the hierarchical social order in general. They were also powerful because Spanish notions regarding sexual and reproductive relations between the three main populations reflected and interacted with other discourses of colonial power. Recurring ideas regarding blood purity and mixture, for example, construed native people—the transmission of their traits—as weak, thereby echoing paternalistic religious and government policies that depicted relations among Spaniards, indigenous people, and blacks in gendered forms. Political, religious, and genealogical discourses in fact mirrored, complemented, and reinforced each other through the use of notions of strength and weakness that by coding different colonial groups as male or female naturalized socially created hierarchies.

Only in the eighteenth century, however, would invocations of nature as the basis of difference between men and women as well as between human groups begin to emerge as a prominent discourse. A growing interest, particularly among natural philosophers, in questions about the origins of different populations and function of men and women in the generation of life influenced how the sistema de castas was represented. As scientific explanations to sexual and racial difference gained ground over religious ones, colonial Mexico's population became subject, like the animals and plants in natural histories, to increasingly elaborate and visual taxonomic exercises that made the gendering of race and racing of gender as well as social hierarchies seem to be ordained by nature. This penchant for classification and naturalization was manifested in "casta paintings," a genre that illustrated and labeled the unions of different "castes" as well as their offspring and that betrayed both how some of Mexico's artists conceived of the appropriate relationship of gender, race, and class and the lingering importance of the discourse of limpieza de sangre.

A third main line of inquiry tracks the importance of the state-sponsored organization of colonial society into two separate commonwealths or "republics"—one Spanish, the other indigenous—to discourses of blood and lineage. Although strict segregation between the two populations was never achieved and some Spanish jurists and legislation allowed for the day when the native people would be fully incorporated into Hispanic colonial society, the dual model of social organization nevertheless had profound repercussions. At least in central Mexico, the republica de indios ("Indian Republic") was not just an ideological device, and it continued to have practical significance well into the eighteenth century. It promoted the survival of pueblos de indios (native communities) with their own political hierarchies

and citizenship regime, the creation of special legal and religious institutions for the indigenous people, and the official recognition of Indian purity. This recognition, which mainly pivoted on the argument that the original inhabitants of the Americas were unsullied by Judaism and Islam and had willingly accepted Christianity, made it possible for some of the descendants of pre-Hispanic dynasties to successfully claim the status of limpieza de sangre, in the long run altering some of their conceptions of blood and history. Their genealogical claims became more frequent in the last third of the seventeenth century, amid increasing efforts to preserve communal lands and histories.

But native nobles and rulers were not the only group to be influenced by the Spanish state's promotion of two polities and corresponding dual citizenship and purity regimes. All colonial identities, after all, were the results of complex colonial processes. Maintaining a system of "proving" purity in the "Spanish republic" necessitated the creation of birth records, classifications, and genealogies and obliged those who wanted access to the institutions or offices with limpieza requirements to submit lineages, produce witnesses, and keep records of their ancestors. Among creoles (Spaniards born and/or raised in the Americas), these administrative and archival practices helped foster a historical consciousness that encouraged their identification with a broader Spanish community of blood even as they developed a strong attachment to the land. By the eighteenth century, they established their purity not so much by stressing their lack of Jewish and Muslim ancestors as by providing evidence of their Spanish descent. Yet this formulation of limpieza de sangre as Spanishness did not entirely undermine the idea that the indigenous people were pure and redeemable because of their acceptance of Christianity. Instead, it produced paradoxical attitudes toward reproduction or mestizaje ("mixture") with Amerindians among Creole elites, particularly as their patriotism intensified and they began to imagine the merger of the two republics in reproductive and biological terms.

[...] Centers on three main issues: the relationship between the Spanish notion of limpieza de sangre and Mexico's sistema de castas; the intersection of notions of purity, gender, and sexuality; and the linkages of religion, race, and patriotic discourses. Framing the exploration of these subjects is an emphasis on the role of the state, church, and archives in promoting a preoccupation with lineage in central Mexico, particularly among Creole and native elites. In other words, one of the [...] thematic threads is how the routinization of genealogical requirements in the secular and religious hierarchies helped shape social practices, notions of self, and concepts of communal belonging. Which is not to say that the Spanish colonial state was powerful and that its laws were always or even frequently obeyed, only that it set guidelines for government and religious institutions and through them shaped the nature of social relations. The term *archival practices* thus generally refers to the record-keeping activities of the state, church, and Inquisition that produced and reproduced categories of identity based on ancestry linked to particular legal statuses (to certain responsibilities, rights, or privileges). These archival practices promoted genealogical ones, including official and unofficial investigations into a person's ancestors—involving examinations of birth records, interrogations of town elders, inspections of tributary lists, and so forth—and the construction of family histories through, among other things, the maintenance, purchase, or falsification of written genealogies, certifications of purity of blood, and copies of baptismal and marriage records.

Another recurring theme [...] is the interaction of metropolitan and colonial notions of purity and, more broadly, discourses about the New Christians—which drew on anti-Semitic tropes—and the converted populations of the Americas. Special attention is drawn to the similarities and differences in Spanish attitudes toward the conversion potential of Jews and native people and especially to how stereotypes that were used to describe one group tended to be mapped onto the other. Finally, [...] underscores the instability of the sistema de castas. It stresses that, like all hegemonic projects, it was a process, powerful and pervasive because it was promoted by the state and the church but fluctuated and was subject to contestation. The relative fluidity of the sistema de castas was partly due to inconsistencies in the discourse of limpieza de sangre, which, for example, characterized native people *as* pure and impure, as both perfect material for Christianization and incorrigible idolaters. Hegemonic discourses tend to derive power from their construction of subjects in a doubled way.

The sistema's fluidity was also a by-product of the Spanish imperial structure, which incorporated Spanish America into the Crown of Castile but failed to clearly outline what that meant in terms of the rights and privileges of different populations. For example, despite the various compilations of laws for the "Indies" *(derecho indiano)* that Spain produced in the seventeenth century, it did not issue a legal code specifically for the castas and did not entirely clarify the status of Creoles as "natives" of a particular jurisdiction. The political vagueness of imperial space and piecemeal nature of colonial legislation prompted individuals and groups to attempt to challenge or redefine statuses, policies, and classifications. These features also resulted in unexpected political imaginaries, ones that a rigid distinction between a metropolitan core and colonial periphery cannot begin to capture.

Limpieza De Sangre, Race, and Colonialism in the Early Modern Period

Scholars of early modern Spain have not paid much attention to the relationship between the concept of limpieza de sangre and Spanish American racial ideology. Their disinterest in the problem can be blamed on the lamentably persistent tendency within the profession to treat the histories of the Iberian Peninsula and colonial Latin America *as* separate analytical fields. But it is also indicative of a broader Spanish denial about certain aspects of Spain's colonial past. I first encountered this denial when I arrived at the Archivo General de Indias (AGI) in Seville to conduct research [...]. After I explained the purpose of my visit, the director of the archive informed me that I would not find any sources on limpieza de sangre there. The response took me aback because I had a list of references for documents related to my topic that other historians had found at that archive. But after being in Spain for a few months, I realized that it was part of a general reluctance among contemporary Spaniards to recognize the importance that the concept of purity of blood had in the Americas, namely because of what it implies for their national history, which has tended to minimize (if not deny) the role of processes of racialization in Castile's overseas territories. This reluctance cannot simply be attributed to ignorance, for even some Spanish historians of colonial Latin America tried to convince me, when at the onset of my research I presented at a reputable research institution in Seville, that the problem of purity of blood was one that never spilled out of the borders of the Iberian Peninsula and that the concept was used exclusively against converted Jews and Muslims. It soon became clear that the organization of archives—the way that many limpieza de sangre documents were classified or not classified, subsumed under other records, or mislabeled—was intimately connected to this national historical narrative.

That the same historians who tried to convince me of the irrelevance of the concept of limpieza de sangre outside of Spain were well acquainted with purity documents produced in Spanish America only added a surreal quality to the discussion that followed my presentation in Seville. But the strangeness of the experience did not end there. To bolster his case, a specialist in Andean history offered the observation that many Spanish colonists had reproduced with native women and, in cases where acquiring land was at stake, even married them! A people concerned with blood purity would not be willing to "mix" with the Amerindians was his point, one that clearly echoed the arguments made by some scholars in the first half of the twentieth century regarding Iberians' relatively benign attitudes toward native people and Africans. This current of thought, which had among its many flaws the propensity to see early colonial sexual relations not as acts of power but as signs of a more gentle or open approach to colonization (sometimes attributed to the history of Spanish and Portuguese "commingling" with Jews and Muslims) is part of the white Legend of Spanish history, an apologetic view of Spain's actions in the Americas. The view to some extent surfaced in reaction to the body of propagandistic literature that began to be produced by Spain's European rivals (especially the British and Dutch) in the late sixteenth century and which gave rise to the Black Legend. Seeking to discredit Castile's claims to the Americas, this legend focused attention on the conquerors' cruelty toward indigenous peoples, their unbridled greed, and their hypocritical use of religion as justification for their deeds.

The Black Legend survived into the twentieth century and colored Anglophone scholarship on both Spain and Spanish America. Its influence is evident, for example, in the modernization studies of the 1950s that compared Latin America's apparent continuity in political, social, and economic forms—its history of authoritarianism, sharp inequalities, and financial dependency—with the more democratic and capitalist trajectory of the United States. These studies tended to blame the "feudal" and "absolutist" foundations of Spanish colonial societies for the region's troubled path to modernity. Many framed the problems associated with the latifundia (the absence of a yeomanry), the Inquisition (the suppression of freedom of political and religious thought), and the church's collusion with the state (the clergy's ongoing support of absolutism) as medieval holdovers that Castilians took to the Americas, where they obstructed economic entrepreneurship, individualism, and democratic ideals, among other things. The causes of Spain's inability to modernize à la other parts of Western Europe and the United States also explained Latin America's "backwardness."

In the past few decades, the Black Legend has taken on a new twist. Some of the scholarship on the history of race and racism has been casting early modern Iberia as the site of a precocious elaboration of racial concepts and practices. A recent historical overview of the problem, for example, begins by discussing developments in Spain, "the first great colonizing nation and a seedbed for Western attitudes toward race." Iberia's pioneering role in the development of racial ideologies is sometimes linked to its participation in the early stages of the transatlantic African slave trade and in the colonization of the Americas. But it is more often associated with the Spanish statutes of limpieza de sangre. Indeed, particularly in the literature that seeks to excavate the "origins" of race, it has become almost commonplace to postulate that the Castilian concept of blood purity was the first racial discourse produced by the West or at least an important precursor to modern notions of difference. Anti-Semitism was endemic in late medieval Europe, and in the two centuries preceding Spain's 1492 expulsion of its Jews. France and England had on repeated occasions tried to do the same with their Jewish populations, but it apparently makes for a much more satisfying narrative when race and racism can be given a single starting point and a linear trajectory. Thanks to its contribution to racism via the purity statutes and Inquisition, early modern Spain can finally make a claim to modernity. It was ahead of its time in something.

Whether the intention of its proponents or not, the argument that credits Spain with establishing the first modern system of discrimination fits neatly into the package of the Black Legend, which might help to explain why Spanish historians would be less than enthusiastic about studying the extension of the concept of limpieza de sangre to the other side of the Atlantic. To acknowledge that a discourse of purity of blood surfaced in the Americas would be to risk adding yet another dark chapter to a history that includes the expulsion of the Jews, the establishment of the Inquisition, the forced exile of Muslims *and moriscos* (Muslim converts to Christianity), and the conquest and colonization of native peoples. Given that the concept of purity of blood was relevant in all of these developments, how does one approach the subject in ways that avoid presenting historical actors in terms of simplistic

dichotomies and, more generally, the politicization of history? Perhaps, as the historian Steve Stern has stressed, the conquest and colonization of the Americas can never be disentangled from politics—from the politics of the past and the present, the history and historiography—but the point here is not to vilify Spaniards or suggest that they were worse, as the Black Legend would have it, than other colonial powers, or for that matter better, as the White Legend camp claimed. No expansionist European country could claim the moral high ground with respect to their attitudes toward and treatment of the peoples they colonized and/or enslaved, only some differences in timing, methods, and guiding principles. This [...] does not intend, therefore, to provide material for the perpetuation of the Black Legend (whether it is used as such is another matter) or to reinforce the tendency in recent studies on the origins of race and racism to single out early modern Iberia, as if those phenomena were unknown in other parts of Europe or somehow spread from the peninsula to the rest of the continent. Its main concern is not with the history of Spain but with that of New Spain, although the two are clearly interrelated, and that in itself is a point that the study tries to reiterate as it charts the transatlantic paths of the problem of limpieza de sangre.

If Spanish historians can be criticized for their failure to recognize the importance of limpieza de sangre in the colonial context, U.S. scholars of Spanish America can be accused of not having paid adequate attention to the complexity of the uses and meanings of the concept in Iberia, which has tended to result in oversimplified and at times anachronistic renditions of the ways in which it shaped racial discourses in the American context. For their part, Mexican and other Latin American academics can be taken to task for their general aversion to treating race as a legitimate subject of inquiry for understanding their region's history. It is fair to say that they tend to regard it as an issue that mainly has had relevance in the United States and other former slave societies (as opposed to "societies with slaves"), whereas they see class as much more salient for understanding the Iberian American past (even when it comes to regions in which slavery was extremely important, such as Brazil and Cuba). Thus, although some Mexican specialists of the colonial period might agree that the notion of limpieza de sangre was of some significance (it is hard to miss references to it in the archives), they commonly dismiss the problem of race by stressing that social organization was based on an estate model. If different groups had distinct rights, privileges, and obligations, it was because of the hierarchical nature of Spanish society, which at the time of the conquest continued to consist of three main estates and numerous corporations with specific functions within the social body, not because of modern notions of biological difference.

The argument that using the notion of race to study the period prior to the nineteenth century is anachronistic has of course not been made exclusively by Latin Americans. Indeed, the standard chronology (and teleology) of the concept is that it had not yet crystallized—assumed its full essentializing potential—in the early modern period because attitudes regarding phenotype usually combined or competed with ideas of cultural or religious difference. According to this account, race did not appear until the nineteenth century, when pseudoscience anchored it in biology, or rather, when biology anchored it in the body much more effectively than natural philosophy and natural history ever did. It is true that the concept of race generally became more biologistic in that period, and it is of course important not to project its modern connotations to previous eras. But arguing that racial discourses took a particular form in the nineteenth century is one thing; contending that they did not operate in the early modern period, quite another. In the past three decades, a number of scholars have demonstrated that the meanings and uses of the concept of race have varied across time, space, and cultures and that even in modern times, it has not relied exclusively on biological notions of difference but rather has often been intertwined with culture and/or class. To elevate "race as biology" to an ideal type is to set up a false dichotomy—to ignore that racial discourses have proven to be remarkably flexible, invoking nature or biology more at one point,

culture more at another. The shifting meanings and uses of race simultaneously underscore its social constructedness and suggest that there is no single, transhistorical racism but rather different types of *racisms,* each produced by specific social and historical conditions. The historian's task is precisely to excavate its valences within particular cultural and temporal contexts, study the processes that enable its reproduction, and analyze how it rearticulates or is "reconstructed as social regimes change and histories unfold."

Several historians of colonial Latin America have argued that it is necessary to keep limpieza de sangre and race analytically distinct for the sake of historical specificity and in particular to attempt to be faithful to the ways in which people of that time and place understood their social identities. Some scholars fear that equating notions of lineage, blood, and descent with race would mean characterizing all pre-modern societies, and those studied by anthropologists, as racially structured. The argument is compelling, and it is certainly difficult to dispute the point that there is a significant difference between the racial discourses that European colonialism unleashed and indigenous kinship systems. But attempting to draw a rigid analytical line between purity of blood and race is tricky, first, because the two concepts gained currency at about the same time and appear side by side in virtually all *probanzas* (certificates) of limpieza de sangre, and second, because the former influenced the latter in no small ways. Indeed, there was no neat transition from early modern notions of lineage to race. In the Hispanic Atlantic world, Iberian notions of genealogy and purity of blood—both of which involved a complex of ideas regarding descent and inheritance (biological and otherwise)—gave way to particular understandings of racial differences.

There is nothing original about asserting that there was a link between European genealogical notions and racial discourses. As the anthropologist Ann Laura Stoler has observed, both Michel Foucault and Benedict Anderson alluded to this link, albeit in different ways. Foucault, who viewed the problem of race mainly as part of Europe's "internal and permanent war with itself" and therefore did not consider colonialism's relevance to it, implied that a discourse of class had emerged from the "racism" of the European aristocracy. For his part, Anderson suggested that race had its origins in ideologies of "class" sprung from the landed nobility. Thus, for one scholar, the aristocracy's racism informed class; for the other, its elitism shaped race. To some extent, these two different formulations stem from confusion over how to characterize the nobility's obsession with "blood," which more often than not was accompanied by concerns with biological inheritance, anxieties about reproduction outside the group, and a series of insidious assumptions about the inferiority and impurity of members of the commoner estate. Medieval representations of peasants, for example, rendered them as a lower order of humanity and associated them with animals, dirt, and excrement. The beastialization of the peasantry could reach such extremes that a historian of slavery has suggested that it was an important precursor to the early modern racialization of Jews and blacks.

Whether medieval and early modern concerns with blood and lineage—in Europe and elsewhere—can be classified as racism will most likely continue to be debated, especially by those who favor using a loose definition of race that makes it applicable to most naturalizing or essentializing discourses and those who opt for a narrow one that basically limits its use to the nineteenth century and beyond. The debate is important but frankly less pressing than analyzing the historical significance of those concerns—the social tensions that produced them, the terms people used to express them, and the ways in which they were reproduced or rearticulated over time and across geocultural contexts. This [...] therefore uses the word *race* in relation to the discourse of limpieza de sangre but does so with caution, stressing that both concepts were strongly connected to lineage and intersected with religion. Through much of the early modern period, they remained part of a grid of knowledge constituted not by scientific (biologistic) discourses but by religious ones and operated through an "episteme of resemblance" in which similitude dominated the organization of

symbols and interpretations and representations of the universe. The book also emphasizes that concepts of blood purity and race were neither contained in Europe nor simply a consequence of the continent's "internal war with itself." They operated in a transatlantic context, and their continued salience and fluctuating meanings over the centuries were partly, if not greatly, determined by colonialism.

In sum, by underscoring the interrelated nature of discourses of purity of blood in Iberia and the Americas, this study undermines the view (especially prominent among Spanish historians) that the problem of limpieza de sangre was primarily an Iberian phenomenon as well as the contention (made by some scholars of Spanish America) that it can be separated from that of race. Furthermore, it problematizes the conceptual division that the literature on race sometimes makes between colonial racism and anti-Semitism. Some studies have argued that the two types of discriminatory regimes are manifestly different: that whereas the former has been characterized by the construction and maintenance of (colonial) hierarchies, the latter has typically promoted exclusion or outright extermination (as in the case of Nazi Germany). But as Etienne Balibar has stressed, a stark distinction between an "inclusive" colonial racism and an "exclusive" (usually anti-Semitic) one is untenable because historically, the two forms have not only exhibited similar characteristics but have depended on each other; rather than having separate genealogies, they have a "joint descent." Few historical phenomena demonstrate this close relationship between anti-Semitic and colonial discourses of difference better than the ideology of purity of blood, which spread while Spain was forging its overseas empire. Like the ships, people, and merchandise moving to and from Europe, Africa, and the Americas, the ideas and practices associated with the notion of limpieza de sangre circulated within, and helped forge, the Hispanic Atlantic world.

If the area to which this [...] most directly contributes is the study of race in Spanish America, it also has implications for a number of other topics, including ones related to periodization, nationalism, and comparative colonialisms. For one, the centrality of the seventeenth century to the development of the sistema de castas places the focus on a period that historians of colonial Latin America have tended to understudy. Perhaps unduly influenced by anthropologist George Foster's characterization of colonial Latin American culture as having "crystallized" or acquired its basic social institutions by 1580, the historiography has generally regarded the years between that decade and 1750 as largely uneventful. Neglect of this "long seventeenth century" or middle phase of Spanish colonialism might also be explained by its shortage of events as dramatic as those of the conquest and its aftermath. How can the period compete, for example, with the years that witnessed the early evangelizing campaigns and their inspiration in biblical, messianic, and eschatological interpretations of history; the Spanish "debates" about the humanity of the Amerindians; and the civil war that erupted among some of Peru's conquerors? It may also be that the seventeenth-century's difficult paleography and less extensive secondary literature have made studying other eras more appealing.

Whatever the case, the period was anything but static. Seventeenth-century Spanish America not only had strong connections with Spain but underwent crucial social and cultural transformations. Included among these changes was the rise of Creole patriotism, a topic that has been explored by David Brading, Bernard Lavalle, and others and which is analyzed in the present study in relation to the ideology of limpieza de sangre. By interrogating the complex relationship of patriotic, religious, and blood discourses, the book makes an intervention in discussions of nationalism in Latin America. Nationalism, however, is not an explicit subject of inquiry, in part because it did not appear until the end of the colonial period, if then. The region's independence movements were primarily triggered by Napoleon's invasion of Spain in 1808 and imposition of his brother Joseph as the new king, which on both sides of the Atlantic led to political assemblies and discussions that quickly became much more than about the restitution of Ferdinand VII to

the throne. Thus, Latin American nationalism seems to have been the result, not the cause, of the independence movements, and to speak of eighteenth-century "creole nationalism" is to walk on shaky argumentative ground. Furthermore, as a number of historians who responded to Benedict Anderson's thesis about its rise in Spanish America have pointed out, not only was creole patriotism compatible with continued loyalty to the Spanish Crown, but the early modern notion of "nation" (nation) was exceedingly ambiguous with regard to territory and bloodlines.

That a strong identification with the local community existed prior to independence does not mean that there was a causal connection between the two or between criollismo (creolism) and nationalism. Assuming such a connection amounts to "doing history backwards," that is, projecting modern categories onto a world in which those forms of thinking had not yet come about. It also forecloses the possibility of studying Creole patriotism on its own terms—its meanings, motivations, and political effects at different points in time. But if patriotism and nationalism should not be conflated, examinations of colonial political ideology, social developments, and cultural movements are necessary to understand the form that Mexican nationalism took after independence. By exploring the relationship between the religiously inflected concept of limpieza de sangre and notions of citizenship (vecindad) in New Spain, this study seeks to provide a basis for further discussions about how the particularities of colonialism in Mexico shaped its postindependence political projects, gendered and racialized imaginings of the nation, and legal formulations of the citizen.

It also aims to highlight some of the specificities of Spanish colonialism. Although there are continuities and similarities between different colonial projects, colonialism cannot be reduced to a single model; it has multiple historicities. The Spanish colonial project, the earliest in the Americas, was driven by historically and culturally specific forces, and its course was determined by early modern dynamics on both sides of the Atlantic. It differed most from modern imperial projects. For example, unlike Britain and France when they launched the second major phase of European colonialism starting in the second half of the eighteenth century, when Spain invaded the Americas, it was not an industrial power seeking raw materials and markets for its manufactured goods. Its expansion west was initially propelled by the search for gold (increasingly important as a medium of exchange in international commerce), and its economic project came to be based primarily on the exploitation of mineral wealth and on state-controlled systems of extracting labor and tribute from native populations that had few parallels.

Furthermore, Spanish colonialism began long before the emergence of the politics of nationhood, liberalism, and Enlightenment-inspired universalist concepts of freedom, equality, rights, progress, and citizenship. Together with the expansion of capitalist relations, these modern developments generated new ideological frameworks for justifying colonial rule as well as a deep tension between the particularism of colonialism (predicated on the creation and perpetuation of colonial hierarchies) and the universalism of western European political theory. Spanish colonialism in the Americas, based more on the concept of status than on the notion of rights, did not have to contend with this tension, at least not at first. During its first two centuries, its main ideological contradiction stemmed from, on one hand, universalist Christian doctrines that touted the redemptive powers of baptism and the equality of all members of the church and, on the other, the construction of different categories of Christians. The extent to which religion played a role in justifying expansion and colonial rule was another aspect of the early modern Spanish colonial project that distinguished it from modern ones.

Readily distinguishable in certain respects from nineteenth- and twentieth-century imperialism, Spanish colonialism becomes less distinctive when it is compared to other formative or early colonial projects in the Americas. Contrary to what the Black Legend would have us believe, during the initial phase of European expansion, Spaniards did not have a monopoly on the unbridled use of violence against native peoples. The British and Dutch amply demonstrated their capacity for barbarity. Furthermore, Spanish, Portuguese, English, and French colonial projects shared a number of features, including expansion through settlement; efforts to recreate European ways of life; and religious Utopias, Catholic and Protestant alike. But similarities among these "settler-type" colonialisms can be overstated, among other reasons because each power had its own economic, political, and religious agendas, even if at certain historical moments some of these overlapped. The Spanish state's control over some systems of labor, its transformation of large indigenous populations into tributaries, and its collective incorporation of native people as Christian vassals of the Crown of Castile were exceptional, especially when compared to British policies in Anglo North America. And although efforts to convert native people to Christianity were by no means exclusive to Spaniards, no other European colonial power, not even the other Catholic ones of Portugal and France, relied on the church to spread the faith, support the government, and structure colonial society as much as Castile. The historical moment and cultural context were both crucial. That religion was integral to Spanish colonialism was due in large measure to its importance in sixteenth-century Spain itself, where Catholicism was the only religion allowed, where the church and state had developed an extraordinarily strong relationship, and where the twin notions of "Old Christian blood" and genealogical purity had emerged as powerful cultural principles and exclusionary weapons. Religion, lineage, and blood would in turn be used to organize the Spanish colonial world.

In conclusion, Spanish colonialism was shaped by particular economic, political, and religious goals; by historical circumstances in early modern Spain and Spanish America; and by distinctive principles of social organization. As a result, its categories of discourse, mechanisms of inclusion and exclusion, and forms of establishing the boundaries of the Spanish community were unique or, at the very least, substantially different from modern colonial projects in Africa and Asia.

Study Terms

Critical Race Theory
Black Legend
White Legend
Limpieza de Sangre
Sistema de Castas
derecho indiano
mestizaje
pueblo de indios
Archival Practices
probanzas
conversos
Genealogy

Scientific Racism and Politics

Race and IQ

Arthur Jensen and Cyril Burt

By Alexander Alland, Jr.

• •

Editor's Introduction to Race and IQ

One of the longest-standing tenets of racism is the assumption or perception that non-whites are biologically inferior, and, by extension, less intelligent than whites. This essay on Race and IQ closely examines and refutes the findings of a study conducted in 1969 by Arthur Jensen. One controversial finding was "an average genetic deficit in IQ among people of black ancestry when compared to whites."[1] Jensen's report was immediately utilized as "proof" that remedial educational programs should cease because if IQ was hereditary, then time and money was being wasted.

In the 1990s, a polarizing book, *The Bell Curve*, claimed that its empirical studies agreed with the Jensen Report, and had expanded upon it. However, the book's claimed empirical studies were thoroughly picked apart by the late Stephen Jay Gould and other scholars.[2] Nonetheless, the "Jensen Report" resurfaces from time to time as an argument to cut federal spending, often camouflaged as an "austerity" measure, or reduction in the size of government.

Notes

1. Arthur Jensen and Cyril Burt. *Race in Mind: Race, IQ, and other Racisms*. New York: Palgrave, 2002, 79.
2. Stephen Jay Gould. *The Mismeasure of Man*. New York: W.W. Norton, 1996.

This chapter deals primarily with race and IQ in the work of Arthur Jensen, the author of a 1969 report on race and IQ that was essentially an attack on the governmental program known as Project Head Start. The program's goal was to help children from poor neighborhoods prepare for their entry into the regular school system through attendance at free government-supported preschools. The assumption behind Head Start was that the children of the poor suffered a learning deficit in their early formative years due to an impoverished intellectual environment. For those who believed that IQ and, therefore, performance was hereditary, Head Start was seen as a waste of federal monies.

Jensen is an educational psychologist specializing in psychological statistics who, after many years as a professor at Teachers College, Columbia University, moved to the University of California at Berkeley. His highly controversial article "How Much Can We Boost IQ and Scholastic Achievement?" published in the *Harvard Educational Review* in 1969, made a case for the preponderance of heredity in the production of intelligence as measured by IQ tests, and an average genetic deficit in IQ among people of black ancestry when compared to whites. Although the argument had been made before, Jensen's article drew a vast amount of positive attention from the press and among some educators and strong criticisms from many, but by no means all, professional psychologists and anthropologists. It is important to note that the "Jensen Report" came shortly after the Supreme Court decision banning segregation in public schools and the successes of the civil rights movement to desegregate schools in the South. Therefore, it should come at no surprise that Jensen's conclusions were seized upon immediately by those who opposed remedial educational programs, such as Project Head Start, for young poor children and, in particular, poor black children. In a nutshell their argument was: If, as Jensen has proved, IQ is largely hereditary, it is a waste of money and time to develop and pursue programs for children in order to enhance their intelligence. Because even today this article stands as a model for those who continue to believe the IQ argument concerning race, this chapter will focus on its major shortcomings. [...]

In discussions concerning hereditary group differences in IQ, race has not always been the crucial variable. In Great Britain, for example, the focus has been on class rather than race. The man most associated with modern work on class and IQ in Britain, and who had a significant impact on Jensen's methods of research, was Cyril Burt. Burt attempted to prove that heredity played a major role in intelligence by studying identical twins reared apart. Because such twins are genetically identical, any differences in IQ found among them must be due to environment. However, because no one has ever argued that genetics plays the

only role in the determination of IQ, such studies are putatively used to determine the proportional contributions of genetics and environment to a trait that varies among populations with different genetic profiles and brought up under different environmental conditions. Since at the time that Cyril Burt did his work class and not race was a major concern in Britain, he set out to prove that IQ was the *major* variable in *class* differences in intelligence.

This idea was not new with Burt. It was first proposed in the middle of the nineteenth century by Darwin's brilliant cousin, one of the founders of mathematical statistics, Francis Galton. Galton warned that class differentials in fertility, with the lower class having more children than the upper classes, would inevitably produce a gradual decrease in the average IQ of the entire British population. Burt represented a modern version of Galton's hypothesis and provided what he claimed was solid evidence of the phenomenon that would bring about the decline in IQ predicted by his predecessor.

Before I criticize Jensen's and Burt's work in detail let me turn to the concept of race and its purported relation to behavioral traits including—but not exclusive to—IQ. As we have already seen, the concept of race is often confused with ethnic, cultural, or religious identity. People speak of the French race, the Irish race, or the Jewish race. In societies where racism is current, individuals of mixed ancestry are usually assimilated into whichever part of their ancestry is downgraded by society. Thus, in the United States even individuals who are phenotypically white may be classed as black if it is known that they have even a small degree of black ancestry. It is fair to say, therefore, that even if race is a false concept in biology it is *real* from a sociological perspective. When members of a society classify an individual by race then that person *is by definition* a member of that race!

Racial identity is by no means a neutral concept. Wherever used it implies superiority or inferiority. Which "racial" groups are esteemed or denigrated is determined by subjective factors linked to historical and sociological factors.

During the middle of the nineteenth century the Protestant establishment in New England tended to characterize the Irish as a distinct race. At that time the Irish were said to display a range of primarily negative biological characteristics. Later, as the Irish gained in population and political power, this attitude changed.

One of the favorite and eternal arguments of dominant groups is that they *merit* their place in the social hierarchy [...]. In times of absolutist royal power kings and nobles ruled through the doctrine of hereditary power. Ever since the enlightenment and the rise of industrial capitalism in the West, large segments of the middle class have rested their claim to social and political dominance on "social selection," a process said to be akin to natural selection. People might rise to the top from humble social origins, but if they did so it was on the basis of *merit* According to this theory, merit was linked directly to heredity. Since the beginning of the twentieth century merit has come to be objectified as intelligence *plus* socially acceptable hard work.

Meanwhile, the somewhat vague concept of intelligence was converted into a supposedly measurable entity through the statistical concept of IQ. It is common for people to believe not only that IQ is hereditary but also that whole "racial" groups differ in average IQ. This has led to what is known as the "IQ argument." As noted above, the IQ argument was originally associated with class relations, particularly in Europe, and with race in the United States. In discussing the assumed link between race and IQ it must be made clear that we are about to deal with two nebulous concepts. We have already seen that race has no firm reality in biology. Now we need to examine the pitfalls in the concept of IQ as well as the notion that whole groups have different *hereditary* averages for intelligence.

What is intelligence? It should be obvious that tests designed to measure it are structured in relation to some theory, but I wish to delay discussion of this problem for the moment. Let us begin with test results and work backward to their origin and the concepts they reflect. Suffice it to say here that intelligence is a comparative phenomenon. Tests are standardized on the basis of a mean average in a population of test takers. Once this has been established individuals can be ranked above, at, or below the mean. It is also possible to give IQ tests to different groups of people, compare average scores, and rank one group against another. When such rankings are made in this country the data show that some sociological categories consistently score lower than the standard white American rage. These groups include American Indians, African Americans, and other ethnic groups, such as Latinos of various origin. Class breakdown of scores shows that middle- and upper-class whites score better than lower-class whites and that people in the North score higher than those in the South. Much has been made of the fact that African Americans from the *North* scored better on one type of test (the army alpha given around the time of World War I), than *Southern* whites. When compared to *Northern* whites, however, they scored below the mean. The lower scores for African Americans in the North when compared to northern whites have been attributed to differences in social environment and education. It is important to note, however, that these results were couched in terms of differences among biological groups. But data actually concern four distinct *sociological* categories. These are: Southern *sociologically* defined whites, Southern *sociologically* defined African Americans, Northern *sociologically* defined whites, and Northern *sociologically* defined African Americans. In no case do any of these groups represent a distinct biological population, although it *is* fair to say that the gene pools of each group differs from the others to some un-quantifiable degree.

It must be stressed as well that IQ data is subject to variation in two ways. First, they depend on particular test protocols (many different kinds of IQ tests exist), and second, tests are given under varying conditions. It has been shown that *different* IQ tests produce *different* results and the *same* tests can produce *different* results when the testing conditions are varied.

Let us return to the concept of intelligence for a moment. What is it? The French psychologist Alfred Binet and his colleague, Theodore Simon, developed a set of tests between 1905 and 1911 that were meant to predict success in French middle-class elementary schools. They suggested that in intelligence there is a fundamental mental facility, the alteration or the lack of which is of utmost importance for practical life. That facility is judgment, or good sense, initiative, the faculty of adapting ones self to circumstances, judging well, comprehending well, and reasoning well. The concept of intelligence became a major preoccupation of American educational psychologists in the first half of the twentieth century. This led to various modifications of the definition. For example, Spearman (1904) reduced it to the ability to deduce relations and correlations. Thorndike (1927) regarded it as the power to make good responses from the standpoint of truth and fact. Terman (1937) defined it as the ability to think in abstract terms. All three definitions imply that intelligence can be measured as the rapidity of accommodation or adaptation to unique environmental situations through learning and conceptualization.

As the attention of psychologists turned to the concept of intelligence and how to test it, a debate began to emerge over the degree to which it is genetically determined. None of the definitions imply directly that IQ is genetic nor does anyone concerned with it claim that it is 100 percent hereditary. Rather, as I have already noted, arguments center over the relative contributions of heredity and environment to individual and group intelligence and how to measure objectively the contribution of each. Not so curiously, given the history of discrimination in the United States, most scholars who take a strong hereditarian position on IQ also assume that group differences in measured IQ are hereditary and that whites are genetically superior in intelligence to blacks. These arguments comfort the "racial" situation in the United States and have strong backing from many politicians and, unfortunately, psychologists [...], who have a strong academic stake in testing. The "new" field of evolutionary psychology (another name for sociobiology) reinforces the simplistic notion that most of human behavior is genetic in origin and that differences among cultural groups are biological in nature (see Wilson 1975).

Here it should be clear that we are concerned with two different problems. It is *not* the same thing to say that (1) genetics are responsible for individual differences in IQ within populations and (2) that population differences in IQ are due to genetics. The human species is highly *polymorphic*. Thus all human populations display wide internal variation in genetic traits, not to mention cultural variation. I have already noted that genetic differences *within* populations are wider than genetic differences among different populations. It is also true that, in the case of the human species, it is difficult, if not impossible, to separate genetic from environmental factors in the expression of phenotypic behavioral traits. Experiments designed to do this are impossible for both ethical and cultural reasons. We cannot breed humans in the laboratory the way we can breed rats. As we shall see in this chapter [...], so far all attempts to empirically separate environmental from genetic factors in behavioral testing have been seriously flawed.

There are other problems as well. The selection and maintenance of a definite goal and the ability to criticize one's own behavior contain elements that are surely subject to environmental modification. No two children ever grow up under the same conditions. In addition, individual psychological differences other than intelligence may affect the way an individual responds to new situations. A hesitant, demurring child might do less well on tests than a more confident one even though both might have the same potential capacities. And, of course, when we deal with test results the testing situation must be considered, for these conditions are bound to be influenced by an individuals cultural and psychological background. Although intelligence tests are supposed to be self-contained units, that is, units that contain all the information necessary to make judgments within the context of the test, the intellectual background, interests, and experience of the individuals tested appear to have significant effects on the responses of test takers. In addition different cultures have a tendency to treat "truth" or "fact" in very different ways. In American society Aristotelian logic is imposed early on children, while in the East not only is a paradoxical type of logic taught in some areas, but some intellectuals there strive to change their basic thought patterns so that they can come to accept a kind of inversion of what Westerners would call truth: The obvious is always false; truth often lies in opposites.

IQ tests themselves are subject to artifactual errors that render interpretation difficult. Among these are such cultural factors as attitudes toward testing in general, the amount of test sophistication an individual brings to a particular experiment, and the structure of the tests themselves. Thus the tests may or may not actually measure what the experimenter assumes they do. For example, such tests are poor measures of biologically based *group* differences. The *independent* variable (the group being tested) is most frequently more *social* than biological. There are major problems with the *dependent* variable (what is being tested) as well. In addition to whatever that is, such items as motivation to take the test, intellectual background based on prior learning, and many other psychological factors affect test results.

Let me summarize those factors that go into an intelligent (successful) response to environmental stimuli. First, the nature of the stimulus must be considered. While there is evidence that the ability to respond to specific cues is partially inherent (humans in general have good vision and hearing and a relatively poor sense of smell), there is also evidence that a good deal of learning goes into the process. Perceptions are always selective (even when the process of selection is unconscious). The response to a cue involves such psychological factors as perceptual acuity, ability to discriminate among stimuli (which is partly hereditary and partly learned), and the ability to generalize, that is, to form classes of data from a range of sense perceptions. The latter is also clearly a process involving both learning and heredity. Accurate responses involve memory and the ability to retrieve necessary bits of information to be employed in

problem solving. Interest and span of attention, both of which are highly dependent upon social and psychological factors, speed of response, and effectiveness of feedback from behavior are all important variables. No single gene, of course, could underlie all of these (and other) psychological processes. In addition each variable, dependent as it may be on a hereditary base, would be subject to environmental modification in different ways. Divergent behavioral phenotypes could emerge from the same basic genotype. This would arise through environmental shaping in the same way that similar phenotypes are derived from different genotypes.

Let us return to those "bright" and "dull" rat strains developed by Tryon. Later experimentation demonstrated that the rats were reacting to specific tests. Environmental factors had a strong effect on the performance of these inbred (and thus genetically pure) strains. More specifically, in three out of five maze measures "dulls" were either equal in performance or better than the "brights." The "brights" were more food-driven, low in motivation to escape water, timid in open field situations, more purposive, and less destructive. "Dulls" were not highly food-driven, were better on average in motivation to escape water, and were fearful of mechanical apparatus features. Note how important these additional facts are to a full understanding of Tryon's results.

Intelligence tests are designed to measure a series of abilities: for example, spatial relations, reasoning, verbal fluency, and facility with numbers. But these are no more culture-free than the concepts behind them. For although it is possible to define intelligence *operationally* as the ability to achieve high scores on IQ tests, we must never forget that certain socially significant concepts lie behind the operational definition. The major concept relates IQ to academic performance under existing forms of education. Our system of education, however, is geared to middle-class success, not necessarily innate ability. Arthur Jensen (1969a) has pointed out that many of the psychological properties that contribute to response potential intercorrelate, even though specific tasks such as spatial relationships, verbal analogies, and numerical problem solving might bear no resemblance to one another. In this he follows Spearman, who separated out a factor ("g") that he believed accounted for "general intelligence." This conclusion led Spearman to define intelligence as the ability to deduce relations and correlates. Nonetheless, Jensen, himself unsatisfied with a unidimensional concept of intelligence, delineated two *genotypically* (genetically based) distinct basic processes that he called level one (associational ability) and level two (conceptual ability). Jensen related level one to the formation of associations between related stimuli, red with danger, for example, and level two to concept learning and problem solving, for him by far the most important factor in intelligence.

Another author, Rosalind Cohen (1969), identified two conceptual styles that she called "relational" and "analytic":

> The analytic cognitive style is characterized by a formal or analytic mode of abstracting salient information from a stimulus or situation and by a stimulus-centered orientation to reality and is parts-specific (i.e., parts or attributes of a given stimulus have meaning in themselves). The relational cognitive style, on the other hand, requires a descriptive mode of abstraction and is self-centered in its orientation to reality; only the global characteristics of a stimulus have meaning to its users, and these only in reference to some total context. (Cohen 1969, 829–30)

For what I hope are obvious reasons, the analytic style is clearly correlated with success in the academic context. While they are perhaps not identical, the analytic style is certainly close to what Jensen (1969a, 114) refers to as level two learning, or conceptual ability. Cohen, however, rejects a genetic hypothesis and substitutes one in which socialization and group structure constitute the independent variables in the formation of cognitive style. I would claim that Cohen's arguments are more convincing than Jensen's.

> Observation indicated that relational and analytic cognitive styles were intimately associated with shared-function and formal styles of group organization. … When individuals shifted from one kind of group structure to the other, their modes of group participation, their language styles, and their cognitive styles could be seen to shift appropriately to the extent that their expertise in using other approaches made flexibility possible. It appeared that certain kinds of cognitive styles may have developed by day-today participation in related kinds of social groups in which the appropriate language structure and methods of thinking about self, things, and ideas are necessary components of their related styles of group participation and that these approaches themselves may act to facilitate or impede their "carriers" ability to become involved in alternate kinds of groups. (Ibid., 831)

As long ago as the 1930s C. C. Brigham, who had been convinced that IQ differences between immigrant groups could be objectively tested, offered this strong renunciation of his own past theoretical bias. "This review has summarized some of the most recent test findings, which show that comparative studies of national and racial groups may not be made with existing tests, and which show, in particular, that one of the most pretentious of these comparative racial studies—the writer's own—was without foundation" (Brigham 1930,165).

Such candor is rare even in science. Once Brigham had reversed himself on culture-free testing he was able offer the following analysis for differential responses to tests. Note how his discussion parallels the analysis of behavioral responses of animals to test situations.

The assumption is made that people taking the alpha test [a U.S. Army test used during World War I] adopted two different attitudes or sets, viz., a "directions attitude"—an attitude of careful attention to the examiner's instructions without looking at the test questions while the directions were read; and "reading attitude"—partially or completely ignoring the examiners instructions while studying the test questions during the time in which the examiner was reading. The adoption of the first attitude would tend to give the individual higher scores in test 1 (entirely oral directions), test 6 (an unusual form of mathematical test), and 7 (a novel type of verbal test). On the other hand a person adopting the second attitude might quickly find out what was required in tests 3, 4, 5, and 8, and his score would be better if he ignored what the examiner was reading and studied the test questions during the period of instruction. (Brigham 1930, 162–63)

To my knowledge this analysis was the first published indication that the problem of constructing a "culture-free" test is not the only one in testing. The procedures themselves appear to have strong and differential effects on the responses of individuals taking the tests.

As I have noted above, in the United States, for what are clearly social and historical reasons, the argument over IQ and heredity has centered around black-white differences. By 1966 Audrey Shuey could publish a heavy tome with the tide *The Testing of Negro Intelligence.* Her summary of this issue ended with the conclusion not only that African Americans scored lower on most tests but also that the studies reviewed confirmed the hypothesis that differences between whites and blacks were largely due to heredity.

A search of the literature shows that this issue has been with us almost since IQ testing was invented. It was of course of great concern during the integration battles of the 1960s. Those who fought to maintain the status quo in the South argued that ending segregation would lower standards in the public schools through an influx of genetically inferior students. Those in favor of integration claimed that the poor showing of African Americans in the school system was an effect of segregation. This, they believed, was true in the North as well as in the South. Under then-president Lyndon Johnson in the middle 1960s, segregation as law was abolished officially in the entire country but continued de facto through residential patterns and educational inequality.

In an attempt to improve educational opportunity and to prepare young children for school, Project Head Start was begun in poor neighborhoods in the middle of the 1960s. Head Start nursery schools were designed to provide cultural stimulus for children before they entered kindergarten. While this project was welcomed by many in the country, there were those who felt that it was a waste of federal monies. Then, in 1969 a media bombshell struck. It was an article by Arthur Jensen, "How Much Can We Boost IQ and Scholastic Achievement?" published in what the press referred to as the "prestigious" *Harvard Educational Review.* By this time a new administration had taken over the White House. The country was in the midst of the Vietnam War, begun under Johnson, and priorities had shifted from domestic programs to foreign relations. Jensen's article, soon to be known as the "Jensen Report," argued that Head Start and programs like it were bound to fail. IQ was, he claimed, primarily hereditary, and African Americans were genetically inferior in IQ to whites. The Jensen article was reported in *Time* magazine to have shown up on the President's desk only a week after its publication. It was certainly taken seriously among those holding political power in the country.

I shall attempt to show below that in my opinion Jensen's paper fails the test of scientific validity. First, however, I should like to call attention to a point that has been overlooked by many on both sides of the IQ argument. Suppose, for a moment, that Jensen was completely right. He claimed that the total deficit between whites and blacks translated into 15 IQ points of difference and that of these, seven or seven and one-half points could be attributed to a genetic deficit among blacks. Now what could this seven to seven and one-half points mean in terms of educability? It should be clear that the answer must be: "Not much and probably nothing!"

Now to the failures of the report itself: Technically Jensen committed a major error when he claimed that his data concerning the degree to which IQ was hereditary, drawn as it was from white populations, could be used to speak about black populations. The genetic factor in IQ, estimated at 80 percent, was taken largely from studies by a well-known British psychologist, Cyril Burt. Burt based his conclusions on data from identical twins reared apart. Such twins are rare and important finds. They *are* identical genetically. Because they are raised in different environments, what measurable differences in behavioral traits occur between each individual in a set of twins can be attributed to the effects of the environment. If the difference between twins is 20 percent on a behavioral measure, for example, then one can say that the maximum effect of the environment is 20 and that the trait is, therefore, 80 percent genetically determined. The problem is that Burt's studies, even if they were correct (see below), were based exclusively on white twins. Additionally, one cannot say that the environments of identical twins reared apart are different enough to reveal genetic similarities as opposed to environmental ones. It is the general practice of adoption agencies to place children in homes that are similar in many respects to the homes of birth parents, except in cases where the birth parents maintained dysfunctional homes. It is even more likely that adoption agencies would go out of their way to place twins to be reared apart in similar homes regardless of the home situation of the birth parents.

The major statistic used in the Jensen Report is known technically as the *heritability* of a trait. The term can be very misleading. In fact, in biology it is employed in two contradictory ways. First, it is sometimes used loosely to indicate that a trait is genetic in origin. In this usage, when a trait is said to be "heritable" it simply means that it is in some way genetic. In the second, more correct and technical usage, heritability is *exclusively* a measure of *variance*. This means that it applies only when *variation* of some kind is present in a population. For example, the condition is satisfied when a population is made up of both blue-eyed and brown-eyed individuals. One can then ask the question: "What percentage of the variance (between blue and brown eyes) is due to heredity and what percentage is due to the environment?" The answer in this case is that the observed variation is 100 percent hereditary. Now if we are faced with a situation in which *everyone* is blue eyed, *then* there is *no* variance in the population (every individual is the same in reference to the trait in question, all have blue eyes). Because in this second case the trait does *not vary* among individuals the heritability is *zero* even though the trait is *100* percent genetic! This is a crucial point since laypeople are often confused by the term "heritability," and it is also misused even by some professional psychologists.

Because the concept of heritability deals with two variables, genetic *and* environmental, as a *statistic* it is subject to a very important restriction. No two populations ever live in exactly the same environment. If a trait with a genetic component is subject to environmental effects, as most are, these effects may differ in value from one environment to another. In other words the *penetrance* of the gene can be different in different environments. The genetic factor in height in humans is certainly based in large measure on heredity. But average height between two different populations might differ for such an environmental reason as nutrition (the degree to which proteins are found in the average diet of each population, for example). For this reason a measure of heritability in one population, let us say .80, is no guarantee that the heritability will be the same (for the same trait) in another population in another environment. It is always possible that the environment has acted differently on the same genetic potential.

Thus the problem is that all the heritability figures available to Jensen came from white populations. What this means is that he had no right (from an experimental point of view) to extrapolate this figure for African Americans. Even in the most integrated parts of American society it is not possible to say that the environment for African Americans is identical to that of whites. IN FACT it is most likely that there are significant environmental differences for the two groups. Therefore, we have no idea what the heritability of IQ might be among African Americans. As the population geneticist James Crow put it in a response to Jensen published in 1969:

> It can be argued that being white and being black in our society changes one or more aspects of the environment so importantly as to account for the difference [in IQ]. For example, the argument that the American Indians score higher than Negroes on IQ Tests—despite being lower on certain socioeconomic scales—can and will be dismissed on the same grounds: some environmental variable associated with being black is not included in the environmental ratio. (Crow 1969, 308)

Did Jensen know any of this when he wrote his report? Yes, he did. In an article published one year before his report he said the following:

> The inventors and developers of intelligence tests—such men as Galton, Binet, Spearman, Burt, Thorndike and Terman—clearly intended that their tests assess as clearly as possible the individuals innate brightness or mental capacity. If this is what a test attempts to do, then clearly the appropriate criterion for judging the test's "fairness" is the *heritability* of the test scores in the population in which the test is used. The quite high value of *H* for tests such as the Stanford-Binet attests to the success of the test-makers aim to measure

innate ability. ... However, I would be hesitant to generalize this statement beyond the Caucasian population of the United States and Great Britain, since nearly all the major heritability studies have been performed in these populations. At present there are no really adequate data on the heritability of intelligence tests in the American Negro population. (Jensen 1968, 94)

The problem does not end here. Jensen's major heritability estimates were drawn from data provided by Cyril Burt (born 1883, died 1971). In 1972 and 1973 a Princeton University professor, Leon Kamin, began to speak out concerning what he saw as problems in Burt's data. Scientific models and the experimental data to support them rarely, if ever, show absolute statistical uniformity. Kamin became suspicious of Burt's material on heritability and IQ because it was just too good to be true. Burt published several studies of twins both reared apart and reared together. The correlation between IQ scores of the twins reared *apart* was given as 0.771. In addition Burt used a single statistic, 0.94, for twins reared *together,* again in every study. Kamin's criticisms were aired verbally in 1972. While Kamin had accused Burt of fraud, in a 1978 article published in *American Psychologist* Jensen attempted to excuse Burt by saying that the peculiarities in Burt's data were probably due to carelessness. Jensen also claimed that whatever the reasons for Burt's data, they were no longer necessary to support his own arguments.

Kamin is not the only one to believe that Burt intentionally skewed the data to support his hypothesis. L. S. Hearnshaw (1979), an avowed fan of Burt's who gave the memorial address at the University of Liverpool on the occasion of Burt's death and who was chosen by the Burt family to write Burt's definitive biography, admits in that book that the evidence points to fraud, at least in the case of IQ: "The verdict must be, therefore, that at any rate in three instances, beyond reasonable doubt, Burt was guilty of deception. He falsified the early history of factor analysis. ...; he produced spurious data on MZ twins; and he fabricated figures on declining levels of scholastic achievement. Moreover, other material on kinship correlations is distinctly suspect" (Hearnshaw 1979, 259).

A stronger argument, published in the *British Journal of Psychology* in 1983, was made against Burt by James Hartley and Donald Rooum. In a survey of Burt's work in the field of typographical research (one less likely to be controversial than heredity and IQ) they concluded:

> Sir Cyril Burt contributed to five main areas of typographical research: spacing words and text; the use of serifs; the effects of typefaces, type sizes and line-lengths on reading comprehension; and aesthetic preferences. Hearnshaw (1979) assessed this contribution as worthy of "well merited acclaim." In this article we examine what Burt had to say on each of these issues, and how far what is said is applicable to typographic practice today. It appears, despite the wisdom of some of the sentiments expressed, that many of them were opinions that were not supported by the data that Burt presented. Indeed there is possible evidence of deceit. We conclude, therefore (and Hearnshaw accepts) that Burt's contribution to typographic practice was marred by the same defects that one can find in his other work. (Hartley and Rooum 1983, 203)

Michael McAskie also disagrees with Jensen in reference to Burt. In a May 1978 article published in *American Psychologist* he argued that Burt's data "points more to invention than to genuine derivation." McAskie concluded by saying:

> It is a great pity that Jensen chose to write so ill-prepared a reply to the fraud allegations concerning Burt. Jensen does not even appear to have applied some of the tools of his trade in trying to distinguish between fraud

and carelessness. He had no right to suppose that people suggesting fraud were merely speculating, nor was he particularly informed about the background of the *Sunday Times* article by Oliver Gillie or the political persuasions of those involved, "Sheer surmise and conjecture, and perhaps wishful thinking" are words that Jensen was not in a strong position to throw accusingly at others on this issue. (McAskie 1978, 498)

Perhaps one of the problems here is that Jensen was a post-doctoral student of Hans Eysenck [...] who himself was a student of Burt's. What we have here is a (nongenetic) family connection. Beyond the fact that Jensen's work was based on Burt's statistics, Jensen's defense may, at least in part, be due to family loyalty.

It is apparent that Jensen accepts race as a valid biological division. Yet when Jensen talks about African Americans, the genes he is talking about (or better, a good percentage of them) come from a huge and varied continent. Thus, some analysis of ethnic and genetic diversity in Africa must be germane to the discussion.

Irving Gottesman (1968) in a book edited by Jensen (!) and others, discussed the geographic range of populations in Africa from which slaves were imported to Charleston during the period 1733 to 1807. His figures, taken from a study by William Pollitzer, show the following percentages: Senegambia 20 percent, Winward Coast 23 percent, Gold Coast 13 percent, Whydah-Bennin-Calibar 4 percent, and Angola 23 percent. Such a distribution covers more than a thousand miles of coastline and a territory extending for six hundred miles inland. The range of genetic and ethnic groups tapped was extensive.

In the United States itself, it is a vast simplification to speak of a single black or white genetic population. According to Gottesman: "The variation observed in the studies reviewed ... are probably valid and reflect the genetic heterogeneity of Negro Americans living in different geographical and social distances away from their white neighbors. Such heterogeneity prevents us from speaking validly of an average Negro American with x percentage of white genes" (Gottesman 1968, 20).

In sum, genetic studies of black versus white intelligence (whatever that is) based upon undifferentiated U.S. samples are naive in the extreme because they do not consider distributions of genetic variation in either Africa or the United States.

The problem does not end here. As we have seen, Jensen found an overall intelligence deficit of 15 percentage points among African Americans. He was willing to attribute about half of this difference to environmental influences. The other 7.5 points were then assumed in the report to be due to genetic factors. Yet on page 100 of his 1969a article Jensen states:

> In addition to these factors, something else operates to boost scores five to ten points from first to second test, provided the first test is really the first. When I worked in a psychological clinic, I had to give individual intelligence tests to a variety of children, a good many of whom came from an impoverished background. Usually I felt these children were really brighter than their IQ would indicate. They often appeared inhibited in their responsiveness in the testing situation on their first visit to my office, and when this was the case I usually had them come in on two to four different days for half-hour sessions with me in a "play therapy" room, in which we did nothing more than get acquainted by playing ball, using finger paints, drawing on the blackboard, making things out of clay, and so forth. As soon as the child seemed to be completely at home in this setting, I would retest him on a parallel form of the Stanford-Binet, a boost in IQ of 8 to 10 points or so was the rule; it rarely failed, but neither was the gain very often much above this.

Was Jensen unaware that these are the conditions that are not met by the majority of studies he cites in his report, particularly those drawn together by Shuey (1966)? If the deficit he notes is consistent in disadvantaged children, then all the IQ differences noted between whites and blacks in the United States may be subsumed under a combination of testing errors and environmental effects.

The Jensen Report contains other distortions and misinformation concerning cited data. The following material was extracted by Dr. Carol Vance and myself from a close reading of the Jensen Report and a comparison of his citations with what was actually said in the original sources.

On page 23 of the report, Jensen refers to an article by Cyril Burt (1963). He says that in the general Negro population there is an excess of IQs in the 70–90 range (see Jensens illustration on page 25 of the Report). This excess is explained as the combined effects of severe environmental disadvantage and emotional disturbance, both of which act to depress test scores. On page 27 Jensen says that Burt corrected for this bulge by eliminating scores of those having depressing factors. However, according to the original Burt article there is a lack rather than an excess in 70–90 range (see figure 1 in Burt 1963, 180).

On page 40–41, Jensen cites Cooper and Zubek (1958). He stresses the effects of rearing bright rats in normal and enriched environments and says, "While the strains differ greatly when reared under 'normal' conditions … they do not differ in the least when reared in a 'restricted' environment and only slightly in a 'stimulating environment.'"

Our reading of the same article puts things the other way around. Cooper and Zubek stress the benefits of stimulation to dull animals. "A period of early enriched experiences produces little or no improvement in the learning of the bright animals, whereas dull animals are so benefited by it that they become *equal* to bright animals. On the other hand dull animals raised in a restricted environment suffer no deleterious effects, while bright animals *are* retarded to the level of the dulls in learning ability" (Cooper and Zubek

1958, 162). This result extrapolated to humans supports the hypothesis that deprived environments such as those known to exist for the poor and particularly black Americans should have an effect on IQ scores.

If one compares Jensen's figure 6 on page 50 of the Report with figure 1 of Erlenmeyer-Kimling and Jarvik's (1963) article, from which some of Jensen's data is drawn, we find that Jensen shows only the midpoints for correlations between relatives reared together and reared apart. This emphasis stresses the discreteness and difference among the correlational scores while the original diagram, which shows the range and the median, demonstrates the overlap of correlational range and hence an overlap in the strength of genetic inheritance.

On page 63 Jensen cites a study by Wheeler (1942) of IQ among Tennessee mountain children and notes that environmental improvements do not counteract a decline in IQ of "certain below average groups." Jensen neglects to mention Wheeler's discovery that the decline in IQ is due to the large percentage of held-back children. This factor raised the age level in every grade and therefore depresses IQ scores because these are always correlated with age. When Wheeler separated out the scores of older children in each grade he found that the other children performed normally. Comparing chronologically "true" members of each grade over time (with those overage weeded out) he found that in most years there was no decline. Wheeler says that the chronological IQ drop of 20 points is accounted for by children being repeatedly held back, which means more older children will be found as the grades get higher. Their presence depresses IQ scores most in the higher grades. If Wheeler's logic is followed the decline that Jensen presents as ranging from 103 to 80 points of IQ is reduced to the range 102.76 to 101.00 points!

On page 74 Jensen says that on the average first-born children are superior mentally and *physically* to their siblings. His citation here is Altus (1966). Altus, however, presents no evidence about physical superiority. Altus does cite a study by Huntington showing differences in birth order and achievement that suggests that the differences are caused by superior physical strength of the first born. Altus has the following to say about Huntington's hypothesis: "While his finding is typical of all those reported thus far, his explanation of the linkage is *not* typical: He argued that the first born probably tend to be physically stronger and healthier. … *One may safely accept his data on the birth order of the eminent without accepting his explanation* (Altus 1966, 45; italics mine).

On page 76 Jensen cites Burt's (1961) contention that the inheritance of intelligence conforms to a Mendelian, polygenic model. Yet, he fails to note the wide variety of intelligence within a social class and the fact that children's scores are not as narrow as those of their parents. In fact, if there were no social mobility at all and class were totally static, the result of breeding over five generations would be a disappearance of class means. "After about five generations the differences between the class-means would virtually vanish, and the proportional range within each class would spread out almost as widely as the proportional range of the population as a whole" (Burt 1961, 15).

Other British studies show that IQ scores within social classes have been remarkably stable over the past hundred years. This is because bright lower-class children have moved up the social scale while less bright upper-class children have moved down. Burt's study appears to bear this out for England. Needless to say the notions of bright and less bright used here do not necessarily imply genetic differences, although they might.

Now if the same model is applied to African Americans, intelligence would have remained constant by class if social mobility operated as it is supposed to operate in England. But even in the lowest class, there would be children of above-average intelligence who would rise so that the range of child intelligence would be much wider than adult intelligence. This is the process known to statisticians as "regression to the mean." In any case, Jensen does not mention this aspect of African American performance, that is, unexpected *over* performance.

In any case the model cannot be applied in the United States, because when Jensen published his report little real social mobility existed for African Americans. Even today, in spite of some increased social mobility, African Americans do not experience the same degree of social mobility as whites. Additionally, it is necessary to stress yet again that from the point of view of genetics, blacks in America do not constitute a homogeneous population.

On page 83 Jensen cites research by Heber and Dever on education and habitation of the mentally retarded. While we did not have access to Jensen's original source for this citation (a paper read at the Conference on Sociocultural Aspects of Mental Retardation), we did read a paper by the same authors entitled "Research on Education and Habilitation of the Mentally Retarded." It appeared in *Social-Cultural Aspects of Mental Retardation,* edited by H. C. Haywood (1968).

Jensen says that Heber has estimated that IQs below 75 have a much higher incidence among African American children than among white children at every level of socioeconomic status (Jensen 1969a, 83). We found no statement by the cited authors that African Americans have a higher frequency of IQs under 75 than whites. Furthermore, Heber's study was not a study of race and intelligence but rather a study of a special group of mentally retarded children from a specific neighborhood in Milwaukee that was:

> Characterized by having the city's highest known prevalence of mental retardation among school age children. The nine census tracts which compose this area, known as the "inner core," also have the city's highest rate of dilapidated housing, the greatest population density per living unit, the lowest median income level, and the greatest rate of unemployment. Though comprising no more than five percent of Milwaukee's population it yields about one-third of the mentally retarded known to the schools. (Heber, et al. 1968, 35)

While it is a good bet that this population is composed primarily of African Americans given its socioeconomic profile, the point of Heber's study was to show that much of what passes for mental retardation is caused by *cultural* rather than genetic factors. One might also wish to take into account the degree to which slum dwellers in urban America are exposed to a high percentage of lead poisoning due to the ingestion of lead dust in old, poorly cared for housing. It is a well-known fact that lead poisoning has a strong effect on mental capacity, particularly in children.

On page 86 Jensen cites a study by Geber (1958) that discusses precocity of African American infants. Jensen mentions motor precocity but neglects to mention intellectual development as well. Geber says, "The result of tests showed an all round advance of development over European standards which was greater the younger the child. The precocity was not only in motor development; *it was found in intellectual development also*" (Geber 1958, 186).

The main thrust of Jensen's paper, which has been somewhat buried by popular accounts, is that there is a wide diversity of mental abilities in humans and that educational programs should be tailored to meet the needs of all children. It is difficult to disagree. It is most unfortunate, however, that Jensen pleads this case in the context of a report centered on a flawed discussion of genetics and IQ. In his report Jensen took a fairly safe, if as yet unproved hypotheses—that intelligence is heritable (that it varies among individuals by genetics and environment)—and forced it to carry the burden of a second argument for which there is no acceptable evidence at all.

In 1977, Jensen published an article in *Developmental Psychology* ("Cumulative Deficit in IQ of Blacks in the Rural South"). Here evidence *is* offered in support of an environmental explanation for IQ deficit! In this study Jensen finds substantial decrements in IQ as a linear function of age and relates it to educational differences. This study did not lead Jensen to change his mind, however. Instead he compares his new data with a previous study of children in Berkeley, California. (In the Berkeley study Jensen found no significant decrements in IQ in either his white or black sample.) This led him to conclude:

> However, the present results on Georgia blacks, when viewed in connection with the contrasting results for California blacks, would seem to favor an environmental interpretation of the progressive IQ decrement [in Georgia]. If the progressive IQ decrement were a genetic racial effect per se, it should have shown up in the California blacks as well as in the Georgia blacks, even if one granted that the California blacks have a somewhat larger admixture of Caucasian ancestry than do blacks in Georgia. ... But the California blacks showed a slight, though significant decrement only in verbal IQ, which one might expect to be more susceptible to environmental or cultural effects than nonverbal IQ. The blacks of rural Georgia, whose environmental disadvantages are markedly greater than in the California sample, show considerable decrements in both verbal and nonverbal IQ. (Jensen 1977, 190)

Apparently Jensen refuses to consider the possibility that even in Berkeley, California, the social and educational environments for whites and blacks might be different and have an effect upon IQ test scores. It might be useful, therefore, before closing this chapter to look at some of the sociological situations that affect the performance of children on IQ tests in American society.

Two studies dating from the 1960s (Cohen's work cited above is also relevant) have amplified the role of culture and social group in both test results and academic performance. Katz (1968) varied test conditions for samples of African American students in relation to "subjective probability of success"—that is, how the individual taking the test feels about how he or she will score. Differences in this attitude were then measured against different types of testing situations in which the race of the tester was varied

as well as the kinds of attitude expressed during the testing situation. The theoretical basis for this study comes from the psychological concept of "need achievement" in which "the strength of the impulse to strive for success on a given task is regarded as a joint function of the persons motives to achieve, the subjective problems of success, and the incentive value of success. According to the model, on a test that has evaluative significance (e.g., a classroom test) motivation is maximal when the probability of success is at the .50 level."

Katz notes that in a number of experiments with black college students, individuals tend to underperform on intellectual tasks in the presence of whites. Katz speculates:

> ... that for Negroes who find themselves in predominantly white academic achievement situations, the incentive value of success is high but the expectance of success is low because white standards of achievement are perceived as higher than own-race standards. By the same token, the perceived value of favorable evaluation by a white adult authority is high, but the expectancy of receiving it is low. Therefore, by experimentally controlling Negro subjects' expectancy of success on cognitive tasks it should be possible to produce the same, if not higher, levels of performance in white situations as in all-Negro situations. (Katz 1968, 134)

A group of freshmen were given a test that was described to them as part of a scholastic aptitude test. They were told that their scores would be evaluated in comparison to scores achieved in predominantly white colleges. The students were given a pretest and then told what their chances of success on the actual test would be. One-third were led to believe that they had little chance of meeting the standards for their group, one-third were told that they had an even chance, and one-third were told that they had a good chance. Each of these three groups was then divided into subunits, one given a white tester, the other a black tester. "The results showed that in the low and intermediate probability conditions, performance … was better with a Negro tester, but when the stated probability of achieving the white norm was high, the performance gap between the two tester groups closed" (Katz 1968, 134).

Another test, in which a college with no admission standards other than high school graduation was compared to a college with high relative standards, demonstrated that the effects of varying the race of the tester were the same as in the controlled experiment described above. On the other hand, the scores achieved by students at the selective college were higher when the testers were white, no matter what the probability of success. Katz explained these differences:

> In summary, it appears that Negro students who had been average achievers in high school (the non selective college sample) were discouraged at the prospect of being evaluated by a white person, except when they were made to believe that their chances of success were good. But Negro students with a history of high academic standards (the selective college sample) seemed to be stimulated by the challenge of white evaluation, regardless of the objective probability of success. (Katz 1968, 138)

Katz generalized his results in terms of differences in socialization between lower- and middle-class children. "The present assumption is that lower class children … because they have received less parental approval for early intellectual efforts remain more dependent than middle class children on social reinforcement when performing academic tasks" (Katz 1968, 138).

While Katz's experiments do not relate directly to intelligence testing they do go a long way toward explaining why certain sociological groups respond as they do to education. The problem is complicated since it involves the motivation of the individual, which is partly a product of home experience but also of the students' conception of the expectations of teachers defined partially in terms of race. The common educational experience of lower-class African Americans with white *and* black teachers is often discouraging. This problem is amplified by the environmental setting in which the probability of success is lowered by the experience of daily life. All these factors would act to lower success in any testing situation.

The process of learning in children is even more subtle than Katz's findings would indicate. A study of performance of children in the San Francisco schools supports the hypothesis that a teacher's attitude toward the success of a child will have a profound effect on the outcome of the educational process.

The experimenters established the expectation in teachers that certain children in the school chosen at *random* would show *superior* performance in the coming school year. This expectation was established by testing the children on an intelligence test and informing teachers of the results. The use of this test in the pre-experimental situation had the added advantage of providing a true measure since the children could be reexamined with the same test later in the experiment. A casual method of informing the teachers about the presence of "potential spurters" was used. "The subject was brought up at the end of the first staff meeting with the remark 'By the way, in case you're interested in who did what in those tests they were done for Harvard"' (Rosenthal and Jacobson 1968, 22).

All the children were retested four months after school started, at the end of the school year, and finally in May of the following year. As the children matured, they were given tests appropriate to their level. These were designed to evaluate both verbal skills and reasoning. The results showed that children who were expected to do well by teachers showed the greatest intellectual gains. An unanticipated finding of the study was that when teachers were asked to evaluate the undesignated children, many of whom had gained in IQ during the year, they tended to evaluate them negatively. The more they gained the less favorably they were seen!

Since writing his report Arthur Jensen has continued his work in the field of IQ and race. It seems to me that in these works Jensen ignores all the recent evidence for the nonexistence of racial categories. Among his recent works are Jensen 1974, 1977, 1978a, 1978b, 1980, 1984a, 1984b, 1985, 1986, 1987a, 1987b, 1989, 1990, 1992, 1993a, 1993b. In 1999 he wrote a laudatory comment in the pretext pages of J. Philippe Rushton's book on race, IQ, and brain size [...]. In none of his works that I have seen does Jensen take account of the evidence against the existence of race as a valid category in the classification of humans. Nor does he seriously discuss the many studies that support the flexibility of IQ in the context of environmental differences. Instead he continues to argue as he has always done, relating race to IQ with the persistent claim that the average black is inferior in intelligence to the average white. To my knowledge he has never cleared up the contradiction between his understanding of the concept of heritability, which, as noted above, he admits does not allow for intergroup comparisons, and his consistent use of heritability statistics for samples of whites applied to blacks.

In the next chapter I will discuss the IQ argument from the perspective of Konrad Lorenz and Robert Ardrey. Lorenz was a Nobel Prize winner and internationally acclaimed biologist, and, although his research concerned fish and birds, he ventured well beyond his competence to speculate, in a series of popular books and articles, about human behavior. Robert Ardrey authored three bestsellers, popularizing Lorenz's ideas concerning our species. Although Lorenz's and Ardrey wrote before the official founding of sociobiology by E. O. Wilson, their extreme form of biological determinism, based primarily on extrapolations from nonhuman animal behavior to humans, stands between the vulgar biological determinism, of the nineteenth century and the explosion of a somewhat more scientific form in the last quarter of the twentieth. Both Lorenz and Ardrey preached the doctrine of racial purity and both argued for the inferiority of certain races.

The Impact of Nineteenth-Century Scientific Racism on Adolf Hitler and National Socialism

An Introduction to "Nation and Race"

By D. Paul Sweeney, Jr.

● ●

Nineteenth-Century Trends: The Rise of Scientific Racism

Long before Cyril Burt (1930s–1960), Arthur Jensen (1969), and the controversial book *The Bell Curve* (1994) provided some continuity to the perspective that race and intelligence are inter-correlated, and that intelligence is a hereditary trait, the overt racism of the nineteenth century formulated several of the now tired "arguments" still in use by the late twentieth century to explain racial differences. In particular, what were the motives of these aforementioned studies? Some have pointed out (see the Alland "Race and IQ" reading in this book) that the Jensen Report was really an attack on inner-city school programs in the wake of the Civil Rights Act (1964). The premise was, if intelligence is more or less fixed within a race, with a "few exceptions," then why spend money on education and social programs to elevate social status through education?[1]

In general, these modern studies focused on "class" differences and twins in England (Burt) and black and white differences in intelligence (Jensen) using statistics and an ambiguous concept called the "heritability" of a trait. When Richard Herrstein and Charles Murray published *The Bell Curve*, Stephen Jay Gould commented in his rebuttal that "[t]he argument is old, un-complicated, and familiar; the mathematics, though labored through several hundred pages by iterating example after example, represent *one study* [emphasis added], appropriately simple in concept and easy to understand."[2]

In other words, like so many studies that preceded *The Bell Curve*, bias, however con-scious or unconscious, shaped the "findings." *The Bell Curve* followed on the heels of the Newt Gingrich-led Congress in 1994 that was dead-set on shaving, or even eliminating, social programs for people in genuine need. Another blast from the past? If "lower class" is often a euphemism for poor whites or non-whites who are dependent on welfare, one implication racism posits is that maybe they should learn to "work harder." Finally, refrains from biased writings and social theories such as Oscar Lewis's *Culture of Poverty* (1959)

---

1 Stephen Jay Gould, *The Mismeasure of Man, Revised and Expanded Edition* (New York, NY: W.W. Norton, 1996), 31–33; Alexander Alland, Jr., *Race in Mind: Race, IQ, and Other Racisms* (New York, NY: Palgrave, 2002), 10–11.

2 Gould, *Mismeasure of Man*, 31–33; Alland, *Race in Mind*, 148–152.

still figure heavily in the present dialog on race and are recycled often in political rhetoric.

Where, then, did "science" become a political reality? We have seen previously in this book how Spain, preoccupied with the purity of blood (*limpieza de sangre*), shaped racial laws in the Iberian Peninsula as well as how New Spain was affected by *limpieza de sangre*, genealogies, gender, and religious and racial considerations in the eighteenth century (Martínez). What follows is an overview of how science, pseudo-science, and overt racism created the prevalence of **cultural anti-Semitism** in Europe, thereby paving the way for Adolf Hitler in the twentieth century.

Even before **social Darwinism** was conceptualized, those given to overt racism asked questions about whether there are in fact inborn and unchangeable differences among racial groups.[3] The long-standing belief that a hierarchy of races exists stems at least as far back as the Elizabethan concept of The Great Chain of Being [see Fig. 2 in Ch. 1]. Additionally, the human habit of classification, or **folk taxonomy**, also played a role in how nineteenth-century intellectuals viewed their respective societies and the world. In a backdrop of imperialism, colonial expansion, industrialization, and continuing African slavery in the Americas, was an undercurrent of nationalism and a desire to establish a national identity, often along racial lines. This *zeitgeist* was not limited to Germany, however. Indeed, all of Western Europe, as well as the United States and many other nations, including Cuba, the Dominican Republic, Argentina, Chile, and Brazil, among others, accepted the "science" of the day to varying degrees, which informed their respective social theories. In many cases, the outcomes often had grave consequences for those considered inferior by the dominant group.[4]

Another significant trend in the middle nineteenth century was the archaeological preoccupation with finding "indigenous origins" entertained by many countries. Additionally, the growing field of physical anthropology, for which archaeology

was a companion discipline, applied the concepts of Darwin and others who will be discussed presently. In general, the world was divided into five groups, but later revised into three racial stocks: Whites, Yellows, and Blacks. As is often the case, the tendency to place White on top of the hierarchy stems as far back as the Spanish *Reconquista* and Conquest of the Americas (*sistema de castas*). In Germany by the 1870s, fascination with indigenous origins and archaeological findings to support the myth of a Nordic race led to an amalgam of "scientific" beliefs; these beliefs, mixed with ideology and distributed by early forms of social media, contributed to a phenomenon in Western Europe best described as cultural anti-Semitism.[5]

Toward a Hierarchy of Races in the Nineteenth Century

Gobineau and Scientific Racism. A leading nineteenth-century figure who thought that races could be categorized into a hierarchy came from France. In his extensive writings on race that filled many ponderous volumes, Joseph Arthur Comte de Gobineau (1816–1882) took an unambiguous position that proved to be widely influential, as will be revealed. In his own words, Gobineau stated:

> The idea of an innate and permanent difference in the moral and mental endowments of the various groups of the human species, is one of the most ancient, as well as universally adopted opinions. With few exceptions, and these mostly in our times, it has formed the basis of almost all political theories, and has been the fundamental maxim of government of every nation, great or small. The prejudices of country have no other causes; each nation believes in its own superiority over its neighbors,

---

3 Gould, *Mismeasure of Man*, 379.
4 Richard J. Evans, *The Coming of the Third Reich* (New York, NY: Penguin Press, 2004), 33.

5 Evans, *Coming of the Third Reich*, 33; Bettina Arnold, "'*Arierdämmerung*' Race and Archaeology in Nazi Germany." *World Archaeology* 38, no. 1 (March 2006): 8–31, accessed November 29, 2014, http://www.jstor.org/stable/40023592.

and very often different parts of the same nation regard each other with contempt.[6]

Racism, in short, was an academic position throughout the nineteenth century, and Gobineau influenced Richard Wagner and Frederick Niezsche; he also inspired a social movement known as Gobinism. However, his most significant disciple was the Englishman Houston Stewart Chamberlain (1855–1927), who, in turn, transformed the racial theories developed by Adolf Hitler. What was so significant about Gobineau's perspective that it shaped many social policies and anticipated the racial state that Nazi Germany (1933–1945) later became? What follows next is a brief overview of how "science," informed by racism, became "commonsense" in the minds of racists.[7]

As echoed in the *Mein Kampf* excerpt "Nation and Race," Gobineau's basic premise was this: "the fate of civilizations is largely determined by racial composition, with decline and fall usually attributable to dilution of pure stocks by interbreeding [miscegenation]."[8] Gobineau feared that France, if weakened by interbreeding, would strengthen the hereditary enemy, Germany. Further, "Aryans" (Gobineau's term) could maintain control only if they avoided miscegenation with intellectually inferior stocks of "yellows" and "blacks." Additionally, Gobineau felt that only these three significant races existed, thereby revising Blumenbach's earlier classification of five discrete types, whence the color-based categories. Moreover, in the United States, Gobineau's works are believed to have impacted the *Dred Scott v. Sanford* (1847) case prior to the American Civil War (1860–1865).[9]

How scientific was Gobineau's evidence? In his own words, he explained that "most people" believed in innate inequality, and careful reading should center on the word *opinions* in the block quote above. Further, he, without any data,

wrote that "… unequal in intellectual capacity, in personal beauty, and in physical strength … I am prepared to admit—and to admit without proof—anything of that sort … that, among the chiefs of the rude negroes of Africa, there could be found a considerable number of active and vigorous minds …" that equaled those of the lower class stocks of Europe.[10] If such opinions have no validity scientifically, then how could a measurement be established? Statistics and mathematics then factored into the racist and biased opinions, to "prove" intellectual, moral, and physical differences existed between the races. What is striking, though, is how often this structure of ideas has been similar across the centuries.[11]

While Gobineau sought a mathematical basis for group differences, his work, along with the craniometrical studies of Paul Broca (1824–1880) and others, gave racist-based science a new focus: on the shapes and sizes of skulls, limbs, and other body part measurements. Using craniometry and anthropometry methodology, Gobineau claimed to have located black destiny: "The darker races, are the lowest on the scale. The shape of the pelvis has a character of animalism, which is imprinted on the individuals of that race ere their birth, and seems to pretend their destiny … [and] [t]he negroes' narrow and receding forehead seems to mark him as inferior in reasoning capacity."[12]

One interpretation of this "finding" led to folk notions that blacks (and the Irish) originated from monkeys, and racist caricature often depicted them as such: monkeys and brutish ape men were shown threatening white women, which "proved" to some that they were not of the same race as "whites" or "yellows." For Hitler, Jews also fit into this diminished category of humanity.

Archaeology, Race, and Nationalism

If archaeology under the Nazi regime was farfetched, exaggerated, often misrepresented, or otherwise twisted to fit prevailing mythology, its

---

6 Gobineau, quoted in Gould, *Mismeasure of Man*, 379.
7 Ibid., 379–380.
8 Gobineau, quoted in Gould, *Mismeasure of Man*, 380.
9 Ibid., 380.

10 Ibid., 381.
11 Ibid., 381–382.
12 Gobineau, quoted in Gould, *Mismeasure of Man*, 383.

primary function was to support Hitler's "racial hygiene" agenda, which was central to the ideas expressed in "Nation and Race." As with the many examples that follow, Hitler's ideas predated Hitler, the man. Ultimately, the preoccupation of National Socialism was the assumed inherent inferiority of the Jews and other subhuman groups, or, *untermensch*. Concurrent with the writings of Gobineau, Charles Darwin, Francis Galton, Henry Herbert Goddard, and others, nineteenth-century scientific racism focused primarily on the presumed anthropological differences between races, and that in turn shaped the racial hierarchy concepts, followed by gender-based hierarchies.[13]

The Nordic Type Concept. Emerging from the writings of the period were two concepts near and dear to racists, anti-Semites, and white supremacists: A Nordic race "existed," which was considered to be the most superior, yet vulnerable to all the world's races, *and* the term "Aryan" was used to denote this master race. From these ideas came questions about hereditary traits. For example, how did genetic mutations in human morphological variation contribute to the Nordic archetype: light-skinned and light-eyed? It is here that **polygenist** thought applied erroneously assumed that the differences in races could be explained by separate trajectories, which separated the beautiful, intelligent, blond and blue-eyed Nordic-Aryans from the "ugly dark peoples."[14]

Where Nazism departed slightly from this premise was a pathological preoccupation that outweighed even *limpieza de sangre* in many regards. "Science" mingled with acute anti-Semitism, and while Adolf Hitler is oblique in mentioning Jews in his diatribe, "Nation and Race," the "real enemy" of the Aryan-Germanic race was not simply the Jews, but also the genetic and cultural swamping that "clearly" was a conspiracy between "Catholic Rome, the Romance language-speaking nations and the Slavs ..." Additionally,

and most importantly, the "enemy within" that threatened German racial purity came specifically "from assimilated Jews and other undesirable racial elements."[15]

This story emerged after the formation of a German state after 1815 reawaked the "Jewish question." When combined with prejudice and discrimination, this created the laws and policies enacted to restrict Jewish civic rights, which were the definition of racism: power plus prejudice. Like during the Middle Ages, Jews were once again denigrated as an "alien" race, culturally outside of German stock, but they were separated along racial lines this time, not religious ones. This ambivalence can be termed Judaeophobia or anti-Semitism; in any case, it symbolized the special hatred for Jews that Christian Europe created and nurtured for nearly two thousand years. To "support" scientific views, German archaeology and physical anthropology used the writings of Gobineau, Charles Darwin (1809–1882), and later Ernst Haeckel (1834–1919) and Chamberlain to direct their inquiries on how to maintain a master race.[16]

One fundamental principle of the National Socialist racial theory was *Arierdämmerung der Nordrass* (sole validity of the Nordic Race), a program fixated on the "superior" long skulls and interracial "contamination" caused by the "inferior" round skulls. A humorous jab at the ridiculousness of craniometric pseudo-science is shown in one scene in the film *Europa, Europa* (1991). Next is a discussion on how scientific racism evolved to fit the views of anti-Semites.

The Role of Literature and Social Anti-Semitism

Among the many claims and themes in the writings of nineteenth-century authors, especially if they leaned towards anti-Semitism, was their profound effect and influence on the political mainstream in Europe. As evidenced during the Dreyfus affair (1894–1906) in France, an outbreak

13 Arnold, *"Arierdämmerung,"* 8–9; Amos Morris-Reich, "Project, Method, and the Racial Characteristics of Jews: A Comparison of Franz Boas and Hans F. K. Günther." *Jewish Social Studies: History, Culture, Society, n.s.* 13, no. 1 (Fall 2006): 136–137, 142–143.
14 Ibid., 9.

15 Ibid.
16 Ibid., 9–10.

of virulent popular anti-Semitism spread. Farther afield in Tsarist Russia, pogroms against Jews led to the creation of the Pale of Settlement (see Map 13.1), a vast zone stretching from the Baltic Sea in the north to the Black Sea in the south. There, in this segregated region, Jews were ritually attacked during Holy Week as retribution for one of anti-Semitism's oldest claims, that Jews killed Christ.[17] Taken further, into politics, something called a "Jewish spirit" entered the discourse. The subtext of this alleged "spirit" generally pinned the words "subversive" and "excessive" upon Jews to highlight negative stereotypes. In other words, Jews had too much sway or representation in society, in sectors such as banking, journalism, or legal positions. If this sounds like the long-standing belief of a Jewish plot to take over the world's governments and markets and **blood libel**, it is indeed the premise of these recurring beliefs and stereotypes about Jews since The First Crusade (1096). Sometime in the late nineteenth or early twentieth century, a work emerged from Tsarist Russia that claimed to be "proof" of this old lie. It was the alleged minutes taken at a "secret meeting" of Jewish Sages (Elders) in a plot to disrupt the global markets and subversively take over the Western world's government. Widely distributed and published after the First World War, *The Protocols of the Elders of Zion* was translated into German, French, English, Arabic, and other languages and published in the United Stated by the Henry Ford Press, until it was determined to be a clumsy forgery hatched by Tsarist secret police. Not everyone, however, accepted that its claims were fabricated. It is known that Hitler read the tract after the war, possibly on Alfred Rosenberg's recommendation, and its influence on him is evidenced in the symbiosis of racist literature espoused in *Mein Kampf*.[18]

Map 13.1: Percentage of Jews in the Pale of Settlement

Therefore, the above circumstances and situations, when combined with a selective or simplified understanding of "science" and social Darwinism, led to the escalations of rhetoric by many authors who advocated Jewish exclusion (Wilhelm Marr), vehement violence against Jews along biological lines (Julius Langbehn), or "complete" assimilation into German society (Richard Wagner). All of these mens' writings, and those of Ludwig Schemann, who was influenced by them, helped popularize Gobineau's term "Aryan," so important to popular German indigenous national myths and Wagner's operas. Schemann, a devotee of Gobinism, founded the Gobineau Society in 1894.[19] What is important to understand is that this background is relevant not only to the concept of race shown in Chapter One, or the justification of slavery, but also to how words and ideas can be synthesized into a race-based ideology of hate. Hitler's collecting and reading of "scientific" works and his adaptation of radical anti-Semitism will be traced next, inasmuch as it is possible.

In his 1873 pamphlet *The Victory of Jewdom over Germandom viewed from a Non-Consensional Standpoint*, Wilhelm Marr made a contribution to future anti-Semitic thought he did not live to see. Like other popular writers and intellectuals,

17   Ronald Takaki, *A Different Mirror: A History of Multicultural America* (New York, NY: Back Bay Books, 2008), 262–263; Evans, *Coming of the Third Reich*, 31.
18   Evans, *Coming of the Third Reich*, 31, 178; Robert G. L. Waite. *The Psychopathic God: Adolf Hitler* (New York, NY: Signet, 1978), 140-147; Jacob Katz, *From Prejudice to Destruction: Anti-Semitism, 1700–1933* (Cambridge, MA: Harvard University Press, 1980), 313.

19   Evans, *Coming of the Third Reich*, 33.

Marr desired German art to return to its racial or indigenous roots, which also preoccupied archaeologists at the time. Additionally, as the age of Industrialization hit its first economic downturn in the 1880s–1890s, the turmoil spawned much "domestication of anti-Semitism," according to the historian Richard J. Evans. Further, this rise of vitriolic language regarding Jews had an imprint on German society, and it eventually opened the door for National Socialism.[20]

Chamberlain's Vision of a Religious and Racial Struggle. As mentioned above, Schemann founded the Gobineau Society, but it proved to be a failure as an organization and political movement. However, its influence can be found in Chamberlain's book *The Foundations of the Nineteenth Century* (1900). Chamberlain synthesized the many racial perspectives that crisscrossed the Atlantic and pitched a perspective that history was "a struggle for supremacy between German races and Jewish races." His belief that only these two groups had been able to keep a semblance of "racial purity" "in a world of miscegenation" can be seen clearly in Hitler's chapter on "Nation and Race."[21]

For Hitler, and others of like mind, Chamberlain had the greatest impact, according to Evans, on pitting "heroic and cultured Germans" (Aryans) against the "ruthless and mechanistic Jews."[22] In this regard, by elevating Jews into a cosmic threat against human society, Chamberlain's hyperbole linked a religious struggle to a racial struggle. Also endemic to his reasoning, Christianity was quintessentially German, and Jesus, despite all the evidence to the contrary, was *Aryan*, not Jewish. Readers of his work were impressed by the appeal to "science" to support the racist views. However, for the purposes of this study, Chamberlain's greatest contribution was fusing anti-Semitism and racism with social Darwinism, which deeply embedded cultural anti-Semitism in Western Europe to greater degrees than before.[23]

In essence, Darwin's law of natural selection, where the fittest animals and plants survived and the weakest or less well adapted died off, led to the notion of improving the species. When social Darwinism was applied to humans, it is easy to see how miscegenation could be viewed as harmful to a dominant "master race." Ultimately, Chamberlain's book made a tremendous impact on Adolf Hitler, and it articulated some of the key ideas assembled by National Socialism and contributed to the Final Solution of the Jewish Question during the Second World War (1939–1945).[24]

Hitler in Vienna and Munich, 1908–1914

While no attempt is made to supplant existing biographies about Adolf Hitler, it is important to look at his personal life and period of identity crisis during his late adolescence to fully grasp how the preceding discussion can be applied. While much has been written about Hitler since 1945, not all of the stories or knowledge professed can be fully considered creditable, in part because of his outlier existence in Vienna after the death of his mother, Klara, in 1908.

Toward a Psychoanalysis of Hitler. The "psychohistorian" Robert G. L. Waite described the 1908–1918 period in Hitler's life as an identity crisis, which fits Erik Erikson's human life-cycle studies' emphasis on personality development. Unlike with traditional psychoanalysis, people are not on a fixed course in life by the age of four or five, nor even affected by one period in their lives. Nevertheless, some periods do indeed shape a person more than others. In particular, the late adolescent to early adulthood span is where an "identity crisis" *and* "identity formation" takes form. They are not to be used interchangeably, however, because in the late teenage years

---

20 Ibid., 32.
21 Ibid., 33.
22 Ibid., 33–34.
23 Evans, *Coming of the Third Reich*, 33–34; Lucy S. Dawidowicz, *The War Against the Jews, 1933–1945* (New

York, NY: Bantam Books, 1986), 44–45.
24 Evans, *Coming of the Third Reich*, 34–35; Alan Bullock, *Hitler: A Study in Tyranny* (New York, NY: Harper & Row, 1962), 374.

individuals experience a *crisis*, but identity *formation* continues to develop.[25]

Relevant to this survey is the period associated with Hitler's growing pains. Associated behaviors in this stage of life *could* include doubts about sexual effectiveness, a desire to dominate someone completely, and a period of torturous self-consciousness and inability to work. Additionally, snobbish disdain for others can be a symptom, and even a sense of alienation and a desire to drop out or disappear so no one can see whether the individual has succeeded or failed in life. Moreover, music can become extremely important for someone going through an identity crisis, because music can express unarticulated feelings and focus emotions. It is this latter factor that is especially relevant to Hitler during his life in Vienna.[26]

As noted previously, the composer Richard Wagner exemplified the Indo-Germanic mythology, with its fantastic tales of gods, demi-gods, heroes, and knights in shining armor. Wagner's anti-Semitism too was on display in his writings, but for Hitler, it was the music that fulfilled his inner turmoil like a religious experience. The uplifting exhilaration he felt when attending Wagner performances at the Vienna opera later gave credence to his sentiment "that Wagner was one of the few people who ever understood him."[27]

Taking Erikson further, one key element of the identity crisis is the "moratorium," a period of withdrawal that precedes the individual's career path or destiny. For Hitler, the moratorium period had duality: his life in Vienna and Munich and serving on or near the front lines during the First World War (1914–1918). Often, a moratorium period is paradoxical. For example, many great figures of history had disparate temperaments and accomplishments, and while all had historic achievements of some kind, there was little in their early lives and careers to suggest future greatness.[28]

After the death of his mother, and other difficult life events still to come, Hitler demonstrated an unusual toughness and resilience. Because of this personality trait, it was a good example of how his will triumphed over adversity. Along the way, however, development of a sense of purpose must occur, according to Erikson. As is often the case, a hunger for ideology shapes the preoccupation of a person in the identity crisis of late adolescence. In Hitler's case, this drive for purpose in life centered on two things: anti-Semitism and racial nationalism.[29] Recent scholarship has challenged this time frame, but at some point Hitler did tie the two concepts together.

Hitler's new direction during his years in Vienna would, on the surface, appear to be the pipedreams of a layabout who lived on the fringe of the Bohemian movement in that city. With all of the bravado of a Wagnerian fantasy, it appears that at some point Hitler adopted a "messianic" notion of self-importance, except instead of focusing on saving souls, it evolved into a desire to single-handedly destroy the "Jewish Peril" and create a racially pure Germany. Not content with racial purity alone, Hitler believed Germany needed a "living space," or *Lebensraum*, which would be acquired largely at the expense of the Slavic peoples in the east. It is this last point especially that Hitler borrowed heavily from Chamberlain.[30] When one door closes, another opens, the saying goes. In Hitler's case, the door that slammed hard and fast in his face was the rejection of his application to the Viennese Academy of Fine Arts. Thwarted in his hopes to become an artist, he experienced the double tragedy of his mother's death to breast cancer. In the best estimation of the literature about Hitler in this period, it was in Vienna, around 1908, that he became a fanatical anti-Semite.[31] However, this period is now in dispute because recent research downplays some

---

25 Waite, *Psychopathic God*, 222.
26 Ibid., 222–223.
27 Ibid., 223.
28 Waite, *Psychopathic God*, 223–224; Brendan Simms, "Against 'a world of enemies': The Impact of the First World

War on the Development of Hitler's Ideology." *International Affairs* 90, no. 2 (2014): 319, 326–327.
29 Waite, *Psychopathic God*, 224; Bullock, *A Study in Tyranny*, 38–40.
30 Waite, *Psychopathic God*, 224; Evans, *Coming of the Third Reich*, 34; Simms, "Against 'a world of enemies,'" 334–336.
31 Waite, *Psychopathic God*, 224–225; Simms, "Against 'a world of enemies,'" 318–319, 327–331.

of Hitler's claims in *Mein Kampf* and places this manifestation around late 1919.

Nonetheless, one significant factor in Hitler's embrace of virulent anti-Semitism is that it was cathartic for him and deeply satisfying psychologically. About this highly vulnerable point in his life, he later reflected in *Mein Kampf* that "[t]his was the time ... in which the greatest change I ever was to experience took place in me. From a cosmopolite I had turned into a fanatical anti-Semite."[32] At the age of nineteen Hitler claimed that he cultivated and devoured anything and everything that smattered of racist, nationalist, and scientific explanations of differences between the races, but books on architecture have also been documented. As summarized earlier, the significant scientific racists and their derivatives featured heavily in his reading time. It is noteworthy that Hitler focused most heavily on the "differences" between the Nordic-Aryan race and the "lesser races," as well as the perceived threat of Jewish conspiracies to take over the world, especially between August and November 1919, when the first recorded speech on capitalism and the Jewish question was given.[33]

Anti-Semitism and Self-Discovery

Amongst others, one of the pamphlets that especially attracted and inspired Hitler's fantasy world of subhuman predators threatening racially pure white women included an illustrated, lurid, semi-pornographic series called *Ostara: Briefbucherei der blonden Mannessechtler* (*Newsletter of the Blond Champions of Man's Rights*), also translated as (*Newspaper for Blond People*). His vision, or maybe it was still a fantasy at this stage, of killing all or some of the Jews seemed to go beyond the current trend advocating exclusion or expulsion that was prevalent in most anti-Semitic discourse. Whatever the case may have been, *Ostara* was published in Vienna by Lanz von Liebenfels, and

the recurring theme from issue to issue was an epic struggle between blond Aryan archetypical heroes and dark, ethnically ambiguous hairy ape-men who symbolized the threat to racial purity. Like much inflammatory art about racial matters, it depicted scantily clad Aryan women constantly needing to be saved from the hairy menace with demonic countenances and bad intent. *Ostara* was widely available in Vienna's newsstands, and Hitler started to collect each forthcoming issue; nevertheless, its appeal was not widespread. In 1909 Hitler contacted Liebenfels directly to obtain missing back issues. Flattered, the publisher complied, free of charge.[34]

While *Ostara* made the existential struggle of races tangible in comic book style, another plausible aspect of Hitler's transformation from a moratorium phase to one of commitment (to an ideology) is that this was one way he dealt with Klara's death. Escaping into a fantasy world of Wagnerian-*Ostara* proportions can be reasonably viewed as two defense mechanisms at play: displacement and projection. First, Jews (dark, hairy ape-men) provided a convenient scapegoat and could be blamed easily for all of his teenage angst and suffering, guilt and despair. Jews were to blame for everything that was wrong in his life: his failure as an artist, the Jewish doctor who failed to save his dying mother, and later, the German defeat in the First World War.[35] However, as Simms noted, there was no overt outward reflection of this anti-Semitism until at least 1919.

It is important to mention that the sexually charged ape-men in *Ostara* were *not* always portrayed as Jews. Nevertheless, Liebenfels editorialized anti-Semitic messages in each issue.

For instance, one issue contained the following sentiment: "we would never dream of preaching pogroms, because they will come without encouragement." Moreover, *sterilization* was the method advocated by the publisher; in particular, the "castration knife" alone would resolve the Jewish question. After all, if a species cannot

---

32 Hitler, quoted in Waite, *Psychopathic God*, 225.

33 Waite, *Psychopathic God*, 225; Dawidowicz, *War Against the Jews*, 16, 20; Simms, "Against 'a world of enemies,'" 326–330.

34 Dawidowicz, *The War Against the Jews*, 19; Evans, *Coming of the Third Reich*, 37.

35 Waite, *Psychopathic God*, 228–229; Simms, "Against 'a world of enemies,'" 326–330.

reproduce, then in time it will become extinct. In other words, social Darwinism combined with a little assistance would hasten natural selection.[36]

As discussed previously, Hitler's private library contained a significantly large percentage of anti-Semitic works. As he later wrote in *Mein Kampf*, terms that clearly came from his influences regularly appear, such as Jews being a "mongrelized breed," amongst others. Vienna, it seems, was a hotbed for anti-Semitism. What is uncertain, however, is whether Hitler actually looked high and low to absorb everything he could as his fanaticism flourished.[37]

Growing Nationalism and Political Awakening

During his residency in Vienna, Hitler was also exposed to two particular political movements that held significant sway in the pre-war years: Georg Ritter von Schönerer's Pan-Germans and Karl Lueger's Christian Socials. While the Pan-Germans were played out by 1908, anti-Semitism was a prerequisite for their ideology.[38] Similarly, Lueger put anti-Semitism at the forefront of his party, which originally formed in the turbulent 1880s in Austria and Germany. While neither group remained long in Hitler's favor, he did gain something from their philosophies. For example, in *Mein Kampf* he mentioned that the Pan-Germans were correct about one thing: they understood the "importance" of the "racial problem" between Germans and Jews, not the lesser consideration of differences between religious ideas.[39]

Regarding Lueger's Christian Socials movement, Hitler liked their tactics, but felt that they had the "wrong" approach to anti-Semitism because the "danger" that Jews posed was too rooted in early nineteenth-century thought (discussed in the chapter on Nazi Germany). To summarize, early thinking about the Jewish question centered on their religious differences from Christians and advocated conversion followed by assimilation into German society. Moreover, Hitler disliked the way Lueger either downplayed or overlooked the "obvious" racial factor. In essence, Hitler felt the Christian Socialists were fake anti-Semites, not nearly extreme enough for his liking.[40] Again, this appears to be a later, possibly exaggerated view expressed to impress his followers with how long and fully committed he was to National Socialism before it was a reality.

Munich and the First World War. After the period of claimed indoctrination in Vienna (currently in dispute and revision by historians), Hitler wandered to Munich, the capital of Bavaria in Germany, to complete his self-styled destiny and crisis of identity. In May 1913 he turned twenty-four, alone, with no friends or family, nor even a career or occupation. His racist "studies" continued, but in Munich he began the transformation from a passive "armchair racist" to an aggressive and passionate public speaker for anyone who would listen in beer halls and taverns. By this point in his psychosexual development, Hitler left the world of fantasy somewhat and tried his hand as a fledgling messianic prophet who preached that Germany's redemption would only come if Germandom was "saved" from the inferior races, including, but not limited to the Jews. Therefore, the influences of *Ostara*, Chamberlain, Gobineau, and others are evident in his long-winded rants and raves. Eventually the police in Munich took notice and concluded that although his message was consistent, it was non-threatening.[41]

Munich and Military Service: The Final Phase of the Identity Crisis

Between 1913–1914, before the outbreak of war, Hitler affirmed his support of the National Socialist concept, but another object of hate manifested itself, which led to the conclusion that

---

36 Liebenfels quoted in Dawidowicz, *The War Against the Jews*, 9.
37 Ibid.
38 Ibid., 10.
39 Dawidowicz, *The War Against the Jews*, 11; Bullock, *A Study in Tyranny*, 44–46.

40 Dawidowicz, *The War Against the Jews*, 11; Bullock, *A Study in Tyranny*, 45–46.
41 Dawidowicz, *The War Against the Jews*, 12; Simms, "Against 'a world of enemies,'" 318–320.

Germany should crush Marxism. After all, Karl Marx was a "Jewish subversive" in his worldview. This was prior to the Bolshevik Revolution (1917), however, but Marx and Bolshevism already equated to "Jewish Peril" in many minds, not just Hitler's. This aspect of his sociopolitical development is also challenged, but that Hitler did feel that way later on cannot be doubted. The real mystery is when exactly this connection was made. Hitler claimed that it was in Vienna, where he longed for a strong leader, a *Führer* who would restore Germany's racial purity, but the point at which Hitler decided that *he* was destined to be a savior seems to have taken place after the war. Did Hitler, in his head, believe that he was Germany's future hero?[42]

The reality, though, was that in 1914 National Socialism did not exist, and Hitler did not have even one friend or follower. Nonetheless, his young mind was still receptive to ideology and symbolism. In Munich especially he absorbed the Teutonic vocabulary and symbols such as the swastika. Before Nazism, the swastika was already in use by nationalist parties to symbolize Nordic-Aryan racial purity, so it is clear that Hitler identified and assimilated all racist and political rhetoric, along with numerology, neo-pagan imagery, and the power of propaganda.

It is not certain which of the extremist anti-Semitic groups he may have joined, if any, because his tendency to walk away before making lasting relationships was still a characteristic of his personality in 1914.[43]

Whatever it was he hoped to accomplish in Munich was placed on hold when the First World War started on August 1, 1914. War came because the assassination of Arch-Duke Ferdinand in Sarajevo by a radical Serbian nationalist broke an uneasy peace. A combination of nationalism, imperialism, colonial expansion, and alliances pitted Europe against itself. An old photograph shows Hitler smiling in the crowd and supportive of the war announcement in Munich. Ultimately, Hitler, an Austrian citizen by birth, was granted admittance to the German military, and he joined a Bavarian regiment that saw extensive combat on the Western Front.[44]

Post-War Political Upheaval in German: The Weimar Republic Begins

Hitler's combat record was evidently resplendent if his medals are any indication. Wounded in France, he received the Iron Cross Second Class. Upon his return to the front he was wounded again and promoted by his Jewish commander to the rank of lance corporal. Later in the war, on the night of October 13–14, 1918, the British preceded an attack with an artillery barrage containing poison gas. Hitler fell victim and was temporarily blinded. As he convalesced in a military hospital, he read about the German capitulation on November 11. That same month, Bavaria revolted because of how the war ended: the monarchy was overthrown, the unfair armistice imposed terms of unconditional surrender, and democracy was forced upon the country by the victors. As the horror of the catastrophe resonated across Germany, in Hitler's mind this was all the work of the Jews and Freemasons, and as new scholarship indicates, anti-capitalism as represented by the United States (which he believed was under Jewish control).[45]

Post-war Germany was anything but peaceful because the humiliating terms of the armistice emasculated the proud Prussian military tradition. Forbidden were a German navy over a certain tonnage, submarines, an air force, and an army, except for a small national guard. Worst of all, however, were the large annual payments imposed to serve as war reparations, and this drained the already weak economy. In the aftermath, political upheaval and political assassinations were rampant in the Weimar years, and of all the German states, Bavaria was the most radical and violent, as

---

42 Dawidowicz, *The War Against the Jews*, 12–13; Simms, "Against 'a world of enemies,'" 318–320.

43 Dawidowicz, *The War Against the Jews*, 13.

44 Dawidowicz, *The War Against the Jews*, 13; Bullock, *A Study in Tyranny*, 50–52; Simms, "Against 'a world of enemies,'" 320.

45 Dawidowicz, *The War Against the Jews*, 13–14; Bullock, *A Study in Tyranny*, 52–53; Simms, "Against 'a world of enemies,'" 320–327.

Figure 13.2: Hitler in the Early 20s

well as shifting far-right politically. One organization that Hitler associated with somewhat was the Thule Society. "Thule" meant Nordic in the racial-homeland sense along with the swastika symbol they adopted, and the group advocated its perpetuation by appealing to the common *volk* (people) by promoting anti-Semitism and destroying political enemies. Here, Hitler made his first real friend, one who would serve him faithfully (at least until the Second World War broke out). His name was Rudolf Hess.[46]

Hitler met many men of like mind between 1919–1924. All of them hated what Germany had become, and nearly all blamed the Jews for personal and national setbacks. While some of his new friends and co-conspirators would later be enemies or despised, Hitler clearly embraced violence as a

means to an end. His rhetoric began anew, in beer halls especially. Its message? Jewish removal from German lands, but only *after* the systematic removal of Jewish civil liberties was accomplished.[47]

The Birth of Nazism: National Socialism and the Volk

An important factor considered in this context is that the First World War (or Great War as it was known then) legitimized violence on a level the modern world had never before seen. Prior to the war, Germans could discuss their political differences without resorting to violence, but returning unemployed soldiers and the national malaise at the unexpected defeat changed something fundamental. Street violence occurred almost daily, and all movements, parties, and organizations created paramilitary squads with one express purpose: beat up or kill the rivals. This was not limited to ex-soldiers; teenagers too flocked to legitimize themselves in the eyes of the older, seasoned veterans.[48]

Before long, numerous political groups formed: The Steel Helmets for veterans, including Jewish veterans, the Nationalists, the Social Democrats, the Communists, and many others. Frequent clashes and murder were the hallmarks of most groups, and in this violent melee another important group emerged called the Free Corps (Feikorps). What distinguished them was almost pathological aggression with a tendency for revenge, and among their favorite targets was anyone they suspected of being a traitor to the nation. There, in the midst of national trauma and political extremism, Nazism was born.[49]

Like most democracies, the Weimar Republic had an elected president and an assembly of elected officials, similar to a parliament-style government. Skipping ahead somewhat in the timeline to elaborate how the tension ultimately led to extremism, by the time the popular war hero Field Marshall Paul von Hindenburg was elected president in 1930, the country

---

46   Dawidowicz, *The War Against the Jews*, 16–17; Evans, *Coming of the Third Reich*, 159–161; Joachim C. Fest, *The Face of the Third Reich* (New York, NY: Penguin, 1983), 289–290.

47   Dawidowicz, *The War Against the Jews*, 16–17.
48   Evans, *Coming of the Third Reich*, 72–73.
49   Evans, *Coming of the Third Reich*, 74–76.

had already slid into chaos. More importantly, Hindenburg paved the way for Hitler's National Socialism movement because he too felt that only a conservative dictatorship could lead the nation out of crisis.[50] Moreover, democracy had been imposed upon Germany, which effectively ended the Second Reich, the great Germanic state founded by Bismarck. Additionally, it was inevitable that Germany would default yet again on its reparation payments, and the situation went from bad to worse when the Great Depression hit. "Killing" democracy was a goal shared by Hitler, Hindenburg, and the disaffected lower classes. Therefore, conditions were ripe psychologically and socially to help explain why Nazism ascended and took over German politics in 1933.[51]

In his psychological study *Escape From Freedom* (1941), Erich Fromm concluded that too much had been placed historically on Western man's desire for freedom, individuality, and liberty. Rather, when life takes a bad turn, people desire *authority* more than freedom (including democracy). Stated another way, a shift to the far right of the political spectrum is characteristic of Fromm's thesis. People want authority to alleviate economic hardships and other social woes. After all, the collapse of the Second Reich also erased *all* of Germany's overseas colonies, but when combined with the freedom to run their own government, things fell apart quickly. Pushed to the breaking point economically and spiritually, the lower class desired a strong conservative, authoritarian leader, a *Führer*, to lead them back from the abyss. Adolf Hitler and National Socialism fit the bill, but in late 1923 their time had not yet come.[52]

The Kapp Beer Hall Putsch and Langsden Prison, 1923–1924

In 1923 Hitler's message only advanced to a few adjacent states outside of Bavaria, so his status as a politician was quite low. He also made mistakes, but he never doubted that success was obtainable. One lesson he did take to heart from the Thule Society was to go to the masses, or, in his case, the lower class (*volk*). Why? Hitler was not shy about explaining how he was later so successful: "[T]he receptive power of the masses are very restricted, and their understanding is feeble. On the other hand, they quickly forget. Such being the case, all effective propaganda must be confined to a few bare necessities and then must be expressed in a few stereotyped formulas."[53] If Hitler loathed the upper middle class, elites, and intellectuals as hindrances to his upward mobility, he banked on the low or uneducated working class because "[o]nly constant repetition will finally succeed in imprinting an idea on the memory of a crowd." Lying was not beneath him, and in effect, the entire premise of nation and race is par for the course. For Hitler, all was fair because "when you lie, tell big lies, this is what Jews do ..."[54]

Hitler and his growing entourage needed regional representation before they could run for positions of power at the national level. However, his ability to excite audiences as a speaker was now almost perfected. The charisma he exuded hypnotized crowds, but oddly enough, few could actually recall exactly what he said, just that his emotional appeal affected them deeply. Nevertheless, his contempt for the state and law (democracy) could only be appeased if he got elected.[55] Until that day came, propaganda fit Hitler's agenda perfectly. It had, as stated previously, to be simple enough for the lower class to digest it, appeal to the emotions, not reason, and "[f]inally, propaganda had to be continuous and unvarying in its messages. It should never admit a glimmer of doubt in its own claims, or concede the tiniest element of right in the claims of the other side."[56]

By 1920, many of Hitler's new followers were former Free Corps thugs, and the new counter-ideology to socialism preferred the connotation of a "movement" because "party" sounded like it was

---

50 Evans, *Coming of the Third Reich*, 82–83.
51 Waite, *Psychopathic God*, 398; Evans, *Coming of the Third Reich*, 82–83.
52 Waite, *Psychopathic God*, 398–399.

53 Hitler quoted in Bullock, *A Study in Tyranny*, 69
54 Ibid., 69–70.
55 Evans, *Coming of the Third Reich*, 165–166.
56 Hitler, quoted in Evans, *Coming of the Third Reich*, 168.

part of the despised democratic process. Therefore, "National Socialists" did the upmost to unite the left and right, and while working initially within the conventional political system it intended to overthrow. Then, a subtle shift in the rhetoric began. The word "*race*" replaced "*class*," and other terminology changes effectively reversed the usual terms of socialist ideology. This synthesis was symbolized best in the official flag, personally selected by Hitler: "the field was bright red, the color of socialism, with the swastika, the emblem of racist nationalism, outlined in black in the middle of a white circle at the center of the flag so that the whole ensemble made a combination of black, white and red, the colors of the official flag of the Bismarckian Empire."[57] In effect, the German Worker's Party officially transformed into the National Socialist German Worker's Party (where the abbreviation Nazi came from) on April 1, 1920.[58]

Hitler was not the first politician hoping to take over a democratic government in Europe. His personal hero and role model of that era was Benito Mussolini, the fascist leader of Italy, who led his brown shirt followers in a march on Rome that resulted in his taking over the political system there. Hitler copied the brown shirt concept for his paramilitary division, the S.A., commanded by his number two, Herman Göring. He too envisioned a march, but on Berlin; however, neither he nor the fledgling party was ready to lead anything yet in 1923, much less a country in turmoil. In the fall of the same year, Hitler and his top leaders planned a *putsch*, an overthrow of Bavarian government in Munich. The S.A. were supposed to take over the security if the plan succeeded, but on the evening of November 8 at the Kapp beer hall, Hitler fired a gunshot into the air and shouted, "the National Revolution has begun," but it never got off the ground, and sixteen followers died in the aborted coup. Defeated, Hitler surrendered and was tried for treason in early 1924.[59]

Although his first bid for power failed badly, Hitler still saw an opportunity. National Socialism was rapidly gaining membership, but the S.A.'s influence was not significant outside of Bavaria. Through it all, Hitler intensified his anti-Semitism by reminding his audience often that the real enemy of Germany was not the French, who were unyielding in their demand for reparation payments to continue; rather, it was the "Jews" in the Weimar government because they sought to ruin the nation for their personal gain. What is clear about Nazism, though, is that it was a phenomenon that could only occur if societal conditions were disorderly and an extreme state of insecurity existed.[60] Indeed, the economic conditions were so bad before the *putsch* attempt that the Weimar government announced that defaulting on the annual payment was going to be a reality and requested a moratorium. The French flatly refused and instead responded by sending troops to occupy the Ruhr region along the Rhine, further embarrassing the beleaguered Weimar government in 1923.[61]

At his trial in early 1924, Hitler appealed to sensibilities by citing the good of the nation, but he also owned his accusation, saying, "I alone bear the responsibility." Additionally, Hitler defended his revolutionary vision and denied all guilt, because "… I feel myself the best of Germans who wanted the best for the German people." It seems that not everyone present saw it this way, though, and Hitler was issued a five-year prison sentence for treason. The failed coup attempt led to a brief period outside of politics, but he felt an important lesson was learned. Failure had occurred because too few individuals couldn't coordinate a popular revolt; therefore, he needed the masses to support Nazism: "I believe that the hour will come when the masses, who today stand in the street with our swastika banner, will unite with those who fired upon them …"[62]

57   Ibid., 174.
58   William L. Shirer, *The Rise and Fall of the Third Reich: A History of Nazi Germany* (New York, NY: Touchstone, 1990), 50.
59   Shirer, *Rise and Fall of the Third Reich*, 66–69; Evans, *Coming of the Third Reich*, 192–195; E. J. Passant, *A Short*

History of Germany, 1815–1945 (London: Cambridge University Press, 1960), 161–162; Bullock, *A Study in Tyranny*, 106–115.
60   Bullock, *A Study in Tyranny*, 89.
61   Ibid., 90.
62   Hitler quoted in Bullock, *A Study in Tyranny*, 115–120.

Landsberg Prison and *Mein Kampf*, 1924

Located fifty miles west of Munich lay the town of Landsberg. It was there that Hitler served his sentence. He received five years, but it was reduced to a nine-month term. With him in the prison, though, were forty of his National Socialist comrades. Apparently this prison was nothing like Jackson, MI or Chino, CA because the men ate well and lived in relative comfort. Hitler received regular visits by admirers and supporters, who showered him with gifts and food—so much so that he grew fat. On his thirty-fifth birthday (1924), he decided to isolate himself in order to dictate *Mein Kampf* (My Struggle), which he began in prison. Rudolf Hess and Emil Maurice served as his transcribers and secretaries. Hitler's original title was as long-winded as his text and speeches: *Four and a Half Years of Struggle against Lies, Stupidity, and Cowardice.* Wisely, his publisher, Max Amann, reduced it to *Mein Kampf.* Amann was not alone in disappointment once the text was made available, however, because the book contained very little autobiographical matter. Instead, it was filled with Hitler's meandering discourse, which is simultaneously as difficult to read as it is dull.[63]

The Significance of *Mein Kampf*

For all its neo-pagan nationalism, Nazism could not refrain from paralleling Catholicism at times. National Socialism too had its prophets, saints, and martyrs, and above all, holy days, especially Hitler's birthday (April 20). Further, *Mein Kampf* served as the Holy Scriptures for the quasi-religious phenomenon called Nazism. The *Bible* was superseded by his book on coffee tables in German homes, and also made an appropriate wedding gift for young couples. The unanswered question, though, is did people actually read it? This is unknown, especially before Hitler seized power on January 30, 1933 (a holy day, naturally),

but after his ascendancy, it sold like hotcakes. Surprisingly, though, by the 1940s it had been translated into sixteen languages, including French, English, and Arabic, and was amongst the most published books in the world.[64]

Ultimately, the cult of personality that surrounded Adolf Hitler spread after 1933, and his ascension to power was manipulated in German schools to resemble that of the Messiah, albeit in a more dictatorial worship manner. An important book even in the United States, *Mein Kampf* was published and republished several times. Ironically, it was a bestseller that no one could tolerate reading cover to cover, which is why the following excerpt, "Nation and Race," was selected and edited accordingly.

Bibliography

Alland, Jr., Alexander. *Race in Mind: Race, IQ, and Other Racisms.* New York, NY: Palgrave, 2002.

Arnold, Bettina. "'*Arierdämmerung*' Race and Archaeology in Nazi Germany." *World Archaeology* 38 [March 2006]: 8–31.

Bullock, Alan. Hitler: *A Study in Tyranny, Completely Revised Edition.* New York, NY: Harper & Row, 1962.

Dawidowicz, Lucy S. *The War Against the Jews, 1933–1945.* 1975. Reprint, New York, NY: Bantam, 1984.

Evans, Richard J. *The Coming of the Third Reich.* New York, NY: Penguin Press, 2004.

Fest, Joachim C. *The Face of the Third Reich.* 1963. Translated by Michael Bullock. Reprint, New York, NY: Penguin Books, 1983.

Gould, Stephen Jay. *The Mismeasure of Man, Revised and Expanded Edition.* New York, NY: W.W. Norton, 1996.

Hitler, Adolf. *Mein Kampf.* Translated by Ralph Manheim. New York, NY: Houghton Mifflin, 1943.

Jacobs, Steven Leonard. "Revisiting Hateful Science: The Nazi 'Contribution' to the Journey of

---

63 Bullock, *A Study in Tyranny*, 121; Fest, *Face of the Third Reich*, 288–289; Waite, *Psychopathic God*, 84–85.

---

64 Waite, *Psychopathic God*, 34–35.

Anti-Semitism." *Journal of Hate Studies* 7, no. 1 [2008/2009]: 47–75.

Katz, Jacob. *From Prejudice to Destruction: Anti-Semitism, 1700–1933*. Cambridge: Harvard University Press, 1980.

Morris-Reich, Amos. "Project, Method, and the Racial Characteristics of Jews: A Comparison of Franz Boas and Hans F. K. Günther." *Jewish Social Studies: History, Culture, Society, n.s.* 13, no. 1 [Fall 2006]: 136–169.

Passant, E. J. *A Short History of Germany, 1815–1945*. 1959. Reprint, London: Cambridge University Press, 1960.

Rupnow, Dirk. "Racializing Historiography: Anti-Jewish Scholarship in the Third Reich." *Patterns of Prejudice* 42, no. 1 [2008]: 27–60.

Shanklin, Eugenia. *Anthropology & Race*. Belmont, CA: Wadsworth Publishing, 1994.

Shirer, William L. *The Rise and Fall of the Third Reich: A History of Nazi Germany*. 1959. Reprint, New York, NY: Touchstone, 1990.

Simms, Brendan. "Against 'a world of enemies': The Impact of the First World War on the Development of Hitler's Ideology." *International Affairs* 90, no. 2 [2014]: 317–336.

Takaki, Ronald. *A Different Mirror: A History of Multicultural America, Revised Edition*. New York, NY: Back Bay Books, 2008.

Waite, Robert G. L. *Adolf Hitler: The Psychopathic God*. 1977. Reprint, New York, NY: Signet, 1978.

Zeman, Z. A. B. *Nazi Propaganda*. New York, NY: Oxford University Press, 1964.

Glossary of Terms

Blood Libel: Dating to medieval times and recirculated after the First Crusade, the premise is that around Passover Jews killed Christian children and used their blood to make unleavened bread. The implication is associated with another old anti-Semitic message stipulating that Jews killed Christ, as Passover is associated with Holy Week.

Cultural anti-Semitism: When Judaeophobia is racialized in society, it becomes generational, with frequent and recurring anti-Semitic messages in literature, or even through acts of violence against the Jews in Europe during the nineteenth and early twentieth centuries.

Folk Taxonomy: The human habit of classification that is characteristic of any given society.

Polygenist: The theory of human origins that posits multiple human races have different origins (polygenesis); the opposite of monogeny.

Social Darwinism: Based on survival of the fittest, but when applied to racial theory, it is biased toward "pure" races being dominant and progressive while inferior groups are regressive.

For Discussion

1. What continuity can you identify between the Alland reading about Race and IQ and the first section of this chapter, which discusses how methodology and interpretation of findings has perpetuated bad science and promoted racist views that humans can be ranked socially and intellectually?

2. After reading Adolf Hitler's "Nation and Race," identify his influences as they are shown in this introductory chapter. Who does he seem to reiterate the most? Is it clear, or is Hitler's diatribe a composite of numerous nineteenth-century sources? What does Hitler say specifically about the master race and its survival?

3. How did anti-Semitism become apparent in Hitler's political development, and what are some of his contributions to the historic discrimination against the Jews?

4. How did Hitler use propaganda to further his agenda? What did he say about the political messages and how they should be formatted? Do you see any similarities today as to how propaganda is utilized in politics?

5. What external and psychological factors can you identify in this chapter that helped Hitler gain power in 1933? Is this something purely of the past, or could it happen again based on your findings?

Image Credits

- Fig. 13.1: The Jewish Encyclopedia, https://commons.wikimedia.org/wiki/File:Map_showing_the_percentage_of_Jews_in_the_Pale_of_Settlement_and_Congress_Poland,_The_Jewish_Encyclopedia_(1905).jpg. Copyright in the Public Domain.
- Fig. 13.2: https://commons.wikimedia.org/wiki/Adolf_Hitler#/media/File:Hitler_as_young_man.jpg. Copyright in the Public Domain.

Nation and Race

from *Mein Kampf*

By Adolf Hitler

• •

Editor's Introduction
Adolf Hitler on Nation and Race

Although his views on race and the biological are a pastiche of nineteenth- and early twentieth-century views, Adolf Hitler quickly devised a way to unify a depressed Germany as he rose to power. His National Socialist Party (Nazi) seized power in 1933, and while rebuilding the nation, he plotted a war against the Jews and other peoples he considered inferior, or *untermensch* (subhuman). What is clear, however, is that Hitler fully understood there is no scientific basis for different races. Instead, his political treatise and manifesto, *Mein Kampf* (my struggles or my battle), places the concept of nation ahead of all else, and envisioned a world led by the superior Aryan race (racially pure Germans) at the expense of Germany's enemies, real or imagined.

References

Bullock, Alan. *Hitler: A Study in Tyranny.* New York: Bantam Books, 1961.
Hitler, Adolf. *Mein Kampf.* Translated by Ralph Manheim. New York: Houghton Mifflin, 1943.
Shanklin, Eugenia. *Anthropology and Race.* Belmont, CA: Wadsworth, 1994.
Waite, Roger G.L. *The Psychopathic God: Adolf Hitler.* New York: Da Capo Press, 1993.

There are statements of truth which are so obvious that just for this reason the common world does not see, or at least does not recognize, them. At times the world passes these well-known truisms blindly and it is most astonished if now suddenly somebody discovers what everybody ought to know. The Columbus eggs' are lying about by the hundreds of thousands, only the Columbuses are rarely seen.

Thus, without exception, people wander about in Nature's garden; they think they know almost everything, and yet, with few exceptions, they walk blindly by one of the most outstanding principles of Nature's working: the inner seclusion of the species of all living beings on earth.

Even the most superficial observation shows, as an almost brazen basic principle of all the countless forms of expression of Nature's will to live, her limited form of propagation and increase, limited in itself. Every animal mates only with a representative of the same species. The titmouse seeks the titmouse, the finch the finch, the stork the stork, the field mouse the field mouse, the common mouse the common mouse, the wolf the wolf, etc.

Only exceptional circumstances can change this; first of all the compulsion of captivity, as well as any other impossibility of mating within the same species. But then Nature begins to resist this with the help of all visible means, and her most visible protest consists either of denying the bastards further procreative faculty, or she limits the fertility of the coming offspring; but in most cases she takes away the capacity of resistance against disease or inimical attacks.

This is then only too natural.

Any crossing between two beings of not quite the same high standard produces a medium between the standards of the parents. That means: the young one will probably be on a higher level than the racially lower parent, but not as high as the higher one. Consequently, it will succumb later on in the fight against the higher level. But such a mating contradicts Nature's will to breed life as a whole towards a higher level. The presumption for this does not lie in blending the superior with the inferior, but rather in a complete victory of the former. The stronger has to rule and he is not to amalgamate with the weaker one, that he may not sacrifice his own greatness. Only the born weakling can consider this as cruel, but at that he is only a weak and limited human being; for, if this law were not dominating, all conceivable development towards a higher level, on the part of all organically living beings, would be unthinkable for man.

The consequence of this purity of the race, generally valid in Nature, is not only the sharp limitation of the races outwardly, but also their uniform character in themselves. The fox is always a fox, the goose a goose, the tiger a tiger, etc., and the difference can lie, at the most, in the different measure of strength, force, cleverness, skill, perseverance, etc., of the various specimens. But there will never be found a fox which, according to its inner nature, would perhaps have humane tendencies as regards the geese, nor will there be a cat with a friendly disposition towards mice.

Therefore also, here the fight amongst one another originates less from reasons of inner aversion than from hunger and love. In both cases, Nature looks calm and even satisfied. The fight for daily bread makes all those succumb who are weak, sickly, and less determined, while the males' fight for the female gives the right of propagation, or the possibility of it, only to the most healthy. But the fight is always a means for the promotion of the species' health and force of resistance, and thus a cause for its development towards a higher level.

If it were different, every further development towards higher levels would stop, and rather the contrary would happen. For, since according to numbers, the inferior element always outweighs the superior element, under the same preservation of life and under the same propagating possibilities, the inferior element would increase so much more rapidly that finally the best element would be forced to step into the background, if no correction of this condition were carried out. But just this is done by Nature, by subjecting the weaker part to such difficult living conditions that even by this the number Is restricted, and finally by preventing the remainder, without choice, from increasing, but by making here a new and ruthless choice, according to strength and health.

This appeal to the sacred norm of the 'survival of the fittest'—customary in Pan-German literature—had been resorted to as well by critics of Socialism. The 'tearful sentimentality' of the humanitarians, forever attempting to salvage what had better be left to die, is denounced by Spengler and many others. But the application of 'fitness' to mating is something else entirely, deriving from Plato through a number of intermediaries some of whom can be sought out in modern anti-Semitic literature. There are considerable differences. Thus, Ludwig Schemann thinks that Nature does not mean the same thing by 'fitness' that man does, and that therefore any vigorous recourse to eugenics—except in so far as purely negative matters (health, etc.) are concerned—would prove impossible and impractical. Others have gone the whole way and advocated rigid public regulation of procreation.

Just as little as Nature desires a mating between weaker individuals and stronger ones, far less she desires the mixing of a higher race with a lower one, as in this case her entire work of higher breeding, which has perhaps taken hundreds of thousands of years, would tumble at one blow.

Historical experience offers countless proofs of this. It shows with terrible clarity that with any mixing of the blood of the Aryan with lower races the result was the end of the culture-bearer. North America, the population of which consists for the greatest part of Germanic elements—which mix only very little with the lower, colored races—displays a humanity and a culture different from those of Central and South America, where chiefly the Romanic immigrants have sometimes mixed with the aborigines on a large scale. By this example alone one may clearly and distinctly recognize the influence of the race mixture. The Germanic of the North American continent, who has remained pure and less intermixed, has become the master of that continent, he will remain so until he, too, falls victim to the shame of blood-mixing.

The result of any crossing, in brief, is always the following:

1.   Lowering of the standard of the higher race.
2.   Physical and mental regression, and, with it, the beginning of a slowly but steadily progressive lingering illness.

To bring about such a development means nothing less than sinning against the will of the Eternal Creator.

This action, then, is also rewarded as a sin.

Man, by trying to resist this iron logic of Nature, becomes entangled in a fight against the principles to which alone he, too, owes his existence as a human being. Thus his attack is bound to lead to his own doom.

Of course, now comes the typically Jewish, impudent, but just as stupid, objection by the modern pacifist: 'Man conquers Nature!'

Millions mechanically and thoughtlessly repeat this Jewish nonsense, and in the end *they* imagine that they themselves represent a kind of conqueror of Nature; whereas they have no other weapon at their disposal but an 'idea,' and such a wretched one at that, so that according to it no world would be conceivable.

But quite apart from the fact that so far man has never conquered Nature in any affair, but that at the most he gets hold of and tries to lift a flap of her enormous, gigantic veil of eternal riddles and secrets, that in reality he does not 'invent' anything but only discovers everything, that he does not dominate Nature, but that, based on the knowledge of a few laws and secrets of Nature, he has risen to the position of master of those other living beings lacking this knowledge; but quite apart from this, an idea cannot *conquer* the presumptions for the origin and the existence of mankind, as the idea itself depends only on man. Without men there is no human 'idea' in this world; thus the idea is always caused by the presence of men, and, with it, of all those laws which created the presumptions for this existence.

The argument has been put another way by Professor Carl Schmitt (cited by Kolnai): 'A universal organization in which there is no place for warlike preservation and destruction of human life would be neither a State nor an Empire: it would lose all political character.' Yet this is not Jewish but Christian teaching that is under criticism. Cardinal Faulhaber, meeting the objection that the Old Testament is filled with 'hymns of hate,' responded that Christianity had indeed changed those hymns into canticles of love, and added: There is no alternative: either we are disciples of Christ, or we lapse into the Judaism of antiquity with its hymns of hate.' The letter which the evangelical churches addressed to Hitler in June, 1936, contained these words: 'When blood, race, creed, nationality and honor are thus raised to the rank of qualities that guarantee eternity, the Evangelical Christian is bound, by the first commandment, to reject the assumption.'

And not only that! Certain ideas are even tied to certain men. This can be said most of all of just such thoughts the content of which has its origin, not in an exact scientific truth, but rather in the world of feeling, or, as one usually expresses oneself so nicely and 'clearly' today, which reflects an 'inner experience.' All these ideas, which have nothing to do with clear logic in itself, but which represent mere expressions of feelings, ethical conceptions, etc., are tied to the existence of those men to whose spiritual force of imagination and creation they owe their own existence. But precisely in this case the preservation of these certain races and men is the presumption for the existence of these 'ideas.' For example, he who actually desires, with all his heart, the victory of the pacifistic idea in this world would have to stand up, with all available means, for the conquest of the world by the Germans; for if it should come about the Other way round, then, with the last German, the last pacifist would die off, as the other part of the world has hardly ever been taken in so deeply by this nonsense, adverse to nature and to reason, as unfortunately our own people. Therefore, whether one wanted to or not, if one had the serious will, one would have to decide to wage war in order to arrive at pacifism. This and nothing else was what the American world-redeemer [President Woodrow] Wilson wanted to have done, at least our German visionaries believed in this. With this, then, the purpose was fulfilled.

Indeed, the pacifist-humane idea is perhaps quite good whenever the man of the highest standard has previously conquered and subjected the world to a degree that makes him the only master of this globe. Thus the idea is more and more deprived of the possibility of a harmful effect in the measure in which its practical application becomes rare and finally impossible. Therefore, first fight, and then one may see what can be done. In the other case, mankind has passed the climax of its development, and the end is not the rule of some ethical 'idea,' but barbarism, and, in consequence, chaos. Naturally, here the one or the other may laugh, but this planet has driven on its course through the ether for millions of years without men, and the day may come when it will do so again, if people forget that they owe their higher existence, not to the ideas of some crazy ideologists, but to the knowledge and the ruthless application of Nature's brazen laws.

The foregoing passages are derived in the main from Houston Stewart Chamberlain, but with *nuances* that suggest the influence of Rosenberg, or at least of the Free Corps which imported so much militaristic anti-Semitism into Germany after the War. For Chamberlain the moral superiority of the disappointed when 1918 seemed to mean perpetual moral degradation for the human race. In his famous letter to Hitler, following their meeting in 1923, he wrote, therefore: 'At one blow you have transformed the state my soul was in. Germany's vitality is proved if in this hour of its deepest need it can produce a Hitler.' Perhaps the basis of this attitude as a whole must be sought in those fears of an eventual 'war between races' which were aired as early as the eighteenth century, but reached a kind of apogee during the nineteenth. Then the inferiority of the 'colored races' was taken for granted, though the interest taken in a newly discovered Indian literature, ascribed in theory to an 'Indo-Germanic invasion' of Asia, tended to make many place the Brahmins on a somewhat higher level. Later on the 'negroid characteristics' of the Mediterranean races were stressed by Pan-German writers. The Latin, the Catholic, was of highly questionable value. The Germanic Aryan had a right to dominate, and eventually he surely would. After the War the stress was shifted to the Jew, partly because French 'inferiority' had not been satisfactorily demonstrated, after all, and partly because the Free Corps encouraged the view that Jewry was responsible for Germany's acquiescence in Allied demands.

Everything that today we admire on this earth—science and art, technique and inventions—is only the creative product of a few peoples and perhaps originally of one race. On them now depends also the existence of this entire culture. If they perish, then the beauty of this earth sinks into the grave with them.

No matter how much the soil, for instance, is able to influence the people, the result will always be a different one, according to the races under consideration. The scanty fertility of a living space may instigate one race towards the highest achievements, while with another race this may only become the cause for the most dire poverty and ultimate malnutrition with all its consequences. The inner disposition of the peoples is always decisive for the way in which outward influences work themselves out. What leads one people to starvation, trains the other for hard work.

All great cultures of the past perished only because the originally creative race died off through blood-poisoning.

The ultimate cause of such a decline was always the forgetting that all culture depends on men and not the reverse; that means, that in order to save a certain culture the man who created it has to be saved. But the preservation is bound to the brazen law of necessity and of the right of the victory of the best and the strongest in this world.

He who wants to live should fight, therefore, and he who does not want to battle in this world of eternal struggle does not deserve to be alive.

Even if this were hard, this is the way things are. But it is certain that by far the hardest fate is the fate which meets that man who believes he can 'conquer' Nature, and yet, in truth, only seems to mock her. Misery, distress, and diseases are then her answer!

The man who misjudges and disdains the laws of race actually forfeits the happiness that seems destined to be his. He prevents the victorious march of the best race and with it also the presumption for all human progress, and in consequence he will remain in the domain of the animal's helpless misery, burdened with the sensibility of man.

It is a futile enterprise to argue which race or races were the original bearers of human culture and, with it, the actual founders of what we sum up with the word 'mankind.' It is simpler to put this question to oneself with regard to the present, and here the answer follows easily and distinctly. What we see before us of human culture today, the results of art, science, and techniques, is almost exclusively the creative product of the Aryan. But just this fact admits of the not unfounded conclusion that he alone was

the founder of higher humanity as a whole, thus the prototype of what we understand by the word 'man'. He is the Prometheus of mankind, out of whose bright forehead springs the divine spark of genius at all times, forever rekindling that fire which in the form of knowledge lightened up the night of silent secrets and thus made man climb the path towards the position of master of the other beings on this earth. Exclude him—and deep darkness will again fall upon the earth, perhaps even, after a few thousand years, human culture would perish and the world would turn into a deserts.

This idyl of 'Aryan' pre-history is interesting because: of the definition of 'culture' that is involved. For 'culture' in this sense is once again become the principal concern of Europe. The 'Aryan' succeeds in pushing his way onward and upward by conquering lesser peoples and using them as 'helping forces' (slaves). Then, however, master and slave intermarry, and the 'culture' decays. Perhaps this is only an analogy borrowed from some pictorial history of European colonizing effort: perhaps it is more philosophical. Spengler had taught—in the *Decline of the West*—that cultures arise and fall cyclically; and Hitler here provides a convenient illustration of why they fall. Therewith the riddle proposed by Spengler is solved; the 'culture-making' folk is that which, obeying the law that only the fittest survive, embarks on conquest and exploitation; and the 'culture-destroying folk' is the slave breed which tempts the aristocratic group into intermarriage. This is Nietzsche materialized.

If one were to divide mankind into three groups: culture-founders, culture-bearers, and culture-destroyers, then, as representative of the first kind, only the Aryan would come in question. It is from him that the foundation and the walls of all human creations originate, and only the external form and color depend on the characteristics of the various peoples involved. He furnishes the gigantic building-stones and also the plans for all human progress, and only the execution corresponds to the character of the people and races in the various instances. In a few decades, for instance, the entire east of Asia will call a culture its own, the ultimate bases of which will be Hellenic spirit and Germanic technique, just as is the case with us. Only the *external* form will (at least partly) bear the features of Asiatic character. It is not the case, as some people claim, that Japan adds European techniques to her culture, but European science and techniques are trimmed with Japanese characteristics.

But the basis of actual life is no longer the special Japanese culture, although it determines the color of life (because outwardly, in consequence of its inner difference, it is more visible to European eyes), but it is the enormous scientific and technical work of Europe and America, that is, of Aryan peoples. Based on these achievements alone the East is also able to follow general human progress. This creates the basis for the fight for daily bread, it furnishes weapons and tools for it, and only the external makeup **is** gradually adapted to Japanese life.

But if, starting today, all further Aryan influence upon Japan should stop, and supposing that Europe and America were to perish, then a further development of Japan's present rise in science and technology could take place for a little while longer; but in the time of a few years the source would dry out, Japanese life would gain, but its culture would stiffen and fall back into the sleep out of which it was startled seven decades ago by the Aryan wave of culture. Therefore, exactly as the present Japanese development owes its life to Aryan origin, thus also in the dim past foreign influence and foreign spirit were the awakener of the Japanese culture. The best proof of this is the fact that the latter stiffened and became completely paralyzed later on. This can only happen to a people when the originally creative race nucleus was lost, or when the external influence, which gave the impetus and the material for the first development in the cultural field, was lacking later on. But if it is ascertained that a people receives, takes in, and works over the essential basic elements of its culture from other races, and if then, when a further external influence is lacking, it stiffens again and again, then one can perhaps

call such a race a '*culture-bearing*' one but never a '*culture-creating*' one.

An examination of the various peoples from this viewpoint evidences the fact that in nearly all cases one has to deal, not with originally *culture-creating*, but rather always with *culture-supporting* peoples.

It is always about the following picture of their development that presents itself:

Aryan tribes (often in a really ridiculously small number of their own people) subjugate foreign peoples, and now, stimulated by the special living conditions of the new territory (fertility, climatic conditions, etc.) and favored by the mass of the helping means in the form of people of inferior kind now at their disposal, they develop the mental and organizatory abilities, slumbering in them. Often, in the course of a few millenniums or even centuries, they create cultures which originally completely bear the inner features of their character, adapted to the already mentioned special qualities of the soil as well as of the subjected people. Finally, however, the conquerors deviate from the purity of their blood which they maintained originally, they begin to mix with the subjected inhabitants and thus they end their own existence; for the fall of man in Paradise has always been followed by expulsion from it.

Often, after a thousand and more years, the last visible trace of the one-time overlords is shown in the fairer complexion which their blood has left, in the form of the color, to the subjected race, and in a petrified culture which they had founded as the original creators. For, just as the actual and spiritual conqueror lost himself in the blood of the subjected, thus also the fuel for the torch of human culture progress was lost! As through the blood the color of the former masters keeps a faint glimmer as a memory of them, thus also the night of the cultural life is faintly brightened by the creations that remained of the erstwhile bearers of light. These now shone through all the barbarism that has returned, and in the thoughtless observer of the moment they awaken only too frequently the opinion that he sees the picture of the present people, whereas it is only the mirror of the past at which he is looking.

Then it may happen that such a people for a second time, nay, even more often in the life of its history, comes into touch with the race of its one-time suppliers of culture, without a memory of former meetings necessarily being present. The remainder of the blood of the one-time masters will unconsciously turn to the new apparition, and what first was only possible by compulsion will now succeed with the help of their own will. Then a new culture wave makes its entrance and lasts until its bearers have once more been submerged in the blood of foreign peoples.

It will be the task of a future culture and world history to make researches in this sense and not to suffocate by reflecting external facts, as this is unfortunately only too often the case with our present science of history.

Merely from this sketch of the development of 'culture-bearing' nations results also the picture of the origin, the work, and—the decline of the true culture-creators of this globe, the Aryans themselves.

Just as in daily life the so-called genius requires a special cause, often even a real impetus in order to be made conspicuous, the same is also the case with the ingenious race in the life of the peoples. In the monotony of everyday life even important people often seem unimportant and they hardly stand out over the average of their surroundings; but as soon as they are faced by a situation in which others would despair or go wrong, out of the plain average child the ingenious nature grows visibly, not infrequently to the astonishment of all those who hitherto had an opportunity to observe him, who had meanwhile grown up in the smallness of *bourgeois* life, and therefore, in consequence of this process, the prophet has rarely any honor in his own country. Never is there a better opportunity to observe this than during war. In the hours of distress, when others despair, out of apparently harmless children, there shoot suddenly heroes of death-defying determination and icy coolness of reflection. If this hour of trial had never come, then hardly anyone would ever have been able to guess that a young hero is hidden in the beardless boy. Nearly always such an impetus is needed in order to call genius into action.

No definition of the word 'Aryan' is acceptable. German lexicographers were hard pressed to hit upon an accurate description. The term itself is probably of Sanskrit origin, and seems to have meant 'friends.' It was next assumed that these 'friends' were Indo-Germans, who (it was further assumed) had invaded India and subjugated the 'lesser breeds.' Finally 'Aryan' became just a synonym for 'Indo-German.' The 1931 edition of the *encyclopedia Der grosse Herder* said: 'Recently some have used (ethnologically, in an incorrect way) 'Aryan;' to indicate Indo-Germans in general. In this case, the term is used as in the nature of a slogan in the struggle over the self-determination and preservation of our race against Jewry, which is of a different order.' For this and similar definitions (surely discreet enough), the earlier volumes of this encyclopedia were ordered withdrawn from circulation. In practice the word is officially used today as a racial term excluding Jews and negroes. The second are frowned upon because (i.a.) they are admitted into the French army; and because, it is hoped, sympathy for the Nazi cause may be thus awakened among Southerners in the United States. Delegations of 'Brahmins' have, however, been cordially welcomed to the New Germany.

Parallels to this can be found in the writings of Pan-Germans like Heinrich Class and Count Reventlow. In an address delivered during 1932, Hitler declared; 'Let them call us inhuman! If we save Germany, we shall have done the greatest deed in the world. Let them call us unjust! If we save Germany, we shall have repaired the greatest injustice in the world. Let them say that we are without morality! If our people is saved, we shall have paved the way for morality!'

Fate's hammer stroke, which then throws the one to the ground, suddenly strikes steel in another, and while now the shell of everyday life is broken, the erstwhile nucleus lies open to the eyes of the astonished world. The latter now resists and does not want to believe that the apparently 'identical' kind is now suddenly supposed to be a 'different' being; a process which repeats itself with every eminent human being.

Although an inventor, for instance, establishes his fame only on the day of his invention, one must not think that perhaps his genius in itself had entered the man only just at this hour, but the spark of genius will be present in the forehead of the truly creatively gifted man from the hour of his birth, although for many years in a slumbering condition and therefore invisible to the rest of the world. But some day, through an external cause or impetus of some kind, the spark becomes fire, something that only then begins to stir the attention of other people. The most stupid of them believe now in all sincerity that the person in question has just become 'clever' whereas in reality they themselves now begin at last to recognize his greatness; for true genius is always inborn and never acquired by education or, still less, by learning.

This, however, may be said, as already stressed, not only for the individual man, but also for the race. Creatively active peoples are creatively gifted from the very bottom and forever, although this may not be recognizable to the eyes of the superficial observer. Here, too, external recognition is always only possible as a consequence of accomplished facts, as the rest of the world is not able to recognize genius in itself, but sees only its visible expressions in the form of inventions, discoveries, buildings, pictures, etc.; but even here it often takes a long time till it is able to struggle through to this knowledge. Exactly as in the life of the individual important man his genius or extraordinary ability strives towards its practical realization only when urged on by special occasions, thus also in the life of the peoples the real use of creative forces and abilities that are present can take place only when certain presumptions invite to this.

We see this most clearly in that race that cannot help having been, and being, the supporter of the development of human culture—the Aryans. As soon as Fate leads them towards special conditions, their latent abilities begin to develop in a more and more rapid course and to mold themselves into tangible forms. The cultures which they found in such cases are nearly always decisively determined by the available soil, the climate, and—by the subjected people. The latter, however, is the most decisive of all factors. The more primitive the technical presumptions for a cultural activity are, the more necessary is the presence of human auxiliary forces which then, collected and applied with the object of organization, have to replace the force of the machine. Without this possibility of utilizing inferior men, the Aryan would never have been able to take the first steps towards his later culture; exactly as, without the help of various suitable animals which he knew how to tame, he would never have arrived at a technology which now allows him to do without these very animals. The words *Der Mohr hat seine Schuldigkeit getan, er kann gehen* [The Moor has done his duty, he may go] has unfortunately too deep a meaning. For thousands of years the horse had to serve man and to help in laying the foundations of a development which now, through the motor-car, makes the horse itself superfluous. In a few years it will have ceased its activity, but without its former co-operation man would hardly have arrived at where he stands today.

Therefore, for the formation of higher cultures, the existence of inferior men was one of the most essential presumptions, because they alone were able to replace the lack of technical means without which a higher development is unthinkable. The first culture of mankind certainly depended less on the tamed animal, but rather on the use of inferior people.

Only after the enslavement of subjected races, the same fate began to meet the animals, and not vice versa, as many would like to believe. For first the conquered walked behind [in later editions read: before] the plow—and after him, the horse. Only pacifist fools can again look upon this as a sign of human baseness, without making clear to themselves that this development had to take place in order to arrive finally at that place from where today these apostles are able to sputter forth their drivel into the world.

The progress of mankind resembles the ascent on an endless ladder; one cannot arrive at the top without first having taken the lower steps. Thus the Aryan had to go the way which reality showed him and not that of which the imagination of a modern pacifist dreams. The way of reality, however, is hard and difficult, but it finally ends where the other wishes to bring mankind by dreaming, but unfortunately removes it from, rather than brings it nearer to, it.

Therefore, it is no accident that the first cultures originated in those places where the Aryan, by meeting lower peoples, subdued them and made them subject to his will. They, then, were the first technical instrument in the service of a growing culture.

With this the way that the Aryan had to go was clearly lined out. As a conqueror he subjected the lower peoples and then he regulated their practical ability according to his command and his will and for his aims. But while he thus led them towards a useful, though hard activity, he not only spared the lives of the subjected, but perhaps he even gave them a fate which was better than that of their former so-called 'freedom.' As long as he kept up ruthlessly the master's standpoint, he not only really remained 'master' but also the preserver and propagator of the culture. For the latter was based exclusively on his abilities, and, with it, on his preservation in purity. But as soon as the subjected peoples themselves began to rise (probably) and approached the conqueror linguistically, the sharp separating wall between master and slave fell.

The Aryan gave up the purity of his blood and therefore he also lost his place in the Paradise which he had created for himself. He became submerged in the race-mixture, he gradually lost his cultural ability more and more, till at last not only mentally but also physically he began to resemble more the subjected and aborigines than his ancestors. For some time he may still live on the existing cultural goods, but then petrifaction sets in, and finally oblivion.

In this way cultures and realms collapse in order to make room for new formations.

The blood-mixing, however, with the lowering of the racial level caused by it, is the sole cause of the dying-off of old cultures; for the people do not perish by lost wars, but by the loss of that force of resistance which is contained only in the pure blood.

All that is not race in this world is trash.

All world historical events, however, are only the expression of the races' instinct of self-preservation in its good or in its evil meaning.

That is, security is better than freedom. And security, carried to its ultimate in the 'total mobilization' of the nation, is very well analyzed by Rauschning. The masses still cling to the residue of personal liberty, of self-determination, which has been left to them. Yet all such things must disappear completely before the absolute 'security' which is the inherent objective of the Hitlerite revolution has been reached.

Extremism and White Supremacy

Contemporary Aryan Hate and Aryan Hate in the Home

American Swastika: Inside the White Power Movement's Hidden Spaces of Hate

By Pete Simi and Robert Furtell

• •

What is the character of Aryan organization and ideology? Observers of white power activity offer two distinct answers to this question. One answer suggests that Aryans are an irrational and disorganized subculture rife with internal conflict. For instance, Mattias Gardell says, "The level of discord, mutual enmity, organizational fragmentation, and ideological division characterizing the world of white racism [is] far too high to be able to speak of a white racist movement in any meaningful way." From this point of view, it appears that ideological schisms threaten to divide Aryans into politically innocuous and fragmented factions. Yet Gardell also affirms, "If there is not a 'movement,' there is still a 'something' that all or most of the different networks, channels of communication, organizations, activists, and tendencies may be seen as parts of." An emphasis on the disorganized aspects of Aryanism obscures its strategic and structured dimensions.

We advocate a second perspective that sees racist activism as "a social movement, a 'family' of overlapping groups organized to spread racist and anti-Semitic ideas and terrorist tactics." To be sure, most Aryan activity does not closely resemble the standard depiction of social movements with traditional, centralized organizations that mobilize insurgents to action. Aryan organization is anchored in fluid, transitory, and informal "submerged networks" that periodically coalesce in Aryan free spaces. But Aryan free spaces require deliberate, calculated organization and sustained commitments among participants to persist. Aryan free spaces are *movement spaces* where white power advocates congregate to reinforce their dedication to the cause and draw others into the ranks of Aryan activism.

The Aryans who connect in free spaces manifest white power ideology in four distinct branches: the Ku Klux Klan, Christian Identity and neo-Pagan racists, neo-Nazis, and racist skinheads. We discuss each of these branches below in some detail, specifying their history and core ideological principles. The ideological and stylistic differences across the branches can be a source of discord and power struggle. But Aryans from across these branches also embrace basic doctrines that transcend their ideological differences and create points of general agreement. We conclude by describing each Aryan branch, their common doctrines, and the solidarity Aryans build with these beliefs.

Ku Klux Klan

The Ku Klux Klan (KKK) has persisted through several eras of change in America's political climate. A small cadre of young Confederate veterans organized the first Klan group in Pulaski, Tennessee, in 1866. Ku Klux refers to the Greek word *kuklos,* meaning circle or band. Original Klan members conceived of the group as a fraternal order where Confederates could continue to meet after the Civil War.

Klan members quickly developed a doctrine based on the defense of white supremacy in the era of Reconstruction. The KKK's ranks swelled in 1868, and the organization grew more political as Southern whites reacted against black civil rights policies. The Klan expanded from outposts in half a dozen Tennessee counties to multiple groups in nearly every Southern state. Klan activity became violent, and numerous members were implicated in whippings, beatings, and murders of Southern blacks. Klan groups assassinated black Republican politicians and murdered voters during the 1868 election. Allen Trelease estimates that more than 1,000 racial murders occurred in Louisiana alone.

This wave of Klan violence was the impetus for the federal government's adoption of the Civil Rights Act of 1871, then known as the Ku Klux Klan Act. In response, Klan officials formally disbanded to avoid federal sanctions, although many local groups continued to meet regularly.

The KKK reemerged in 1915 when Alabama native William J. Simmons founded the Second Era Klan in Stone Mountain, Georgia. Simmons implored all white Americans to join "The World's Greatest Secret, Social, Patriotic, Fraternal, Beneficiary Order." Simmons emphasized a doctrine of "100% Pure Americanism" to preserve the racial purity of white Anglo-Saxon Protestant Americans. White mobs targeted African American communities across the United States and anti-Semitism flourished as the KKK cast Jews and other "mongrel" groups as "outsiders" who threatened white America's racial integrity.

KKK membership reportedly reached between 2 and 5 million people nationwide by 1925. Such high numbers reflected the extent to which early-twentieth-century Americans accepted the Klan's explicit racist and anti-Semitic views. The KKK also gained political strength and became one of the largest and most powerful political organizations in U.S. history.

Klan-sponsored candidates won U.S. Senate races in Alabama, Colorado, Georgia, Indiana, Oklahoma, and Texas, and in 1924 a Klan-endorsed candidate won the Kansas governorship. Klan membership crossed class lines and included influential Americans, such as Supreme Court Justice Hugo Black and presidents Harry Truman (who resigned after attending one meeting) and Warren Harding. By the late 1920s, however, membership numbers began plummeting as various scandals, including stories of indiscriminate terrorism and brutality, tarnished the Klan's self-righteous image. By the 1930s, the Klan was active in limited areas, such as Florida, where membership topped 30,000.

Klan activism reemerged again in response to civil rights protests in the 1950s and 1960s. Klan members carried out arson and numerous bombings and assassinations, including the murder of three civil rights workers in Philadelphia, Mississippi, in 1964, which became the topic of the motion picture *Mississippi Burning* (1988). Federal authorities responded with Operation White Hate Group, infiltrated Klan organizations, and arrested and prosecuted many leading members in Alabama, Mississippi, and other Southern states.

Government pressure led to a precipitous drop in KKK official membership numbers during the 1970s and 1980s. By the late 1980s most KKK groups were fragmented and in dire financial straits. By 1995, about 60 splintered Klan groups remained in the United States and membership had declined to well below 10,000. However, KKK numbers rose again a decade later. The Southern Poverty Law Center estimates that 143 Klan chapters were active in 2008.

Immigration fears and economic concerns, along with a "new racist discourse" of white victimization and loss of white cultural heritage, have combined to rejuvenate the modern KKK. The Anti-Defamation League asserts that Klan participation has grown over the past decade in several areas where the Klan has not been strong for many years, such as Iowa, as well as traditional Klan strongholds, such as Florida, Louisiana, and Indiana. The largest and most active Klan groups today are the Empire Knights of the Ku Klux Klan, active in eighteen states in the South, Northeast, and Western United States; the Church of the National Knights of the Ku Klux Klan, headquartered in Indiana with chapters in twenty states; and Brotherhood of Klans, with fifteen state chapters.

Today's Klan members are active in the white power scene, organizing events such as Nordic Fest, which draws several hundred Aryans to the heavily guarded, gated compound of the Imperial Klans of America. These events have driven the "Nazification" of the Klan. KKK networks increasingly overlap with neo-Nazi racists, and Klan members are integrating neo-Nazi symbolism and rituals into long-standing KKK traditions. The German swastika has become a familiar symbol at KKK-sponsored gatherings along with the German Iron Cross emblazoned on traditional Klan robes and hoods.

The Klan's greatest impact on the white power movement may be its historic legacy. The Ku Klux Klan has now persisted for more than 140 years. Radical groups in addition to the KKK have emerged in the landscape of racist extremism. The Klan remains a symbol of perseverance alongside these groups and continues to inspire Aryan vigilantism and devotion to white power. We turn next to discuss Christian Identity and neo-Pagan racists, neo-Nazis, and racist skinheads.

Christian Identity and Neo-Paganism

Christian Identity and neo-Paganism make up a branch of Aryan extremists anchored in religion and mythology. Christian Identity is a movement that espouses a theological justification for white superiority through interpretations of the Judeo-Christian Bible. Neo-Pagans combine pre-Christian pagan myths with Aryan racist and anti-Semitic ideals.

Christian Identity

Christian Identity believers define nonwhites as evil incarnate and promote racial violence as acts ordained by God. They see blacks, Latinos, Asians, and other nonwhites as lower-order subspecies of "pre-Adamic mudpeople" and, therefore, not fully human. These beliefs are rooted in British Israelism, a nineteenth-century English theology that posits the true Israelites were Anglo-Saxons. Christian Identity adds to this interpretation the notion that Jews are descended from Satan and resulted from Eve's copulation with the serpent. Identity believers imagine they are warriors in a righteous battle against the Jewish conspiracy to eradicate the white race.

Historically, the most prominent Christian Identity group has been Aryan Nations/Church of Jesus Christ Christian, founded by Richard Butler in 1974. Under Butler's leadership, Aryan Nations grew to include chapters in twenty-six states with multiple chapters in Louisiana, New Jersey, and Ohio. Butler hosted a number of annual gatherings on his compound in Hayden Lake, Idaho. The most notorious were the Aryan Nations World Congresses, which brought together members from other white power branches.

Aryan Nations was bankrupted in 2000 when the Southern Poverty Law Center (SPLC) won a $6.3 million lawsuit against Butler. The Aryan Nations compound was transferred to the plantiffs in 2001 and the group splintered following Butler's death in 2004. Now three separate Aryan Nations organizations claim to be the rightful heirs to Butler's legacy. August Kreis leads one faction, currently in Lexington, South Carolina. Kreis is well known among Aryans for advocating an alliance between Islamic jihad and the white power struggle. Jonathon Williams leads the second Aryan Nations faction based in Lincoln, Alabama. Williams holds annual Aryan Nations gatherings that bring WPM activists together from across the country. Both factions are struggling to match the resources, membership, and notoriety Aryan Nations enjoyed under Butler's leadership. In 2009, Jerald O'Brien emerged to lead a third Aryan Nations faction claiming rightful inheritance of Butler's legacy. Located in Coeur d'Alene, Idaho, members have leafleted the Coeur d'Alene area announcing the return of Aryan Nations to Idaho.

Christian Identity also persists in many small, independent cells of believers. Christian Identity members meet in Aryan free spaces such as small Bible study groups, independent churches, and cultural heritage organizations linked by a range of websites devoted to the cause.

Neo-Paganism

Racist neo-Pagans celebrate the ancient pre-Christian, proto-Germanic spiritual traditions of Odinism and its Icelandic cousin, Asatru. Odinism and Asatru share a social Darwinist philosophy that defines the survival of pure whites as a goal to be achieved at all costs.

Racist neo-Pagans draw upon Norse mythology to emphasize the mystical and heroic nature of European folk heritage. Neo-Pagans construct racial consciousness and solidarity around the worship of Odin, the chief Norse god of wisdom; Thor, the Norse god of strength; and Freyja, the Norse goddess of fertility and love.

Racist neo-Pagans see these gods as pure white deities that stand apart from the bastardized spirituality of mainstream Christianity. They also tend to "biologize spirituality" through the belief that their white gods and goddesses are "encoded in the DNA of their descendants." Gardell explains, "Blood is thought to carry memories of the ancient past, and divinities are believed to be genetically engraved upon or reverberate from deep down within the abyss of the collective subconscious or 'folk soul'" of true Aryans.

As they are interspersed throughout the larger Aryan networks of the neo-Nazi and skinhead faithful, neo-Pagans have spread their motifs to other factions of the white power movement. Thus, Aryan websites, racist literature, white power musicians, and racist music lyrics feature "muscular heathens, pagan gods and goddesses, runes and symbols, magic, and esoteric themes in abundance." The warrior imagery appeals to Aryans across all branches because warrior imagery symbolizes the righteous, combatant ideal with which many contemporary Aryans identify. Not all Aryans are devout followers of Pagan rituals and spiritual beliefs, but neo-Paganism provides modern-day Aryans with a collection of symbols, images, and ideals that amplify white power ideology.

Neo-Nazis

Neo-Nazi networks persist through parties, crashpads, the white power music scene, and the Internet. Neo-Nazis embrace traditional Nazi symbolism, such as the swastika; describe themselves as National Socialists; revere Adolf Hitler and the Third Reich; and promote eugenics to ensure the existence of a pure white race. George Lincoln Rockwell formed one of the earliest versions of neo-Nazis in 1958 with the American Nazi Party (ANP). The ANP popularized Holocaust denial among the American racist right and encouraged followers to join forces with Christian Identity churches.

The National Alliance, White Aryan Resistance, and the National Socialist Movement (NSM) have been three of the most influential sources of American neo-Nazism. William Pierce founded the National Alliance in 1974 after he became involved with Rockwell and the American Nazi Party during the 1960s. In 1978, Pierce, a former physics professor, authored the *Turner Diaries,* which depicts a racist guerrilla war and a truck bombing of a federal building. Timothy McVeigh reportedly used the *Turner Diaries* as an inspirational blueprint for the 1995 bombing of the Alfred P. Murrah Building in Oklahoma City.

Pierce established the National Alliance headquarters in 1985 on his 346-acre farm in Mill Point, West Virginia. He and a small cadre of members used the headquarters to publish white power books and other propaganda, operate the white power music company Resistance Records, and organize Internet activities. In 2001, the Alliance claimed thirty-five groups in thirty different states. Pierce's death in 2002 dealt a severe blow to the group, resulting in a substantial drop in the number of Alliance units and members. Recent evidence points to a shift in the National Alliance from a relatively large membership organization toward a small, loosely organized clique of white supremacists with long histories of violence and other criminal offending.

Since Pierce's death, several groups have splintered from the National Alliance. One of the most prominent neo-Nazi groups is Billy Roper's White Revolution. Roper, a former high school history teacher with a master's degree in anthropology, founded White Revolution in 2002. White Revolution draws upon Nazi-era ideals of *volk* to celebrate an ideal of Aryan racial kinship. Roper is noted for his efforts to pull together factions from across the movement for rallies, music shows, and other Aryan gatherings. White Revolution has an extensive Web presence and active chapters in sixteen states.

Tom Metzger's White Aryan Resistance (WAR) is a popular multimedia clearinghouse for neo-Nazi ideology. Metzger founded WAR in the 1980s after traveling a circuitous route through several white power branches. Metzger began his career in right-wing extremism during the 1960s and joined the John Birch Society. He quickly left the organization dissatisfied with their unwillingness to openly advocate anti-Semitism. In 1975, Metzger joined David Duke's Knights of the Ku Klux Klan and ascended to the rank of grand dragon, the KKK's highest-ranking state officer in California. Eventually Metzger and Duke parted ways and after an unsuccessful Congressional bid in 1980, Metzger founded the White American Political Association, which he eventually renamed the White Aryan Resistance. WAR has been in the forefront of the white power movement's Internet presence and aggressively recruits younger generations to the cause.

The National Socialist Movement formed in 1974 as an off-shoot of the American Nazi Party, but remained on the periphery of U.S. neo-Nazi groups until the mid-1990s when Jeff Schoep took over NSM leadership. Schoep has stepped into the vacuum created by William Pierce's death to recruit new members into the NSM. The fifty-six NSM groups in the United States periodically sponsor public rallies against illegal immigration and gay marriage. The NSM also sponsors an armed border watch unit that patrols the U.S./Mexican border in Southern California.

Racist Skinheads

Racist skinheads are the youngest branch of the white power movement. They derive from a distinct youth subculture, and since the late 1980s racist skinheads have synthesized neo-Nazi ideals and symbolism. Racist skinheads persist in loosely organized gangs and activist networks that congregate in skinhead crash-pads and white power music gatherings. The largest organized groups, such as the Hammerskin Nation, produce white power concerts and festivals and have active cells around the world and an extensive Web presence.

Racist skinhead groups formed in the United States during the late 1970s as a response to increased economic pressures, Latino and Asian immigration, and the growth of minority street gangs. The early U.S. racist skinheads in the 1970s and 1980s drew inspiration from disaffected British skinheads associated with the extreme right-wing National Front and the British National Party. Prior to the mid-1980s, skinhead racism was limited mainly to intermittent local conflicts with nonwhites and minority street gangs. In the late 1980s, however, WAR leader Tom Metzger, along with Aryan Nations' Richard Butler and other white power groups, began vigorously recruiting skinheads into the cause of global Aryan activism.

Racist skinheads organize themselves in a variety of ways. There are racist skinhead gangs with state-level affiliations, such as the West Virginia Skinheads; county affiliations, such as Orange County Skins; and city affiliations, such as the Las Vegas Skins.

The two most prominent American skinhead groups are Hammerskin Nation and Volkfront. The Hammerskins claim six regional chapters in the United States—Northwest Hammers, Midland Hammers, Confederate Hammers, Western Hammers, Northern Hammers, and Eastern Hammers—and official chapters in twelve other countries.

Hammerskins hosted dozens of white power music shows in 2008, along with Aryan barbeques. mixed martial arts viewing parties, and a "Fuhrer's Birthday Party" to commemorate Adolf Hitler's birthday. In December 2008, more than 100 Aryans from five states attended a "Martyrs Day" party in Florida to commemorate the Silent Brotherhood founder Robert Mathews, an Aryan terrorist who was killed in a 1984 shoot-out with federal authorities in Whidbey Island, Washington. Martyrs Day was cosponsored by the Confederate Hammerskins, Volksfront, and the American Front, and featured a keynote address by Richard Kemp, an imprisoned member of the Silent Brotherhood, who phoned in from federal prison.

Volksfront is one of the fastest growing and most active racist skinhead groups. Founded in an Oregon state penitentiary by Randal Lee Krager and Richard Arden in 1994, Volksfront calls itself "The Independent Voice of the White Working Class" and claims chapters in sixteen states and eight countries. Volksfront members are closely linked with Hammerskins and Blood & Honour, and Aryans from across the movement's branches attend its annual music festivals and participate in their Web forums. One of Volksfront's main goals is to create an all-white private community, and the group has reportedly purchased land for this purpose in Oregon, Washington, and Missouri. Volksfront uses their Missouri property to host an Aryan summit and music festival called Althing, dedicated to Samuel Weaver, martyred son of Christian Identity adherent Randy Weaver who was killed by federal authorities in an Idaho standoff in 1992.

Our sorting of Aryan branches overstates the lines of distinction among these networks, which in reality are much more blurred and porous. The white power movement encompasses contradictory realities. Some Aryans hold hard-line stances against other believers, which creates the basis for schisms. However, many Aryans collaborate across ideological lines to sustain the Aryan cause. Aryans of all stripes move back and forth across racist networks that meet in Aryan free spaces and uphold some basic white power doctrines on which all Aryans agree.

Aryan Doctrine and Collective Identity

Aryans sustain a sense of solidarity anchored in fundamental aims and ideological doctrines shared across the different white power branches. Their free spaces nourish and reinforce a sense of group unity around these doctrines and certain elemental beliefs about what it means to be an Aryan.

First and foremost, Aryans across all branches believe that they possess a unique ancestry that links them literally as racial brothers and sisters. That is, Aryans imagine that they are all connected by an innate biogenetic superiority. This presumed racial superiority is used to justify their belief in Aryan cultural superiority. Aryan doctrine claims that race mixing and intercultural exchange threaten their superior genetic and cultural lineage. In this way, Aryans see themselves as victims of a society that not only fails to acknowledge the natural superiority of whites but also suppresses and destroys all things Aryan. This view is summed up in the Aryan mantra known as the "14 Words": *We must secure the existence of our people and a future for white children.*

Aryans idealize traditional male-dominant families in which women are meant for domesticity, particularly for rearing white children who will become the early risers of the racial revolution. Aryans desire a racially exclusive world where nonwhites and other subhumans are vanquished, segregated, or at least subordinated to Aryan authority.

These beliefs are amplified by the emotions that accompany them. While it is easy to imagine that hate is the sole emotion underlying Aryan solidarity, it is only part of the picture. Expressions of intense hatred, anger, frustration, and outrage toward racial others do permeate Aryan networks. These "reactive emotions" are prominent in the relationships that galvanize white power members against their enemies. But Aryans also express a range of "vitalizing" and "reciprocal" feelings of pride, pleasure, solidarity, loyalty, solicitude, affection, gratification, and love directed toward one another. These sorts of convictions are the "glue of solidarity." They transcend ideological and stylistic differences among Aryan branches and help link members around the common goal of white power.

*

Constructing solidarity is a major accomplishment for members of such an extreme and marginalized ideology as white power. Aryan free spaces are the primary contexts where white power members fashion a sense of unity around core beliefs and the emotions they arouse.

We now turn to discuss *how* Aryans build solidarity in their free spaces. We begin with the family as the most intimate of Aryan free spaces. Aryan families are the clearest and most direct representation of white racial kinship. The family home is meant to be a pure white space offering escape from mainstream society. Aryan parents use this space to envelope their children in white power hate culture, to socialize new recruits for the movement.

> We all know the movement begins with the family. If you can't save your family, then what's the point? Keeping your families pure and raising your kids among your kin is what we fight for.
> —Darren, SWAS member

Aryan homes are the most private, guarded, and valued of the white power movement's free spaces. Homes offer Aryans control over what they say and do, and they are the spaces where Aryans can close the doors and draw the blinds to hide their subversive acts from those who oppose them. Aryan parents use the home as a place to raise their children as tomorrow's warriors who will defend the white race against genocide.

I stood in the doorway to Erik and Andi's living room and watched the scene unfold. Four Aryan mothers sat around the room chatting about their children. Two toddlers played on a blanket in the middle of the floor. Andi busied herself with the birthday cake in the kitchen behind me. It all seemed rather unremarkable, except for the white power themes that dominated the occasion.

Seven Aryan families had gathered to celebrate Erik and Andi's son Hunter's birthday. Erik and Andi named Hunter for the fictional killer of Jews and interracial couples in the infamous white power fantasy novel *Hunter*. This was only Hunter's fourth birthday, but he and his friends already appeared to embrace an Aryan attitude.

I stepped quickly out of the doorway as two young boys, Turner and William, came stomping through in their black Doc Marten boots, arms raised in salute, repeatedly shouting, "White power!" Turner wore a white power music T-shirt, while William wore a red T-shirt emblazoned with "88," the Aryan code for "Heil Hitler."

The parents watched Turner and William's display. As Turner passed his mother, she patted his head, looked at the others, smiled, and said proudly: "He's already racially aware."

Throughout the afternoon, Hunter and friends played tag and hide and seek, and wrestled in the yard. As the children prepared to play hide and seek, Erik helped them decide who was "it": "Eeny, meeny, miny, moe. Catch a nigger by the toe … ."

The most shocking white power symbol was Hunter's birthday cake. Erik called the kids and parents into the dining room, and then Andi walked out of the kitchen carrying a red-and-white birthday cake in the shape of a swastika. A lit candle topped each arm of the swastika. The group sang the happy birthday song followed by a *"Sieg heil"* chant and Nazi salutes.

I lingered at the edge of the group, watching in amazement as Aryans transformed one of the most common family rituals into a deeply racist experience.

Aryan parents normalize racist extremism among their children by making white power culture central to family life. They fill their homes with racist and anti-Semitic symbols and name their children after icons of the movement. They use white supremacist stories to teach hatred and homeschool to immerse their children in Aryan ideology.

But homes are not completely free. The degree to which Aryans can explicitly fashion their homes and family life to normalize extreme racism varies, in part, by where they live. While some isolated rural families live very private lives that allow them to openly display their extremist beliefs, most Aryans reside in urban and suburban settings surrounded by those they hate. Prying neighbors and landlords pose the risk of exposure and confrontations. It is therefore important for Aryans to balance their desire for white power purity and expression in the home with the need to conceal their extremism from outsiders.

In this chapter, we focus on white power parents' socialization styles. Socialization refers to the process by which humans learn the norms, values, and ideals of a culture and community. Socialization strategies can vary among members of the same culture. We discuss three distinct Aryan family types—hard-core, newly respectable, and communitarian—to describe how Aryans use the home as a free space.

Seth and Jessie are a hard-core family that mirrors popular stereotypes of extremely dysfunctional, raucous, violent, and impoverished Aryans with criminal histories. Kate and Todd represent a newly respectable family, maintaining a façade of mainstream normality that masks their home's racist and anti-Semitic hate culture. Darren and Mindy raise their family as part of a rural communitarian network of Aryans who meet regularly, share resources, and collaborate to raise their children in a private setting saturated with Aryan idealism.

Although Aryan family styles differ, the common factor across Aryan families is that they use their homes as free spaces where Aryan culture survives through child socialization and family rituals. Aryans agree that rearing white children is a righteous task essential for strengthening the movement.

Seth and Jessie's Hard-Core Home Life

Seth and his wife, Jessie, are staunchly committed racist skinheads. Seth is thirty-four years old, and his short and stocky build, shaved head, goatee, and tattoos create an intimidating public persona. He earned his veteran skinhead status during his nearly two decades with the group White Aryan Resistance, or WAR Skins, and later as a Hammerskin. Seth grew up in what he describes as a "pretty typical everyday family" and calls his father a "traditional conservative who was racist but never put race as the most important factor."

When Seth was a teenager, he met racist skinheads at punk music concerts. Despite the tensions that carousing with racists caused with his father, Seth talks fondly of his recruitment into white power groups, getting inked with racist tattoos, and playing in racist bands.

Jessie, a year older than Seth, is tall and slender with dark red hair. She has a volatile personality shaped by a life on the streets as a member of the white power criminal gang Nazi Lowriders and two stints in prison for drug dealing. Her life has been steeped in racism. Her father, a successful attorney, taught Jessie about racial hatred as a young child. He advocated pseudo-scientific theories of racial supremacy and trained Jessie to believe in a natural order of white dominance. Although Jessie came from an affluent family, after dropping out of school in her teens, she turned to street life and befriended skinhead gang members.

Seth and Jessie live in an ordinary-looking three-bedroom apartment in a small working-class city in Southern California with Jessie's three young children from two earlier marriages, Ronnie (age five), Sven (four), and Ethan (three). Seth's daughter, Amber (twelve), from his first marriage, regularly visits them. Jessie is jobless and stays at home with the kids. The family struggles to get by on Seth's job as a credit collection agent.

Seth and Jessie both talk passionately of their deep commitment to Aryanism and saving the white race from genocide. They claim their main goal in life is to raise their children as young white power warriors. Seth has been active in the Southern California white power music scene for more than a decade, playing in a number of bands and organizing white power concerts. Despite their low income, he takes leave from work several times a year to play with his band at Aryan festivals around the United States and Europe.

Seth and Jessie's home is a far cry from Seth's classic skinhead crashpad where he lived prior to their marriage. The crashpad was constantly filled with Seth's skinhead friends and Aryan musicians. Walls were covered with signs of the movement, including white power music posters, a Hitler portrait, and a swastika flag displayed in the living room. White power books, pamphlets, and CDs littered the tables and floors.

The white power symbolism throughout Seth's old crashpad is like the accessory items in other Aryan family homes we had seen. Religious Aryans fill their homes with the Christian cross along with spiritual movement messages. Neo-Nazi, Christian Identity, and Klan families display statuettes and paintings of Hitler, swastika flags, and images of Nazi Germany, along with Confederate flags and wall hangings to mark their local group affiliation. Iconic Nordic imagery appears commonly in homes across Aryan branches.

Seth and Jessie avoid openly brazen signs of Aryanism in their home. They fear exposure to their Hispanic neighbors, who vastly outnumber whites in their complex, and the apartment manager, who sometimes enters unannounced. They hide the most obvious signs of their beliefs, but they are not happy about these constraints. Seth says they are just biding their time in the apartment as they save money for a house where they can be free to "live as we please."

Seth and Jessie express their Aryan beliefs in some inconspicuous ways. Seth wears T-shirts, many emblazoned with the insignia of his favorite white power bands. To the uninitiated, Aryan band logos can be difficult to decipher as white power symbolism, but to the Aryans like Seth who wear them, band logos are very meaningful symbols of resistance.

Jewelry is a staple in the wardrobes of activist parents and children. The first time we met Jessie, a necklace of tiny swastikas dangled loosely around her neck. She later showed us Waffen-SS lightning-bolt earrings and a Celtic ring with "HH" and "88" stamped around it.

This is not to say, however, that Aryan clothing is always subtle in its meaning. We observed Aryans whose around-the-house clothing choices displayed images that are impossible to misconstrue: Nazi soldiers, swastikas, and hooded Klansmen, as well as messages such as "Supreme White Power." Kathy, a Southwest Aryan Separatist, wearing a "Hitler World Tour" T-shirt as she cooked breakfast one morning, explained: "At work I can't wear a shirt like this. So I feel pretty good around here to be able to put it on and be myself. I like that a lot."

Around their apartment, Seth and Jessie typically dress their two oldest boys to mimic their father's skinhead uniform of Doc Marten boots, jeans, and T-shirt. Their youngest son sometimes sports infant bodysuits covered with swastikas and German iron crosses. Their children also play dress up in Nazi uniforms and wear more covert clothing styles that include ordinary jersey shirts that bear the numbers "14" to represent the "14 Words" mantra, "88" for "Heil Hitler," and "18," which is code for the first and eighth letters of the alphabet, A and H, Adolf Hitler's initials.

While Seth and Jessie's home decor did not scream "white power," they did create displays infused with Aryan themes. Like many families, Seth and Jessie displayed family photographs around their home. After Jessie pointed at a photo of her oldest son, Ronnie, giving a *Sieg heil* salute, we realized that in several pictures their children wore movement clothing and were surrounded by racist symbols.

Raising "Little Hitler"

Seth and Jessie's hard-core parenting style encourages an acidly racist and anti-Semitic culture among their children. We found their tactics painful to watch. Seth and Jessie were under supervision by Child Protective Services. Jessie was on parole. Their oldest son, Ronnie, was undergoing psychiatric therapy. Jessie was particularly vicious at times, cursing, yelling, and hitting the kids at the slightest provocation. The violence carried over into constant fights among their three young boys. Seth and Jessie paid little attention to these fights, except when they encouraged the battles so their boys would, according to Seth, "learn self-defense." The effects of racist socialization in this hard-core environment were clearly visible on Ronnie, whom Seth and Jessie's friends nicknamed "Little Hitler."

Ronnie was born while Jessie was incarcerated and spent the first three years of his life living with his biological father, Lars, an active Nazi Lowrider. Lars and his friends reportedly forced Ronnie to drink malt liquor and abused him physically, sexually, and psychologically. When Ronnie was three years old, Lars was convicted of murder and sentenced to life in prison. Ronnie lived with Lars's parents until Jessie was released from prison.

Ronnie had just turned five years old when we met him. Psychologists had recently diagnosed him with several mental health problems including attachment disorder and oppositional defiance disorder. Ronnie is physically aggressive. He constantly fights with his brothers and his peers, and he killed a small bird and tried to kill a kitten with his bare hands. Ronnie is also sexually aggressive and brags about "sticking his ding-a-ling in girls' mouths."

Seth and Jessie are adamant about turning Ronnie into a neo-Nazi. Seth and Jessie have taught him movement slogans such as *Sieg heil*, which he frequently yells at his parents and anyone else around him. When Seth puts Aryan music on the stereo, Ronnie dances excitedly around their living room singing the lyrics. Ronnie has learned to call himself a skinhead and to label all dark-skinned people he sees as niggers and muds.

He watches a lot of television, mostly violent cartoons and movies. Seth and Jessie tell Ronnie to mimic the violence in the shows as practice for fighting their racial enemies. When watching television, Seth and Jessie point out the "darkies," "faggots," and "Jewbags" to remind Ronnie about his racial enemies.

Like other Aryan families we studied, Seth and Jessie use birthday celebrations as ritual initiations for their children to embrace white power culture. For Ronnie's fifth birthday, Seth and Jessie presented him with a cake decorated with swastikas and iron crosses. Aryan parents often use phrases like "14 Words" or "white power" along with figurines of robed Klansmen or Nazi guards on their children's birthday cakes. During the parties, parents and friends racialize the happy birthday song by substituting the child's name with phrases like "young Aryan" and "white warrior" and infuse entire celebrations with *Sieg heil* salutes and choruses of "White power!" and "Rahowa!"

Parents also infuse gift-giving at birthdays and holidays with racial themes. Seth and Jessie transformed a G.I. Joe action figure into "G.I. Nazi" complete with swastika arm bands and SS emblazoned on the doll's forehead. As they gave the doll to Ronnie, Seth and Jessie explained to him that G.I. Nazi will help save the white race. Other parents gave blond, blue-eyed Barbie dolls they called "Aryan girls" to their young daughters. We also saw gifts of clothing with racist symbols, Aryan comics, white power coloring books, neo-Nazi video games, Aryan music, and SS knives among other weapons.

Seth and Jessie also commemorate Aryan holidays, such as the birthdays of Hitler and his deputy, Rudolph Hess. They use these celebrations to help Ronnie imagine an Aryan legacy that extends beyond his own family. Seth and Jessie also join with other Aryan families to memorialize the death of Ian Stuart Donaldson, the "godfather" of white power rock music. Similar ritual commemorations occur in Christian Identity families. We witnessed families praying for martyred Aryans such as Gordon Kahl, a tax evader and founder of a Texas Posse Comitatus cell, and Silent Brotherhood founder Robert Mathews, who led a terrorist cell in murder, counterfeiting, and armed robberies.

Aryan parents control their children's environment in these ways to expose them to role models and experiences that affirm the attitudes and aspirations they think are best for their children. This socialization style is no different in families of other cultural backgrounds, except that Aryans emphasize violent, racist white power fantasies that must be kept hidden from outsiders.

The home is one of the places where Aryans are able to sustain their racist visions in the most unrestricted manner. Seth and Jessie's hard-core Aryan home life reflects a style we also saw with other skinhead families. But Aryan families are varied. The next type of family racializes the home in more subtle ways.

The Newly Respectable: Todd and Kate

Todd is thirty-two years old, short and slender. Tattoos of Aryan warriors, Celtic crosses, and swastikas cover his chest, stomach, and back. Todd's parents divorced when he was twelve years old, and he spent much of his youth on the streets of Los Angeles.

> My mom was all fucked up and there was nobody else to take care of me and my brothers, so my aunt took us. They were pretty racist … . She would say. "I don't want you hanging out with niggers. I don't want you hanging out with beaners." [She] dated the grand dragon of the local KKK. They were adamant about [extreme racism].

In his early teens, Todd followed his older brother Jason into the notorious Southern California Aryan criminal gang Public Enemy Number One (PEN1). Todd spent fourteen years with PEN1 committed to the group's hard-core racism, which couples a "mercenary and criminal nature" with white power ideology.

At thirty, Todd began to distance himself from PEN1's hard-core lifestyle of drugs, crime, and gangbanging. He felt burned out from his hard-driving lifestyle and wanted to settle down with his new wife, Kate. He did not completely exit white power activism, however. He is a regular in the Southern California white power music scene, often visits his friends' crashpads, attends Aryan house parties, and keeps in close contact with PEN1 leaders.

Todd's wife, Kate, is thirty years old and a veteran Orange County Skin. In high school, she rebelled from her middle-class upbringing by befriending a group of local racist skinheads. Kate said, "I made some bad choices when I was young, doing drugs and helping skinhead friends break into some homes." She was arrested for one burglary, served three months in jail, then "cleaned up her life" after her release.

Kate met Todd at a white power concert when she was twenty-five. Todd and Kate dated and married three years later. Like Todd, Kate remains committed to the white power movement. She closely follows the movement through Aryan websites, but each year limits her face-to-face contact to just a few white power music shows or parties.

Todd and Kate's attitude about raising their Aryan family reflects the new respectability ideal advocated by White Aryan Resistance leader, Tom Metzger. Metzger and other prominent Aryans encourage activists to strategically hide their Aryanism in order to blend into the mainstream. The rationale is that clandestine Aryans are not easy to detect and can therefore infiltrate the social system; rise to positions of wealth, power, and respectability; give resources back to the movement; and become role models for future Aryans. This strategy encourages racist skinheads to grow out their hair, cover their tattoos, stay out of trouble, earn college degrees, find good jobs, and raise children in a stable environment filled with potent Aryan idealism.

Judging only by outward appearance, Todd and Kate live a rather ordinary, solidly middle-class way of life. Todd works full-time as a welder; Kate as a paralegal. They have two young boys, Teddy and Alex, whom they see as their foremost responsibility. Their freshly painted, well-landscaped house looks no different from others in their attractive middle-class neighborhood. Signs of the white power movement are hard to find inside the home as well. Todd stashes his swastika flag and other racist paraphernalia in a closet, hides his Aryan tattoos, and lowers the volume when he plays white power music. Yet their home is an Aryan enclave.

Todd and Kate hope to shield their kids from the street life they experienced. They reject the hustling, gangbanging, and drugs of their youth, but not their commitment to white power ideology. They are still devoted racists and steadfast in their plans to raise Aryan children. They imagine their boys attending college, taking professional jobs, and rising to influential positions where they can change society with their white power vision.

Like most Aryan parents we studied, Kate and Todd talk of strikingly familiar parental worries. We listened as they spoke about many of the same anxieties as other doting parents, such as their children's health and nutrition and what they learn in school. They fret about Teddy and Alex's future, but these worries are sifted through the filter of white power ideology.

When Teddy and Alex are sick, Todd and Kate worry about the care they will receive from doctors and nurses who might be secret agents of ZOG. They also worry that their children might be brainwashed in public school by ZOG-controlled teachers. ZOG could turn them against white power ideals and control their future.

Todd and Kate expose Teddy and Alex to home-based white power culture in several ways. They pepper their talk with matter-of-fact statements about "niggers," "spies," "Jew-dogs," and "muds." They clothe their boys with covert Aryan symbols, such as football jerseys numbered "88." Todd and Kate read their sons bedtime stories about Aryan heroes, give toys that purportedly reflect their Aryan values, and emphasize Aryan superiority. Todd tells Teddy and Alex about the white power music shows he attends, describes in detail the meaning of song lyrics, and emphasizes that they are among the enlightened few engaged in a struggle against ZOG. If Teddy and Alex embrace Aryan ideals, Todd and Kate are convinced that they will be among the chosen few who are prepared for the race war that will come.

Todd and Kate teach their children more than Aryan hatred. They also emphasize love, camaraderie, and kinship among Aryans. Kate says: "I'm raising our kids so they understand that racialism isn't just about hate and violence. I want them to only have white friends and understand their white heritage. I plan to teach them to be proud of their ancestors and to love their whiteness."

Todd and Kate stress racial kinship with other Aryans. As Randall Collins says, these sentiments are the "the 'glue' of solidarity" that really binds all people to one another. Kate and Todd hope that by nurturing these same feelings in their young children, they will imagine themselves as part of a larger Aryan family.

Soft-Sell Socialization

Todd and Kate also use an indirect socialization strategy to teach their children white power ideas. Quietly persuasive, soft-sell tactics favor a subtler tone that serves to normalize Aryan beliefs. Such methods reflect the hard reality that Aryans cannot totally exorcise mainstream influences from their children's lives.

Todd and Kate direct their kids' mainstream exposure toward experiences that are consistent with Aryan ideals. They surround their kids with white people and white culture, hoping to make nonwhites seem odd and undesirable social contacts. This tactic is relatively easy for them now, since the boys do not yet attend school, but the difficulty will increase as they grow up and become exposed to a greater number of outside influences.

This strategy is a popular topic of conversation in many Aryan circles. We listened as a group of Aryan parents at a party related how they limited their children's contact with nonwhites. Ryan, a Colorado Skin, said: "I surround them with white culture, friends, and family ... . We don't discuss race much, but my kids only attend birthday parties and play groups with white children. They have white parents, white children, and white friends and that's what they know."

Other Aryans emphasize their Eurocentric cultural heritage to subtly accentuate white culture without pushing young children too early to confront explicit and extreme styles of racial hatred. Brandy, a Christian Identity mother, explained:

> I just teach them about their Irish heritage. I teach them to be loyal to their kin. I don't want my children to ruin their lives by hating everything like I've seen happen. My six-year-old goes to school, and I volunteer for class parties and field trips. I just allow my kids to have their own ideas and I do my best to instill white pride in them. I think this works a lot better than force feeding them.

Television, films, and other media are a major thorn in the side of Aryan parents, so they closely monitor what children watch. Beth, a Christian Identity disciple, ended one of her daughter's favorite shows when a black character was shown. "She used to watch *Clifford the Big Red Dog* all the time, but then we saw an episode where he had a black friend and we said no more. *Little Mermaid's* not too bad, but it's got some multicultural crap too."

Aryan parents that we studied did not totally ban popular media from the home, but, like Beth, they screened the content of television shows and movies for how many nonwhite characters would be shown, whether nonwhites were villains or heroes, and if plot lines promoted race-mixing or homosexuality. Michelle, a Colorado Skin, blocks channels, such as Nickelodeon, Cartoon Network, and PBS, to ensure that her daughters are not inadvertently exposed to culturally diverse shows. "The media is so antiwhite, so we have to use what we can to our advantage. We use white books and movies that have the right message. We block the cable channels that have antiwhite kid shows."

Some Aryan parents allow their children to watch shows with ethnically diverse casts and then use those shows to teach their kids about racial doctrine. Seth and Jessie used movie characters to teach their son Ronnie about racial enemies.

In one instance, Ronnie asked, "Mommy, is that guy [the Rock's character in the movie *Scorpion King*] on our side or is he one of our enemies?" Jessie replied, "Honey it's hard to tell, but he's not white. Those other guys are on our side [pointing at two, clearly white, protagonists]."

Soft-sell socialization strategies attempt to address the dichotomy between Aryans' desire for a purified white-only existence and the reality that such racial purity is almost impossible to achieve. Like other newly respectable Aryan families, Kate and Todd try to bring their children along gradually, decreasing the confusion youngsters may feel as they are taught extremist values that conflict so starkly with the mainstream norms that also surround them. They try to cloak their radical beliefs in the appearance of mainstream normality while simultaneously rejecting mainstream anti-Aryan ideas. But living a veiled resistance inevitably creates dissonance and a double bind.

Todd and Kate worry about their kids being co-opted by mainstream culture and drifting away from white power ideals. Their worries reflect those of some hard-core white power members who criticize the new respectability strategy for creating soft, uncommitted Aryans. But, if Todd and Kate were to be more open about their Aryanism they would run the risk of jeopardizing their middle-class success, leading to the downward mobility so common among Aryan activists. They fear that exposing their true identities would bring critical scrutiny and stigma, possible job loss, and disruptions to their home life and to many of the relationships they use to mask their Aryan beliefs.

Hiding under the veil of normality may not create the kind of powerful socialization experiences that white power parents hope will ensure their children become Aryan warriors. But public exposure of parents' racial extremism might well weaken the movement's goal of gaining a foothold in mainstream society. The power of Aryan free spaces is that they allow Aryans to retreat into contexts that challenge multicultural ideology and experiences. Newly respectable families adopt mainstream appearances while mixing explicit and implicit racialized messages in their homes.

Communitarian families, to which we now turn, are not as encumbered, although, as with all Aryans, there are also limits to their expression of hate in the home.

Darren and Mindy's Communitarian Family Life

Darren and Mindy are parents in a communitarian white power network in rural Nevada. They both grew up near Reno, Nevada, and describe their parents as "patriots but not white power." Raised as Mormons in the Church of Jesus Christ of Latter Day Saints (LDS), Darren and Mindy also experienced socialization into a narrow worldview. They now reject the LDS Church for straying from white supremacist beliefs.

Mindy is twenty-six years old and traces her white power extremism to high school confrontations with blacks and Polynesian girls. These confrontations drove her toward white groups, where she took up with skinheads and immersed herself in white power ideology. Darren, twenty-nine, turned to Aryanism in high school. "I felt there was a lot of racial bullshit in school. I got tired of all these niggers walking around doing whatever they wanted and the skinheads weren't having any of that shit. We stood up to people and kicked ass."

Darren and Mindy married soon after high school and, fearing a race war, joined a small communitarian white power group, the Southwest Aryan Separatists (SWAS) to avoid the major cities, where the racial fighting would begin. Darren learned from his Aryan friends about the rural hotbed for racism where SWAS was located. The dozen families that made up SWAS welcomed them. SWAS families live within twenty miles of one another and meet regularly for events, such as weekly dinners, Bible study meetings, homeschooling, camping, and birthday celebrations.

After several years renting a home, Darren and Mindy bought twelve acres with another Aryan couple, Erik and Andi. During our fieldwork both families were building a solar-powered home, growing their own food, and stockpiling weapons and supplies in preparation for the government collapse and racial battles they anticipated.

Darren and Mindy talk enthusiastically about the freedom they experience living with other Aryans in a communitarian style. Darren wants to "just live off the land, live by the scripture, raise my family, raise my crops." They see their secluded homestead as a fortress to defend against ZOG. "I want to see 'em coming. I know eventually they will. When they do we'll be ready."

When we met them, Darren and Mindy were living in a mobile home parked on their land. They spent much of their free time in the afternoons and weekends working on their new home and a barn. Darren erected a Confederate flag outside their trailer and decorated the inside with a portrait of Hitler and a Klan painting in the living room. White power children's books, movement pamphlets, and other paraphernalia were scattered throughout their home.

Cultural Isolation

SWAS parents like Darren and Mindy romanticize the idea of total societal withdrawal to create a pure Aryan lifestyle for their children. They go to great lengths to try to ensure a purified existence, free from anti-Aryan society, by carving out private family spaces where they can be submerged in white power culture.

Such social-geographic isolation is an extreme measure, which is relatively uncommon among WPM families, who often reside in urban and suburban areas. But SWAS members see a purification effect in their seclusion. Withdrawal shields the family from mainstream authorities and anti-Aryan culture, they say, and helps nurture the survivalist skills and sensibilities required for the inevitable race war.

Daily life at Darren and Mindy's reflects a pastoral ideal. They are transforming their land into a sustainable homestead. Their kids play carefree in the woods that cover their property, participate in chores, and help to build their solar home. The SWAS families in the area trade hosting duties for gatherings such as bonfire parties, birthday celebrations, and Bible study meetings. They also trade labor, such as carpentry, gardening, and babysitting, within the SWAS network.

Mindy and Darren's isolation means that their children are not directly exposed to much mainstream culture as compared to families like Seth and Jessie who live in urban areas surrounded by what they define as mainstream filth. Yet Mindy and Darren's socialization style is still fueled by the fantasy vision of a coming race war, which all SWAS families are gearing up to survive. Mindy and Darren encourage their children to explore the woods as a way to become familiar with the land they will protect with their lives from "niggers, ZOG, and the bad, evil government." They work together as a family on their building projects, as well as hunting, fishing, and other survivalist skills, to ready themselves for the apocalyptic race war. Bill, a SWAS parent, explained: "Our youth are going to be responsible for securing our race. Everything we do, it's not just for fun, it's very serious and he needs to know what he's up against."

SWAS children are ensconced in their closed society and know little about the outside world. Their lives are dominated by the specter of race war and survival. But it is hard to predict whether exposure to inevitable outside non-Aryan influences will reshape their intense childhood Aryan socialization experiences.

Gender Lessons

SWAS kids learn that Aryan men and women in the movement have distinct roles. Like most Aryan families, Darren and Mindy idealize the patriarchal structure in which men are esteemed protectors of family and race, and women are relegated to the subordinate, albeit vital, roles of motherhood and homemaker.

Aryan ideology prescribes that men must be warrior combatants. In their role as fathers, men are expected to prepare themselves and their family for the enduring racial struggle. SWAS men like Darren fancy themselves as outdoorsmen. They camp, hike, and hunt to hone their survivalist skills, and they stockpile weapons, food, and water. SWAS men lead backcountry outings as survivalist training missions to prepare families against ZOG attacks.

Families are the core Aryan fighting unit. Homes are their defensive refuge in the race war. SWAS boys quickly learn their roles in this mythic battle. Darren explicitly models the dominant male role for his sons, repeatedly reminding them of their responsibility to family and race. He prepares them to fight to the death to repel ZOG. "All my kids, you know, we're shooting it out; we're staying. My boys, they say, 'Dad, we're going to hold our guns and shoot back, and if you and Mom get killed we're gonna shoot it out.'"

Urban neo-Nazi men also play out warrior fantasies in their gangbanging and bar fights. But frequent fighting is a young man's game. Older veteran skinheads like Todd and Seth typically stay out of brawls they once instigated. Todd and Seth own weapons, however, and practice combat at shooting ranges.

The main role of SWAS women is to procreate. Women encourage one another to have children for the movement and talk to their own young girls about the responsibility to have Aryan babies when they are grown. The women's prodding of one another comes with the tacit assumption that the Aryan community of women will support one another by trading child care, dinners, hand-me-down clothes, and domestic help. The mutual support moderates the expense of rearing children, making it possible to have more than they could otherwise afford alone.

White power ideology defines procreation as Aryan women's main contribution to the racial struggle. Mindy explained: "I love having white babies! I love the fact that I can contribute in that way, helping my people by helping produce the next generation. When you look in your white baby's eyes you can see the world you're creating."

Kathy, a fellow Southwest Aryan Separatist, proudly showed us her newest child and spoke of the honor of motherhood. "Look at him [her newborn son], he's so special. He's white and that just makes it even more special. That's what's so amazing, knowing that I'm helping save my race. It's an honor to raise white babies."

In their role as movement mothers, women do more than procreate and raise their own little Aryans. For example. Mindy and other SWAS women operated an outreach program called Operation White Care to send care packages to Aryans in the U.S. military stationed in the Middle East.

Mothers in hard-core and newly respectable Aryan families also connect with one another for support and camaraderie. Jessie takes her kids to the beach with other skinhead families and trades hand-me-down clothes and toys. Kate is an Aryan soccer mom, carting her kids along with two others from Aryan families to soccer games on their all-white teams. While these activities may look like typical family activities, each mother ensures that their children's experiences are situated in a context where racial extremism bubbles just below the surface.

Aryan Names

SWAS racial socialization begins at birth with the choice of baby names drawn directly from Aryan symbolism. Darren and Mindy's eight-year-old daughter is named Liberty, symbolizing white power commitment to freedom from ZOG and patriotism to America, which they envision as a pure white nation. Forrest, their five-year-old son, is named for the first Ku Klux Klan imperial wizard, Nathaniel Bedford Forrest. As mentioned earlier, Erik and Andi named their son Hunter after the fictional character in William Pierce's infamous white power fantasy novel, *Hunter,* who guns down interracial couples and Jews to cleanse America and save the future of white civilization. Their daughter's name, Ariana, derives from the word Aryan.

Aryan parents use these names to link children to a racist tradition, which they expect will help instill in their children a racialized identity. White power parents commonly look to Nordic mythology or to German culture, which they associate with the Nazis, for names that symbolize their beliefs. We did not meet anyone named Adolf, but parents do use less notorious German names. Randy, a SoCal Skin and friend of Seth and Jessie's, told us, "I'll probably name my child Dieter if I have a son. That would be in honor of my grandfather, who was SS, and because it's a

good German name and that'll help my son stay in touch with his roots."

Parents reinforce the significance of names with stories and admonitions about their meaning. Cal, a SoCal Skin, said, "Aryan names won't start a revolution or anything, but names are like a lot of other things; it's what they symbolize that's important. [Names] tell you something about what's in a person's heart. It's kind of like the '14 Words'; they may just be words, but they're also a lot more than that." Baxter, a father of four and veteran neo-Pagan believer, agreed. "The name is very important; it defines the spirit of a newborn, and parents should think carefully about their decision of what to name their child. Think of anyone you know. Their name represents everything about that person."

White power parents choose names explicitly to instill their children with racial extremism. The act of naming a child with some meaningful referent is not unique to Aryans. Parents of all cultures do it. But unless those Aryan names reflect the most infamous historical figures, like Hitler, they are not likely to be noticed. To the uninitiated, the meaning of Hunter, Forrest, Ariana, and other common white power names is not clear, which helps children pass in mainstream settings. For those in the know, however, such names may represent a significant, lifelong symbolic attachment to the white power movement. Parents' goal is to convert the Aryan-named child into a person committed to a white power identity.

Homeschooling Hate

Aryan homeschooling systematically transmits white power culture to kids. Mindy homeschools her children, focusing on the fundamentals of reading, writing, and math, but her makeshift curriculum is saturated with Aryan themes. History and social studies lessons concentrate on European cultures and Western civilization while vilifying Asian, Middle Eastern, and African cultures. Her lessons are historical accounts of Nordic nations, Anglo-British experiences, and Nazi Germany. Mindy uses these narratives to emphasize white accomplishments that convey

Aryan superiority. She says homeschooling gives her the chance to transmit Aryan truth.

SWAS and other Aryan communitarian networks divide teaching responsibility across parents to ease each family's burden and draw on complementary skills of the parents. The mothers who teach come together to plan lessons, organize supplies, and discuss teaching strategies to insure that all SWAS children receive well-rounded white power instruction. Carrie, a SWAS mother with two boys, said, "We completely control the environment where they're raised, and this means we can exclude nonwhites from their childhood, which is excluding them from their worldview."

Another SWAS mother, Brenda, reflected on the purity of homeschooling. "Homeschool is the best. You provide the information: they live it. Homeschool allows me to know that my children will get the truth and not all this liberal propaganda."

Homeschooling is not limited to communitarian families like SWAS. Aryan parents worry about their children's education, and many see homeschooling as a way to control their children's political indoctrination. Homeschooling gives parents the direct and systematic power to racialize the content of their child's learning and to keep their children out of the public school system, which Aryans see as a brainwashing tool to perpetuate lies about race mixing and to force-feed students with liberal Jewish propaganda.

The white power website, Stormfront.org, declares:

> Education is a key component to our survival, however, the conventional idea of education is not sufficient, because of the liberal, Jewish bias that is imposed on most learning materials. ... For our children to be properly educated we must have places to teach them the accomplishments of white Europeans and the importance of staying true to one's race. If we don't take the time to show them the way, they will be brainwashed by ignorant liberal teachers ... that encourage race mixing and degeneracy.

Aryan parents also fear for their children's safety in public schools, imagining schools as playgrounds for nonwhite gangs who have declared open season on white students, bullying, beating, and murdering them as school officials sit idly by. Homeschooling resolves the problems of public school and guarantees that Aryan children will remain immersed in racist culture. Melanie, a SoCal Skin, summed up the attitude of the Aryan homeschoolers we studied:

> We need to educate our children. They're being indoctrinated into a society that has no morals, no responsibility. To survive, we need to teach our children that there's more to life than the garbage they're feeding us. Our kids shouldn't be afraid to walk the streets and schools without being preyed upon; they should be able to enjoy being white kids. I've worked hard to be a mother and a teacher.

White power lessons saturate children with ideals that stress biological and cultural attachment to their Aryan racial kin. Cal, a SoCal Skin with a three-year-old son, uses themes of white heritage and cultural preservation to justify his child's racist education. "My son is homeschooled. I teach him to be proud of his people ... that he's part of the race that created civilization. I just want to make sure he inherits what is rightfully his and what our forefathers fought so hard to pass on."

Similarly, Janine, a SoCal Skin and mother of three, homeschools her children to stress sacred cultural knowledge that public school would deny them. "European culture is fading; our tradition is being stripped away so we have to do something to fight the assault. I think with the public schools just promoting filth and hypocrisy, I can't imagine sending my kids there, so I teach them here."

Despite its appeal, however, homeschooling remains an unattainable luxury for most Aryan parents. With a few exceptions, the families we studied sent their children to public schools.

Homeschooling requires a support network that is absent for many Aryans. Seth and Jessie want to homeschool but do not know other Aryans near them who homeschool and do not feel prepared to do it alone. Thus, Seth and Jessie's socialization prepares their kids to stand up and fight the "niggers and spies" who, they imagine, will threaten Ronnie and his brothers in public schools.

Aryans like Kate and Todd take a different approach to school. They acknowledge the virtues of homeschool, but they both work and do not have the time to spare. They moved to their neighborhood precisely so their children could attend a predominantly white public school. They view public school as a place where their kids will learn to exist as Aryans in settings that champion anti-Aryan attitudes. They also talk about public school as an essential experience for their children prior to college. College, they believe, will guarantee their children the credentials for getting a good job in a mainstream setting.

In accord with the newly respectable creed that a poor Aryan is an ineffective one, Kate and Todd plan for their kids to blend into the mainstream and secretly contribute to the Aryan cause. Their choice of public schools adds risk and exposes their children to precisely the type of social influences that hinder extreme racism and blind hatred. Yet Kate and Todd believe that they can saturate their children's experiences in the home with enough Aryanism to combat the normalizing tendencies of the public school experience and harden their children against mainstream, anti-Aryan culture.

*

Aryan families—hard-core, newly respectable, and communitarian—live diverse styles while sharing a fundamental commitment to white power. Debates rage inside the white power movement over which style is most effective for the movement's survival. Hard-core parents and activists claim that newly respectable families

have sold out and do little more than play act as Aryans. Likewise, hardcore Aryans see many communitarian groups, especially those ensconced in rural hideaways, as shirking from the front lines of the racial struggle occurring in urban zones. Aryans committed to the newly respectable strategy dismiss hardcore families as rogues of the movement who lend little to the ultimate goal of preparing to take the reins of political and social power. Newly respectable families offer another route into Aryanism that does not require self-denial of society's fruits. All Aryan families imagine that it is only a matter of time before whites will take over society.

What white power adherents all agree on is the importance of the family to anchor and sustain the white power movement. Aryan homes provide a private setting where white power members trace in-group/out-group boundaries and attempt to create the next generation of believers. Their weaving of white power ideological messages into the mundane routines of daily life reduces the psychological distance between everyday life and virulent racist hate.

Homes are white power sanctuaries that affect both children and parents. By nourishing their children on Aryan ideas, parents hope to create budding little soldiers committed to carrying on the fight against ZOG for white supremacy. But the devotion to raising Aryan children also gives white power parents a strong sense of purpose and direction that sustains their own commitment to the cause. White power parents identify an intense responsibility to use their children to keep alive the racist and anti-Semitic ideology of violence and hate that anchors the white power movement.

Racial socialization in the free space of homes is part of Aryans' constant struggle against ZOG and multicultural ideals. Aryan resistance in the home makes no headlines, but each seemingly inconsequential act helps sustain white power ideas in the family and makes possible the persistence of the white power movement. [...]

Bibliography for the Medieval Suite

Asbridge, Thomas. *The First Crusade: A New History, the Roots of Conflict Between Christianity and Islam.* 2004. Reprint, New York, NY: Oxford University Press, 2005.

Bennett, Matthew. "The Crusaders' 'Fighting March' Revisited," *War in History* 8:1 (2001): 1–18. Accessed February 16, 2017.

Berger, David, ed. *History and Hate: The Dimensions of Anti-Semitism.* Philadelphia, PA: The Jewish Publication Society, 1986.

Bonner, Michael David. *Jihad in Islamic History: Doctrines and Practice.* Princeton, NJ: Princeton University Press, 2006.

Burkholder, Mark A. and Lyman L. Johnson. *Colonial Latin America, Seventh Edition.* New York, NY: Oxford University Press, 2010.

Burns, Robert I. "Interactive Slave Operations: Muslim-Christian-Jewish Contracts in Thirteenth-Century Barcelona," *Medieval Encounters* 5:2 (1999): 135–155. Accessed August 17, 2016.

Caestecker, Frank and David Fraser. "The Extraterritorial Application of the Nuremberg Laws: *Rassenchande* and "Mixed" Marriages in European Liberal Democracies," *Journal of the History of International Law* 10 (2008), 35–81. Accessed on June 6, 2016.

Chazan, Robert. "Medieval Anti-Semitism." In *History and Hate: The Dimensions of Anti-Semitism*, edited by David Berger, 49–65. Philadelphia, PA: The Jewish Publication Society, 1986.

Chazan, Robert. *European Jewry and the First Crusade.* Berkeley, CA: University of California Press, 1987.

Chazan, Robert. *In the Year 1096: The First Crusade and the Jews.* Philadelphia, PA: The Jewish Publication Society, 1997.

Christie, Niall. "Jerusalem in the *Kitab Al-Jihad* of 'Ali ibn Tahir Al-Sulami," *Medieval Encounters* 13 (2007): 209–221. Accessed February 16, 2017.

Collins, Roger. *The Arab Conquest of Spain, 710–797.* Oxford, UK: Basil Blackwell, 1989.

Coope, Jessica A. "An Etiquette for Women: Women's Experience of Islam in Muslim Spain," *Essays in Medieval Studies* 29 (2013): 75–83. Accessed August 17, 2016.

Crowley, Roger. *1453: The Holy War for Constantinople and the Clash of Islam and the West.* New York, NY: Hyperion, 2005.

Domínguez García, Javier. "St. James the Moor-Slayer, A New Challenge to Spanish National Discourse in the Twenty-First Century," *International Journal of Iberian Studies* 22:1 (2009): 69–78. Accessed August 17, 2016.

Fernandez, Sonya. "The Crusade Over the Bodies of Women," *Patterns of Prejudice* 43:3–4 (2009): 269–286. Accessed February 16, 2017.

Fernandez-Morera, Dario. "The Islamic Warriors' Destruction of a Nascent Civilization: The Catholic Kingdom of the Visigoths in Spain (A.D. 589–711)," *Modern Age* 53:1/2 (2011): 6–19. Accessed August 17, 2016.

Florean, Dana. "East Meets West: Cultural Confrontation and Exchange After the First Crusade," *Language and Intercultural Communication* 7:2 (2007): 144–151. Accessed March 2, 2017.

Fuente, María Jesús. "Christian, Muslim and Jewish Women in Late Medieval Iberia," *Medieval Encounters* 15 (2009): 319–333. Accessed August 17, 2016.

Fulcher of Chartres. *A History of the Expedition to Jerusalem, 1095–1127.* Translated by Frances Rita Ryan. New York, NY: W.W. Norton, 1969.

Gilbert, Martin. *The Routledge Atlas of Jewish History, Eighth Edition.* New York, NY: Routledge, 2010.

Glick, Thomas F. *Islamic and Christian Spain in the Early Middle Ages.* Princeton, NJ: Princeton University Press, 1979.

Green, Toby. "Policing the Empires: A Comparative Perspective on the Institutional Trajectory of the Inquisition in the Portuguese and Spanish Overseas Territories in the Sixteenth and Seventeenth-Centuries," *Hispanic Research Journal* 13:1 (Feb. 2012). Accessed January 11, 2017.

Guerson, Alexandra. "Seeking Remission: Jewish Conversion in the Crown of Aragon, c. 1378–1391," *Jewish History* 24 (2010): 33–52. Accessed June 8, 2016.

Harris, Max. *Arabs, Moors, and Christians: Festivals of Reconquest in Mexico and Spain.* Austin, TX: University of Texas Press, 2000.

Hitchcock, Richard. "Christian-Muslim Understanding(s) in Medieval Spain," *Hispanic Research Journal* 9:4 (2008): 314–325. Accessed August 17, 2016.

Hourani, Albert. *A History of the Arab Peoples.* Cambridge, MA: Harvard University Press, 1991.

Housley, Norman. "The Crusades and Islam," *Medieval Encounters* 13 (2007): 189–208. Accessed February 16, 2017.

Katz, Jacob. *From Prejudice to Destruction: Anti-Semitism, 1700-1933.* Cambridge, MA: Harvard University Press, 1980.

Kertzer, David I. *The Popes Against the Jews: The Vatican's Role in the Rise of Modern Anti-Semitism.* New York, NY: Knopf, 2001.

Krow-Lucal, Martha G. "Marginalizing History: Observations on the Origins of the Inquisition in Fifteenth-Century Spain by B. Netanyahu," *Judaism* 46 (1997): 47–52. Accessed June 8, 2016.

Lapina, Elizabeth. "The Mural Paintings of Berzé-la-Ville in the Context of the First Crusade and the *Reconquista*," *Journal of Medieval History* 31 (2005): 309–326. Accessed February 16, 2017.

Lewis, Bernard. *The Muslim Discovery of Europe.* 1982. Reprint, New York, NY: W.W. Norton, 2001.

Lewis, Bernard. *Semites and Anti-Semites: An Inquiry into Conflict and Prejudice.* 1987. Reprint, New York, NY: W.W. Norton, 1999.

Lock, Peter. *The Routledge Companion to the Crusades.* New York, NY: Routledge, 2006.

Lowney, Chris. *A Vanished World: Muslims, Christians, and Jews in Medieval Spain.* 2005. Reprint, New York, NY: Oxford University Press, 2006.

Maalouf, Amin. *The Crusades Through Arab Eyes.* Translated by Jon Rothschild. New York, NY: Schocken Books, 1985.

Madden, Ronald. "The Passion of the Christ: A Modern Mystery Play," *Journal of Religion and Health* 43:3 (2004): 247–252. Accessed February 7, 2015.

Malkiel, David. "Destruction or Conversion: Intention and Reaction, Crusaders and Jews, in 1096," *Jewish History* 15 (2001): 257–280. Accessed June 8, 2016.

Mallett, Alex. "Islamic Historians of the Ayyubid Era and Muslim Rulers from the Early Crusading Period: A Study in the Use of History," *Al-Masaq* 24:3 (2012): 241–252. Accessed February 16, 2017.

Martínez, María Elena. *Genealogical Fictions: Limpieza de Sangre, Religion, and Gender in Colonial Mexico.* Stanford, CA: Stanford University Press, 2008.

Martz, Linda. "Relations Between Conversos and Old Christians in Early Modern Toledo: Some Different Perspectives." In *Christians, Muslims, and Jews in Medieval and Early Spain: Interaction and Cultural Change,* edited by Mark D. Meyerson and Edward D. English, 220–240. Notre Dame, IN: University of Notre Dame Press, 2000.

Megoran, Nick. "Towards a Geography of Peace: Pacific Geopolitics and Evangelical Christian Crusade Apologies," *Transactions of the Institute of British Geographers* 35:3 (2010): 382–398. Accessed February 16, 2017.

Meyerson, Mark D. and Edward D. English, eds. *Christians, Muslims, and Jews in Medieval and Early Spain: Interaction and Cultural Change.* Notre Dame, IN: University of Notre Dame Press, 2000.

Morton, Nicholas. "The Saljug Turks' Conversion to Islam: The Crusading Sources," *Al-Masaq* 27:2 (2015): 109–118. Accessed February 16, 2017.

Nirenberg, David. "Religious and Sexual Boundaries in the Medieval Crown of Aragon." In *Christians, Muslims, and Jews in Medieval and Early Spain: Interaction and Cultural Change,* edited by Mark D. Meyerson and Edward D. English, 141–160. Notre Dame, IN: University of Notre Dame Press, 2000.

Nirenberg, David. "Conversion, Sex and Segregation: Jews and Christians in Medieval Spain," *American Historical Review* 107:4 (2002): 1065–1093. Accessed June 8, 2016.

Pérez, Joseph. *History of a Tragedy: The Expulsion of the Jews from Spain.* Translated by Lysa Hochroth. Urbana and Chicago, IL: University of Illinois Press, 2007.

Peters, Edward. "The American Encounter with Islam: The *Firanji* Are Coming-Again," _____ (2004): 3–17. Accessed February 16, 2017.

Popkin, Richard H. "Jewish Christians and Christian Jews in Spain, 1492 and After," *Judaism* 41:3 (1992): 248–267. Accessed June 8, 2016.

Restall, Matthew. *Seven Myths of the Spanish Conquest.* New York, NY: Oxford University Press, 2003.

Rogozen-Soltar, Mikaela. "Al-Andalus in Andalusia: Negotiating Moorish History and Regional Identity in Southern Spain," *Anthropological Quarterly* 80:3 (2007): 863–886. Accessed June 8, 2016.

Roth, Norman. "The Jews and the Muslim Conquest of Spain," *Jewish Social Studies* 38:2 (1976): 145–158. Accessed November 15, 2016.

Roth, Norman. "The Jews of Spain and the Expulsion of 1492," *Historian* 55:1 (1992): 17–29. Accessed June 8, 2016.

Rubiera Mata, Maria Jesús and Mikel de Epalza. "Al-Andalus: Between Myth and History," *History and Anthropology* 18:3 (2007): 269–273. Accessed June 8, 2016.

Said, Edward. *Orientalism*. 1978. Reprint, New York, NY: Vintage, 1994.

Salameh, Jala. "European Women During the First Crusade in the Holy Land," _____ 12:28 (2014): 2733–2748. Accessed February 16, 2017.

Schmidt-Nowara, Christopher. *The Conquest of History: Spanish Colonialism and National Histories in the Nineteenth Century*. Pittsburgh, PA: University of Pittsburgh Press, 2006.

Seidenspinner-Núñez, Dayle. "Conversion and Subversion: Converso Texts in Fifteenth-Century Spain." In *Christians, Muslims, and Jews in Medieval and Early Spain: Interaction and Cultural Change*, edited by Mark D. Meyerson and Edward D. English, 241–264. Notre Dame, IN: University of Notre Dame Press, 2000.

Shagrir, Iris and Nitzan Amitai-Preiss. "Michaud, Montrond, Mazloun and the First History of the Crusades in Arabic," *Al-Masaq* 24:3 (2012): 309–312. Accessed February 16, 2017.

Shepkaru, Shmuel. "The Preaching of the First Crusade and the Persecutions of the Jews," *Medieval Encounters* 18 (2012): 93–135. Accessed June 8, 2016.

Shepkaru, Shmuel. "Christian Resurrection and Jewish Immortality During the First Crusade," *Speculum* 89:1 (2014): 1–34. Accessed August 17, 2016.

Soyer, François. "Faith, Culture and Fear: Comparing Islamophobia in Early Modern Spain and Twenty-First-Century Europe," *Ethnic and Racial Studies* 36:3 (2013): 399–416. Accessed June 8, 2016.

Soyer, François. "Enforcing Religious Repression in an Age of World Empires: Assessing the Global Reach of the Spanish and Portuguese Inquisitions." *History* (2015): 331–353. Accessed 3/21/2017.

Stark, Rodney. *God's Battalions: The Case for the Crusades*. New York, NY: Harper Collins, 2009.

Steffen, Lloyd. *Holy War, Just War: Exploring the Meaning of Religious Violence*. Lanham, MD: Rowman & Littlefield, 2007.

Stephens, Thomas M. *Dictionary of Latin American Racial and Ethnic Terminology, Second Edition*. Gainesville, FL: University of Florida Press, 1999.

Talmon-Heller, Daniella and Benjamin Z. Kedar. "Did Muslim Survivors of the 1099 Massacre of Jerusalem Settle in Damascus? The True Origins of the al-Salihiyya Suburb." *Al-Masaq* 17:2 (2005): 165–169.

Trachtenberg, Joshua. *The Devil and the Jews: The Medieval Conception of the Jew and Its Relation to Modern Anti-Semitism*. Philadelphia, PA: The Jewish Publication Society, 1993.

Tyerman, Christopher. *God's War: A New History of the Crusades*. Cambridge, MA: Harvard University Press, 2006.

Webster, Yehudi O. *Racialization of America*. 1992. Reprint, New York, NY: St. Martin's Press, 1993.

Wegman, Andrew N. "The Vitriolic Blood of a Negro: The Development of Racial Identity and Creole Elitism in New Spain and Spanish Louisiana, 1763–1803." *Journal of Transatlantic Studies* 13:2 (2015): 204–225. Accessed August 29, 2017.

Wolf, Kenneth Baxter. "Muhammad as Antichrist in Ninth-Century." In *Christians, Muslims, and Jews in Medieval and Early Spain: Interaction and Cultural Change*, edited by Mark D. Meyerson and Edward D. English, 3–19. Notre Dame, IN: University of Notre Dame Press, 2000.

Woodson, Carter G. "Attitudes of the Iberian Peninsula," *The Journal of Negro History* 20:2 (1935): 190–243. Accessed 5/21/2008.

Glossary

Agnatic: A variation of patrilineal principle where inheritance favors the leader's younger brother over his sons, and the younger sons succeed only after the elder male(s) have expired.

Al-Andalus: The accurate name for Islamic Spain after the 711 Islamic Conquest. It was corrupted to *Andulasia* after the reconquista in 1492.

Al-hurub al-salbiyya: Arabic term for "the wars of the cross."

Andalusia: The term used today in Spain to describe the former Islamic State *al-Andalus*.

Anti-Semitism: A hatred for Jews; The term emerged in the late nineteenth century and incorporates all aspects of cultural anti-Semitism.

Assimilation: The process of fitting into the dominant society, usually associated with immigrants. In some historical contexts, assimilation required converting to Christianity in Western countries.

Blood libel: Dating to medieval times and recirculated after the First Crusade, the premise that around Passover, Jews killed Christian children and used their blood to make unleavened bread. The accusation is associated with another old anti-Semitic message stipulating that Jews killed Christ, as Passover is associated with Holy Week.

Caliph: An Islamic leader who claimed to be a descendant of the Prophet Muhammad.

Caliphate: A confederation of multiethnic regions under one centralized Islamic state, similar to empires. They came and went over time and could be either Sunni or Shia.

Casta: Spanish for "caste."

Convenvincia: Spanish for "toleration" or "relative peace" between Christians, Muslims, and Jews in al-Andalus. Some scholars consider this the "myth of al-Andalus" and take a more critical view of Islam.

Conversos: The term used to denote converted Jews in Spain.

Cruce signati: Latin for "cross insignia", the symbol of the crusaders sewn onto clothing.

Crypto-Judaism: Literally, secret practitioners of Judaism, who stood accused by the Inquisition of not being genuine Christians and were under investigation.

Cultural anti-Semitism: When Judaeophobia is racialized in society, it becomes generational, with frequent and recurring anti-Semitic messages in literature. It is often associated with acts of violence against the Jews in Europe during the nineteenth and early twentieth centuries.

Economic anti-Semitism: Disparaging Jews based on their practices with money and in the world market.

Political anti-Semitism: Often associated with socialism, it disparages Jews, with an emphasis on their quest for power.

Racial anti-Semitism: Hatred of Jews most associated with Nazi Germany, but it may have originated with the *limpieza de sangre* policies in fifteenth century Spain.

Religious anti-Semitism: Hatred of Jews that uses religious differences to discriminate.

Dhimmi: Arabic for "protected people." The protected people were citizens afforded religious and cultural rights conditional on a special tax and following of codes. It put the *dhimmi* in second-class status in Islamic societies.

Displacement: The psychological concept where anger or hate is conferred towards another, often weaker person or animal, as a substitute for the object of hate.

Emir: A localized Islamic leader in a large city or town.

Endogamy/Endogamous: To marry only within a proscribed group to maintain kinship lines, and in some cases, racial integrity.

Ethnic Cleansing: The elimination of an unwanted ethnic group from society by legislating expulsion, exclusion, forced migration, or genocide.

Exogamy/Exogamous: To marry outside the immediate kinship group, a cross-cousin marriage for example, to enhance alliances and keep the genetic pool varied to avoid the incest taboo.

Feudal System: The medieval societal model where below the king was a descending hierarchy of princes, dukes, and manor lords, who owed allegiance and tribute to the king, but received tribute from the peasants bound to their tracts of land (*fiefs*).

Fideles: Latin for "faithful," it connoted vassalage to papal authority in the times of Gregory VII and Urban II, in the eleventh century.

Franj/Firanj: The Arabic term for "Franks," a generic word applied to the crusaders who originally stemmed from France during the First Crusade.

Great Chain of Being: The medieval and early modern belief that humans and the natural world were ranked, with God at the top and Satan at the bottom, and much stratification in between.

Holy War: The concept of sanctified warfare against an enemy of Christendom where participants are absolved of sins committed during the prosecution of the war.

Infideles: Latin for "unfaithful," and often used as a pejorative term: 'infidel.'

Islamophilia: Literally, "love for Islam and Muslims."

Islamophobia: Literally, "fear of Islam and Muslims," although not all Arabs are Muslims and not all Muslims are Arabs.

Jihad: Literally to strive, its meaning has changed over time to mean "holy war," especially the offensive form most associated today with Islamic extremism. Its more peaceful connotations are largely ignored in the Western literature.

Jizya: The head tax mandated by shariah codes on the dhimmi; in return the dhimmi were protected, and allowed to worship in their traditional manner.

Judaeophobia: The form of anti-Jewish sentiment that was originally based on doctrinal and religious differences, especially that Jews killed Christ. This is most similar in concept to *religious anti-Semitism*.

Judaizing: The term used by the Inquisition to accuse conversos of secretly practicing Judaism, which meant the conversion was not genuine. The accused were referred to as marranos.

Juderias: The Jewish quarters and neighborhoods in Christian kingdoms, which were essentially segregated living spaces with corresponding dress codes to enforce social and sexual boundaries.

Limpieza de Sangre: Spanish for "purity of blood." The concept first emerged with the Purity of Blood Statutes in 1448 and 1467 in Toledo. "Race" was defined by blood and created racial differences between Old Christians, Jews, and New Christians.

Linaje: Spanish for "lineage."

Matrilineal: Tracing lineage and establishing social rank through the mother's family.

Miscegenation: The "mixing of races," especially between whites and non-whites through marriage or sexual intercourse.

Millenarian: The spiritual awakening that precedes significant periods of time (e.g., Y2K), which is tied to the belief that the Second Coming of Christ is near at hand.

Moieties: Two social or ethnic groups into which people are divided, especially in tribal or clan organizations.

Moriscos: Spanish term used for Muslims who converted to Christianity.

Moros: Spanish term that first appeared in the lexicon of *Poema o Mio Cid*, and denoted "Moors" as a catchall term to mean Muslims.

Mozarabs: Christians in Toledo who adopted Arabic surnames and language, but were discriminated against as a separate 'race.'

Mudejar: Spanish term for Muslim communities in Christian kingdoms as they gained territories from al-Andalus.

Mystery plays: Liturgical and public performance of biblical scenes, especially the Passion of the Christ. These were popular by the late thirteenth century in Spain and sometimes promoted Judaeophobia by laying blame on Jews for the death of Jesus.

New Christians: A term to denote the newly converted to Christianity that applied to both converted Jews (conversos) and Muslims (moriscos). It also implied less purity of blood and served a class distinction from Old Christians.

Occident(al): An old term used to mean "the West," or Western Civilization.

Old Christians: A socially separated group, determined by purity of blood, it created social and racial distinctions posited on the Christian faith being most pure if the mother or father never had any Jewish or heretical antecedents, and never converted to Islam for at least four generations.

Orient: An old term used to mean "the East," especially Turkish or Persian culture, but not limited to the Far East.

Orientalism: A movement of scholars who viewed the East (Orient) as both beautiful, exotic, but also backwards regarding religion and technology.

Orientalist: Any scholar who researches or writes about the East, particularly between the late Nineteenth-Century and 1940s.

Patrilineal: Tracing lineage and establishing social rank through the father's family.

People's Crusade: Five in total, these were individually led groups by notable figures such as Peter the Hermit and Walter the Penniless. Arriving in Anatolia first, the group led by Peter was almost completely annihilated by the Turks.

Poema o Mio Cid: The influential epic poem that shaped the reconquista and introduced the term *moros* (Moors) to the lexicon to mean any enemy who was Muslim.

Protocols of the Elders of Zion: The infamous forgery and anti-Semitic tracts that were alleged to be secret minutes from a meeting where plotting to take over the world's governments and markets. It came from Czarist Russia, and although debunked, it still influences anti-Semitic tropes and thought.

Purity of blood statutes: Laws in Toledo Spain issued to place conversos and Jews in a lesser social position based on assumed contamination of their blood from Jewish antecedents.

Racialization: a mode of racial classification created via a social process that creates a privileged status for those in power. Also referred to in the text as *racialized*.

Rassenschande: German for "race pollution," or "race defilement."

Raza: Spanish for "race." The word is a corruption of the Arabic term *raz*.

Rum/Rumi: Arabic for "Roman," a term used to designate the Byzantine Empire.

Santiago Matamoros: St. James the "Moor Slayer" or "Muslim Killer." The association with violence and the reconquista are presently a source of conflict in Spain's cultural identity because of conflict with social inclusion policies.

Santiago Peregrino: Saint James the Pilgrim, patron saint of Santiago de Campostela, Spain.

Sistema de castas: The complex typological organization by race and caste in New Spain and other Spanish colonies until the late eighteenth century. The measure used *limpieza de sangre* to determine degrees of whiteness.

Typological frameworks: A form of classification using linguistic theory to create meaning in a given society, but which is a fallacy when applied to racial classifications.

Visigoths: A Germanic group (Goths) that invaded Spain and assumed control over the Hispano-Romans until the Islamic Conquest in 711 C.E.

For Discussion

Part One

1. What effect did the rapid spread of Islam have on global markets and what did it mean for East/West trade? Did the conquests open or close historically established trade routes?

2. How did each of the three ethno-religious groups deal with the inevitable tensions between power and powerlessness? What were the social and intellectual boundaries between groups in al-Andalus, and how were they enforced or observed?

3. From the case studies given, how or when were boundaries crossed and how did this heighten tensions socially? Did these conditions last indefinitely? Or were they confined to particular situations?

4. Episodes of anti-Semitism often blamed the Jews for tragic losses in war and economic downturns. How did this pattern manifest in the narrative about the fall of the Visigoths in Spain after the Islamic invasion in 711? What patterns and evidence were used to support and refute the "treachery at Toledo" myth? How does this myth resemble others in the book, or from outside sources? Consider the concept of cultural anti-Semitism and its four manifestations in a detailed analysis.

5. Islamophobia is tied not only to differences of belief, but characterizations that it is a violent religion that subjugates women and wishes to impose sharia law on different societies. How do these feelings take form today when compared to how they shaped al-Andalusan society during Islamic rule? What aspects of the past are found in the "Clash of Civilizations" narrative today? How do prejudice, stereotyping and cultural racism play a role in this narrative?

6. What are dress codes and why have they maintained such importance as a form of social control? Consider power + prejudice and the system of advantages based on race to help distinguish the principles of dress codes. How was this tied to sexual honor in Spain? Do dress codes still play a role today? If so, explain in detail.

Part Two

1. What were the social conditions in Europe during Pope Urban II's lifetime, and how might this have influenced his decision to proclaim a holy war in late 1095? What specific reasons or motivations, both religious and secular, are cited in the text? What evidence was presented in the proclamation to support the claims, and was it justified?

2. What are the three prerequisites for holy wars and just wars, and who influenced them, according to the text? How can the three conditions for holy war be applied to the proclamation by Urban II at Clermont? What

did Urban say, based on the block quotation and supporting quotes through the section from various period sources?

3. What long-term affects did the First Crusade have on East-West relations? How did the binary good versus evil or us versus them doctrines come into play? How were the Muslims and Turks turned into "others"? What language was used to describe this in 1095 and do you see it reflected in the rhetoric today regarding Islam?

4. The Rhineland Jews were the first victims of the First Crusade. How did the three-part process of religious differences, demonization, and dehumanization play a role in those attacks? What other specific cultural anti-Semitic views may have contributed to violence and attempts to convert the Ashkenazi Jews? Why did the Ashkenazi Jews resist? How does the literature discuss the events from the Hebrew and Christian perspectives?

5. How did Arab historians interpret the arrival of the People's Crusade in Turkish lands in 1096? How did Arab historians define the crusaders' mission? What contributed to differences of opinion between chroniclers of the crusade? How was the violence justified or explained?

6. The campaign through Syria and the capture of Jerusalem led to not only in fighting by the crusader princes, but it also created instability in the region by violating agreements and attacking allies of the Greek emperor. How so the collective memories of Arabs and Christians explain these events and their consequences? In what ways does each group propagandize? How do they describe each other as the "other"? What else can you surmise from the summary? Outside sources could be used for this exercise, but be sure to cite accordingly and list them correctly in references.

Part Three

1. The image of St. James (Santiago) is a powerful symbol in Spanish traditions. He is the patron saint of the nation and also represents two manifestations: The Pilgrim (*Santiago Perigrino*) and the Moor Slayer (*Santiago Matamoros*). What processes led to this almost bipolar perspective and how was it reinforced throughout the reconquista? How did the poem *El Cid* affect perceptions of Islam?

2. In Part One, despite being Christians, the mozarabs were singled out for discrimination by the Church and legislation to isolate them from regular Christian society reflects how racialization works. What were the reasons for, and processes of racialization used to elevate some members of society above others deemed unfit? Who carried out these processes?

3. Although there were different circumstances in Spain, compared to Northern Europe, the Jews in Toledo and other Christian lands were violently attacked, and in many cases, forced to convert. What are the patterns that preceded those events from 1391 onward? How did attitudes towards Jews change and what social or legal measures were implemented? How did segregated living and dress codes factor into boundaries of sexual honor for those who considered themselves Old Christians?

4. The conversos were suspected of converting to avoid persecution, but many Old Christians did not believe they were genuine converts. What laws and concepts were applied to distinguish them? How did the term New Christians emerge, and what social benefits and exclusions faced the newly converted? What were the Purity of Blood Statutes? How did limpieza de sangre become the first documented case of racial distinction and its subsequent notions of inferiority, based on blood contamination? Explain how power + prejudice and a system of advantages based on race applies to this case study?

5. The Inquisition was formed to police the Christian territories and appointments to positions of power in the government and Church. What was their approach to

conversos? Once accused, what processes and legacy did the Inquisition acquire? When and why were unconverted Jews drawn into the spotlight, and what led to their expulsion in 1492?

Part Four

1. Modern Spain presents itself as a Christian nation, particularly after the expulsion of the unconverted Jews in 1492 and the moriscos later in the sixteenth century. How do the symbols of the medieval past and legacy conflict with ideas of modernity and the European Unions' policies of social inclusion and immigration? What similarities does this have with the attitudes of the United States regarding Islam, Muslims, and immigration? How do racism and prejudice merge with stereotypes of "others"?

2. Cultural festivals are historic events that celebrate one or more traditions. In Spain many such festivals have similar counterparts in Latin America to celebrate the reconquista and Spanish Conquest of the Americas. After 500 years, why are these events presently coming under fire for Islamophobic and anti-Semitic imagery? What are the arguments for and against the celebrations?

3. Regarding literature associated with Orientalism, how do scholars today view the convivencia? To what extent does the concept fit a modern narrative of Andalusia? Why would some scholars view the concept as an elaborate myth? Are they hostile to social inclusion? What do you think the motivations to attack multicultural concepts are? Consider nationalism and racism as possible factors. You may have to draw on more outside sources to frame the arguments, particularly the controversial "myth of al-Andalus" thesis.

4 Colonialism's Long Shadow

Discourse on Colonialism

By Aimé Césaire

● ●

Editor's introduction

Described as "… a declaration of war … [and] a 'third world manifesto …,'"[1] Aimé Césaire, raised in the French Caribbean colony Martinique, lashed out against colonialism, the colonizer, and the "deciviliz[ing]"[2] methods employed to subjugate the populace. A central message throughout this reading is that "the colonizer's sense of superiority, their sense of mission as the world's civilizers, depends on turning the Other into a barbarian."[3] Students will find many similarities of thought in the Frantz Fanon passage contained in this anthology.

Notes

1. Aimé Césaire. *Discourse on Colonialism.* Trans. Joan Pinkham. New York: Monthly Review Press, 2000.
2. Ibid., 89.
3. Ibid., 9.

A civilization that proves incapable of solving the problems it creates is a decadent civilization.

A civilization that chooses to close its eyes to its most crucial problems is a stricken civilization.

A civilization that uses its principles for trickery and deceit is a dying civilization.

The fact is that the so-called European civilization—"Western" civilization—as it has been shaped by two centuries of bourgeois rule, is incapable of solving the two major problems to which its existence has given rise: the problem of the proletariat and the colonial problem; that Europe is unable to justify itself either before the bar of "reason" or before the bar of "conscience"; and that, increasingly, it takes refuge in a hypocrisy which is all the more odious because it is less and less likely to deceive.

Europe Is Indefensible.

Apparently that is what the American strategists are whispering to each other.

That in itself is not serious.

What is serious is that "Europe" is morally, spiritually indefensible.

And today the indictment is brought against it not by the European masses alone, but on a world scale, by tens and tens of millions of men who, from the depths of slavery, set themselves up as judges.

The colonialists may kill in Indochina, torture in Madagascar, imprison in Black Africa, crack down in the West Indies. Henceforth the colonized know that they have an advantage over them. They know that their temporary "masters" are lying.

Therefore that their masters are weak.

And since I have been asked to speak about colonization and civilization, let us go straight to the principal lie that is the source of all the others.

Colonization and civilization?

In dealing with this subject, the commonest curse is to be the dupe in good faith of a collective hypocrisy that cleverly misrepresents problems, the better to legitimize the hateful solutions provided for them.

In other words, the essential thing here is to see clearly, to think clearly—that is, dangerously—and to answer clearly the innocent first question: what, fundamentally, is colonization? To agree on what it is not: neither evangelization, nor a philanthropic enterprise, nor a desire to push back the frontiers of ignorance, disease, and tyranny, nor a project undertaken for the greater glory of God, nor an attempt to extend the rule of law. To admit once and for all, without flinching at the consequences, that the decisive actors here are the adventurer and the pirate, the wholesale grocer and the ship owner, the gold digger and the merchant, appetite and force, and behind them, the baleful projected shadow of a form of civilization which, at a certain point in its history, finds itself obliged, for internal reasons, to extend to a world scale the competition of its antagonistic economies.

Pursuing my analysis, I find that hypocrisy is of recent date; that neither Cortez discovering Mexico from the top of the great teocalli, nor Pizzaro before Cuzco (much less Marco Polo before Cambuluc), claims that he is the harbinger of a superior order; that they kill; that they plunder; that they have helmets, lances, cupidities; that the slavering apologists came later; that the chief culprit in this domain is Christian pedantry, which

laid down the dishonest equations *Christianity = civilization, paganism = savagery,* from which there could not but ensue abominable colonialist and racist consequences, whose victims were to be the Indians, the Yellow peoples, and the Negroes.

That being settled, I admit that it is a good thing to place different civilizations in contact with each other; that it is an excellent thing to blend different worlds; that whatever its own particular genius may be, a civilization that withdraws into itself atrophies; that for civilizations, exchange is oxygen; that the great good fortune of Europe is to have been a crossroads, and that because it was the locus of all ideas, the receptacle of all philosophies, the meeting place of all sentiments, it was the best center for the redistribution of energy.

But then I ask the following question: has colonization really *placed civilizations in contact?* Or, if you prefer, of all the ways of *establishing contact,* was it the best?

I answer *no.*

And I say that between *colonization* and *civilization* there is an infinite distance; that out of all the colonial expeditions that have been undertaken, out of all the colonial statutes that have been drawn up, out of all the memoranda that have been dispatched by all the ministries, there could not come a single human value.

First we must study how colonization works to *decivilize* the colonizer, to *brutalize* him in the true sense of the word, to degrade him, to awaken him to buried instincts, to covetousness, violence, race hatred, and moral relativism; and we must show that each time a head is cut off or an eye put out in Vietnam and in France they accept the fact, each time a little girl is raped and in France they accept the fact, each time a Madagascan is tortured and in France they accept the fact, civilization acquires another dead weight, a universal regression takes place, a gangrene sets in, a center of infection begins to spread; and that at the end of all these treaties that have been violated, all these lies that have been propagated, all these punitive expeditions that have been tolerated, all these prisoners who have been tied up and "interrogated," all these patriots who have been tortured, at the end of all the racial pride that has been encouraged, all the boastfulness that has been displayed, a poison has been distilled into the veins of Europe and, slowly but surely, the continent proceeds toward *savagery*.

And then one fine day the bourgeoisie is awakened by a terrific boomerang effect: the gestapos are busy, the prisons fill up, the torturers standing around the racks invent, refine, discuss.

People are surprised, they become indignant. They say: "How strange! But never mind—it's Nazism, it will pass!" And they wait, and they hope; and they hide the truth from themselves, that it is barbarism, the supreme barbarism, the crowning barbarism that sums up all the daily barbarisms; that it is Nazism, yes, but that before they were its victims, they were its accomplices; that they tolerated that Nazism before it was inflicted on them, that they absolved it, shut their eyes to it, legitimized it, because, until then, it had been applied only to non-European peoples; that they have cultivated that Nazism, that they are responsible for it, and that before engulfing the whole edifice of Western, Christian civilization in its reddened waters, it oozes, seeps, and trickles from every crack.

Yes, it would be worthwhile to study clinically, in detail, the steps taken by Hitler and Hitlerism and to reveal to the very distinguished, very humanistic, very Christian bourgeois of the twentieth century that without his being aware of it, he has a Hitler inside him, that Hitler *inhabits* him, that Hitler is his *demon,* that if he rails against him, he is being inconsistent and that, at bottom, what he cannot forgive Hitler for is not *the crime* in itself, *the crime against man,* it is not *the humiliation of man as such,* it is the crime against the white man, the humiliation of the white man, and the fact that he applied to Europe colonialist procedures which until then had been reserved exclusively for the Arabs of Algeria, the "coolies" of India, and the "niggers" of Africa.

And that is the great thing I hold against pseudo-humanism: that for too long it has diminished the rights of man, that its concept of those rights has been—and still is—narrow and fragmentary, incomplete and biased and, all things considered, sordidly racist.

I have talked a good deal about Hitler. Because he deserves it: he makes it possible to see things on a large scale and to grasp the fact that capitalist society, at its present stage, is incapable of establishing a concept of the rights of all men, just as it has proved incapable of establishing a system of individual ethics. Whether one likes it or not, at the end of the blind alley that is Europe, I mean the Europe of Adenauer, Schuman, Bidault, and a few others, there is Hitler. At the end of capitalism, which is eager to outlive its day, there is Hider. At the end of formal humanism and philosophic renunciation, there is Hitler.

And this being so, I cannot help thinking of one of his statements: "We aspire not to equality but to domination. The country of a foreign race must become once again a country of serfs, of agricultural laborers, or industrial workers. It is not a question of eliminating the inequalities among men but of widening them and making them into a law."

That rings clear, haughty, and brutal, and plants us squarely in the middle of howling savagery. But let us come down a step.

Who is speaking? I am ashamed to say it: it is the Western *humanist,* the "idealist" philosopher. That his name is Renan is an accident. That the passage is taken from a book entitled *La Reforme intellectuelle et morale,* that it was written in France just after a war which France had represented as a war of right against might, tells us a great deal about bourgeois morals.

> The regeneration of the inferior or degenerate races by the superior races is part of the providential order of things for humanity. With us, the common man is nearly always a declasse nobleman, his heavy hand is better suited to handling the sword than the menial tool. Rather than work, he chooses to fight, that is, he returns to his first estate. *Regere imperiopopulos,* that is our vocation. Pour forth this all-consuming activity onto countries which, like China, are crying aloud for foreign conquest, Turn the adventurers

who disturb European society into a *vet sacrum,* a horde like those of the Franks, the Lombards, or the Normans, and every man will be in his right role. Nature has made a race of workers, the Chinese race, who have wonderful manual dexterity and almost no sense of honor; govern them with justice, levying from them, in return for the blessing of such a government, an ample allowance for the conquering race, and they will be satisfied; a race of tillers of the soil, the Negro; treat him with kindness and humanity, and all will be as it should; a race of masters and soldiers, the European race. Reduce this noble race to working in the *ergastulum* like Negroes and Chinese, and they rebel. In Europe, every rebel is, more or less, a soldier who has missed his calling, a creature made for the heroic life, before whom you are setting *a task that is contrary to his race,* a poor worker, too good a soldier. But the life at which our workers rebel would make a Chinese or a fellah happy, as they are not military creatures in the least. *Let each one do what he is made for, and all will be well.*

Hitler? Rosenberg? No, Renan.

But let us come down one step further. And it is the long-winded politician. Who protests? No one, so far as I know, when M. Albert Sarraut, the former governor-general of Indochina, holding forth to the students at the Ecole Coloniale, teaches them that it would be puerile to object to the European colonial enterprises in the name of "an alleged right to possess the land one occupies, and some sort of right to remain in fierce isolation, which would leave unutilized resources to lie forever idle in the hands of incompetents."

And who is roused to indignation when a certain Rev. Barde assures us that if the goods of this world "remained divided up indefinitely, as they would be without colonization, they would answer neither the purposes of God nor the just demands of the human collectivity"?

Since, as his fellow Christian, the Rev. Muller, declares: "Humanity must not, cannot allow the incompetence, negligence, and laziness of the uncivilized peoples to leave idle indefinitely the wealth which God has confided to them, charging them to make it serve the good of all."

No one.

I mean not one established writer, not one academic, not one preacher, not one crusader for the right and for religion, not one "defender of the human person."

And yet, through the mouths of the Sarrauts and the Bardes, the Mullers and the Renans, through the mouths of all those who considered—and consider—it lawful to apply to non-European peoples "a kind of expropriation for public purposes" for the benefit of nations that were stronger and better equipped, it was already Hitler speaking!

What am I driving at? At this idea: that no one colonizes innocently, that no one colonizes with impunity either; that a nation which colonizes, that a civilization which justifies colonization—and therefore force—is already a sick civilization, a civilization which is morally diseased, which irresistibly, progressing from one consequence to another, one denial to another, calls for its Hitler, I mean its punishment.

Colonization: bridgehead in a campaign to civilize barbarism, from which there may emerge at any moment the negation of civilization, pure and simple.

Elsewhere I have cited at length a few incidents culled from the history of colonial expeditions.

Unfortunately, this did not find favor with everyone. It seems that I was pulling old skeletons out of the closet. Indeed!

Was there no point in quoting Colonel de Montagnac, one of the conquerors of Algeria: "In order to banish the thoughts that sometimes besiege me, I have some heads cut off, not the heads of artichokes but the heads of men."

Would it have been more advisable to refuse the floor to Count d'Herisson: "It is true that we are bringing back a whole barrelful of ears collected, pair by pair, from prisoners, friendly or enemy."

Should I have denied Saint-Arnaud the right to profess his barbarous faith: "We lay waste, we burn, we plunder, we destroy the houses and the trees."

Should I have prevented Marshal Bugeaud from systematizing all that in a daring theory and invoking the precedent of famous ancestors: "We must have a great invasion of Africa, like the invasions of the Franks and the Goths."

Lastly, should I have cast back into the shadows of oblivion the memorable feat of arms of General Gerard and kept silent about the capture of Ambike, a city which, to tell the truth, had never dreamed of defending itself: "The native riflemen had orders to kill only the men, but no one restrained them; intoxicated by the smell of blood, they spared not one woman, not one child. … At the end of the afternoon, the heat caused a light mist to arise: it was the blood of the five thousand victims, the ghost of the city, evaporating in the setting sun."

Yes or no, are these things true? And the sadistic pleasures, the nameless delights that send voluptuous shivers and quivers through Loti's carcass when he focuses his field glasses on a good massacre of the Annamese? True or not true? And if these things are true, as no one can deny, will it be said, in order to minimize them, that these corpses don't prove anything?

For my part, if I have recalled a few details of these hideous butcheries, it is by no means because I take a morbid delight in them, but because I think that these heads of men, these collections of ears, these burned houses, these Gothic invasions, this steaming blood, these cities that evaporate at the edge of the sword, are not to be so easily disposed of. They prove that colonization, I repeat, dehumanizes even the most civilized man; that colonial activity, colonial enterprise, colonial conquest, which is based on contempt for the native and justified by that contempt, inevitably tends to change him who undertakes it; that the colonizer, who in order to ease his conscience gets into the habit of seeing the other man as *an animal,* accustoms himself to treating him like an animal, and tends objectively to transform *himself into* an animal. It is this result, this boomerang effect of colonization that I wanted to point out.

Unfair? No. There was a time when these same facts were a source of pride, and when, sure of the morrow, people did not mince words. One last quotation; it is from a certain Carl Siger, author of an *Essai sur la colonisation* (Paris, 1907):

> The new countries offer a vast field for individual, violent activities which, in the metropolitan countries, would run up against certain prejudices, against a sober and orderly conception of life, and which, in the colonies, have greater freedom to develop and, consequently, to affirm their worth. Thus to a certain extent the colonies can serve as a safety valve for modern society. Even if this were their only value, it would be immense.

Truly, there are sins for which no one has the power to make amends and which can never be fully expiated.

But let us speak about the colonized.

I see clearly what colonization has destroyed: the wonderful Indian civilizations—and neither Deterding nor Royal Dutch nor Standard Oil will ever console me for the Aztecs and the Incas.

I see clearly the civilizations, condemned to perish at a future date, into which it has introduced a principle of ruin: the South Sea Islands, Nigeria, Nyasaland. I see less clearly the contributions it has made.

Security? Culture? The rule of law? In the meantime, I look around and wherever there are colonizers and colonized face to face, I see force, brutality, cruelty, sadism, conflict, and, in a parody of education, the hasty manufacture of a few thousand subordinate functionaries, "boys," artisans, office clerks, and interpreters necessary for the smooth operation of business.

I spoke of contact.

Between colonizer and colonized there is room only for forced labor, intimidation, pressure, the police, taxation, theft, rape, compulsory crops, contempt, mistrust, arrogance, self-complacency, swinishness, brainless elites, degraded masses.

No human contact, but relations of domination and submission which turn the colonizing man into a classroom monitor, an army sergeant, a prison guard, a slave driver, and the indigenous man into an instrument of production.

My turn to state an equation: colonization = "thingification."

I hear the storm. They talk to me about progress, about "achievements," diseases cured, improved standards of living.

I am talking about societies drained of their essence, cultures trampled underfoot, institutions undermined, lands confiscated, religions smashed, magnificent artistic creations destroyed, extraordinary *possibilities* wiped out.

They throw facts at my head, statistics, mileages of roads, canals, and railroad tracks.

I am talking about thousands of men sacrificed to the Congo-Océan. I am talking about those who, as I write this, are digging the harbor of Abidjan by hand. I am talking about millions of men torn from their gods, their land, their habits, their life—from life, from the dance, from wisdom.

I am talking about millions of men in whom fear has been cunningly instilled, who have been taught to have an inferiority complex, to tremble, kneel, despair, and behave like flunkeys.

They dazzle me with the tonnage of cotton or cocoa that has been exported, the acreage that has been planted with olive trees or grapevines.

I am talking about natural *economies* that have been disrupted—harmonious and viable *economies* adapted to the indigenous population—about food crops destroyed, malnutrition permanently introduced, agricultural development oriented solely toward the benefit of the metropolitan countries; about the looting of products, the looting of raw materials.

They pride themselves on abuses eliminated.

I too talk about abuses, but what I say is that on the old ones—very real—they have superimposed others—very detestable. They talk to me about local tyrants brought to reason; but I note that in general the old tyrants get on very well with the new ones, and that there has been established between them, to the detriment of the people, a circuit of mutual services and complicity.

They talk to me about civilization, I talk about proletarianization and mystification.

For my part, I make a systematic defense of the non-European civilizations.

Every day that passes, every denial of justice, every beating by the police, every demand of the workers that is drowned in blood, every scandal that is hushed up, every punitive expedition, every police van, every gendarme and every militiaman, brings home to us the value of our old societies.

They were communal societies, never societies of the many for the few.

They were societies that were not only ante-capitalist, as has been said, but also *anti-capitalist.*

They were democratic societies, always.

They were cooperative societies, fraternal societies.

I make a systematic defense of the societies destroyed by imperialism.

They were the fact, they did not pretend to be the idea; despite their faults, they were neither to be hated nor condemned. They were content to be. In them, neither the word *failure* nor the word *avatar* had any meaning. They kept hope intact.

Whereas those are the only words that can, in all honesty, be applied to the European enterprises outside Europe. My only consolation is that periods of colonization pass, that nations sleep only for a time, and that peoples remain.

This being said, it seems that in certain circles they pretend to have discovered in me an "enemy of Europe" and a prophet of the return to the pre-European past.

For my part, I search in vain for the place where I could have expressed such views; where I ever underestimated the importance of Europe in the history of human thought; where I ever preached a *return* of any kind; where I ever claimed that there could be a *return.*

The truth is that I have said something very different: to wit, that the great historical tragedy of Africa has been not so much that it was too late in making contact with the rest of the world, as the manner in which that contact was brought about; that Europe began to "propagate" at a time when it had fallen into the hands of the most unscrupulous financiers and captains of industry; that it was our misfortune to encounter that particular Europe on our path, and that Europe is responsible before the human community for the highest heap of corpses in history.

In another connection, in judging colonization, I have added that Europe has gotten on very well indeed with all the local feudal lords who agreed to serve, woven a villainous complicity with them, rendered their tyranny more effective and more efficient, and that it has actually tended to prolong artificially the survival of local pasts in their most pernicious aspects.

I have said—and this is something very different—that colonialist Europe has grafted modern abuse onto ancient injustice, hateful racism onto old inequality.

That if I am attacked on the grounds of intent, I maintain that colonialist Europe is dishonest in trying to justify its colonizing activity *a posteriori* by the obvious material progress that has been achieved in certain fields under the colonial regime—since *sudden change* is always possible, in history as elsewhere; since no one knows at what stage of material development these same countries would have been if Europe had not intervened; since the introduction of technology into Africa and Asia, their administrative reorganization, in a word, their "Europeanization," was (as is proved by the example of Japan) in no way tied to the European *occupation;* since the Europeanization of the non-European continents could have been accomplished otherwise than under the heel of Europe; since this movement of Europeanization was in progress; since it was even slowed down; since in any case it was distorted by the European takeover.

The proof is that at present it is the indigenous peoples of Africa and Asia who are demanding schools, and colonialist Europe which refuses them; that it is the African who is asking for ports and roads, and colonialist Europe which is niggardly on this score; that it is the colonized man who wants to move forward, and the colonizer who holds things back.

One of the values invented by the bourgeoisie in former times and launched throughout the world was *man*—and we have seen what has become of that. The other was the nation.

It is a fact: the *nation* is a bourgeois phenomenon.

Exactly; but if I turn my attention from *man* to *nations,* I note that here too there is great danger; that colonial enterprise is to the modern world what Roman imperialism was to the ancient world: the prelude to Disaster and the forerunner of Catastrophe. Come, now! The Indians massacred, the Moslem world drained of itself, the Chinese world defiled and perverted for a good century; the Negro world disqualified; mighty voices stilled forever; homes scattered to the wind; all this wreckage, all this waste, humanity reduced to a monologue, and you think all that does not have its price? The truth is that this policy *cannot but bring about the ruin of Europe itself,* and that Europe, if it is not careful, will perish from the void it has created around itself.

They thought they were only slaughtering Indians, or Hindus, or South Sea Islanders, or Africans. They have in fact overthrown, one after another, the ramparts behind which European civilization could have developed freely.

I know how fallacious historical parallels are, particularly the one I am about to draw. Nevertheless, permit me to quote a page from Edgar Quinet for the not inconsiderable element of truth which it contains and which is worth pondering.

Here it is:

> People ask why barbarism emerged all at once in ancient civilization. I believe I know the answer. It is surprising that so simple a cause is not obvious to everyone. The system of ancient civilization was composed of a certain number of nationalities, of countries which, although they seemed to be enemies, or were even ignorant of each other, protected, supported, and guarded one another. When the expanding Roman Empire undertook to conquer and destroy these groups of nations,

the dazzled sophists thought they saw at the end of this road humanity triumphant in Rome. They talked about the unity of the human spirit; it was only a dream. It happened that these nationalities were so many bulwarks protecting Rome itself ... Thus when Rome, in its alleged triumphal march toward a single civilization, had destroyed, one after the other, Carthage, Egypt, Greece, Judea, Persia, Dacia, and Cisalpine and Transalpine Gaul, it came to pass that it had itself swallowed up the dikes that protected it against the human ocean under which it was to perish. The magnanimous Caesar, by crushing the two Gauls, only paved the way for the Teutons. So many societies, so many languages extinguished, so many cities, rights, homes annihilated, created a void around Rome, and in those places which were not invaded by the barbarians, barbarism was born spontaneously. The vanquished Gauls changed into Bagaudes. Thus the violent downfall, the progressive extirpation of individual cities, caused the crumbling of ancient civilization. That social edifice was supported by the various nationalities as by so many different columns of marble or porphyry.

When, to the applause of the wise men of the time, each of these living columns had been demolished, the edifice came crashing down; and the wise men of our day are still trying to understand how such mighty ruins could have been made in a moment's time.

And now I ask: what else has bourgeois Europe done? It has undermined civilizations, destroyed countries, ruined nationalities, extirpated "the root of diversity." No more dikes, no more bulwarks. The hour of the barbarian is at hand. The modern barbarian. The American hour. Violence, excess, waste, mercantilism, bluff, conformism, stupidity, vulgarity, disorder.

In 1913, Ambassador Page wrote to Wilson: "The future of the world belongs to us. ... Now what are we going to do with the leadership of the world presently when it clearly falls into our hands?"

And in 1914: "What are we going to do with this England and this Empire, presently, when economic forces unmistakably put the leadership of the race in our hands?" This Empire. ... And the others. ...

And indeed, do you not see how ostentatiously these gentlemen have just unfurled the banner of anti-colonialism?

"Aid to the disinherited countries," says Truman. "The time of the old colonialism has passed." That's also Truman.

Which means that American high finance considers that the time has come to raid every colony in the world. So, dear friends, here you have to be careful!

I know that some of you, disgusted with Europe, with all that hideous mess which you did not witness by choice, are turning—oh! in no great numbers—toward America and getting used to looking upon that country as a possible liberator.

"What a godsend!" you think.

"The bulldozers! The massive investments of capital! The roads! The ports!"

"But American racism!"

"So what? European racism in the colonies has inured us to it!"

And there we are, ready to run the great Yankee risk.

So, once again, be careful!

American domination—the only domination from which one never recovers. I mean from which one never recovers unscarred.

And since you are talking about factories and industries, do you not see the tremendous factory hysterically spitting out its cinders in the heart of our forests or deep in the bush, the factory for the production of lackeys; do you not see the prodigious mechanization, the mechanization of man; the gigantic rape of everything intimate, undamaged, undefiled that, despoiled as we are, our human spirit has still managed to preserve; the machine, yes, have you never seen it, the machine for crushing, for grinding, for degrading peoples?

So that the danger is immense.

So that unless, in Africa, in the South Sea Islands, in Madagascar (that is, at the gates of South Africa), in the West Indies (that is, at the gates of America), Western Europe undertakes on its own initiative a policy of *nationalities*, a new policy founded on respect for peoples and cultures—nay, more—unless Europe galvanizes the dying cultures or raises up new ones, unless it becomes the awakener of countries and civilizations (this being said without taking into account the admirable resistance of the colonial peoples primarily symbolized at present by Vietnam, but also by the Africa of the Rassemblement Democratique Africain), Europe will have deprived itself of its last *chance* and, with its own hands, drawn up over itself the pall of mortal darkness.

Which comes down to saying that the salvation of Europe is not a matter of a revolution in methods. It is a matter of the Revolution—the one which, until such time as there is a classless society, will substitute for the narrow tyranny of a dehumanized bourgeoisie the preponderance of the only class that still has a universal mission, because it suffers in its flesh from all the wrongs of history, from all the universal wrongs: the proletariat.

On Violence

By Frantz Fanon

● ●

Editor's Introduction

Like his countryman, Aimé Césaire, Frantz Fanon delivers a damning condemnation on those who colonized the world, and instructions on how the colonized could liberate themselves physically and psychologically. Fanon's works appealed to Pan-African movements as well as Malcolm X, the Black Panther leaders, and many others who recognized his diagnosis. A psychiatrist, he advocated the role of violence in historic change as inevitable. This excerpt, "On Violence," should be compared with Césairé's reading, and any studies on white bias, internalized racism, and self-hatred.

References

Fanon, Frantz. *The Wretched of the Earth*. Translated by Richard Philcox. New York: Grove Press, 2004.

_____. *Black Skin, White Masks*. Translated by Richard Philcox. New York: Grove Press, 2008.

National liberation, national reawakening, restoration of the nation to the people or Commonwealth, whatever the name used, whatever the latest expression, decolonization is always a violent event. At whatever level we study it—individual encounters, a change of name for a sports club, the guest list at a cocktail party, members of a police force or the board of directors of a state or private bank—decolonization is quite simply the substitution of one "species" of mankind by another. The substitution is unconditional, absolute, total, and seamless. We could go on to portray the rise of a new nation, the establishment of a new state, its diplomatic relations and its economic and political orientation. But instead we have decided to describe the kind of tabula rasa which from the outset defines any decolonization. What is singularly important is that it starts from the very first day with the basic claims of the colonized. In actual fact, proof of success lies in a social fabric that has been changed inside out. This change is extraordinarily important because it is desired, clamored for, and demanded. The need for this change exists in a raw, repressed, and reckless state in the lives and consciousness of colonized men and women. But the eventuality of such a change is also experienced as a terrifying future

Frantz Fanon, "On Violence," *The Wretched of the Earth*, trans. Richard Philcox, pp. 1-21. Copyright © 2004 by Grove/Atlantic Press. Reprinted with permission.

in the consciousness of another "species" of men and women: the *colons,* the colonists.

* * *

Decolonization, which sets out to change the order of the world, is clearly an agenda for total disorder. But it cannot be accomplished by the wave of a magic wand, a natural cataclysm, or a gentleman's agreement. Decolonization, we know, is an historical process: In other words, it can only be understood, it can only find its significance and become self coherent insofar as we can discern the history-making movement which gives it form and substance. Decolonization is the encounter between two congenitally antagonistic forces that in fact owe their singularity to the kind of reification secreted and nurtured by the colonial situation. Their first confrontation was colored by violence and their cohabitation—or rather the exploitation of the colonized by the colonizer—continued at the point of the bayonet and under cannon fire. The colonist and the colonized are old acquaintances. And consequently, the colonist is right when he says he "knows" them. It is the colonist who *fabricated* and *continues to fabricate* the colonized subject. The colonist derives his validity, i.e., his wealth, from the colonial system.

Decolonization never goes unnoticed, for it focuses on and fundamentally alters being, and transforms the spectator crushed to a nonessential state into a privileged actor, captured in a virtually grandiose fashion by the spotlight of History. It infuses a new rhythm, specific to a new generation of men, with a new language and a new humanity. Decolonization is truly the creation of new men. But such a creation cannot be attributed to a supernatural power: The "thing" colonized becomes a man through the very process of liberation.

Decolonization, therefore, implies the urgent need to thoroughly challenge the colonial situation. Its definition can, if we want to describe it accurately, be summed up in the well-known words: "The last shall be first." Decolonization is verification of this. At a descriptive level, therefore, any decolonization is a success.

* * *

In its bare reality, decolonization reeks of red-hot cannonballs and bloody knives. For the last can be the first only after a murderous and decisive confrontation between the two protagonists. This determination to have the last move up to the front, to have them clamber up (too quickly, say some) the famous echelons of an organized society, can only succeed by resorting to every means, including, of course, violence.

You do not disorganize a society, however primitive it may be, with such an agenda if you are not determined from the very start to smash every obstacle encountered. The colonized, who have made up their mind to make such an agenda into a driving force, have been prepared for violence from time immemorial. As soon as they are born it is obvious to them that their cramped world, riddled with taboos, can only be challenged by out and out violence.

The colonial world is a compartmentalized world. It is obviously as superfluous to recall the existence of "native" towns and European towns, of schools for "natives" and schools for Europeans, as it is to recall apartheid in South Africa. Yet if we penetrate inside this compartmentalization we shall at least bring to light some of its key aspects. By penetrating its geographical configuration and classification we shall be able to delineate the backbone on which the decolonized society is reorganized.

The colonized world is a world divided in two. The dividing line, the border, is represented by the barracks and the police stations. In the colonies, the official, legitimate agent, the spokesperson for the colonizer and the regime of oppression, is the police officer or the soldier. In capitalist societies, education, whether secular or religious, the teaching of moral reflexes handed down from father to son, the exemplary integrity of workers decorated after fifty years of loyal and faithful service, the fostering of love for harmony and wisdom, those aesthetic forms of respect for the status quo, instill in the exploited a mood of submission and inhibition which considerably eases the task of the agents of law and order. In capitalist countries a multitude of sermonizers, counselors, and "confusion-mongers" intervene between the exploited and the authorities. In colonial regions, however, the proximity and frequent, direct intervention by the police and the military ensure the colonized are kept under close scrutiny, and contained by rifle butts and napalm. We have seen how the government's agent uses a language of pure violence. The agent does not alleviate oppression or mask domination. He displays and demonstrates them with the clear conscience of the law enforcer, and brings violence into the homes and minds of the colonized subject.

The "native" sector is not complementary to the European sector. The two confront each other, but not in the service of a higher unity. Governed by a purely Aristotelian logic, they follow the dictates of mutual exclusion: There is no conciliation possible, one of them is superfluous. The colonist's sector is a sector built to last, all stone and steel. It's a sector of lights and paved roads, where the trash cans constantly overflow with strange and wonderful garbage, undreamed-of leftovers. The colonist's feet can never be glimpsed, except perhaps in the sea, but then you can never get close enough. They are protected by solid shoes in a sector where the streets are clean and smooth, without a pothole, without a stone. The colonist's sector is a sated, sluggish sector, its belly is permanently full of good things. The colonist's sector is a white folks' sector, a sector of foreigners.

The colonized's sector, or at least the "native" quarters, the shanty town, the Medina, the reservation, is a disreputable place inhabited by disreputable people. You are born anywhere, anyhow. You die anywhere, from anything. It's a world with no space, people are piled one on top of the other, the shacks squeezed tightly together. The colonized's sector is a famished sector, hungry for bread, meat, shoes, coal, and light. The colonized's sector is a sector that crouches and cowers, a sector on its knees, a sector that is prostrate. It's a sector of niggers, a sector of towelheads. The gaze that the colonized subject casts at the colonist's sector is a look of lust, a look of envy. Dreams of possession. Every type of possession:

of sitting at the colonist's table and sleeping in his bed, preferably with his wife. The colonized man is an envious man. The colonist is aware of this as he catches the furtive glance, and constantly on his guard, realizes bitterly that: "They want to take our place." And its true there is not one colonized subject who at least once a day does not dream of taking the place of the colonist.

This compartmentalized world, this world divided in two, is inhabited by different species. The singularity of the colonial context lies in the fact that economic reality, inequality, and enormous disparities in lifestyles never manage to mask the human reality. Looking at the immediacies of the colonial context, it is clear that what divides this world is first and foremost what species, what race one belongs to. In the colonies the economic infrastructure is also a superstructure. The cause is effect: You are rich because you are white, you are white because you are rich. This is why a Marxist analysis should always be slightly stretched when it comes to addressing the colonial issue. It is not just the concept of the precapitalist society, so effectively studied by Marx, which needs to be reexamined here. The serf is essentially different from the knight, but a reference to divine right is needed to justify this difference in status. In the colonies the foreigner imposed himself using his cannons and machines. Despite the success of his pacification, in spite of his appropriation, the colonist always remains a foreigner. It is not the factories, the estates, or the bank account which primarily characterize the "ruling class." The ruling species is first and foremost the outsider from elsewhere, different from the indigenous population, "the others."

The violence which governed the ordering of the colonial world, which tirelessly punctuated the destruction of the indigenous social fabric, and demolished unchecked the systems of reference of the country's economy, lifestyles, and modes of dress, this same violence will be vindicated and appropriated when, taking history into their own hands, the colonized swarm into the forbidden cities. To blow the colonial world to smithereens is henceforth a clear image within the grasp and imagination of every colonized subject. To dislocate the colonial world does not mean that once the borders have been eliminated there will be a right of way between the two sectors. To destroy the colonial world means nothing less than demolishing the colonist's sector, burying it deep within the earth or banishing it from the territory.

Challenging the colonial world is not a rational confrontation of viewpoints. It is not a discourse on the universal, but the impassioned claim by the colonized that their world is fundamentally different. The colonial world is a Manichaean world. The colonist is not content with physically limiting the space of the colonized, i.e., with the help of his agents of law and order. As if to illustrate the totalitarian nature of colonial exploitation, the colonist turns the colonized into a kind of quintessence of evil.[1] Colonized society is not merely portrayed as a society without values. The colonist is not content with stating that the colonized world has lost its values or worse never possessed any. The "native" is declared impervious to ethics, representing not only the absence of values but also the negation of values. He is, dare we say it, the enemy of values. In other words, absolute evil. A corrosive element, destroying everything within his reach, a corrupting element, distorting everything which involves aesthetics or morals, an agent of malevolent powers, an unconscious and incurable instrument of blind forces. And Monsieur Meyer could say in all seriousness in the French National Assembly that we should not let the Republic be defiled by the penetration of the Algerian people. Values are, in fact, irreversibly poisoned and infected as soon as they come into contact with the colonized. The customs of the colonized, their traditions, their myths, especially their myths, are the very mark of this indigence and innate depravity. This is why we should place DDT, which destroys parasites, carriers of disease, on the same level as Christianity, which roots out heresy, natural impulses, and evil. The decline of yellow fever and the advances made by evangelizing form part of the same balance sheet. But triumphant reports by the missions in fact tell us how deep the seeds of alienation have been sown among the colonized. I am talking of Christianity and this should come as no surprise to anybody. The Church in the colonies is a white man's Church, a foreigners' Church. It does not call the colonized to the ways of God, but to the ways of the white man, to the ways of the master, the ways of the oppressor. And as we know, in this story many are called but few are chosen.

Sometimes this Manichaeanism reaches its logical conclusion and dehumanizes the colonized subject. In plain talk, he is reduced to the state of an animal. And consequently, when the colonist speaks of the colonized he uses zoological terms. Allusion is made to the slithery movements of the yellow race, the odors from the "native" quarters, to the hordes, the stink, the swarming, the seething, and the gesticulations. In his endeavors at description and finding the right word, the colonist refers constantly to the bestiary. The European seldom has a problem with figures of speech. But the colonized, who immediately grasp the intention of the colonist and the exact case being made against them, know instantly what he is thinking. This explosive population growth, those hysterical masses, those blank faces, those shapeless, obese bodies, this headless, tailless cohort, these children who seem not to belong to anyone, this indolence sprawling under the sun, this vegetating existence, all this is part of the colonial vocabulary. General de Gaulle speaks of "yellow multitudes," and Monsieur Mauriac of the black, brown, and yellow hordes that will soon invade our shores. The colonized know all that and roar with laughter every time they hear themselves called an animal by the other. For they know they are not animals. And at the very moment when they discover their humanity, they begin to sharpen their weapons to secure its victory.

As soon as the colonized begin to strain at the leash and to pose a threat to the colonist, they are assigned a series of good souls who in the "Symposiums on Culture" spell out the specificity

---

1 We have demonstrated in *Black Skin, White Masks* the mechanism of this Manichaean world.

and richness of Western values. But every time the issue of Western values crops up, the colonized grow tense and their muscles seize up. During the period of decolonization the colonized are called upon to be reasonable. They are offered rock-solid values, they are told in great detail that decolonization should not mean regression, and that they must rely on values which have proved to be reliable and worthwhile. Now it so happens that when the colonized hear a speech on Western culture they draw their machetes or at least check to see they are close to hand. The supremacy of white values is stated with such violence, the victorious confrontation of these values with the lifestyle and beliefs of the colonized is so impregnated with aggressiveness, that as a counter measure the colonized rightly make a mockery of them whenever they are mentioned. In the colonial context the colonist only quits undermining the colonized once the latter have proclaimed loud and clear that white values reign supreme. In the period of decolonization the colonized masses thumb their noses at these very values, shower them with insults and vomit them up.

Such an occurrence normally goes unseen because, during decolonization, certain colonized intellectuals have established a dialogue with the bourgeoisie of the colonizing country. During this period the indigenous population is seen as a blurred mass. The few "native" personalities whom the colonialist bourgeois have chanced to encounter have had insufficient impact to alter their current perception and nuance their thinking. During the period of liberation, however, the colonialist bourgeoisie frantically seeks contact with the colonized "elite." It is with this elite that the famous dialogue on values is established. When the colonialist bourgeoisie realizes it is impossible to maintain its domination over the colonies it decides to wage a rearguard campaign in the fields of culture, values, and technology, etc. But what we should never forget is that the immense majority of colonized peoples are impervious to such issues. For a colonized people, the most essential value, because it is the most meaningful, is first and foremost the land: the

land, which must provide bread and, naturally, dignity. But this dignity has nothing to do with "human" dignity. The colonized subject has never heard of such an ideal. All he has ever seen on his land is that he can be arrested, beaten, and starved with impunity; and no sermonizer on morals, no priest has ever stepped in to bear the blows in his place or share his bread. For the colonized, to be a moralist quite plainly means silencing the arrogance of the colonist, breaking his spiral of violence, in a word ejecting him outright from the picture. The famous dictum which states that all men are equal will find its illustration in the colonies only when the colonized subject states he is equal to the colonist. Taking it a step further, he is determined to fight to be more than the colonist. In fact, he has already decided to take his place. As we have seen, it is the collapse of an entire moral and material universe. The intellectual who, for his part, has adopted the abstract, universal values of the colonizer is prepared to fight so that colonist and colonized can live in peace in a new world. But what he does not see, because precisely colonialism and all its modes of thought have seeped into him, is that the colonist is no longer interested in staying on and coexisting once the colonial context has disappeared. It is no coincidence that, even before any negotiation between the Algerian government and the French government, the so-called "liberal" European minority has already made its position clear: it is clamoring for dual citizenship, nothing less. By sticking to the abstract the colonist is being forced to make a very substantial leap into the unknown. Let us be honest, the colonist knows perfectly well that no jargon is a substitute for reality.

The colonized subject thus discovers that his life, his breathing and his heartbeats are the same as the colonist's. He discovers that the skin of a colonist is not worth more than the "native's." In other words, his world receives a fundamental jolt. The colonized's revolutionary new assurance stems from this. If, in fact, my life is worth as much as the colonist's, his look can no longer strike fear into me or nail me to the spot and his voice can no longer petrify me. I am no longer uneasy in his presence. In reality, to hell with him.

Not only does his presence no longer bother me, but I am already preparing to waylay him in such a way that soon he will have no other solution but to flee.

The colonial context, as we have said, is characterized by the dichotomy it inflicts on the world. Decolonization unifies this world by a radical decision to remove its heterogeneity, by unifying it on the grounds of nation and sometimes race. To quote the biting words of Senegalese patriots on the maneuvers of their president, Senghor: "We asked for the Africanization of the top jobs and all Senghor does is Africanize the Europeans." Meaning that the colonized can see right away if decolonization is taking place or not: The minimum demand is that the last become the first.

But the colonized intellectual introduces a variation on this demand and in fact, there seems to be no lack of motivation to fill senior positions as administrators, technicians, and experts. The colonized, however, equate this nepotism with acts of sabotage and it is not unusual to hear them declare: "What is the point of being independent then …?"

Wherever an authentic liberation struggle has been fought, wherever the blood of the people has been shed and the armed phase has lasted long enough to encourage the intellectuals to withdraw to their rank and file base, there is an effective eradication of the superstructure borrowed by these intellectuals from the colonialist bourgeois circles. In its narcissistic monologue the colonialist bourgeoisie, by way of its academics, had implanted in the minds of the colonized that the essential values—meaning Western values—remain eternal despite all errors attributable to man. The colonized intellectual accepted the cogency of these ideas and there in the back of his mind stood a sentinel on duty guarding the Greco-Roman pedestal. But during the struggle for liberation, when the colonized intellectual touches base again with his people, this artificial sentinel is smashed to smithereens. All the Mediterranean values, the triumph of the individual, of enlightenment and Beauty turn into pale, lifeless trinkets. All those discourses appear a jumble of dead words. Those values which seemed to ennoble the soul prove worthless because they have nothing in common with the real-life struggle in which the people are engaged.

And first among them is individualism. The colonized intellectual learned from his masters that the individual must assert himself. The colonialist bourgeoisie hammered into the colonized mind the notion of a society of individuals where each is locked in his subjectivity, where wealth lies in thought. But the colonized intellectual who is lucky enough to bunker down with the people during the liberation struggle, will soon discover the falsity of this theory. Involvement in the organization of the struggle will already introduce him to a different vocabulary. "Brother," "sister," "comrade" are words outlawed by the colonialist bourgeoisie because in their thinking my brother is my wallet and my comrade, my scheming. In a kind of auto-da-fe, the colonized intellectual witnesses the destruction of all his idols: egoism, arrogant recrimination, and the idiotic, childish need to have the last word. This colonized intellectual, pulverized by colonialist culture, will also discover the strength of the village assemblies, the power of the people's commissions and the extraordinary productiveness of neighborhood and section committee meetings. Personal interests are now the collective interest because in reality *everyone* will be discovered by the French legionnaires and consequently massacred or else *everyone* will be saved. In such a context, the "every man for himself" concept, the atheist's form of salvation, is prohibited.

Self-criticism has been much talked about recently, but few realize that it was first of all an African institution. Whether it be in the *djemaas* of North Africa or the palavers of West Africa, tradition has it that disputes which break out in a village are worked out in public. By this I mean collective self-criticism with a touch of humor because everyone is relaxed, because in the end we all want the same thing. The intellectual sheds all that calculating, all those strange silences, those ulterior motives, that devious thinking and secrecy as he gradually plunges deeper among the people. In this respect then we can genuinely say that the community has already triumphed and exudes its own light, its own reason.

But when decolonization occurs in regions where the liberation struggle has not yet made its impact sufficiently felt, here are the same smart alecks, the sly, shrewd intellectuals whose behavior and ways of thinking, picked up from their rubbing shoulders with the colonialist bourgeoisie, have remained intact. Spoiled children of yesterday's colonialism and today's governing powers, they oversee the looting of the few national resources. Ruthless in their scheming and legal pilfering they use the poverty, now nationwide, to work their way to the top through import-export holdings, limited companies, playing the stock market, and nepotism. They insist on the nationalization of business transactions, i.e., reserving contracts and business deals for nationals. Their doctrine is to proclaim the absolute need for nationalizing the theft of the nation. In this barren, national phase, in this so-called period of austerity, their success at plundering the nation swiftly sparks anger and violence from the people. In the present international and African context, the poverty-stricken and independent population achieves a social consciousness at a rapidly accelerating pace. This, the petty individualists will soon find out for themselves.

In order to assimilate the culture of the oppressor and venture into his fold, the colonized subject has had to pawn some of his own intellectual possessions. For instance, one of the things he has had to assimilate is the way the colonialist bourgeoisie thinks. This is apparent in the colonized intellectual's inaptitude to engage in dialogue. For he is unable to make himself inessential when confronted with a purpose or idea. On the other hand, when he operates among the people he is constantly awestruck. He is literally disarmed by their good faith and integrity. He is then constantly at risk of becoming a demagogue. He turns into a kind of mimic man who nods his assent to every word by the people, transformed by him into an arbiter of truth. But the fellah, the unemployed and the starving do not lay claim to truth. They do not say they represent the truth because they are the truth in their very being.

During this period the intellectual behaves objectively like a vulgar opportunist. His maneuvering, in fact, is still at work. The people would never think of rejecting him or cutting the ground from under his feet. What the people want is for everything to be pooled together. The colonized intellectual's insertion into this human tide will find itself on hold because of his curious obsession with detail. It is not that the people are opposed to analysis. They appreciate clarification, understand the reasoning behind an argument and like to see where they are going. But at the start of his cohabitation with the people the colonized intellectual gives priority to detail and tends to forget the very purpose of the struggle—the defeat of colonialism. Swept along by the many facets of the struggle, he tends to concentrate on local tasks, undertaken zealously but almost always too pedantically. He does not always see the overall picture. He introduces the notion of disciplines, specialized areas and fields into that awesome mixer and grinder called a people's revolution. Committed to certain frontline issues he tends to lose sight of the unity of the movement and in the event of failure at the local level he succumbs to doubt, even despair. The people, on the other hand, take a global stance from the very start. "Bread and land: how do we go about getting bread and land?" And this stubborn, apparently limited, narrow-minded aspect of the people is finally the most rewarding and effective working model.

The question of truth must also be taken into consideration. For the people, only fellow nationals are ever owed the truth. No absolute truth, no discourse on the transparency of the soul can erode this position. In answer to the lie of the colonial situation, the colonized subject responds with a lie. Behavior toward fellow nationalists is open and honest, but strained and indecipherable toward the colonists. Truth is what hastens the dislocation of the colonial regime, what fosters the emergence of the nation. Truth is what protects the "natives" and undoes the foreigners. In the colonial context there is no truthful behavior. And good is quite simply what hurts *them* most.

We have seen therefore that the Manichaeanism that first governed colonial society is maintained intact during the period of decolonization. In fact the colonist never ceases to be the enemy, the antagonist, in plain words public enemy number 1. The oppressor, ensconced in his sector, creates the spiral, the spiral of domination, exploitation and looting. In the other sector, the colonized subject lies coiled and robbed, and fuels as best he can the spiral which moves seamlessly from the shores of the colony to the palaces and docks of the metropolis. In this petrified zone, not a ripple on the surface, the palm trees sway against the clouds, the waves of the sea lap against the shore, the raw materials come and go, legitimating the colonist's presence, while more dead than alive the colonized subject crouches for ever in the same old dream. The colonist makes history. His life is an epic, an odyssey. He is invested with the very beginning: "We made this land." He is the guarantor for its existence: "If we leave, all will be lost, and this land will return to the Dark Ages." Opposite him, listless beings wasted away by fevers and consumed by "ancestral customs" compose a virtually petrified background to the innovative dynamism of colonial mercantilism.

The colonist makes history and he knows it. And because he refers constantly to the history of his metropolis, he plainly indicates that here he is the extension of this metropolis. The history he writes is therefore not the history of the country he is despoiling, but the history of his own nation's looting, raping, and starving to death. The immobility to which the colonized subject is condemned can be challenged only if he decides to put an end to the history of colonization and the history of despoliation in order to bring to life the history of the nation, the history of decolonization.

A world compartmentalized, Manichaean and petrified, a world of statues: the statue of the general who led the conquest, the statue of the engineer who built the bridge. A world cocksure of itself, crushing with its stoniness the backbones of those scarred by the whip. That is the colonial world. The colonial subject is a man penned in; apartheid is but one method of compartmentalizing the colonial world. The first thing the colonial subject learns is to remain in his place and not overstep its limits. Hence the dreams of the colonial subject are muscular dreams, dreams of action, dreams of aggressive vitality. I dream I am jumping, swimming, running, and climbing. I dream I burst out laughing, I am leaping across a river and chased by a pack of cars that never catches up with me. During colonization the colonized subject frees himself night after night between nine in the evening and six in the morning.

The colonized subject will first train this aggressiveness sedimented in his muscles against his own people. This is the period when black turns on black, and police officers and magistrates don't know which way to turn when faced with the surprising surge of North African criminality. We shall see later what should be made of this phenomenon.[2] Confronted with the colonial order the colonized subject is in a permanent state of tension. The colonist's world is a hostile world, a world which excludes yet at the same time incites envy. We have seen how the colonized always dream of taking the colonist's place. Not of becoming a colonist, but of replacing him. This hostile, oppressive and aggressive world, bulldozing the colonized masses, represents not only the hell they would like to escape as quickly as possible but a paradise within arm's reach guarded by ferocious watchdogs.

The colonized subject is constantly on his guard: Confused by the myriad signs of the colonial world he never knows whether he is out of line. Confronted with a world configured by the colonizer, the colonized subject is always presumed guilty. The colonized does not accept his guilt, but rather considers it a kind of curse, a sword of Damocles. But deep down the colonized subject acknowledges no authority. He is dominated but not domesticated. He is made to feel

---

2 *Colonial Wars and Mental Disorders*, chapter 5.

inferior, but by no means convinced of his inferiority. He patiently waits for the colonist to let his guard down and then jumps on him. The muscles of the colonized are always tensed. It is not that he is anxious or terrorized, but he is always ready to change his role as game for that of hunter. The colonized subject is a persecuted man who is forever dreaming of becoming the persecutor. The symbols of society such as the police force, bugle calls in the barracks, military parades, and the flag flying aloft, serve not only as inhibitors but also as stimulants. They do not signify: "Stay where you are." But rather "Get ready to do the right thing." And in fact if ever the colonized subject begins to doze off or forget, the colonist's arrogance and preoccupation with testing the solidity of the colonial system will remind him on so many occasions that the great showdown cannot be postponed indefinitely. This impulse to take the colonist's place maintains a constant muscular tonus. It is a known fact that under certain emotional circumstances an obstacle actually escalates action.

The relationship between colonist and colonized is one of physical mass. Against the greater number the colonist pits his force. The colonist is an exhibitionist. His safety concerns lead him to remind the colonized out loud: "Here I am the master." The colonist keeps the colonized in a state of rage, which he prevents from boiling over. The colonized are caught in the tightly knit web of colonialism. But we have seen how on the inside the colonist achieves only a pseudo-petrification. The muscular tension of the colonized periodically erupts into bloody fighting between tribes, clans, and individuals.

At the individual level we witness a genuine negation of common sense. Whereas the colonist or police officer can beat the colonized subject day in and day out, insult him and shove him to his knees, it is not uncommon to see the colonized subject draw his knife at the slightest hostile or aggressive look from another colonized subject. For the colonized subject's last resort is to defend his personality against his fellow countryman.

Internecine feuds merely perpetuate age-old grudges entrenched in memory. By throwing himself muscle and soul into his blood feuds, the colonized subject endeavors to convince himself that colonialism has never existed, that everything is as it used to be and history marches on. Here we grasp the full significance of the all too familiar "head-in-the-sand" behavior at a collective level, as if this collective immersion in a fratricidal bloodbath suffices to mask the obstacle and postpone the inevitable alternative, the inevitable emergence of the armed struggle against colonialism. So one of the ways the colonized subject releases his muscular tension is through the very real collective self-destruction of these internecine feuds. Such behavior represents a death wish in the face of danger, a suicidal conduct which reinforces the colonist's existence and domination and reassures him that such men are not rational. The colonized subject also manages to lose sight of the colonist through religion. Fatalism relieves the oppressor of all responsibility since the cause of wrong-doing, poverty, and the inevitable can be attributed to God. The individual thus accepts the devastation decreed by God, grovels in front of the colonist, bows to the hand of fate, and mentally readjusts to acquire the serenity of stone.

In the meantime, however, life goes on and the colonized subject draws on the terrifying myths that are so prolific in underdeveloped societies as inhibitions for his aggressiveness: malevolent spirits who emerge every time you put one foot wrong, leopard men, snake men, six-legged dogs, zombies, a whole never-ending gamut of animalcules or giants that encircle the colonized with a realm of taboos, barriers, and inhibitions far more terrifying than the colonialist world. This magical superstructure that permeates the indigenous society has a very precise function in the way the libido works. One of the characteristics, in fact, of underdeveloped societies is that the libido is primarily a matter for the group and family. Anthropologists have amply described societies where the man who dreams he has sexual intercourse with a woman other than his own must publicly confess his dream and pay the penalty in kind or in several days' work to the husband or the injured family party—which proves, by the way, that so-called prehistorical societies attach great importance to the unconscious.

In scaring me, the atmosphere of myths and magic operates like an undeniable reality. In terrifying me, it incorporates me into the traditions and history of my land and ethnic group, but at the same time I am reassured and granted a civil status, an identification. The secret sphere in underdeveloped countries is a collective sphere that falls exclusively within the realm of magic. By entangling me in this inextricable web where gestures are repeated with a secular limpidity, my very own world, our very own world, thus perpetuates itself. Zombies, believe me, are more terrifying than colonists. And the problem now is not whether to fall in line with the armor-plated world of colonialism, but to think twice before urinating, spitting, or going out in the dark.

The magical, supernatural powers prove to be surprisingly ego boosting. The colonist's powers are infinitely shrunk, stamped by foreignness. There is no real reason to fight them because what really matters is that the mythical structures contain far more terrifying adversaries. It is evident that everything is reduced to a permanent confrontation at the level of phantasy.

In the liberation struggle, however, this people who were once relegated to the realm of the imagination, victims of unspeakable terrors, but content to lose themselves in hallucinatory dreams, are thrown into disarray, re-form, and amid blood and tears give birth to very real and urgent issues. Giving food to the mujahideen, stationing lookouts, helping deprived families, and taking over from the slain or imprisoned husband—such are the practical tasks the people are asked to undertake in the liberation struggle.

In the colonial world, the colonized's affectivity is kept on edge like a running sore flinching from a caustic agent. And the psyche retracts, is obliterated, and finds an outlet through muscular spasms that have caused many an expert to classify the colonized as hysterical. This overexcited affectivity, spied on by invisible guardians who constantly communicate with the core of the personality, takes an erotic delight in the muscular deflation of the crisis.

Another aspect of the colonized's affectivity can be seen when it is drained of energy by the ecstasy of dance. Any study of the colonial world therefore must include an understanding of the phenomena of dance and possession. The colonized's way of relaxing is precisely this muscular orgy during which the most brutal aggressiveness and impulsive violence are channeled, transformed, and spirited away. The dance circle is a permissive circle. It protects and empowers. At a fixed time and a fixed date men and women assemble in a given place, and under the solemn gaze of the tribe launch themselves into a seemingly disarticulated, but in fact extremely ritualized, pantomime where the exorcism, liberation, and expression of a community are grandiosely and spontaneously played out through shaking of the head, and back and forward thrusts of the body. Everything is permitted in the dance circle. The hillock, which has been climbed as if to get closer to the moon, the river bank, which has been descended whenever the dance symbolizes ablution, washing, and purification, are sacred places. Everything is permitted, for in fact the sole purpose of the gathering is to let the supercharged libido and the stifled aggressiveness spew out volcanically. Symbolic killings, figurative cavalcades, and imagined multiple murders, everything has to come out. The ill humors seep out, tumultuous as lava flows.

One step further and we find ourselves in deep possession. In actual fact, these are organized seances of possession and dispossession: vampirism, possession by djinns, by zombies, and by Legba, the illustrious god of voodoo. Such a disintegration, dissolution or splitting of the personality, plays a key regulating role in ensuring the stability of the colonized world. On the way there these men and women were stamping impatiently, their nerves "on edge." On the way back, the village returns to serenity, peace, and stillness.

During the struggle for liberation there is a singular loss of interest in these rituals. With his back to the wall, the knife at his throat, or to be more exact the electrode on his genitals, the colonized subject is bound to stop telling stories.

After years of unreality, after wallowing in the most extraordinary phantasms, the colonized subject, machine gun at the ready, finally confronts the only force which challenges his very being: colonialism. And the young colonized subject who grows up in an atmosphere of fire and brimstone has no scruples mocking zombie ancestors, two-headed horses, corpses woken from the dead, and djinns who, taking advantage of a yawn, slip inside the body. The colonized subject discovers reality and transforms it through his praxis, his deployment of violence and his agenda for liberation.

We have seen that this violence throughout the colonial period, although constantly on edge, runs on empty. We have seen it channeled through the emotional release of dance or possession. We have seen it exhaust itself in fratricidal struggles.

The challenge now is to seize this violence as it realigns itself. Whereas it once reveled in myths and contrived ways to commit collective suicide, a fresh set of circumstances will now enable it to change directions.

From the point of view of political tactics and History, the liberation of the colonies poses a theoretical problem of crucial importance at the current time: When can it be said that the situation is ripe for a national liberation movement? What should be the first line of action? Because decolonization comes in many shapes, reason wavers and abstains from declaring what is a true decolonization and what is not. We shall see that for the politically committed, urgent decisions are needed on means and tactics, i.e., direction and organization. Anything else is but blind voluntarism with the terribly reactionary risks this implies.

5 Chinese Immigration and Resistance in the United States and Mexico

"A Distinct and Antagonistic Race"

Constructions of Chinese Manhood in the Exclusionist Debates, 1869–1878

By Karen J. Leong

● ●

They are bringing plague and pestilence
In fever-laden ships,
And taking gold and silver back
On their returning trips.
They are-bringing hordes of prostitutes
To ply their trade of shame,
And breeding vice and foul disease
Too horrible to name.
In fetid lanes and alleys
They are like a festering sore.
They are coming, they are coming,
Every week a thousand more.

       (Sam Booth, "They Are Coming")[1]

Throughout the 1860s, politicians and labor leaders in California and other western states sounded the alarm at the prospect of thousands of Chinese male laborers descending like a plague, a "yellow peril," upon the United States. The image of the Chinese female prostitute proved a key rhetorical device not only in Booth's poem, but also in western states' efforts to restrict the immigration of Chinese male laborers through federal legislation. The Chinese Exclusion Act of 1882 denied entry to Chinese laborers for ten years. The first enacted piece of federal legislation to restrict immigration to the United States explicitly based on nationality, Chinese exclusion was symptomatic of heightened sensitivity to issues of race and citizenship as well as a depressed economy and labor conflicts after the Civil War. Depictions of Chinese prostitutes and the illicit sexuality associated with Chinese laborers implicated the Chinese male as immoral, uncivilized, and fundamentally unfit for American citizenship. The architects of the anti-Chinese movement and subsequent exclusion laws expanded this theme into a broad-ranging, gendered argument against the Chinese as a race. Proponents of Chinese exclusion would measure Chinese men against normative standards of Anglo-American masculinity and find them wanting.

The argument that Chinese men did not meet the ideal of Anglo-American masculinity and thus could not be virtuous republican citizens ideologically justified restricting Chinese immigrant labor. Scholars have examined how gendered arguments for exclusion relied on the image of the Chinese prostitute, yet largely have neglected complementary constructions of Chinese and Anglo-American working-class masculinity.[2] Gendered rhetoric circumvented the obstacles posed by federal constitutional law and diplomacy to states' attempts to enact anti-Chinese legislation on a racial basis. The anti-Chinese movement thus shifted emphasis from the racial threat posed by Chinese male laborers to the moral threat posed by "aberrant" Chinese gender relations. The reconstruction of racial difference as cultural difference suggested the inability of Chinese to maintain American cultural values as evidenced in the lack of a home, family, and "appropriate" relations between men and women. This strategy also allowed western state representatives to successfully situate their regional economic interests within the post-Reconstruction national discourse of race, gender, sexuality, and morality, which ultimately transcended the sectionalism of the antebellum period.

The anti-Chinese movement established itself nationally in the United States by the end of the 1870s, advocating the exclusion of the Chinese male laborer because of his fundamental difference from the Anglo-American male citizen. Perceptions that a majority of Chinese women immigrants had been forced into prostitution helped to justify the United States' rejection of Chinese manhood. Chinese men's alleged exploitation of women betrayed their lack of manhood—in this case, a failure to protect female virtue—and revealed their unsuitability as Americans. Describing the Chinese trade in women, Senator Higby of California declared in 1870, "That is their character. You cannot make citizens of them."[3] A poem printed in the *San Francisco Chronicle*, "How He Sold Her Short," told a tragic tale of a young Chinese woman, Ching Lee, who was courted by a young man in China and traveled to join him in the United States, only to be sold on arrival to another man. The poet ended this epic with a "MORAL. Now all you Chinese maidens who have lovers far away, / Be careful of your characters, and don't be led astray, / Don't leave your native rice fields to join a moon-eyed sport, / For fear you be, like poor Ching Lee, sold very badly short."[4] In 1878, a speaker in New York similarly distinguished Chinese from American men: "They consider the wife a slavish chattel; we consider her a sacred partner."[5] The conclusions

drawn from these images of degraded women, of "female slaves," enabled American men and women to judge Chinese standards of morality as inferior to their own.

This moral argument crystallized in the national political consciousness when, in February 1878, the House Committee on Education and Labor issued a special report addressing the question of Chinese immigration. The committee provided three reasons why the Chinese male would be an "undesirable citizen": his effect on labor, his debilitating effect on society, and his inability to assimilate. The Chinese laborer was inferior to his Anglo-European counterpart because the American laborer "shall possess courage, self-respect and independence. To do this he must have a home." Exclusionists implied that Chinese workers depressed wages to the point where property ownership became impossible. Second, the Chinese evidenced peculiar moral habits in "their treatment of women" by profiting from their sexual servitude. In other words, by organizing prostitution, Chinese men reneged on their duty as providers. Chinese women faced lives full of "privation, contempt and degradation from the cradle to the tomb." Third, Chinese men failed to establish nuclear family households. Chinese males distinguished themselves from other immigrants because "[t]hey bring with them neither wives nor families, nor do they intermarry with the resident population. ... Mentally, morally, physically, socially and politically *they have remained a distinct and antagonistic race.*"[6] All three reasons focus on the aberration of Chinese gender roles as perceived by the American public.

According to these perceptions, the Chinese male laborer failed to fulfill the gendered, cultural requirements of American citizenship. As several feminist historians have demonstrated, American citizenship relied upon and perpetuated the economic and moral dimensions of Anglo masculine identity. The American male demonstrated his independence and self-sufficiency by providing economically for his dependents—his wife and children—and upheld social morality by protecting the virtue of his dependents and others. The ability to provide for a family constituted an integral component of citizenship.[7] As Stephanie McCurry has noted in her study of antebellum South Carolina yeomen, maintaining dominance over dependents has constituted an integral yet often overlooked aspect of how republican ideology defined the independent male American citizen.[8] Increasingly after Reconstruction, citizenship was equated with a masculinity and whiteness that were maintained by policing the racial, class, and gendered boundaries of middle-class Anglo-American behavior.[9] Those males who neither formed families nor supported them thus undermined the assumed heterosexual, nuclear household basis of the national economy.

Similarly, anti-Chinese rhetoric also centered around the Chinese laborers' lack of wives, family, and homes, and the danger "inassimilable aliens" posed to the republic and its families. Without a home, a "Chinaman" had no reason to defend the country; without a family, a "Chinaman" had no reason to invest in the future well-being of the nation; without a wife, a "Chinaman" was simply barbaric and uncivilized.[10] Based on definitions of American masculinity, the "Chinaman" was no man at all. This argument developed after the mid-1870s to encompass relationships in which gender identities were central: marriage, family, and even the republic itself. In 1878, Senator Jones of Nevada succinctly explained the danger Chinese men posed by citing both their effect on wages and their responsibility for Chinese prostitutes: "They debauch our men by their virtues and our boys by their vices."[11]

Constructions of the Chinese as a race and culture alien to all things American focused upon the ways Chinese male behavior deviated from Anglo-American social norms. One magazine article described the Chinese as a "community of males, without the humanizing influences of women and children." According to this interpretation, "no such principle in the Chinese make-up as filial, connubial or any other form of affection" existed because Chinese men spent their money buying sexual favors from prostitutes as opposed to investing in their homes and families.[12] Women, as this article implies, were considered civilizing forces in American society. The lack of virtuous females offered little hope that Chinese men would change. Without their civilizing influence, Chinese men could not be expected to become true citizens. The apparent fact that most Chinese women were immoral only amplified the extent to which Chinese men were wicked and debased.

Standards of masculinity, femininity, sexuality, and morality were central to the construction of working-class Anglo-American masculinity and also defined the working-class "Chinaman."[13] Rather than solely protecting the livelihood of the white male worker and thus maintaining the rights associated with American masculinity, anti-Chinese agitators also asserted their own masculine roles as protectors of the nation's morality and families. This paralleled a similar development in the Reconstruction South where, according to Martha Hodes, the prospects of political equality and economic mobility for freedmen were expressed in fears about sexual intimacy between black men and white women, resulting in the sexualization of politics.[14] Emerging norms of sexuality and morality, then, helped to maintain a racial division between Euro-American citizenry and "others," including African-American freedmen and Chinese immigrants, at the end of Reconstruction.[15]

Further examination of the gendered rhetoric of the movement to restrict Chinese immigration illustrates how issues of sexuality and gender became integral to projections of racial difference. At this particular moment, when many Americans sought to avoid the divisive issue of racial difference in Reconstruction politics, gender norms critically expressed and contributed to the national definition of American citizenry as male and of Anglo-European descent. The image of the Chinese female immigrant as enslaved, abused, and sexually exploited provided a key means through which Anglo-American working men on the West Coast could read gender and race onto the foreign body of the Chinese male worker. By articulating their own white, American masculinity in opposition to the Chinese foreigner, they thereby claimed their own political and moral dominance within the sphere of national politics.

The Chinese question emerged on a national level at a crucial time in U.S. history. In the aftermath of the Civil War, radical Republicans sought to reshape the nation. They envisioned an ideal society based on equal rights, free labor, and the continued civilizing of the frontier. One Republican declared, "My dream is of a model republic, extending equal protection and rights to all men. ... The wilderness shall vanish, the church and school-house will appear; ... the whole land will revive under the magic touch of free labor."[16] Reconstruction legislated equality in terms of race and class but excluded gender.[17] Male politicians described the model republic from the very end of the Civil War and the beginnings of Reconstruction in masculine terms: the republic would include all men, who would manifest not only their destiny but also their manhood by extending the republic geographically. Women had roles in what Amy Kaplan has termed *manifest domesticity*—the civilizing efforts that accompanied the spread of free labor and government not only across the expanse of what constituted the United States, but abroad as well.[18] During radical Reconstruction, however, the gendered construction of the republic remained subordinate to the question of race that had underlain the issue of free labor during the antebellum period.

Debates over the immigration of Chinese labor during Reconstruction revived unresolved concerns about race and the specter of slavery. Proponents of restricting Chinese labor evoked the free labor argument: Chinese wage labor would have the same effect as slavery on American labor and industry, undermining the possibility of free men to provide for their families. Opponents of restrictions, on the other hand, warned against restricting a group of immigrants on the basis of race. Indeed, opponents successfully rejected an 1869 bill that restricted the entry of Chinese contract labor and Chinese women on the grounds that the bill was motivated by race prejudice.[19] In 1869, Senator Williams proposed a bill that would deny entry to Chinese contract laborers, and would require any Chinese woman immigrant to be accompanied by her husband or father.[20] Williams presented this secondary provision in

Congress as a form of slavery on par with that of Chinese contract labor. During the open debate on this bill, Senator Pomeroy of Kansas quibbled with the largess of Senator Howard from Oregon. Pomeroy noted Howard's claims "that this [bill] is only to discriminate against a certain class; but the objection is that in that effort we discriminate against the whole." Pomeroy further disputed Howard's argument that his bill would prevent a type of slavery: "I am for the suppression of the slave trade ... but I am not for discriminating against persons who propose to become American citizens, whether they are white or black; whether they are from China or from Africa."[21]

The agitation on the part of western states to exclude all Chinese based on race conflicted ideologically with attempts to transform the slave economy in the South to that of free labor based on the equality of all men. The passage of both the Fourteenth Amendment and the Civil Rights Bill of 1870 extended rights of equality before the law, in principle, to all naturalized or native-born peoples in the United States.[22] Some radical Republicans attempted to extend rights explicitly to Native Americans and Chinese, not solely blacks. By 1870, however, California Republicans recognized that supporting legislation granting rights to the Chinese would alienate voters and significantly erode their party's representation in that state. Subsequently, California politicians united across party lines as well as with other western representatives to ensure that the Fifteenth Amendment would not interfere with individual states' suffrage qualifications.[23]

However, western politicians who sought to exclude Chinese immigrants from America's shores still faced particularly formidable legal obstacles posed by the U.S. Constitution and international diplomacy. State laws could be overruled by both the federal and state court systems and Chinese immigrants successfully challenged many anti-Chinese laws in court.[24] The California Supreme Court and the Federal District Court ruled various state and San Francisco anti-Chinese laws unconstitutional, based largely on the 1868 Burlingame Treaty, which extended to Chinese the equal protection enjoyed by American citizens under the Fourteenth Amendment as part of a free trade and migration agreement between the United States and China.[25] California's right to self-protection was deemed subordinate to federal law in 1874, when the California Supreme Court struck down California's law prohibiting the importation of prostitutes. State protection could be ensured only by passing legislation that protected western interests on the federal level.

Meanwhile, the growing disparity between working men and industrialists resulted in class antagonism that in itself reflected norms of American manhood.[26] The self-made man celebrated by American liberal ideology demonstrated his self-sufficiency in part by his property. Working-class men in the western states feared that they might never attain this goal in the wake of the 1873 economic depression and increasing competition for jobs. During the Reconstruction era, however, their complaints—often phrased in terms of Chinese inferiority to whites—were dismissed on the whole as racist and self-seeking. One unidentified Californian complained, "It has even been asserted, and prominent men and journals in the East have repeated it, that the opposition to Chinese immigration in California is confined to a few demagogues and discontented communists."[27]

Western politicians and newspapers frequently expressed frustration that other states did not fully understand the effects of Chinese immigration. East Coast newspapers and journals regularly derided the West Coast as paranoid, reactionary, and ungrateful for the contributions of Chinese labor to the industrialization of California. Scribner's declared with exasperation, "In the East, the prejudice against our heathen brother John in California, seems a little unreasonable and we want more light."[28] California newspapers, in turn, deplored the "perverted condition of opinion in the East," where for months "the newspapers ... have been filled with the grossest misrepresentations of every phase of the [Chinese] question, all proceeding from poisoned and interested sources."[29] Several newspapers reprinted commentaries from national papers concerning the reaction to the Chinese on the West Coast. West Coast

papers and politicians often pointed out that if large numbers of Chinese were arriving on the East Coast the easterners would react as the West had; an argument that probably contained more truth than those in the East cared to admit. The frustrated Californian suggested that the Pacific states vote on the Chinese question and that their Congressmen, "armed with these credentials, say to their brethren, of the East: 'The people of the Pacific Coast have been so far the only people exposed to Chinese immigration. They are strongly and bitterly opposed to it. ... If they are wrong you can easily prove it. ... Amend the treaty and confine the Chinese to the Atlantic ports. If this immigration suits you, you are welcome to it.'"[30]

What Californians perceived as an East-West polarization also involved issues of class. Newspapers outside of the West Coast frequently noted that a lower class of citizen inhabited most of California. The San Francisco Chronicle quoted the Louisville Courier-Journal claiming that the politicians were working on behalf of "the vast rabble of hoodlums in San Francisco," while the Chronicle itself implied that those "poisoned and interested sources" included corporations relying on cheap labor.[31] So long as they continued to dismiss the Chinese as racially inferior, laborers' demands were easily dismissed as lower-class resentment of more productive Chinese labor. By the late 1870s, however, national opinion began to accept the interpretation that the Chinese immigrating to the States were undesirables.[32] Increased attention in the national press and Congress evidenced a growing concern over Chinese immigration. This shift also reflected both the western states' greater importance in national politics and the changing rhetoric against the Chinese from issues of race to more nebulous and persuasive issues of morality and gender.[33]

West Coast representatives increasingly sought to persuade the national public that their actions were motivated not by base self-interest but by national interest. California politicians and the press consciously manipulated gendered images of Chinese in opposition to the ideal Anglo-American family unit in order to gain national sympathy and electoral support.

The policing of sexual disease, prostitution, and Chinese females proved an effective way to ultimately exclude Chinese male labor. By 1874 President Ulysses S. Grant in his annual address to Congress introduced the possibility of limiting the influx of Chinese prostitutes. Motivated by his party's viability in the western United States, Grant acknowledged the powerful images of Chinese slavery and prostitution in addressing the "problems" of the particular class of Chinese entering the United States:

> In relation to this subject I call the attention of Congress to a generally-conceded fact—that the great proportion of the Chinese immigrants who come to our shores do not come voluntarily to make their homes with us and their labor productive of general prosperity, but come under contracts with head-men who own them almost absolutely. In worse form does this apply to Chinese women. Hardly a perceptible percentage of them perform any honorable labor, but they are brought for shameful purposes, to the disgrace of the communities where settled and to the great demoralization of the youth of those localities. If this evil practice can be legislated against, it will be my pleasure as well as duty to enforce any regulation to secure so desirable an end.[34]

President Grant focused on the unfree status of both Chinese laboring men and prostitutes and its effects on American morality and productivity: unfree labor undermined the economy and political system upon which the American republic rested. If California came to rely too heavily upon Chinese contract labor, a system of unfree labor such as that in the antebellum South might result. The president implicitly appealed to the nation's conceptions of the republic, family, and female virtue. American citizens—native-born or naturalized immigrant males—constituted, protected, and perpetuated the nation; but American manhood could be weakened economically by Chinese labor and morally by Chinese prostitutes.

Western politicians, led by Horace Page and other California representatives, willingly obliged. On March 3, 1875, "An Act Supplementary to Acts in Relation to Immigration" entered the federal statutes as law.[35] The bill's purpose purportedly was to end Chinese slavery and prostitution: it required "free and voluntary immigration" from "China, Japan, or any Oriental country"; increased the fine levied on those importing contract labor; made illegal any contracting of unfree labor; prohibited the "importation into the United States of women for the purposes of prostitution"; and, lastly, denied entry to criminals or "women imported for the purposes of prostitution." Any "such obnoxious person or persons" would be returned to their own country.[36] This act, commonly referred to as the Page Act or Page Law, added a new element to Chinese immigration legislation, supplementing an 1862 bill that had attempted to halt the transportation of Chinese contract labor to the United States. Whereas the 1862 bill withheld landing permits from ships transporting Chinese for "lewd and immoral purposes," the Page Act sought to directly prevent the importation of female prostitutes and refused entry to any woman suspected of immigrating for this purpose.[37] Significantly, this legislation established at the federal level the connection between unfree labor, prostitutes, and Chinese immigrants.

The president's strong endorsement of the issues covered in the Page Act left little room for dissent among his fellow Republicans, who traditionally opposed legislation that might discriminate on the basis of race. President Grant assumed that many Chinese immigrants entered the United States against their will, under contract to someone else who profited from their labor as workers and prostitutes. According to this widely held assumption, the bill's enactment would curtail most of the undesirable elements of Chinese immigration to the United States. Indeed, immigration officials' conviction that the majority of Chinese female immigrants to the United States were prostitutes, combined with the difficulty

Chinese wives faced in proving otherwise, appear to have discouraged some Chinese women from even attempting to emigrate to the United States. As George Anthony Peffer has demonstrated, the lack of wives and families accompanying the Chinese males partly resulted from institutionalized discrimination against Chinese women immigrants by U.S. immigration officials and the Page Law of 1875.[38] The number of Chinese female immigrants to the United States significantly declined as a result of the indiscriminate enforcement of the Page Law.[39]

The Page Law of 1875 also effectively established grounds for further and broader exclusion legislation. By convincing the president and the people of the United States that a portion of the immigrants were undesirable based on moral grounds, the proponents of the Page Act opened the possibility that *all* Chinese immigrants could be categorized as undesirable. Within less than a year western politicians sought to exploit further the fears and prejudices of the American public in order to gain ready acceptance not only of the Page Act but also the necessity of revising the Burlingame Treaty.

In 1876 Senator Aaron Sargent of California spoke in favor of the resolution to renegotiate the Burlingame Treaty to allow for the further restriction of Chinese immigration. He contended that the ineffectiveness of the Page Law necessitated a policy of "general exclusion":

> The importation of females for immoral purposes is also forbidden by statute. But the law is a dead-letter, because of the impossibility of obtaining proof of its violation. And yet it is the almost universal conviction of Californians that nine-tenths of the Chinese male immigration is in violation of the former [coolie slavery], and ninety-nine hundredths of the female immigration in violation of the latter statute. There can be no remedy but general exclusion; and the policy, justice, and necessity of that supreme measure I purpose to discuss.[40]

Senator Sargent clearly admitted he had no proof of any violations and that his argument was based on Californians' *perceptions* of these violations. Californians opposed to Chinese immigration perceived the majority of Chinese male immigrants—90 percent—as enslaved.[41] More important, they were able to persuade national opinion that these perceptions were for the most part accurate. The image of the enslaved Chinese male preempted the condemnation of racial prejudice and appealed to free labor ideology while also calling into question the fitness of Chinese men to become naturalized citizens.

Establishing a link between Chinese male labor and female sexual servitude constituted an essential part of attempts to exclude Chinese immigrants. Comparing Chinese male and female immigrants to slaves conveyed both the economic threat posed by the Chinese men and the moral threat posed by Chinese women. Perceptions of Chinese as unfree justified Americans' desires to deny them entry. Free immigration, the exclusionists argued, should be restricted to those people who came freely. As U.S. Minister to China Benjamin P. Avery explained to a Chinese diplomat who questioned the immigration restrictions on Chinese, "This system of free immigration and equal privileges has had a large share in making the United States prosperous and strong and has been encouraged and protected by very careful laws which are strictly enforced."[42]

In his legal history of Chinese immigration, Hudson Janisch observed wryly, "If the South fought to protect white womanhood, the West fought to protect white manhood."[43] The West generously extended its protection to the nation's future generations of manhood as well. Images of the "Chinaman" and the diseased Chinese prostitute converged with national concerns about the stability of American social institutions. The amoral sexuality displayed by the Chinese threatened to pollute the virtues upon which American society and civilization rested. The Congregational Churches of America adopted a resolution urging the government to revise the Burlingame Treaty and to pass measures to "prevent the importation of Chinese prostitutes, and so relieve us from impending peril to our republican and Christian institutions."[44] Urban American masculine youth especially appeared vulnerable to this threat. Testimony before the Joint Special Committee that boys seven to twelve years old visited Chinese prostitutes shocked the national audience even more than the lurid descriptions of diseased prostitutes left to die on the streets of Chinatown. The Order of Caucasians, an anti-Chinese club, warned Congress that Chinese prostitution existed in many cities and that American male youth were "enticed thither by Chinese women—and who, for a few cents, can acquire a loathsome disease, ruin their constitutions and render themselves unfit to become the progenitors of a healthy and moral race."[45] Law enforcement officers, religious leaders, and local politicians, in their testimony before Congress, assumed that young boys were less likely to resist overt sexuality, especially at such bargain prices. The direct correlation between the constitution of American male youth and institutions of American society strikingly exemplifies the gendered basis of American national identity.

Concerns about the effects of perverse Chinese sexuality on the national body further illuminate the ideological relationships between virility and economic health, morality and industry. The dangers of sexually transmitted diseases graphically and concretely illustrated the danger embodied by Chinese immigrants to the nation's morality. Wherever Chinese settled, one editorial declared, "progress staggers and halts, industry withers, and public morals and public decency decay and die. … They are the embodiment of the plague, pestilence, famine and death."[46] Several San Francisco physicians quoted in the San Francisco *Medico-Literary Journal* attributed such diseases in that city to the Chinese prostitutes because they, "unlike the white women, use no preventative measures." This article further warned that Chinese women would spread a plague that could "sink this nation into effeminacy and political death."[47]

Disease and immorality were physical manifestations of corruption and vice that would not only ruin the constitutions of young men but also undermine the Constitution of the United States, which depended upon a healthy civic life of virtuous male participants. The Chinese, claimed one pamphlet, "corrupt the morals and undermine [sic] the framework of our social structure."[48] A California anti-Chinese convention memorial in 1886 explicitly spelled out the threat to white masculinity—and thus to the nation as a whole—posed by Chinese men. While Chinese labor thrived on low wages,

> the white laboring man, to whom the nation must, in the long run, look for the reproduction of the race and the bringing up and educating of citizens to take the place of the present generation as it passes away, and, above all, to defend the country in time of war, is injured in his comfort, reduced in his scale of life and standard of living, necessarily carrying down with it his moral and physical stamina.[49]

Chinese working men and immoral Chinese women would erode the foundations of Anglo-American masculinity: work, self-sufficiency, and virility.

Discussions about the Chinese question relied upon constructions of gender and sexuality that supported America's implicitly masculine and heterosexual national identity.[50] The virtues ascribed to Anglo-American women increased their political visibility in opposition to Chinese males (working women also participated in anti-Chinese demonstrations).[51] Anti-Chinese sentiment even entertained the possibility of political franchise. If Chinese men were to gain the vote, white women's votes would be needed to "overbalance the Chinese power and give us the majority. … Republics and Empires have been saved through different causes, but not one yet has had the honor of having been saved by women. Well, let California have the glory of having been saved by them."[52] This appeal to American domesticity and womanhood was reminiscent of the race and gender logic expressed in the debates over the Fifteenth Amendment: when threatened by nonwhite masculinity, a common ethnic culture would transcend gender identity. Anglo-American women presumably would vote according to the same cultural values as Anglo-American men, just as Chinese men's votes would reflect their (inferior) racial and cultural identities.

Some anti-Chinese agitators sought moral protection through the American female as mother in opposition to the corrupted morality of Chinese women and the fallibility of male youth. The aforementioned article in the *Medico-Literary Journal* asked, "If it is through the Chinese women that our nation is threatened with destruction, why [do] not the American women at least raise their voices to repel them?" The article ended by appealing to mothers "to be more watchful of their sons."[53] Representing the highest virtues of Anglo-American civilization, white women had the power to protect American morality, even as their sexuality had the power to undo it.[54] The Chinese prostitute and the Anglo-American wife or mother emphasized the manhood and strength of character of American masculinity, and the "absence" of these traits in Chinese males.

By the late 1870s, anti-Chinese rhetoric shifted its primary focus from Chinese threats to morality to the ways Chinese men disrupted Anglo-American patterns of gender segregation in the workforce. After the completion of the transcontinental railroad in 1870, Chinese males increasingly competed with Anglo working men as well as women. They owned laundries and found employment as house servants. Because Chinese males apparently made few gender distinctions in the labor they performed—they did not care whether they were doing work traditionally assigned to females or males—they challenged the norms regarding accepted gendered divisions of labor in American society.

Politicians and rally speakers now warned that Chinese males threatened the economic basis of the American woman's virtue. Testimony persuaded members of the Joint Special Committee that Chinese males monopolized employment in traditionally female occupations by working for low wages, and that the "hardships resulting from these causes bear with especial weight upon women."[55] One witness testified that Anglo-American working women, who had lost their jobs at a sewing factory due to the influx of Chinese labor, could be found in places "where I presume you would not wish your sisters, mothers, or wives to be."[56] A pamphlet comparing contemporary evils to the "greatest curse" of intemperance deplored the fact that, although "the Chinaman" had once "filled a place and performed the labor which was not so agreeable to Anglo-Saxon masculinity," he now entered a domain hitherto occupied by virtuous Anglo women. As a result, "good, honest intelligent women" were forced to "decide between a short and wretched life of infamy and shame, or a life of starvation."[57] Chinese male laborers blurred the gendered division of labor in western cities, economically forcing Anglo-American women into prostitution, where their moral position would sink to that of Chinese women. The effects of Chinese labor manifested themselves in "domestic help, where the honest, virtuous and trustworthy females have been ousted and driven into dens of infamy and prostitution."[58] Thus Chinese males inevitably corrupted the female sex regardless of racial background, because they displaced Anglo-American women from the only respectable jobs available to them.

According to exclusionists, the Chinese male's ability to work for lower wages and in feminine occupations endangered American families. The congressional committee declared, "Family-life is a great safeguard of our political institutions."[59] This pervasive rhetoric indicates that the metaphor of family and home was a concept accepted as normative, and that it transcended class divisions in Anglo-American society. The Anglo-American nuclear family ensured the production of American institutions and represented a virtuous cause, one that could overshadow racist overtones. Senator Booth of California asserted that the "source of civilization in which we live, of the institutions we believe to be its highest outgrowth, is the family."[60] An article in *The Argonaut*

(1877) characterized the intricate relationships among family, nation, and the economy:

> With us the family is not only the most sacred of our relationships, but is also the unit of nationality. Each family constitutes a little Republic. A collection of States, the nation. The nation is a collection of families. The "family relation" is, among our race sacredly regarded as the foundation of government. Society has been organized with reference to it. ... The assumption that every man among us is to have a family and a house enters into all our calculations.[61]

The relationship of family, government, and private property—owning a house—found expression not only in masculinity but in the primary role assigned to males within the republic, that of citizen. Thus, the Chinese immigrants, most of whom lacked family and private property, could not be expected to enjoy the same privileges of government protection extended to Anglo-American males or even male immigrants from other European countries. Representative James G. Blaine said as much in his February 1879 speech before the Senate: "You cannot work a man who must have beef and bread, alongside of a man who can live on rice. In all such conflicts, and in all such struggles, the result is not to bring up the man who lives on rice to the beef-and-bread standard, but it is to bring down the beef-and-bread man to the rice standard."[62]

By blurring feminine and masculine roles and undermining the Anglo working male's ability to provide for his dependents, Chinese male labor threatened to expose the arbitrary division of American society into separate domains based on gender, the public, and the private, which thus far had restricted women from public political institutions, including citizenship. As leaders of the Workingman's Party complained, the Chinese "seem to have no sex."[63] The Chinese threat to Anglo-American manhood extended beyond economic livelihood and morality to the ideological underpinnings of American society. The

Chinese laborer's willingness to do "feminine" work was perceived as unnatural, outside the gendered division of labor that reinforced masculine citizenship in American society.

As anti-Chinese rhetoric shifted to a gendered moral argument, national opinion about the Chinese question also changed. The *San Francisco Post* attributed this to a more elevated argument:

> Heretofore the anti-chinese [*sic*] agitation has been sporadic and violent in character. It assumed the tone of race antagonism—an attitude sure to arouse feeling against those who take it. When the venue was changed and the non-assimilative and aggressive attitude of this people shown towards, not only our labor, but our commerce and manufactures, our institutions and civilization, the plane of statesmanship was reached and that of bitter race hostility abandoned forever.[64]

According to the *Post*, issues of assimilation and civilization, culture and morality, transcended racism and caste prejudice. Furthermore, the argument was framed proactively: rather than reacting to perceived racial and economic threats to the American male's livelihood, American masculinity sought to protect American institutions.

Anti-Chinese rhetoric also expressed larger social tensions regarding class status, race relations, and gender and sexual norms. Cultural definitions of whiteness and masculinity became the ideological focal point for political organization nationwide: politicians seized upon anti-Chinese sentiment to mobilize political support of the working-class electorate among the developing urban areas along the West Coast. As Mary P. Ryan demonstrates, western urban politics shared a critical transformation with other urban centers nationwide. Normative definitions of race, gender, and class increasingly circumscribed American civic participation in the post-Reconstruction era. "Gender ... provided the sexual prohibitions, codes of segregation, and rhetorical power with which to mortar the rising wall of segregation," which replaced those sectional barriers that had hitherto dominated American politics.[65] Western politicians and union leaders succeeded in developing a refined political rhetoric and strategy with which to fit a blatantly racist exclusionary argument into the larger national political trend of maintaining social order and exploiting white middle-class fears of urban disarray.[66]

Indeed, the shift from class- and race-based arguments against the Chinese from the western states to ever more sophisticated arguments for exclusion based on gender at the national level took place through trial and error between the 1860s and 1882, when Congress passed the first exclusion act. Ryan's work suggests several avenues for further analysis of the ways in which exclusion legislation was part of larger national trends. It is apparent, however, that western politicians increasingly adapted their presentation of regional concerns to the evolving concerns of the North and South to persuade northern and southern politicians of the necessity of exclusion.

The political use of gender, and the issue of sexuality associated with gender roles, emphasized the necessity of ultimately excluding Chinese as a race from America's shores. During the era of Reconstruction, a racial argument still evoked suspicion and fears of division; a moral argument based on gender and sexuality that implicitly substantiated racial difference, however, was pursued with success.[67] The race argument, or the "caste prejudice" as it was frequently referred to in Congress, found expression and subsequent acceptance within a more positive ideology affirming Anglo-American manhood.

Presuming to protect both the Chinese and Americans from slavery, western leaders could deflect criticisms of racial intolerance. On the hierarchy of race, Californians referred to the Chinese laborer as "below the most degraded specimen of the American Indian, and but very little above the beast."[68] Chinese females were the most abject of immigrants, existing in "a state of servitude beside which African slavery was a beneficent captivity."[69] Employing these comparisons enabled other regions to comprehend the West Coast situation. Many southern politicians already supported the right of California and other western states to protect their population from a Chinese invasion. The nature of the Chinese slavery argument, however, also appealed to Republicans who had worked to abolish slavery and protect the rights of newly freed African Americans but also needed political support from California voters. The resulting strategy rephrased the Chinese question as one of assimilation. This argument encompassed the ideology of equality while addressing racial and labor tensions on the West Coast.[70] Significantly, it also reinforced white masculine superiority: the Anglo-American could continue to claim paternal benevolence toward immigrants in the name of exclusion, while protecting the national body from imagined harm.

Notes

1. Sam Booth, "They Are Coming," in *The Chinese Invasion,* comp. Henry Josiah West (San Francisco: Bacon and Company, 1873). This is one stanza of the poem, most of which considers the effects of the Chinese on American labor.

2. Thomas Almaguer is one of the few scholars who has examined the development of a hierarchy of race, class, gender, and sexuality in California politics and society. His analysis of how whiteness and masculinity were constructed against the hypersexualized Chinese male and female, however, overlooks the critical role of the Page Act in this process. Mary P. Ryan's work also has examined how gender relations and sexuality were critical to urban political discourse. See Thomas Almaguer, *Racial Faultlines: The Historical Origins of White Supremacy in California* (Berkeley and Los Angeles: University of California Press, 1994); and Mary P. Ryan, *Civic Wars: Democracy and Public Life in the American City during the Nineteenth Century* (Berkeley and Los Angeles: University of California Press, 1997), as well as Mary P. Ryan, *Women in Public: Between Banners and Ballots, 1825–1880* (Baltimore: Johns Hopkins University Press, 1990).

3. *Congressional Globe,* February 21, 1866.

4. [D. O'C], "How He Sold Her Short," *San Francisco Chronicle*, January 11, 1878.

5. *Daily Morning Call*, February 25, 1878.

6. *San Francisco Chronicle*, February 26, 1878 (emphasis mine).

7. See, for example, Martha Hodes, *White Women, Black Men: Illicit Sex in the 19th-century South* (New Haven: Yale University Press, 1997); Stephanie McCurry, "Proslavery Politics in Antebellum South Carolina," *Journal of American History* 78 (1992): 1245–64; and Jacqueline Jones, *American Work* (New York: W.W. Norton, 1998).

8. McCurry, 1253 and 1259.

9. Hodes, 177.

10. This argument was popular in speeches. See, for example, *Report from the House Committee on Education and Labor*, February 25, 1878, by Senator Willis (Kentucky).

11. *San Francisco Post*, November 1, 1878.

12. "The Chinese in California," *Lippincott's Magazine* 2 (July 1868).

13. James Leroy Evans, *The Indian Savage, the Mexican Bandit, the Chinese Heathen: Three Popular Stereotypes* (Ph.D. diss., University of Texas at Austin, 1967); Lucie Cheng Hirata, "Free, Indentured, Enslaved: Chinese Prostitutes in Nineteenth-Century America," *Signs* 5 (1979): 27. Further work on nineteenth-century Chinese-American women has shown the fundamental impact of the Page Act on the formation of Chinese-American families and the community. See Judy Yung, *Unbound Feet* (Berkeley and Los Angeles: University of California Press, 1994); Sucheng Chan, "Immigration of Chinese Women under the Page Law," in *Entry Denied*, ed. Sucheng Chan (Philadelphia: Temple University Press, 1991); George Anthony Peffer, "Forbidden Families: Emigration Experience of Chinese Women under the Page Law, 1875–1882," *Journal of American Ethnic History* 6 (1986): 28–46; and Peffer, *If They Don't Bring Their Women Here: Chinese Female Immigration before Exclusion* (Urbana: University of Illinois Press, 1999).

14. Hodes, 151–71.

15. For an extended discussion of this process, see Ryan, *Civic Wars*. Ryan's ambitious comparative study of urban political culture in nineteenth-century New York, New Orleans, and San Francisco illuminates the development of each region's racial, gendered, and class politics within the larger national discourses of democracy.

16. An unidentified Republican in 1866, *Congressional Globe*, 39th Cong., 2nd sess., 118, Appendix, 78, as quoted and cited in Eric Foner, *Reconstruction: America's Unfinished Revolution, 1863–1877* (New York: Harper & Row, 1988), 235.

17. Ryan, *Civic Wars*, 297.

18. Amy Kaplan, "Manifest Domesticity," *American Literature* 70 (1998): 581–606.

19. A similar bill, proposed by James A. Johnson in 1870, also was denied because of concerns about racial prejudice. James A. Johnson, *Chinese Immigration: A Speech Made in the House of Representatives, January 25, 1870* (Washington, D.C.: Government Printing Office, 1870). Johnson proposed a joint resolution to discourage the immigration of "Chinese laborers and debased and abandoned females," and notes that Senator Williams had introduced a similar "anti-coolie, anti-harlot bill" in December 1869.

20. *Congressional Globe*, 41st Cong., 2nd Sess., December 22, 1869, 299.

21. *Congressional Globe*, 41st Cong., 2nd Sess., December 22, 1869, 300.

22. Foner, 256.

23. Hudson N. Janisch, *The Chinese, the Courts, and the Constitution: A Study of the Legal Issues Raised by the Chinese Immigration to the United States, 1850–1902* (JSD thesis, University of Chicago, 1971), 184. Some politicians even requested the insertion of an exclusive clause declaring that the right to vote never was intended to apply to the Chinese or Mongolian races, but this was defeated 106 to 42 in the House. Senators Trumbull and Sumner each introduced an amendment allowing Chinese to become naturalized citizens in 1870. Both were rejected, with nearly half of the Senate not voting. See Stuart Creighton Miller, *Unwelcome Immigrant: The American Image of the Chinese, 1785–1882* (Berkeley and Los Angeles: University of California Press, 1969), 160.

24. See Charles McClain and Laurene Wu McClain, "The Chinese Contribution to the Development of American Law," in Chan, ed., *Entry Denied*.

25. San Francisco's Cubic Air Ordinance, for example, sought to limit the number of persons inhabiting a room based on cubic feet per person. See McClain and McClain.

26. Alexander Saxton, *The Indispensable Enemy: Labor and the Anti-Chinese Movement in California* (Berkeley and Los Angeles: University of California Press, 1971).

27. "The Chinese Question," in *Chinese Immigration Pamphlets*, Special Collections, Bancroft Library. University of California at Berkeley, 15.

28. *Scribner's Monthly*, January 1877, as reprinted in *San Francisco Daily Alta*, December 26, 1878. The "John" referred to is "John Chinaman."

29. *San Francisco Chronicle*, February 28, 1878.

30. "The Chinese Question," 16.

31. *San Francisco Chronicle*, January 14, 1878.

32. Gwendolyn Mink, *Old Labor and New Immigrants in American Political Development: Union, Party, and State, 1875–1920* (Ithaca, N.Y.: Cornell University Press, 1986).

33. See Saxton and Mink.

34. Message from the President, *Journal of the House of Representatives of the United States*, 43rd Cong., 2nd Sess., December 7, 1874, 12.

35. The Committee on Foreign Affairs originally introduced the Page Act to the House on February 18, 1875, with unanimous consent. Four days later, the House passed the bill. It then proceeded to the Senate Committee of Foreign Relations, which reported it to the Senate without amendment on March 3, 1875. President Ulysses S. Grant signed the Page Act into law that evening. The San Francisco newspapers merely mention the law's passage and comment no further. No records or reports remain from the committee that deliberated upon and produced this bill. See *Congressional Record*, 43rd Cong., 2nd sess., Mar. 3, 1875, 1454, 1599, and 2161; and *Journal of the House of Representatives of the United States*, 43rd Cong., 2nd sess., March 3, 1875, 487, 640, 652, and 679–80.

36. "An Act Supplementary to the Acts in Relation to Immigration," March 3, 1875, *United States Statutes at Large*, 477.

37. The Page Law was the first law to prevent women from entering the United States as immigrants on the explicit assumption that they may be prostitutes; only with the Immigration Act of 1907 would Congress authorize the deportation of foreign-born prostitutes of any race. For an extended discussion about the passage of the Page Law, its effects on the Chinese-American community, and its role in the debates on Chinese exclusion, see Peffer, *If They Don't Bring Their Women Here.*

38. Peffer, "Forbidden Families."

39. See Chan; and Peffer, "Forbidden Families."

40. Aaron A. Sargent, *Immigration of Chinese, Speech of Hon. Aaron A. Sargent, of California, in the Senate of the United States, May 2, 1876* (Washington, D.C.: Government Printing Office, 1876).

41. Almaguer, 160–62. Almaguer argues that Chinese males in service industries also were hypersexualized as threats to young women and girls, but, interestingly, these depictions did not take on the significant role of the Chinese prostitute (perhaps because they too uncomfortably paralleled racial tensions in the South).

42. Benjamin P. Avery to Prince Kung, May 28, 1878, Despatch no. 64, Inclosure I, *Despatches from United States Ministers to China 1843–1906*, vol. 38, March 31– July 31, 1875.

43. Janisch, 81. He continues, "So far did this go that legislation was proposed, making seduction by a Chinese woman of a member of the California legislature or minister 'in good standing' a criminal offense."

44. *Resolutions Adopted by the General Association of Congregational Churches of California*, *Chinese Immigration Pamphlets*, vol. 1, Special Collections, Bancroft Library, University of California at Berkeley.

45. Petition to Congress from the Chico Encampment of the Order of Caucasians, *The Pacific*, December 1877.

46. Editorial from the *Cincinnati Enquirer* as reprinted in the *San Francisco Chronicle*, January 4, 1878.

47. "How the Chinese Women Are Infusing a Poison Fate into the Anglo-Saxon Blood," reprinted from the *Medico-Literary Journal* in the *San Francisco Chronicle*, November 21, 1878.

48. Henry Josiah West, *The Chinese Invasion* (San Francisco: Bacon and Company, 1873).

49. The memorial from the anti-Chinese convention of 1886 is quoted in Samuel Gompers and Herman Gutstadt, *Meat vs. Rice: American Manhood against Asiatic Coolieism, Which Shall Survive?* Published by American Federation of Labor and printed as Senate document 137, 1902. Reprinted with introduction and appendixes by Asiatic Exclusion League.

50. Jennifer Ting, "Bachelor Society: Deviant Heterosexuality and Asian American Historiography," in *Privileging Positions*, ed. Gary Y. Okihiro, et al. (Pullman, Wash., 1995), 271–80.

51. Ryan, *Women in Public*, 163.

52. *Sacramento Record Union*, February 23, 1879.

53. *San Francisco Medico-Literary Journal*, reprinted in *San Francisco Chronicle*, November 21, 1878.

54. Ryan, *Women in Public*, 163.

55. *Report of the Joint Special Committee to Investigate Chinese Immigration*, iv.

56. Testimony of Mrs. Sophronia Swift, *Report of the Joint Special Committee to Investigate Chinese Immigration*, 246.

57. Jennett Blakeslee Frost, *California's Greatest Curse* (San Francisco: J. Winterburn & Co., 1879), 15, 18.

58. Patrick Stephen Fox, Letter to the Editor, *San Francisco Daily Mail*, November 25, 1877.

59. *Report of the Joint Special Committee to Investigate Chinese Immigration*, viii.

60. *San Francisco Chronicle*, August 12, 1878.

61. " 'Caucasian' vs. 'Mongolian,' " *The Argonaut*, October 27, 1877.

62. Excerpt from the Speech of James G. Blaine in the Senate, February 14, 1879, as quoted in Gompers and Gutstadt, 22.

63. *San Francisco Chronicle*, December 28, 1877.

64. *San Francisco Post*, June 22, 1878.

65. Ryan, *Civic Wars*, 296.

66. Ryan's description of municipal attempts, through legislation and police force, to "discipline occupants of public space" in the postbellum period highlights changing expressions of masculinity in public space as well. American masculinity thus was disciplined at the same time that Chinese masculinity was disciplined (and rejected) through the ever evolving contestation and definition of American citizenship. Ryan, *Civic Wars*, 217–18.

67. This increasingly sophisticated use of gender, race, and sexuality to justify nativism would manifest itself yet again in justification of imperialism and racial eugenics toward the turn of the century. For example, see Kristin Hoganson, *Fighting for American Manhood; How Gender Politics Provoked the Spanish-American and Philippine-American Wars* (New Haven: Yale University Press, 1998), and Kaplan.

68. Memorial and Joint Resolution in Relation to the Chinese Immigration to the State of California, *Journal of Senate and Assembly of the 17th Session of the Legislature of the State of California*, vol. II (Sacramento: 1868), 3.

69. Memorial of the Senate of California to Congress of United States, April 3, 1876.

70. See Mink, esp. chap. 3, "Meat vs. Rice (and Pasta): Discovering Labor Politics in California, 1875–85."

Crossing Boundaries, Claiming a Homeland

The Mexican Chinese Transpacific Journey to Becoming Mexican, 1930s–1960s

By Julia María Schiavone Camacho

In 2004 Alfonso Wong Campoy, a Mexican Chinese man from the northern Mexican town of Navojoa in Sonora, reflected on his life, saying, "I love Mexico, I love Navojoa."[1] His father, Alfonso Wong Fang, and his mother, Dolores Campoy Rivera, had traversed racial and cultural boundaries by marrying and forming a family during the 1920s. These cultural crossings eventually pushed the family across political borders. Expelled from Navojoa by the Sonoran government during the early 1930s, they entered the United States, whose immigration agents then deported them to China. After living briefly in Guangdong (Canton) Province and nearly thirty years in the Portuguese colony of Macau, Alfonso Wong Campoy ultimately returned to Mexico, the homeland he had longed for since his childhood.[2]

This work is a journey. It follows the paths of Mexican Chinese families from northern Mexico, across the Mexican-U.S. border, to southeastern China, and back to Mexico. Chinese men increasingly arrived in Mexico after the United States passed a series of Chinese Exclusion Acts beginning in 1882. These men concentrated in northern Mexico because of its proximity to the

United States and the existence of opportunities in the developing economy. Integrating into local society, Chinese men forged a variety of relationships with Mexicans, including romantic unions and marriages with Mexican women. During the Mexican Revolution of 1910, an anti-Chinese campaign emerged in Sonora. Although this movement spread across the nation during the 1920s and early 1930s, anti-Chinese organizing was strongest in the Mexican north, owing partially to its location near the United States and the circulation of anti-Chinese ideology in the border region.[3] Only the states of Sonora and its coastal neighbor, Sinaloa, carried out mass expulsions of Chinese men and their families, including even those of Mexican origin, during the early 1930s. While some were deported directly from Mexican ports, others passed through the United States after Mexican officials literally pushed Chinese men and Mexican Chinese families through gaps in the international boundary fence. After taking their testimony and holding them in immigration jails in the Southwest, the United States deported them to China. Once in China, Mexican Chinese families confronted drastic changes. They formed local networks in Guangdong Province and,

Julia María Schiavone Camacho, "Crossing Boundaries, Claiming a Homeland The Mexican Chinese Transpacific Journey to Becoming Mexican, 1930s–1960s," *Race and Immigration in the United States: New Histories*, pp. 178-202. Copyright © 2012 by Taylor & Francis Group. Reprinted with permission.

over time, an enclave in Portuguese Macau. Nevertheless, many Mexican Chinese sought to return to Mexico and appealed to Mexican authorities between the 1930s and 1960s. Two official Mexican repatriations took place, the first under the administration of President Lázaro Cárdenas in 1937–1938 and the second under President Adolfo López Mateos in 1960. From the early 1930s until at least the 1980s, smaller groups also returned outside the two official repatriations.[4]

On the cultural and geographic fringes of the nation, these Mexican Chinese became "Mexican" only after they struggled from abroad for years with federal authorities for the official acknowledgment of the legitimacy of their racially mixed families. In the process, the identities they formed as Mexicans were both heartfelt and strategic, born in the context of conflict in mid-twentieth-century China. Confronting political and economic hardship, Mexican Chinese claimed Mexico as their homeland and argued that their families belonged in that nation because they wanted to leave China. Mexico became increasingly desirable as they were forced to compare their memories of it with their lives in China. The concept of a "Mexican homeland" became ever more salient among the Mexican Chinese as China experienced invasion by Japan, the Sino-Japanese War, World War II, the Communist Revolution, and the Cold War. Over the years, as they grew to love and miss Mexico, they romanticized the nation and developed a diasporic Mexican citizenship.[5]

In making a case for the *Mexicanness* of their families, the Mexican Chinese pushed the concept of *mestizaje*—the ideology of the nation's heritage of racial and cultural mixture—to include them. *Mestizaje* is the centerpiece of Mexican nationalism but has historically excluded Chinese and other Asians. Following Mexican Chinese families across borders and oceans as they left northern Mexico, developed a Mexican national identity, and repatriated decades later, this article complicates the literature on postrevolutionary and postwar Mexico by placing the nation in a larger transpacific context and addressing the understudied question of gendered citizenship.

This article also contributes to scholarship on Borderlands history, moving beyond the U.S. Southwest and focusing instead on northern Mexico. Chinese concentrated in the Mexican north, and anti-Chinese campaigns were most successful on the northern border. Moreover, the expulsion of Chinese from Sonora and Sinaloa (1931–1934) partially coincided with the massive forced repatriation of Mexicans from the U.S. Southwest (1929–late 1930s). The return of Mexican workers, who had become scapegoats for the Great Depression in the United States, added momentum to anti-Chinese campaigns in Mexico that had called for the removal of Chinese residents since the 1910s.

The Mexican-U.S. border region is linked with the rest of the Pacific Rim not only by migration but also by transpacific ties and by the complex, hybrid, diasporic identities that Mexican Chinese individuals and families created and maintained over time. Mexican Chinese families developed a "diasporic citizenship," imbued with a strong sense of Mexican nationalism and a longing for the homeland, which they cultivated across three decades. I use Lok C. D. Siu's concept of "diasporic citizenship" to highlight the interstitial status of the Mexican Chinese in China and the loyalty they felt toward Mexico while they were abroad.[6] Like other peoples on the fringes of nation-states who did not fit by virtue of their race, gender, class, language, culture, or affiliative ties, the Mexican Chinese sought to negotiate a place in the Mexican nation.

Chinese Migration to Mexico and the Anti-Chinese Movement

This story begins in southeastern China during the mid-nineteenth century when Chinese men left their villages and towns and began to form overseas communities around the world.[7] The discovery of gold drew many Chinese, and others, to northern California. They began to arrive in northern Mexico after the Chinese Exclusion Act of 1882 forbade the entry of Chinese laborers into the United States. On the U.S.-Mexican border, Sonora was among the Mexican states that attracted the highest numbers of Chinese.[8] Some came with the intention of entering the United States illegally. Others had learned of local prospects and found commercial niches in the growing economy of northern Mexico.[9]

Among the Cantonese newcomers to Sonora was Wong Fang, Wong Campoy's father. Wong Fang left Guangdong Province with his brother and arrived in San Francisco in the early 1900s. While his brother remained in San Francisco, Wong Fang moved to Sonora where he worked and learned Spanish. Adapting to local society, Wong Fang became Alfonso Wong Fang by adding a familiar Mexican first name and using his Chinese names as surnames, a common practice among Chinese in Latin America.[10] He eventually became an associate of Ching Chong y Compañía and met Dolores Campoy Rivera, whose father worked in the local post office in Navojoa. They ultimately married and formed a family. Their eldest child, Alfonso Wong Campoy, was born in Navojoa on October 12, 1928. In keeping with Mexican custom, the parents named their first-born son after his father and gave him one of his father's and one of his mother's surnames.[11]

Other Chinese also integrated into Sonoran communities; they learned Spanish and became naturalized Mexicans. Individual Chinese and Mexicans—mainly from the working and middle classes—developed an array of everyday social, economic, and neighborly ties, including romantic unions and marriages. At times, Chinese men and Mexican women formed relationships without eliciting much reaction from their families or communities. They got to know one another in the businesses Chinese men established. Families also arranged marriages, and Mexican and indigenous fathers who worked for Chinese landowners sometimes encouraged their daughters to marry their Chinese bosses for economic stability. In other cases, however, women's families did not approve, and Chinese men and Mexican women had to maintain secret relationships.[12]

Chinese played an important and visible role in the Sonoran economy and society despite their relatively small numbers. Although they comprised only between 1 and 2 percent of Sonora's overall population between 1910 and 1930, Chinese concentrated in particular towns and gained disproportionate attention because of their commercial activities.[13] Fulfilling a variety of needs, they brought merchandise and services to towns throughout Sonora. They lived and labored on the haciendas, ranchos, and fields of Mexican as well as Chinese landowners. Chinese also created businesses, either individually or jointly with other countrymen. They often hired compatriots who had just arrived to work in their stores, but at times they also employed Mexican women. Initially, Chinese businessmen enjoyed the protection of municipal authorities because they brought revenue and necessary goods to local communities. While some were large-scale operations, most Chinese businesses were small, including street peddling. Selling goods house by house, street by street, they made frequent contact with their clientele. North American and European immigrants, many of whom were businessmen and possessed far larger sums of capital, were simply not a part of Sonoran working people's day-to-day lives. Chinese laborers, peddlers, and shopkeepers, on the other hand, were visible on a daily basis.[14]

Owing to their visible presence, Chinese had experienced prejudice since they first arrived in Sonora. Negative attitudes and jokes abounded, and some people perceived Chinese as different and foreign. North American and European immigrants were insulated from this pattern by the legacy of Spanish colonialism, which privileged the lighter skinned. Nevertheless, anti-Chinese sentiment was neither widespread nor organized in Sonora until the period between the Mexican Revolution of 1910 and the Great Depression.[15] During this time, especially when Mexican workers began to return from the United States, Chinese ethnic distinctiveness generated Mexican scorn for Chinese as foreigners who took jobs from "real" Mexicans—a mirror of the treatment that Mexicans received in the United States.

The Mexican Revolution set notions of race, citizenship, and *mestizaje* in flux. Revolutionaries argued that the nation needed to embrace its indigenous character and repudiate the Porfirian tradition of privileging foreigners and light-skinned Mexicans. In this period, resentment of Chinese and perceptions of their purportedly undeserved economic success became increasingly pronounced among some working-class and middle-class Mexicans in Sonora. In 1916 about twenty people founded the Commercial Association of Businessmen in the small northern mining town Magdalena.[16] Led by José María Arana, the group proposed to defend "Mexican" merchants and rid Sonora of Chinese business owners. This action signaled the beginning of an organized anti-Chinese movement in Mexico. It is significant that the movement began in Sonora, and more specifically Magdalena, which is very near the Mexican-U.S. border. Many Mexican men had left Magdalena to fight in the revolution or work in the United States. Pointing to the "shortages" of Mexican men, some local people complained that Chinese men had filled the void, stealing both capital and women that rightfully belonged to Mexican men. Spreading quickly, anti-Chinese campaigns in Sonora, like those in California during the 1860s and 1870s, portrayed the Chinese as dangerous outsiders who infringed on the domain of the Mexican poor and working classes.[17] The people who organized these campaigns—working-class and middle-class Mexicans—came from the same social and economic classes as those who had formed bonds with Chinese. Antichinistas (anti-Chinese activists) focused on Mexican Chinese relationships, and on romantic unions and marriages in particular, arguing that these threatened the integrity of the Mexican race and nation. They chastised Mexicans who maintained ties with or were friendly toward Chinese by labeling them "chineros" and "chineras." The particularly hateful nature of the Sonoran movement against Chinese reverberated in their published propaganda.[18]

Anti-Chinese ideology infiltrated state politics over time. The movement succeeded in passing several anti-Chinese laws, including one in 1923 that banned Mexican Chinese marriages or unions, which antichinistas called "illicit friendships." In order to help enforce the law, anti-Chinese activists used sexual policing tactics. Antichinista newspapers such as El Intruso (The Intruder) printed the names and photographs of Mexican women who engaged in sexual liaisons with Chinese men. Anti-Chinese activists targeted Mexican women with a special fervor, casting them as dangerous traitors to the race and nation.[19]

The movement peaked by the early 1930s. The Great Depression and the return of Mexican laborers from the United States provided the final impetus that anti-Chinese activists needed to rid Sonora of the vast majority of Chinese.[20] Some people had drawn connections between the situations of Chinese in Mexico and Mexicans in the United States before the expulsion of Chinese from Sonora and Sinaloa. For example, in 1926 Francisco Martínez wrote to President Plutarco Elías Calles from Nogales, Arizona, and attached a newspaper article entitled "Mexicans Will be Kicked out of California." According to the piece, 75 percent of Mexicans in California had entered the United States illegally; a campaign to return them to Mexico was to begin immediately. Although the United States would not conduct a massive deportation of Mexicans until the depression years, U.S. newspapers reported on the formation of smaller deportation campaigns in California during this time. Using this anti-Mexican backlash to call for the expulsion of Chinese from Mexico, Martínez wrote, "If the Americans can do this to a neighboring country, to Mexicans, why don't we take advantage of this idea—using it against Chinese?" The Chinese "plague," he argued, "infested and threatened" Mexico.[21]

Martínez's wish was fulfilled a few years later when Sonora and Sinaloa haphazardly drove out Chinese and their families en masse through mob violence, arrests, deportations, and exit deadlines. Anti-Chinese proponents justified the expulsion by asserting that eradicating Chinese would facilitate the reintegration of Mexican workers who had returned from the United States.[22] Several U.S. states forcibly "repatriated" approximately 1 million Mexicans, among them many U.S. citizens, between 1929 and the latter 1930s, but the majority arrived in Mexico between 1931 and 1933, precisely the years when Sonorans and Sinaloans evicted most of their Chinese residents.[23]

Only Sonora and Sinaloa carried out mass expulsions; nevertheless, Chinese elsewhere in Mexico also were driven out or fled. As a result, the population of Chinese in Mexico fell drastically. In 1930 there had been close to 18,000 Chinese in Mexico. By 1940 fewer than 5,000 remained. Not surprisingly, population decline was most dramatic in the two northern states, where the numbers of Chinese were reduced from 3,571 to 92 in Sonora and from 2,123 to 165 in Sinaloa during the 1930s.[24]

Mexican women, as well as Mexican Chinese children, accompanied Chinese men out of Sonora and Sinaloa for various reasons. Women chose to go out of love and to keep their families together. Fear that they would not be able to support their families without their spouses or that anti-Chinese hatred would be directed at their racially mixed children motivated women to leave as well. In some instances, local and state authorities or mobs simply rounded up entire Mexican Chinese families and drove them out.

Faced with a vicious anti-Chinese climate, Mexican Chinese families in Sonora and Sinaloa used a variety of tactics. Some hid and waited out the expulsion period with the support of complicit families, friends, and communities.[25] Others fled to the states of Baja California Norte or Chihuahua, where anti-Chinese movements were not as strong.[26] Mexican Chinese families also chose to leave Mexico altogether. They exited via Mexican ports such as Mazatlán in Sinaloa or crossed into the United States, often landing in the custody of U.S immigration agents.

The passage of Chinese men and Mexican Chinese families through U.S. territory during the early 1930s complicated U.S.-Mexican relations. The United States accused the governor of Sonora and other officials of violating the U.S. Chinese Exclusion Act by forcing Chinese to cross the border. Sonoran Governor Rodolfo Elías Calles repeatedly denied this charge. Attempting to prove it in court, the Immigration and Naturalization Service (INS) tried Alcadio García, a police officer from Nogales, Sonora, and Alejandro Ungson, a "Chinese smuggler," for bringing Chinese into the United States. Immigration agents held Chinese men and Mexican Chinese families in jails in the Southwest and took the men's testimonies to try to establish that Sonoran officials' accounts were deceitful.[27] U.S. immigration agents perceived the Chinese men and Mexican Chinese families whom they apprehended through the lens of racial exclusion that had framed border enforcement since 1882.[28] They created still another category, classifying even Mexican women and Mexican Chinese children as "Chinese Refugees from Mexico." Handling 4,317 cases, the INS reported that it spent $530,234.41 to maintain and deport the "refugees" between mid-1931 and early 1934. Included in these figures were at least 574 people who were members of 114 Mexican Chinese families traveling as units. Immigration agents kept itemized records that showed names, costs, and dates of train passage to San Francisco for ultimate deportation to China.[29]

It is striking that Mexican women and Mexican Chinese children were deported to China rather than to Mexico, for the latter would have cost the agency less money; moreover, the United States already had a practice of deporting Mexicans within its borders. The United States even deported to China Mexican women who were not legally married to Chinese men. With few exceptions, U.S. immigration agents did not take Mexican women's testimonies, even though they interviewed hundreds of Chinese men who had entered the United States from Mexico. The accepted wisdom of men's control over women and gendered citizenship policies made it possible for the United States to send Mexican women, whether married or unmarried, to China along with their companions. The Wong Campoys were among the Mexican Chinese families from Sonora who traveled through the United States. INS records listed them as a family group consisting of Wong Fang, Dolores C. [Campoy] Wong Fang, and their children, Alfonso Wong, Irma Wong, and Hector Manuel Wong. This family traveled to

San Francisco to be deported with other refugees on April 3, 1933.[30]

At least 500 families arrived in China either via the United States or directly from Mexico during the expulsion period. Since they included numerous children, these families numbered at least 2,000 people.[31] These figures speak to the significance of this history. Moreover, the experience of expulsion and the sense of displacement, loss, and pain that accompanied it, as well as the struggle to survive abroad and restore a space for their racially and culturally mixed families in the Mexican nation, make this a broader story about movement, identity, and humanity. The history of these Mexican Chinese tells us about the strategies that diasporic peoples have employed to claim a place for themselves where they did not fit in automatically.

Mexican Chinese Families in China

Life in China led to new family arrangements. Mexican women often had trouble with gender norms in their companions' Cantonese and Taishanese communities. Some wrote to Mexican consuls and other authorities that their men had not told them they had already been married in China. Accustomed to being the only wives or the primary spouses in Mexico, they complained about being relegated to secondary wife or concubine status in China. In particular, women objected to having to live with or nearby Chinese wives and concubines. Although many Mexican men have historically maintained multiple households (gender customs in China and Mexico overlapped in some ways), it was not normative in Mexico for such households to be in close proximity. Owing to ruptures in gender expectations, some women separated from their companions, either temporarily or permanently. Chinese men occasionally kept one or more of their Mexican Chinese children with them and included them in their Chinese households. Sometimes parents or children moved back and forth between two households.

Although many families separated, some Chinese men remained with their Mexican-origin families after leaving Mexico, and some even raised their Mexican Chinese children alone. For instance, Roberto M. Fu arrived in China a widower with seven children. He had married Ana María Domínguez in Sonora in 1919, but she died shortly after their youngest child was born in 1933, just before Sonoran authorities expelled the family. Roberto Fu, whose Chinese name was Fu Gui, and his children, Roberto Fu, Jr., Manuela Fu, Jacinto Fu, Tomás Fu, Ventura Fu, Amelia Fu, and Maximiliano Fu, passed through U.S. territory in October 1933.[32] After their deportation to China, the family settled in Macau, where the father earned a meager income as a porter at the San José Seminary. In 1937 six of the children returned to Mexico as part of the official Cárdenas repatriation. Cárdenas had broken with his anti-Chinese predecessors and brought at least 400 Mexican women and countless Mexican Chinese children back to Mexico in 1937–1938.[33] Nevertheless, the Cárdenas administration also maintained a limited vision of who belonged in the nation-state; repatriation under Cárdenas denied entry to Chinese men who wanted to return with their families. Thus, Roberto Fu and his youngest child, Maximiliano Fu, who was too little to travel without his father, remained in Macau. Split apart during the Cárdenas repatriation, the Fu family formed new kinds of transpacific ties as they worked from both Macau and Mexico for at least two decades to be united again. The older children struggled for years to secure documents for their father and brother but met obstacle after obstacle. After the tragic death of his youngest son during the early 1950s, Roberto Fu waited in Macau even more anxiously to return to Mexico to reunite with his other children.[34]

The Wong Campoy family was among those that remained united in China. They lived first in a Cantonese village but eventually settled in Macau. The eldest child, Alfonso Wong Campoy, was four years old when his family was expelled from Sonora and then deported from the United States. In an interview, he remembered learning that his mother had decided to follow her husband to keep their family together. Once in China, however, she had a difficult time with the stark linguistic and cultural differences and was very unhappy. Another son, Antonio René Wong Campoy, was born in 1934, and the family left Guangdong Province for Macau by the mid-1930s. After they moved to Macau, Wong Fang conducted business and his wife did domestic service in people's homes where she was much more at ease. Their youngest child, Raquel Wong Campoy, was born in the Portuguese colony. The father died in the late 1930s. Forming friendships with other Mexican and Latin American women in Macau comforted Campoy Wong Fang after her husband died.[35]

The Mexican Chinese Community in Macau

Mexican Chinese in a variety of family situations forged a vibrant, coherent community in Macau between the 1930s and 1950s. They found Macau attractive for its distinct status as a colony with a cosmopolitan atmosphere, which offered them space to blend in as people with mixed racial and cultural identities. Founded by merchants in the sixteenth century, Macau was under the control of a Portuguese colonial administration in the 1930s. Early in the twentieth century, many refugees from China resided in Macau, whose population doubled from about 75,000 in the early 1900s to 150,000 by the early 1930s. Among other groups, Peruvian women who had married Chinese men and traveled with them to China during the late nineteenth and early twentieth centuries had a presence in the colony.[36] In an interview, Alfonso Wong Campoy recounted that ships constantly docked there, bringing people from all over the world. Exemplifying this cosmopolitanism, he became fluent not only in Spanish and Cantonese but also in Portuguese and Italian, having attended an Italian school in Macau.[37]

The colony's Latin, Iberian, and Catholic traditions gave Mexican Chinese people a sense of familiarity. Catholic institutions, moreover, became critical to the community, for they offered places to meet, connections with Mexico through foreign

clergy, emotional and spiritual support, economic assistance, and even jobs. Churches and other organizations were bases from which Mexican Chinese conducted the struggle for repatriation to Mexico. Catholic organizations also linked the Macanese enclave with Mexicans and other Latin Americans in British Hong Kong. People traveled between the two colonies to celebrate Catholic and Mexican (or Latin American) traditions and to strategize for the repatriation effort. Revealing the significance of Catholic symbols, the Latin American Association of Hong Kong was known in Spanish as the Asociación Hispano-Americana de Nuestra Señora de Guadalupe. People from Macau and Hong Kong gathered at Santa Teresa Church, which houses a shrine to the Virgen de Guadalupe, in Kowloon, Hong Kong.[38] This name, Nuestra Señora de Guadalupe (Our Lady of Guadalupe), indicates the strong ties to Catholic traditions specific to the Americas, for this indigenous icon of the Virgin Mary had originated in colonial Mexico.[39]

The size of the Mexican Chinese community in Macau fluctuated over the years, as some moved elsewhere in China and others returned to Mexico. In 1959 the enclave consisted of 24 households with 121 people in total. Sons and daughters born of Mexican Chinese unions formed their own families in Guangdong Province or Macau, at times choosing marital partners from within the Mexican Chinese community. Some Mexican and Mexican Chinese women such as Campoy Wong Fang performed domestic service in homes or religious institutions. Chinese and Mexican Chinese men were businessmen (Wong Fang and Alfonso Wong Campoy), held positions in the colonial government (the latter did this for a time as well), and worked as police officers, servants for the local captaincy, painters, mechanics, porters at the Catholic seminary (Fu), and scribes for the Ecclesiastic Chamber (Ramón Lay Mazo and his brother Francisco Lay Mazo). During this time, Mexican Chinese households ranged from three to nine people; most had several children. Some families were spread between Macau, Hong Kong, and villages in Guangdong Province. People in these situations often moved between these places.

Travel to the mainland became more complicated after the Chinese Communist Revolution of 1949, yet people continued to move back and forth. In doing so, the Mexican Chinese traversed various metaphoric and geographic borders; these areas were quite distinct political and cultural entities even though they were in close proximity.[40]

Chinese and Mexican culture and language fused in interesting ways over the decades. Embodying such hybridity, Ramón Lay Mazo's complex Mexican Chinese identity emerged in his letters. Born in Mocorito, Sinaloa, he arrived in Taishan County in Guangdong Province with his family when he was four years old, around 1933, and moved to Macau after World War II.[41] Writing letter upon letter on behalf of the Mexican Chinese while he was employed as a scribe in Macau's Ecclesiastic Chamber, he became the leader of the repatriation movement. Associated with the church, he was an important figure in the community. His Spanish was formal and well written, and he articulated a strong sense of Mexican nationalism.[42]

Yet, Ramón Lay Mazo also invoked Chinese language and culture. In letters to compatriots in Mexico, he transliterated Chinese phrases into Spanish. A gesture of cross-cultural communication, his transliterations offered aspects of Chinese culture to people he hoped to enlist in the repatriation struggle. For example, in a letter to a sympathetic Mexican widow, Concepción Rodríguez Viuda de Aragón, he opened by stating that he had his hands in a fist over his chest, in the ancient Chinese fashion, in order to ask her "sek-pau-fan-mei-a?" ("¿ya está llena de arroz?" or "have you had your fill of rice?"). He reminded her that this phrase was a Chinese greeting as well as a wish for good health, since basic subsistence was always on people's minds in China. After sharing this cultural practice, however, he wrote that he would set aside the greeting, which to a Westerner might have seemed like a joke, and move on to the discussion they had begun when she visited Macau in 1960. Aware of the deep divisions between East and West, he exhibited his own Chineseness but then made light of it. He was careful not to paint himself or his compatriots in

China as too Chinese, since their long-term goal was to return to Mexico. Renouncing or disregarding their Chineseness was part of the rhetoric of nationalism that Mexican Chinese individuals elaborated as they attempted to return to Mexico in the Cold War era. In a letter to President López Mateos in 1959, Ramón Lay Mazo wrote that, even though they had been in China so long, Mexicans living there knew neither the language nor the "exotic practices and customs of these people whose mentality is so opposite ours." He declared that his community, which he presented as *Mexicans* trapped in a foreign land, had the right to return to their homeland. Although he had a Chinese father, was fluent in Cantonese dialects, and had lived in Guangdong Province and Macau for most of his life, he emphasized his Mexicanness and separated himself and his compatriots from the Chinese.[43]

While there were both real and imagined divisions between Mexicans and Chinese, mixed-race people participated in the local culture and challenged existing social and political borders. For instance, Ramón Lay Mazo's nephew, Antonio León Sosa Mazo, the son of his cousin Valeriana Sosa Mazo, became a respected dancer in Guangdong Province where he lived with his family through the 1950s.[44] The young man taught ballet and classic Chinese dances in Cantonese social and cultural centers and was recognized as one of the five best dancers and instructors in South China. After the Communist Revolution, however, his mixed-race status became a liability. León Sosa Mazo had wanted to study medicine at a university but was barred because his father was a "well-off property owner" who had arrived from foreign lands, and his mother was a "Mexican devil." After his rejection from the university, he wrote a controversial book, whose title his uncle transliterated as *Chaut'in-lui-tek-tung-t'in* (and translated into Spanish as *El invierno de otoño* or "The Winter in the Fall"). The book described a student's experiences of the sudden changes in government and in private and public life, and how texts, materials, professors, and discipline at the university had been transformed. The book went through Communist Party censorship without incident, and the government published 50,000 copies. Nevertheless, during a campaign to purge intellectuals a few months later, authorities denounced the book as damaging to the mental health of the people because it espoused capitalist and bourgeois ideology. Communist officials condemned him as a traitor to the party and an agent of North American imperialists and their puppet Chiang Kai-shek.[45] Associating the book with the imperialist-supported Nationalist regime in Taiwan, Communist Party authorities ordered all copies of the book to be burned and the author to be confined in a mental institution.[46]

León Sosa Mazo escaped to Macau in April 1958 after his friends in the government informed him of the order for his arrest. After he fled, he told his uncle that communist authorities had written to him in Macau offering money and other material benefits if he returned to Guangdong Province, where people missed him at popular dance festivals and social worker centers. The government letters became threatening when he did not return. Concerned about his nephew's safety, Ramón Lay Mazo wrote to Ambassador Carlos Gutiérrez-Macías at the Mexican embassy in Manila during 1958 and 1959. He pled with authorities to allow his nephew to return to Sinaloa to live with his extended family. The Reverend Lancelote Miguel Rodríguez, the National Catholic Welfare Conference representative in Macau, offered to pay León Sosa Mazo's passage once he secured the proper documentation. Sadly, he was never able to obtain permission to enter Mexico and was killed in Macau sometime in 1959.[47]

By the late 1950s the plight of the Mexican Chinese in the two foreign colonies had become so well known that it penetrated the local vernacular. A proverbial generalization in Cantonese as spoken in Macau and Hong Kong, the phrase "being like a Mexican" came to signify being poor and stateless. Calling this linguistic turn "a disgraceful ridicule of the sacrosanct name of our beloved Nation, of our adored Mexico," Ramón Lay Mazo argued that pride in their country should move Mexican authorities to rescue their compatriots in China so that neither Mexicans nor Mexico could be characterized in such degrading ways.[48] In their

struggle to repatriate, the Mexican Chinese community in China played on Mexico's newfound concern for its image abroad during the Cold War.

Repatriation to Mexico

Many of the Mexican Chinese who had been drawn to Macau in the 1930s and 1940s were able to return to Mexico either during the Cárdenas repatriation or in small groups after World War II. Some of those who remained in Macau were unable to establish Mexican citizenship. They incessantly appealed to individuals, organizations, and governmental agencies in Mexico and abroad between the 1930s and 1950s to return to Mexico. Ramón Lay Mazo's work from Macau brought various actors into the struggle.[49]

By the late 1950s the Lions Club in Mexico had become involved in the repatriation effort. In Mexico, this organization was historically conservative; indeed, between 1910 and 1930 it drew the bulk of its membership from middle-class professionals, businessmen, and local officials—the same segment of society that led the anti-Chinese campaigns.[50] By mid-century, however, conservatism in Mexico, as in many parts of the world, had become synonymous with anti-communism. Thus, it became possible for this traditional association to take on the project of "liberating" Mexican women, Mexican Chinese children, and even some Chinese men from Communist China. The Lions Club in Tampico, Tamaulipas, began the national campaign to help the Mexican Chinese return to Mexico. Officers and leading members of branches in various states, including Tamaulipas, Guerrero, Jalisco, Nayarit, Chihuahua, and Coahuila, wrote letters during late 1959 and early 1960 pressuring federal officials to document and repatriate Mexican citizens in China.[51]

The Lions Club used three tactics. The first appealed to Mexican patriotism. Invoking ideas of sameness, President Dr. Javier Elizondo Otañez and Secretary Antonio López Alatorre of the Lions Club in San Blas, Nayarit, wrote to President López Mateos on behalf of the Mexican "families that long to be in the Nation, who share our language and religion, and find themselves far away, sad, and bitter, but nevertheless continue to be our compatriots." Utilizing concepts of Mexican citizenship embedded in the Mexican Constitution of 1917, Lions Club members argued that the women and their children, even if they were born in foreign lands, were Mexican and had the right to protection by their government. For instance, in their letter to the national leader, President Armando C. Flores Peña and Secretary Professor Alejo Carrillo Sánchez of the Lions Club in Monclova, Coahuila, cited Article 30, Section 2a of the Mexican Constitution that "Those who are born in foreign lands of a Mexican father and foreign mother or a Mexican mother and unknown father are Mexicans," in order to persuade the Mexican government to grant citizens in China the proper documentation so that they might be able to return to their homeland.[52]

The second strategy turned on Mexican gender norms and the importance of guarding Mexican women. For example, Dr. Luis G. López O. wrote to President López Mateos on behalf of the Lions Club in Hermoso, Tamaulipas, concerning the tragedy of the "abandoned Mexican women who live in China alone." He called on the president to urge the appropriate government offices to open "the doors of our nation to those Mexican women." Also writing to the Mexican president, Dr. Alfredo Ortega Rivera of the Lions Club in Pachuca, Hidalgo, argued that Mexican women had been "faithful to hearth and home" when they chose to accompany their husbands to China after they were expelled from Mexico. Alluding to the role of Mexican women in the nation to form families, Ortega Rivera pointed out that, when women chose to fulfill these duties with Chinese men, Mexican authorities had punished them by forcing them out of the country if they wanted to keep their families intact.[53]

The third tactic evoked the poverty that Mexican compatriots faced in China and the fear of communism abroad. Dr. Ildefonso Lozano Bosque and Roberto Santos Ibarra of the Lions Club in Ciudad Acuña, Coahuila, wrote to the president that the Mexican Chinese in Macau and Hong Kong lived in misery and worked in the worst jobs—an embarrassment to Mexico. Ortega Rivera used the same line of reasoning, adding that the Mexican government should seek to save its citizens who lived in mainland China, along with those who had sought refuge in the colonies, from communism. Suggesting that Chinese men had contributed to the development of several Mexican states, Ortega Rivera included them in his vision of the nation-state as well. Because many of these men had been businessmen in Mexico, he contended, the communist regime persecuted and excluded them for their capitalist ideas. Jorge B. Cuellar Arocha and Leopoldo S. Villarreal Corona of the Lions Club in Sabinas, Coahuila, wrote to López Mateos on behalf of Mexican women in China, stating that, in Hong Kong and Macau, "they are disliked for being Mexican" and "persecuted by communism": They needed to return to the homeland.[54]

Despite their exclusion from the nation for so many years, the Mexican Chinese maintained a strong sense of Mexican nationalism and kept alive the hope that they would one day repatriate. Their unrelenting pleas, the work of their supporters (particularly the Lions Club campaign), and the internationalist politics of López Mateos together finally triggered the official Mexican repatriation of 1960. López Mateos, who came to power in 1958, sought to establish Mexico as a modern, democratic nation on the world scene. Not coincidentally, he was the first Mexican president to make a diplomatic trip to Asia.[55] Under López Mateos, the Secretaría de Relaciones Exteriores authorized the official in charge of business relations at the Mexican embassy in Manila to travel to Hong Kong and Macau by June 1959 to interview Mexican Chinese families who lived there. By early 1960 the Mexican government permitted Ambassador Gutiérrez-Macías to document people who could prove Mexican nationality. That spring Rodríguez Viuda de Aragón, whose husband had been a prominent citizen of Tampico, visited Macau and Hong Kong shortly after the Lions Club campaign began in her hometown. She had connections with Mexican government officials to whom she conveyed information about the Mexican Chinese community that she had gathered during her trip. A series of official communications on the matter ensued, and by May 1960 the government publicly announced that it would document and repatriate its citizens in China in one sweep.[56]

News of the repatriation brought hope to families who had been split by the expulsion and stages of repatriation. For instance, on May 24, 1960, Juana Trujillo Viuda de Chiu wrote to the office of the president from Coatzacoalcos, Veracruz, that she had heard López Mateos's repatriation order on the radio. She urged the government to consider her sons, Juan Chiu Trujillo, in Macau, and Emmanuel Chiu Trujillo, in Hong Kong, when the repatriation took place. They had been waiting to reunite with her for a long time. Similarly, on June 30, 1960, Lorenzo Alvarado and other family members in Pichucalco, Chiapas, appealed to the president on behalf of their elderly relative, Mercedes Alvarado Méndez, who had lived in Hong Kong for many years.[57]

Publicity around the repatriation also elicited negative reactions. In Sonora, where anti-Chinese elements were still active, some people spoke out against the return of the Mexican Chinese. On June 28, 1960, Alfredo G. Echeverría, Professor Eduardo Reyes Díaz, and other members of the Campaña Nacionalista (Nationalist Campaign) in Hermosillo, the capital, wrote to the office of the president about the "problem" that repatriating these families represented for the nation. Echeverría had been a leader in the anti-Chinese movement in Sonora as a young man during the 1920s and 1930s.[58] He and the others sought to convince authorities to confine the repatriates to La Isla del Tiburón, an island off the coast of Sonora traditionally occupied by the racially excluded and marginalized Seri, an indigenous people. They argued that there were economic possibilities within the *ejido* (community land and farming) system and the fishing industry on the island.[59] Perhaps these men feared that those who returned would become economically successful in Sonora, as their Chinese relatives had been prior to the expulsion. Continuing to

define Mexican Chinese families as non-Mexican, the Campaña Nacionalista had kept alive anti-Chinese ideology for over four decades, and it outweighed, in this case, anti-communism. The influence of the Lions Club campaign and the larger repatriation effort, however, trumped the work of these Sonorans.[60]

By the fall of 1960 the Mexican government had set up a special repatriation commission and appointed Dr. Bernardo Bátiz as its head commissioner. Bátiz arrived in Hong Kong to document and repatriate Mexican Chinese living in the two colonies. The government circulated a notice in Spanish, Portuguese, Chinese, and English advertising the repatriation. Stating that repatriation would occur "without intervention or contribution from anyone," the flyer announced that this was the final opportunity for people who wished to repatriate to Mexico, vowing to "finish definitively the repatriation and naturalization problem of Mexicans residing in the East."[61] Although various groups had appealed to the government on behalf of the Mexican Chinese community and the National Catholic Welfare Conference had offered to pay travel expenses, the Mexican government wanted sole responsibility for the return of its citizens in the effort to build Mexico's international reputation.

During this time, Mexican and Mexican Chinese women appealed to Bátiz so that their Chinese husbands could also travel to Mexico. On October 3, 1960, Ramón Lay Mazo wrote to López Mateos that some women were very uneasy because Bátiz had responded that he was there to "repatriate Mexicans, not insert foreigners into the country." If the case had involved Mexican men with Chinese spouses, there would not have been an issue, since foreign women married to Mexican men could be considered citizens under the law. Over the decades, however, gendered citizenship policies caused numerous challenges for women who formed romantic ties with Chinese men. Begging the president to allow Chinese husbands to enter Mexico with their wives, Lay Mazo noted that there were merely nine such men in Macau and a few more in Hong Kong. With the exception of two, the men in Macau were now over the age of sixty. To allay any fears that they would compete with Mexicans for jobs, he pointed out that the men were well above the normative working age. Drawing on Mexican family and gender norms, as well as those in China, he wrote that, if husbands were allowed to accompany their wives, families would not have to break up. There would be no need for the "painful and atrocious sacrifice of the wife, or a son, or perhaps the entire family, remaining in China, simply because a part of the family, or more accurately, the chief member, cannot go along."[62] Alfonso Wong Campoy remembered that some Chinese husbands and fathers were able to return to Mexico during this time, unlike the earlier repatriation that had separated families. He recalled that the Chinese men who traveled to Mexico as part of this repatriation lived the rest of their lives there and eventually died in Mexico.[63]

Finally returning to Mexico, two groups repatriated in November 1960. On November 7, thirteen repatriates left Hong Kong. Their leader, A. Vargas, informed the newspaper *Excélsior* that they were happy to return to Mexico and hoped to be well received. A group of 113 more repatriates, this time from Macau, arrived in Mazatlán, Sinaloa, via Hong Kong, on November 16.[64] Grateful to President López Mateos for facilitating their return, Lay Mazo told *Excélsior* that the repatriates "would work 'to make the nation greater.' "[65] After all his labor, he was finally able to return to his homeland, along with the compatriots he had assisted. Among the repatriates, Dolores Campoy Wong Fang and her three sons returned to Sonora. Alfonso Wong Campoy relayed that he and his brothers, who by then were adults, chose to accompany their mother because they wanted to be in the country of their birth and become acquainted with their extended family.[66]

Reintegrating into Mexican Society

Life was not easy for those who returned to Mexico in 1960. They had to adapt to the changing society they had left, often abruptly in the expulsion, almost thirty years earlier. Children whose families had been expelled when they were very young, as well as those born in China, integrated into Mexican society for the first time. Among other trials, the repatriates had to contend with the ways Mexicans in their home states received them. Alfonso Wong Campoy described returning to Navojoa as "a little strange." The family experienced difficulties readjusting, so Campoy Wong Fang wrote to the president requesting assistance on December 7, 1960. She told López Mateos that her sons, who were ages thirty-two, twenty-seven, and twenty-six, had been unable to find jobs, even though officials had promised the family support upon returning. She urged the government to help her sons secure employment or offer the family economic aid.[67]

It was not the government that assisted the Wong Campoys after they repatriated, however. Rather, family members and Mexican Chinese compatriots provided them with the support they needed. Alfonso Wong Campoy recounted that they lived with their maternal uncle, Pedro Campoy, for nearly a month. Upon hearing of their repatriation, compatriots they had met in Macau went to visit Campoy Wong Fang (or "Lolita," as they affectionately called her) and her sons. One such family was the Chons from Bacobampo, a small town near Navojoa, who had also been expelled in the early 1930s. They had returned to Mexico during the Cárdenas repatriation, and the Wong Campoys were delighted to see the Chons again. Having suffered the expulsion and been together in Macau, the two families formed strong, deep bonds. The Wong Campoys soon went to live with the Chons in Bacobampo where Campoy Wong Fang worked making *aguas* (water-based fruit drinks) at the Chons' store. Things were easier for the family, her son remembered, after they reunited with their *paisanos* or compatriots.[68] His use of the term "paisanos" is significant. Both Mexican Chinese families had been expelled from Sonora and came to reside in Macau, where they met. They were compatriots in a profound sense of the word: Not wanted in Mexico but not fully Chinese either, they were mixed, in-between, without a country.[69] They had made each other *paisanos* in the new community they created abroad. Mexican Chinese families like the Wong Campoys and the Chons formed relationships that persisted over years and across oceans. Familiar only through a brief period in Macau in the 1930s, the two families renewed their close ties in Sonora in the 1960s after living far apart from each other for over twenty years. The assistance of the Chons was critical for the reintegration of the Wong Campoy family into Sonoran society. It was because their compatriots treated them well, Alfonso Wong Campoy noted, that they stayed in Bacobampo for years, returning to Navojoa only later in the decade when it began to grow into a larger town.[70]

Conclusion

Mexican Chinese families crossed borders and became diasporic in a number of ways. They traversed racial, gender, and cultural boundaries in Mexico, which pushed them across physical and symbolic lines to the United States and China. Chinese men were already diasporic citizens in Mexico, where they established links with their Chinese countrymen and maintained connections with the communities from which they had emigrated. They simultaneously became integral to local communities and formed myriad ties with Mexicans. Mexican women defied anti-Chinese attitudes by establishing romantic associations with Chinese men, even after the movement succeeded in making such unions illegal. Upon leaving Mexico with expelled Chinese husbands, companions, and fathers, Mexican women and Mexican Chinese children became diasporic citizens. In China, Mexican Chinese families, whether they remained unified or not, developed different relationships and adapted to their new contexts to survive. During their years abroad, they longed for the Mexican homeland and worked to reclaim a space for themselves in it. Some Chinese men who had been part of local Mexican communities also sought to be reincorporated into the nation. Mexican Chinese families, however, began to imagine a Mexican homeland only after they left Sonora, Sinaloa, and elsewhere. Before the expulsion, they were identified with particular local communities or regions, rather than the larger entity of Mexico. This new diasporic sense of a Mexican national homeland emerged as the Mexican Chinese experienced the tumult that characterized China during the mid-twentieth century.

Alfonso Wong Campoy, Dolores Campoy Wong Fang, Ramón Lay Mazo, Roberto Fu, members of the Asociación Hispano-Americana de Nuestra Señora de Guadalupe, and other Mexican Chinese sustained an ardent Mexican nationalism during their years in southeastern China. Upholding Mexican identity and culture for over three decades helped people like Alfonso Wong Campoy, who had left as a boy, become part of Mexican society as an adult. A businessman like his father, he has sold fruits, vegetables, salsas, honey, and nuts, among other goods, at his stand in the Navojoa Mercado (central market) for nearly fifty years. After living in Guangdong Province briefly and then Macau for almost thirty years, he always wanted to return to the land of his birth. He and his wife, Conchita Castañeda Wong, have taught their son, Alfonso Wong Castañeda, about his family's experiences and his father's love for Mexico. They plan to do the same for their young grandchildren. In so doing, they will help keep alive the history of the Mexican Chinese. [71]

Notes

1. Oral history interview with Alfonso Wong Campoy, Oct. 10, 2004, Navojoa, Sonora, in author's possession. The oral history interviews conducted for this project will eventually be available to other researchers at the Oral History Institute of the University of Texas at El Paso. All translations from Spanish into English are by the author; the original recordings or copies of the archival documents and unpublished papers are available from her.

2. *Ibid.*

3. See Erika Lee, "Orientalisms in the Americas: A Hemispheric Approach to Asian American History," *Journal of Asian American Studies*, 8 (2005), 235–256.

4. I address these movements in my as-yet unpublished book manuscript, Julia María Schiavone Camacho, "Becoming Mexican Across the Pacific: Expulsion, Gendered Citizenship, and Diasporic Imaginings, 1930s–1960s."

5. It is difficult to estimate how much of their love for Mexico was heartfelt and how much was strategic. A seemingly genuine love for the homeland emerges in the many communications of the Mexican Chinese, as well as the oral history interviews I conducted. I explore this further in my book manuscript. Relations between China and Japan became increasingly hostile in the early 1930s as Japan seized control of parts of northern China, beginning with Manchuria in September 1931. Such actions eventually led to the second Sino-Japanese War in 1937–1945 (the first Sino-Japanese War was in 1894–1895). See Hsi-Sheng Ch'i, *Nationalist China at War: Military Defeats and Political Collapse, 1937–1945* (Ann Arbor, Mich., 1982), 27, 40, 42–43; Yun-han Li, "The Origins of the War: Background of the Lukouchiao Incident, July 7, 1937," in Paul K. T. Sih, ed., *Nationalist China during the Sino-Japanese War, 1931–1945* (Hicksville, N.Y., 1977), 3–5.

6. See Lok C. D. Siu, *Memories of a Future Home: Diasporic Citizenship of Chinese in Panama* (Stanford, Calif., 2005); Jeffrey Lesser, ed., *Searching for Home Abroad: Japanese Brazilians and Transnationalism* (Durham, N.C., 2003); Lesser, *A Discontented Diaspora: Japanese Brazilians and the Meanings of Ethnic Militancy* (Durham, N.C., 2007); William Safran, "Diasporas in Modern Societies: Myths of Homeland and Return," *Diasporas*, 1 (1991), 83–99; and James Clifford, "Diasporas," *Cultural Anthropology*, 9 (1984), 302–338.

7. Wang Gungwu, *China and the Chinese Overseas* (Singapore, 1991); Wang, "Sojourning: The Chinese Experience in Southeast Asia," in Anthony Reid, ed., *Sojourners and Settlers: Histories of Southeast Asia and the Chinese* (Honolulu, 1996), 1–14; Wang, *Community and Nation: Essays on Southeast Asia and the Chinese* (Singapore, 1981). The Chinese who traveled to the Americas emigrated largely from the city of Canton (today Guangzhou) and surrounding areas in Guangdong Province, not only because of population growth, economic transformation, political turmoil, religious persecution, and natural disaster in the region, but also owing to this region's key role in Chinese history, especially China's relationship with the external world. Chinese emigrated from Taishan County in particular. See Sucheng Chan, *Asian Americans: An Interpretive History* (Boston, 1991), 5–8; Madeline Yuan-yin Hsu, *Dreaming of Gold, Dreaming of Home: Transnationalism and Migration between the United States and South China, 1882–1943* (Stanford, Calif., 2000), 1–5; and June Mei, "Economic Origins of Emigration: Guangdong to California, 1850–1882," *Modern China*, 5 (1979), 463–501. Until 1960 over half of all Chinese in the United States came from Taishan County. See Hsu, *Dreaming of Gold, Dreaming of Home*, 3, and Mei, "Economic Origins of Emigration," 465.

8. Sonora was the Mexican state with the highest numbers of Chinese in every census year between 1900 and 1930, with the exception of 1927, when the state had the second-highest Chinese population. The following are the numbers of Chinese men in Sonora listed for each census year: 1900: 850; 1910: 4,486; 1921: 3,639; 1927: 3,758; 1930: 3,571. See José Jorge Gómez Izquierdo, *El movimiento antichino en México (1871–1934): Problemas del racismo y del nacionalismo durante la Revolución Mexicana* [The anti-Chinese movement in Mexico (1871–1934): problems of racism and nationalism during the Mexican Revolution] (Mexico City, 1991), 77, 78, 109, 127, 150, and Kif Augustine-Adams, "Making Mexico: Legal Nationality, Chinese Race, and the 1930 Population Census," *Law and History Review*, 27 (2009), at ssrn.com/abstract=1033061, accessed June 1, 2009.

9. Erika Lee, *At America's Gates: Chinese Immigration During the Exclusion Era, 1882–1943* (Chapel Hill, N.C., 2003); Evelyn Hu-DeHart, "La comunidad china en el desarrollo de Sonora" [The Chinese community in the development of Sonora], in Cynthia Radding de Murrieta, ed., *Historia General de Sonora, Tomo IV, Sonora Moderno, 1880–1929* [General history of Sonora, Vol. 4, 1880–1929] (6 vols., Hermosillo, Mex., 1997), 4: 198–202; Hu-DeHart, "Coolies, Shopkeepers, Pioneers: The Chinese of Mexico and Peru (1849–1930)," *Amerasia*, 15 (1989), 91–116.

10. Evelyn Hu-DeHart, "Latin America in Asia-Pacific Perspective," in Arif Dirlik, ed., *What is in a Rim?*

Critical Perspectives on the Pacific Region Idea (New York, 1998), 251–282; Hu-DeHart. "Coolies, Shopkeepers, Pioneers"; Siu, *Memories of a Future Home*; Isabelle Lausent-Herrera, "Mujeres olvidadas: Esposas, concubinas, e hijas de los inmigrantes chinos en el Perú republicano" [Forgotten women: wives, concubines, and daughters of Chinese immigrants to republican Peru], in Scarlett O'Phelan Godoy and Margarita Zegarra Florez, eds., *Mujeres, familia y sociedad en la historia de América Latina, siglos XVIII–XXI* [Women, family, and society in Latin American history, eighteenth to twenty-first centuries] (Lima, 2006), 287–312.

11. Wong Campoy interview.

12. Gerardo Rénique, "Race, Region, and Nation: Sonora's Anti-Chinese Racism and Mexico's Postrevolutionary Nationalism, 1920s–1930s," in Nancy P. Appelbaum, Anne S. Macpherson, and Karin Alejandra Rosemblatt, eds., *Race and Nation in Modern Latin America* (Chapel Hill, N.C., 2003), 219–226; Rénique, "Anti-Chinese Racism, Nationalism and State Formation in Post-Revolutionary Mexico, 1920s–1930s," *Political Power and Social Theory*, 14 (2000), 95, 97, 102; Robert Chao Romero, "The Dragon in Big Lusong: Chinese Immigration and Settlement in Mexico, 1882–1940" (Ph.D. dissertation, University of California, Los Angeles, 2003); Chao Romero, " 'El destierro de los Chinos' [The exile of the Chinese]: Popular Perspectives on Chinese-Mexican Intermarriage in the Early Twentieth Century," *Aztlan: A Journal of Chicano Studies*, 32 (2007), 113–144; Augustine-Adams, "Making Mexico." See also Julia María Schiavone Camacho, "Traversing Boundaries: Chinese, Mexicans, and Chinese Mexicans in the Formation of Gender, Race, and Nation in the Twentieth-Century U.S.-Mexican Borderlands" (Ph.D. dissertation, University of Texas at El Paso, 2006).

13. When Chinese first migrated to Sonora during the last quarter of the nineteenth century, they were concentrated in Guaymas, the port of entry, and in Hermosillo, the capital. They later moved to other areas. See Hu-DeHart, "Coolies, Shopkeepers, Pioneers," 99; Hu-DeHart, "La comunidad china"; Hu-DeHart, "Immigrants to a Developing Society: The Chinese in Northern Mexico, 1875–1932," *Journal of Arizona History*, 21 (1980), 275–312;

Grace Peña Delgado, "In the Age of Exclusion: Race, Religion, and Chinese Identity in the Making of the Arizona-Sonora Borderlands, 1863–1943" (Ph.D. dissertation, University of California, Los Angeles, 2000); Peña Delgado, "At Exclusion's Southern Gate: Changing Categories of Race and Class among Chinese Fronterizos," in Samuel Truett and Elliott Young, eds., *Continental Crossroads: Remapping U.S.-Mexico Borderlands History* (Durham, N.C., 2004); and Schiavone Camacho, "Traversing Boundaries."

14. Rénique, "Race, Region, and Nation"; Rénique, "Anti-Chinese Racism"; Hu-DeHart, "Racism and Anti-Chinese Persecution in Sonora, Mexico, 1876–1932," *Amerasia*, 9 (1982), 1–28; Chao Romero, "The Dragon in Big Lusong"; Chao Romero, " 'El destierro de los Chinos.' "

15. *Ibid.*

16. The original name of the group was the Junta Comercial y de Hombres de Negocios de Magdalena. See Rénique, "Región, raza y nación en el antichinismo sonorense. Cultura regional y mestizaje en el México posrevolucionario" [Region, race, and nation in Sonoran anti-Chinese activism. Regional culture and mestizaje in post-revolutionary Mexico], unpublished paper, in author's possession.

17. On anti-Chinese campaigns in California, see Alexander Saxton, *The Indispensable Enemy: Labor and the Anti-Chinese Movement in California* (Berkeley, 1971); Saxton, *The Rise and Fall of the White Republic: Class Politics and Mass Culture in Nineteenth-Century America* (London, 1990).

18. Papers of José María Arana, Special Collections, University of Arizona Library, Tucson; Rénique, "Race, Region, and Nation"; Rénique, "Anti-Chinese Racism."

19. *Ibid.*; Schiavone Camacho, "Traversing Boundaries," 83–84. Although I never saw a reference to La Malinche in the documents, it is possible that the popular Mexican discourse that sees women as potential traitors influenced anti-Chinese ideology and activity. See, for example, Octavio Paz, *The Labyrinth of Solitude: Life and Thought in Mexico*, trans. Lysander Kemp (New York, 1961); Cristina González Hernández, *Doña Marina, la Malinche y la formación de la identidad mexicana* [Doña Marina, la Malinche, and the formation of Mexican identity] (Madrid, 2002); and Rolando Romero and Amanda

Nolacea Harris, eds., *Feminism, Nation, and Myth: La Malinche* (Houston, 2005).

20. On the expulsion of Chinese from Mexico, see Hu-DeHart, "Racism and Anti-Chinese Persecution"; Hu-DeHart, "La comunidad china"; Chao Romero, "The Dragon in Big Lusong"; Chao Romero, " 'El destierro de los Chinos' "; Philip A. Dennis, "The Anti-Chinese Campaigns in Sonora, Mexico," *Ethnohistory*, 26 (1979), 65–80; Gómez Izquierdo, *El movimiento antichino en México*; Patricia Irma Figueroa Barkow, "El movimiento antichino en México de 1916–1935; Un caso de 'racismo económico' " [The anti-Chinese movement in Mexico of 1916–1935: a case of economic racism] (M.A. thesis, Universidad Nacional Autónoma de México, 1976), 53–57; Alan Knight, "Racism, Revolution, and *Indigenismo*: Mexico, 1910–1940," in Richard Graham, ed., *The Idea of Race in Latin America, 1870–1940* (Austin, Tex., 1990); Moisés González Navarro, "Xenofobia y xenofilia en la Revolución Mexicana" [Xenophobia and xenophilia in the Mexican Revolution], in González Navarro, ed., *México: el capitalismo nacionalista* [Mexico; nationalist capitalism] (Guadalajara, Mex., 2003); Charles C. Cumberland, "The Sonora Chinese and the Mexican Revolution," *Hispanic American Historical Review*, 40 (1960), 191–211; Leo Michael Dambourges Jacques, "The Anti-Chinese Campaign in Sonora, Mexico, 1900–1931" (Ph.D. dissertation, University of Arizona, 1974); and Schiavone Camacho, "Traversing Boundaries."

21. Exp. [folder] 104-CH-l, caja [box] 28, Fondo [collection] Obregón-Calles, Archivo General de la Nación, Mexico City. This archive has collections divided by presidential administrations, and card catalogs describe the contents of folders in each collection.

22. Trueba Lara, *Los chinos en Sonora: Una historia olvidada* [The Chinese in Sonora: a forgotten history] (Hermosillo, Mex., 1990), 51–60.

23. Francisco E. Balderrama and Raymond Rodríguez, *Decade of Betrayal: Mexican Repatriation in the 1930s* (Albuquerque, 1995), 202. See also Mercedes Carreras de Velasco, *Los Mexicanos que devolvió la crisis, 1929–1932* [The Mexicans the crisis sent back, 1929–1932] (Mexico City, 1974).

24. Gómez Izquierdo, *El movimiento antichino en México*, 150, 161; Rénique, "Race, Region, and Nation," 230.

25. For example, the fathers of Luis Chan Valenzuela and Marta Elia Lau de Salazar hid in Sonora. See Schiavone Camacho, "Traversing Boundaries"; oral history interview with Luis Chan Valenzuela, Oct. 11, 2004, Hermosillo, Sonora, in author's possession; and oral history interview with Marta Elia Lau de Salazar by Berenice Barreras Ayala (for the author), Aug. 19, 2004, Bacobampo, Sonora, in author's possession.

26. It is hard to quantify these movements. My book manuscript investigates them further.

27. File 55771, folders 718 A–D, boxes 514 and 515, Subject Correspondence, 1906–1932, Records of the Central Office, Records of the Immigration and Naturalization Service (INS), Record Group 85 (RG 85), National Archives, Washington, D.C.; Case 6381, box 143, and Cases 6461–6462, box 145, Case Files, 1914–1947, District of Arizona, Tucson Division, Criminal, Records of the National Archives, Pacific Region, Laguna Niguel, Calif.

28. Lee, *At America's Gates* ; Mae M. Ngai, *Impossible Subjects: Illegal Aliens and the Making of Modern America* (Princeton, N.J., 2004).

29. INS records set apart members of Mexican Chinese families by case numbers and naming patterns.

30. File 55771; Wong Campoy interview. Even though Alfonso Wong Campoy and his siblings used one of their father's and one of their mother's surnames, U.S. immigration agents recorded only their father's name, imposing on the family the dominant U.S. naming practice. INS records reveal other biases, which I treat in my book manuscript.

31. These are conservative figures based on INS files and Mexican consular and government records. The numbers of Mexican Chinese families, and the individuals they comprised, were probably higher. Archival sources suggest that between 400 and 600 Mexican women arrived in China with Chinese men. The records consistently point to the numerous children in these families. For example, those included in INS lists had an average of three to four children per family. Mauricio Fresco, a businessman and Honorary Mexican Vice Consul in Shanghai, noted in his reports that Dollar Line records accounted for at least 600 Mexican women and innumerable children who arrived in China on the steamship company's ships between 1931 and 1933 alone.

The Mexican government later repatriated about 400 Mexican women and a high but unspecified number of their children in 1937–1938. Given the various figures, I have estimated that 500 families, which consisted of a minimum of 2,000 people, arrived in China. See file 55771; IV-341–13, Archivo Histórico Genaro Estrada, Secretaría de Relaciones Exteriores, Mexico City; exp. 546/3, caja 899, Fondo Lázaro Cárdenas del Río, Archivo General de la Nación, Mexico City; exp. 546.2/1, caja 714, Fondo Adolfo López Mateos, in *ibid.*; OM-149–5, 1960 [this is the file number], Archivo de Concentraciones, Secretaría de Relaciones Exteriores, Mexico City; and Felipe Pardinas, *Relaciones diplomáticas entre China y México, 1898–1948, Caja 1* [Diplomatic relations between China and Mexico, 1898–1948, box 1] (Mexico City, 1982), 428–430, 461–465, 466–468, 471, 474, 475–476, 478–479.

32. File 55771; exp. 546.2/1. INS records and Ramón Lay Mazo's letters included the identical names for the children, without discrepancy, except for Lay Mazo's spelling of "Bentura" and the INS listing "Ventura." In this case, the children apparently used only their father's surname.

33. The outbreak of the second Sino-Japanese War during the summer of 1937 prompted Cárdenas to repatriate Mexicans from China. On Cárdenas and the Sino-Japanese conflict, see Friedrich E. Schuler, *Mexico Between Hitler and Roosevelt: Mexican Foreign Relations in the Age of Lázaro Cárdenas, 1931–1940* (Albuquerque, 1998), 57, 94.

34. Exp. 546.2/1.

35. Wong Campoy interview.

36. Lausent-Herrera, "Mujeres olvidadas."

37. Wong Campoy interview. Similar to the relationship between Britain and Hong Kong, Macau remained a Portuguese colony until 1976, when it became a Chinese territory with a Portuguese administration. At the end of 1999, Macau came under China's sovereign control. R. D. Cremer, ed., *Macau: City of Commerce and Culture* (Hong Kong, 1987), 1, 103, 115, 119–120, 125; Steve Shipp, *Macau, China: A Political History of the Portuguese Colony's Transition to Chinese Rule* (Jefferson, N.C., 1997), 78.

38. Exp. 546.2/1 and 546.2/12, caja 714, Fundu Adolfo López Mateos; oral history interview with José Serafín Anaya, Aug. 10, 2007, Kowloon, Hong Kong, in author's possession.

39. See, for example, D. A. Brading, *Mexican Phoenix: Our Lady of Guadalupe, Image and Tradition, 1531–2000* (New York, 2001).

40. IV-352–28, Archivo Histórico Genaro Estrada; OM-149–5, 1960. China was in profound economic, social, political, and cultural transformation during most of the twentieth century. The changing dynamics of Macau, Hong Kong, and Guangdong Province during the Sino-Japanese War, World War II, the Communist Revolution, and the Cold War created complex boundaries for the Mexican Chinese to negotiate. According to Chen Jian, Chinese Communist leader Mao Zedong utilized "anti-foreign-imperialist propaganda . . . to mobilize the Chinese masses" in the 1940s. Many Chinese probably viewed Mexicans and Mexican Chinese as foreigners during this time. Chen Jian, *Mao's China and the Cold War* (Chapel Hill, N.C., 2001), 13.

41. The populations of Macau and Hong Kong grew as refugees flooded into the colonies owing to war and revolution in the mid-twentieth century. When the Sino-Japanese War broke out in the summer of 1937, Macau in particular experienced an overwhelming influx of refugees, especially after the fall of Shanghai in late 1937. The colony's population increased from 150,000 in the early 1930s to 350,000 by 1940. These trends continued during World War II, as thousands more refugees descended upon Macau, bringing the population to 600,000 by 1945. Although Japan occupied Hong Kong, forcing the British colony to surrender in 1941, Japanese leaders decided not to do the same in Macau. Unlike Great Britain, Portugal took a neutral stance in the war. Nonetheless, Japanese soldiers maintained a presence in Macau, and Japan's policy toward the colony became harsher as World War II progressed. During the Communist Revolution, refugees continued to enter the colony, which became a key sanctuary for people who wanted to escape communist rule. See Shipp, *Macau, China*, 81; John Hunter Boyle, *China and Japan at War, 1937–1945: The Politics of Collaboration* (Stanford, Calif., 1972), 54; Tsung-han Shen, "Food Production and Distribution for Civilian and Military Needs in Wartime China, 1937– 1945," in Sih, ed., *Nationalist*

China during the Sino-Japanese War, 168; and Chen, *Mao's China*, 17, 20, 26–34, 41.

42. OM-149-5, 1960.

43. *Ibid.*; exp. 546.2/1.

44. Ramón Lay Mazo referred to León Sosa Mazo as his nephew in his letters. It is common in Mexico to consider the children of first cousins as nephews and nieces. Many Mexican Chinese upheld informal Mexican social and familial practices such as these in China, which is part of why I view them as diasporic citizens.

45. Chiang Kai-shek had come to power in China during the late 1920s. The Franklin D. Roosevelt administration had supported Chiang unilaterally during the period of Sino-American conflict in the late 1930s and early 1940s. Subsequent U.S. administrations would also support Chiang, against whose Nationalist forces Communists struggled during the Chinese Civil War (1945–1949). In 1949 the Communists defeated the Nationalists, who fled to Taiwan. This put the Chinese Communist Party (CCP) and the Guomindang (GMD), or Nationalist Party, in constant conflict across the Taiwan Strait, as the CCP wanted to include Taiwan in its new Chinese Communist state. See Joseph A. Camilleri, *Chinese Foreign Policy: The Maoist Era and its Aftermath* (Seattle, 1980), 7–8, 12, 31–34, 41, 197; Chen, *Mao's China*, 17, 165; and Boyle, *China and Japan at War*, 9–10, 20–21.

46. OM-149-5, 1960; exp. 546.2/1.

47. *Ibid.*

48. OM-149-5, 1960.

49. Exp. 546.2/1.

50. On conservative organizations and the rise of reactionary movements in Mexico, see Ricardo Pérez Montfort, *Estampas de nacionalismo popular mexicano: diez ensayus sobre cultura popular y nacionalismo* [Imprints of popular Mexican nationalism: ten essays on popular culture and nationalism] (Mexico City, 2003), and Brígida Von Mentz, Ricardo Pérez Montfort, and Verena Radkau, eds., *Fascismo y antifascismo en América Latina y México (apuntes históricos)* [Fascism and antifascism in Latin America and Mexico (historical notes)] (Mexico City, 1984).

51. Exp. 546.2/1; OM-149-5, 1960.

52. *Ibid.*

53. *Ibid.*

54. *Ibid.*

55. Enrique Suárez Gaona, *¿Legitimación revolucionaria del poder en México? Los presidentes, 1910–1982* [Revolutionary legitimization of power in Mexico? The presidents, 1910–1982] (Mexico City, 1987), 75–77, 81–84; Héctor Aguilar Camín and Lorenzo Meyer, *A la sombra de la Revolución Mexicana: Un ensayo de historia contem-poranea de México, 1910–1989* [In the shadow of the Mexican Revolution: an essay on contemporary Mexican history, 1910–1989] (Mexico City, 1989), 98–99, 102, 187–235; Agustín Yáñez, *Proyección universal de México; crónica del viaje realizado por el Presidente de México, ALM [Adolfo López Mateos], a India, Japón, Indonesia, y Filipinas, el año 1962* [Mexico's universal projection; Chronicle of the trip realized by Mexican president, ALM (Adolfo López Mateos), to India, Japan, Indonesia, and the Philippines, the year 1962] (Mexico City, 1963), 8; Yáñez, *Misión económica, politica y social en el Oriente: Una gira de trabajo y buena voluntad en favor de la amistad y la solidaridad por la India, el Japon, Indonesia y Filipinas, con base en los principios de la democracia, de la cultura y de la paz/ALM [Adolfo López Mateos]* [Economic, political, and social mission in the Orient: a work and good relations tour in favor of friendship and solidarity in India, Japan, Indonesia, and the Philippines, based on the principles of democracy, culture, and peace/ALM (Adolfo López Mateos)] (Mexico City, 1962); Jörg Faust and Uwe Franke, "Attempts at Diversification: Mexico and the Pacific Asia," *Pacific Review*, 15 (2002), 299–324.

56. OM-149-5, 1960.

57. Exp. 546.2/12.

58. Schiavone Camacho, "Traversing Boundaries," 63–111. See also, Juán Ramón Gutiérrez, "José María Arana y el comercio chino de Magdalena" [José María Arana and Magdalena's Chinese commerce], *Historia de Sonora*, 91 (1994), 2–3. Alfredo G. Echeverría's organization continued to exist well after the expulsion of Chinese in the early 1930s. Indeed, the Campaña Nacionalista celebrated its thirtieth anniversary in 1955. A banner commemorating the event is housed at the Museo de la Universidad de Sonora in Hermosillo. See oral history interviews with Leo Sandoval, Nov. 14 and 17, 2003, Hermosillo, Sonora, in author's possession. Sandoval began the

interviews by showing me the banner and discussing what it represented. See also Sandoval, *La Casa de Abelardo* [Abelard's house] (Hermosillo, Mex., 1990).

59. When I gave a paper on this topic in Hermosillo, Sonora, numerous persons in the audience laughed boisterously at the absurdity of the suggestion because of the island's limited resources and historic lack of good land. Schiavone Camacho, " 'Aunque vayamos a escarbar camotes amargos a la sierra, queremos México': nacionalismo mexicano en China, 1930–1960, y la repatri-ación de la década de 1960" ['Even if we have to scrape bitter sweet potatoes in the sierra, we want Mexico': Mexican nationalism in China, 1930–1960, and repatriation during the 1960s], paper presented at the Simposio de Historia y Antropología de Sonora: Treinta años escribiendo la historia del noroeste de México [Sonoran history and anthropology symposium: thirty years writing the history of northwestern Mexico], Hermosillo, Sonora, Feb. 23–26, 2005. On La Isla del Tiburón, see Miguel Tinker Salas, *In the Shadow of the Eagles: Sonora and the Transformation of the Border during the Porfiriato* (Los Angeles, 1997), 61.

60. Exp. 546.2/12.

61. OM-149–1 and OM-149–5, 1960; Exp. 546.2/1.

62. Exp. 546.2/1.

63. Wong Campoy interview.

64. Approximately 300 people repatriated in 1960. Alberto Antonio Loyola noted that 267 people repatriated in 1960 and 70 more remained in Communist China hoping to repatriate. Monica Cinco Basurto's father, Jorge Cinco, remembered that there were 365 repatriates in total. See Alberto Antonio Loyola,

Chinos-mexicanos cautivos del comunismo: su repatriación fue una gran proeza [Mexican-Chinese captives of communism: their repatriation was a great exploit] (Mexico City, 1961); and Monica Cinco Basurto, "China in Mexico: Yesterday's Encounter and Today's Discovery," in Roshni Rustomji-Kerns, ed., *Encounters: People of Asian Descent in the Americas* (New York, 1999), 13–18.

65. "De Hong Kong vuelven mexicanos en avión" [Mexicans return from Hong Kong by plane]; "Repatriación de chinomexicanos" [Mexican Chinese repatriation]; and "Más repatriados de China, regresaron" [More repatriates from China, returned], *Excélsior* (Mexico City), Nov. 8, 16, 17, 1960.

66. Exp. 546.2/1; Wong Campoy interview. Dolores Campoy Wong Fang's two daughters stayed in Macau, making their homes there and later moving away. Irma Wong Campoy married a Brazilian in Macau and currently lives in San Francisco. Raquel Wong Campoy also married in Macau and later moved to Lisbon, Portugal, where she lives with her husband. Having established their own families, the women considered Macau their home at the time of the repatriation and did not desire to travel to Mexico with their mother and brothers.

67. Wong Campoy interview; exp. 546.2/1.

68. Wong Campoy interview.

69. Cinco Basurto vividly described the feeling of being between cultures. See Basurto, "China in Mexico," 13–18.

70. Wong Campoy interview.

71. *Ibid.*

The Foreignness of Germs

The Persistent Association of Immigrants and Disease in American Society

By Howard Markel and Alexandra Minna Stern

During the 20th century the United States witnessed sweeping social, political, and economic transformations as well as far-reaching advancements in medical diagnosis and care. Despite the dramatic changes in demography, the meaning of citizenship, and the ability to treat and cure acute and chronic diseases, foreigners were consistently associated with germs and contagion. In this article we explore why, at critical junctures in American history, immigrants have been stigmatized as the etiology of a wide variety of physical and societal ills. Anti-immigrant rhetoric and policy have often been framed by an explicitly medical language, one in which the line between perceived and actual threat is slippery and prone to hysteria and hyperbole.

Our examination focuses on three periods of immigration history: (1) the late 19th century to the passage of the National Origins Act in 1924 when millions of newcomers arrived in the United States and increasingly stringent quotas were enacted; (2) an era of retrenchment and exclusion from 1924 to 1965 when far fewer immigrants entered, yet their identification with disease and contamination remained intact; (3) and the period from 1965 to the present, when family reunification laws became the centerpiece of immigration policy and spawned the migration of millions of Asians and Latin Americans to this country.

In each of these phases, even as the political and social currents shifted, a series of interrelated factors shaped immigrant health and health care in American society. First, the social perception of the threat of the infected immigrant was typically far greater than the actual danger. Indeed, the number of "diseased" immigrants has always been infinitesimal when compared with the number of newcomers admitted to this country. Second, Americans have tended to view illness among immigrants already settled in the United States as an imported phenomenon. Third, policymakers have employed strikingly protean medical labels of exclusion. If authorities and anti-immigration advocates found that one classification failed to reject the "most objectionable," they soon created a new one that emphasized contagion, mental disorder, chronic disability, or even a questionable physique. Although such labels never became the primary reason for debarring specific immigrant groups, their widespread use contributed to durable biological metaphors that explained, usually in catastrophic terms, the potential risks of unrestricted immigration to the nation's social health. The association of immigrants with disease persisted even as health care improved substantially with the introduction of vaccines that all but eliminated age-old scourges such as cholera, yellow fever, and smallpox;

broad-spectrum antibiotics that quelled previously devastating bacterial infections; and the development of lifesaving procedures.

As we enter the 21st century and confront a microbial universe in which epidemic diseases such as tuberculosis and HIV are becoming more prevalent and drug resistant, we need to be aware of Americans' propensity to blame outsiders for the spread of dangerous pathogens. Maintaining and protecting the public health in our current era of globalization require an ecumenical, pragmatic, and historically informed approach to understanding the links between immigration and disease.

Racial Labels and Medical Exclusion, 1880–1924

Recent scholarship has shown that public health and medicine have been crucial to immigration and the immigrant experience in American society (Kraut 1994; Markel 1997). For the most part, these studies have concentrated on the period from 1890 to the mid-1920s, when more than 25 million newcomers arrived at U.S. ports and borders. They came primarily by sea, across the Atlantic from eastern, southern, and central Europe; across the Pacific from China, Japan, and South Asia; and also by foot across the Canadian and Mexican borders. For those who climbed aboard a steamship to their future in a faraway land, the journey was often an ordeal and, at times, risked the health of even the heartiest travelers.

In his history of the American Jewish immigration experience, *World of Our Fathers*, Irving Howe asked, "Was the Atlantic crossing really as dreadful as memoirists and legend have made it out to be? Was the food as rotten, the treatment as harsh, the steerage as sickening?" (Howe 1976, 39). To be sure, memory plays tricks on even the most logically minded, and harrowing events often become more so in the retelling. But as several immigration historians and, more important, actual participants have noted, the steerage compartments of most oceangoing vessels of this era, which carried the bulk of the passengers, offered only cramped and unsanitary quarters consisting

of long tiers of berths on either side of the ship and a central area for benches and tables where immigrants took their meals. Bedding and linen were rarely provided; well-prepared immigrants brought their own. The food served onboard was often unpalatable at best and downright inedible at worst. Seasickness and its all too common companion, vomiting, were habitual features of the voyage, and open troughs and rudimentary water closets served as toilets. Sporadically flushed clean with buckets of saltwater, the facilities aboard many of these ships were foul, disgusting, and, to say the least, an imminent health hazard. Indeed, the risks of malnourishment and the prolonged debilitation brought about by these arduous conditions made these travelers susceptible to a host of medical problems. Although many immigrants were inspected by physicians before leaving Europe and Asia, especially after the passage of a series of immigration acts beginning in 1891—a time in which many now-forgotten diseases were everyday occurrences and the average life expectancy across the globe hovered at 40 years of age—few left their host country in solid health (U.S. Immigration Commission 1911).

Beginning in the 1880s and 1890s, as the pace of urbanization and industrialization quickened, many native-born Americans became alarmed at the huge numbers of immigrants arriving daily at Ellis Island and similar, but smaller, reception centers around the country. Between 1881 and 1884, approximately 3 million newcomers set foot in the United States, almost the same number of immigrants who entered the country during the entire decade of the 1870s. Between 1885 and 1898, 6 million immigrants landed, followed by 18 million between 1898 and 1924 (U.S. Immigration Bureau 1890–1924). These figures are even more significant when comparing the size of annual admissions with the size of the host society (rate of immigration). This rate reached its zenith in the first decade of the 20th century (10 to 11 immigrants arriving per 1,000 residents per year) and dropped off sharply in the aftermath of the restrictive admission policies of the 1920s, the Great Depression, and World War II. By contrast, today's wave of immigration, while in absolute numbers approximates that of the early 20th century, runs at a rate of about four immigrants per 1,000 residents per year (*Statistical Abstract of the United States* 1992).

In order to distinguish the thousands who began to disembark from steerage compartments on Ellis Island in the 1890s from earlier migrations of the English, Scots, and Irish, many turn-of-the-century American commentators began to make judgmental distinctions between "old" and "new" immigrants. The early 20th-century term *new immigrant* referred to those originating from eastern, central, and southern Europe (e.g., Russia, Poland, Austria-Hungary, the Balkans, Greece, Italy, Spain, Portugal, and Turkey), whereas *old immigrants* encompassed those coming from northern Europe (e.g., Great Britain, Ireland, Scotland, Belgium, Denmark, France, Germany, the Netherlands, Sweden, Norway, and Switzerland). Many Americans considered the "new" immigrants such as east European Jews and southern Italians, many of whom were destitute and uneducated, to be less assimilable and far more troublesome than their "old" counterparts. Between 1819 and 1880, more than 95 percent of all immigrants to the United States originated from the "old" immigrant regions, but by 1892, the peak year of immigration during the 19th century, "old" immigrants made up less than 50 percent of the total immigration. This trend intensified during the first two decades of the 20th century. For example, in 1914, the peak year of the 20th century, when 1,218,480 newcomers arrived in the United States at all ports of entry, 158,370 came from the "old" countries, in contrast to 1,051,181 from the "new," or an 86 percent rise in "new" over "old" immigrants (U.S. Department of Labor 1916, chart 2).

Several factors converged in the late 19th century to make immigration—leaving one's native land, enduring the transoceanic passage, and being processed upon arrival in the United States—a journey increasingly mediated by the language and practice of medicine and public health. First, the rise of bacteriology, which for the first time in human history identified microscopic organisms as the culprits of specific diseases, galvanized existing public health programs and encouraged medical authorities to believe that germs could be contained and controlled through direct intervention (Leavitt 1996). Second, during a period in which evolutionary doctrines upheld a belief in the racial degeneracy of most nonwhite groups, it was relatively easy to attribute the weary condition of some immigrants—whether impoverished, malnourished, or suffering from a particular ailment—to their biological inferiority. This circular logic meant that "new" immigrants were described alternately as swarthy, squalid, pestilent, or of "bad stock" (Higham 1988; Kraut 1994). Third, the broader medical surveillance of immigrants was part and parcel of a more over-arching expansion of the federal government that entailed the subsumption of local and state public health agencies by the United States Public Health Service (USPHS) 1 (Marcus 1979). Furthermore, politicians and physicians alike began to consider a comprehensive public health apparatus as essential to making America a modern nation and inoculating the future of the country against unwanted germs from both within and without (Rosen 1993).

With the passage of the Immigration Act of 1891, a permanent foundation for the federal government's oversight of immigration began. This and subsequent laws included detailed regulations governing eligibility for entry. In addition to bans on those with criminal records, polygamists, contract laborers, and prostitutes, this legislation excluded those persons suffering from a "loathsome or contagious disease" and required steamship companies to inspect and disinfect all immigrants before leaving foreign docks as well as bear the costs of returning immigrants who were found to be afflicted (Higham 1988; Hutchinson 1981). At the turn of the century, as the reach of the federal government extended even further, the USPHS began to occupy a more central role at the ports of entry throughout the nation, displacing local authorities. On the West Coast, for example, although the USPHS met resistance from the San Francisco Board of Health when it tried to claim jurisdiction over matters related to immigrant health inspections, the federal government eventually established control in 1910 with the opening of the Angel Island immigration station and hospital (Daniels 1997; Shah 2001). Whether entering the United States via land or water, immigrants passed through an elaborate set of medical and psychological criteria that were quite real and frightening as the clinical gaze and diagnostic equipment of the public health physicians sized up their physical and mental condition. The overwhelming majority of immigrants passed their medical examinations and settled gradually into life in a new country. A small number, however, were turned back or detained for weeks, months, or even years at USPHS hospitals as they underwent observation and treatment for illnesses ranging from trachoma to ringworm. If not cured within a reasonable period of time, deportation—adjudicated by the immigration authorities with the input of the USPHS physicians—was typically the recommendation (Markel and Stern 1999). Nevertheless, all excludable immigrants were entitled to make their case before the Board of Special Inquiry, where immigration and public health officials offered their opinions of the desirability of the individual in question. And while a USPHS physician did not have the legal authority to prohibit entry, a diagnosis of a "loathsome or dangerous contagious disease" almost always meant deportation.

The procedure of medical inspection at New York Harbor, which from 1891 to 1924 received more than 75 percent of all immigrants, and at the other processing centers along the nation's perimeter warrants comment. Not surprisingly, during an era in which the lines of Jim Crow segregation were being etched across the South, xenophobia against ethnic minorities was mounting, and the working class was regularly blamed for the seething class tensions and outspreading slums in American cities, the USPHS's approach to assessing newcomers was often predicated on the prevailing racial and class stereotypes. For example, Mexican and Chinese laborers, who donned work clothes and did not display the fashionable dress of more affluent immigrants, were subjected to harsher medical scrutiny, more frequently poked for blood and urine samples,

and disinfected with chemical agents (Markel and Stern 1999; Shah 2001). Indeed, it was nearly always the case that travelers in first, and most in second, class on ships and trains entering the country underwent a much more cursory appraisal than did those in steerage. In order to avoid more invasive and traumatic medical examinations, the wealthier immigrants, especially before 1907, were encouraged by European and Asian shipping agents to purchase a first- or second-class ticket in order to keep clear of the intrusive eyes of the American doctors (Fishberg 1905). Recent research regarding the Mexican border found that after the erection of medical inspection and disinfection stations from California to Texas in the 1910s, many working-class immigrants, including Chinese, Syrians, and Mexicans, began to cross into the United States along unwatched stretches of desert or remote points along the Rio Grande in order to evade public health authorities (Markel and Stern 1999).

At Ellis Island and other stations, USPHS physicians monitored the steady stream of immigrants filing through the labyrinth of fenced-in areas, on the lookout for a list of medical and psychiatric conditions that grew longer each year (Birn 1997; Dwork 1981; Yew 1980). For example, one physician was stationed near an entryway, accessible only by stairs, where he could scrutinize newcomers hauling their suitcases and possessions for signs of shortness of breath and cardiac problems. Another physician carefully inspected the neck size and shape of those queuing before him for evidence of goiter. Yet another examined newcomers for rashes on the skin, nails, and scalp that might indicate ringworm, favus, and other fungal infections (Reed 1913a,b). Most vividly recalled by immigrants, however, was the dreaded eye examination for trachoma, which involved everting the eyelid with either the physician's fingers or an implement akin to a buttonhook (Markel 2000). Commonly used instruments were stethoscopes and, after 1910, X-rays, which aided in the identification of pulmonary tuberculosis. Similarly, the tools of the bacteriology laboratory, such as microscopes, slides, stains, and culture methods, were regularly used at American immigration centers during the first two decades of the 20th century. These apparatus were crucial to the diagnosis of sexually transmitted diseases, like gonorrhea and syphilis, and parasitic infections, like hookworm. USPHS physicians also looked for insanity, hernias, rheumatism, senility, malignancies, varicose veins, poor eyesight or blindness, and a range of other infirmities (Kraut 1994).

In any year between 1891 and 1924, less than 3 percent of the total number of immigrants seeking entry to the United States were rejected for reasons of a contagious, infectious, or loathsome disease; mental disorder; or physical disability. What did change during this period was the percentage of those immigrants debarred for medical reasons out of the total number debarred for any reason (e.g., being a contract laborer, criminal, or prostitute; showing evidence of an untoward political belief system; or being deemed "likely to become a public charge"). For example, in 1898, of the total number of immigrants excluded, only 2 percent were shut out based on medical criteria. In 1913, this percentage rose to 57 percent, and by 1915, it was 69 percent. More significantly, this proportional increase was not the result of a higher incidence of contagious or infectious disease; rather, it was due to a growing list of ailments, physical disabilities, and, over time, determinations of moral status (Kraut 1994; U.S. Department of the Treasury 1891–1901, 1902–1911; USPHS 1912–1930; Yew 1980). In other words, the creation and application of categories of medical exclusion outpaced the actual presence of disease among the newly arrived, reflecting the shift away from acute and short-lived ailments, such as typhoid and cholera, to chronic, mental, or moral conditions, such as feeblemindedness, constitutional psychopathic inferiority, or hookworm, which began to be interpreted as likely to make an immigrant a "public charge" and an economic and social drain on the nation (Markel and Stern 1999).

Medical rejection rates varied from region to region and reflected the racial and ethnic segregation that characterized the Progressive Era. For example, between 1890 and 1924, approximately 15 million newcomers, primarily European, arrived at Ellis Island. Although as "new" immigrants they were perceived negatively by many Americans, an average of only 1 percent of them were turned back each year for medical reasons. Conversely, at Angel Island, where approximately 100,000 Chinese, Japanese, and Korean immigrants landed between 1910 and 1940, about 17 percent of all immigrants were debarred, and one-third of those were rejected because of a diagnosis of trachoma (Daniels 1997; Salyer 1995; USPHS 1912–1930; Shah 2001). Indeed, although the Chinese comprised only 1 percent of the nation's immigrants during this period, they accounted for more than 4 percent of *all* immigrants deported each year (Daniels 1997). These USPHS interventions were based on epidemiological surveys of the region of Canton and South China, the provenance of many who set out for "Gold Mountain" and a part of the world recognized in public health studies as the globe's foremost "hookworm belt." Once merged with the Sinophobic attitudes of the day, however, this medical knowledge meant that stool specimens were demanded—in an atmosphere of much animosity—from almost all Asian immigrants coming into West Coast ports, but only sporadically from newcomers arriving on the Atlantic seaboard or via Mexico and Canada (Heiser 1936; Shah 2001).

Along the 2,000-mile border between Mexico and the United States, the tension between the constant demand from southwestern growers and industrialists for cheap labor and the USPHS's mandate to protect the nation's health created an unusual form of medical inspection and quarantine. Until the early 1900s, Mexicans were accustomed to moving freely across the border; indeed, many considered the southwestern United States as part of their homeland (Sánchez 1993; Stern 1999). However, after the outbreak of the Mexican Revolution in 1910, U.S. immigration and health officials became uncomfortably aware of the openness of the border and the swelling circulation of insurgents, refugees, and temporary laborers. Besides being cast as transient and uprooted, Mexicans also began to be categorized as diseased and dirty. News of a typhus epidemic in Mexico's interior in 1915 and the discovery of several cases of the fever in El Paso, Texas, in late 1916 led the USPHS to launch a full-scale quarantine in January 1917. According to the USPHS physician in charge at the time, the purpose of the quarantine, which started in El Paso and soon extended to all border stations, was to disinfect and delouse all persons "considered as likely to be vermin infested" (Pierce 1917, 426). Under the constant gaze of attendants, entrants were stripped naked, showered with kerosene, examined for lice and nits, and vaccinated against smallpox. At the end of this process, the scoured clothing was returned to its owners, who also received a USPHS certificate verifying that the bearer had "been deloused, bathed, vaccinated, clothing and baggage disinfected" (Pierce 1917, 428). Several months after the quarantine had been in effect, officials reported that the threat of typhus had all but disappeared. Despite this, however, medical inspections remained in force until the late 1930s; a public health response to a manageable epidemic had metamorphosed into a protracted quarantine along the entire U.S.–Mexican border (Stern 1999). Although over time a sizable number of Mexicans—especially recognized commuters, those who were well dressed, and those who rode first class on the train—were exempted from the disinfection drill, the harsh reality and duration of the quarantine helped generate and underscore stereotypes of Mexicans as impure and infectious (Sánchez 1993; Stern 1999).

Finally, along the vast Canadian–American border, where immigrants entering the United States typically underwent medical examinations along the eastern seaboard before proceeding inland and an amicable relationship existed between American and Canadian officials, the immigrant traffic was relatively light. When the newcomers in question were of British descent, questions of assimilation were easily dismissed. For those of French heritage, however, entering New England could sometimes be more difficult (Stern and Markel 1999). Frictions did arise between federal and local authorities and between USPHS officers and immigrants, and entrants deemed "unfit" were excluded. However, for the most part, along the Canadian border, quiescence reigned: the protocol in place throughout the country was followed, but in terms of public health concerns, the situation never approached the intensity of the two coasts or the Mexican border, nor were nativist voices nearly as vociferous (Markel and Stern 1999).

Perhaps the most striking feature of the medical inspection of immigrants at different ports and borders during this era was the fluidity of the exclusionary labels themselves. Although some of the classifications were more popular in specific regions of the country, an underlying premise colored them all: immigrants threatened the health of the nation. Asians were portrayed as feeble and infested with hookworm, Mexicans as lousy, and eastern European Jews as vulnerable to trachoma, tuberculosis, and—a favorite "wastebasket" diagnosis of nativists in the early 1900s—"poor physique" (Markel and Stern 1999).

Fast-moving epidemics, such as typhoid or cholera, requiring immediate action preoccupied medical authorities from the mid-1800s to the onset of the 20th century (Rosenberg 1987). By the 1920s, however, in part due to public health campaigns, the growing popularity of personal hygiene, and for reasons that still puzzle historians, epidemics were on the wane (Rosen 1975; Tomes 1998). In order to legitimate a more enduring restriction against the menace of germs and foreigners that the rapid rise and fall of a typhus, yellow fever, or plague epidemic could not justify, immigration restrictionists began to mine the language of eugenics (Allen 1986; Kevles 1995). Relying on simplistic Mendelian theories of dominant and recessive traits, eugenicists asserted that not only did potentially infectious newcomers threaten the present with their propensity toward contagion, poverty, and alien beliefs but also their admission endangered the future of American society. Long after the admission to American ports and borders of the "neurasthenic" Jew, the "criminally minded" Italian, the grimy Mexican, or the parasite-ridden Asian, their defective genes would multiply and defile the national body (Laughlin 1923; Markel 1997).

With a protean vocabulary that connected foreign germs and genes to fears of societal disruption and the mongrelization of the American race, nativists were instrumental in the passage of the 1924 National Origins Act, which imposed exceedingly strict quotas on so-called new immigrants and debarred all Asian entrants (Higham 1988; Ngai 1999). A quota system based on national origins that clearly ranked immigrant groups in order of desirability was inaugurated with the Immigration Act of 1921, which allowed for the entrance of 3 percent of foreign nationalities as recorded in the 1910 census. Most severely affected by these limits were the "new" immigrants, whom the vocal eugenicists of the era claimed harbored innumerable deleterious and inheritable traits. The quota system was further restricted in 1924, when the National Origins Act decreed that based on the 1890 census, only 2 percent of the foreign born of a given nationality would be admitted. Moving the source of the quota's numerical determination back two decades, when "new" did not yet outnumber "old" immigrants, ensured only a trickle of immigrants from eastern and southern Europe, Asia, the Indian subcontinent, and the Mediterranean. One of the bill's key sponsors, Congressman Albert Johnson (Washington) emphatically upheld the rationale behind the National Origins Act:

> The United States is our land. If it was not the land of our fathers, at least it may be, and it should be the land of our children. We intend to maintain it so. The day of unalloyed welcome to all peoples, the day of indiscriminate acceptance of all races, has definitely ended.
>
> (Bernard 1980, 493)

Following on the heels of a series of progressively detailed laws dictating the entry of the foreign born—such as the 1882 Chinese Exclusion Act, the 1891 Immigration Act, and the 1893 Quarantine Act—the 1924 act represented both a crescendo of nativism and the start of a new era of immigration and racial exclusion in American society. As several scholars have argued, while still stigmatizing and severely limiting "new" immigrants, the National Origins Act nonetheless symbolically permitted them to enter the realm of white America by classifying them as Caucasian while categorically defining Mexicans and Asians as outsiders (Jacobson 1998; Ngai 1999). Whichever the group in question, however, categories of medical exclusion had become closely entwined with racial labels and perceptions of foreigners as inassimilable and diseased.

Illegal Aliens and Anticommunism, 1925–1964

After the passage of the 1924 National Origins Act and its more carefully articulated interpretations in 1927 and 1929, the rhetoric of the biological hierarchy of races trumped all other medicalized rationales for shutting the doors to the foreign born. These laws favored immigrants whose external physical appearance most resembled the majority of white American faces and were believed to possess the greatest potential for assimilation into mainstream society. During this period, for example, northern and western European countries received 85 percent of the annual admissions visas, a number striking in both its size and its favoritism of those people that immigration restrictionists had long preferred. Nonetheless, the implementation of the quota regulations meant that only 150,000 individuals, less than 15 percent of the pre–World War I average, were eligible to come into the United States each year from all the countries covered by the National Origins Act (Ngai 1999).

As the pace of newcomers slowed, so did the patterns and perceptions of immigration. On one hand, the medical inspection process of the Progressive Era became outdated as previously frightful scourges like smallpox and plague slowly disappeared. In addition, the development and growth of air travel meant that by the end of this period, most immigrants—especially those from Europe and Asia—boarded a plane, not an ocean liner, when they set out for the United States. On the other hand, the enforcement of the quota system meant an unprecedented concern with unauthorized entry, which soon became linked to the concept of the illegal alien and, by the 1950s, to fears of Communist infiltration and subversion. Largely ignored by scholars and interpreted as uneventful, a closer examination of the period between 1924 and 1965 reveals that rather than evaporating completely, associations between immigrants and disease remained intact, albeit overshadowed by depictions of outsiders as a menace to the nation's political stability.

Immigration, of course, did continue during these decades. In all, some 7 million immigrants and another almost 5 million guest workers entered the United States between 1925 and 1964. The most significant drop in numbers occurred during the Great Depression and World War II, and for a brief time during the 1930s, more people left the United States than entered. Between 1930 and 1945, fewer than 700,000 immigrants arrived, in contrast to the more than 5 million immigrants who came to the United States between 1915 and 1930. The paucity of entrants is evidenced by the fact that even with the reductions enforced by the National Origins Act, between 1930 and 1947 only 23 percent of all available immigrant quota slots were used (Ueda 1994; U.S. Congress 1950). During this period, the densest immigrant traffic flowed along the Canadian and Mexican borders, not into the once crowded buildings of Ellis Island and Angel Island. And while the USPHS authorities continued their inspections, public health became a secondary issue and imported disease a more latent concern.

Instead, the economic and political demands brought on by the pressures of World War II and the Cold War came to the forefront of immigration policy. By the late 1930s, for example, the quarantine procedures along the U.S.–Mexican border, prompted by the typhus outbreak in 1917, were terminated, and as was the case across the board, the responsibility of examining immigrants was transferred to contracted doctors and consular offices in the sending country. So many Mexicans had left the United States during the Great Depression that in 1942, when industrial and agricultural laborers were needed during the war, a novel binational guest worker arrangement was established to lure Mexicans back. Lasting until 1964 and designed to fill shortages in the factories and on the fields, the Bracero Program sought simultaneously to monitor the movement of Mexican transmigrants and to place them in factories and fields to aid the war mobilization. Critics of this program derided it as nothing more than a vehicle for an "endless army" of cheap labor for American growers (Calavita 1992). Most Mexicans who stayed in the United States settled in California and the Southwest, with smaller yet substantial numbers migrating to the great industrial cities of the Midwest and Northeast. Not subjected to the quotas of the National Origins Act and allowed to enter the United States under the Bracero Program, yet tracked and often harassed by the Border Patrol, Mexican immigrants were in an exceedingly vulnerable and ambiguous position. During this period they gradually came to be identified as the quintessential "illegal aliens" and, when McCarthyism reached its apex in the early 1950s, were subjected to the militaristic purges of Operation Wetback, an undertaking in which nearly 4 million Mexicans, both documented and undocumented, were rounded up in factories, restaurants, bars, and even private domiciles and then expelled (Jacobson 1996; Massey 1986; Ngai 1999; Ueda 1994).

During these years, European immigration, above all from the "old" countries, fell sharply, and disease ceased to be one of the primary considerations for evaluating recent arrivals. Nevertheless, this era's immigration policy did have unforeseen deadly consequences as the Third Reich rose and fell. The American response to the refugee crisis created by Hitler's genocidal rampage was appalling in its impotence, yet the Roosevelt administration's disinterest in saving Jews was rarely couched in metaphors of disease and biological inferiority, in contrast to those of the governments in countries like Brazil and Argentina (Lesser 1995; Wyman 1968, 1985). Occasional appeals to save the lives of Jews and other victims of Nazi persecution were made during the late 1930s and early 1940s, but relief efforts were minuscule in proportion to the need. More often than not, Americans simply ignored the problem. After the end of World War II and the "discovery" of Nazi atrocities, U.S. refugee policies became somewhat more liberalized, particularly for displaced refugees and those aliens who were either children or spouses of American service men and women. As a result, these years witnessed a small rise in European entrants and after 1943, when the Chinese Exclusion Act was rescinded, in Chinese immigrants now able to claim their quota allotments.

One significant change that had a major impact on both the public health and the immigrant experience during this period was the transformation in modes of travel. Angel Island closed in 1940 after a devastating fire, and Ellis Island shut down in 1954. Following World War II, as air transportation became the norm, travel time was markedly shortened, causing public health officials to worry about the risks of passengers introducing diseases, especially infections. Given the incubation periods of many dangerous conditions, which range from a few days for cholera to days or two weeks for typhus fever, steamship travel at least gave medical inspectors a week for an infection to manifest itself in the lapse between an immigrant's departure and his or her arrival. Consequently, in the early 20th century, it was expected that the most acutely ill immigrants would be readily apparent to the USPHS physician. But with the advent of air travel, it was now possible for an asymptomatic yet highly infectious person to set foot in the United States and, in less than 48 hours, become deathly ill and spread germs to an unsuspecting American public. As a result, a number of federal agencies, civil aviation boards, physicians, public health experts, and representatives of the airlines began meeting and holding hearings to update the medical inspection process. Not unlike the countless hearings and discussions held between members of Congress and the steamship companies at the turn of the 20th century, the airlines cooperated with immigration officials at the same time as they guarded their burgeoning industry (National Archives 1946).

Moreover, by this time, most medical inspections were conducted well before the immigrant left his or her country of origin, as a chain of checkpoints was instituted for long flights, with frequent stopovers to ensure that a passenger who became acutely ill en route was quickly examined and, if necessary, isolated. Such was the case of Guido Castro Quesado, a 43-year-old immigrant from Costa Rica who flew to Texas in late 1943 seeking treatment for neurosyphilis. He was barred from entry and returned by January 1944 (National Archives 1944). During these years, the risks of swift travel and the transmission of germs from one part of the globe to another became pressing considerations for public health officials and citizens at large. An awareness of the new mobility of germs, however, also coincided with a striking worldwide diminution in the incidence of the classic and most rapidly lethal epidemic diseases equated with earlier waves of immigration. After the development of antibiotics and a host of preventive vaccines in the postwar years, the hue and cry about imported scourges became moot when compared with the fears earlier expressed by nativists and public health.

Above all else, the perceived threat of Communism and other political ideologies considered "un-American" framed immigration policy in the late 1940s and 1950s as a number of laws were passed, most infamously the Internal Security Act of 1950, which prohibited the entry or settlement of immigrants who either were or had been Communists. Indeed, the Cold War facilitated a close partnership between those advocating immigration restriction and national security (Divine 1957; Ngai 1998; Schrecker 1998). While never a major chord, the themes of diseased immigrants, inferior races, and other biological explanations did insinuate themselves into the rationales behind ongoing immigration restriction. This was illustrated by both popular representations of disease and public health in American film and the hallmark piece of immigration legislation of this period, the Walter-McCarran Act.

In August 1950—just six months after Senator Joseph McCarthy of Wisconsin set in motion the era that bears his name by announcing before the Republican Women's Club of Wheeling, West Virginia, that he had in his hand a list of more than 200 Communists working in the U.S. State Department—the film *Panic in the Streets* was released. Directed by Elia Kazan, who two years later stood before the House Un-American Activities Committee and "named names" of purported Communists working in Hollywood, this film captures the tenacious association between germs and foreignness in American society. Set in the humid port city of New Orleans, *Panic in the Streets* tells the story of an outbreak of pneumonic plague that is being spread by a low-class and gambling outsider who is described alternately as Armenian, Argentine, or Greek (Murphy 1950). The hero in this film noir is a USPHS officer, Dr. Clinton Reed, played by Richard Widmark, who is portrayed as the classic family man of the 1950s, torn between the exhausting demands of his civil service job and his desire to be a more devoted father and husband. Following the script of American individualism, Widmark is the only character who can steer the correct course, safeguard the public, and insulate New Orleans, the nation, and the world from a devastating and fatal epidemic. In his quest to eliminate the source of the bacteria, he incinerates the body of the deceased plague carrier; wages a fierce battle of sterilization, inoculation, and serum injections; and combs the city's seedy underworld of dock workers, gamblers, and gangsters looking for those who came in contact with the sick and shady foreigner. In this film, plague is depicted as an alien disease brought into the United States by non-natives speaking with thick accents. Indeed, Widmark refers to an earlier USPHS effort, in 1924, to quarantine plague in Los Angeles when it broke out in a Mexican community (Deverell 1999; Viseltear 1974). In the end, Widmark triumphs despite jurisdictional clashes with the local police and municipal authorities, and the film's primary villain, the brutal gangster Blackie, is trapped like vermin by a rat catcher on a ship's mooring line and plunges into the water. Like the ideal Cold War husband, Widmark returns home to the arms of his adoring, pregnant wife and admiring son.

With regard to immigration policy, by the close of World War II, it was clear to policymakers that the relentlessly amended collection of laws enacted between 1891 and 1950 was unwieldy and confusing and required serious revision or, at least, clarification. Taking the lead in crafting a new omnibus immigration bill was Senator Patrick McCarran of Arizona. An ardent anti–New Dealer and a staunch conservative who viewed himself as a bona fide defender of American society from unwanted intrusion and infiltration, McCarran collaborated closely with McCarthy in the campaign against the alleged Communist subversion. In 1950, McCarran spearheaded sponsorship of the Internal Security Act. Two years later, he and Congressman Francis Walter of Pennsylvania embarked on the elaboration of what ultimately became the Immigration and Nationality Act, or the McCarran-Walter Act, of 1952.

The solution they reached was a revamped code of immigration laws that introduced selective admission categories based on job expertise and the permanent residence of the immigrant's immediate family members in the United States. The bill retained the quota system for European immigrants, which numerically favored western and Nordic Europeans over eastern and southern Europeans; released some additional slots for Asians; and widened the grounds for debarring immigrants with criminal records and chronic diseases. As historian Robert A. Divine noted, implicitly embedded in the McCarran-Walter Act were two opposing philosophies. Restrictionists like McCarran and Walter believed that immigration was a source of danger to the United States and that laws were needed to guard American institutions and traditions. Their opponents argued that immigration was a source of strength and urged a policy that expressed generosity and a helping hand to the oppressed people of the world (Divine 1957).

In McCarran's anti-immigration rhetoric against east European Jews, southern Italians, Asians, and other so-called undesirables were deep-seated metaphors of disease and contagion. As floor manager of the bill during its final debate in the Senate in mid-May 1952, McCarran made an impassioned plea to save the United States from imported ruin:

> Today ... as never before, a sound immigration and naturalization system is essential to the preservation of our way of life, because that system is the conduit through which a stream of humanity flows into the fabric of our society. If that stream is healthy, the impact on our society is salutary; but if that stream is polluted our institutions and our way of life becomes infected.
>
> (*Congressional Record*,
> May 13, 1952, 5089)

More significantly, this language of exclusion revealed the continuing malleability of the "undesirable immigrant" classification and the resurrection of the association between germs and foreigners that marked the Progressive Era. For example, in the law's general categories of ineligible aliens, we find—in no explainable order of actual threat—the feebleminded; the insane; people with epilepsy or other mental defects; drug addicts and alcoholics; those with leprosy or contagious diseases; aliens found to have a physical defect, disease, or disability that would restrict their ability to earn a living; the impoverished; criminals; polygamists; prostitutes; homosexuals; contract laborers; and Communists, anarchists, or those subscribing to totalitarian political ideologies (U.S. Immigration and Nationality Act of 1952). The McCarran-Walter Act defined undesirability along a spectrum that was both specific enough to keep out those identified as minatory and loose enough to encircle newer perceived threats to the American way of life. This formula of this series of analogies could be summarized as

> Disease = Criminal Behavior = Poverty = Addiction = Immoral Behavior = Communism

The law was vetoed by President Harry Truman, who contended that the bill would not successfully modernize American immigration policy, admonishing its reliance on a national origins quota system designed to keep immigration at a low level:

> We do not need to be protected against immigrants from these countries. On the contrary, we want to stretch out a helping hand ... . The greatest vice of the present quota system ... is that it discriminates, deliberately and intentionally, against many of the people of the world ... . It is incredible to me that, in the year 1952, we should again be enacting into law such a slur on the patriotism, the capacity, and the decency of a large part of our citizenry.
>
> (*Congressional Record*,
> June 25, 1952, 8083)

Despite the presidential warning, Truman's veto was overridden, and the bill became law on June 27, 1952 (*Congressional Record*, June 26–27, 1952). Although from this moment on, American presidents—from Truman and Eisenhower to John F. Kennedy—began advocating a more liberal and fair-minded immigration policy, this did not become a reality until Lyndon Johnson signed the Hart-Celler Immigration Act of 1965.

The Newest Immigrants and the Recrudescence of Old Fears, 1965–Present

Speaking from a podium at Liberty Island in New York Harbor in October 1965, just under the outstretched arm that had both welcomed and shunned newcomers, President Johnson explained to his audience that while

> the days of unlimited immigration are past ... the immigration policy of the United States has been twisted and distorted by the harsh injustice of the national origins quota system ... [according to which people] of needed skill and talent were denied entrance

because they came from southern or eastern Europe or from one of the developing countries.

(Johnson 1966, 1038–9)

This philosophy bolstered a much more relaxed attitude toward immigration in the latter third of the 20th century and reopened the gates to new generations of arrivals, especially from Latin America and Asia. This period was punctuated, however, by a resurgence of nativism in the 1980s that was sparked by the advent of AIDS, tied to worries about the browning of America, and drawn from decades-old stereotypes of outsiders as either acutely or chronically ill (Nelkin and Michaels 1998; Perea 1997). In the 1990s, federal and state chambers debated the need to restrict state services, particularly health care, to the under- and undocumented (Markel 1999). More recently, the emergence of multidrug resistant strains of HIV and tuberculosis have reignited the persistent association between foreigners and germs, which works against the effective and judicious management of global public health (Brimelow 1995; Edwards 2001; Farmer 1999).

The Immigration Act of 1965 was cosponsored by Senator Philip A. Hart of Michigan and Congressman Emmanuel Celler, who represented New York City's ethnically diverse Tenth Congressional District in Brooklyn. It constituted one facet of a larger trend of social activism that encompassed the Civil Rights Act of 1964 and the Voting Rights Act of 1965, as well as the beginning of the Vietnam War. The center of the Hart-Celler Act was an immigration policy that emphasized reuniting immediate family members of already settled immigrants and attracting highly educated and occupationally skilled immigrants. An initial ceiling of 290,000 admissible immigrants per year was instituted, with 170,000 slots for the Eastern Hemisphere and 120,000 for the Western Hemisphere, marking the first time that Latin American and Caribbean immigrants were subject to numerical limitations. Nonetheless, the Hart-Celler Act's abolition of the national origins quota system had an unexpected consequence: a large increase in U.S. immigration rates (Reimers 1992; Ueda 1994).

Each year after 1965 the number of immigrants entering the United States rose as family reunification enlarged, almost exponentially, the pool of eligible visa applicants. While the 1970s averaged 450,000 newcomers annually, by the 1980s, this figure had risen to 730,000, along with an estimated 200,000 undocumented entrants. These newest immigrants were more heterogeneous than their former counterparts, coming, literally, from every corner of the world and representing greater socioeconomic diversity (Ueda 1994). Whereas the majority of the "new" immigrants of the Progressive Era were working class, the post-1965 generation was composed of both laborers, often with scant education, and skilled professionals and trained workers. Seventy-five percent of the newest immigrants settled in six states: California, New York, Texas, New Jersey, Florida, and Illinois (U.S. Select Commission on Immigration and Refugee Policy 1981). Intensely concentrated settlement patterns in the largest American cities made many of the latest—particularly the unskilled and Latino—arrivals much more visible and prompted many Americans to assert that unwanted foreigners were inundating the country. In 1986, in order to gauge the tangible quantity of illegals, especially Mexicans, and absorb those who had resided unlawfully in the United States since 1982, Congress passed the Immigration Reform and Control Act, which offered amnesty to many undocumented workers and attempted to prosecute the American employers who had wittingly hired them (Zolberg 1990).

During this period, large international airports such as John F. Kennedy in New York, O'Hare in Chicago, Miami International, San Francisco International, and Los Angeles International consolidated their position as the nation's principal ports of entry, just as Ellis Island, Angel Island, and El Paso's immigration station had been in times past. Moreover, by this time, immigrants coming to the United States were generally healthier people. After World War II, many countries built hospitals and rural clinics and spearheaded campaigns to combat endemic diseases, and many parts of the world benefited from reductions in childhood mortality and various infectious diseases as well as improved standards of nutrition as a result of hygiene and maternity programs. In addition, organizations like the United States Peace Corps and the United Nations World Health Organization brought modern sanitary techniques, public health administration, vaccines, and medical treatments to areas that had neither the financial nor human resources to afford them. But these enhanced living conditions and lowered mortality rates had the ironic outcome of skyrocketing populations. People facing overcrowding and few opportunities now had powerful incentives to immigrate, especially to the United States. And come they did, whether by jet, rickety boat, plane, or foot. In 1990, for example, more than 1.8 million legal and approximately 300,000 illegal newcomers entered the United States. Immigration was now truly global, primarily from Asia, Mexico, and the Caribbean; the majority of the newest immigrants were people of color and far more likely than their predecessors to settle permanently in the United States.

One thing had not changed, however: the assumption that many infectious diseases originated beyond American borders and were trafficked in by foreigners. This perception was supported by immigration health policy, which required only potential immigrants and visa solicitors, not visiting travelers or American citizens returning from abroad, to undergo medical examinations before leaving their countries of origin. Thus, the realistic menace of imported germs—which scorn all boundaries and can incubate just as elusively and easily in an American tourist heading back from a vacation in the Bahamas as in a Russian visa applicant seeking to join her relatives in Chicago—was eclipsed by the recalcitrant connection between foreigners and disease.

In the context of resurgent anti-immigrant sentiment in the 1980s, calls to protect the public health from external hazards began to be sounded in tandem with the escalating AIDS epidemic. For example, in 1986, the USPHS suggested adding AIDS to the list of infections that would automatically debar a prospective newcomer. Senator Jesse Helms of North Carolina, a noted opponent of both gay rights and AIDS research, treatment, and prevention, subsequently introduced a bill that made AIDS an excludable disease for immigrants. President George H.W. Bush's secretary of health and human services, Louis Sullivan, a physician, publicly stated that only tuberculosis should be defined as a "communicable disease of public health significance," yet the regulation, passed in 1987, remained in effect until 1991 when the policy was changed only slightly. HIV-positive "travelers" could enter the United States, but immigrants wishing to take up permanent residence were banned. The message was clear: tourists with money were welcome, but impoverished and potentially ill immigrants, "likely to become a public charge," were not (Federal Register 1986, 1987; Markel 1990). All newcomers seeking refugee status at a U.S. embassy in their nation of origin were tested for HIV; those seeking asylum were allowed to live in the United States for a year, but if they wished to stay longer, they had to submit to an HIV test.

The actual number of immigrants sent back for being HIV positive was not particularly high. In 1989, for instance, the National Commission on AIDS estimated that fewer than 1,000 immigrants with HIV/AIDS would seek entry into the United States during that calendar year. At the same time, Dr. June Osborn, the chairperson of the commission, observed that the current policies "fly in the face of strong opinion and practice and lead to unconscionable infringement of human rights and dignity, and they reinforce a false impression that AIDS and HIV infection are a general threat when in fact they are sharply restricted in their mode of transmission" (Cohen 1989; Farmer 1992; National Commission on Acquired Immune Deficiency Syndrome 1989).

The AIDS regulations reiterated a recurrent theme in American immigration policy, that specific "undesirable" groups were labeled as being "high risk" whether or not they actually posed a threat of transmitting disease. Given the policy of more than a century of regulating the entry of people with identified infectious or contagious diseases, it was hardly surprising that HIV-positive status could be used to reject an entrant. However, when AIDS appeared suddenly in the 1980s, it was quickly conflated with deviant sexuality and several minority groups, ranging from gays and intravenous drug abusers to Haitians and Africans. As a disease category, it shared much with the feared killers of the past, such as tuberculosis and syphilis, could be understood in terms of the labels of moral undesirability articulated in the McCarran-Walter Act, and, moreover, was racially tainted by fantastical theories tracing the etiology of HIV/AIDS to Haitian voodoo rituals and animal sacrifice (Fairchild and Tynan 1994; Farmer 1992).

More than five years after it was scientifically established that HIV could be transmitted only through bodily fluids such as blood and semen—as opposed to casual contact—the potency of AIDS stereotypes nevertheless led the Immigration and Naturalization Service (INS) to quarantine HIV-positive Haitian immigrants at the U.S. Marine Base at Guantanamo Bay, Cuba (Annas 1993). From 1990 to 1993, these detainees were separated from other Haitian émigrés who had been intercepted at sea and held in unsanitary conditions far worse than those of their predecessors at Ellis Island (Hilts 1992). In fact, the situation was so severe that in 1993, a federal district court judge, Sterling Johnson of Brooklyn, ruled that the Immigration and Naturalization Service had denied these immigrants adequate medical care and legal consul (*Haitian Centers Council v. Sale* 1993).

Once faced with this judicial reprimand, supporters of the HIV ban on immigrants replicated a pattern of the early 20th century when nativists turned toward eugenics and arguments of cost to explain why admitting foreigners would, over time, drain America's coffers. Now less focused on the panic that outsiders would spread AIDS throughout the United States and aware also that 650,000 to 900,000 American citizens were HIV positive, they emphasized instead the fiscal burden of having to care for sick newcomers (Gostin et al. 1990). Accordingly, in February 1993, Senator Don Nickles of Oklahoma introduced

a bill prohibiting the entry of HIV-positive immigrants on economic grounds, which passed in the U.S. Senate, 76 to 23, with an even larger show of support in the U.S. House of Representatives a few weeks later. Despite the opinion of many immigration and public health experts that the migration of HIV-positive persons to America would be minimal, Senator Nickles's warning in a well-publicized speech of the need to guard the nation from a "communicable disease" rang true for many Americans: "If we change this policy, it will almost be like an invitation for many people who carry this dreadful, deadly disease, to come into the country because we do have quality health care in this country ..." and will "jeopardize the lives of countless Americans and will cost U.S. taxpayers millions of dollars" (*Congressional Record*, February 17, 1993, 2865).

On June 10, 1993, President Bill Clinton signed into law the National Institutes of Health Revitalization Act, which amended the Immigration and Nationality Act of 1988, adding HIV infection as a criterion to keep out immigrants. The reasoning behind this law was to shield the United States against external pathogens and the expense of providing medical care to foreigners, concerns that also were evident in the logic of the contemporaneous California Illegal Alien Statute, approved in 1994 by a majority of California voters who resented the putative taxpayer burden of public and country medical care (Reimers 1998). Known colloquially as "Proposition 187," this state law required publicly funded health care facilities to refuse care to illegal immigrants and mandated that health care workers who suspected that one of their patients might be an illegal alien report him or her to the Immigration and Naturalization Service, the state attorney general, and the state director of health services (Ziv and Lo 1995).

Contested to this day in the courts at the insistence of a number of immigrant advocacy groups, the law has never been formally implemented (Purdum 1999). Nevertheless, this kind of proposition not only imperils the frank discussion vital to a doctor-patient relationship, and if it were ever successfully enforced, it would seriously undermine the public's health. Consider, for example, the plight of undocumented citrus pickers in the California valleys. Lured across the Mexican border in the hopes of earning higher wages in the United States, these laborers live and work in difficult and unsanitary conditions, which put them at significantly greater risk of contracting tuberculosis and other ailments. With the sword of deportation hanging over him, an undocumented immigrant with tuberculosis and a productive cough—whether he contracted it in his native country or the United States—would be reticent to seek medical attention (Markel 1999; McKenna, McCray, and Onorato 1995). Indeed, legal and illegal immigrants in California avoided health care providers during the months immediately after the passage of Proposition 187, a predicament that puts all American citizens in jeopardy (Asch, Leake, and Gelberg 1994). Some recent studies of the public health risks of tuberculosis around the world recommend that instead of forcing undocumented immigrants to hide from physicians, the United States and other industrialized nations create user-friendly tuberculosis detection and treatment programs for the hundreds of millions of people who cross international boundaries each year (Bloom 2002; Bloom et al. 1999; Farmer 1999; Geng et al. 2002; Reichman 2002; Sachs 2002). Such an arrangement was recently implemented by the U.S.–Mexican Border Health Commission to track and care for Mexican transmigrants afflicted with HIV/AIDS, hepatitis A, or tuberculosis (Smith 2001). Especially novel is the creation of a confidential binational tuberculosis card that allows patients to obtain treatment in both the United States and Mexico without fearing deportation or long-term detention in one of the many TB screening centers along the border (Sachs 2000). As Dr. Lincoln Chen, a public health expert from the Rockefeller Foundation, stated, such initiatives make the U.S.–Mexican border a model for other possible multinational efforts and "the cutting edge of health in the 21st century ... this is the front line of global health" (Smith 2001, A19).

Protecting the Public Health in a Global Millennium

In order to protect the public health of Americans today, the all too common tendency to conflate disease with foreigners and/or specific ethnic, racial, or sexual minorities must be held in check by discovering where the risk factors for public health threats actually lie. At many points over the past century, some people have wanted to exclude persons perceived as foreign, inassimilable, and dangerous to the country's social, political, or economic fabric. Metaphors of germs and contagion have never lurked far beneath the surface of such rationales. As we have shown, more often than not these arguments have been motivated by, and closely intertwined with, ideologies of racialism, nativism, and national security rather than substantiated epidemiological or medical observations. Not surprisingly, these attitudes have deterred rather than encouraged many immigrants from seeking medical care. As the 20th century came to a close, the associations between immigration and disease remained powerful and prevalent.

The world we inhabit today is essentially a global village. Ideas, goods, and people can now travel long distances in a matter of hours. More compelling, microbes are not required to carry passports and can easily escape the best-laid plans to block their entry. Safeguarding America's health means safeguarding the world's health. If any concept in this brief history of immigration and public health is antiquated, it is the idea that infectious diseases can be controlled by targeting certain populations based on apparent ethnic or national background. The Ellis Island model of medical inspection is not appropriate to our current era, and it is fitting that this symbol of American immigration history is now a museum. Moreover, economists and experts in global public health have demonstrated that the most humane, effective, and fiscally sound approaches are those in which wealthy nations, organizations, and corporations come to the assistance of poorer nations in order to protect all the world's citizens. In the 21st century it is no longer acceptable or wise to consider that an epidemic brewing in

Zaire is either remote or irrelevant (Garrett 1994, 2000; Markel 2003).

The presence of serious public health risk factors—including soaring rates of tuberculosis, malaria, and emergent or poorly understood infectious diseases; shrinking economic resources for epidemiological surveillance and the delivery of primary care; and the recognition of the profound mental health disorders generated by genocidal practices in the war-torn countries of Africa, the Middle East, and eastern Europe, not to mention the prospects of bioterrorism—all point to potential episodes in which the appearance of a specific epidemic disease may again be associated with foreigners (Drexlar 2002; Miller, Engelberg, and Broad 2001; Tucker 2001). While we should never expect that our responses to such potential crises will be perfect, we can learn from the mistakes of the past in order to better balance between combating and containing specific diseases and scapegoating a particular group.

Note

1. Before 1902, the Public Health Service was the United States Marine and Hospital Service. After 1902, it was designated the United States Marine Hospital and Public Health Service, and, in 1912, it became the United States Public Health Service. For simplicity's sake, we refer to it as the U.S. Public Health Service, or USPHS, throughout this article.

References

Allen, G. 1986. The Eugenics Record Office at Cold Spring Harbor, 1910–1940: An Essay in Institutional History. *Osiris* 2 (2nd series):225–64.

Annas, G.J. 1993. Detention of HIV-Positive Haitians at Guantanamo. *New England Journal of Medicine* 329:589–92.

Asch, S., B. Leake, and L. Gelberg. 1994. Does Fear of Immigration Authorities Deter Tuberculosis Patients from Seeking Care? *Western Medical Journal* 161:373–76.

Bernard, W.S. 1980. Immigration: A History of U.S. Policy. In *The Harvard Encyclopedia of American Ethnic Groups*, edited by S. Thernstrom, 486–95. Cambridge, Mass.: Harvard University Press.

Birn, A-E. 1997. Six Seconds per Eyelid: The Medical Inspection of Immigrants at Ellis Island, 1892–1914. *Dynamis* 17:281–316.

Bloom, B.R. 2002. Tuberculosis: The Global View. *New England Journal of Medicine* 346(19): 1434–35.

Bloom, B.R., D.E. Bloom, J.E. Cohen, and J.D. Sachs. 1999. Investing in the World Health Organization. *Science* 284:911.

Brimelow, P. 1995. *Alien Nation: Common Sense about America's Immigration Disaster.* New York: Random House.

Calavita, K. 1992. *Inside the State: The Bracero Program, Immigration, and the I.N.S.* New York: Routledge.

Cohen, G.S. 1989. National AIDS Panel Government Urged to Travel Policy. *San Francisco Chronicle* (December 13). Available at http://www.aegis.com/news/sc/1989/SC891209.html (accessed August 19, 2002).

Congressional Record. 1952. (May 13):5089.

Congressional Record. 1952. (June 25):8082–5.

Congressional Record. 1952. (June 26 and 27):8254–8.

Congressional Record. 1993. (February 17):2865.

Daniels, R. 1997. No Lamps Were Lit for Them: Angel Island and the Historiography of Asian American Immigration. *Journal of American Ethnic History* 17:2–18.

Deverell, W. 1999. Plague in Los Angeles, 1924: Ethnicity and Typicality. In *Over the Edge: Remapping the American West*, edited by V.J. Matsumoto and B. Allmendinger, 172–200. Berkeley and Los Angeles: University of California Press.

Divine, R.A. 1957. *American Immigration Policy, 1924–1952.* New Haven, Conn.: Yale University Press.

Drexlar, M. 2002. *Secret Agents: The Menace of Emerging Infections.* Washington, D.C.: Joseph Henry Press/National Academy Press.

Dwork, D. 1981. Health Conditions of Immigrant Jews on the Lower East Side of New York, 1880–1914. *Medical History* 25:1–40.

Edwards, J.R. 2001. TB: Coming to America. *National Review Online* (June 1). Available at http://www.nationalreview.com/comment/comment-edwardsprint060101.html (accessed July 24, 2002).

Fairchild, A.L., and E.A. Tynan. 1994. Policies of Containment: Immigration in the Era of AIDS. *American Journal of Public Health* 84(12):2011–22.

Farmer, P. 1992. *AIDS and Accusation: Haiti and the Geography of Blame.* Berkeley and Los Angeles: University of California Press.

Farmer, P., ed. 1999. *The Global Impact of Drug-Resistant Tuberculosis.* Boston: Harvard Medical School/Open Society Institute.

Federal Register. 1986. Medical Inspection of Immigrants (AIDS). 51 (April 23):15354–5.

Federal Register. 1987. Medical Inspection of Immigrants. 52 (June 8): 21607–8.

Fishberg, M. 1905. Report to the Commissioner-General of Immigration, Frank P. Sargent. In *Annual Report of the Commissioner-General of Immigration to the Secretary of Commerce and Labor for 1905.* Washington, D.C.: U.S. Government Printing Office.

Garrett, L. 1994. *The Coming Plague: Newly Emerging Diseases in a World Out of Balance.* New York: Farrar, Straus & Giroux.

Garrett, L. 2000. *Betrayal of Trust: The Collapse of Global Health.* New York: Hyperion.

Geng, E., B. Kreiswirth, C. Driver, J. Li, J. Burzynski, P. DellaLatta, B.A. LaPaz, and N. Schluger. 2002. Changes in the Transmission of Tuberculosis in New York City from 1990 to 1999. *New England Journal of Medicine* 346(19):1453–8.

Gostin, L.O., P.D. Cleary, K.H. Mayer, A.M. Brandt., and E.H. Chittenden. 1990. Screening Immigrants and Internal Travelers for the Human Immunodeficiency Virus. *New England Journal of Medicine* 322:1743–6.

Haitian Centers Council vs. Sale. 1993. 823, F. Suppl. 1028. E.D.N.Y.

Heiser, V. 1936. *An American Doctor's Odyssey: Adventures in 45 Countries.* New York: Norton.

Higham, J. 1988. *Strangers in the Land: Patterns of American Nativism, 1860–1925* . New Brunswick, N.J.: Rutgers University Press.

Hilts, P.J. 1992. *New York Times* (December 10):A13.

Howe, I. 1976. *World of Our Fathers. The Journey of the East European Jews to America and the Life They Found and Made.* New York: Harcourt Brace Jovanovich.

Hutchinson, E.P. 1981. *Legislative History of American Immigration Policy, 1798–1965.* Philadelphia: University of Pennsylvania Press.

Jacobson, D. 1996. *Rights across Borders: Immigration and the Decline of Citizenship.* Baltimore: Johns Hopkins University Press.

Jacobson, M.F. 1998. *Whiteness of a Different Color: European Immigrants and the Alchemy of Race.* Cambridge, Mass.: Harvard University Press.

Johnson, L.B. 1966. Remarks at the Signing of the Immigration Bill, Liberty Island, New York, October 3, 1965. In *Public Papers of the Presidents of the United States. Containing the Public Messages, Speeches, and Statements of the Presidents. Lyndon B. Johnson, 1965.* Book II, June 1–December 31, 1965. Washington, D.C.: U.S. Government Printing Office.

Kevles, D. 1995. *In the Name of Eugenics: Genetics and the Uses of Human Heredity.* Cambridge, Mass.: Harvard University Press.

Kraut, A.M. 1994. *Silent Travelers: Germs, Genes and the Immigrant Menace.* New York: Basic Books.

Laughlin, H.H. 1923. *Analysis of America's Melting Pot.* U.S. House of Representatives Committee on Immigration, 67th Cong., 3rd sess. Washington, D.C.: U.S. Government Printing Office.

Leavitt, J.W. 1996. *Typhoid Mary: Captive to the People's Health.* Boston: Beacon Press.

Lesser, J. 1995. *Welcoming the Undesirables: Brazil and the Jewish Question.* Berkeley and Los Angeles: University of California Press.

Marcus, A. 1979. Disease Prevention in America: From a Local to a National Outlook, 1880–1910. *Bulletin of the History of Medicine* 53(2):184–203.

Markel, H. 1990. A U.S. Agency Shuts the Gates on AIDS Victims. *Baltimore Evening Sun* (June 6):A13.

Markel, H. 1997. *Quarantine! East European Jewish Immigrants and the New York City Epidemics of 1892.* Baltimore: Johns Hopkins University Press.

Markel, H. 1999. When Germs Travel. *The American Scholar* 68:61–9.

Markel, H. 2000. "The Eyes Have It": Trachoma, the Perception of Disease, the United States Public Health Service, and the American Jewish Immigrant Experience, 1897–1924. *Bulletin of the History of Medicine* 74:525–60.

Markel, H. 2003. *When Germs Travel: American Stories of Imported Disease*. New York: Pantheon Books.

Markel, H., and A.M. Stern. 1999. Which Face? Whose Nation? Immigration, Public Health, and the Construction of Disease at America's Ports and Borders, 1891–1928. *American Behavioral Scientist* 42(9):1313–30.

Massey, D.S. 1986. The Social Organization of Mexican Immigration to the United States. *Annals of the American Academy of Political and Social Science* 487:102–13.

McKenna, M.T., E. McCray, and I. Onorato. 1995. The Epidemiology of Tuberculosis among Foreign-born Persons in the United States. *New England Journal of Medicine* 332:1071–6.

Miller, J., S. Engelberg, and W. Broad. 2001. *Germs: Biological Weapons and America's Secret War*. New York: Simon & Schuster.

Murphy, R. 1950. *Panic in the Streets*. Motion Picture Copyright #LP417 (July 3). Collections of the Library of Congress, Motion Picture Division. Washington, D.C.

National Archives. 1944. INS, RG 85, Accession 58A/734, File 56055/499C, Box 1938, National Archives Records Administration, Washington, D.C.

National Archives. 1946. International Standards and Recommended Practices on Customs, Immigration, Sanitary and Related Matters Facilitating International Air Transport, February 2, PICAO Subcommittee on Facilitation of International Civil Aviation, RG 85, INS, Accession 58A/734, File 56055/4990, Box 1939, National Archives Records Administration, Washington, D.C.

National Commission on Acquired Immune Deficiency Syndrome. 1989. *Background Paper. AIDS and Immigration: An Overview of United States Policy*. Washington, D.C.

National Institutes of Health Revitalization Act of 1993. Pub. L., No. 103–143, sec. 2007, 107 Stat. 210 (codified as amended at U.S.C., section 1182, (a) (1) (A) (I), suppl. 1993).

Nelkin, D., and M. Michaels. 1998. Biological Categories and Border Controls: The Revival of Eugenics in Anti-Immigration Discourse. *International Journal of Sociology and Social Policy* 18(5/6):35–63.

Ngai, M.M. 1998. Legacies of Exclusion: Chinese Illegal Immigration during the Cold War Years. *Journal of American Ethnic History* 18(1):3–36.

Ngai, M.M. 1999. The Architecture of Race in American Immigration Law. *Journal of American History* 86(1):67–92.

Perea, J.F., ed. 1997. *Immigrants Out! The New Nativism and the Anti-Immigrant Impulse in the United States*. New York: New York University Press.

Pierce, C.C. 1917. Combating Typhus on the Mexican Border. *United States Public Health Service Reports*. Washington, D.C.: U.S. Government Printing Office.

Purdum, T. 1999. Fight on Immigrant Measure Splits California Democrats. Lieutenant Governor Breaks with Governor. *New York Times* (April 25):A18.

Reed, A.C. 1913a. Going through Ellis Island. *Popular Science Monthly* 82:5–18.

Reed, A.C. 1913b. Immigration and the Public Health. *Popular Science Monthly* 83:320–28.

Reichman, L.B., with J.H. Tanne. 2002. *Timebomb: The Global Epidemic of Multi-Drug Resistant Tuberculosis*. New York: McGraw-Hill.

Reimers, D.M. 1992. *Still the Golden Door: The Third World Comes to America*. 2nd. ed. New York: Columbia University Press.

Reimers, D.M. 1998. *Unwelcome Strangers: American Identity and the Turn against Immigration*. New York: Columbia University Press.

Rosen, G. 1975. *Preventive Medicine in the United States, 1900–1975: Trends and Interpretations*. New York: Prodist/Science History Publications.

Rosen, G. 1993. *A History of Public Health*. Baltimore: Johns Hopkins University Press.

Rosenberg, C.E. 1987. *The Cholera Years: The United States in 1832, 1849, and 1866*. Chicago: University of Chicago Press.

Sachs, J.D. 2002. Investing in Health for Economic Development. *Project Syndicate* (January). Available at http://www.project-syndicate.org (accessed July 24, 2002).

Sachs, S. 2000. More Screening of Immigrants for TB Sought. *New York Times* (January 3):A5.

Salyer, L.E. 1995. *Laws Harsh as Tigers: Chinese Immigrants and the Shaping of Modern Immigration Law*. Chapel Hill: University of North Carolina Press.

Sánchez, G.J. 1993. *Becoming Mexican American: Ethnicity, Culture, and Identity in Chicano Los Angeles, 1900–1945*. New York: Oxford University Press.

Schrecker, E. 1998. *Many Are the Crimes: McCarthyism in America*. Boston: Little, Brown.

Shah, N. 2001. *Contagious Divides: Epidemics and Race in San Francisco's Chinatown*. Berkeley and Los Angeles: University of California Press.

Smith, J.F. 2001. U.S., Mexico Team up on Health Care. *Los Angeles Times* (October 17):A119.

Statistical Abstract of the United States. 1992. Rate of Immigration by Decade, 1821–1992. Table 5:10. Washington, D.C.: U.S. Government Printing Office.

Stern, A.M. 1999. Buildings, Boundaries, and Blood: Medicalization and Nation-Building on the U.S.-Mexico Border. *Hispanic American Historical Review* 79(1):41–81.

Stern, A.M., and H. Markel. 1999. All Quiet on the Third Coast: Medical Inspection of Immigrants in Michigan. *Public Health Reports* 114(2):178–82.

Tomes, N. 1998. *The Gospel of Germs: Men, Women and the Microbe in American Life*. Cambridge, Mass.: Harvard University Press.

Tucker, J. 2001. *Scourge: The Once and Future Threat of Smallpox*. New York: Atlantic Monthly Press.

Ueda, R. 1994. *Postwar Immigrant America: A Social History*. Boston: Bedord's Books of St. Martin's Press.

U.S. Congress, Senate Committee on the Judiciary. 1950. *The Immigration and Naturalization Systems of the United States*. Table 4:889. Washington, D.C.: U.S. Government Printing Office.

U.S. Department of Labor, Bureau of Immigration. 1916. *Annual Report of the Commissioner General of Immigration to the Secretary of Labor, 1916*. Chart 2: Immigration into the United States from the Different Countries and Total from All Countries, 1820–1926, inserted between pp. 140 and 141. Washington, D.C.: U.S. Government Printing Office.

U.S. Department of the Treasury. 1891–1901. *Annual Reports of the Surgeon General of the Marine and Hospital Service of the United States*. Washington, D.C.: U.S. Government Printing Office.

U.S. Department of the Treasury. 1902–1911. *Annual Reports of the Supervising Surgeon General of the United States Marine Hospital and Public Health Service*. Washington, D.C.: U.S. Government Printing Office.

U.S. Immigration Bureau. 1890–1924. *Annual Reports of the U.S. Immigration Bureau*. Washington, D.C.: U.S. Government Printing Office.

U.S. Immigration Commission (1907–1910). 1911. *Reports of the U.S. Immigration Commission on Steerage Legislation, 1819–1908*. Senate Document no. 758, 61st Cong., 3rd sess., 336–485. Washington, D.C.: U.S. Government Printing Office.

U.S. Immigration and Nationality Act of 1952. 66 Stat 163, sec. 212. *U.S. Statutes at Large* 66:163–282.

U.S. Public Health Service (USPHS). 1912–1930. *Annual Reports of the Surgeon General of the USPHS*. Washington, D.C.: U.S. Government Printing Office.

U.S. Select Commission on Immigration and Refugee Policy. 1981. *U.S. Immigration Policy and the National Interest: Final Report and Recommendations of the Select Commission on Immigration and Refugee Policy*. Washington, D.C.: U.S. Government Printing Office.

Viseltear, A. 1974. The Pneumonic Plague Epidemic of 1924 in Los Angeles. *Yale Journal of Biology and Medicine* 47:40–54.

Wyman, D. 1968. *Paper Walls: America and the Refugee Crisis, 1938–1941*. Amherst: University of Massachusetts Press.

Wyman, D. 1985. *The Abandonment of the Jews*. New York: Pantheon Books.

Yew, E. 1980. Medical Inspection of Immigrants at Ellis Island, 1891–1924. *Bulletin of the New York Academy of Medicine* 56(5):488–510.

Ziv, T.A., and B. Lo. 1995. Denial of Care to Illegal Immigrants: Proposition 187 in California. *New England Journal of Medicine* 332:1095–8.

Zolberg, A.R. 1990. Reforming the Back Door: The Immigration Reform and Control Act of 1986. In *Immigration Reconsidered: History, Sociology, and Politics*, edited by V. Yans-McGlaughlin, 315–39. New York: Oxford University Press.

6 Race and Ethnicity Issues in Latin America

The Leather Strap

By Jorge Amado

●●

Editor's Introduction

Situated in the late 1960s or early 1970s, Brazil was in the midst of a twenty-one-year military dictatorship. The conservative element in Brazilian society emanated from the strong influence of the Catholic Church and the government that sought to restrict land reforms and curtail socialist movements during the Cold War. One conflict, however, is the presence of Afro-Brazilian religions, such as *candomblé*, in Salvador de Bahia, a legacy of the slave trade that officially ended in 1888. Other themes that arise from this excerpt by Jorge Amado are issues of mixed race, religious prejudices, self-hatred, and internalized racism. Today in Brazil a new element of religious discrimination toward the Afro-Brazilian faiths is evident from the growth of evangelical and Pentecostal churches that actively seek to weaken the Catholic traditions and "pagan idolatry."

References

Amado, Jorge. *The War of the Saints.* Translated by Gregory Rabassa. New York: Dial Press, 2005.
Chestnut, R. Andrew. *Competitive Spirits: Latin America's New Religious Economy.* New York: Oxford University Press, 2007.

Adalgisa at the Street Door with the Five Wounds of Christ

Adalgisa's yell shook the foundations of the Avenida da Ave-Maria: "Inside, right now, filthy brat! Slut!"

Manela scurried off, fleeing her aunt so that when Adalgisa lifted her arm for the slap, the girl was nowhere to be seen. She must have gone through the always wide-open door of Damiana's house. To Adalgisa it even looked like a brothel, with all that coming and going of people, in and out.

Damiana was a candy-maker, and in the morning she prepared pots of dough for the cakes of cassava, corn, and sweet manioc that an insolent troop of black urchins peddled from door to door in the afternoons to regular customers. A masterful sweets-maker, Sweet-Rice Damiana was famous—oh! Damiana's sweet rice, just thinking about it makes your mouth water—not just in the Barbalho district; her clientele was spread throughout the four corners of the city.

During June, the month of the festivals of Saint John and Saint Peter, she couldn't fill all the orders for corn and coconut mush, tamales, and honey-corn cakes. It was a happy, hard-working house. Comparing it to a brothel showed an excess of ill will, but Adalgisa wasn't one for halfway measures. Besides, Adalgisa knew nothing about brothels, outside or in. If she chanced to pass a woman of pleasure on the street, she would spit to the side to show her disgust and disapproval. She considered herself a lady, not just an ordinary woman: Ladies have principles, and they demonstrate them.

An expert in amplified speech, she didn't lower her voice but yelled so the neighbor woman would hear her:

"I swear by the Five Wounds of Christ that I'm going to put an end to that love affair if it's the last thing I do in my life! God will give me the strength to stand up to such lowlifes trying to take a young girl down the wrong road, the road to perdition! The Lord is with me—I'm not afraid, nothing can touch me, that nigger business won't get anywhere with me. I'm cut from better cloth, don't need to mix with any common people. I'll get the sin out of that girl if it costs me what health I've got left."

Adalgisa was always complaining about her fragile health, because in spite of her healthy appearance, she was subject to recurring migraines, continuing headaches that often persisted day and night, turning her mood bitter, driving her out of her mind. She blamed her acquaintances and relatives, not to mention the whole neighborhood, but especially her niece and her husband, for all the migraine attacks that persecuted and plagued her. Dona Adalgisa Perez Correia, of touted Spanish blood on her father's side and whispered African blood on her mother's, was the nightmare, the terror of her street.

Adalgisa's Hips, and the Rest of Her Body

It wasn't even a street: The Avenida da Ave-Maria was nothing but a blind alley, a cul-de-sac, to use Professor Joao Batista de Lima e Silva's pedantic phrase. Still a bachelor in his forties, the professor lived in the last little house on the alley, also the smallest. Whenever he heard Adalgisa's ill-tempered echoes, he went to the window, lowered his reading glasses, and rested his eyes on his irritable neighbor's hips.

Adalgisa was certainly irritating—but she was a knockout in looks. Everything has its compensation. In the mediocre setting of the alley, bereft of lawns and gardens, of trees and flowers, the real compensation was Adalgisa's derriere, which reaffirmed the beauty of the universe. The fanny of a Venus, Aphrodite's bottom, worthy of a painting by Goya—so meditated the professor. He, too, exaggerated somewhat, as can be seen.

The rest of Adalgisa's body was nothing to be sneezed at either—quite to the contrary, the professor allowed, feasting his eyes: full, firm breasts, long legs, black braids encircling an oblong Spanish face with eyes of fury, burning dramatically. A pity she had such an aggressive demeanor. On the day Adalgisa lost her arrogant, mocking, and disdainful ways, her air of superiority, on the day Adalgisa left the Five Wounds of Christ in peace and smiled without rancor, without affectation—oh! on that day her beauty would transfix the heart, inspire the poets' verses.

From her father's side, the Perez y Perezes, Adalgisa got her pious and penitent behavior, displayed in Holy Week processions in Seville, carrying the cross of Christ. She acknowledged only that side of her family, not wishing to know anything about her mother's. She took no pride in her Goya hips, and if she knew about Venus, beautiful but missing both arms, she'd never heard tell of Aphrodite.

The Junior Partner

The angry cavalcade of threats reached its peak of rage when Adalgisa recognized, sitting behind the wheel of the taxi parked by the entrance to the alley, Miro. The mangy dog was waving at her, that cynical, cheeky, insolent pauper! But then, noticing that she was also being observed by the professor, a solid citizen, teacher, journalist, she nodded courteously, feeling obliged to explain her fury and bad manners:

"I'm bearing my cross, paying for my sins," she said. "That's what comes of raising other people's children: blame and mortification. That wretched girl is leaving me all skin and bones, ruining my health, driving me to my grave. Never seen anything like it, a girl barely seventeen."

"That's youth." The professor tried to make excuses without knowing exactly what Manela's crime was. He suspected that she'd been fooling around with her boyfriend—could she have actually done it already? A girl of seventeen? The aunt was blind; she hadn't noticed that Manela was all woman, headstrong and wiggly, an appetizing body, ready for bed. Wasn't she a candidate for Miss Something-or-Other? "You've got to be patient with young people."

"More patient than I've been?" Adalgisa was horrified. "You don't know the half of it, professor! If I were to tell you—"

If Manela still hadn't, the professor thought, she was wasting her time. Drugstores sold the Pill without requiring any prescription. Freed from the fears of pregnancy, the girls of today live it up, in a wild hurry, their tails on fire. They don't follow Adalgisa's ideal of chastity and honor.

As everyone was tired of hearing, Adalgisa had had no gentlemen friends until she met Danilo, her first and the only one, the man who had led her to the altar a virgin and pure. Well, a virgin, maybe—pure is more doubtful. There's no morality capable of passing through a yearlong engagement unscathed; a few daring things, minimal as they might be, always end up happening: a hand on the breast, a tool between the thighs. Danilo Correia was a modest but enterprising clerk in the notary office of the Wilson Guimaraes Vieira, and a former soccer star; he was the worthy opponent of the professor at checkers and backgammon, fortunate husband, exclusive master of those sumptuous hips and the rest of Adalgisa's body, that chaste, virtuous woman—what a pity! the professor thought.

Actually, Professor Joao Batista de Lima e Silva was mistaken. He knew Adalgisa was chaste, but he hadn't guessed she was prudish. Danilo at the very most was a junior partner. The one who actually mastered Adalgisa's body, who determined the rules in her bed, was Christ our Lord.

This is a solemn promise. In a little while we'll return to the burning and controversial subject of Adalgisa's prudishness, her Catholic bed, governed by her father confessor each Sunday in the confessional of the Church of Sant'Ana, before ten o'clock mass and holy communion. We will also get to the Spartan personality of her confessor, the Reverend Father Jose Antonio Hernandez, a Falangist, incorruptible, master of the fires of hell, missionary to Brazil—*me cago en Dios,* what a painful, rotten mission!—custodian of Adalgisa's purity. When we do, we will recount, with all the necessary details, the bitter vicissitudes of the clerk Danilo Correia, her noncompliant victim.

First, however, the figure of Manela must come to the fore, now only barely glimpsed as she disappeared from her aunt's sight into the wide-open door of fat Damiana's house. From Damiana's house emerged the appetizing smell of spices mixed with coconut milk and grated lemon cooking in the oven: vanilla and clove, cinnamon, ginger, almonds, and cashew nuts.

In Professor Joao Batista's ponderings, doubts about Manela have been raised. Why did her aunt Adalgisa want to punish her? Was she still a virgin, or did she already know the taste of what's good? Was she or wasn't she running for Miss Something-or-Other? It's important to clear up such uncertainties because a few pages back it was announced that it was to free Manela from captivity that Oya Yansan, the *iaba* who has no fear of the dead and whose very cry lights up the craters of volcanos on the summits of mountains, was visiting the City of Bahia, her sack of thunder and lightning strapped over her shoulder. So in the end, what was the question of Manela?

Her name was Manela, just as it's written—not Manuela, as was asked whenever her name was seen or heard, as if to correct a spelling mistake or mispronunciation. It was a name she inherited from her Italian ancestor, whose memory was kept within the family because the beauty of that first Manela, a scandalous and fatal beauty, had become legendary. Two dashing and foolish lieutenant colonels, in disrespect of orders, had fought a duel over this earlier Manela; one governor of a province had conceived a passion and killed himself for her; one priest on his way to the honors of a bishopric had committed a sacrilege, reneged on his eminence, tossed his cassock aside, and run off to live with her.

In order to familiarize oneself with the extensive and lively chronicle of Manela Belini, with the precise details of names and dates, titles and offices, a reading of the chapter in *Supplement to the History of the Province of Bahia,* by Professor Luis Henrique Dias Tavares, is recommended. It records the triumphs of this diva in the theater, who sang operatic arias for ecstatic audiences; the deadly duel with swords in which the honor of La Belini was bathed in blood—only a few drops, but sufficient; the rumors about the governor's suicide; and the concubinage with the priest, which resulted in the Bahian family and the tradition of the name Manela. It's pleasant reading, in spite of the title.

Luis Henrique Dias Tavares, historian, is the alter ego of the fiction writer Luis Henrique, or Luis Henrique *tout court,* as his colleague and intimate friend Joao Batista de Lima e Silva would say. The fiction writer used the episode of the priest to create a charming picaresque novel. It's difficult to say who deserves greater praise, the historian or the novelist—it would be best to read both.

Eufrasio Belini do Espirito Santo, the descendant of the sacrilege, liked retelling stories about his great-grandmother during rounds of beer and conversation—a gorgeous Italian woman she was, whose hair blew in the wind. The day he had a daughter he gave her the name Manela. He was a romantic and a reveler.

Manela's Procession

Our Manela did not come from Seville; nor did she participate in any Procession of the Dead Lord on Good Fridays. No, her procession was that of Bomfim Thursday or if you will, the washing festival, the waters of Oxala, the most important festival in Bahia, unique in all the world. Nor did our Manela wrap herself in atonement and penitence, cover herself with a black mantilla, or recite the litany to the sinister sound of rattles: *"Mea culpa! Mea culpa!"* Her aunt Adalgisa so repented, pounding her chest. But Manela came wrapped in joy and merriment, dressed in the dazzling traditional white dress of a Baiana, a Bahian woman. On her head, balanced over her torso, she carried the jug of scented water for washing the Church of Bomfim, and she went along dancing and singing Carnival songs to the irresistible sounds of the music truck.

That year, for the first time, Manela took her place among the Baianas on Bomfim Thursday. In order to walk in the procession—unbeknownst to her aunt, needless to say—she had played hookey from her English class in the intersession program at the Americans' institute. She played hookey in a proper fashion, however, because the day before the procession the class had unanimously informed Bob Burnet, the teacher, of their decision not to attend that day in order to take part in the washing festival Curious about Bahian customs, young Bob not only went along with the idea but proposed that he keep them company, and he did so with his well-known thoroughness: he *samba-ed* ceaselessly under the burning January sun, bloating himself with beer. He was what you'd call a nice guy.

Manela changed her clothes at the house of her other aunt, Gildete, who lived nearby in Tororo. Manela's parents, Dolores and Eufrasio, had died in an automobile accident several years ago, while returning in the early morning hours from a wedding party in Feira de Sant'Ana. Eufrasio, who was behind the wheel, hadn't had time to get out of the way of a truck loaded with cases of beer. After the funeral, Adalgisa had taken charge of thirteen-year-old Manela, while Gildete took charge of Marieta, Manela's sister, who was a year younger. Although Gildete was a widow and mother of three children, she had wanted to keep both girls, but Adalgisa wouldn't allow it: The sister of Dolores, she was just as much an aunt to the girls as Eufrasio's sister was. She took on her responsibilities, fulfilled her duty. God had not given her children, so she dedicated herself to making a lady out of Manela—a lady of principle.

Adalgisa kept to herself her opinion of the fate that had been awarded Marieta, relegated as she had been to an environment whose customs she considered censurable—and Adalgisa never passed up an occasion to censure them. Gildete was the widow of a shopkeeper at the market and a public schoolteacher. She was not a lady, although she was a very good person. So that we keep everything out in the open, it's worth quickly mentioning the general opinion of all their friends and acquaintants, who agreed that in the lottery of orphanhood, it was Marieta who had won the grand prize.

On Bomfim Thursday, Manela had arrived at the steps of the Church of the Conceicao da Praia, the dwelling of Yemanja, to begin the revelry. She'd come early in the morning in the company of Aunt Gildete, Marieta, and Cousin Violeta, and they mingled with dozens of Baianas as they waited for the procession to form. What do we mean, dozens? Actually, there were hundreds of Baianas gathered on the steps of the church, all in the elegance of their ritualistic white costume: the wide skirt, the starched petticoat, the smock of lace and embroidery, the low-heeled sandals, On their arms and necks they displayed silver *balanganda* bracelets and necklaces, jewelry and armbands in the colors of their saints. The pot, jug, or jar on the turban atop their heads carried scented water for their obligation. *Maes de santo* and *filhas de santo* of all Afro-Bahian nations were there—Nago, Jeje, Ijexa, Angola, Congo—and copper-colored beauties of the mulatto nations, full of coquetry and merriment. Manela, perhaps the prettiest of all, was blooming with excitement. Up on the trucks the *atabaque* drums were throbbing, calling the people together. Suddenly music exploded from a Carnival truck, and the dancing began.

The procession wound all the way from the Church of the Conceicao da Praia, along the Lacerda Elevator, up to the Church of Bomfim on Sacred Hill, for a distance of six miles, more or less, depending on the quantity of devotion and cane liquor consumed by the participants. Thousands of people—the procession was a sea of people—it stretched out of sight. Cars, trucks, carriages, and donkeys festooned with flowers and sprigs, carrying full barrels on their backs; all ensured there would be no lack of scented water for the ceremony. In the trucks were lively groups, whole families, *samba* clubs, and *afoxes.* Musicians clutched their instruments: guitars, accordions, ukeleles, tambourines, *capoeira berimbaus.* Popular singers and composers were there, like Tiao the Chauffeur, River Man, Chocolate, and Paulinho Camafeu. The voices of Jeronimo, of Moraes Moreira were heard. In riding breeches, white jacket, dandified, kinky cotton hair, Batatinha, "Small Potatoes," smiled while crossing the street. People shook his hand, shouted his name, "Batatinha!" embraced him. A blond—American, Italian, from Sao Paulo?—ran over and kissed him on his black and beautiful face.

Rich and poor mingled, rubbing elbows. In the mixed-blood city of Bahia, all shades of color exist in the flesh of its inhabitants, ranging from a black so dark it's blue, to milky white, the color of snow, and in between the infinite gamut of mulattos. Who isn't a devotee of Our Lord of Bomfim, with his countless miracles; who doesn't cling to Oxala, bearing the unfailing *ebos?*

Also present were the commanding general of the region, the admiral of the naval base, the brigadier of the air force, the president of the Assembly, the presiding judge of the Superior Court, the president of the Honorable Chamber of Aldermen, bankers, cacao barons, entrepreneurs, executives, senators, and deputies. Some paraded in black limousines. Others, however— the governor, the mayor, and the head of the tobacco industry, Mario Portugal—followed on foot along with the people. There followed a mob of demagogues—that is, candidates in the upcoming elections—canvassing every mile, butting in, distributing fliers and embraces, kisses, smiles, and pats on the back to potential voters.

The procession swayed to the music from the trucks: religious hymns, folk songs, Carnival *sambas,* and *frevos.* The accompaniment swelled along the way, the multitude expanded; people clambered down the hillsides, the Sao Joaquim market emptied out, latecomers disembarked from ferryboats and launches or arrived in sloops. When the front of the procession reached the foot of Sacred Hill, a voice well known and loved rose from the music truck of Dodo and Osmar—a hush descended over everyone, the procession halted, and Caetano Veloso intoned the hymn to Our Lord of Bomfim.

Then the march up the hillside resumed to the beating of the drums, to the singing of the *afoxes* about the waters of Oxala. The mass of people headed for the Church of Bomfim, which had been closed by a decision of the Curia. In years past, the procession would wash the whole church and honor Oxala on the altar of Jesus. Someday it will go back to being that way. Today the Baianas occupied the steps and the entrance to the church; the washing began, and the obligation of the *candomble* is fulfilled: *"Exe-e-babd!"*

Our Lord of Bomfim arrived in Bahia from Portugal during colonial times riding on the mournful Catholic vow of a shipwrecked Portuguese sailor; Oxala arrived from the coast of Africa, during the time of the traffic in blacks, riding on the bloody back of a slave. Today they hovered over the procession, Our Lord and Oxala, fused in the breasts of the Baianas, plunged into the scented water, and mingled. Together they are a single uniquely Brazilian divinity.

The Two Aunts

That Bomfim Thursday was decisive in Manela's life. The procession, a happy time of singing and dancing, the ceremonious Baianas, the square on Sacred Hill festooned with paper streamers and decorated with fronds of coconut palms, the washing of the steps of the basilica, the possessed women receiving the enchanted ones, the sacred ritual, and having lunch with her cousins at a table of love, eating and drinking, dende oil running from her mouth down her chin, her hands licked, cold beer, *batidas* and the warmth of cane liquor, cinnamon and clove, prancing around the square with her sister, her cousin, and the boys, parties in family homes and the public dance in the street, the music trucks, the lighting of the footlights, the colored bulbs on the facade of the church, she wandering amid the crowd with Miro beside her,

leading her by the hand. With a sense of lightness, Manela felt capable of taking flight, a free swallow in the euphoria of the festival.

That morning, when she had first arrived at the Church of the Conceicao da Praia, she had been a poor, unhappy girl—oppressed, lacking a will of her own, always on the defensive: timid, deceiving, disheartened, submissive. Yes, Auntie. I heard, Auntie. I'm coming, Auntie. Well behaved. She'd attended the procession because Gildete had demanded it with an ultimatum of fearsome threats:

"If you're not here bright and early," her aunt had said, "I'm coming to get you, and I'm a woman capable of slapping that so-and-so right in the face if she so much as dares say you can't come with me. Where did anyone ever hear tell of such a thing? She thinks she's carrying the king in her belly, but she's nothing but a stuck-up bitch. I don't know how Danilo puts up with all that crap—it takes balls."

Hands on hips, on a war footing, Gildete finished:

"I've got some accounts to settle with that busybody, going around talking about me, treating me like a street walker or some hoodooer. She'll pay me for that someday."

Yet, big-hearted, cordial, loving, a piece of coconut sweet, Aunt Gildete held no rancor; the threatened revenge, the promised vengeance, never went beyond words. On the rare occasion when she lost her temper, she would become transformed, capable of uttering the worst absurdities.

Wasn't Gildete the one who had stormed wildly into the office of the secretary of education like a crazy woman, when the government attempted to cancel student lunches in order to save money? "Calm down, my dear teacher!"—that was all the secretary had said to her. He lost his composure in fear of physical assault as he faced Gildete's robust figure, itching for a fight, her harsh accusations defending the poor children, her imperious figure—and he hastily left the room. Panicky stenographers tried to restrain her, but Gildete had pushed them away; all determination, ignoring protests and warnings, she crossed through anterooms until she got to the sanctum sanctorum where the secretary issued his orders. Her photograph later appeared in the newspapers with an expose about the plan to do away with elementary school lunches—it had been a carefully guarded secret until then—resulting in such a wave of protests, including the threat of a strike and a demonstration, that the measure was canceled, and Gildete even escaped a negative report in her service file. Instead of a reprimand, she was praised; for the governor took advantage of what had happened to get rid of the secretary, whose political loyalty he had doubted anyway. The governor attributed the authorship of the disastrous idea to the secretary, then threw him to the wolves.

Along with the praise came a certain notoriety: Newton Macedo Campos, a combative opposition deputy, referred to the incident in a speech in the State Assembly, praising Gildete to the skies, calling her an "ardent patriot and distinguished citizen, paladin of children, paragon of teachers." In addition the union tried to co-opt her for its leadership, but she refused: She enjoyed the praise but had no ambitions to be a paladin or a paragon.

On Bomfim Thursday, Manela turned her weakness into strength and did as Gildete had instructed her. Early in the morning, she set out for Gildete's, taking advantage of the fact that Adalgisa was gone for the morning—she and Danilo had left to attend the seventh-day mass for the wife of one of his co-workers. Manela carried her English books and notebooks so that when she came home for lunch, they would think she had been off at her class. To be back for lunch, Manela planned to check her watch, leave the procession in time to pick up her dress and her books, and catch the bus—the whole thing was well orchestrated in her mind. Trembling inside, astounded by her own audacity, she had changed her clothes had put on the petticoat and wide skirt, her breasts naked under the Baiana smock—oh, if Aunt Adalgisa ever saw such a thing!

To say that Manela wasn't sorry she had come, that she was in love, would be to say very little. By the time she finally did take the road back home that day, poorly timed rather than according to her schedule, she was a different Manela. The real Manela, the one who'd hidden herself away ever since the death of her parents, had almost extinguished herself in fear of punishment—the punishment of God who, omnipresent, sees everything and makes note of all for a settling of final accounts on the Day of Judgment. And she had lived in fear of the punishment of Aunt Adalgisa, who reared and educated her. Auntie, ever watchful and nosy, had collected her dues for whatever she saw or found out with a good tongue-lashing and the leather strap, too!

As the twig is bent, so grows the tree. Manela had been thirteen and a half when she came to live with her aunt and uncle, so she wasn't that young. But according to Adalgisa, her parents had brought her up very poorly: She was a teenager full of wiles and will, accustomed to bad company, consorting with trash, loose with her schoolmates at movie matinees, only pretending to take part in programs for children, running off to festivals on the square. Why, her parents had even taken her to *candomble* temples, that was how irresponsible …

Adalgisa had taken her in hand, put a leash on her. She'd laid down strict hours: She couldn't let her set foot on the street, and as for festivals and movies, she could go only if accompanied by her aunt and uncle. *Candombles?* Not even to be mentioned: Adalgisa had a horror of *candombles*—a *sacred* horror, the adjective imposes itself. A short rein and a strong wrist would bring Manela under control. Adalgisa would punish her with no misgivings or pity. She was fulfilling her duty as an adoptive mother—and one day, established in life, Manela would thank her for it.

The Hour of Noon

"Exe-e-baba!" The palms of her open hands at chest level, Manela greeted Oxolufa, Qxala the elder, as he arrived at the entrance to the Church of Bomfim. Bending over in front of Aunt Gildete, she watched Gildete quiver, close her eyes, and bend her body over her knees, possessed. Leaning on her broom as an improvised *paxoro*, Gildete came out doing the dance of the enchanted one: Oxala, old, debilitated, but free from captivity at

last, from the jail where he'd been punished without any trial or sentence, was celebrating his freedom. When he showed himself on the square, the bells were ringing, announcing the hour of noon.

Noon was the hour when Manela was expected back at the Avenida da Ave-Maria for lunch, dressed again as a student, skirt and blouse, her breasts held in by a brassiere, carrying the schoolbag with her English text and her notebooks, as if she were coming from her class at the institute. Good afternoon, Auntie, how was the mass?

But she must have forgotten, or decided not to, and when she heard the bells, it was no longer any use if she remembered, because at half-past noon on the dot, Uncle Danilo was sitting at the table and Aunt Adalgisa was serving him his repast. Whenever Manela happened to be late, her prepared plate would grow cold waiting in the kitchen. That day Adalgisa didn't even fix up the cold plate, and she herself barely tasted the beef stew with dwarf beans—she stopped with the first forkful, choking with surprise and indignation. Her mouth was as bitter as bile, her head was bursting, mute. She did not want to believe what her eyes had seen—she'd rather go blind.

The Waters of Oxalá

Anyone who moves backward is a crab, Aunt Gildete had stated the night before, using proverbial phrases, popular tales, and folk wisdom to sum up her diatribe against Adalgisa. Returning to her normal self, sitting with her nieces, stroking the head of her daughter Violeta who was crouching at her feet, she'd mentioned the legend of the waters of Oxala and recounted it—if you'd like to hear it, I'll tell it to you. She cleared her throat and spoke what follows, perhaps a word more, a word less:

"The ancients tell, I heard from my granny, a Grunci black woman, that Oxala went out one day through the lands of his kingdom and the kingdoms of his three sons, Xango, Oxossi, and Ogum, to find out how the people were getting along, with the intention of correcting injustices and punishing evildoers. In order not to be recognized, he covered his body with the rags of a beggar and set out, asking questions. He didn't get very far; accused of vagrancy, he was taken to jail and beaten. Just on suspicion they tossed him into the clink where, forgotten, he spent years on end in solitude and filth.

"One day, happening to pass by the miserable jail, Oxossi recognized his missing father, who had been given up for dead. Quickly freed, he was loaded down with honors, and before he returned to the royal palace, Oxala was bathed and perfumed. Singing and dancing, the women brought water and balm and bathed him. The most beautiful among them warmed his bed, his heart, and his parts for him.

"'I have learned with my own flesh the conditions under which the people of my kingdom live, and of the kingdoms of my sons. Here, there, everywhere, whim and violence reign, rules of obedience and silence: I carry the marks on my body. The waters that put out the fire and washed the wounds are going to extinguish despotism and fear. The lives of the people are going to change.' Oxala was true to his word, he put his power as king into play. That's the story of the waters of Oxala. It passed from mouth to mouth, crossed the ocean, and so it reached our Bahian capital city. A lot of people who walk along in the procession, carrying jugs and jars of scented water to wash the floor of the church, don't know why they're doing it. Now you know, and you can pass it on to your children and grandchildren when you have them; it's a pretty good story, and it bears a lesson."

Oxala didn't manage to change the lives of the people—that was easy to see. Even so, we have to recognize that no word spoken against violence and tyranny is entirely vain and useless: Somebody who hears it just might overcome fear and start to rebel. Just look at Manela following the path of Oxala in front of the Church of Bomfim, just at that moment when she should have been hightailing it home.

The *Ekede*

When the noon bells rang, in her affliction at the lost hour, Manela clung to Our Lord of Bomfim, for whom nothing is impossible. On the upper floor of the sacristy was a whole tier filled with thanks and exvotos, the awesome museum of miracles, attesting to and proving the power of the patron saint.

At the same time that she was invoking a divine protection—Have I mercy, my Lord of Bomfim!—with an instinctive hereditary gesture, Manela joined in the ritual of the *ekedes,* the acolytes of possessed women who are under the care of the *orixas* who have revealed themselves. She took off her immaculate sash to wipe the sweat from Gildete's face; hands on hips, fists clenched, Oxala was muttering commands.

Manela began to sense the enormity of her transgression, the size of her sin—it couldn't have been greater, alas, it couldn't! She'd have to invent a plausible explanation, figure out an acceptable excuse that would restrain Aunt Adalgisa's pitiless arm and shut her cursing mouth—some insults wound deeper than a couple of slaps. It was normally difficult for Manela to get around her aunt, who was mistrustful and speculative, but sometimes Manela managed to convince her and escape a sermon, a bawling out, and the leather strap. Not that she was deceitful by nature, but in times of panic and humiliation, there was nothing she could do but lie. Worse still was when nothing came to mind, and all that was left for her to do was confess her error and ask forgiveness: I'm sorry, Auntie, I won't do it again, ever again. I swear by God, by the soul of my mother. Today, Manela knew, such an entreaty for forgiveness couldn't forestall punishment; the best it could do was soften it—and would that even be worthwhile?

Manela wiped Aunt Gildete's face, and without thinking, as if obeying orders—orders muttered by Oxala, perhaps—she followed Gildete through the entire triumphal dance of the enchanted one, commemorating his regained freedom—the end of his solitude and filth. She was getting dizzy, she felt a tingling in her arms and legs, she tried to keep her balance, was unable to, bent her body over, let herself go. As if in a dream, she saw herself as someone else, soaring in the air, and she realized that she didn't have to invent excuses or make up lies to tell her aunt because she wasn't

committing any crime, misdemeanor, or error, any sin. There was nothing to confess, no reason to beg forgiveness and deserve punishment. With a leap of freedom, Manela danced in front of Oxala, *Baba Oke,* father of the Sacred Hill of Bomfim—she and Aunt Gildete went on in front of the church in the midst of the cadenced clapping of the Baianas. How did she know those steps, where had she learned that dance, acquired those fundamentals? Sprightly and light-footed, standing up against captivity, guilt and fear no longer weighed on her shoulders.

Oxolufa, or Oxala the elder, the greatest of all, the father, came for her and embraced her and held her, hugging her against his chest, trembling and making her tremble. As he went off, he shouted quite loud so they would know: *"Eparrei!"* and the Baianas repeated, bowing before Manela: *"Eparrei!"*

Once this change had come over Manela, Yansan, who had been present, left as suddenly as she had come. She carried away all the accumulated filth, all that dirt, to bury in the jungle: hesitation and submission, ignominy and pretense, the fear of threats and shouts, of slaps in the face, of the leather strap hanging on the wall, and worst of all, the pleas for forgiveness. Oya had cleansed Manela's body and straightened out her head.

So it was that the fright and mortification that had overcome Manela when the bells marked the hour of noon were followed by complete release: Filled with joy, in the rejection of yoke and harness, Manela was reborn. That was how the waters of Oxala flowed on that Bomfim Thursday. They had put out the fires of hell, *axé.*

The *Coup de Foudre*

On that Bomfim Thursday, under the scalding and luminous January sun, at the end of the washing ceremony, Manela met Miro.

It was a *coup de foudre,* as Adalgisa's dear and esteemed neighbor, Professor Joao Batista de Lima e Silva, familiar with the French language and its literature, would have said upon learning about the case. But it was love at first sight only as far as Manela was concerned, because if one could believe Miro, he'd had his eye on her for some time and was only waiting for a chance to state his intentions.

Manela was busy on the steps of the church, scattering scented water over the delirious crowd—*filhas de santo* in trance were receiving *orixas;* seventeen Oxalas were hanging about the entrance, ten Oxolufas, and seven Oxaguinhas— when she heard someone say her name, calling her insistently:

"Manela! Manela! Look, here I am!"

She looked and she saw him, squeezed in along the steps, his pleading eyes fastened on her. His open mouth displayed white teeth against his black face, and unbelievable as it might seem in that horrible crush, his feet were dancing a *samba.* Manela leaned over and emptied the last drops from her clay jar over the big-mouth's kinky hair. His hair was combed out in an Afro, a symbol of the world struggle against racism made popular by American Black Panthers. Manela couldn't remember seeing him before, but what difference did that make?

Miro reached out his hand and said:
"Come."

Racism in a Racialized Democracy and Support for Affirmative Action Policy in Salvador and São Paulo, Brazil

By Gladys Mitchell-Walthour

University affirmative-action policies in Brazil have come under attack from a number of scholars who believe the program is inappropriate for Brazil's multiracial population. Peter Fry et al.'s *Dangerous Divisions: Racial Politics in Contemporary Brazil* (2007) includes a number of opinion pieces by both scholars and activists against university affirmative action. On the other hand, sociologists such as Antonio Guimarães (2001) and Sales Augusto dos Santos (2006) support the programs. North American scholar Seth Racusen (2010) proposes a novel approach with a schema that would consider both class and race in university affirmative action. Much of the debate focuses on Brazilian racial identity and why the policy is inappropriate. There is also a focus on class, and the fact that Brazil's primary and secondary public schools are inadequate, and most of those attending these schools are Afro-Brazilian. For this reason, opponents of affirmative action believe resources should be allocated to improving public schools rather than supporting university affirmative action.

What is lost in most scholarship concerned with affirmative action is an examination of political opinions of those who would potentially benefit from such policies. This chapter examines determinants of Afro-Brazilian support of affirmative action. I focus on respondents in Salvador and São Paulo. My hypothesis is that Afro-Brazilians who believe blacks (*negros*) face difficulties in society due to racism and discrimination claim a black identification, and the highly educated are more likely to support affirmative-action policy than those who do not acknowledge racism as a major problem for blacks, who claim nonblack identifications, and are less educated. Previous research has shown that Afro-Brazilians who claim a black identification are more likely to vote for black candidates (G. Mitchell 2010a), and that those who identify as a black racial group tend to vote for black candidates (G. Mitchell 2009). Because Black Movement activists tend to be middle-class (Hanchard 1994; Burdick 1998), I believe those with higher education will support the policy more than those with lower education. The alternative hypothesis is that Afro-Brazilians with higher levels of education are more likely not to support affirmative-action policies than those with lower levels of education. Perhaps people with higher education believe they were success-ful based on merit, and that merit only should be considered for university admission rather than one's racial background. In fact, Stanley R. Bailey and Edward E. Telles (2006) find that among *negros* (*pretos* and *pardos*) and *brancos* there is less support for quotas in employment and in universities as education increases. Those with higher education are less likely to support affirmative action than those with lower education. Bailey and Telles use large-scale survey data collected in 2000 in the state of Rio de Janeiro.

Gislene Aparecida dos Santos's (2008) interviews reveal that Afro-Brazilian high school students are less supportive of affirmative-action programs for Afro-Brazilians, and most prefer that the policy be class-based. However, she also finds that Afro-Brazilian university students, through outreach, encourage Afro-Brazilian high school students to consider university admission under affirmative-action programs because it is a right granted to them as citizens. These students oftentimes begin to claim a black identification after attending university. Andrew Francis and Turrini-Pinto (2009) find that at the University of Brasilia, candidates for admission misrepresent their color to be considered for university affirmative action. However, using a survey, Bailey (2008) finds that nearly half of racially mixed Brazilians would choose white over black racial classifications if forced to choose one. He also finds that using photographs where respondents can determine if an individual is eligible for quotas for blacks (*negros*), most respondents do not believe those of lighter and medium skin tones deserve inclusion in the quotas. In fact, for the photographs of individuals with medium skin tone, 60 percent of mulattos do not find them deserving of quota inclusion. Nonetheless, Bailey also finds that in an experiment, simply mentioning a racial policy for *negros* increases the percentage of those identifying as such. These findings appear counterintuitive, but I believe that as in the University of Brasília case, when faced with the real-life choice of benefiting from affirmative action, some candidates for university admission will in fact change or misrepresent

their identification to benefit from the program. I do not intend to contribute to the literature on changing racial identification to benefit from affirmative action. Rather, I am interested in the determinants of support for affirmative action among Afro-Brazilians, and hope to contribute to social-science literature on political opinion and behavior of Afro-Brazilians.

This chapter focuses on Afro-Brazilians in Salvador and São Paulo, Brazil, exclusively. I examine whether support of affirmative-action policy is related to sociodemographic factors such as Afro-Brazilians' educational level, age, gender, income, color identification, and opinions about the major problems blacks (*negros*) face in Brazil. Presumably, respondents attributing blacks' problems to racism and discrimination might support racial policies aimed at reducing discrimination. Juliet Hooker, in *Race and the Politics of Solidarity* (2009), notes that political solidarity is racialized and shaped by race despite the fact that scholars of multicultural theories often do not discuss racialized solidarity. In the case of the United States, there are huge disparities between whites' and blacks' political opinions regarding racial injustice and racial inequality, Hooker posits that there are also differences in support for racial policies because of differential sympathy. She states, "As a result of racialization, the pain and suffering of nonwhites are either rendered invisible or, when visible, are seen as less deserving of empathy and redress than those of whites (2009, 40). While Hooker's work is largely theoretical and focuses on Afro-descended and indigenous communities in Nicaragua, her point regarding empathy and solidarity is well taken. This chapter only focuses on Afro-descendants and does not presume solidarity. On the contrary, I assume differences exist among Afro-Brazilians in terms of racial identification and political opinion. Examining responses about the major problem of blacks allows me to analyze differential sympathy, especially when noted by acknowledging difficulties blacks face because of race rather than simply class. More importantly, I will examine how a respondent's opinion about the major problem of blacks and sociodemographic factors impact their support for affirmative action. Throughout this chapter Afro-Brazilians are synonymous with Afro-descendants. All survey respondents identify as Afro-descendants, although they self-identify as belonging to various color or racial categories.

Race, Racism, and Racial Politics in Brazil

In the past, Brazilians viewed their country as distinct from the United States because of conceptions of race and racism. American racism is viewed as explicit, whereas Brazilian racism and discrimination are characterized as hidden and less clear because of class inequality and a racially mixed population. Social relations in Brazil appear to be fairly integrated and racially harmonious among racial groups (Telles 2004). Edward Telles (2004) notes in his explanation of vertical and horizontal relations that there are huge gaps in educational attainment, income, and mortality rates between white Brazilians and nonwhite Brazilians; yet social relations appear to be racially integrated or less rigid in terms of intermarriage and residential segregation than in the United States and South Africa. Brazilian racism has been documented by various scholars, such as Florestan Fernandes's (1965) UNESCO-sponsored research documenting racial inequality in the 1950s; Carlos Hasenbalg's (1978) research showing differences in social mobility by race in the late 1970s; France Winddance Twine's (1998) anthropological research on racism in the 1990s; and Michael Mitchell and Charles Wood's (1998) work on police abuse of browns and blacks. Such research, along with Black Movement activists who have long acknowledged racism in Brazilian society, proves that Brazil has not been immune to racism in its society.

Traditionally, white Brazilian political elites promoted the idea that Brazil was a racial democracy where racism did not exist, because of its mixed-race citizenry; however, today the idea of racial democracy is often referred to as a myth among scholars and activists. Brazilian racial politics have changed dramatically. Affirmative-action

policies in universities were first implemented in 2001. Federal Law 10.639/03, passed in 2003, requires public schools to teach African and Afro-Brazilian history. Black Movement activists supported and pushed for such policies, while at the same time encouraging Afro-Brazilians to embrace blackness. In addition, Black Movement activism has expanded the traditional boundaries of volunteer organizations and are now formal nongovernmental and nonprofit organizations (S. Santos 2010), nontraditional routes of activism are present in hip-hop organizations and activity (Reiter and Mitchell 2010; S. Santos 2010; Pardue 2004), "prevestibular" courses also serve as avenues for disseminating racial consciousness (S. Santos 2010), and political campaigns serve as a means of mobilization and teaching racial consciousness (G. Mitchell 2009). Given that much of the work of Black Movement activism continues to push for affirmative-action policies and encourage Afro-Brazilians to embrace blackness and contemporary activism, and is disseminated in these nontraditional ways, one must ask, how do Afro-Brazilians perceive such programs? Do they embrace a black identification, and does this impact their support for affirmative action? Does acknowledging racism as a problem blacks face, as opposed to simply a class problem, result in differential support for affirmative-action policies? This chapter seeks to answer these questions. Before my analysis, I briefly review the literature on Brazilian racial politics. Second, I define key terms such as racism, and racial and color identification. Lastly, I follow with analyses of my quantitative study.

Current Literature

The goal of this chapter is not to outline the specifics of affirmative-action policies throughout Brazil, nor do I seek to give a thorough review of scholarship on affirmative action. Rather, I situate my work in research on Brazilian politics and political behavior, and research on racial attitudes and racial politics. On the one hand, scholars do not consider race as significant to Brazilian politics (von Metteinheim 1986; Hagopian 1996; Mainwaring et al. 2000). On the other hand, racial politics and the role of race in Brazilian politics have been studied since the 1970s (de Souza 1971; M. Mitchell 1977, 2007; Pereira 1982; Soares and Silva 1987; Valente 1986; Câstro 1993; Hanchard 1994; Prandi 1996; Oliviera 1997, 2007; Johnson 1998, 2006; Nobles 2000; S. Santos 2000; Guimarães 2001; Telles 2004; Bailey 2009). My research contributes to this body of work with the hope of broadening knowledge on political opinion, racial identification, and racial attitudes of Afro-Brazilians.

Ethnographic and sociological scholarship differs in findings concerning black group identity. Robin Sheriff (2001), in her ethnographic work in a slum community in Rio de Janeiro, finds that Afro-Brazilians essentially have a bipolar view of race as white and black, but use various color gradations to soften the effect of color. In an effort to be polite, color gradations are used to describe a person, rather than the term "black." Stanley Bailey (2009) claims that racial group identity does not exist among Afro-Brazilians. Citing the 2002 PESP survey in which only 7 percent of respondents chose to self-classify as *negro*, Bailey concludes that "Brazil clearly lacks the sense of black racial group membership and many of the types of participation in antiracism found in the U.S. context (2009, 121)." Drawing from a 2000 racial-attitudes study conducted in the state of Rio de Janeiro, Bailey finds little difference in color categories between whites and Afro-Brazilians who agree that the *negro* movement is right, and that prejudice must be the object of a struggle to overcome it (126). He finds that *pretos* are most willing to participate in antiracism activities (127), and that *morenos* and whites differ significantly from browns, *pretos*, *negros*, and all others in the choice of "a lot" over "no" in willingness to become a member of an antiracism organization (131). Bailey notes this difference, and posits that differences between *moreno* attitudes and other Afro-Brazilian attitudes toward the *negro* movement may serve as a barrier for mobilization. Because the focus of these findings is to show that white and "nonwhite" Brazilian racial attitudes are not distinctly different, in contrast to clear differences between whites and blacks in the United States, there is no exclusive focus on Afro-Brazilians. I hope to contribute to the growing body of work on racial attitudes by exclusively focusing on Afro-Brazilians and trends within cities, using city surveys rather than state and national surveys. These trends may not be revealed in state and national surveys.

Key Terms

"Color" and "racial identification" refer to the color or racial group a respondent self-identifies as, Brubaker and Cooper (2000) note the processual nature of identification, making this term preferable to identity. In this article, *preto* and *negro* are considered separate categories. *Preto* is considered a color category, while *negro* is considered a politically charged racial category. Because *negro* was and continues to be promoted by the Black Movement, it is politically charged. Mainstream media use the term *negro* as the sum of *pardos* and *pretos*; however, I consider it a racialized identification because of its historical usage.

As Melissa Nobles (2000) demonstrates, during specific time periods political elites, academics, and census officials were motivated to use the census to further their political agendas, and at other times they were not. The addition of more mixed-race categories helped political elites empirically show that Brazil was becoming less black and more white. This was important as Brazil searched for a national identity in the early twentieth century. In contrast, political activists involved in the Black Movement pushed for a change of the color categories for the 2000 census. They were concerned with the use of the term *pardo*. They preferred that *moreno* be used in place of *pardo*. *Moreno* is used more in social settings than *pardo*, so members of the Black Movement believed more people would choose this term. The Brazilian Institute of Geography and Statistics (IBGE) did not replace *pardo* with *moreno*. In the most recent (2000) census, categories include white, black (*preto*), brown (*pardo*), yellow, and indigenous. In sum, it is important to note that categorization depends on political agendas and *who* categorizes. At different historical periods, white political elites categorized and constructed race to further their political and social agendas (Nobles 2000). On the other hand, Afro-Brazilian activists also had political agendas and wanted to identify people of African descent in ways that were politically beneficial to their agenda. My study relies on self-identification in an open-ended question that can be especially revealing considering the Black Movement's goals.

Racism and *racial discrimination* throughout the article are synonymous terms. Racism is negative differential treatment or perceptions of people based on one's perceived color or racial categorization of that individual. Telles (2004) documents racial inequality in occupational mobility, income, and educational attainment due to racial discrimination. He also discusses how discrimination operates as negative stereotypes in the Brazilian context. Negative stereotypes of blacks are often disseminated as humor through jokes in daily life (154), and in the media, blacks and browns are virtually nonexistent. When they do appear, they are portrayed with certain behaviors while whites are seen as beautiful, happy, and middle-class (155). In schools, teachers give more preference to lighter children and invest more in them (158).

Statistical comparisons of infant mortality show that in 2005, infant mortality was higher for blacks and browns than whites: 24.4 percent for *pretas* and *pardas*, and 23.7 percent for *brancas* (Paixão and Carvano 2008, 38). In 2006 the number of whites attending university was over four times the number of blacks and browns attending university (81). Despite inequalities in health and education, some argue that these are class inequalities. This is often the argument made in debates about university affirmative action. Those against affirmative action believe that public school education should be improved because poorer children attend such schools. Yet, Paixão and Carvano (2008) show that *pretos* and *pardos* who have finished college are 1.2 times

more likely to be unemployed compared to whites with the same schooling. This difference can be attributed to racial discrimination.

Racism is explicitly practiced as police brutality—a problem Afro-Brazilians face. Michael Mitchell and Charles H. Wood (1998) find that the likelihood of assault by police officers on men increases depending on skin color and age. Younger black and brown men are more likely to be assaulted by the police than whites. Although income and education decrease one's chance of assault, it is important to note color differences. The darker one's skin color, the higher likelihood of assault by police officers. In my study, I am concerned with whether or not respondents cite discrimination as a hindrance in blacks' lives rather than simply acknowledging class barriers.

Methodology

I rely on an original survey carried out in Salvador and São Paulo, Brazil, in 2006. The survey has 674 respondents. Salvador is located in the northeast, a poor region, and is known as the "mecca" of Afro-Brazilian culture. It is nearly 70 percent African-descendant. São Paulo is in the south, a wealthier region of Brazil. Its population is nearly 30 percent African-descendant. According to the 2000 census, 20 percent of Salvador's population considered themselves *preto*. In São Paulo, 5 percent considered themselves *preto*. Black Movement activity has occurred in São Paulo since the 1930s (Hanchard 1994; Covin 2006), making it an interesting site of comparison. São Paulo is also home to the first university specifically for African descendants in Latin America.

In consultation with experts in survey methods from the Federal University of Bahia (UFBA), I chose the Salvador neighborhoods Federação, Peri peri, and Itapoãn. Federação is socioeconomically heterogeneous.[1] Part of the campus of UFBA, a prestigious public university, is located in Federação, which includes middle-class households. There are also very low-income households. Itapoãn is also socioeconomically diverse, but has a large proportion of low-income households. Peri peri is located in the suburbs. It is a low-income neighborhood. It is relatively easy to find African descendants in these neighborhoods. A total of 346 interviews were conducted in Salvador. Brazilian undergraduate students conducted interviews. They were trained in interviewing methods. Interviewers in São Paulo were affiliated with a student group that focuses on racial issues. All interviewers in São Paulo self-identify as *negro/a*. In Salvador, one interviewer self-identifies as white, one as *parda*, and the others identify as *negra*. Interviewers told potential interviewees that the study was with Afro-descendants and asked if any lived in the household. The respondent ultimately determined their selection to participate in the study. The survey does not include respondents who are self-identified whites *and* who were identified as white by interviewers. Thus when reporting results, white Afro-descendants are those who self-identified as white but were not identified as such by interviewers. Unlike large-scale Brazilian national surveys that include whites, *pretos*, and *pardos*, this survey is restricted to Afro-descendants in select neighborhoods.

In São Paulo, along with experts of research on race in Brazil, I identified neighborhoods with high populations of Afro-descendants, but that were also socioeconomically diverse. Neighborhoods chosen were Cidade Tiradentes, Casa Verde, Brasilândia, Campo Limpo, and Capão Redondo. Cidade Tiradentes is a low-income neighborhood located in the far east of São Paulo. Casa Verde is mostly middle-class in the northeast of São Paulo. Campo Limpo is located in the southwest and is known for its large social divisions. Capâo Redondo is located on the periphery in the south. I obtained neighborhood maps from the Institute of Brazilian Geography and Statistics (IBGE) in São Paulo, and randomization was introduced by randomly selecting streets where students conducted face-to-face interviews, and through interviewer selection. A total of 328 interviews were conducted.

Students were assigned to at least two neighborhoods. Randomization was also introduced as interviewers used a skip-number method and conducted interviews at every fifth house, or third house if the street did not contain many houses. Respondents were of voting age. Voting is mandatory for those who are 18 to 70 years old. However, citizens can begin voting at the age of 16. A total of 674 interviews were conducted in Salvador and São Paulo.

Selection Bias

Since 2007, blacks and browns have outnumbered whites, and this was due to an increase in Afro-Brazilians identifying as black (*preto*). Nonetheless, nationally most Afro-Brazilians identify as brown (*pardo*). In the 2000 census, 45 percent of the population identified as white, 39 percent as brown, 6 percent as black, and less than 1 percent as yellow or indigenous. In Salvador, in the census, 66 percent of the population consider themselves black or brown. In São Paulo, 30 percent of the population consider themselves black (*preto*) and brown (*pardo*). In both cities, most Afro-Brazilians consider themselves brown. It is impossible to know how many Afro-Brazilians self-identify as white. My Salvador and São Paulo samples are biased because of the large number of respondents identifying as black (*preto* or *negro*).

These biases are accounted for because my sample includes a significant percentage of young people. Livio Sansone (2004) finds that younger people self-identify more as black. Stanley R. Bailey and Edward E. Telles (2006) find that younger and educated people are more likely to choose the *negro* category than older people. People with higher education are more likely to choose the *negro* category rather than the *moreno* category (Bailey and Telles 2006). They claim that for younger people, *negro* is associated with a modern identity that is influenced by black American culture dispersed by music. They also concur that educated Afro-Brazilians claiming the *negro* identity are more exposed to black activists' rhetoric than those who are less educated. This rhetoric encourages a collective black identity. Although my sample is biased, the study is especially useful as respondents were able to freely choose a color or racial identification without being restricted to census categories. This survey is not generalizable to the country of Brazil, because it is restricted to neighborhoods in the cities of Salvador and São Paulo. The survey is intended to add to existing literature restricted to other states or local communities.

Telles (2004) finds that the black and brown isolation index from whites in neighborhoods in Salvador is 82, which is close to Chicago's index of 83—Chicago being the most segregated city in the United States. An index of 100 indicates full isolation from whites. However, in the Salvador case, this is due to the large population of blacks rather than housing discrimination as present in the United States. This result is telling because it highlights the fact that neighborhoods in my Salvador sample are quite representative of Afro-descendant neighborhoods, considering that most black and brown neighborhoods are isolated from white neighborhoods. The segregation index for São Paulo is only 37, and the population percentage of blacks and browns is 25 percent (Telles 2004, 203). However, it must be again noted that isolation indexes are affected by the population percentage. Telles also shows that, with the exception of five districts, the districts in the center of São Paulo city are mostly white, and almost all of them are less than 16 percent black and brown (199). Larger percentages of blacks and browns are found in districts in the periphery, where most of my survey interviews were conducted, making the survey useful in highlighting racial-opinion dynamics in such neighborhoods.

Descriptive Results of the 2006 Survey

Color and Race

Negro is a racial category. *Preto* is a color category denoting black, and *pardo* denotes brown or mixed-race people. *Moreno* is a term that Brazilians of all colors may identify as, and includes dark-skinned and light-skinned people with tans. Respondents were asked to identify their color in an open-ended and closed-ended question. In the open-ended question, they could identify in a color category with no choices given. In the closed-ended question, they were asked to choose a census color category. The census categories in the 2000 census were white (*branco*), brown (*pardo*), black (*preto*), yellow (*amarelo*), and indigenous (*indígena*). Yellow denotes people of Asian descent. Considering the open-ended color categories in both cities, 2 percent of Afro-Brazilians identified as white, 62 percent as black (*preto, negro, negão*), and 36 percent as brown (*mulato, moreno, pardo, moreno claro, marrom*). In my surveys, in both cities, more Afro-Brazilians chose a "brown" color or racial category in the open-ended question than interviewers classified them as (see table 22.1). In Salvador, interviewers classified 102 respondents as brown (*pardo*), whereas 121 respondents identified themselves as brown (*mulato, moreno, pardo, moreno claro, marrom*). In São Paulo, interviewers classified 119 respondents as brown and 143 respondents identified themselves as brown (*mulato, moreno, pardo, moreno claro, moreno escuro, moreno jambo, marrom*). There is a tendency to identify as brown because it acknowledges racial mixture, part of Brazil's national identity. I consider *marrom, moreno*, and *pardo* brown color categories. *Moreno claro* translates as light brown. The English translation of *moreno escuro* and *moreno jambo* is dark brown. *Mulato* is mixed-race. Table 22.1 gives the results in absolute numbers of respondents identifying in the open-ended and close-ended questions and how they were classified by the interviewer. I focus on respondents' self-identification in the open-ended question.

Overall, the color and racial category most claimed was black (*preto* and *negro*). Considering the open-ended color categories, the Afro-Brazilian sample in Salvador is made up of 2 percent of Afro-Brazilians who identified as white, 62 percent who identified as black (*preto, negro, negão*), and 36 percent who claimed some type of brown (*mulato, moreno, pardo, moreno claro,*

Table 22.1. Number of Afro-Brazilian Respondents Self-Identified in Census And Open Color Categories; and Respondents Classified in Census Color Categories by Interviewers

Salvador

Census Category	Open-Ended Color Category	Interviewer Classified Census Color Category			
White (*branco*)	12	White (*branco*)	8	White (*branco*)	2
Black (*preto*)	208	Black (*negro, negão,* preto*)	210	Black (*preto*)	230
Brown (*pardo*)	104	Brown (*mulato, moreno, pardo, moreno claro, moreno*)	121	Brown (*pardo*)	102
Other	6	Other		Other	0

São Paulo

Census Category	Open-Ended Color Category	Interviewer Classified Census Color Category			
White (*branco*)	21	White (*branco*)	20	White (*branco*)	4
Black (*preto*)	141	Black (*negro, negão,* preto*)	150	Black (*preto*)	191
Brown (*pardo*)	131	Brown (*mulato, moreno, pardo, moreno claro, moreno escuro, moreno jambo marrom*)	143	Brown (*pardo*)	119
Other	0	Other	3	Other	3

*Negão literally means big black or really black. In Brazilian Portuguese, one can emphasize that an object or person is large by adding *ão* to the word: thus *negro* becomes *negão*.

Table 22.2. Monthly Family Income in Salvador and São Paulo (%)

	Salvador	São Paulo
No income	3	3
< 2 times the minimum salary* (R$700)	40	26
2 to 5 times the minimum salary (R$700–1,750)	44	46
5 to 10 times the minimum salary (R$1,750–3,000)	12	22
10 to 20 times the minimum salary (R$3,500–7,000)	1	3
Total	100	100

*The minimum monthly salary is R$350. Rather than an hour minimum wage, in Brazil one considers minimum monthly salary.

marrom) identification. Considering the open-ended color categories in São Paulo, 6 percent of Afro-Brazilians self-identified as white (*branco*), 47 percent identified as black (*preto, negro, negão*), 45 percent identified as brown (*mulato, moreno, pardo, moreno claro, moreno escuro, moreno jambo,* and *marrom*), and 2 percent identified as "other." In both cities, the number of blacks (*pretos*) interviewers classified as such exceeds the number of self-identified blacks (*pretos* and *negros*). Afro-Brazilians identifying as brown have fundamentally different political behavior than those who identify as black (G. Mitchell 2009). This leads to my conclusion that Afro-Brazilians identifying as black may be more likely to support affirmative-action policy than those who self-identify in nonblack categories. I note these are the categories respondents chose for the survey and in everyday life; color categories can change by the minute depending on a person's social situation.

Gender, Education, Income, and Age

In Salvador, 52 percent of respondents were male and 48 percent female. In São Paulo, 57 percent were female and 43 percent were male. In both cities, the average age was 33. In Salvador, respondents ages ranged from 17 to 67, and in São Paulo, from 16 to 83.

Educationally, 45 percent of the sample in Salvador and 36 percent of the sample in São Paulo had some high school education or had finished high school. In Salvador, 15 percent did not complete middle school, and in São Paulo, 24 percent did not. There were 19 percent of respondents in Salvador and 14 percent in São Paulo who were pre-college. In Salvador, 40 percent of respondents had a monthly family income of two minimum salaries or R\$700 (approximately \$350 USD).[2] I consider this low-income. About 44 percent of the sample had an average family income of R\$700 to R\$1,750 (\$350 to \$875 USD) per month. Only 13 percent of the sample had a high monthly family income, ranging from R\$1,750 to R\$7,000 (\$1,875 to \$3,500 USD) (see table 22.2). In São Paulo, 26 percent of respondents had a monthly family income of approximately R\$700 (approximately \$350 USD), 46 percent had a monthly family income between R\$700 and R\$1,750 (\$350 and \$875 USD), and 25 percent had a monthly family income between R\$1,750 and R\$7,000 (\$875 and \$3,500 USD). Although the sample in São Paulo was less educated than the Salvador sample, they earned more money—likely due to it being a more developed city. Now that I have examined descriptive statistics of relevant variables of the data, I turn to my analysis.

Logistic Regression Analysis

Hypothesis and Variables

My hypothesis is that Afro-Brazilians who believe blacks (*negros*) face difficulties in society due to racism and discrimination, claim a black identification, and are highly educated are more likely to support affirmative-action policy than those who believe blacks' problems are due to social or class inequality, claim nonblack identifications, and are less educated. As stated earlier, previous research shows that Afro-Brazilians who identify as black are more likely to vote for black candidates. For this reason, it is likely that blacks would support racial policies for blacks. Presumably, Afro-Brazilians with higher incomes do not face class discrimination; thus it is plausible that when facing discrimination, they will attribute this to racial discrimination rather than class discrimination. Angela Figueiredo's (2010) work on middle-class Afro-Brazilians in Salvador show that they face racial discrimination but do not confront the perpetrators, because they simply believe these people have bad manners, and they do not want to cause problems for people less well off than themselves. Nonetheless, Figueiredo's work is illustrative of the fact that middle-class Afro-Brazilians face racial discrimination. It is likely that Afro-Brazilians with lower incomes will attribute discrimination to their class rather than race. Gladys Mitchell (2010b) finds that Afro-Brazilians who self-identify as *negro* and *preto* are more likely to claim they have experienced racism than those claiming nonblack identities. For this reason, it is possible that self-identifying as black will positively correlate with support of affirmative-action policies.

The alternative hypothesis is that Afro-Brazilians with higher levels of education are not more likely to support affirmative-action policies than those with lower levels of education. As noted earlier, Telles and Bailey (2002) find that among all color groups, support for affirmative action decreases as education increases. It is noteworthy that the survey they use was restricted to the state of Rio de Janeiro and was conducted in the year 2000, before the implementation of affirmative-action policies in universities.

To test my hypotheses, I use a logistic regression model. The dependent variable is support for affirmative action in employment and university admissions, and the independent variables are racial/color identification, gender, age, income, education, city, and opinion of the major problem of blacks (*negros*). The survey question regarding affirmative action states: "Affirmative action is a program that focuses on the problem of discrimination against blacks (*negros*) and browns (*pardos*). It encourages universities and workplaces to have a higher percentage of blacks and browns. Do you believe affirmative action programs are important?"[3] Respondents could answer yes or no. In the sample, 70 percent of respondents support affirmative action and 30 percent do not. Thus an overwhelming percentage of Afro-Brazilians in the Salvador and São Paulo samples support affirmative action.

Respondent ages were grouped in the following cohorts: 16–25; 26–40; 41–55; and 56 years and older. The variable city is a dichotomous variable and includes Salvador and São Paulo. The color/racial identification variable is how the respondent self-identifies in an open-ended question asking about their color or race. The categories are: white (*branco*), light brown (*moreno claro*), mixed-race (*mulato*), brown (*moreno, pardo, marrom*), dark brown (*moreno jambo*), the racial category black (*negro*), and the color category black (*preto*). The education categories are: did not complete middle school, completed middle school, some high school or completed high school, pre-college, in college or completed college, and graduate level education. The monthly family income categories are: zero; up to two minimum salaries or $350 USD; between two and five minimum salaries or between $350 and $875 USD; between five and ten minimum salaries or between $875 and $1,750 USD; and between ten and twenty minimum salaries or between $1,750 and $3,500 USD.

The independent variable, "major problem of blacks," is operationalized with the question "What do you think is the major problem of blacks

(*negros*)?" I grouped these responses into eight categories. Those categories are (1) racism/discrimination/prejudice/exclusion; (2) lack of opportunity/lack of opportunity to study; (3) racism or discrimination from blacks themselves/blacks do not vote for blacks; (4) lack of education, lack of money/low education/poverty/hunger/lack of places to live/not prepared; (5) before they did not have space, now they do; (6) social inequality; (7) lack of unity, lack of knowledge about black people, lack of consciousness; and (8) blacks are not interested/accustomed to their situation/ blacks do not like to study/lack of courage. These responses are quite telling, as some respondents blame blacks (*negros*) for their situation, while others blame racism or social inequality for the obstacles blacks face. Because of the open-ended format, answers are useful for examining if a respondent is sympathetic with blacks. Empathy can be demonstrated by acknowledging structural obstacles blacks face, rather than blaming victims of discrimination, or attributing difficulties blacks face to social inequalities.

Noteworthy is that most (50 percent) of the self-identified white Afro-Brazilian respondents cited a lack of education, lack of money, or poverty as the major problem of blacks. Most blacks and browns cited racism or discrimination as the major problem of blacks. About 36 percent of browns cited racism as the major problem of blacks, while 40 percent of *negros* cited racism. Roughly 43 percent of *pretos* cited discrimination as the major problem of blacks. Afro-Brazilians self-identifying as white were more likely to attribute black problems to class inequality, whereas most black and brown respondents discussed blacks' problems as racialized problems of racism and discrimination.

Pretos Versus *Negros*, And The Major Problem Of Blacks (*Negros*)

John Burdick (1998) noted that *pretos* as compared with *negros assumidos*, or Afro-descendants who later in life identified as black, more often recalled personal experiences of

Table 22.3. "Major Problem of Blacks" Cited by Self-Identified Negro and Preto Respondents in Salvador and São Paulo, Brazil.

Major Problem of Blacks	Negro	Preto
Racism/discrimination/prejudice/exclusion	40	43
Lack of unity, lack of knowledge about black people, lack of consciousness	5	7
Social inequality	1	0
Before they did not have space, now they do	7	7
Lack of education, lack of money/low education/poverty/hunger/lack of place to live	28	32
Racism or discrimination from blacks themselves/blacks don't vote for blacks	5	1
Lack of opportunity/lack of opportunity to study	11	6
Blacks aren't interested/accustomed to their situation/blacks don't like to study; lack of courage	3	3
Total	100%	100%

*Rounding affected the tally in this column.

racial discrimination. Slightly more *pretos* cite racism and discrimination as a major problem of blacks. About 43 percent of *pretos* cite discrimination and racism, and 40 percent of *negros* cite racism and discrimination as the major problem of blacks (see table 22.3). Some 32 percent of *pretos* cite either a lack of education or money, or poverty as the major problem of blacks, while 28 percent of *negros* cite these same problems. Thus there are slight differences between *pretos* and *negros* in explaining the difficulties blacks (*negros*) face, but they are not overwhelming differences. It is noteworthy that 1 percent of *negros* claimed that the major problem of blacks is social inequality, and no *pretos* cited social inequality. It is also noteworthy that 5 percent of *negros* claimed that the major problem of blacks

is racism from blacks, while only 1 percent of *pretos* claimed this.

Logistic Regression Analysis Results

I have discussed general trends of the independent variables. I now turn to my analysis. In the logistic regression model, support for affirmative action is the dependent variable, and the independent variables are age, city, gender, education, income, and the "major problem of blacks." In the logistic regression analysis, where support for affirmative action is the dependent variable, age, city, and opinion of the major problem of blacks are all statistically significant at the 99 percent confidence interval (see table 22.4). Income is

Table 22.4. Logistic Regression of Support for Affirmative Action (N 613)

Independent Variable	Coefficient	Standard Error
Age	−0.97	0.31
Gender	−0.20	0.18
City	−0.52	0.19
Color	0.22	0.38
Education	−0.32	0.45
Income	1.21	0.50
Black problems	0.74	0.28
Constant	0.60	0.42

statistically significant at the 95 percent confidence interval. As age increases, the likelihood a respondent will support affirmative action decreases. Afro-Brazilians in the age cohort of 16–25 years old are 78 percent likely to support affirmative action, holding the independent variables income, gender, city, education, color identification, and major problem of blacks constant (see table 22.5). Those in the age cohort of 26–40 years old are 73 percent likely to support affirmative action, holding income, gender, city, education, color identification, and major problem of blacks constant. This likelihood decreases to only 58 percent for those 56 years or older. Thus a respondent in the youngest cohort is 1.3 times more likely to support affirmative action than a respondent in the oldest cohort, holding income, gender, city, education, color identification, and major problem of blacks constant. It is likely that younger cohorts support affirmative action more than older cohorts because of their accommodation to the discourse of racism and the need for redress through racial policies. As noted earlier, the discourse of race in Brazil has significantly changed from denying racism to acknowledging racism in Brazilian society, and younger cohorts have been more exposed to the rhetoric of acknowledging racism than older cohorts.

Respondents in São Paulo are more likely to support affirmative action than respondents in Salvador. Holding the independent variables education, income, gender, age, color identification, and major problem of blacks constant, respondents in São Paulo are 77 percent likely to support affirmative action, as compared to those in Salvador, who are only 67 percent likely to support

the policy. I believe Afro-Brazilians in Salvador are less willing to support affirmative-action policies than respondents in São Paulo because the percentage of Afro-Brazilians in Salvador is more than double the percentage in São Paulo. As a result, racial dynamics in the two cities are different. There is a much larger white population in São Paulo. Because Salvador is overwhelmingly Afro-descendant, respondents may believe racial policies aimed at blacks (*negros*) are not needed in a city where they compose a majority of the population. In contrast, Afro-Brazilians in São Paulo are a minority, and thus may be more likely to acknowledge the need for racial policies for Afro-Brazilians. Much Black Movement activism began in São Paulo (Hanchard 1994), and São Paulo is home to South America's only university geared toward Afro-descendants. Thus activism has played a significant role in São Paulo despite the smaller percentage of Afro-descendants when compared to Salvador.

In this sample, education is not statistically significant; thus the alternative hypothesis that higher-educated respondents are more likely to oppose affirmative-action policy than lower-educated respondents is rejected. Although education is not statistically significant, income is. As income increases, the likelihood of support for affirmative action increases. Respondents who claim the major problem of blacks is discrimination are more likely to support affirmative action than respondents who believe the major problem of blacks is that they are accustomed to their situation, or that problems are due to social inequality. Thus my hypothesis is in part correct, but not entirely. Color or racial identification is

Table 22.5. Probability of Supporting Affirmative Action by Age Cohort (Income, Gender, City, Education, Color Identification, and "Major Problem of Blacks" Constant)

Age	Yes	No
16–25	0.78	0.22
26–40	0.73	0.27
41–55	0.66	0.34
56+	0.58	0.42

not statistically significant. This is surprising, yet one explanation is that the survey question asks if respondents support affirmative action for blacks (*negros*) and browns (*pardos*). In the mainstream media and among Black Movement activists, the term *negro* is used to denote blacks and browns. Using the term *negro* includes browns, in addition to their specific mention with the term *pardo* in the survey question. Using the term *preto* or *negro* without the mention of *pardo* would likely have yielded different results. In a similar vein, Bailey (2008) finds that simply mentioning a racial policy for blacks results in an increase in respondents identifying as such. Thus the racial or color terminology in the survey question can influence survey results.

As predicted, those with higher incomes are more likely to support affirmative action than those with lower incomes. I posit that Afro-Brazilians with higher incomes are more likely to interpret challenges in the workplace or in society as challenges due to their race or color, rather than their class, because class is less of an issue. In fact these data show that of those stating the major problem of blacks is racism, 44 percent have a monthly family income between $350 and $850 USD, or two to five times the minimum salary. Thirteen percent of those citing racism and discrimination have a monthly family income between $875 and $1,750 USD, or five and ten monthly salaries. Education is not statistically significant. This finding is in contrast to Bailey and Telles's (2006) finding that education has a

negative impact on support for affirmative action. This could be due to sample differences. A key difference is that my sample is restricted to Afro-Brazilians and limited to neighborhoods in Salvador and São Paulo. Telles and Bailey's data includes white, brown, and black Brazilians and is based on a state survey.

Fifty-nine percent of respondents who admit the major problem of blacks is racism and discrimination have monthly family incomes in the middle income category ($350 to $850 USD) and two highest income categories (see table 22.6). Only 4 percent of those claiming racism is the major problem of blacks come from the lowest income bracket of no earnings. However, 38 percent of those admitting racism is a major problem of blacks come from the next to lowest income bracket.

As predicted, respondents who cited racism or discrimination as a major problem of blacks, rather than blaming blacks or citing class inequality, had a higher predicted probability of supporting affirmative action (see table 22.7). Because many in the sample support affirmative-action policies, the predicted probabilities are high for all responses; yet there are some differences. Examples of responses that blame blacks are: racism or discrimination from blacks themselves, or blacks are not interested and are accustomed to their situation. In the first case, holding the variables age, gender, income, education, color identification, and city constant, the predicted probability of support for affirmative action for

Table 22.6. Percentage of Respondents Citing Racism and Discrimination as a Major Problem of Blacks (Negros), by Monthly Family Income Bracket

Income	Percent
No income	4
Up to $350 USD	38
$350 to $875 USD	44
$875 to $1,750 USD	13
$1,750 to $3,000 USD	2
Total	*100%*

Table 22.7. Predicted Probability of Supporting Affirmative Action Considering Responses to "Major Problem of Blacks" (Age, Gender, Income, Education, Color Identification, And City Constant)

Major Problem of Blacks	Predicted Probability of Support of Affirmative Action
Racism/discrimination/prejudice/exclusion	0.80
Lack of unity, lack of knowledge about black people, lack of consciousness	0.75
Social inequality	0.73
Before they did not have space, now they do	0.71
Lack of education, lack of money/low education/poverty/hunger/lack of places to live	0.69
Racism or discrimination from blacks themselves/blacks don't vote for blacks	0.66
Lack of opportunity/lack of opportunity to study	0.64
Blacks aren't interested/accustomed to their situation/blacks don't like to study; lack of courage	0.62

a respondent who believes the major problem of blacks is racism from blacks themselves is 0.66. Similarly the predicted probability for a respondent who claims blacks are not interested or are accustomed to their situation is 0.62. This is the lowest predicted probability of support for affirmative action of all responses. In contrast, holding the variables age, gender, income, education, color identification, and city constant, the predicted probability of support for affirmative action for a respondent who claims the major problem of blacks is racism and discrimination is 0.80. This lends credence to my hypothesis that respondents sympathetic to blacks (*negros*) by admitting the barrier of racial exclusion are more likely to support affirmative-action policies than those blaming victims of discrimination for the problems they face. Similarly, the predicted probability of support for affirmative action for a respondent who claims that blacks' problems are due to social inequality is 0.73, while the predicted probability of support is only 0.69 for those who claim blacks' problems are due to poverty or a lack of education. These results are demonstrative of the role that acknowledging racism as a problem of blacks, or claiming these problems are simply class-based problems play on support for affirmative-action policies.

Age, City, Income, Major Problem of Blacks, and Support for Affirmative Action

To highlight the interaction of the independent variables age, city, income, and the major problem of blacks, which are all statistically significant in a logistic regression model where support for affirmative action is the dependent variable, I examine predicted probabilities. Holding the variables gender, color identification, and education constant, the predicted probability of supporting affirmative action for a respondent in the oldest age cohort (56 years and older) in Salvador with no income who believes the major problem of blacks is that blacks are not interested or are accustomed to their situation is only 0.28 percent. In contrast, holding the independent variables gender, education, and color identification constant, the predicted probability of support of affirmative action by a respondent in the youngest age cohort (16–25 years old) in the city of São Paulo, in the highest income bracket that admits the major problem of blacks is racism, is 0.92. This is a difference of 0.64. Thus the respondent in Sao Paulo in the youngest age cohort, highest income bracket admitting the major problem of blacks is racism is 3.3 times more likely than a Salvador respondent in the lowest income bracket who blames blacks for their problems to support affirmative action.

Conclusion

In this chapter, I find that Afro-Brazilian respondents in São Paulo are more likely than respondents in Salvador to support affirmative-action policies. I also find that younger respondents are more likely to support the policy than older respondents, and that as income increases, the likelihood that a respondent will support affirmative action increases. Beyond these demographic variables, an important finding is that Afro-Brazilian respondents who cite racism and discrimination as a major problem of blacks are more likely to support affirmative action than those citing social inequality or who blame Afro-Brazilians for their problems by claiming they are accustomed to their situations.

Scholars studying political opinion and racial attitudes of Afro-Brazilians cannot assume that racial solidarity leads to overwhelming support of affirmative-action policy. Yet it is important to consider that changing racial politics in Brazil may influence Afro-Brazilians to acknowledge racism in Brazilian society. While Brazil is a multiracial society seeking redress for the ills of racism, it is important to note how potential beneficiaries of policies aimed at them interpret these programs. It is ultimately up to individual Afro-Brazilians to interpret exclusion against them in society. As Afro-Brazilians increasingly acknowledge the role of both racial and class discrimination rather than simply class discrimination, it is likely they will support and seek the implementation of such programs.

Notes

1. The author thanks the following for their assistance in Brazil: Edson Arruda, Paula Barreto, Magda Lorena, Cloves Oliveira, Leon Padial, Rosana Paiva, Jacqueline Romio, Kledir Salgado, Thabatha Silva, Gislene Santos, Darlene Sousa, Ricardo Summers, Jaqueline Santos, Gabriela Watson, Neusa, and Gloria Ventapane.

2. For an idea of the class standing of respondents, I report average monthly family incomes for various occupations. My statistical analyses concern monthly family income, which combines all incomes of those working in the household. A maid has a monthly family income of 386 *reais*, a bus driver of 964 *reais*, an engineer of 5,246 *reais*, and a construction worker 637 *reais* (www.worldsalaries.org/brazil.shtml).

3. Ação afirmativa é um programa que enfoca o problema da discriminação contra negros e pardos. Ela tenta incentivar que nas universidades e no trabalho tenha uma porcentagem maior de negros e pardos. Você acredita que programas de ação afirmativa são importantes?

References

Bailey, Stanley R. 2008. "Unmixing for Race Making in Brazil." *American Journal of Sociology* 114(3):577–614.

———. 2009. *Legacies of Race: Identities, Attitudes, and Politics in Brazil.* Palo Alto, CA: Stanford University Press.

Bailey, Stanley R. and Edward E. Telles. 2006. "Multiracial vs. Collective Black Categories: Census Classification Debates in Brazil." Ethnicities 6(1): 74–101.

Brubaker, Rogers, and Frederick Cooper. 2000. "Beyond 'Identity.'" *Theory and Society* 29.

Burdick, John. 1998. "The Lost Constituency of Brazil's Black Movements." *Latin American Perspectives* 25:136–155.

Castro, Mônica. 1993. "Raça e comportamento político." *Dados* 36:469–491.

Covin, David. 2006. *Unified Black Movement in Brazil, 1978–2002.* Jefferson, NC: McFarland & Company.

Fernandes, Florestan. 1965. *A integração do negro na sociedade de classes.* São Paulo: Dominus Editora.

Figuereido, Angela. 2010. "Out of Place: The Experience of the Black Middle Class." In *Brazil's New Racial Politics*, ed. Bernd Reiter and Gladys Mitchell. Boulder, CO: Lynne Rienner Publishers.

Francis, Andrew, and Maria Tannuri-Pinto. 2009. *Using Brazil's Racial Continuum to Examine the Short-Term Effects of Affirmative Action in Higher Education.* Unpublished manuscript.

Fry, Peter, Yvonne Maggie, Marcos Chor Maio, Simone Monteiro, Ricardo V. Santos. 2007. *Divisões perigosas: Políticas raciais no Brasil contemporâneo.* 1st ed. Rio de Janeiro: Civilização Brasileira.

Guimarães, Antonio Sergio. 2001. "The Race Issue in Brazilian Politics (The Last Fifteen Years)." Fifteen Years of Democracy in Brazil Conference. University of London, London, England, 15–16 February.

Hagopian, Francis. 1996. *Traditional Politics and Regime Change in Brazil.* New York: Cambridge University Press.

Hanchard, Michael. 1994. *Orpheus and Power: The Movimento Negro of Rio de Janeiro and São Paulo, Brazil, 1945–1988.* Princeton, NJ: Princeton University Press.

Hasenbalg, Carlos. 1978. "Race Relations in Post-Abolition Brazil: The Smooth Preservation of Racial Inequalities." PhD dissertation, University of California, Berkeley.

Hooker, Juliet. 2009. *Race and the Politics of Solidarity.* New York: Oxford University Press.

Johnson III, Ollie. 1998. "Racial Representation and Brazilian Politics: Black Members of the National Congress, 1983–1999." *Journal of Interamerican Studies and World Affairs* 40:97–118.

———. 2006. "Locating Blacks in Brazilian Politics: Afro-Brazilian Activism, New Political Parties, and Pro-Black Public Policies." *International Journal of Africana Studies* 12: 170–193.

Mainwaring, Scott, et al. 2000. "Conservative Parties, Democracy, and Economic Reform in Contemporary Brazil." In *Conservative Parties, the Right, and Democracy in Latin America*, by Kevin Mid-dlebrook, 164–222. Baltimore: Johns Hopkins University Press.

Mitchell, Gladys. 2009. "Black Group Identity and Vote Choice in Brazil." *Opinião Pública* 15(2).

———. 2010a. "Politicizing Blackness: Afro-Brazilian Color Identification and Candidate Preference." In *Brazil's New Racial Politics*, ed. Bernd Reiter and Gladys Mitchell. Boulder, CO: Lynne Rienner Publishers.

———. 2010b. "Racism and Brazilian Democracy: Two Sides of the Same Coin?" *Ethnic and Racial Studies* 33(10).

Mitchell, Michael. 1977. "Racial Consciousness and the Political Attitudes and Behavior of Blacks in São Paulo, Brazil." PhD dissertation, Indiana University.

———. 2007. "Race and Democracy in Brazil: The Racial Factor in Public Opinion." Paper presented at the National Conference of Black Political Scientists, San Francisco, CA, 21–24 March.

Mitchell, Michael, and Charles Wood. 1998. "The Ironies of Citizenship: Skin Color, Police Brutality, and the Challenges to Brazilian Democracy." *Social Forces* 77:1001–1020.

Nobles, Melissa. 2000. *Shades of Citizenship: Race and the Census in Modern Politics.* Stanford, CA: Stanford University Press.

Oliveira, Cloves. 2007. A Inevitável Visibilidade de Cor: Estudo comparativo das campanhas de Benedita da Silva e Celso Pitta às prefeituras do Rio de Janeiro e São Paulo, nas eleições de 1992 e 1996. PhD dissertation, Instituto Universitário de Pesquisa do Rio de Janeiro (Iuperj).

Oliveira, Cloves Luiz P. 1997. *A Luta por um Lugar: Gênero, Raça, e Classe: Eleições Municipais de Salvador-Bahia, 1992.* Salvador: Serie Toques Programa A Cor da Bahia-UFBA.

Paixão, Marcelo, and Luiz M. Carvano. 2008. *Relatório anual das desigualdades raciais no Brazil, 2007–2008.* Rio de Janeiro: Editoria Garamond Ltda.

Pardue, Derek. 2004. "Putting Mano to Music: The Mediation of Race in Brazilian Rap." *Ethnomusicology Forum* 13:253–286.

Pereira, João Baptista Borges. 1982. "Aspectos do comportamento político do negro em São Paulo." *Ciência e Cultura* 34:1286–1294.

Prandi, Reginaldo. 1996. "Raça e boto na eleição presidencial de 1994." *Estudos Afro-Asiaticos* 30:61–78.

Racusen, Seth. 2010. "Affirmative Action and Identity." In *Brazil's New Racial Politics*, by Bernd Reiter and Gladys Mitchell. Boulder, CO: Lynne Rienner Publishers.

Reiter, Bernd, and Gladys Mitchell, eds. *Brazil's New Racial Politics.* 2010. Boulder, CO: Lynne Rienner Publishers.

Sansone, Livio. 2004. *Negritude sem Etnicidade: O Local e o Global Nas Relações Raciais e na*

Produção Cultural Negra do Brasil. Salvador, BA: EDUFBA.

Santos, Gislene A. 2008. "Racism and Its Masks in Brazil: On Racism and the Idea of Harmony." In *Race, Colonialism, and Social Transformation in Latin America and Caribbean*, ed. Jerome Branch, 91–115. Gainesville: University Press of Florida.

Santos, Sales Augusto dos. 2000. *A ausência de uma bancada suprapartidária afro-brasileira no Congreso Nacional (Legislatura 1995/1998).* 2 vols. Brasília: Centro de Estudos Afro-Asiaticos.

———. 2006. "Who is Black in Brazil? A Timely or a False Question in Brazilian Race Relations in the Era of Affirmative Action?" *Latin American Perspectives* 33:30–48.

———. 2010. "Black NGOs and 'Conscious' Rap: New Agents of the Antiracism Struggle in Brazil." In *Brazil's New Racial Politics*, ed. Bernd Reiter and Gladys Mitchell. Boulder, CO: Lynne Rienner Publishers.

Sheriff, Robin. 2001. *Dreaming Equality: Color, Race, and Racism in Urban Brazil.* New Brunswick, NJ: Rutgers University Press.

Soares, Glaucio, Ary Dillon, and Nelson da Valle Silva. 1987. "Urbanization, Race, and Class in Brazilian Politics." *Latin American Research Review* 22:155–176.

Souza, Amaury de. 1971. "Raça e política no Brasil urbano." *Revista de Administração de Empresas* 11:61–70.

Telles, Edward. 2004. *Race in Another America: The Significance of Skin Color in Brazil.* Princeton, NJ: Princeton University Press.

Twine, France Winddance. 1998. *Racism in a Racial Democracy: The Maintenance of White Supremacy.* New Brunswick, NJ: Rutgers University Press.

Valente, Ana Lúcia E. F. 1986. *Política e relações raciais: Os negros e às eleições paulistas de 1982.* São Paulo: FFLCH-US.

Von Mettenheim, Kurt. 1986. *The Brazilian Voter: Mass Politics in Democratic Transition, 1974–1986.* Pittsburgh, PA: University of Pittsburgh Press.

A Region in Denial

Racial Discrimination and Racism in Latin America

By Ariel E. Dulitzky

● ●

Editor's Introduction

Denials and a legacy of class struggle and revised history within imagined spaces are rampant in many Latin American nations, such as Cuba, Brazil, and Argentina, to name but a few. In this selection, readers will learn where and how racism and racial discrimination exist; the notion of "racial democracy" in Brazil is challenged as evidence reveals many imbalances in Brazilian society. This reading is a good place to start on this complex issue, and allows students to see that the United States is not unique with regard to race relations.

References

Anderson, Benedict. *Imagined Communities: Reflections on the Origin and Spread of Nationalism*. New York: Verso, 2006.

Applebaum, Nancy P., Anne S. Macpherson, and Karin Alejandra Rosenblatt, eds. *Race and Nation in Modern Latin America*. Chapel Hill: University of North Carolina Press, 2001.

Dulitzky, Ariel E. "A Region in Denial: Racial Discrimination and Racism in Latin America." In *Neither Enemies Nor Friends: Latinos, Blacks, Afro-Latinos,* edited by Anani Dzidzienyo and Suzanne Oboler, 39–59. New York: Palgrave Macmillan, 2005.

Racism (and racial discrimination) is, to a certain extent, alive and well in every society, country, and region of the world.[1] It can appear in a variety of forms depending on the culture or context in which it occurs and the period of history during which it rears its head. Nonetheless, one common thread that seems to be woven throughout almost every culture, country, and region is that people deny that racism even exists.

In this article we attempt to delve into the different forms of denying the existence of racial discrimination in Latin America. The crux of our argument is that the people of our region are prone to conceal, twist, and cover up the fact that racism and racial discrimination exists in our part of the world. This phenomenon of denial stands in the way of acknowledgment of the problem and, consequently, hampers effective measures that could be taken to eliminate and prevent racial discrimination. In order to identify the best strategies for combating racism, we must first take a close look at the different forms and manifestations of the phenomenon itself.

A kind of presumption of moral superiority vis-à-vis the United States of America is quite widespread throughout our region. Rarely does a conversation on this issue among Latin Americans take place without mentioning the serious incidence of racism and racial discrimination that exists in the land of our neighbors to the north, a claim that is altogether true. As the Brazilian scholar Antonio Sergio Guimaraes (1999:37; 2001) notes, we point out with nationalistic pride that racial segregation of the type that exists in the United States does not exist in our countries. We pompously tout our "racial democracies," "racial melting pots," "racial harmony," complete *mestizaje*, or mixing of races.

Nothing epitomizes Latin Americans' view on this issue as well as the declaration of the presidents and heads of state of South America that was issued in 2000 at a meeting in Brasilia. This statement reads: "The Presidents [of South America] view with concern the resurgence of racism and of discriminatory manifestations and expressions in *other parts of the world* and state their commitment to preserve South America from the propagation of said phenomenon."[2] Or as the Mexican government put it: "The government of Mexico opposes any form of discrimination, institutionalized or otherwise, as well as the new forms of discrimination, xenophobia and other forms of intolerance that have emerged in several parts of the world, particularly in the developed countries."[3]

In short, these leaders concur that racism and racial discrimination are practices that take place in other regions and that Latin Americans possess a moral fortitude that cannot and does not allow any discrimination to be practiced in their countries. Moreover, these statements echo the widespread sentiment of the region.

Our aim here is to encourage a debate on what we feel is a widespread and outright misrepresentation of Latin America as a region that is respectful of racial mobility and more tolerant toward racial identities than it really is. These misguided impressions are merely a reflection of the absence of a deep, sincere, and open political debate on the issue of race in our region. With regard to this point, the Mexican government is right when it states, "In Mexico, the indigenous issue is never approached as a problem of racial discrimination but as a matter related to the right to development and to their situation of economic and social marginalization (exclusion)."[4] This same government would also state that racial discrimination "is not even a issue of national debate."[5]

But to point out that this phenomenon is not part of the national debate, or that it is not viewed as racial discrimination, by no means erases or negates the fact that racism and racial discrimination do exist, and that the countries of the region refuse to admit and combat.

In reality, racial discrimination and racism, like the failure to recognize these phenomena and the absence of a debate on these issues in Latin America, are simply part and parcel of what could be dubbed the "democratic deficit" that we are experiencing in the region. Equality, as it relates to race, gender, ethnicity, or anything else, is still far from being viewed in the region as an essential and basic requirement for democracy. Equality cannot exist without democracy; nor can democracy exist without equality. Hence, the struggle to solidify democracy is a fundamental step in the struggle against racism and racial discrimination.

This article is partly based on a study conducted by Stanley Cohen (1996), which looked at different governments' responses to reports denouncing violations of human rights. In this study, three different types of denial are posited: literal denial (nothing has happened); interpretive denial (what is happening is actually something else); and justificatory denial (what's happening is justified).[6] Sometimes these types of denial appear in sequence; when one type is struck down, it is replaced by another type. For example, literal denial may prove ineffective because the facts may simply bear out that the black population is indeed more disadvantaged than the white population. Therefore, strategy shifts toward use of another type of denial such as a legalistic reinterpretation or a political justification (522).

Before delving into the subject at hand, we would first like to make a point of clarification.

This article focuses primarily on the plight of the Black or Afro-Latin American population, with very little discussion on racial discrimination against indigenous peoples or other ethnic groups. It is by no means our intent to ignore or fail to recognize that indigenous peoples are victims of racial discrimination as well. We have chosen to center our analysis on this particular social group, for the most part, because Blacks have been the most low-visibility victims of racial discrimination in Latin American society today.

A Look at the Current Situation in the Region

We must first make sure that readers understand what we mean by racism or racial discrimination. Even though it is true that forms, types, or definitions of "racism" or "racial discrimination" may vary widely, for the purposes of this article we use the definition provided by article 1(1) of the International Convention on the Elimination of All Forms of Racial Discrimination (referred to hereinafter as the "Convention against Racism" or the "Convention"):

> In this Convention the expression "racial discrimination" shall denote any distinction, exclusion, restriction or preference based on motives of race, color, lineage or national or ethnic origin whose purpose or result is to nullify or diminish the recognition, enjoyment or exercise, in equal conditions, of human rights and fundamental liberties in the political, economic, social, cultural or any other sphere of public life.

The true state of affairs in Latin American societies, nonetheless, stands in stark contrast with the objectives pursued by the International Convention. Although very few statistics are available on the phenomenon, the small amount of data we have at our disposal shows how racial discrimination permeates each and every realm of life in our region: from the social to the political,

education,[7] labor,[8] cultural, and public health sectors.[9] In countries like Colombia, the Afro-Colombian population is disproportionately a victim of political violence.[10] In other countries of Latin America, access to land has eluded the descendents of African peoples.[11] In many countries of the region, judicial (Adorno, 1999:123) and law-enforcement (Oliveira, 1998:50) systems provide less protection to Blacks and, at the same time, punish them more severely.

For example, a recent study by the UN Economic Council for Latin America shows that Afro-Latin Americans have little or no job security, which is proof of racial segregation throughout the region. Racial discrimination in the labor market stems from inequities in the education sector. Consequently, whites have more of a chance of successfully climbing the corporate ladder, so to speak, or making it to positions of power or upper management. Distribution of income in the region is revealed to be even more unfair when it is viewed by ethno-racial origin of the inhabitants. The Black population has a harder time gaining access to education; they are more likely to fall behind in their studies, to fail to make progress, to drop out of school, and to attend schools of inferior quality.[12]

The government of Colombia, one of the few governments that at least has clearly acknowledged, in written documents, the problem of discrimination, has described the plight of the Afro-Colombian population in the following terms:

> They are among the group of Colombians with the highest indices of unmet needs. Their health conditions are precarious, their sanitation conditions are the most deficient in the entire nation, and coverage of education services is poor. Housing in Afro-Colombian communities, in addition to [having] poor coverage of public utilities, shows problems in the legalization of property and lots, a high rate of overcrowding, and poor quality. It is estimated that the per capita income of [the members of]

these communities is $500 per year, less than one-third of the national average. Afro-Colombian women are facing conditions of poverty, high unemployment rates, low-quality jobs, deficient health care, and a high incidence of domestic violence. Afro-Colombian teens do not have optimal guarantees and opportunities to gain access to higher or vocational education, good jobs, and development in keeping with their world vision and with their sociocultural reality. The territorial entities where the Afro-Colombian population creates settlements are characterized by their poor ability to govern, plan, and manage.[13]

This scenario, which is identical to the situation in several countries of Latin America, makes it all the more necessary to take a closer and more honest look at our region in order to be able to adopt the necessary measures to overcome this crisis. Even so, there are still strong currents of thought in political, academic, and social circles, which deny that racial discrimination even exists or try to explain away these differences as a function of other variables, rather than as a function of race or ethnic origin. In the following section we look closely at some of these variables.

"There Is No Racism or Racial Discrimination": Literal Denial

Literal denial is simply to say *"nothing has happened"* or *"nothing is happening."* What is of concern to us here is that this type of denial is synonymous with saying that there has never been any racial discrimination or racism in the past nor is there any at the present time. Over the past few years, different governments of Latin America have made statements to the Committee on the Elimination of Racial Discrimination (CERD) claiming, among other things, that "racial prejudice"[14] does not exist, "in our country problems of discrimination do not exist,"[15] "racial discrimination does not exist,"[16] "today racial problems practically do not exist any longer,"[17] "this phenomenon does not appear in our country,"[18] or "in society at the present time racial prejudices are practically negligible."[19]

This type of discourse is typical not only of governments that have a well-known history of insensitivity to racial issues, but also of governments that have a track record of being committed, at least rhetorically, to racial equality. Paradoxically, these so-called racially sensitive governments are often the ones who most categorically deny the existence of the problem. It would not be entirely farfetched to hear the following argument brandished in discussing the issue with a Latin American: *"Our government would never allow something like that to happen, and therefore it could never have happened?"*

A pseudo sophisticated way of denying that racial discrimination exists is to argue that it could not have taken place because discrimination is illegal in the countries of the region and the governments have even ratified every appropriate international instrument related to the subject. This legalistic version of denial of racial discrimination is based on the following specious claim: "Since racial discrimination is prohibited by law, our government would never allow it and, therefore, it could not have ever occurred" (Cohen, 1996:254).

The most syllogistic form of literal denial is the widespread myth that the region boasts a racial democracy because the concept of race has been officially rejected by government institutions. This type of denial has many variations but essentially amounts to saying that if races do not officially exist, then racism cannot exist either. Nevertheless, erasing the concept of race from laws and other official documents has by no means led to the end of race as a key factor in determining how the benefits of society are distributed, nor does it negate the fact that Latin American society is predicated upon a clearly pyramidal structure with Blacks and indigenous people at the bottom and whites at the top.

"What Goes On in Latin America Is Not Racism or Racial Discrimination but Something Else": Interpretive Denial

At this point in time, it is hard, if not ludicrous, to categorically deny that racial discrimination and racism exist in Latin America. This is because groups that have been discriminated against have become more visible and have begun to engage in activism to address their plight. Additionally, a limited but growing number of studies and statistics, which bear out that racism and racial discrimination still exist in Latin America, are now available. Consequently, people resort to slightly more sophisticated explanations. Instead of denying that economic and social indicators show a wide gap between races, they commonly give reasons other than racism to account for the disparities among Blacks, indigenous peoples, and whites. These disparities, attitudes, and prejudices are framed in far less pejorative or stigmatizing theoretical terms than racism or racial discrimination.

The true story of the racial issue in Latin America is doctored in many different ways. In the following section we identify some of the ways in which the facts are distorted such that they do not fit the definition of racism or racial discrimination.

Euphemisms

One of the most common ways of putting a spin on the facts is the use of euphemistic expressions to mask the phenomenon, confer a measure of respectability on the problem, or paint a picture of neutrality in the face of discriminatory practices. A variety of terms are used to negate or cloud the racist side of certain social conduct or government policies: "ethnic minority,"[20] "restrictions on immigration,"[21] "customer screening or selection" (*selección de clientes*),[22] "reservation of rights to refuse admission" *(reserva de admisión)*,[23] "proper attire" *(Buena presencia)*.[24]

Probably the most common euphemism attributes the differences among races to poverty. The syllogism goes something like this: People discriminate against Blacks or indigenous people *not* because they are black or indigenous, but because they are poor.

The government of Haiti, for example, cited economic reasons for the disparities between whites and other groups: "Even though it is true that in the private sphere prejudices related to color are sometimes expressed, in reality its origin lies in the social inequities that exist in Haitian society."[25] Similarly, the government of Peru claimed, "Today practically every Peruvian is of mixed blood and a racial problem no longer exists. Instead, there exists a problem of economic underdevelopment in certain sectors of the population."[26] Mexico has developed the most explicit arguments on this point: The indigenous issue is not "a problem of racial discrimination"; rather it has to do with "forms of discrimination derived from the socioeconomic reality."[27]

The myth of a *racial democracy*, which is defined as harmony between ethnic and racial groups and, therefore, the absence of racial discrimination, would lead people to believe that any display of racism and discrimination that may occur is usually a result of social and economic rather than racial prejudice. Once again we cite the official version of the Mexican government: "some forms of discrimination are a result of socioeconomic differences more than a distinction between ethnic groups, and they [the differences] have been addressed by means of a variety of government social development programs targeted toward the most vulnerable groups."[28] This way of thinking is so widespread and has endured for so long throughout Latin America that, regardless of a persons race, the population for the most part is unwilling to explain current social disparities among racial groups in terms of racial inequities. Yet, our societies quite readily accept explanations based on economic disparities (Minority Rights Group, 1999:23).

These interpretations are marred by faulty logic. First, they fail to explain why in our region even though not all people of color are poor, almost all poor people are colored.[29] One government did not have any problem acknowledging "a clear correlation between proportion of the indigenous population and poverty and marginalization indices."[30] Second, several statistical studies on economic disparities in Latin America have shown that even when all possible variables are factored out of the equation, including indicators of poverty, one variable, which can only be attributed to a persons race, always carries over.[31] Moreover, according to this specious argument, it would be lawful to discriminate against poor people. As far as we are aware, there is no provision of human rights law currently on the books that legitimizes unequal treatment of persons based on social class or economic status.[32] Justification of class-based over race-based discrimination, once again, is simply a corollary to the assumption that we live in racial democracies in Latin America. It is also a corollary to the ideological basis for that assumption, which is that societies in the region are monolithically mestizo or mixed raced and, therefore, allegedly free of prejudice and discrimination. If Latin America indeed lives in racial harmony and there is really only one race in our societies (the mestizo race), then it would follow that any disparities between population groups could never be explained by a persons race but rather would have to be explained as a function of poverty, social status, or education.

Legalisms

Most interpretive denials of racism are laced with some sort of legalistic or diplomatic language to negate the existence of discriminatory practices. Many different legal defenses have been used to counter charges of racial discrimination. To take stock of every single one would far exceed the scope of this article, so in this section we offer only a few examples.

One form of legalistic argument is to maintain that racial discrimination is nonexistent in Latin America because the laws in the countries of the region do not establish rules of segregation or apartheid as is the case in certain other parts of the world. The claim is thus put forth that "never in history has any legal text been in effect that establishes racial discrimination even in a veiled way."[33] The implication of this statement is that discrimination can only exist when it is established by law, and not when sectors of the population are discriminated against by deed or when laws are applied or enforced in a discriminatory way.

Nevertheless, international conventions require our countries to do much more than simply erase discriminatory laws from the books. International treaties call for the adoption of specific laws in support of each provision of these conventions, egalitarian and nondiscriminatory enforcement of laws and conventions, and, particularly, the prevention, punishment, and elimination of discrimination in all its forms, whether by law or by deed. The CERD, therefore, has expressly mentioned the obligation of states to repeal any law or *practice* whose effect it is to create or perpetuate racial discrimination.[34]

The Convention against Racial Discrimination requires nations to adopt comprehensive legislation to prevent, eliminate, punish, and remedy racial discrimination. Such legislation does not exist at the present time in Latin American countries, as the CERD has been pointing out over the past two years.[35] Instead, the respective constitutions contain basic provisions that prohibit racial discrimination; yet the appropriate legislative structures to fully enforce those provisions are not in place.[36] Specifically, the Convention requires enactment of certain criminal laws, which prohibit and adequately penalize any act of racial discrimination that may be committed by individuals, organizations, public authorities, or institutions. To date, in many countries of the Americas, such laws are yet to be passed.[37] In other countries, even though legal provisions designed to eliminate unequal treatment based on racial factors may have already been enacted, express provisions making it unlawful to discriminate on the basis of national or ethnic origin have not been written into the laws.[38] Such specificity is necessary because these types of discrimination are the most prevalent forms of intolerance and bigotry in many nations of the region. In many countries in Latin America, there are no laws preventing racial discrimination in the private sector, despite the fact that section d, paragraph 1, of article 2 of the Convention provides that signatories shall prohibit any racial discrimination practiced not only by public authorities or institutions but also by private "groups or organizations."[39] Lastly, in many of our countries legislation currently in force has proven to be inadequate, either because the ban on discrimination does not go hand in hand with the appropriate punishments[40] or because punishments provided for by law are so lenient that they do not serve as an effective means to prevent, prohibit, and eradicate all practice of racial segregation.[41]

Another way people attempt to prove that racial discrimination does not exist in the region is to point to the fact that Latin American courts receive very few complaints of racial discrimination. As the government of Mexico stated, the absence of racial discrimination "can be corroborated by the absence of both domestic and international complaints"[42]—the logic being that an absence of court convictions for racial discrimination means that the phenomenon is non-existent. Nevertheless, this argument ignores important questions such as whether victims of racism are aware of the legal recourse available to them for their defense; whether laws are effective in combating racial discrimination; or whether the courts properly apply antidiscrimination laws. The low number of complaints may very well be attributable to "unawareness of existing legal remedies available for cases of racial discrimination, and to the public in general perhaps not being very aware of the protection against racial discrimination provided for in the Convention."[43] The small number of complaints and, consequently, convictions may also be due to a lack of confidence in law enforcement and judicial authorities.[44] Lastly, the low incidence of racial discrimination cases brought before the court may also stem from the fact that judicial or police officers do not rate this type of behavior as a display of racism or discrimination.[45]

In a variation of the argument that the absence of legislation making racial discrimination a crime is in itself proof that racial discrimination does not exist, the government of Venezuela stated: "Even though it is true that very few laws are in force against racial discrimination and any defense or support *(apologia)* that may foment it, we can say that there is no practical need to legislate on this subject, given that problems of discrimination or defense thereof do not exist in our country. … [Such a] situation, fortunately unknown in our milieu, would be different if there were violent clashes between ethnic groups or if certain persons were alienated or left out on the basis of physical characteristics, since in explosive situations such as these would be, the Parliament, which cannot turn its back on the social reality, would issue laws on this subject. It has not done so because there has not been a need for it."[46]

In an extreme variation of this argument, governments respond to allegations of racism and racial discrimination by rattling off a long list of domestic laws enacted, international treaties ratified, and a host of legal mechanisms designed to punish those responsible for discrimination and racism. With such prohibitions in place, racial discrimination cannot possibly exist.

Denials of Responsibility

Many times governments deny any type of state responsibility for racism and racial discrimination, although they acknowledge that such acts may indeed take place.

The argument is that even though some acts of racism and racial discrimination have occurred, such acts are events that cannot be attributed to the government, are out of its control, and are the product of deeply rooted social practices or private actors. The Dominican government, for example, has only accepted that "there exists the possibility that individually, someone in the country, with the utmost discretion supports racial discrimination."[47] Or as the government of Haiti has stated, in the event that there are incidents of racial discrimination, these "are in no case the work of the state."[48]

In any case, under the Convention against Racial Discrimination, these arguments are not a valid justification. Every state must guarantee effective application of the Convention. "Inasmuch as the practices of private institutions influence the exercise of rights or the availability of opportunities, the State Party must ensure that the result of these practices does not have as a purpose or effect the creation or perpetuation of racial discrimination."[49]

Just Isolated Incidents

One of the most common ways in which governments respond to charges of racism or racial discrimination is to accept that a specific act has indeed taken place, but to deny that such acts are systematic, routine, or representative of a pattern of behavior. Typical responses in this category include:

> "Such acts arise in an isolated way and are the result of the motivation of individuals or very small groups."[50]
>
> Incidents of racial discrimination occur only "episodically and selectively."[51]
>
> "In present-day society racial prejudices are practically negligible and are manifested in the most intimate spheres of life."[52]
>
> What occurred was an *"isolated incident"*, such events never occurred in the past, and since they have not happened again, it is unfair to brand our government as racist on the basis of this single event.

Justificatory Denial

Justificatory denial has countless variations, which, generally speaking, involve either an attempt to justify the argument that racism does not exist or an attempt to show that in some hypothetical situations, racism or racial discrimination is in fact justifiable. Some of these denials are offered in good faith; others are simply excuses, fabrications, ideological defenses, or attempts to neutralize allegations.

Camouflaging Racism

We focus here on one of the most pernicious forms of denial—blaming the victim for his or her situation or making the victim of racism and racial discrimination invisible.

In perhaps its most extreme form, whole sectors of the population are simply said not to be victims of racism. Witness the popular Argentine saying: "We Argentines are not racist because we don't have any Blacks." The collective conscience in that country of the Southern Cone, however, refuses to ask key questions such as why today there is no Black population in Argentina, whereas in 1850, 30 percent of the population of Buenos Aires was Black.[53]

Governments throughout Latin America have engaged in a campaign to officially do away with any racial identification by claiming that the population is of mixed race *(mestizaje)*. This view is evident, for example, in the way censuses are conducted in the countries of the region. The census of almost every country in Latin America does not include any question on racial identity.[54] The exceptions are Brazil and a few other countries, which are halfheartedly beginning to inquire into these distinctions.[55] This practice only serves to camouflage a highly representative sector of Latin American populations. The absence of official statistics on the true makeup of the population has a most serious consequence: it prevents the true plight of sectors that are victims of discrimination from being known. This practice also makes it impossible to implement public policies to overcome these inequities.

This drastic negation of any racial distinctions within the population makes it impossible to question the prevailing norm in Latin America of a persons color being a decisive factor in determining chances and opportunities to succeed in society. In Latin America, the whiter you are, the better and greater your chances are; while the darker you are, the lesser and worse your chances are. The chromatic social scale is blatant throughout Latin America, and social surveys have begun to corroborate these disparities.[56]

While it is true that racial categories in Latin America differ from those of other parts of the world in that they are not exclusively of a dual nature, that is, Black and white,[57] this by no means does away with the disparities among races or with the fact that the darker the skin, the fewer the economic, cultural, educational, employment, and social opportunities. We could say that a "strong pigmentocracy" prevails throughout Latin America, in which a negative value is attached to darker skin color, thus relegating races other than the white race to the lower echelons of society (Casaus Arzu, 1998:138).

The idea that we are all mestizos,[58] we are all cafe-au-lait-colored, we all have some indigenous or black blood in us, is an obstacle to identifying and developing the concept of specific racial groups. This myth is used to prevent nonwhites from developing their own identity and demands; however, it is not used to attain a higher degree of equality and social integration for these sectors of the population. The official notion of a mixed race (*mestizaje*)[59] camouflages diversity and denies nonwhites the right to dissent, while making conditions ripe for excluding anyone who falls outside the "norm" of mestizo or mixed (Arocha Rodriguez, 1992:28).

Furthermore, the concept of a mixed race also undermines or weakens the political and social struggle against racial discrimination. If we are all mestizos, then there are no racial distinctions, and mere discussion of the racial issue is therefore viewed by many as foreign to the region. By raising such matters in Latin America, the thinking goes, people are only trying to bring problems into the region that belong to other countries.

Moreover, the mixed-race theory covers up the official racist policy of whitening or infusing white blood into society, which has been attempted in almost every single country of Latin America. Many Latin American countries made a concerted effort to bring down the number of Blacks and indigenous people in the population and, as a last resort, to camouflage these racial groups by encouraging miscegenation, or marriage between nonwhites and whites, to make the population whiter. For example, almost every country in the region has developed at one time or another immigration policies that restrict or deny entry to Black people while strongly promoting European immigration.

The mixed-race claim not only serves to camouflage or make the Black or indigenous population invisible but is also used as proof that racism does not exist. Mexico has explained the situation in the following way:

> Additionally, our historical experience and the makeup of the Mexican population—90 percent mestizo (mixed race), a product of the mix between Spaniards and indigenous people—give rise to an indisputable fact: the denial of either [one of these] origin[s] does not take place in our country, which is why there has been no need to legislate in this regard, unlike what goes on in other countries where the phenomenon of *mestizaje* did not occur.[60]

Mestizaje is also used as proof of harmony among different racial and ethnic groups. In other words, if there are mestizos, it is because there are mixed marriages between whites and Blacks or indigenous people. As the government of Cuba stated, the fact that there are a high number of racially mixed families on the island is a sign of how limited racial prejudice is.[61] Nonetheless, not even the magical force of *mestizaje* has managed to completely do away with racial prejudice when such marriages take place. Furthermore, many people in Latin America try to keep mixed marriages from ever taking place in their families.

The mixed raced/mixed marriage theory, however, is unable to conceal the fact that the Latin American population in general and the Black/indigenous population in particular feel that whitening ones lineage is the only route to improving ones standing on the social scale. This view is at the root of racism in Latin America; this attitude denies the Black or indigenous presence and identity and stresses the "white" side of the mixed race as the essential ingredient to obtain better social, employment, and education opportunities in a white-dominated world (Minority Rights Group, 1995:28). In reality, more than a democratizing force behind society, *mestizaje* constitutes, for the most part, one of the most masterful forms of racism in Latin America. In order to climb the social ladder, one must be as white as possible and the blending of races is the way to attain it.

In Latin America, as has been correctly pointed out, "the white/mestizo [person] forswears or abjures his or her indigenous [and, we add, Black] part and must constantly demonstrate his or her 'superiority,' even when these displays only illustrate that it is impossible for mestizos to accept their white and Indian humanity" [or the Black side of their humanity, we add once again] (de la Torre, 1997:7).

Even though Latin American governments have officially denied or done away with the different racial identities that exist throughout the region, such an action has not done away with informal racial designations, which in fact have a decisive effect on the social structure in Latin America. Even at the risk of making a sweeping generalization, we feel compelled to call attention to a common fact that has persisted throughout Latin America independently of the social, political, historical, and cultural peculiarities of the different countries: there is discrimination based on skin color (Early, 1999).

Another way of saying that nonwhites are not victims of racism in Latin America is to reduce their sphere of action in society. Accordingly, it is socially acceptable to acknowledge that Blacks excel only in sports, music, and dance; indeed Black equates with soccer: to be Black is to be good at soccer or even to be a soccer player. In keeping with this same line of thinking, the victims of racism are excluded from other sectors, for example, the media, in order to "project the image of a racially white country" (Oscategui, 1998:31). For example, the CERD has stated its "concern for the information that the media provide regarding minority communities, including the consistent popularity of television programs in which stereotypes based on race or ethnic origin are promoted. The Committee states that those stereotypes contribute to reinforcing the cycle of violence and marginalization that has already had

serious repercussions on the rights of traditionally disadvantaged communities in Colombia."[62] The labor market is another place where there is a clear demarcation of the types of jobs that nonwhites may gain access to or not. Nonwhite populations in Latin America usually have access to the lowest-level and poorest-paid jobs.[63]

The last form of this type of denial involves turning the story around to pin the blame on the victims. This takes place when a Black or indigenous person denounces racially discriminatory practices. Many times, the person is branded a victim of unfounded complexes, without even the slightest consideration that he or she may instead be the victim of racial discrimination.

Convenient Comparisons

One of the most common ways of attempting to justify the racial situation in Latin America is to compare the region with other countries of the world. Four countries, South Africa, the United States, Rwanda, and Bosnia, are old standbys that are often used for such comparisons. With regard to each instance, respectively, Latin Americans state, "we never had apartheid in our region"; "nor was there ever any legalized racial segregation";[64] and "we never had racially motivated, violent armed conflicts."[65]

In the report submitted by a government to the CERD, the only time the xenophobia, racism, and racial discrimination are mentioned is in reference to the plight of nationals from that country living in the United States.[66] Discrimination always takes place on the other side of the border.

The intellectual and political elite, in many ways, has made the United States the paragon of racial hatred against which all other societies must be measured. The specious claim goes something like this: since the segregationist laws and practices of the country to the north have not been applied in Latin America, there is no need to look at other forms of racial exclusion and alienation.

None of the above-mentioned comparisons are untrue and this ought to be a source of pride for Latin Americans. However, the people of the region, or anyone else for that matter, should not read anything more into these facts than what they say on the face of things. It is true that there has been no apartheid regime in the region; it is true that no racist legislation has ever existed in the region either; and it is also true that no Latin American government has implemented policies of ethnic cleansing.[67] Nonetheless, these are not the only manifestations of racism and racial discrimination. A myriad of phenomena can be found throughout Latin America that fits the definition of racial discrimination and racism.

Conclusion: Is There a Future Without a Past?

A racist way of thinking has endured throughout our region over the years. Today it is not even entirely far-fetched to hear out of the mouths of Latin Americans such statements as: "The only solution for Guatemala is to improve the race, bring in Aryan studs to improve it. I had a German administrator on my farm for many years and for every Indian girl he got pregnant, I'd pay him an extra fifty dollars."[68]

The existence of racial discrimination and racism, however, continues to be denied or ignored by Latin American societies and governments alike. Very few studies have been conducted on the topic to date, very few statistics have been gathered, and no public debate on the issue is taking place. This grim picture constitutes a roadblock to the development of public policies to combat racial discrimination and racism on the national, regional, and international levels.

In recent years, the advent of democratically elected governments in the majority of the countries of Latin America has paved the way for the improvement of the human rights situation of the region in many ways. Most notably, most countries have no policies of serious state-planned violations. Nevertheless, our democracies still have not been successful at fulfilling their implicit promise and the basic tenet of ensuring full, formal, and effective equality for all segments of society. Consequently, the consolidation of democracy is looming over us both as an unavoidable challenge in Latin America

and as the path we must follow in order to combat racism and racial discrimination effectively.

The World Conference against Racism, Racial Discrimination, Xenophobia, and Related Forms of Intolerance (WCAR), which was convened by the United Nations in 2001, may yet spur on the inhabitants of the region to deal with an issue that has long been consigned to oblivion.

A regional meeting in preparation for the WCAR was held for the Americas in Santiago, Chile, from December 3 to December 7, 2000. Two parallel meetings were organized: the governmental conference, the Americas Preparatory Conference Against Racism, Racial Discrimination, Xenophobia and Related Forms of Intolerance (Regional PrepCom), and the parallel NGO forum, titled the Conference of Citizens Against Racism, Xenophobia, Intolerance and Discrimination (the Citizens Conference).

There were several positive outcomes from these meetings. The massive presence of civil society organizations should be highlighted. More than 1,700 people participated. There is still some hope that this significant mobilization could give birth to a strong regional movement to fight racism. The Santiago meetings also contributed to enhancing the dialogue among Afro-descendants throughout the region, bringing international attention to the challenges that they face. The Chile meetings represented a unique, and probably the first, opportunity for Afro-Latin Americans to appear as significant actors functioning in regional groups on the international level. Participating with a burgeoning collective identity that demonstrated enormous potential for bringing the fight against racism to the fore, they successfully heightened both their own visibility and that of the problems they face throughout the entire hemisphere.

On the governmental side, and at least in the declaratory documents, the Regional PrepCom allowed decisive actions to be taken to fight racial discrimination in the region. For the first time, all the governments of the Americas accepted that racial discrimination exists throughout the region and that it should be strongly combated. Some themes, which appeared in the Regional

PrepComs Final Declaration, deserve mention as they point to important changes in the official position of many states in the region highlighted through this article. The Final Declaration includes a clear recognition that the history of the hemisphere has often been characterized by racism and racial discrimination, and that these phenomena persist in the region (preamble). Moreover the governments of the region stated that the denial of the existence of racism and racial discrimination on the part of states and societies directly or indirectly contributes to their perpetuation (para. 2). The documents also included a positive call for governments to include ethnic or racial criteria in order to give visibility to diverse sectors of the population (para. 18).

It is important to note that the presidents and heads of state of the thirty-four countries of the hemisphere expressly endorsed this document. Similarly, the Inter-American Democratic Charter, adopted by the OAS General Assembly in Lima, Peru, on September 11, 2001, in its Article 9, established that "The elimination of all forms of discrimination, especially gender, ethnic and race discrimination, as well as diverse forms of intolerance, the promotion and protection of human rights of indigenous peoples and migrants, and respect for ethnic, cultural and religious diversity in the Americas contribute to strengthening democracy and citizen participation."

The WCAR was held shortly after the Regional PrepCom, during the first week of September 2001, in Durban, South Africa. While the objective of the WCAR was to address issues of discrimination and intolerance around the world and formulate recommendations and action-oriented measures to combat these evils in all their forms, most of the discussions focused on two issues: the conflict in the Middle East and the question of reparations. Notwithstanding the diplomatic hurdles, the event allowed Afro-Latin Americans to continue raising the level of public awareness on a number of important issues, thus replicating their Chilean success. For Latin America, the most important development is that the governments of the region did not retract their prior

recognition that the region faces important racial discrimination issues.

The mobilization of civil society groups was quite significant, resulting in a number of positive, tangible developments. Beyond highlighting the problems Afro-Latinos confront, the conference also acted as a welcome catalyst to put in motion the long-overdue debate on how to effectively address racial inequality. The progress here lies in the discussion itself. Perhaps for the first time in Latin America, governments and civil society began to debate racial inequality. At last, the debate over race seemed to have moved beyond the discrete circles of academics and activists to find an incipient place in the regions agenda. As an example, the OAS decided to start discussions on the adoption of an Inter-American convention against racism and any other form of discrimination and intolerance. For a region that, as the first part of this article suggests, denies the existence of racism and racial discrimination, this is an important development.

There have also been some promising institutional developments in the last couple of years in terms of creating public institutions charged specifically with addressing allegations of discrimination or helping in the definition and implementation of public policies for the prevention and combating of racial discrimination. Some examples of this trend are the creation of the National Institute against Discrimination, Xenophobia and Racism in Argentina,[69] the National Council for the Prevention of Discrimination in Mexico,[70] the Presidential Commission against Racism and Discrimination against Indigenous People in Guatemala[71] and the Special Secretariat on Policies for the Promotion of Racial Equality in Brazil[72] The creation of new institutions, in countries that traditionally did not officially address the problems of exclusion and marginalization in terms of discrimination, could signal a departure from some of the positions highlighted earlier in this article.

Perhaps the most important development in recent years is that the Brazilian government has begun imposing racial quotas for government jobs, contracts,[73] and university admissions.[74] As expected, these measures have unleashed an acrimonious debate in a country that has traditionally prided itself on being a "racial democracy." There is also a racial equality statute pending now before Congress that would make racial quotas obligatory at all levels of government and even in casting television programs and commercials. The debate is broad and very complex, covering questions such as the definition of who is black, a puzzling process in a country where more than 300 terms are used to designate skin color. It has also prompted a discussion on national identity where critics of the measures say the government is importing a solution from the United States, a country in which racial definitions and relations are very different.[75] Others say that racial quotas are not needed, since racism is not a feature of Brazilian society and conditions for Blacks will improve as poverty is gradually eliminated. The issue probably will be partially settled in the near future when the Brazilian Federal Supreme Court rules on the constitutionality of racial quotas being challenged by white applicants to federal universities. The decision could have an impact in Brazil and also in the rest of Latin America comparable to that of Brown v. Board of Education in the United States (Rohter, 2003).

In order to capitalize on the momentum created by the WCAR, it is indispensable to keep race and racial inequality in the forefront of Latin American political and legal debate. This is not an easy task and the region faces many challenges. While the Latin American governments took a crucial first step by formally acknowledging at the international level the existence of racial discrimination, this is just the beginning rather the end of the struggle. Despite some of the positive changes that have taken place in the last two years, it remains to be seen whether governments will start laying the groundwork for formulation of effective public policies, including legal reforms needed to address racial disparities. There are signs that officials in some Latin American governments are slowly incorporating diplomatic recognition of the existence of racism and racial discrimination into their official domestic discourse. But throughout the region whether Latin American governments will turn their rhetoric into action remains to be seen.

Notes

1. The views expressed in this article are solely those of the author and do not reflect the official position of the Organization of American States or the Inter-American Commission on Human Rights. I wish to express my gratitude to Flavia Modell for her support in researching this article. I would also like to thank James Early and Ruthanne Deutsch for their input in an earlier version of this article,

2. Meeting of the presidents of South America, communique, Brazil, September 1, 2000.

3. 10th periodical report that the states parties were required to submit in 1994: Mexico. 30/03/95. CERD/C/260/Add. 1, paragraph 155.

4. 10th periodical report that the states parties were required to submit in 1994: Mexico. 30/03/95. CERD/C/260/Add. 1, paragraph 161.

5. 10th periodical report that the states parties were required to submit in 1994: Mexico. 30/03/95. CERD/C/260/Add. 1, paragraph 157. Nevertheless, there are authors who have begun to conduct studies on the situation of the indigenous peoples from a racial perspective. See Gall (1998 and 2000).

6. The method used in this study is somewhat limited, mainly because it is of a general nature and, therefore, does not cover specific aspects of racism or racial discrimination. The article is not meant to be a complete study of the significance of race in Latin America, the different manifestations of racial discrimination in the hemisphere, or all of the ways that the existence of racism is denied. We use the paper as a preliminary theoretical framework to draw out debate on the persistence of racism in our region.

7. For example, in Uruguay Black people have a lower level of education and a higher school dropout rate. 12th, 13th, and 14th Consolidated Report of Uruguay to the Committee on the Elimination of Racial Discrimination, &: 203 et seq.

8. In Brazil, the Black population shows a higher level of unemployment than the white population, earns at least 40% less salary, and holds the lowest-grade and most unstable jobs on the labor market, which

also provide the least benefits. See Inter-American Trade Union Institute for Racial Equality (2000).

9. In Nicaragua, for example, even though 32.3% of the nations population has access to potable water, the percentage drops off sharply to 8.8% for the population living on the Atlantic coast, where the majority of the indigenous and Afro-Caribbean populations in the country are concentrated. See International Human Rights Law Group (2000).

10. See chapter 11 of the English version of Inter-American Commission on Human Rights (1999).

11. As is the case of the remaining survivors of the Quilombos in Brazil, the Garifunas in Honduras, or the Afro-Caribbean peoples in Nicaragua.

12. CEPAL, Etnicidad, Raza y Equidad en America Latina y el Caribe, LC/R. 1967, March 8, 2000, 36 et seq.

13. 9th periodical report that the states parties were required to submit in 1998: Colombia. 17/11/98. CERD/C332/Add. I (State Party Report). See on this same topic, Plan Nacional de Desarrollo de la Poblacion Afrocolombiana, Departamento Nacional de Planeacion, 1998.

14. CERD/C331/Add. 1, 02/11/99, and 6 (Dominican Republic).

15. 13th periodical report that the signatories were required to submit in 1994: Venezuela. 13/05/96. CERD/C263/Add. 8/Rev 1, 77.

16. 13th periodical report that the signatories were required to submit in 1998: Haiti. 25/05/99. CERD/C/336/Add. 1 and 15 and 17.

17. Summary of the minutes of the 1317th session: Peru. 16/03/99. CERD/C/SR. 1317, 78.

18. 10th periodical report that the signatories were required to submit in 1994: Mexico. 30/03/95. CERD/C/260/Add. 1, paragraph 157.

19. 13th periodical report that the signatories were required to submit in 1997: Cuba. 07/10/97. CERD/C/319/Add. 4 and 16.

20. In order to cover up exclusion of minorities such as indigenous people in Guatemala or the Black population in Brazil.

21. Immigration policies in our region are highly racist. Uruguay, Paraguay, Honduras, Costa Rica, and Panama prohibited people of African origin from immigrating. Venezuela and the Dominican Republic placed restrictions on the immigration of individuals of African extraction. Quoted in Carlos Hasenbalg (1998:168).

22. *For* example, this was the criterion used by dance clubs or discos in Peru to discriminate. See Law 27049, Un Gesto Politico contra la Discrimination Racial, Ideele. Lima, February 1999, *no.* 115, p. 57.

23. This is the criterion that is used in Uruguay to prevent entry into certain establishments or clubs. See Mundo Afro (1999:12, 35).

24. One of the most widely used devices in Brazil to keep Afro-Brazilians out of the labor market or to make access difficult for them.

25. 13th periodical report that the signatories were required to submit in 1998: Haiti. 25/05/99. CERD/C336/Add. 1.

26. Summary proceedings of the 1317th session: Peru. 16/03/99. CERD/C/SR. 1317, 78.

27. Final Observations of the Committee on the Elimination of Racial Discrimination: Mexico. 22/09/95. A/50/18, paragraphs 353–398.

28. Summary proceedings of the 12306th session: Mexico. 21/10/97. CERD/C/SR. 1206, paragraph 5. The following day, the same representative of the government would admit that when certain practices act as an obstacle to the application of Articles 2 to 5 of the Convention, that constitutes ethnic, if not racial, discrimination. Summary proceedings of the 1207th session: Bulgaria, Mexico. 21/10/97. CERD/C/SR. 1207, paragraph 3.

29. "In Peru, not every *cholo* (mestizo, mixed race, black, or Indian) is poor, but almost every poor person is *cholo*" (Oscatequi, 1998:31).

30. 10th periodical report that the signatories were required to submit in 1994: Mexico. 20/03/95. CERD/C/260/Add. I, paragraph 40. In response to this argument, the CERD stated its "particular concern for the fact that the signatory does not seem to realize that the latent discrimination that the 56 indigenous groups that live in Mexico are experiencing is covered by the definition of racial discrimination that appears in Article 1 of the Convention. The description of the difficult situation of those groups as mere unequal participants in socioeconomic development is inadequate." Final Observations of the Committee on the Elimination of Racial Discrimination: Mexico. 22/09/95. A/50/18, paragraphs 353–398.

31. See Telles and Lim (1998:465–474) and Lovell (2000:85), showing how equally qualified Afro-Brazilians who are defined as both Black and brown Brazilians earn less than white Brazilians.

32. The American Convention of Human Rights states: "The States Parties to this Convention pledge to respect the rights and liberties [that are] recognized therein and to guarantee their free and full exercise to any person who may be subject to their jurisdiction, without any discrimination whatsoever due to reasons of origin, social and economic position or any other social condition" (Article 1.1). The International Covenant on Civil and Political Rights states: "Each one of the States Parties to this Covenant pledge to respect and guarantee all individuals who may be found in their territory and may be subject to their jurisdiction, the rights [that are] recognized in this Covenant, without any distinction whatsoever of social origin, economic position, any other social condition" (Article 2.1).

33. 8th periodical report that the signatories were required to submit in 1998. Addition, Dominican Republic, CERD/C/331/Add. 1, 02/11/99 and 27.

34. Compilation of General Recommendations: 11/02/99. CERD/C/365, General Recommendation XIV pertaining to paragraph 1 of Article 1 of the Convention (42nd Period of Sessions. El enfasis nos pertenece).

35. See, for example, Final Observations of the Committee on the Elimination of Racial Discrimination: Chile. 20/08/99. A/54/18, paragraphs 365–383.

36. See, for example, Final Observations of the Committee on the Elimination of Racial Discrimination: Colombia. 20/08/99. A/54/18, paragraphs 454–481.

37. See, for example, Final Observations of the Committee on the Elimination of Racial Discrimination: Uruguay. 19/08/99. A/54/18, paragraphs 454–435.

38. See, for example, Final Observations of the Committee on the Elimination of Racial Discrimination: Costa Rica. 07/04/99. CERD/C/304/Add. 71 and CERD/C/SR/1317, (Peru), 03/16/99, paragraph 35.

39. See, for example, Final Observations of the Committee on the Elimination of Racial Discrimination: Costa Rica. 07/04/99. CERD/C/304/Add. 71.

40. Final Observations of the Committee on the Elimination of Racial Discrimination: Peru. 12/04/99. CERD/C/304/Add. 69 (hereafter referred to as CERD, Peru).

41. CERD, Costa Rica.

42. 10th periodical report that the signatories were required to submit in 1994: Mexico. 30/03/95. CERD/C260/Add. 1, paragraph 157.

43. Final Observations of the Committee on the Elimination of Racial Discrimination: Haiti. A/54/18, paragraphs 253–271.

44. A point made in Brazils report, CERD/C/SR.1157, 10/23/96, paragraph 55.

45. For example, in Brazil most complaints alleging the crime recognized as racism according to the Constitution, as well as Law 7716/89, amended by Law 9459/97, are described as "crimes against honor."

46. 13th periodical report that the signatories were required to submit in 1994: Venezuela. 13/05/96. CERD/C/263/Add. 8/Rev. 1, paragraph 77.

47. 8th periodical report that the signatories were required to submit in 1998: Dominican Republic. 02/11/99. CERD/C331/Add. 1, paragraph 6.

48. 13th periodical report that the signatories were required to submit in 1998: Haiti. 25/05/99. CERD/C/336/Add.1.

49. Compilation of General Recommendations: 11/02/99. CERD/C/365, General Recommendation 20 (48th period of sessions, 1996).

50. 12th, 13th, and 14th Consolidated Report of the Oriental Republic of Uruguay to the Committee on the Elimination of Racial Discrimination, paragraph 56.

51. Ibid., paragraph 34.

52. 13th periodical report that the signatories were required to submit in 1997: Cuba. 07/10/97. CERD/C/319/Add. 4, paragraph 16.

53. Someone once called Afro-Argentines the first "desaparecidos" in the history of the country. See Goldberg (2000:36).

54. There is a widespread sentiment that data collection on racial makeup constitutes a form of discrimination. The government of Uruguay, for example, recognized this practice as being discriminatory in its 12th, 13th, and 14th Consolidated Report to the Committee on the Elimination of Racial Discrimination, paragraph 3. To cite examples, Argentina has not included questions on race or color since 1914; Bolivia, since 1900; Peru, since 1961; Ecuador, since 1950; Venezuela, since 1876; Nicaragua, since 1920; Honduras, since 1945; and the Dominican Republic, since 1950. (Quoted in Hasenbalg, 1998:166.)

55. For example, Bolivia.

56. See Telles and Lim (1998) in which the authors look at how *pardos* (brown people) are closer in terms of social status to the *pretos* (Blacks) than to *brancos* (whites) in Brazil.

57. In fact, there are over 100 different categories in Brazil. See an interesting article by Eugene Robinson (1999), recounting the experience of an African American in Brazil in terms of racial identity.

58. For example, an article that appeared in Peru states that "there is a broad spectrum of interpretive possibilities on the origin, function, and destiny of Black people in Peru, but none of them separates their future from the mixed race {*mestizo*) complex that characterizes the nation" (Millones, 1996:16).

59. In this article, we shall not analyze how the origin of *mestizaje* in Latin America hearkens back to the sexual violence perpetrated by the Spanish and Portuguese conquistadors against indigenous women and later by slave traders against women brought from Africa as slaves.

60. 10th periodical report that the signatories were required to submit in 1994: Mexico. 30/03/95. CERD/C/260/Add. 1, paragraph 157.

61. CERD/C/319/Add. 4, 10.07.97, paragraph 16.

62. Final Observations of the Committee on the Elimination of Racial Discrimination: Colombia. 20/08/99. A/54/18, paragraphs 454–481.

63. Santiago Bastos y Manuela Camus, La exclusion y el desafio. Estudios sobre segregacion etnica y empleo en la ciudad de Guatemala (1998).

64. "To speak of racism in Venezuela is somewhat complex, since it is not a very accepted topic, especially if we use the forms of racism that exist in the United States, Germany or in the Republic of South Africa as a point of reference" (Mijares, 1996:52),

65. It would be possible to take exception to this statement by considering the cases of the *politica de tierra arrasada* (scorched earth policy) in Guatemala or the many policies of extermination that were implemented against indigenous populations in different countries of Latin America.

66. 10th periodical report that the signatories were required to submit in 1996: Mexico. 30/09/96. CERD/C/296/Add. 1, paragraph 73 ("feeling of xenophobia and racial discrimination in some sectors of American society") and paragraph 75 ("at the present time, it is relatively easy to inflame racist and xenophobic sentiments in some sectors of American society against the streams of migrant labor or refugees"). The report only mentioned the indigenous people as constituting one of the most vulnerable groups to violations of human rights (paragraph 5) or migrant workers on the southern border who face the prospects of fear and uncertainty, and on a few occasions it mentioned the situations of violence, corruption, and vulnerability (paragraph 59), but never did it mention discrimination (within its borders).

67. Of course, with the exceptions noted in the footnote above.

68. Response given in a survey conducted in Guatemala among traditional families in that country, in Casaus Arzu (1998:130).

69. Ley creation del IN AD I Instituto Nacional contra la Discriminacion y la Xenofobia y el Racismo, 23.515, promulgada de hecho, July 28, 1995, Ley 24.515.

70. Decreto por el que se expide la Ley Federal para Prevenir y Eliminar la Discriminacion, June 11, 2003, Diario Oficial de la Federacion.

71. Acuerdo Gubernativo 390–2002 de creacion de la Comision Presidencial contra el Racismo y la Discriminacion contra los Pueblos Indigenas.

72. Law 10.678, May 23, 2003, Cria a Secretaria Especial de Politicas de Promocao da Igualdade Racial, da Presidencia da Republica, e da outras providencias.

73. Presidential decree 4.228 of May 13, 2002, establishing a national program of affirmative action.

74. Law 3.708 of Rio de Janeiro, September 11, 2001 (establishes a quota system of 40% of all the admissions slots for "Black and brown" students in the local universities of Rio de Janeiro).

75. See Carneiro (2003), arguing for the examples from the United States that can be helpful for the Brazilian experience.

References

Adorno, Sergio. 1999. Racial discrimination and criminal justice in Sao Paulo. In *Race in Contemporary Brazil: From Indifference to Inequality*, ed. Rebecca Reichmann. University Park: Pennsylvania State University Press.

Arocha Rodriguez, Carlos. 1992. Afro-Colombia denied. In *NACLA Report on the Americas: The Black Americas, 1492–1992* 25, no. 4 (February).

Bastos, Santiago, and Manuela Camus. 1998. La exclusion y el desafio: Estudios sobre segregacion etnica y empleo en el area metropolitana de Guatemala. *FLACSO* 43.

Carneiro, Sueli. 2003. Amicus curiae. *Correio Braziliense,* January 8.

Casaus Arzu, Marta Elena. 1998. *La metamorfosis del racismo en Guatemala.* Guatemala City: Cholsamaj.

Cohen, Stanley. 1996. Government responses to human rights reports: Claims, denials and counterclaims. *Human Rights Quarterly* 18:3.

de la Torre, Carlos. 1997. La letra con sangre entra: Racismo, escuela y vida cotidiana en Ecuador, Paper presented at the 20th Congress of the Latin American Studies Association.

Early, James. 1999. Reflections on Cuba, race, and politics. *Souls: A Critical Journal of Black Politics, Culture, and Society* 1, no. 2 (Spring).

Economic Commission on Latin America and the Caribbean (ECLAC). 2000. Etnicidad, raza y equidad en America Latina y el Caribe, August.

Gall, Olivia. 1998. Racism, interethnic war and peace in Chiapas. Paper presented at the 21st Congress of the Latin American Studies Association.

———. 2000. Mestizaje-indigenismo and racism in the Mexican state's ideology of national integration. Paper presented at the 23rd Congress of the Latin American Studies Association.

Goldberg, Marta Beatriz. 2000. Nuestros negros, desaparecidos o ignorados? *Todo es Historia* 393 (April).

Guimaraes, Antonio Sergio. 1999. *Racismo e antiracismo no Brasil.* Sao Paulo: Editora 34, Ltda.

———. 2001. The misadventures of nonracialism in Brazil. In *Beyond Racism,* ed. Charles V.

Hamilton, Lynn Huntley, Neville Alexander, Antonio Sergio Guimaraes, and Wilmot James. Boulder, CO: Lynne Rienner Publishers.

Hasenbalg, Carlos. 1998. Racial inequalities in Brazil and throughout Latin America: Timid responses to disguised racism. In *Constructing Democracy: Human Rights, Citizenship, and Society in Latin America,* ed. Elizabeth Jelin and Eric Hershberg. New York: Perseus Books.

Inter-American Commission on Human Rights. 1999. Third Report on the Human Rights Situation in Colombia. OAS/ser. L/V; II. 102, doc. 9, rev. 1, February 26.

Inter-American Trade Union Institute for Racial Equality. 2000. Map of the Black population in the Brazilian labor market.

International Human Rights Law Group. 2000. Submission to the Inter-American Commission on Human Rights, March 3.

Lovell, Peggy A. 2000. Gender, race, and the struggle for social justice in Brazil. *Latin American Perspectives* 27:85–102.

Millones, Luis. 1996–1997. Peruanos de Eban. *Bienvenida Lima,* December-February.

Minority Rights Group. 1995. *No Longer Invisible: Afro-Latin Americans Today.* London: Minority Rights Group.

———. 1999. *Afro-Brazilians: Time fir Recognition.* London: Minority Rights Group.

Mijares, Maria Marta. 1996. Racismo y endoracismo en Barlovento: Presencia y ausencia en Rio Chico: Autoimagen de una poblacidn barloventena. *Caracas: Fundacidn Afroamerica.*

Mundo Afro. 1999. Situacidn de discriminacion y racismo en el Uruguay.

Oliveira, Barbosa e dos Santos. 1998. *A cor do medo: O medo da cor.*

Oscategui, Jose. 1998. Poblacion, crecimiento economico y racismo en el Peru. *Actualidad Economica* (Lima), May.

Robinson, Eugene. 1999. On the beach at Ipanema. *Washington Post Magazine,* August 1.

Rodriguez, Romero Jorge. 2000. La discrimination racial en la epoca de la globalizacion economica. *Mundo Afro.*

Rohter, Larry. 2003. Racial quotas in Brazil touch off fierce debate. *New York Times,* April 5.

Telles, Edward, and Nelson Lim. 1998. Does it matter who answers the race question?: Racial classification and Income inequality in Brazil. *Demography* 35 (4):465–474.

UNITED NATIONS. 1995. Committee on the Elimination of Racial Discrimination. 10th periodical report that the signatories were required to submit in 1994: Mexico. March 30, CERD/C/260/ Add. 1.

———. Committee on the Elimination of Racial Discrimination. 12th, 13th, and 14th Consolidated

Report of Uruguay to the Committee on the Elimination of Racial Discrimination.

———. 1998. Committee on the Elimination of Racial Discrimination. 9th periodical report that the signatories were required to submit in 1998: Colombia. November 17, '98. CERD/C332/Add. 1 (State Party Report).

———. 1999. Committee on the Elimination of Racial Discrimination. Dominican Republic CERD/C331/Add. 1, November 3 and 6.

———. 1996. Committee on the Elimination of Racial Discrimination. 13th periodical report that the signatories were required to submit in 1994: Venezuela. May 13, CERD/C263/Add. 8/Rev. 1.

———. 1999. Committee on the Elimination of Racial Discrimination. 13th periodical report that the signatories were required to submit in 1998: Haiti. May 25, CERD/C/336/Add. 1.

———. 1999. Committee on the Elimination of Racial Discrimination Summary of the minutes of the 1317th session: Peru. March 16. CERD/C/SR, 1317, & 78.

———. 1997. Committee on the Elimination of Racial Discrimination 13th periodical report that the signatories were required to submit in 1997: Cuba. October 7. CERD/C/319/Add. 4, & 16.

———. 1995. Committee on the Elimination of Racial Discrimination. Final observations of the Committee on the Elimination of Racial Discrimination: Mexico. September 22, A/50/18.

———. 1995. Committee on the Elimination of Racial Discrimination. Final observations of the Committee on the Elimination of Racial Discrimination: Mexico. September 22, A/50/18, paragraphs 353–398.

———. 1997. Committee on the Elimination of Racial Discrimination. Summary proceedings of the 12306th session: Mexico. October 21, CERD/C/SR. 1206, paragraph 5.

———. 1997. Committee on the Elimination of Racial Discrimination. Summary proceedings of the 1207th session: Bulgaria, Mexico. October 21, CERD/C/SR. 1207, paragraph 3.

———. 1999. Committee on the Elimination of Racial Discrimination. 8th periodical report that the signatories were required to submit in 1998. Addition: Dominican Republic, CERD/C/331/Add. 1, November 2.

———. 1999. Committee on the Elimination of Racial Discrimination. Final observations of the Committee on the Elimination of Racial Discrimination: Chile. August 20, A/54/18.

———. 1999. Committee on the Elimination of Racial Discrimination. Final observations of the Committee on the Elimination of Racial Discrimination: Colombia. August 20, A/54/18.

———. 1999. Committee on the Elimination of Racial Discrimination. Final observations of the Committee on the Elimination of Racial Discrimination: Uruguay. August 19, A/54/18.

———. 1999. Committee on the Elimination of Racial Discrimination. Final observations of the Committee on the Elimination of Racial Discrimination: Costa Rica. April 7, CERD/C/ 304/Add. 71.

———. 1999. Committee on the Elimination of Racial Discrimination. Final observations of the Committee on the Elimination of Racial Discrimination: Peru. April 12, CERD/C/304/Add. 69.

———. 1999. Committee on the Elimination of Racial Discrimination. Final observations of the Committee on the Elimination of Racial Discrimination: Haiti. A/54/18, paragraphs 253–271.

———. 1999. Committee on the Elimination of Racial Discrimination. Final observations of the Committee on the Elimination of Racial Discrimination: Colombia. August 20, A/54/18.

CPSIA information can be obtained
at www.ICGtesting.com
Printed in the USA
LVHW061947080419
613404LV00008B/14/P